SANDS OF TIME

THE HISTORY OF BEACH VOLLEYBALL
VOLUME #3

2004
BY
ARTHUR R. COUVILLON

FIRST EDITION
ALL RIGHTS RESERVED.
THIS BOOK, OR PARTS THEREOF,
MAY NOT BE REPRODUCED IN ANY FORM
WITHOUT PERMISSION OF THE PUBLISHER
Printed in the United States of America
COPYRIGHT, 2004 BY INFORMATION GUIDES

Library of Congress Cataloging Data:
Couvillon, Art

"Beach Volleyball"

PUBLICATIONS

1. Fire Service: Handbooks, manuals, text books, etc.
2. Firefighter:Handbooks, manuals, text books, etc.
3. Information:Handbooks, manuals, text books, etc.
4. Promotional:Handbooks, manuals, text books, etc.
5. Practice Exams: Fire Service Written and Oral Exams.
6. Winners Series: Beach Volleyball.
7. History of Beach Volleyball.
8. Worlds Best, 20 years of the AVP.

I. Title

LCCN 2002105899
ISBN 0-938329-79-0

FORWARD

When I first began research on the history of beach volleyball, I had no idea as to the amount of history there was attached to the roots of the game. First there was the Outrigger Canoe Club's "Oral-History" accounts that revealed the birth of beach volleyball, in 1915 on the sands of Waikiki Beach in Honolulu Hawaii. Then to the coast of California, in the 1920's, on the beach in Santa Monica, where the first legends of beach volleyball began to develop the growth of beach volleyball. The commitment and interest of these forerunners shaped what became the lifestyle of the players that enjoyed the "Golden" and "Adolescent" years of beach volleyball. The collecting and cataloging of information and photography became endless hours of a fulfilling adventure with the characters, personalities, promoters, enthusiasts, journalists, photographers and legends that have contributed and become part of the history of beach volleyball.

The research proceeded from the 1960's to the 1970's and 1980's with the "Spirited" and "Transitional" years of beach volleyball. In the mid-1980's, the formation of the Association of Volleyball Professionals (AVP), the Women's Professional Volleyball Association (WPVA) as well as the Federation of International Volleyball's (FIVB) beach volleyball tours provided a professional medium for the athletes of beach volleyball. The players and the game continued to progress and develop both domestically and internationally into the 1990's with the "Prosperous" years. During the 1990's, the players and the promoters of beach volleyball could actually accrue a living from the game of beach volleyball. The inclusion of beach volleyball in the 1996 and 2000 Olympics showcased, to the world, the best that the game had to offer. "2000 and Beyond" was escorted in with hard times and then a rebuilding process that has beach volleyball back on track for what looks like a bright and successful "Historical" future.

After nearly ten years of this "Labor of Love" the three volume book series: "Sands Of Time" -The History Of Beach Volleyball is complete for now. But, the history continues with today and tomorrow's beach volleyball characters, personalities, promoters, enthusiasts, journalists, photographers and legends that are continuing to create and record beach volleyball history.

ACKNOWLEDGMENTS

Thanks to all the characters, personalities, promoters, enthusiasts, journalists, photographers and legends of the past, present and future of beach volleyball. And thanks for "Grand-Kids" to fulfill the endless hours of all my future adventures, be it beach volleyball or just playing on the beach!

THE AUTHOR

Arthur "Artie" Couvillon is a retired Firefighter that has published several books relating to the Fire Service. Aside from the Fire Service, "Artie's" greatest interest has been his involvement with the sport of beach volleyball, which began in the early 1960"s. Throughout this period of time, he has accumulated pertinent information, facts, records, stories, anecdotes, and photographs, relating to the sport of beach volleyball.

Since retiring from the Fire Service, "Artie" has been focusing on the history of beach volleyball. He has utilized all of his resources along with assistance from the fans, players, legends, photographers and followers of beach volleyball, to produce the book: "Sands of Time" The History of Beach Volleyball, Volume's #1, #2 and #3.

During his research, "Artie" has accumulated such a vast amount of information along with an awesome collection of photographs, that it became apparent to him that he would not be able to utilize all of it in the "Sands of Time", hence the "Winner's" series. Artie has published the "Winners" series which highlight the careers of various, successful beach volleyball players, both men and women. The series includes pertinent information about each "Winner" and cover each of the "Winners" career championship victories, along with numerous photographs of the "Winner's" as well as other players of the same era. The "Winner's" series includes books covering the careers of Jim Menges, Ron Von Hagen, Matt Gage, Sinjin Smith, Karch Kiraly, Randy Stoklos, Mike Dodd. Holly McPeak, Linda Hanley, Liz Masakayan, and Barbra Fontana. These publications will be followed by additional "Winner's" series publications including, Karolyn Kirby, Jackie Silva, Kathy Gregory, Nina Grouwinkel Matthies, Lisa Arce, Bernie Holtzman, Gene Selznick, Ron Lang, Henry Bergman, Tim Hovland, Mike Whitmarsh, Scott Ayakatubby, Brent Frohoff, Kent Steffes, Adam Johnson, Jose Loiola, and Eric Fonoimoana, just to name a few!

2003 marked the 20th anniversary of the AVP, which inspired Artie to publish the book: "Worlds Best" 20 Years of the AVP. This book covers the formation of the AVP and highlights each of its 20 years with information, anecdotes, tournament records and photographs.

The books: "Sands of Time" The History of Beach Volleyball, The "Winners" series and "Worlds Best" 20 years of the AVP are all available from Information Guides.

Books are available from:
INFORMATION GUIDES
32 Eighteenth Street
Hermosa Beach, CA 90254
1-800-347-3257
E-MAIL: firebks@gte.net
WEB-SITE: www.volleyballbooks.net

TABLE OF CONTENTS
VOLUME #3

CHAPTER #1
"THE PROSPEROUS YEARS OF BEACH VOLLEYBALL"
1990 Through 1999

1990 Beach Volleyball Summary..**1-20**
    Men's Beach Volleyball..1-13
    Men's Tournament Results..5-13
    Women's Beach Volleyball..14-18
    Women's Tournament Results...15-18
    Additional Volleyball Information...19
1991 Beach Volleyball Summary..**21-44**
    Men's Beach Volleyball..21-33
    Men's Tournament Results..25-31
    Women's Beach Volleyball..34-39
    Women's Tournament Results...35-39
    Additional Volleyball Information...40-44
1992 Beach Volleyball Summary..**45-68**
    Men's Beach Volleyball..46-58
    Men's Tournament Results..48-57
    Women's Beach Volleyball..58-66
    Women's Tournament Results...59-65
    Additional Volleyball Information...66-68
1993 Beach Volleyball Summary..**69-94**
    Men's Beach Volleyball..69-81
    Men's Tournament Results..73-79
    Women's Beach Volleyball..82-92
    Women's Tournament Results...85-91
    Additional Volleyball Information...93-94
1994 Beach Volleyball Summary..**95-126**
    Men's Beach Volleyball..95-109
    Men's Tournament Results..99-107
    Women's Beach Volleyball..110-123
    Women's Tournament Results...114-122
    Additional Volleyball Information...124-126
1995 Beach Volleyball Summary..**127-156**
    Men's Beach Volleyball..127-144
    Men's Tournament Results..133-143
    Women's Beach Volleyball..145-154
    Women's Tournament Results...147-153
    Additional Volleyball Information...155-156
1996 Beach Volleyball Summary..**157-206**
    Men's Beach Volleyball..157-172
    Men's Tournament Results..162-171
    Women's Beach Volleyball..173-185
    Women's Tournament Results...177-184
    Olympic Beach Volleyball..186-205
    Additional Volleyball Information...206
1997 Beach Volleyball Summary..**207-240**
    Men's Beach Volleyball..207-226
    Men's Tournament Results..212-225
    Women's Beach Volleyball..227-239
    Women's Tournament Results...230-238
    Additional Volleyball Information...240

TABLE OF CONTENTS
VOLUME #3

1998 Beach Volleyball Summary **241-284**
    Men's Beach Volleyball 241-271
    Men's Tournament Results 246-270
    Women's Beach Volleyball 272-283
    Women's Tournament Results 275-282
    Additional Volleyball Information 284
1999 Beach Volleyball Summary **285314**
    Men's Beach Volleyball 285-300
    Men's Tournament Results 291-299
    Women's Beach Volleyball 301-309
    Women's Tournament Results 304-308
    Additional Volleyball Information 310-314

CHAPTER #2
"BEACH VOLLEYBALL 2000 AND BEYOND"
2000 Through 2004

2000 and Beyond Beach Volleyball Summary, ... **315-317**
    Men's Beach Volleyball 318-330
    Men's Tournament Results 323-329
    Women's Beach Volleyball Summary 331-341
    Women's Tournament Results 335-340
    Additional Volleyball Information 342
2001 Beach Volleyball Summary **343-366**
    Men's Beach Volleyball 343-354
    Men's Tournament Results 346-353
    Women's Beach Volleyball 355-364
    Women's Tournament Results 357-363
    Additional Volleyball Information 365-366
2002 Beach Volleyball Summary **367390**
    Men's Beach Volleyball 367-381
    Men's Tournament Results 370-380
    Women's Beach Volleyball 382-389
    Women's Tournament Results 384-388
    Additional Volleyball Information 390
2003 Beach Volleyball Summary **391-430**
    Men's Beach Volleyball 391-411
    Men's Tournament Results 394-404
    Women's Beach Volleyball 412-425
    Women's Tournament Results 415-422
    Additional Volleyball Information 426-430
2004 Beach Volleyball Summary **431-454**
    Men's Beach Volleyball 431-441
    Men's Tournament Results 434-439
    Women's Beach Volleyball 442-453
    Women's Tournament Results 445-451
    Additional Volleyball Information 454
ALL-TIME BEACH VOLLEYBALL TOURNAMENT RECORDS **555-466**
    Men's All-Time Career Beach Volleyball Tournament Records 455-461
    Women's All-Time Career Beach Volleyball Tournament Records 462-466
USA VOLLEYBALL "ALL-ERA" PLAYERS **467-470**
    Men's "All-Era" Players 467-468
    Women's "All-Era" Players 469-470
ADDITIONAL BEACH VOLLEYBALL BOOKS **471-472**

FRONT COVER PHOTO

The 1990's through 2000 and beyond included the inclusion of beach volleyball in the Olympics. The Olympics have included the best beach volleyball players in the world. The author took this cover photo at the beach volleyball venue for the 1996 Olympiad in Atlanta Georgia, during what many beach volleyball enthusiast consider the most exciting beach volleyball gasme ever played. There are three of beach volleyball's "All-Time" career tournament winner's in this photo. The number-two "All-Time" career winner, with 139 championships to his credit, Sinjin Smith is hitting the ball towards the defense of Kent Steffes (left), number-four on the list with 110 career championships and the "All-Time" career leader, Karch Kiraly (right), still counting with 146 career championships to his credit. In the photo, Sinjin's partner is Carl Henkel, who elevated his play to the level of the three "Hall of Famer's" on the court with him, to nearly pull-off an improbable upset. (Note: the number-three "All-Time" career tournament winner is Randy Stoklos with 122 to his credit).

Photo courtesy of "Couvi"

MEN'S BEACH VOLLEYBALL 1990

AVP

In 1990, there were thirty-two recorded "Pro" Beach Volleyball tournaments. Twenty-seven of these tournaments were staged in the U.S.A. while five were played internationally. Of the twenty-seven U.S. tournaments, twelve were California events, while fifteen were played in thirteen different states. The California tournaments were held in San Jose, Sacramento, Fresno, Santa Cruz, Santa Monica (twice), Venice Beach, Manhattan Beach, Hermosa Beach, Seal Beach, Laguna Beach, and San Diego. The remaining U.S. tournaments were held in Fort Myers Florida, Fort Lauderdale Florida, Clearwater Beach Florida, Honolulu Hawaii, Phoenix Arizona, Dallas/Fort Worth Texas, Boulder Colorado, Baltimore Maryland, Cape Cod Massachusetts, Grand Haven Michigan, Milwaukee Wisconsin, Cleveland Ohio, Chicago Illinois, Indianapolis Indiana, and Seattle Washington. The five international events were held in Rio de Janeiro Brazil, Ste France, Lignano Italy, Enoshima Japan, and Australia.

Sinjin Smith and Randy Stoklos outdistanced all other teams in 1990 by winning 12 tournaments. Five of their wins came in California, at Sacramento, Seal Beach, San Diego, and the U.S. Championships in Hermosa Beach. They had eight more U.S. wins, which came in Clearwater Beach Florida, Honolulu Hawaii, Phoenix Arizona, Boulder Colorado, Milwaukee Wisconsin, Chicago Illinois, and Indianapolis Indiana. They added one international win by winning the FIVB "World Championships in Rio de Janeiro Brazil.

Karch Kiraly and Brent Frohoff won 6 tournaments together in 1990. Three of their victories came in California, at: Venice Beach, Manhattan Beach, and the "World Series of Beach Volleyball" held at Santa Monica's Jonathon Club. Their remaining three wins were obtained in Seattle Washington, Grand Haven Michigan, and Cape Cod Massachusetts. Frohoff also won the Dallas/Fort Worth Texas event with Scott Ayakatubby. Kiraly added the Fort Lauderdale event to his win list when teamed-up with Kent Steffes for a win. Kent Steffes also won three tournaments with Tim Hovland and one with Dan Vrebalovich. With Hovland, Steffes won in Cleveland Ohio, Santa Monica California, and the FIVB event in Lignano Italy. With Vrebalovich he won at the San Jose California event. Vrebalovich also won with John Hanley at the Fort Myers Florida event and at the Australian Open with Tim Walmer.

RANDY STOKLOS & SINJIN SMITH
The top team on the 1990 AVP Tour was Randy Stoklos and Sinjin Smith. In the photo above, Stoklos hits a set from Smith, towards the block of Karch Kiraly. Action took place during the 1990 AVP event in Venice Beach.
Photo Courtesy of the AVP

Additional teams that won in 1990 were Pete Aroncheck and Mike Boehle won the Laguna Beach Open together, while Tim Hovland won the Fresno event with Mike Dodd. Lief Hanson and Eric Wurts won an international event in Enoshima Japan. The Brazilian team of Andre Perlingeiro Lima and and Guilherme Luiz Marquez won the international event in Ste France.

In 1990, Karch Kiraly had started the season with Kent Steffes. After winning only one tournament together, winning only 8 matches while losing 12, Karch went back with Brent Frohoff for the remainder of the 1990 season.

Dodd and Hovland went their separate ways in 1990. Also, there were a lot of people that felt Smith and Stoklos were on the downside of their careers, even though they had fourteen tournament championships and still managed to sweep the "Cuervo Gold Crown" series, along with the win at the U.S. Championships. They may have been on "their downside" but they still were ahead of all the others.

Smith and Stoklos were also able to claim the FIVB World Championship title, in Rio de Janiero Brazil, for the second straight year. This was their third Brazilian championship out of the last four.

1990 AVP PLAYER AWARDS
Most Valuable Player: Karch Kiraly
Best Offensive Player: Karch Kiraly
Best Defensive Player: Sinjin Smith
Most Improved Player: Wally Goodrick
Rookie of the Year: Mike Whitmarsh
Sportsman of the Year: Larry Mear
Most Underrated Player: Roger Clark
(Ron Von Hagen Award)

KARCH KIRALY
In 1990, Karch Kiraly was voted the AVP's "Most Valuable Player" as well as the "Best Offensive Player" Kiraly advanced to 16 finals, winning 7 times In the photo above, Karch hits the ball during an AVP event at the Manhattan Beach Pier.
Photo Courtesy of "Couvi"

WALLY GOODRICK
Wally Goodrick was the AVP's "Most Improved Player" in 1990. Goodrick was very competitive, finishing within the top five six times. In the photo above, Goodrick is in position to make the pass.
Photo Courtesy of Dennis G. Steers

1990 AVP PLAYERS & MONEY EARNED

1.	Sinjin Smith	$221,437
1.	Randy Stoklos	$221,437
3.	Karch Kiraly	$120,125
4.	Brent Frohoff	$114,675
5.	Tim Hovland	$104,168
6.	Kent Steffes	$102,556
7.	Mike Dodd	$ 87,268
8.	Dan Vrebalovich	$ 62,118
9.	John Hanley	$ 57,068
10.	Ricci Luyties	$ 49,581
11.	Scott Ayakatubby	$ 47,825
12.	Scott Friederichsen	$ 43,278
13.	Larry Mear	$ 42,303
14.	Andrew Smith	$ 41,087
15.	Wally Goodrick	$ 40,281
16.	Tim Walmer	$ 39,625
17.	Al Janc	$ 38,650
18.	Craig Moothart	$ 35,928
19.	John Eddo	$ 33,662
20.	Steve Timmons	$ 32,981
21.	Pat Powers	$ 32,450
22.	Adam Johnson	$ 31,862
23.	Jon Stevenson	$ 31,168
24.	Rudy Dvroak	$ 29,418
25.	Sean Fallowfield	$ 27,681
26.	Eric Wurts	$ 26,650
27.	Leif Hanson	$ 26,050
28.	Bruk Vandeweghe	$ 25,243
29.	Mike Whitmarsh	$ 16,643
30.	Jeff Rodgers	$ 15,362
31.	Roger Clark	$ 15,275
32.	Brian Lewis	$ 14,550
33.	Owen McKibbin	$ 14,175
34.	Robert Chavez	$ 11,893
35.	Eugene LeDuff	$ 11,043
36.	Mark Eller	$ 10,418
37.	Eric Boyles	$ 10,143
38.	Steve Krai	$ 8,837
39.	Mike Boehle	$ 8,500
40.	Steve Rottman	$ 8,100
41.	Pete Aronchick	$ 6,768
42.	Bill Bouillianne	$ 6,650
43.	Eric Westcott	$ 5,737
44.	Shawn Davis	$ 5,493
45.	Bob Ctvrtik	$ 5,475
46.	Doug Foust	$ 5,275
47.	Pono Ma'a	$ 5,175
48.	Todd Schaffer	$ 5,125
49.	Steve Obradovich	$ 3,975
50.	Andy Klussman	$ 3,500

1990 INDIVIDUAL AVP TOURNAMENT FINISHES

Player	1st	2nd	3rd	4th	5th
Scott Ayakatubby	1	3	0	1	7
Roger Clark	0	0	0	1	1
Bob Ctvrtik	0	0	0	0	1
Mike Dodd	2	3	9	2	4
Rudy Dvroak	0	0	0	0	3
John Eddo	0	0	0	2	2
Sean Fallowfield	0	0	0	2	0
Scott Friederichsen	0	0	0	2	8
Brent Frohoff	6	10	1	2	3
Wally Goodrick	0	0	2	3	1
John Hanley	1	1	2	4	5
Leif Hanson	0	0	0	0	1
Tim Hovland	4	6	7	2	3
Al Janc	0	0	0	1	2
Adam Johnson	0	0	2	1	3
Karch Kiraly	7	9	5	1	1
Brian Lewis	0	0	0	0	1
Ricci Luyties	0	0	3	4	3
Owen McKibbin	0	0	0	0	1
Larry Mear	0	0	0	2	8
Craig Moothart	0	0	1	1	4
Pat Powers	0	0	0	1	7
Jeff Rodgers	0	0	0	0	1
Andrew Smith	0	0	0	5	3
Sinjin Smith	**11**	**6**	**5**	**1**	**0**
Kent Steffes	5	5	3	3	5
Jon Stevenson	0	0	2	0	4
Randy Stoklos	**11**	**6**	**5**	**1**	**0**
Steve Timmons	0	0	2	1	1
Bruk Vandeweghe	0	0	0	0	3
Dan Vrebalovich	2	1	1	4	8
Tim Walmer	0	0	0	1	2
Mike Whitmarsh	0	0	1	0	1
Eric Wurts	0	0	0	0	1

RANDY STOKLOS & SINJIN SMITH
Randy Stoklos and Sinjin Smith were the top money earners on the 1990 AVP Tour. Smith and Stoklos each earned $221,437.00. In the above photo, Stoklos (left) and Smith (right) are ready to make the defensive play.

Photo Courtesy of the AVP

BRUK VANDEWEGHE
Bruk Vandeweghe provided some skillful competition on the 1990 AVP Tour. Vandeweghe had three top five finishes in 1990. In the photo above, Vandeweghe makes a nice dig on a hard driven ball.

Photo Courtesy of the AVP

FIVB

The first FIVB World Council gathered in Lausanne, Switzerland to discuss and plan the future regulations and calender of the World Series events.

The 1990 FIVB beach volleyball tour included four men's tour sites, in four countries: Rio de Janeiro Brazil, Ste France, Lignano Italy, Enoshima Japan, the total prize money was worth almost $200,000.00.

There was no dominant team on the 1990 FIVB Men's Tour. Each of the four events were won by four different teams. The only dominant factor was the fact that American teams were in all of the finals, winning three of the events.

INDIVIDUAL FIVB TOURNAMENT FINISHES
1990

Player	1st	2nd	3rd	4th	5th
Atila Pereira	0	0	0	0	1
Clovis Freitas	0	0	0	0	1
Fabrizio Bastianelli	0	0	0	0	1
Philippe Blain	0	0	0	1	0
Eduardo Carlos Garrido Dias	0	0	1	0	2
Roberto Moreira Durate Dias	0	0	1	0	2
Mike Dodd	0	1	0	0	0
John Eddo	0	2	0	0	0
Alain Fabian	0	0	0	1	0
Sean Fallowfield	0	2	0	0	0
Emanuele Fracascia	0	0	0	0	1
Leif Hanson	1	0	0	0	0
Tim Hovland	1	1	0	0	0
Al Janc	0	1	0	0	0
Jean Philippe Jodard	0	0	0	1	0
Jan Kvalheim	0	0	0	0	1
Dionisio Dio Lequaglie	0	0	1	1	1
Andre Perlingeiro Lima	1	0	0	1	0
Roberto Costa Lopes	0	0	2	0	2
Bjorn Maaseide	0	0	0	0	1
Luiz Guilherme Marquez	1	0	0	1	0
Jos Franco Vieira Neto	0	0	2	0	2
Christian Penigaud	0	0	0	1	0
Sinjin Smith	1	0	0	0	0
Marco "Sollu" Solustri	0	0	1	1	1
Kent Steffes	1	0	0	0	0
Randy Stoklos	1	0	0	0	0
Tim Walmer	0	1	0	0	0
Eric Wurts	1	0	0	0	0

MIKE DODD
Mike Dodd's best finish on the 1990 FIVB Tour was a second place, with Tim Hovland, at the FIVB event in Rio de Janeireo Brazil. In the above photo, Dodd reaches high to spike the ball.
Photo Courtesy of Frank Goroszko

KENT STEFFES
Along with his 5 AVP championships, Kent Steffes gained a championship win on the 1990 FIVB Tour, paired-up with Tim Hovland, at the FIVB event in Lignano Italy. In the above photo, Steffes reaches high to block the ball.
Photo Courtesy of Frank Goroszko

MEN'S TOURNAMENT RESULTS
1990-AVP

FORT MYERS FLORIDA
March 17th-18th, 1990

The 1990 Miller Lite $60,000.00 AVP Pro-Beach Volleyball event at Fort Myers, was won by John Hanley and Dan Vrebalovich. The winner's split $13,200.00. In the championship final, they edged-out Scott Ayakatubby and Brent Frohoff.

3rd Place: Mike Dodd and Tim Hovland
4th Place: Sinjin Smith and Randy Stoklos
5th Place: Craig Moothart and Jon Stevenson
5th Place: Karch Kiraly and Kent Steffes.

FORT LAUDERDALE FLORIDA
March 24th-25th, 1990

The $60,000.00 Men's Miller Lite 1990 Fort Lauderdale Open was won by the team of Karch Kiraly and Kent Steffes. The winner's split $13,200.00, while the second place team shared $8,400.00. In the championship match, Kiraly and Steffes were able to grab their first 1990 tournament championship together when they defeated Sinjin Smith and Randy Stoklos.

3rd Place: Craig Moothart and Jon Stevenson
4th Place: John Hanley and Dan Vrebalovich
5th Place: Scott Ayakatubby and Brent Frohoff
5th Place: Mike Dodd and Tim Hovland

HONOLULU HAWAII
March 31st-April 1st, 1990

The $75,000.00 Men's Miller Lite 1990 Hawaiian Open was the third stop of the 1990 AVP Tour. The team of Sinjin Smith and Randy Stoklos were the winner's at Fort DeRussey Beach on the shores of Honolulu. The winner's split $16,500.00, for their fourth Hawaiian title in the last five Hawaiian events and it was Smith's career victory number 104. The second place team shared $10,500.00. In the championship match, Smith and Stoklos defeated Karch Kiraly and Brent Frohoff, 15-5.

3rd Place: Mike Dodd and Tim Hovland
4th Place: Scott Friederichsen and Larry Mear
5th Place: Tim Walmer and Al Janc

PHOENIX ARIZONA
April 7th-8th, 1990

The $60,000.00 Men's Miller Lite 1990 Arizona Open was won by the team Sinjin Smith and Randy Stoklos. The winner's split $13,200.00, while the second place team shared $8,400.00. Smith and Stoklos defeated Karch Kiraly and Kent Steffes in the championship match.

3rd Place: Wally Goodrick and Ricci Luyties
4th Place: Mike Dodd and Tim Hovland
5th Place: Scott Ayakatubby and Brent Frohoff
5th Place: John Hanley and Dan Vrebalovich

JOHN HANLEY
John Hanley stepped-up for a championship victory with Dan Vrebalovich at the 1990 AVP event in Fort Myers Florida. In the photo above, Hanley cuts the ball past the block of Rudy Dvorak.
Photo Courtesy of the AVP

DAN VREBALOVICH
Dan Vrebalovich paired-up with John Hanley to start the 1990 AVP season with a championship win at the 1990 Fort Myers event. Above photo, "Vrb" pokes the ball past the block of Tim Hovland.
Photo Courtesy of the AVP

HOUSTON TEXAS
April 14th-15th, 1990

The AVP Pro-Beach Volleyball Tour was in Houston Texas, where Mike Dodd and Tim Hovland were the winner's of this $60,000.00 AVP Miller Lite "Special Olympics" Open. Their share for winning was $13,200.00. In the championship match, they easily defeated Sinjin Smith and Randy Stoklos 15-3 to win the title.

3rd Place: Karch Kiraly and Kent Steffes
4th Place: Scott Ayakatubby and Brent Frohoff
5th Place: Wally Goodrick and Ricci Luyties
5th Place: Scott Friederichsen and Larry Mear

NEW ORLEANS LOUISIANA
April 21st-22nd, 1990

The $60,000.00 Men's Miller Lite 1990 New Orleans Open was won by the team of Karch Kiraly and Kent Steffes. The winner's split $13,200.00, while the second place team shared $8,400.00. In the championship match, Kiraly and Steffes defeated John Hanley and Dan Vrebalovich 15-8.

3rd Place: Sinjin Smith and Randy Stoklos
4th Place: Wally Goodrick and Ricci Luyties
5th Place: Tim Hovland and Mike Dodd
5th Place: Scott Friederichsen and Larry Mear

FORT WORTH/DALLAS TEXAS
April 28th-29th, 1990

The $60,000.00 Men's Miller Lite 1990 Fort Worth Open was won by the team of Scott Ayakatubby and Brent Frohoff. The winner's split $13,200.00, while the second place team shared $8,400.00. In the championship match, Ayakatubby and Frohoff outlasted Mike Dodd and Tim Hovland.

3rd Place: Karch Kiraly and Kent Steffes
4th Place: Wally Goodrick and Ricci Luyties
5th Place: Andrew Smith and Dan Vrebalovich
5th Place: John Eddo and Craig Moothart

CLEARWATER BEACH FLORIDA
May 5th-6th, 1990

The $100,000.00 Jose Cuervo Gold Crown event, in Clearwater Florida, was won by the winningest team on pro beach volleyball history. Sinjin Smith and Randy Stoklos won the biggest prize of their career, when they shared a record first place check in the amount of $50,000.00. In the championship final, they defeated Scott Ayakatubby and Brent Frohoff by a score of 15-5. The runner-ups split $10,300.00.

3rd Place: John Hanley and Ricci Luyties
4th Place: Karch Kiraly and Kent Steffes
5th Place: Scott Friederichsen and Larry Mear

MIKE DODD & TIM HOVLAND
During the early part of the 1990 AVP season, Mike Dodd (left) and Tim Hovland (right) were happy, winning the AVP event in Houston Texas.
Photo Courtesy of the AVP

SINJIN SMITH & RANDY STOKLOS
Sinjin Smith and Randy Stoklos were "As-One" during the entire 1990 AVP season, winning 11 tournament championships. Above photo, Smith (left) and Stoklos (right) celebrate a win.
Photo Courtesy of the AVP

SACRAMENTO CALIFORNIA
May 12th-13th, 1990

The $60,000.00 Men's Miller Lite 1990 Sacramento Open was won by the team of Sinjin Smith and Randy Stoklos. The winner's split $13,200.00, while the second place team shared $8,400.00. In the championship match, Smith and Stoklos came back from an 11-7 deficit to defeat Karch Kiraly and Kent Steffes 15-11.

3rd Place: Mike Dodd and Tim Hovland
4th Place: Roger Clark and Andrew Smith
5th Place: John Eddo and Craig Moothart
5th Place: John Hanley and Dan Vrebalovich

FRESNO CALIFORNIA
May 19th-20th, 1990

The $60,000.00 Men's Miller Lite 1990 Fresno "Beach" Open was won by the team of Mike Dodd and Tim Hovland. The winner's split $13,200.00, while the second place team shared $8,400.00. Fresno provided a $500,000.00 volleyball stadium, with aid from a parks grant, for this event. The stadium was the first of its kind, a unique grassy arena that enclosed the championship court and rivaled something out of the movie "Field of Dreams." In the championship match, 15,000 fans packed around center court as Hovland and Dodd defeated Sinjin Smith and Randy Stoklos, 15-13 and 7-1 in the double final.

3rd Place: Karch Kiraly and Kent Steffes
4th Place: John Hanley and Dan Vrebalovich
5th Place: Pat Powers and Jon Stevenson
5th Place: Scott Friederichsen and Larry Mear

VENICE CALIFORNIA
May 26th-27th, 1990

The $75,000.00 Men's Miller Lite 1990 Venice Beach Open was won by the team of Karch Kiraly and Brent Frohoff. This was the 1990 AVP Pro Beach Volleyball Tour's first Southern California stop. In the championship final, in front of a crowd of about 15,000, Kiraly and Frohoff easily defeated Sinjin Smith and Randy Stoklos by a score of 15-2.

3rd Place: Mike Dodd and Tim Hovland
4th Place: Andrew Smith and Kent Steffes
5th Place: Pat Powers and Jon Stevenson
5th Place: John Hanley and Dan Vrebalovich

SAN JOSE CALIFORNIA
June 2nd-3rd, 1990

The $75,000.00 Men's Miller Lite 1990 San Jose Open was won by the team of Kent Steffes and Dan Vrebalovich. In the championship match, in front of a surprised crowd, Steffes and Vrebalovich bitterly out-battled Karch Kiraly and Brent Frohoff, in a double final, as they pulled out a 15-10 and 7-3 triumph, winning the title and the $16,500.00 first prize. Kiraly and Frohoff shared $10,500.00.

3rd Place: Sinjin Smith and Randy Stoklos
4th Place: Mike Dodd and Tim Hovland
5th Place: Scott Ayakatubby and John Hanley
5th Place: Larry Mear and Scott Friederichsen

BRENT FROHOFF & SCOTT AYAKATUBBY
Brent Frohoff and Scott Ayakatubby stepped-up for a championship victory at the 1990 Dallas-Fort Worth AVP event. Above photo, "Ack" passes the ball to "Fro" during a 1990 AVP event.
Photo Courtesy of the AVP

KENT STEFFES & KARCH KIRALY
Kent Steffes and Karch Kiraly teamed-up for an AVP chamionship at the 1990 Fort Lauderdale event. Above photo, Kiraly passes the ball to Steffes during an AVP event.
Photo Courtesy of Frank Goroszko

BOULDER COLORADO
June 8th-9th, 1990

In Boulder Colorado, the AVP's $125,000.00 Jose Cuervo Gold Crown Series was won by Sinjin Smith and Randy Stoklos. They shared the $60,000.00 pot for first place, in this eight team event. In the championship match, Smith and Stoklos out-pointed Karch Kiraly and Brent Frohoff, by a score of 15-6. Kiraly and Frohoff split $12,000.00 for their second place finish.

3rd Place: Mike Dodd and Tim Hovland
4th Place: Wally Goodrick and Ricci Luyties
5th Place: Scott Friederichsen and Larry Mear

INDIANAPOLIS INDIANA
June 16th-17th, 1990

The AVP Pro-Beach Volleyball Tour went to Indianapolis, Indiana, for the $60,000.00 Men's Miller Lite Indianapolis Open. The winner's of the tournament were Sinjin Smith and Randy Stoklos. In the championship match, Smith and Stoklos defeated Karch Kiraly and Brent Frohoff 15-11. The winners split $13,200.00.

3rd Place: Mike Dodd and Tim Hovland
4th Place: Kent Steffes and Dan Vrebalovich
5th Place: Steve Timmons and Adam Johnson
5th Place: Scott Friederichsen and Larry Mear

CAPE COD MASSACHUSETTS
June 23rd-24th, 1990

The AVP Pro-Beach Volleyball Tour went to Cape Cod Massachusetts, for the $60,000.00 Men's Miller Lite Cape Cod Open on West Dennis Beach. Karch Kiraly and Brent Frohoff won the tournament and first place money of $13,200.00. In the championship match, they defeated Scott Ayakatubby and Tim Hovland, after Ayakatubby spent all of his energy winning the loser's bracket final 15-8 over Sinjin Smith and Randy Stoklos.

3rd Place: Sinjin Smith and Randy Stoklos
4th Place: Andrew Smith and Pat Powers
5th Place: Kent Steffes and Dan Vrebalovich
5th Place: Mike Whitmarsh and Jeff Rogers

MANHATTAN BEACH CALIFORNIA
June 30th-July 1st, 1990

The AVP Pro-Beach Volleyball Tour's 1990 Manhattan Beach Open was won by Karch Kiraly and Brent Frohoff. They split the $13,200.00 first place money. In the championship match, of the $60,000.00 Off Shore Manhattan Open, Kiraly and Frohoff were down 5-10, to the top seeded team of Sinjin Smith and Randy Stoklos, before they were able to tie the match at 11-all. At 10-11, Kiraly got his team even when he faked Stoklos to one side, and dropped a shot into the open court. Kiraly and Frohoff went on to win by a score of 15-13.

3rd Place: Tim Hovland and Mike Dodd
4th Place: Al Janc and Tim Walmer
5th Place: Kent Steffes and Dan Vrebalovich
5th Place: Scott Friederichsen and Larry Mear

SINJIN SMITH
Sinjin Smith won eleven tournament championships, in 1990, with partner Randy Stoklos. Above photo, Smith hits the ball into the block of Brent Frohoff during the 1990 Manhattan Beach Men's Open.
Photo Courtesy of Frank Goroszko

KENT STEFFES
Kent Steffes was successful with several different partners on the 1990 AVP Tour, winning five tournament championships. Above photo, Steffes hits the ball past the block of Wally Goodrick during the 1990 AVP event staged in Fresno California.
Photo Courtesy of Frank Goroszko

LAGUNA BEACH CALIFORNIA
June 30th-July 1st, 1990

The 1990 Laguna Beach Men's Open was the 36th annual staging of the event. The tournament was played the same weekend that the top 32 AVP teams were required to participate in the Manhattan Beach Open. The other 250 or so AVP members were eligible to play in the Laguna Beach Open. The event was won by Pete Aroncheck and Mike Boehle. The winner's split the $13,300.00 first place prize. In the championship match, they defeated the top seeded team of Shawn Davis and Mike Whitmarsh, by a score of 15-12. Aroncheck also won last years Laguna Open with Mark Eller.

3rd Place: Andy Fishburn and Dane Selznick

GRAND HAVEN MICHIGAN
July 7th-8th, 1990

The AVP Pro-Beach Volleyball Tour was in Grand Haven Michigan for the $60,000.00 Men's Miller Lite Michigan Open. In the sudden-death championship final, Kiraly and Frohoff defeated Tim Hovland and Mike Dodd, 7-3, and split the $13,200.00 top prize. Earlier in the tournament, Kiraly and Frohoff had also defeated Dodd and Hovland in the semifinals.

3rd Place: Sinjin Smith and Randy Stoklos
4th Place: Scott Friederichsen and Larry Mear
5th Place: Scott Ayakatubby and Ricci Luyties
5th Place: Kent Steffes and Dan Vrebalovich

MILWAUKEE WISCONSIN
July 14th-15th, 1990

The AVP Pro-Beach Volleyball Tour, went to Bradford Beach, in Milwaukee Wisconsin, for the $75,000.00 Miller Lite Men's Milwaukee Open. Top seeded Sinjin Smith and Randy Stoklos were the winners of the $16,500.00 first place money. In the championship match, Smith and Stoklos defeated second seeded Karch Kiraly and Brent Frohoff. The runner-ups earned $10,500.00 for their efforts.

3rd Place: Steve Timmons and Adam Johnson
4th Place: John Eddo and Sean Fallowfield
5th Place: Scott Ayakatubby and Ricci Luyties
5th Place: Pat Powers and Andrew Smith

CLEVELAND OHIO
July 21st-22nd, 1990

The $60,000.00 Men's Miller Lite 1990 Cleveland Open was won by the team of Tim Hovland and Kent Steffes. The winner's split $13,200.00, while the second place team shared $8,400.00. In the championship match, Hovland and Steffes defeated Sinjin Smith and Randy Stoklos.

3rd Place: Mike Dodd and Dan Vrebalovich
4th Place: John Hanley and Ricci Luyties
5th Place: Pat Powers and Andrew Smith
5th Place: Scott Ayakatubby and Brent Frohoff

JON STEVENSON
Jon Stevenson had six top five finishes on the 1990 AVP Tour. Above photo, Stevenson hits a set from Ricci Luyties, past the block of John Hanley.
Photo Courtesy of the AVP

RICCI LUYTIES
During the 1990 AVP season, Ricci Luyties finished within the top-five on ten occasion. Above photo, Luyties hits the ball into the block of Al Janc.
Photo Courtesy of the AVP

CHICAGO ILLINOIS
July 28th-29th, 1990

The $75,000.00 Men's Miller Lite 1990 Chicago Open was won by the team of Sinjin Smith and Randy Stoklos. The winners split $15,400.00 for their efforts. In the championship match, Smith and Stoklos defeated Tim Hovland and Kent Steffes. The runner-ups split $9,800.00.

3rd Place: Karch Kiraly and Brent Frohoff
4th Place: Wally Goodrick and Craig Moothart
5th Place: Pat Powers and Roger Clark
5th Place: Brian Lewis and Owen McKibben

SEAL BEACH CALIFORNIA
August 4th-5th, 1990

The AVP Pro-Beach Volleyball Tour went to Seal Beach California, for the $100,000.00 Men's Miller Lite Orange County Open. This was the twenty-first stop of the AVP's 1990 Pro-Beach Volleyball Tour. Gusty winds played havoc during play, but Sinjin Smith and Randy Stoklos were able to control the ball as well as the matches. They were the winner's of the $21,000.00 first place check. In the championship match, Smith and Stoklos defeated the new team of Mike Dodd and Brent Frohoff, by a score of 15-6. Dodd and Frohoff split $13,000.00 for their second place finish.

3rd Place: Jon Stevenson and Mike Whitmarsh
4th Place: Andrew Smith and Dan Vrebalovich
5th Place: Rudy Dvorak and Bruk Vandeweghe
5th Place: Leif Hanson and Eric Wurts

SAN DIEGO CALIFORNIA
August 10th-11th, 1990

Sinjin Smith and Randy Stoklos were the winners at the 1990 AVP Pro-Beach Volleyball $150,000.00 "Jose Cuervo Gold Crown" event in San Diego. By winning the event, Smith and Stoklos became the first team in history to win all three Gold Crown events in one season. The pair collected the winner's check in the amount of $70,000.00, while the second place team split $15,000.00. In the championship match, in front of about 8,000 spectators on Mariner's Point, they defeated Tim Hovland and Kent Steffes, by a score of 15-6. Smith and Stoklos started the match strong. They went out to a 9-0 lead as Smith scored time and again with a towering "Skyball" serve.

3rd Place: Karch Kiraly and Brent Frohoff
4th Place: Adam Johnson and Steve Timmons
5th Place: Bob Ctvrtlik and Mike Dodd

SEATTLE WASHINGTON
August 18th-19th, 1990

The AVP made its next tour stop in Seattle, Washington, where Karch Kiraly and Brent Frohoff won the $60,000.00 Men's Miller Lite Seattle "Seafair" Open. They shared their $13,200.00 portion of the purse. In the championship match, Kiraly and Frohoff overcame Kent Steffes and Tim Hovland by a score of 15-9.

3rd Place: Sinjin Smith and Randy Stoklos
4th Place: John Eddo and Sean Fallowfield
5th Place: Rudy Dvorak and Bruk Vandeweghe
5th Place: Pat Powers and Adam Johnson

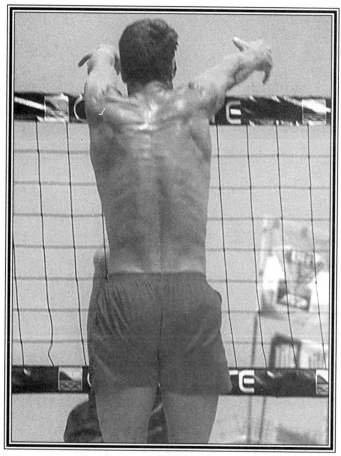

PAT POWERS
During the 1990 AVP Tour, Pat "PP" Powers was a huge force to contend with, especially at the net! Above photo, "PP" covers the "Air-Space" with his formidable block.
Photo Courtesy of the AVP

KARCH KIRALY & BRENT FROHOFF
Karch Kiraly and Brent Frohoff teamed-up for six AVP Tour championships together in 1990. Above photo, Frohoff (right) gets ready to pass the ball to Kiraly (left).
Photo Courtesy of Frank Goroszko

HERMOSA BEACH CALIFORNIA
August 24th-26th, 1990

The AVP went to Hermosa Beach California for the $200,000.00 Miller Lite Men's U.S. Championship. The big winner's were Sinjin Smith and Randy Stoklos, collecting the first place prize of $41,000.00, along with their eleventh title of the season. The $200,000.00 purse was the richest in the history of the tournament. (Note: The first world championship of beach volleyball in 1976 on State Beach in Santa Monica was only worth $5,000.00). In the championship match, in front of over 25,000 spectators, Smith and Stoklos outlasted the team of Karch Kiraly and Brent Frohoff, by a score of 15-11. The match was filled with excitement as Stoklos utilized power and finesse, while Smith utilized his "Skyball" serve for several points including match point. The vast majority of the crowd were pulling for Kiraly and Frohoff, the popular local. Smith and Stoklos won the title, but between play, they were taunted with a barrage of heckling, such as "Sinjin who?" and "locals only" along with chants of "Randolph Piermont Stoklos" directed at Randy. At times Sinjin lost his cool, with several outburst directed to the crowd, and at one point he walked to the sidelines pointing his finger and shouted at hecklers. Of course when he did this the crowd booed every move that he made, while cheering every point and side-out for Frohoff and Kiraly.

Earlier, Kiraly and Frohoff outlasted Steve Timmons and Adam Johnson, in a semifinal match that pitted two Olympic gold medalist (Kiraly and Timmons), on opposite sides. Johnson and Timmons took an early lead at 12-8, but Kiraly and Frohoff came back to win 15-13, after scoring the last five points.

3rd Place: Steve Timmons and Adam Johnson
4th Place: Andrew Smith and John Hanley
5th Place: Mike Dodd and Pat Powers
5th Place: Tim Hovland and Kent Steffes

SANTA MONICA CALIFORNIA
September 29th-30th, 1990

The AVP Pro-Beach Volleyball Tour was in Santa Monica for the $60,000.00 "Hard Rock Café Challenge Cup." Kent Steffes and Tim Hovland were the winner's. In the championship match, Steffes and Hovland defeated the team of Karch Kiraly and Brent Frohoff. The winners split a check for $20,000.00, while the runner-ups shared $9,000.00.

3rd Place: Wally Goodrick and Ricci Luyties
3rd Place: Mike Dodd and John Hanley
5th Place: Adam Johnson and Craig Moothart
5th Place: Scott Ayakatubby and Jon Stevenson
5th Place: Rudy Dvorak and Bruk Vandeweghe
5th Place: Al Janc and Tim Walmer

RICCI LUYTIES & WALLY GOODRICK
Ricci Luyties and Wally Goodrick paried-up for several "top-five" AVP finishes in 1990. Above photo, Luyties passes the ball to Goodrick, during a 1990 AVP Tour event.
Photo Courtesy of the AVP

ADAM JOHNSON
Adam Johnson stepped-up for a third place finish at the 1990 AVP event in Hermosa Beach California. Above photo, Johnson hits the ball during the 1990 AVP Tour event in Hermosa Beach.
Photo Courtesy of Frank Goroszko

MEN'S TOURNAMENT RESULTS
1990-FIVB

RIO DE JANEIRO BRAZIL
February 13th-18th, 1990

The "Beach Volleyball Stadium" at Copacabana Beach in Rio De Janeiro, Brazil was again the site of the $50,000.00 FIVB World Beach Volleyball Championship. The beach grandstands were filled with 15,000 screaming fanatic fans.

There were forty-four teams from 14 different countries that participated, but, It was an- all-U.S.A. final, with Randy Stoklos and Sinjin Smith defeating Tim Hovland and Mike Dodd, 12-10 and 12-3 to snatch the championship. The all American final was created because unlike recent years when the top American teams were put in the same semifinal pools, the top teams were put in separate pools. Stoklos and Smith split the $6,000.00 first place prize money.

3rd Place: Jos Franco Vieira Neto and Roberto Costa Lopes-Brazil
4th Place: Andre Perlingeiro Lima and Luiz Guilherme Marquez-Brazil
5th Place: Eduardo Carlos Garrido Dias-Brazil
5th Place: Atila Pereira and Freitas Clovis-Brazil

BJORN MAASEIDE
Norwegian, Bjorn Maaseide started to show some success on the 1990 FIVB Tour. Above photo, Maaseide shows his passing ability.
Photo Courtesy of the FIVB

STE, FRANCE
July 27th-29th, 1990

Ste, France was the site for the $30,000.00 French FIVB Pro Beach Volleyball tournament. Sixty-three teams from twenty-one countries participated. The Brazilian team of Andre Perlingeiro Lima and Luiz Guilherme Marquez were the winner's. In the championship match, they defeated the U.S.A. team of John Eddo and Sean Fallowfield, to earn the first place check of $7,550.00.

3rd Place: Jose Franco Vieira Neto and Roberto Costa Lopes-Brazil
4th Place: Christian Penigaud and Jean-Philippe Jodard-France
5th Place: Dionisio Lequaglie and Marco "Sollu" Solustri-Italy
5th Place: Jan Kvalheim and Bjorn Maaseide-Norway
The U.S.A. team of Tom Ribarich and Todd Arisson finished in 11th place.

LIGNANO, ITALY
August 1st-5th, 1990

Lignano, Italy was the site of this $50,000.00 FIVB Pro Beach Volleyball event. Sixty-three teams from twenty-one countries participated, but it was an all U.S.A. final, with the team of Tim Hovland and Kent Steffes winning 12-3 and 12-8 over John Eddo and Sean Fallowfield, to capture the championship prize of $12,000.00.

3rd Place: Carlos Eduardo Garrido Dias and Roberto Durate Dias-Brazil
4th Place: Dionisto Dio Lequaglie and Marco Solustri-Italy
5th Place: Jos Franco Vieira Neto and Roberto Costa Lopes-Brazil
5th Place: Emanuele Fracascia and Fabrizio Bastianelli-Italy
Tom Ribarich and Todd Harrison, from the U.S.A., were in the 12th spot.

ENOSHIMA, JAPAN
August 9th-11th, 1990

The FIVB "Pro Beach Volleyball" tour made its next stop in Enoshima Japan where sixty-three teams from twenty-one countries participated. This $50,000.00 event was won by Eric Wurts and Leif Hanson, 15-11 over Al Janc and Tim Walmer, in another all U.S.A. final. Wurts and Hanson each split a check for $6,000.00 along with the victory.

3rd Place: Dionisio Dio Lequaglie and Marco Solustri-Italy
4th Place: Philippe Blain and Alain Fabian-France
5th Place: Jos Franco Vieira Neto and Roberto Costa Lopes-Brazil
5th Place: Eduardo Carlos Garrido Dias and Roberto Durate Dias-Brazil

FIVB CROWDS
By 1990, The FIVB Tour was drawing large crowds as well as some of the best beach volleyball players in the world, to the events. Above photo, a large crowd at an FIVB event in Brazil.
Photo Courtesy of the FIVB

TOP PHOTOS: Left: Andrew Smith hits the ball past the block of Rudy Dvorak. **Center:** Brent Frohoff Hits the ball into the block of Steve Timmons. **Right:** Sinjin Smith hits the ball into the block of Karch Kiraly

MIDDLE PHOTOS: Left: Toa Fonoimoana passing the ball. **Center:** Ricci Luyties hits the ball past the block of Bruk Vandweghe. **Right:** Tim Walmer hits the ball past the block of Ricci Luyties.

1990 MEN'S BEACH VOLLEYBALL ACTION

BOTTOM PHOTOS: Left: Randy Stoklos and Brian Lewis "joust" for control of the ball. **Center:** John Hanley hits the ball into the block of Tim Hovland. **Right:** Karch Kiraly hits the ball past the block of Steve Timmons.

Photo's Courtesy of the AVP

WOMEN'S BEACH VOLLEYBALL
1990

WPVA

The WPVA scheduled 16 events in 1990. They were staged in Phoenix Arizona, Santa Barbara California, San Diego California, Hermosa Beach California, Santa Cruz California, Huntington Beach California, Cleveland Ohio, Honolulu Hawaii, Manhattan Beach California, Tokyo Japan, Pismo Beach California, Redondo Beach California, Laughlin Nevada, Boulder Colorado, Cincinnati Ohio, and one tournament in Mexico. All of the events were televised on ESPN.

In 1990, WPVA president Roxana Vargas promised the best WPVA tour ever. It was the "Flamingo Hilton Women's Pro Beach Volleyball Tour" and there was more prize money, more television exposure, and the first big sponsor, The Flamingo Hilton. The total prize money available on the 1990 WPVA tour was $482,000.00, with a minimum of $25,000.00 per event, a $15,000.00 increase from the previous season. The 1990 World Championship was worth $50,000.00, a $30,000.00 increase from 1989.

Jackie Silva, the 1990 WPVA Tour's top money earner cashed in a total of $47,100.00 along with 10 tournament championships. Karolyn Kirby had arrived on the WPVA Tour, starting the season out with Patti Dodd and finishing with Jackie Silva. Kirby reached the finals of 8 events winning five times. She earned a total of $41,100.00. Janice Opalinski also had a respectable season. She reached 8 finals winning 6 times, earning over $40,000.00 for her efforts.

1990 WPVA PLAYER & MONEY EARNED

1.	Jackie Silva	$47,100
2.	Karolyn Kirby	$41,100
3.	Janice Opalinski	$40,675
4.	Elaine Roque	$31,550
4.	Nina Matthies	$31,550
6.	Linda Carrillo	$27,700
7.	Patty Dodd	$25,950
8.	Lisa Strand	$20,813
9.	Gail Castro	$19,640
9.	Lori Kotas	$19,640
11.	Rita Crockett	$17,950
12.	Linda Hanley	$15,813
13.	Angela Rock	$13,175
14.	Dennie Schupyt-Knoop	$10,424
15.	Gail Stammer	$9,225
16.	Heather Hafner	$9,187
17.	Jeanne Reeves	$7,099
18.	Alison Johnson	$5,662
19.	Kathy Hanley	$5,375
20.	Lori Biller	$5,312
20.	Deb Richardson	$5,312

JACKIE SILVA
Brazilian Jackie Silva was the 1990 WPVA Tour's top money earner, winning a total of $47,100.00 along with 10 tournament championships. In the above photo, Silva makes a diving effort to dig the ball during the 1990 WPVA event in Phoenix Arizona.
Photo Courtesy of Frank Goroszko

INDIVIDUAL WPVA TOURNAMENT FINISHES
1990

Player	1st	2nd	3rd	4th	5th
Linda Chisholm Carrillo	1	2	2	3	1
Gail Castro	0	1	3	1	6
Patty Dodd	1	3	3	2	3
Lori Kotas Forsythe	0	1	4	1	6
Jeanne Goldsmith	0	0	0	0	1
Heather Hafner	0	0	0	1	5
Linda Robertson Hanley	1	2	1	1	0
Janice Opalinski Harrer	6	2	2	2	1
Karolyn Kirby	5	3	3	0	2
Lisa Strand Ma'a	0	0	1	1	4
Nina Grouwinkel Matthies	1	4	1	2	4
Jeanne Reeves	0	0	0	1	1
Nancy Reno	0	0	0	0	1
Angela Rock	0	1	0	3	4
Elaine Roque	1	4	2	2	4
Rita Crockett Royster	0	1	2	3	2
Dennie Schupyt-Knoop	0	0	1	1	3
Jackie Silva	**10**	**2**	**1**	**0**	**1**
Gail Stammer	0	0	0	1	2
Julie Thornton	0	0	0	0	2

WOMEN'S TOURNAMENT RESULTS
1990-WPVA

PHOENIX ARIZONA
May 5th-6th, 1990

First stop of 1990 WPVA Flamingo Hilton Pro Beach Volleyball Season was in Phoenix Arizona. The tournament was won by the team of Jackie Silva and Janice Opalinski. They split the first place prize of $6,000.00. In the championship match, they defeated Patty Dodd and Karolyn Kirby. Silva and Opalinski completed the double elimination tournament without a loss.

3rd Place: Lori Kotas and Gail Castro
4th Place: Linda Carrillo and Angela Rock
5th Place: Heather Hafner and Gayle Stammer
5th Place: Nina Matthies and Elaine Roque

SANTA BARBARA CALIFORNIA
May 12th-13th, 1990

The second stop of the 1990 WPVA Tour was the Santa Barbara Women's Open. The event was dedicated to Judy Bellomo, the rising beach star and former UC Santa Barbara standout who died during surgery at age 23. The tournament was won by the team of Jackie Silva and Janice Opalinski. For the second week in a row, Silva and Opalinski completed the double elimination tournament without a loss. In the championship match, they outlasted Patty Dodd and Karolyn Kirby by a score of 15-13, the most points that any team has scored on this team. The winner's split the first place prize of $6,000.00.

3rd Place: Lori Kotas and Gail Castro
4th Place: Linda Hanley and Jeanne Reeves
5th Place: Heather Hafner and Gayle Stammer
5th Place: Nina Matthies and Elaine Roque

SAN DIEGO CALIFORNIA
May 19th-20th, 1990

The third stop of the 1990 WPVA Tour was in San Diego for the PCH San Diego Women's Open on Pacific Beach. The event was the second stop of the Hilton Flamingo Women's Pro Beach Volleyball Tour. The event was won by the team of Jackie Silva and Janice Opalinski. The winner's were happy to split the $6,000.00 first place check. In the championship match, after falling behind 10-4 and 14-9, Silva and Opalinski outlasted Elaine Roque and Nina Matthies 16-14, forcing a tiebreaker which they won 7-1. Matthies and Roque had served for the match and the $6,000.00 first place prize money five times before they lost the first game.

3rd Place: Patty Dodd and Karolyn Kirby
4th Place: Linda Carrillo and Angela Rock
5th Place: Dennie Knoop and Jeanne Goldsmith
5th Place: Julie Thornton and Lisa Strand Ma'a

HERMOSA BEACH CALIFORNIA
June 2nd-3rd, 1990

The WPVA was on the sands of Hermosa Beach California, where in the championship match, Jackie Silva and Janice Opalinski, after going through the loser's bracket, fell behind to the team of Nina Grouwinkel Matthies and Elaine Roque. But, Silva and Opalinski's stubbornness wouldn't allow them to lose as they clawed back to a 16-14 triumph and then they won the tie-breaker to earn the $6,000.00 first place prize.

3rd Place: Patty Dodd and Karolyn Kirby
4th Place: Linda Carrillo and Angela Rock
5th Place: Dennie Knoop and Rita Crockett
5th Place: Lori Kotas and Gail Castro

JUDY BELLOMO
The 1990 WPVA Tour event staged in Santa Barbara was dedicated to, Judy Bellomo who at age 23 died during surgery. Above photo, Bellomo is ready for action
Photo Courtesy of Dennis G. Steers

GAIL CASTRO
Gail Castro was the number nine money earner on the 1990 WPVA Tour, earning $19,640. In the photo above, Castro passes the ball.
Photo Courtesy of Frank Goroszko

SANTA CRUZ CALIFORNIA
June 9th-10th, 1990

The $25,000.00 WPVA event at Santa Cruz California was won by Jackie Silva and Janice Opalinski. In the double final, Silva and Opalinski defeated Patty Dodd and Karolyn Kirby 15-11 and 7-5. The winner's split another $6,000.00 check.

3rd Place: Nina Grouwinkel Matthies and Elaine Roque
4th Place: Dennie Knoop and Rita Crockett
5th Place: Gail Castro and Lori Forsythe
5th Place: Linda Carrillo and Angela Rock

HUNTINGTON BEACH CALIFORNIA
June 16th-17th, 1990

The 1990 Women's $25,000.00 Huntington Beach Women's Open, next to the Pier, was won by the team of Patty Dodd and Karolyn Kirby. In the championship match, second seeded Dodd and Kirby had no trouble upsetting top-seeded Jackie Silva and Janice Opalinski, 15-6. This was the first career title for Kirby. Dodd and Kirby split the $6,000.00 first place prize, while the runner-ups split $4,500.00.

3rd Place: Linda Carrillo and Linda Hanley
4th Place: Nina Grouwinkel Matthies and Elaine Roque
5th Place: Angela Rock and Julie Thornton
5th Place: Lori Kotas and Gail Castro

FRESNO CALIFORNIA
June 24th-25th, 1990

The next 1990 WPVA event was the "Flamingo Hilton Women's Open" in Fresno California. The team of Linda Hanley and Linda Carrillo moved-up for a tournament win and first place prize of $6,000.00. In the championship match, they defeated Jackie Silva and Janice Opalinski.

3rd Place: Dennie Knoop and Rita Crockett
4th Place: Lori Kotas and Gail Castro
5th Place: Patty Dodd and Karolyn Kirby
5th Place: Nina Matthies and Elaine Roque

LAGUNA BEACH CALIFORNIA
June 30th-July 1st, 1990

On Main Beach, the 1990 Laguna Beach Women's Open was won by the new team of Jackie Silva and Karolyn Kirby. In the championship match, after only six days of playing together, Silva and Kirby, the top seeds, outlasted the sixth-seeded team of Linda Hanley and Linda Chisholm-Carrillo by a score of 15-11. The winner's split $13,300.00, while the runner-ups split 6,300.00.

3rd Place: Lisa Strand Ma'a and Janice Opalinski Harrer
4th Place: Nina Matthies and Elaine Roque
5th Place: Gail Castro and Lori Forsythe
5th Place: Rita Crockett Royster and Dennie Shupryt Knoop

KAROLYN KIRBY
Karolyn Kirby was the number two money earner on the 1990 WPVA Tour, earning $41,100.00 along with her five WPVA Tour championships. In the photo above, Kirby hits the ball past the block of her opponent.
Photo Courtesy of Frank Goroszko

JANICE OPALINSKI
Janice Opalinski was the number three money earner on the 1990 WPVA Tour, earning $40,675.00 along with her six WPVA Tour championships. In the photo above, Opalinski hits the ball past the block of Gail Castro.
Photo Courtesy of Frank Goroszko

HONOLULU HAWAII
July 7th-8th, 1990
On the beach at the Hilton Hotel, in Honolulu, Hawaii, Karolyn Kirby and Jackie Silva defeated Linda Chisholm and Linda Hanley 15-9, to win the championship match of this $25,000.00 WPVA Tour event.
3rd Place: Nina Matthies and Elaine Roque
4th Place: Janice Harrer and Lisa Strand-Ma'a
5th Place: Lori Kotas and Gail Castro
5th Place: Patty Dodd and Jeanne Reeves

TOKYO JAPAN
July 29th, 1990
In Tokyo Japan, Janice Opalinski and Lisa Strand defeated Nina Matthies and Elaine Roque to win the WPVA "Salem Fresh Open".
3rd Place: Patty Dodd and Rita Crockett
4th Place: Heather Hafner and Gayle Stammer
5th Place: Jackie Silva and Karolyn Kirby

PISMO BEACH, CALIFORNIA
August 4th-5th, 1990
Jackie Silva and Karolyn Kirby defeated Nina Matthies and Elaine Roque to win the WPVA "Club Sportswear California Classic" at Pismo Beach, California.
3rd Place: Lori Kotas Forsythe and Gail Castro
4th Place: Patty Dodd and Rita Crockett
5th Place: Janice Harrer and Lisa Strand Ma'a
5th Place: Nancy Reno and Angela Rock

VENICE BEACH CALIFORNIA
August 12th-11th, 1990
The $30,000.00 Coors Light U.S. Women's Open at Venice Beach was the twelfth stop on the 16-city $500,000.00 Flamingo Hilton Women's Pro Beach Volleyball Tour. The Team of Jackie Silva and Karolyn Kirby were back in the winner's circle after they defeated Lori Kotas and Gail Castro. In the championship match they won by the score of 15-8 as they, to captured the WPVA "U.S. Championships."
3rd Place: Janice Opalinski and Linda Chisholm Carrillo
4th Place: Patty Dodd and Rita Crockett
5th Place: Nina Matthies and Elaine Roque
5th Place: Lisa Strand Ma'a and Angela Rock

LAUGHLIN NEVADA
August 17th-19th, 1990
The 1990 $50,000.00 WPVA "World Championships," in Laughlin Nevada, was won by the team of Nina Matthies and Elaine Roque. In the championship match, Matthies and Roque defeated Angela Rock and Rita Crockett.
3rd Place: Jackie Silva and Karolyn Kirby
4th Place: Janice Opalinski and Linda Carrillo
5th Place: Patty Dodd and Lisa Strand Ma'a
5th Place: Gail Castro and Lori Forsythe

ANGELA ROCK
Angela Rock was able to earn $13,175.00 on the 1990 WPVA Tour, putting her in the thirteenth spot. In the photo above, Rock gets up high with her jump-serve.
Photo Courtesy of Frank Goroszko

PATTY DODD
Patty Dodd was able to earn $25,950.00 on the 1990 WPVA Tour, putting her in the seventh spot. In the photo above, Dodd gets up high to spike the ball over Jackie Silva.
Photo Courtesy of Frank Goroszko

TOP PHOTOS: Left: Karolyn Kirby jump-serving. **Center:** Lisa Strand Ma'a gives a big effort for the spike. **Right:** Jackie Silva hits a set from Janice Opalinski, away from the block of Patty Dodd.

MIDDLE PHOTOS: Left: Rita Crockett reaches high to make the block. **Center:** Dennie Schupyt-Knoop reaches over the net to make the block. **Right:** Gail Stammer reaches high to make a cut-shot.

1990 WOMEN'S BEACH VOLLEYBALL ACTION

BOTTOM PHOTOS: Left: Linda Hanley reaches for the tree-tops for a jump-serve. **Center:** Deb Richardson pokes the ball over the block of Linda Hanley. **Right:** Elaine Roque gets down low to make a dig.

Top and Middle Photo's Courtesy of Frank Goroszko. Bottom Photo's courtesy of the AVP

ADDITIONAL VOLLEYBALL INFORMATION
1990

ADDITIONAL "PRO" BEACH TOURNAMENTS

By the 1990's, in addition to the AVP, there were numerous "Pro" beach Volleyball tournaments taking place. These tournaments were not only being staged all across the U.S.A. by the EVA: Eastern Volleyball Association's tour but also in several other countries as well. Australia and Brazil were the countries leading the way outside of the U.S.A. Japan had even staged some tournaments on sand courts that they built on top of buildings.

During this same time frame, some of the top players on the EVA tour included: Manny Agant, Mark Christensen, Frank Hall, Richmond Hall, Andy Butler, Carter Hall, Rick Wood, Kyle West, Henery Daufeldt, Bob Bull, Kirk Mason, Jon Anderson, Dave Morehouse, Matt Sonnichsen, Jim Nichols, Steve Byrd, Paul Ortiz, Andrew Cavanaugh, Glen Brooks, Drake Dvorak, Chris Hannemann, Greg Hatch, Mike Barszcz, Pono Ma'a, Eric Boyles, Kenny Haan, Rick Branson, Christian Dietiker, Doug Diley, Jay Rourke, Kevin Sweat, etc.

EASTERN VBA
BEACH 'n' SPORT SPRING BREAK
Clearwater, Florida

1. Frank Hall and Richmond Hall
2. Jon Anderson and Dave Morehouse
3. Manny Agant and Matt Sonnichsen
4. Jim Nichols and Steve Byrd
5. Paul Ortiz and Andrew Cavanaugh
6. Glen Brooks and Mark Christensen
7. Drake Dvorak and Chris Hannemann
8. Gregg Hatch and Mike Barszcz
9. Pono Ma'a and Eric Boyles
10. Kenny Hann and Rick Branson
11. Christian Dietiker and Doug Dilley
12. Jay Rourke and Kevin Sweat

NESCAFE/PVBA INTERNATIONAL
Hamilton Head

1. Tim Walmer and Dan Vrebalovich
2. Chris Hannemann and Mike Stafford
3. Chris Cochrane and Hadley Carpenter
4. Rande Turner and Mike Whitmarsh
5. John Sneddon and Andrew Sneddon
6. Rod Kinross and Matt Donohoe
7. Stuart Jamesen and Robert Keating
8. Paul Calder and Fulvio DiPrinzio

AUSTRALIAN BEACH VOLLEYBALL

During this same 1990 time frame, some of the top players on the Australian Men's Circuit included: Rod Kinross, Matt Donohoe, Paul Calder, Fulvio DiPrinzio, John Sneddon, Andrew Sneddon, Paul Raudkepp, Andrew Lyell, Rob Wilson, Marty Daly, Don Stazic, Peter Hogan, Rod Pruks, Ron DeJongh, Steve Hansen, Stuart Jamensen, Paul Mounter, and many more.

Also in 1990, some of the top players on the Australian Women's Circuit included: Marino Taylor, Sue Carroll, Jane Howard, Julie-Anne McMahon, Melanie Marshall, Ginny Marshall, Julie-Anne Short, Tara Payne, Jenny Atkinson, Joelle Morin, Allison Cox, Julia Cox, Carla Kinross, Sonja Zollman, Davina Park, Colleen Wald, and many more talented players.

AUSTRALIA

The 1990 Australian Open "Pro" Beach Volleyball event was won by the U.S.A. team of Tim Walmer and Dan Vrebalovich.

AROUND THE WORLD

In 1990, the World League of Volleyball was created. Although this league was created for the promotion of indoor volleyball, it helped develop some of the great beach volleyball players.

CHINA

The 1990 Women's World Indoor Volleyball Championship was played in China. In the championship match, the Soviet Union won the gold medal when they defeated the team representing China. The U.S.A. finished in third place.

PONO MA'A
Some of the AVP Tour players also participated on the Eastern Volleyball Association's Tour. Pono Ma'a entered events on both tours. In the photo above, Ma'a hits the ball past the block of Ricci Luyties during an AVP event.
Photo Courtesy of the AVP

HOLYOKE MASSACHUSETTS

October 25, 1990, the fifth Volleyball Hall of Fame induction took place in Holyoke, Massachusetts. Burt DeGroot, Al Fish, and Mary Jo Peppler were enshrined during the noon ceremony at "VBHF." USVBA became the newest member of "VBHF Court of Honor."

SANTA CRUZ CALIFORNIA

In the 1990's, there was a group of talented players in Northern California, at Cowells Beach in Santa Cruz. The group included:

Mark Anderson	Eric Anderson
Nate Brown	Sean Delapp
Gary Gysin	Kent Kitchel
Mike Morgan	Kjell Neillsen
Ernie Sandidge	Russ Tanner
Mark Tanner	Tate Wathall
Dave Werdmuller	

SAN CLEMENTE CALIFORNIA
September 15th-16th, 1990

On San Clemente Beach, the 14th stop on the sixth annual Jose Cuervo Beach Volleyball Series found a pair of first-time finalist vying for the men's open title. Eddie Carrillo and Dan Vorkink scored the last four points for a 15-11 victory over Kraig Karnazes and Dave Yoder. Beth Engman and Hilary Johnson won the women's division. In the championship match, Engman and Johnson out-pointed DeeDee Greatorex and Chris Porsch, by a score of 15-8.

MIXED-DOUBLE'S TOURNAMENT RESULTS
OCEAN BEACH CALIFORNIA
June 9th, 1990

The 1990 Ocean Beach Mixed Open was won by the team of Butch Miali and Liz Masakayan. In the championship match, they defeated Scott Bailey and Linda Johnson. Third place went to Mark Knudson and Samantha Shaver. Doug Stone and Theresa Butler were in fourth place. Tournament director George Stepanof said that there were only 18 teams entered because of bad weather.

MANHATTAN BEACH CALIFORNIA
August 11th-12th, 1990

Under sun filled skies, the 1990 Bacardi Breezer Marine Street Mixed-Double's Open was won by Doug Foust and Keri Pier. In the championship match, they defeated Dan Slayer and Marie Slayer 15-10. Third place went to Steve Napolitano and Lisa Arce along with John Brajevic and Christina Gage. The four-way fifth place tie went to Ty Lum and Piper Hahn, Paul Cuevas and Lisa Mariotti, Rick Shaw and Danica Djujich along with Mike Doll and Kathy Parucha. There were 31 teams entered in this tournament. Tournament director Mike Cook said that they used "pool-play" on Saturday and single elimination on Sunday. This accounts for the tie in third place and a four-way tie in the fifth spot.

MARY JO PEPPLER
In 1990, Mary Jo Peppler was inducted into the Volleyball Hall Of Fame. Peppler was a top player on both the beach as well as indoors. In the photo above, Peppler gets low to play some defense during a 1970 indoor match.
Photo Courtesy of Holyoke Volleyball Hall of Fame

DOUG FOUST
Doug Foust teamed-up with Keri Pier to win the 1990 Bacardi Breezer Marine Street Mixed-Doubles event in Manhattan Beach CA. In the championship match, they defeated Dan and Marie Sayler by the score of 15-10. Above photo, Foust passing the ball.
Photo Courtesy of the AVP

MEN'S BEACH VOLLEYBALL
1991

AVP

In 1991, there were thirty-two recorded "Pro" Beach Volleyball tournaments. Twenty six of these tournaments were staged in the U.S.A. while six were played internationally. Of the twenty-six U.S. tournaments, nine were California events, while five were played in Florida. There were seventeen events staged in twelve states other than Florida and California. The California tournaments were held in Sacramento, Fresno, Santa Cruz, Santa Barbara, Manhattan Beach, Hermosa Beach, Seal Beach, Laguna Beach, and San Diego. The tournaments in Florida were in Fort Myers, Fort Lauderdale, Clearwater, Orlando, and Daytona. The remaining U.S. tournaments were held in Honolulu Hawaii, Phoenix Arizona, Houston and San Antonio Texas, Boulder Colorado, Philadelphia Pennsylvania, Cape Cod Massachusetts, Belmar New Jersey, Grand Haven Michigan, Milwaukee Wisconsin, Cleveland Ohio, and Chicago Illinois. The six international events were held in Yokohama Japan, Cap de Agde France, Catolica Italy, Almeria Spain, Sydney Australia, and Rio de Janeiro Brazil. In addition to these events, the first beach volleyball tournaments in Switzerland were held in Jona and Lausanne.

By winning fourteen tournaments in 1991, Sinjin Smith and Randy Stoklos, once again, outdistanced all other teams on the pro beach volleyball tour. Three of their wins came in California, at the Sacramento, Fresno, and Seal Beach events. They had eight additional U.S. wins, which came in Honolulu Hawaii, Fort Myers and Fort Lauderdale Florida, Phoenix Arizona, Boulder Colorado, Houston Texas, Philadelphia Pennsylvania, and Cape Cod Massachusetts. Smith and Stoklos added three international wins by winning the FIVB events in Sydney Australia, Catolica Italy, and the "World Championships" in Rio de Janeiro Brazil,

Karch Kiraly and Kent Steffes won six tournaments together in 1991. Two of their victories came in California, at Seal Beach and Santa Cruz. Their remaining four wins were obtained in Orlando Florida, Belmar New Jersey, Grand Haven Michigan, and Chicago Illinois. Steffes also won the Clearwater Beach and San Diego Tournaments with Tim Hovland. Kiraly added the "King of the Beach" title in Daytona Beach Florida.

SINJIN SMITH & RANDY STOKLOS

Sinjin Smith and Randy Stoklos were the top team on the 1991 AVP Tour. As a team, they won 11 domestic and 3 international events. In the above photo, in-front of a large crowd, Smith passes the ball to Stoklos.

Photo Courtesy of the AVP

Additional teams that won in 1991 were Andy Klussman and Jeff Williams, winning the Laguna Beach Open together, while Pat Powers won the Santa Barbara event with Adam Johnson. Johnson also won the Milwaukee and Cleveland events with Ricci Luyties. Luyties also won the San Antonio event with Mike Dodd and the U.S. Championships in Hermosa Beach with Brent Frohoff. Lief Hanson and John Eddo won an international event in Cap de Agde France, while Al Janc and Tim Walmer won the event in Yokohama Japan. The French team of Christian Penigaud and Jean-Philippe Jodard won the event in Almeria Spain.

NBC telecast three AVP tournaments, live, to a National audience in 1991. The 1991 AVP tour gave out $2,000,000.00 in prize money, including $500,000.00 in the Grand Prix bonus pool. The 1991 AVP schedule included six new stops: Atlanta Georgia, San Antonio Texas, Philadelphia Pennsylvania, Jersey Shore, New Jersey, and Denver Colorado.

The AVP Tour schedule for 1991: Honolulu Hawaii, Fort Myers Florida, Fort Lauderdale Florida, Phoenix Arizona, San Diego California, Santa Barbara California, Clearwater Florida, Sacramento California, Fresno California, Houston Texas, Arlington Texas, San Antonio Texas, Boulder Colorado, Philadelphia Pennsylvania, Cape Cod Massachusetts, Belmar Beach New Jersey, Manhattan Beach California, Grand Haven Connecticut, Chicago Illinois, Milwaukee Wisconsin, Cleveland Ohio, Santa Cruz California, Seal Beach California, Hermosa Beach California. The AVP also added the "King of the Beach" event to the tour's schedule.

In 1991 Karch teamed-up with Kent Steffes again and they started their incredible saga of victories. In 1991 they won six out of ten tournaments together, when Karch returned from Italy, where he spent the first part of the beach season playing indoor's with Il Messaggero in the Italian professional league.

Old Spice sponsored the "King of the Beach" tournament, which was won by Karch Kiraly. In this tournament each of the invited players were continually changed and paired, in a "player-round-robin" over the weekend. It made for some interesting team combinations. Nintendo released a video game entitled: "King of The Beach."

In October 1991 Jon Stevenson was re-elected as president of the AVP. Kevin Cleary, the first AVP president was planning a comeback on the AVP tour.

KARCH KIRALY
In 1991, after playing indoors, Karch Kiraly was on top of his beach game, winning 7 AVP Tour events. Above photo, Kiraly gives an all-out effort to dig the ball.
Photo Courtesy of Dennis G. Steers

INDIVIDUAL AVP TOURNAMENT FINISHES
1991

Player	1st	2nd	3rd	4th	5th
Scott Ayakatubby	0	4	5	2	5
Eric Boyles	0	0	1	0	0
Roger Clark	0	0	1	0	5
Shawn Davis	0	0	1	0	1
Mike Dodd	1	0	4	6	8
Rudy Dvorak	0	1	0	0	4
John Eddo	0	0	1	0	1
Mark Eller	0	0	1	0	0
Sean Fallowfield	0	0	1	0	0
Scott Friederichsen	0	0	0	0	1
Brent Frohoff	0	4	8	3	3
John Hanley	0	3	1	3	1
Leif Hanson	0	0	0	0	1
Tim Hovland	2	5	8	1	3
Al Janc	0	0	0	1	3
Adam Johnson	4	2	3	6	5
Karch Kiraly	7	2	0	0	2
Brian Lewis	0	0	0	0	4
Ricci Luyties	4	0	0	4	7
Owen McKibben	0	0	1	1	1
Larry Mear	0	0	0	1	1
Craig Moothart	0	0	0	0	5
Pat Powers	1	2	3	5	6
Andrew Smith	0	1	1	1	2
Sinjin Smith	11	5	2	1	3
Kent Steffes	8	7	3	0	3
Jon Stevenson	0	0	0	2	1
Randy Stoklos	11	6	2	1	2
Steve Timmons	0	1	0	0	2
Bruk Vandeweghe	0	2	1	2	1
Dan Vrebalovich	0	0	0	0	2
Tim Walmer	0	0	1	2	2
Wes Welch	0	0	1	1	0
Mike Whitmarsh	0	2	0	4	3
Eric Wurts	0	0	1	0	5

1991 BEACH VOLLEYBALL ACTION

Top Left photo: Brent Frohoff follows through after spiking the ball in front of a large crowd. **Top Right Photo:** Leif Hanson hits the ball past the block of Steve Krai. **Bottom Left Photo:** Scott Ayakatubby pokes the ball over the block of Kent Steffes. **Bottom Right Photo:** Sinjin Smith hits the ball towards the defense of Adam Johnson.

Photos Courtesy of the AVP

FIVB

The 1991 FIVB beach volleyball tour included 6 men's tour sites with the total prize money worth $350,000.00. The six stops included six countries: Yokohama Japan, Cap de Agde France, Catolica Italy, Almeria Spain, Sydney Australia, and Rio de Janeiro Brazil.

The American team of Sinjin Smith and Randy Stoklos entered and won three events. They won the Rio de Janeiro Brazil, Sydney Australia, and the Catolica Italy events. The American team of John Eddo and Leif Hanson won the event staged in Cap de Agde France while another American team, Tim Walmer and Al Janc, won the event held in Yokohama Japan. The French team of of Christian Penigaud and Jean-Philippe Jodard moved up to win the championship match at the $50,000.00 FIVB Pro Beach Volleyball event in Almeria Spain.

INDIVIDUAL FIVB TOURNAMENT FINISHES
1991

Player	1st	2nd	3rd	4th	5th
Marlos de Almeida	0	0	0	0	1
Andy Burdin	0	0	1	0	0
John Child	0	0	0	0	1
Roger Clark	0	0	0	0	1
Eduardo Carlos Garrido Dias	0	0	0	1	0
Roberto Moreira Durate Dias	0	0	0	1	0
Mike Dodd	0	0	0	1	0
Edward "Eddie" Drakich	0	0	0	0	1
John Eddo	1	1	0	0	1
Sean Fallowfield	0	2	0	0	0
Andrea Ghiurghi	0	1	0	0	1
Wally Goodrick	0	0	0	0	1
Leif Hanson	1	1	0	0	1
Tim Hovland	0	1	0	0	0
Al Janc	1	0	0	0	0
Sixto Jimenez	0	0	0	0	1
Jean Philippe Jodard	1	0	0	2	2
Yasunori "Kuma" Kumada	0	0	0	0	1
Jan Kvalheim	0	0	0	0	1
Dionisio Dio Lequaglie	0	1	0	0	1
Lezaburo	0	0	0	0	1
Andre Perlingeiro Lima	0	3	4	0	0
Roberto Costa Lopes	0	0	1	0	1
Bjorn Maaseide	0	0	0	0	1
Luiz Guilherme Marquez	0	3	4	0	0
Benjamin Vicedo Mayor	0	0	0	0	1
Jos Franco Vieira Neto	0	0	1	0	1
Gianni Mascagna	0	0	0	2	0
Christian Penigaud	1	0	0	2	2
Julien Prosser	0	0	1	0	0
Rossard	0	0	0	0	1
Sinjin Smith	**3**	0	0	0	0
Marco "Sollu" Solustri	0	0	0	2	0
Kent Steffes	0	1	0	0	0
Jon Stevenson	0	0	0	1	0
Randy Stoklos	**3**	0	0	0	0
Tulio Teixeira,	0	1	0	0	1
Tim Walmer	1	0	0	0	0

RANDY STOKLOS
In 1991, Randy Stoklos was an imposing figure on both the AVP and the FIVB beach volleyball Tours. Above photo, Stoklos is ready to block anything that comes his way.
Photo Courtesy of the AVP

JEAN PHILIPPE JODARD
Jean Philippe Jodard, from France, teamed-up with countryman Christian Penigaud to win the 1991 FIVB Tour event in Almeria Spain. Above photo, Jodard passing the ball.
Photo Courtesy of the FIVB

MEN'S TOURNAMENT RESULTS
1991-AVP

HONOLULU HAWAII
February 1st -2nd, 1991

The AVP opened the season with the $75,000.00 "Miller Lite" AVP Men's Hawaiian Invitational, in Honolulu Hawaii. Sinjin Smith and Randy Stoklos won this tournament for the seventh time, earning $16,500.00 for their efforts. This was the 115th career championship for Sinjin and the 96th for Stoklos. In the championship match, Smith and Stoklos defeated the 12th seeded team of Bruk Vandeweghe and Rudy Dvorak, 15-4.

3rd Place: Sean Fallowfield and John Eddo
4th Place: Mike Whitmarsh and Jon Stevenson
5th Place: Mike Dodd and Brent Frohoff
5th Place: Tim Hovland and Kent Steffes

FORT MYERS FLORIDA
March 23rd-24th, 1991

Sinjin Smith and Randy Stoklos won at the 1991 Miller Lite AVP $75,000.00 Fort Myers Open, in Fort Myers Florida, to earn the $15,750.00 first place money. In the championship match, they beat Tim Hovland and Kent Steffes, in a re-match. Smith and Stoklos made it to the finals after an exciting win in the winner's bracket final. In that match, they assumed a 10-0 lead over Hovland and Steffes. Hovland then took over as he orchestrated the large crowd to his advantage. Before long, the 10-0 deficit turned into a 13-12 lead. The game then was at 13-all when Steffes missed a scoring opportunity hitting a spike out-of-bounds. Smith and Stoklos seized the momentum shift and closed out the game at 15-13. In the championship re-match, Smith and Stoklos led at 8-4, when Smith hit a ball just wide. He could not believe that he hit the ball out, as he went over to where the ball landed and ripped the lines out of the ground, drawing a red-card. With the score tied at 10-all, Stoklos came-up with some big blocks. He partially blocked a ball that Smith dug and set for the 14th point and then stuffed Hovland for match point. Beach volleyball legend, Jim "Mingo" Menges, at age 40 years, attempted a comeback at this tournament. Menges ended-up in seventeenth place with partner Wes Welch.

3rd Place: Eric Wurts and Roger Clark
4th Place: Mike Dodd and Brent Frohoff
5th Place: Tim Walmer and Al Janc
5th Place: Pat Powers and Adam Johnson

BRENT FROHOFF
Brent Frohoff was a force to contend with, on the 1991 AVP Tour, advancing to the finals of 4 events, finishing second each time. Above photo, Frohoff hits the ball past the block of Tim Hovland.
Photo Courtesy of the AVP

ROGER CLARK
Roger Clark played well, on the 1991 AVP Tour, finishing within the top five at six events. Above photo, Clark cuts the ball past the block of Randy Stoklos.
Photo Courtesy of the AVP

FORT LAUDERDALE FLORIDA
March 30th-31st, 1991

The $65,000.00 Men's Miller Lite Fort Lauderdale Open was won by Sinjin Smith and Randy Stoklos. They earned $13,650.00 along with the victory. The victory was the 99th for Stoklos, while it was Smith's 118th. At this time, Smith was the only player with more than 100 tour titles. In the championship match, Smith and Stoklos won over Tim Hovland and Kent Steffes, by a score of 15-9.

3rd Place: Brent Frohoff and Mike Dodd
4th Place: John Hanley and Bruk Vandeweghe
5th Place: Dan Vrebalovich and Andrew Smith
5th Place: Tim Walmer and Al Janc

PHOENIX ARIZONA
April 6th-7th, 1991

The $75,000.00 Men's Miller Lite Phoenix Open was won by the team of Sinjin Smith and Randy Stoklos. It was their fourth men's pro beach volleyball title of the season. Smith and Stoklos took home $15,750.00 for their efforts. In the championship match, they beat Tim Hovland and Kent Steffes 15-9. This was the 100th career championship for Stoklos. After Hovland got heat exhaustion on the first day of the event, he "threw-up" and was taken into the players tent where he received an IV and was checked by the doctor. He then went out and advanced all the way back to the championship match.

3rd Place: Pat Powers and Adam Johnson
4th Place: Jon Stevenson and Mike Whitmarsh
5th Place: Scott Ayakatubby and Leif Hanson
5th Place: Brent Frohoff and Mike Dodd

SAN DIEGO CALIFORNIA
April 13th-14th, 1991

At the $75,000.00 Men's Miller Lite San Diego Open, Tim Hovland and Kent Steffes finally stepped into the winner's circle at San Diego's Mariner's Point. Second seeded, Hovland and Steffes were the runners-up in the past three tournaments. With their victory they split $15,750.00. In the championship match, Hovland and Steffes fell behind 5-10, to Sinjin Smith and Randy Stoklos, but after three blocks by Steffes and a hard hit by Hovland, the score was tied at 11. Hovland and Steffes then went ahead at 13-12 when the two teams sided-out fifteen time before Smith was blocked by Hovland to bring the score to 14-12. Steffes then made a nice shot for the 15-12 win. Smith and Stoklos were looking for their 100th win together as a team.

3rd Place: Mike Dodd and John Hanley
4th Place: Adam Johnson and Pat Powers
5th Place: Dan Vrebalovich and Ricci Luyties
5th Place: Eric Wurts and Roger Clark

KENT STEFFES
In 1991, Kent Steffes advanced to the finals of 15 AVP events, winning 8 championships. Above photo, Steffes attempts to slice the ball past the block of Randy Stoklos.
Photo Courtesy of the AVP

PAT "PP" POWERS
Pat "PP" Powers advanced to 3 AVP championship matches, in 1991, winning the Santa Barbara event. Above photo, "PP" gets up high for the block attempt of Sinjin Smith's spike.
Photo Courtesy of the AVP

SANTA BARBARA CALIFORNIA
April 20th-21st, 1991

The $65,000.00 Men's Miller-Lite AVP Pro-Beach Volleyball event in Santa Barbara was won by Adam Johnson and Pat Powers. The AVP Tour returned to Santa Barbara for the first time in five years. In the championship match, under dark cloudy skies and heavy winds, Johnson and Powers held on for a 15-11 victory over Sinjin Smith and Randy Stoklos. Johnson and Powers jumped out to a 9-1 lead, then Stoklos and Smith made it close at 13-11, but Johnson served-up a "spader" to make the score 14-11. "AJ" then ended the tournament on a cross-court kill despite two tournament-saving digs by Sinjin during the final furious rally. Johnson and Powers split the first place prize of $13,650.00. This was Johnson's first pro-beach volleyball tournament championship.

3rd Place: Tim Hovland and Kent Steffes
4th Place: Brent Frohoff and Mike Whitmarsh
5th Place: Scott Ayakatubby and Jon Stevenson
5th Place: Roger Clark and Eric Wurts

CLEARWATER FLORIDA
April 26th-27, 1991

The 1991 "Jose Cuervo $100,000.00 Gold Crown," in Clearwater Florida, was won by Tim Hovland and Kent Steffes. In the championship match, they defeated Sinjin Smith and Randy Stoklos to take home the first place prize of $50,000.00. The second place finishers took home $8,900.00 for their efforts.

3rd Place: Scott Ayakatubby and Brent Frohoff
4th Place: Mike Dodd and John Hanley
5th Place: Adam Johnson and Pat Powers
6th Place: Leif Hanson and Andrew Smith

JON STEVENSON
In 1991, Jon Stevenson was elected as President of the AVP. He was also still playing some competitive beach volleyball on the 1991 AVP Tour. Above photo, Stevenson reaches high to spike the ball.
Photo Courtesy of Dennis G. Steers

STEVE TIMMONS
Steve Timmons enjoyed some success on the 1991 AVP Tour, advancing to the championship match of the 1991 Manhattan Beach Open with Scott Ayakatubby. Above photo, Timmons hits the ball past the block of Karch Kiraly during the 1991 MB event.
Photo Courtesy of Frank Goroszko

SACRAMENTO CALIFORNIA
May 4th-5th, 1991

The $65,000.00 Men's Miller Lite Men's AVP Pro-Beach Volleyball event in Sacramento was won by top-seeded Sinjin Smith and Randy Stoklos. The winners split $13,650.00 for their efforts. In the championship match, they defeated Tim Hovland and Kent Steffes. This was the 100th pro beach volleyball tournament title that Smith and Stoklos had won together as a team.

3rd Place: Scott Ayakatubby and Brent Frohoff
4th Place: Adam Johnson and Pat Powers
5th Place: Brian Lewis and Craig Moothart
5th Place: Mike Dodd and Ricci Luyties

FRESNO CALIFORNIA
May 11th-12th, 1991

The $65,000.00 Men's Miller Lite Fresno Open was won by Sinjin Smith and Randy Stoklos. Smith and Stoklos each took home $6,825.00 for their first place effort. In the championship match, they defeated Tim Hovland and Kent Steffes. After falling behind 2-7, they came back with a winning score of 15-11.

3rd Place: Scott Ayakatubby and Brent Frohoff
4th Place: Adam Johnson and Pat Powers
5th Place: Brian Lewis and Craig Moothart
5th Place: Mike Dodd and Ricci Luyties

HOUSTON TEXAS
May 18th-19th, 1991

The $65,000.00 Men's Miller Texas Special Olympics Open was won by Sinjin Smith and Randy Stoklos. Smith and Stoklos each took home $6,825.00 for their first place effort. In the championship match, they defeated Adam Johnson and Pat Powers. Johnson and Powers split $8,450.00 as the runners-up.

3rd Place: Mark Eller and Wes Welch
4th Place: John Hanley and Mike Whitmarsh
5th Place: Roger Clark and Eric Wurts
5th Place: Rudy Dvorak and John Eddo

SAN ANTONIO TEXAS
June 1st-2nd, 1991

The $65,000.00 Men's Miller Lite Saint Mary's Open, in San Antonio Texas, was won by Mike Dodd and Ricci Luyties. Dodd and Luyties each took home $6,825.00 for their first place effort. In the championship match, Dodd and Luyties outlasted Brent Frohoff and Scott Ayakatubby by a score of 15-13. Ayakatubby and Frohoff split $8,450.00 for their second place effort.

3rd Place: Tim Hovland and Kent Steffes
4th Place: Sinjin Smith and Randy Stoklos
5th Place: Scott Friederichsen and Larry Mear
5th Place: Shawn Davis and Owen McKibben

BOULDER COLORADO
June 7th-8th, 1991

For the second week in a row, Scott Ayakatubby and Brent Frohoff were in second place. This week, at the $150,000.00 Men's Jose Cuervo Gold Crown, in Boulder Colorado, it cost them a lot of money. The first place team of Sinjin Smith and Randy Stoklos split $70,000.00, while Ayakatubby and Frohoff settled for $7,180.00 each. In the championship match, Smith and Stoklos outscored the "young-guns" 15-8 to win the final. Tim Hovland and Kent Steffes finished in third place, while Adam Johnson and Pat Powers settled for the fourth spot. Fifth place went to Mike Dodd and Mike Whitmarsh.

3rd Place: Tim Hovland and Kent Steffes
4th Place: Adam Johnson and Pat Powers
5th Place: Mike Dodd and Mike Whitmarsh
6th Place: Al Janc and Tim Walmer

CRAIG MOOTHART
In 1991, Craig Moothart finished within the top five on five occasions. Above photo, Moothart gets "down-an-dirty" to make a nice dig.
Photo Courtesy of the AVP

KARCH KIRALY
In 1991, Karch Kiraly teamed-up with Kent Steffes at 10 AVP Tour events and won six championship matches. Above photo, Kiraly celebrates one of his many AVP Tour championship moments.
Photo Courtesy of Dennis G. Steers

PHILADELPHIA PENNSYLVANIA
June 15th-16th, 1991

The $65,000.00 Men's Miller Lite Philadelphia Open was won by Sinjin Smith and Randy Stoklos. They split the $13,650.00 first place check. In the championship match, they defeated the surprise team of Andrew Smith and Bruk Vandeweghe. A. Smith and Vandeweghe split the second place check of $8,450.00.

3rd Place: Adam Johnson and Pat Powers
4th Place: Mike Dodd and Ricci Luyties
5th Place: Roger Clark and Eric Wurts

CAPE COD MASSACHUSETTS
June 22nd-23rd, 1991

The $65,000.00 Men's Miller Lite Cape Cod Open was won by Sinjin Smith and Randy Stoklos. They split the $13,650.00 first place check. In the championship final, they defeated John Hanley and Mike Whitmarsh by a score of 15-11.

3rd Place: Brent Frohoff and Tim Hovland
4th Place: Adam Johnson and Pat Powers
5th Place: Karch Kiraly and Kent Steffes
5th Place: Mike Dodd and Ricci Luyties

BELMAR BEACH NEW JERSEY
June 29th-30th, 1991

The $65,000.00 Men's Miller Lite Belmar Open was won by a team that would go on to win over 100 tournaments together. Karch Kiraly and Kent Steffes won the tournament and split the $13,650.00 first place check. In the championship match, Kiraly and Steffes out-pointed Adam Johnson and Pat Powers for the victory. Powers and Johnson split $8,450.00 as the runner-ups.

3rd Place: Brent Frohoff and Tim Hovland
4th Place: Al Janc and Tim Walmer
5th Place: Sinjin Smith and Randy Stoklos
5th Place: Scott Ayakatubby and Steve Timmons

MANHATTAN BEACH CALIFORNIA
July 6th-7th, 1991

The 1991 Manhattan Beach Open Beach was the $75,000.00 Men's Off-Shore Manhattan Beach Open. For the second week in a row, Karch Kiraly and Kent Steffes were the winner's. In the championship final, they defeated Scott Ayakatubby and Steve Timmons. The winner's split $15,750.00, while the runner-ups split $9,750.00.

3rd Place: Sinjin Smith and Randy Stoklos
4th Place: Mike Dodd and Ricci Luyties
5th Place: Rudy Dvorak and Craig Moothart
5th Place: Roger Clark and Eric Wurts

GRAND HAVEN MICHIGAN
July 13th-14th, 1991

The $65,000.00 Men's Miller Lite Grand Haven Open was won by Karch Kiraly and Kent Steffes. This was the third consecutive beach volleyball title for them. They split the $13,650.00 first place check. In the championship final, Kiraly and Steffes defeated Sinjin Smith and Randy Stoklos by a score of 15-7.

3rd Place: Tim Hovland and Pat Powers
4th Place: Andrew Smith and Bruk Vandeweghe
5th Place: Scott Ayakatubby and Steve Timmons
5th Place: Mike Dodd and Ricci Luyties

SCOTT AYAKATUBBY
Scott "Ack" Ayakatubby played some great beach volleyball, on the 1991 AVP Tour, advancing to the championship match of 4 events, finishing in the second spot on each occasion. "Ack" was also gaining a reputation as the "best-dressed" player on the beach, because of his "Primitive-Prints" trunks that he wore. Above photo, the "Primitive-Prince" makes a nice diving dig while wearing "Dingle-Ball" shorts.
Photo Courtesy of the AVP

CHICAGO ILLINOIS
July 20th-21st, 1991

The $100,000.00 Men's Miller Lite Chicago Open was won by Karch Kiraly and Kent Steffes. This was their fourth consecutive beach volleyball title. They split the $20,000.00 first place check. In the championship match, they defeated John Hanley and Brent Frohoff. The runner-ups collected $12,000.00 for their efforts.

3rd Place: Eric Boyles and Shawn Davis
4th Place: Mike Dodd and Ricci Luyties
5th Place: Adam Johnson and Mike Whitmarsh
5th Place: Tim Hovland and Pat Powers

MILWAUKEE WISCONSIN
July 27th-28th, 1991

The $65,000.00 Men's Miller Lite Milwaukee Open, played on Bradford Beach, saw Adam Johnson and Ricci Luyties win the surprising final. They split the $15,750.00 first place check. This was the first win for this team combo. In the championship final, The new team of Johnson and Luyties defeated the upset minded team of Mike Whitmarsh and John Hanley by the score of 14-13 as the time clock ran-out. Whitmarsh and Hanley had taken leads of 5-1 and 9-4 before succumbing.

3rd Place: Sinjin Smith and Randy Stoklos
4th Place: Larry Mear and Wes Welch
5th Place: Scott Ayakatubby and Brent Frohoff
5th Place: Karch Kiraly and Kent Steffes

CLEVELAND OHIO
August 3rd-4th, 1991

The $65,000.00 Men's Miller Lite Cleveland Open, was won by Adam Johnson and Ricci Luyties. They split the $13,650.00 first place check. In the championship match, they defeated top seeds, Karch Kiraly and Kent Steffes, 7-5, in the second game of a double final.

3rd Place: Scott Ayakatubby and Brent Frohoff
4th Place: Owen McKibbon and Tim Walmer
5th Place: Mike Dodd and Tim Hovland
5th Place: Rudy Dvorak and Craig Moothart

SEAL BEACH CALIFORNIA
August 10th-11th, 1991

The $100,000.00 Men's Miller Lite Orange County Open, was staged at Seal Beach California. Sinjin Smith and Randy Stoklos as a team were back in the winner's circle again with their eleventh title of the season and 107th all time. They split the $20,000.00 first place check, and an additional $70,000.00 each for clinching the 1991 AVP point title. In the championship final, Smith and Stoklos lost the first game, 15-7, to Karch Kiraly and Kent Steffes. In the "sudden death" game, of the two-day, double-elimination tournament, they out-pointed Kiraly and Steffes 7-2.

3rd Place: Owen McKibbon and Tim Walmer
4th Place: Scott Ayakatubby and Brent Frohoff
5th Place: John Hanley and Mike Whitmarsh
5th Place: Adam Johnson and Ricci Luyties

SANTA CRUZ CALIFORNIA
August 16th-17th, 1991

The $200,000.00 Men's Jose Cuervo Gold Crown event, in Santa Cruz, was won by the team of Karch Kiraly and Kent Steffes. They split a first place check of $100,000.00. In the championship match, Kiraly and Steffes defeated Sinjin Smith and Randy Stoklos. Smith and Stoklos split $17,960.00 for their 2nd place finish.

3rd Place: Mike Dodd and Tim Hovland
4th Place: Adam Johnson and Ricci Luyties
5th Place: Al Janc and Pat Powers
6th Place: John Hanley and Mike Whitmarsh

HERMOSA BEACH CALIFORNIA
August 23rd-25th, 1991

The AVP's 1991 $750,000.00 Miller Lite "U.S. Pro-Beach Volleyball Championship," in Hermosa Beach, was won by the third seeded team of Adam Johnson and Ricci Luyties. They split $100,000.00 for their 13-11 victory over top-seeded and defending champions, Sinjin Smith and Randy Stoklos, in front of over 15,000 cheering fans at the Hermosa Beach Pier. This was Johnson and Luyties third title on the 1991 AVP Tour.

In the championship final, televised live on NBC, Johnson and Luyties rallied from a 11-10 deficit to Randy Stoklos and Sinjin Smith, in the final 20 seconds. At 11-10, Luyties hit a ball out, but the ref called a touch by Stoklos on the block, and awarded the ball to Luyties and Johnson. Smith then hit the ball out to tie the score at 11-all. Next Johnson dug a spike by Stoklos and put the ball away for a 12-11 lead, with 11 seconds remaining on the time clock. The final point came when Stoklos hit the next ball out as time expired. Smith and Stoklos split $22,500.00 as the runner-ups.

3rd Place: Scott Ayakatubby and Brent Frohoff
4th Place: Mike Dodd and Tim Hovland
5th Place: Brian Lewis and Pat Powers
5th Place: Andrew Smith and Bruk Vandeweghe

ORLANDO FLORIDA
September 4th-5th, 1991

The $100,000.00 Men's Miller Lite World Invitational Tournament was staged in Orlando Florida. This AVP Pro-Beach Volleyball event in was won by Karch Kiraly and Kent Steffes. They earned a check for $12,390.00. In the championship match, Kiraly and Steffes outscored Scott Ayakatubby and Brent Frohoff.

3rd Place: Mike Dodd and Tim Hovland
3rd Place: Andrew Smith and Bruk Vandeweghe
5th Place: Rudy Dvorak and Craig Moothart
5th Place: Brian Lewis and Pat Powers
5th Place: Adam Johnson and Ricci Luyties
5th Place: Sinjin Smith and Randy Stoklos

DAYTONA BEACH FLORIDA
October 6th, 1991

The $250,000.00 Men's Old Spice King of the Beach tournament was staged on the beach in Daytona Beach Florida. The AVP's 1991 "King of the Beach" tournament was won by Karch Kiraly. In the final determining match, Kiraly and Adam Johnson outscored Randy Stoklos and Scott Ayakatubby 14-4. Kiraly collected a total of $71,500.00 along with the crown. Randy Stoklos was the second place finisher. He earned $36,500.00 for his efforts. Adam Johnson was the third place finisher, while Scott Ayakatubby was in fourth place. Fifth place went to Sinjin Smith.

3rd Place: Adam Johnson
4th Place: Scott Ayakatubby
5th Place: Sinjin Smith
6th Place: Tim Hovland

MEN'S TOURNAMENT RESULTS
1991-FIVB

RIO DE JANEIRO, BRAZIL
February 12th-23rd, 1991

The 1991, $50,000.00 FIVB World Championship of Beach Volleyball, took place at Copacabana Beach in Rio de Janeiro Brazil. Sixty-three teams from twenty-one countries participated. This was the fourth FIVB World Series championship in, five years, won by Sinjin Smith and Randy Stoklos. This year it was another all U.S.A. final, with Stoklos and Smith defeating Tim Hovland and Kent Steffes to capture the championship by scores of 14-12 and 12-9. Smith and Stoklos split the $12,000.00 first place check while Hovland and Steffes shared $7,500.00.

3rd Place: Andre Lima and Guilherme Marquez-Bra
4th Place: Mike Dodd and Jon Stevenson-USA
5th Place: Jose Franco Vieira Neto and Roberto Costa Lopes-Bra
5th Place: Marlos De Almeida and Tulio Teixeira-Bra

SYDNEY, AUSTRALIA
March 14th-17th, 1991

The U.S.A. team of Randy Stoklos and Sinjin Smith outlasted the Brazilian team of Andre Perlingeiro Lima and Luiz Guilherme Marquez, 12-6, 9-12, and 15-9, to win the $50,000.00 FIVB Pro Beach event in Sydney Australia. The winner's share of the purse was $6,000.00 each. Sixty-three teams from twenty-one countries participated.

3rd Place: Jose Franco Vieira Neto and Roberto Costa Lopes-Bra
4th Place: Jean Philippe Jodard and Christian Penigaud-Fra
5th Place: Roger Clark and Wally Goodrick-USA
5th Place: Andrea Ghiurghi and Dionsisio Lequaglie-Italy

RANDY STOKLOS & SINJIN SMITH
Randy Stoklos and Sinjin Smith were the top team on the AVP Tour with 11 championships. They were also the top team on the FIVB Tour with 3 championship victories. Above photo, Smith (right) passes the ball to Stoklos (left).
Photo Courtesy of the AVP

YOKOHAMA, JAPAN
July 20th-21st, 1991

Yokohama Japan was the site of the $50,000.00 FIVB Pro Beach Volleyball event, where sixty-nine teams from twenty-one countries participated. The U.S.A. team of Al Janc and Tim Walmer came out with an 8-12, 12-5, and 15-9 victory over the Brazilian team of Andre Perlingeiro Lima and Luiz Guilherme Marquez to capture the championship. The Americans split $12,000.00 for their efforts.

3rd Place: Julien Prosser and Andy Burdin-Aus
4th Place: Marco Solustri and Gianni Mascagna-Italy
5th Place: Jean Philippe Jodard and Christian Penigaud-Fra
5th Place: Yasunori "Kuma" Kumada and Lezaburo-Japan

CAP DE AGDE, FRANCE
July 25th-28th, 1991

Another $50,000.00 FIVB Pro Beach Volleyball event, was held in Cap de Agde France, where sixty-nine teams from twenty-one countries participated. The U.S.A. team of Leif Hanson and John Eddo outlasted the Italian team of Andrea Ghiurghi and Dionisio Dio Lequaglie, 12-2 and 12-9 to snatch the championship. Hanson and Eddo split $12,000.00 for their first place effort.

3rd Place: Andre Lima and Luiz Guilherme Marquez-Bra
4th Place: Jean Philippe Jodard and Christian Penigaud-Fra
5th Place: Jan Kvalheim and Bjorn Maaseide-Nor
5th Place: Gaston and Rossard-Fra
The U.S.A. team of Steve Krai and Doug Foust were able to snatch a ninth place.

CATOLICA, ITALY
July 29th- August 4th, 1991

In an all U.S.A. final, Randy Stoklos and Sinjin Smith defeated John Eddo and Leif Hanson, 12-6 and 12-8, to take the championship match at the $50,000.00 FIVB Pro Beach Volleyball event in Catolica Italy. Smith and Stoklos split $12,000.00 for their efforts. This event hosted sixty-nine teams from twenty-one countries.

3rd Place: Andre Perlingeiro Lima and Luiz Marquez-Bra
4th Place: Smarco "Sollu" Solustri and Gianni Mascagna-Italy
5th Place: Jean Philippe Jodard and Christian Penigaud-Fra
5th Place: John Child and Edward "Eddie" Drakich -Canada
Additional U.S.A. finishers: Bill Suwara and Anthony Curci seventh, Steve Krai and Doug Foust in thirteenth.

ALMERIA, SPAIN
August 7th-11th, 1991

The French team of Christian Penigaud and Jean-Philippe Jodard moved up to win the championship match over the Brazilian team of Marlos de Almeida and Tulio Teixeira, at the $50,000.00 FIVB Pro Beach Volleyball event in Almeria Spain. The final scores were 12-7 and 13-11. The French team split $12,000.00 for their first place effort.

3rd Place: Andre Perlingeiro Lima and Luiz Marquez-Bra
4th Place: Eduardo Garrido Dias and Roberto Duarte Dias-Bra
5th Place: John Eddo and Leif Hanson-USA
5th Place: Sixto Jimenez and Benjamin Vicedo Mayor-Spain

TOP PHOTOS: Left: Scott Ayakatubby hits the ball over the block of Owen McKibbon. **Center:** Sinjin Smith hits the ball towards the block of Adam Johnson, with Ricci Luyties on defense. **Right:** Brent Frohoff chases after the ball.

MIDDLE PHOTOS: Left: Mike Whitmarsh follows-through after spiking the ball. **Center:** Adam Johnson follows-through after spiking the ball. **Right:** Ricci Luyties hits the ball past the block of Wes Welch.

  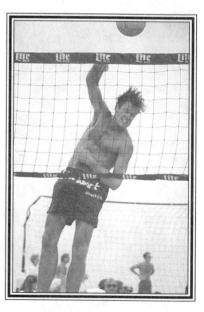

1991 MEN'S BEACH VOLLEYBALL ACTION

BOTTOM PHOTOS: Left: Dan Vrebalovich hits the ball over the net. **Center:** Ricci Luyties reaches high to make a nice block. **Right:** Andy Fishburn was still around to hit the ball in 1991. In this photo Fishburn hits the ball during the 1991 Hermosa Beach event.

Photo's Courtesy of the AVP

TOP PHOTOS: Left: John Hanley follows through after spiking the ball. **Center:** Rudy Dvorak hits the ball past the block of John Hanley. **Right:** Bruk Vandeweghe hits the ball into the block of Rudy Dvorak.

MIDDLE PHOTOS: Left: Andrew Smith gets the ball over the net. **Center:** Leif Hanson reaches over the net to make the block. **Right:** Scott Friederichsen making the pass.

1991 MEN'S BEACH VOLLEYBALL ACTION

BOTTOM PHOTOS: Left: Tim Hovland reaching high to make the block. **Center:** Andy Klussman ready to make the play. **Right:** Wally Goodrick diving for the dig attempt.

Photo's Courtesy of the AVP

WOMEN'S BEACH VOLLEYBALL
1991

The WPVA had five new sites in 1991, they included: Florida, South Carolina, Texas, Washington, and Colorado. These new sites were part of a 19 stop WPVA tour in 1991. The minimum prize money was $40,000.00 per tour event, with the largest tournament prize money was set at $100,000.00 in Tokyo Japan. Total tour prize money for the WPVA in 1991 was $665,000.00.

Karolyn Kirby and Angela Rock dominated the 1991 WPVA Tour. They outclassed the competition, reaching the finals of 14 tournaments, winning 12 of them. Gail Castro with Lori Kotas managed 3 tournament championships.

Two future stars of the women's beach volleyball tour made their entrance in 1991. Liz Masakayan earned her first tour championship while Holly McPeak showed some promise by placing in the top five on 5 occasions, earning "Rookie-of-the-Year" honors.

1991 WOMEN'S PRO BEACH VOLLEYBALL TOUR

DATE	SITE	PURSE
April 6th-7th	Austin TX	$ 40,000.00
April 13th-14th	Daytona FL	$ 30,000.00
April 20th-21st	Clearwater FL	$ 40,000.00
April 27th-28th	Fresno CA	$ 30,000.00
May 4th-5h	Phoenix AZ	$ 40,000.00
May 11th-12th	Hermosa Beach CA	$ 40,000.00
May 18th-19th	San Diego CA	$ 40,000.00
May 25th-26th	Salt Lake City UT	$ 30,000.00
June 1st-2nd	Reno NV	$ 40,000.00
June 8th-9th	Dallas TX	$ 40,000.00
June 15th-16th	Santa Cruz CA	$ 40,000.00
June 22nd-23rd	Manhattan Beach CA	$ 40,000.00
June 29th-30th	Camp Pendleton CA	$ 40,000.00
July 6th-7th	Myrtle Beach SC	$ 30,000.00
July 13th-14th	Venice CA	$ 50,000.00
July 20th-21st	Boulder CO	$ 30,000.00
July 27th-28th	Santa Barbara CA	$ 30,000.00
August 3rd-4th	Tokyo Japan "canceled"	$100,000.00
August 24th-25th	Las Vegas NV	$ 75,000.00

INDIVIDUAL WPVA TOURNAMENT FINISHES
1991

Player	1st	2nd	3rd	4th	5th
Lori Biller	0	0	0	0	2
Linda Chisholm Carrillo	2	3	4	3	3
Gail Castro	3	3	4	2	1
Cammy Ciareilli	0	0	0	1	1
Patty Dodd	0	1	2	0	3
Barbara Fontana.	0	0	0	1	4
Lori Kotas Forsythe	3	3	4	2	1
Janice Opalinski Harrer	0	5	2	5	2
Alison Johnson	0	0	0	0	3
Karolyn Kirby	**12**	**2**	**2**	**1**	**0**
Lisa Strand Ma'a	0	0	2	1	3
Liz Masakayan	1	3	4	2	2
Nina Grouwinkel Matthies	1	0	1	0	4
Holly McPeak	0	0	0	1	4
Charlotte Mitchellll	0	0	0	0	2
Marla O'Hara	0	0	1	1	2
Mary Jo Peppler	0	0	0	0	1
Diane Pestolesi	0	0	0	1	1
Nancy Reno	0	0	1	0	2
Deb Richardson	0	1	2	0	4
Angela Rock	**12**	**2**	**2**	**1**	**0**
Elaine Roque	0	5	2	4	2
Rita Crockett Royster	0	1	0	0	2
Dennie Schupyt-Knoop	0	0	0	1	0
Jackie Silva	0	3	2	0	0
Gail Stammer	0	0	0	0	3
Julie Thornton	0	0	0	0	1
Kelly Van Winden	0	0	1	1	1

ANGELA ROCK
Angela Rock dominated the 1991 WPVA Tour, with her partner Karolyn Kirby, by winning 12 tournament championships. Above photo, Rock gets-up high for a jump serve.
Photo Courtesy of Frank Goroszko

WOMEN'S TOURNAMENT RESULTS
1991-WPVA

AUSTIN TEXAS
April 6th-7th, 1991

The 1991 WPVA $40,000.00 Flamingo Hilton Open, in Austin Texas was won by Karolyn Kirby and Angela Rock. In the championship match, they defeated Gail Castro and Lori Kotas, to earn the $9,600.00 first place prize money. Rock and Kirby won the first game 15-12, then they won the sudden-death game 7-2 for the victory.

3rd Place: Lisa Strand and Kelly Van Winden
4th Place: Janice Harrer and Linda Carrillo
5th Place: Deb Richardson and Marla O'Hara
5th Place: Mary Jo Peppler and Nancy Reno

DAYTONA BEACH FLORIDA
April 13th-14th, 1991

The 1991 WPVA $30,000.00 Coors Light Daytona Beach Open was won by the team of Karolyn Kirby and Angela Rock. In the championship match, they defeated Gail Castro and Lori Forsythe-Kotas 15-12, to earn the $7,000.00 first place prize money.

3rd Place: Janice Harrer and Elaine Roque
4th Place: Lisa Strand and Kelly Van Winden
5th Place: Linda Chisholm Carrillo and Nina Matthies
5th Place: Alison Johnson and Julie Thornton

CLEARWATER BEACH FLORIDA
April 20th-21st, 1991

The 1991, WPVA $40,000.00 Diet Pepsi Clearwater Beach Open was won by the team of Nina Matthies and Linda Carrillo. In the emotional championship double final match, they defeated Janice Harrer and Elaine Roque 7-4, to earn the $9,600.00 first place prize.

3rd Place: Angela Rock and Karolyn Kirby
4th Place: Gail Castro and Lori Forsythe-Kotas
5th Place: Deb Richardson and Marla O'Hara
5th Place: Patty Dodd and Liz Masakayan

FRESNO CALIFORNIA
April 27th-28th, 1991

In near-perfect weather, the 1991 WPVA Flamingo Hilton Fresno Open, in front of 8,000 fans, was won by the team of Gail Castro and Lori Kotas. They collected the first place prize of $7,200.00. In the nail biting championship match, played in front of 8,000 beach volleyball fans, Castro and Kotas defeated Angela Rock and Karolyn Kirby, in overtime. The tie-breaking game to seven points, saw Castro and Kotas go ahead 6-4. After numerous side-outs and match point opportunities, they were finally able to put Rock and Kirby away, 7-5 for the victory.

3rd Place: Nina Matthies and Linda Carrillo
4th Place: Janice Harrer and Elaine Roque
5th Place: Charlotte Mitchell and Gayle Stammer
5th Place: Holly McPeak and Barbara Fontana

KAROLYN KIRBY
Karolyn Kirby "hustled" her way into 14 WPVA Tour championship matches in 1991. Above photo, Kirby "hustles" to make a diving dig.
Photo Courtesy of Frank Goroszko

JANICE OPALINSKI
Janice Opalinski advanced th the championship match five times on the 1991 WPVA Tour, finishing in the second spot each time. Above photo, Opalinski passes the ball to Elaine Roque.
Photo Courtesy of Frank Goroszko

PHOENIX ARIZONA
May 4th-5th, 1991

The "Laguna Sportswear Women's Phoenix Open was won by Karolyn Kirby and Angela Rock. They earned $9,600.00 for their effort. In the championship match, they defeated Gail Castro and Lori Forsythe-Kotas.

3rd Place: Janice Harrer and Elaine Roque
4th Place: Cammy Ciareilli and Diane Pestolesi
5th Place: Holly McPeak and Barbra Fontana
5th Place: Linda Carrillo and Nina Matthies

HERMOSA BEACH CALIFORNIA
May 11th-12th, 1991

The 1991, WPVA $40,000.00 Hermosa Beach Open was won by the top seeded team of Angela Rock and Karolyn Kirby. They went practically untested through the event as they collected the $9,600.00 first place prize. In the championship match, Kirby and Rock outscored Janice Opalinski and Elaine Roque by the score of 15-8.

3rd Place: Liz Masakayan and Nancy Reno
4th Place: Linda Chisholm Carrillo and Nina Matthies
5th Place: Gail Castro and Lori Forsythe-Kotas
5th Place: Marla O'Hara and Deb Richardson

SAN DIEGO CALIFORNIA
May 18th-19th, 1991

The 1991, WPVA $40,000.00 San Diego Open, played near the Crystal Pier in Pacific Beach, was won by the number one seeded team of Angela Rock and Karolyn Kirby. They collected the $9,600.00 first place prize. This was their fifth title in seven events on the 1991 WPVA Tour. In the championship match, Rock and Kirby went out to an 8-6 lead over Lori Kotas and Gail Castro. There were 14 side outs before the top seeds scored again. They went on to win 15-7.

3rd Place: Janice Opalinski and Elaine Roque
4th Place: Liz Masakayan and Linda Chisholm Carrillo
5th Place: Marla O'Hara and Deb Richardson
5th Place: Alison Johnson and Gayle Stammer

SALT LAKE CITY UTAH
May 25th-26th, 1991

The 1991, WPVA $30,000.00 Diet Pepsi Salt Lake City Open was won by Karolyn Kirby and Angela Rock. They shared the $9,600.00 first place prize. In the championship match, they defeated Linda Carrillo and Liz Masakayan.

3rd Place: Gail Castro and Lori Kotas
4th Place: Holly McPeak and Barbra Fontana
5th Place: Janice Harrer and Elaine Roque
5th Place: Nina Matthies and Nancy Reno

RENO NEVADA
June 1st-2nd, 1991

Gail Castro and Lori Forsythe were the winners at the $40,000.00 WPVA Flamingo Hilton Open, in Reno, Nevada. In the championship match, Castro and Forsythe defeated Linda Chisholm and Liz Masakayan 15-13.

LINDA CHISHOLM CARRILLO

Linda Chisholm Carrillo was a force to contend with on the 1991 WPVA Tour. She advanced to five finals, winning two championships. Above photo, Chisholm crushes the ball.
Photo Courtesy of Frank Goroszko

ELAINE ROQUE

Elaine Roque was also a force to contend withon the 1991 WPVA Tour. She advanced to 5 finals, finishing in the second spot each time. Above photo, Roque reaches high to spike the ball.
Photo Courtesy of Frank Goroszko

3rd Place: Karolyn Kirby and Angela Rock
4th Place: Janice Harrer and Elaine Roque
5th Place: Kelly Van Winden and Lisa Strand Ma'a
6th Place: Barbra Fontana and Holly McPeak

SANTA CRUZ CALIFORNIA
June 15th-16th, 1991

The 1991, WPVA $40,000.00 Santa Cruz Open was won by Karolyn Kirby and Angela Rock. In the championship match, they defeated Jackie Silva and Rita Crockett-Royster.

3rd Place: Marla O'Hara and Deb Richardson
4th Place: Elaine Roque and Janice Harrer
5th Place: Liz Masakayan and Linda Chisholm
5th Place: Cammy Ciarelli and Diane Pestoiesi

MANHATTAN BEACH CALIFORNIA
June 22nd-23rd, 1991

The 1991, WPVA $40,000.00 Manhattan Beach Open was won by Karolyn Kirby and Angela Rock. In the championship match, played in front of and estimated crowd of 10,000 beach volleyball fans, Kirby and Rock defeated Linda Chisholm-Carrillo and Liz Masakayan.

3rd Place: Gail Castro and Lori Forsythe
4th Place: Elaine Roque and Janice Harrer
5th Place: Lori Biller and Patty Dodd

CAMP PENDLETON CALIFORNIA
June 29th-30th, 1991

The 1991 Camp Pendleton $40,000.00 Women's Open was won by Karolyn Kirby and Angela Rock. They won $4,200.00 each, for their efforts in this 32-team, double elimination tournament. In the championship match, Kirby and Rock out-pointed Janice Opalinski-Harrer and Elaine Roque, 15-4. Kirby and Rock started out fast with a 5-0 lead that soon was an 11-1 lead. The teams then traded points until Kirby and Rock finished off the 1 hour and 15 minute match with an ace at match point. Kirby had 27 kills, a block and an ace while Rock added 12 kills during the final as they won for the ninth time in 12 tournaments this season.

Earlier, in the winner's bracket final, Kirby and Rock outlasted Harrer and Roque 15-13. As the second place team, Harrer and Roque each took home a check for $3,600.00.

3rd Place: Lisa Strand and Deb Richardson
4th Place: Linda Carrillo and Liz Masakayan
5th Place: Lori Biller and Patty Dodd
5th Place: Kelly Van Winden and Charlotte Mitchell

MYRTLE BEACH SOUTH CAROLINA
July 6th-7th, 1991

The 1991, WPVA $30,000.00 Myrtle Beach Open was won by Karolyn Kirby and Angela Rock. They split the $7,200.00 first place check. In the championship match, they defeated Janice Harrer and Elaine Roque.

3rd Place: Patty Dodd and Jackie Silva
4th Place: Marla O'Hara and Dennie Knoop
5th Place: Lori Kotas and Gail Castro
5th Place: Holly McPeak and Barbara Fontana

LIZ MASAKAYAN
In 1991, Liz Masakayan began to show her beach volleyball skills. She finished in the top five 12 times, adfvancing to the finals 4 times, winning one championship. Above photo, Masakayan looks good passing the ball.
Photo Courtesy of Frank Goroszko

GAIL CASTRO
In 1991, Gail Castro had a good season on the WPVA Tour. She finished within the top five 13 times, advancing to the finals 6 times, winning 3 championships. Above photo, Castro hits a tough jump serve.
Photo Courtesy of Frank Goroszko

VENICE BEACH CALIFORNIA
July 13th-14th, 1991

The top players on the women's pro beach volleyball tour competed for the $50,000.00 Coors Light U.S. Open at Venice Beach. The winner's were Lori Kotas and Gail Castro. They shared $12,000.00 for their efforts. In the championship match, Castro and Kotas defeated Karolyn Kirby and Angela Rock 15-8.

3rd Place: Liz Masakayan and Linda Carrillo
4th Place: Janice Harrer and Elaine Roque
5th Place: Holly McPeak and Barbara Fontana
5th Place: Alison Johnson and Gayle Stammer

BOULDER COLORADO
July 20th-21st, 1991

The 1991, WPVA $30,000.00 Boulder Open was won by Karolyn Kirby and Angela Rock. They split the $7,200.00 first place prize. In the championship match, they defeated Jackie Silva and Patty Dodd.

3rd Place: Linda Carrillo and Liz Masakayan
4th Place: Lori Kotas and Gail Castro
5th Place: Lisa Strand and Deb Richardson
5th Place: Janice Harrer and Elaine Roque

SANTA BARBARA CALIFORNIA
July 27th-28th, 1991

The 1991, WPVA $30,000.00 Santa Barbara Women's Open was won by top-seeded Karolyn Kirby and Angela Rock. Kirby and rock earned $7,200.00 for the victory, their 12th in 16 tour stops this season. The 12 victories surpassed the tour record of 11, in 1989, by Jackie Silva and Patty Dodd. In the championship match, on Leadbetter Beach, Kirby and Rock defeated Elaine Roque and Janice Opalinski-Harrer by a score of 15-9. Earlier, in the winner's bracket final, Kirby and Rock sent Roque and Harrer into the consolation bracket with a 15-7 win.

3rd Place: Jackie Silva and Patty Dodd
4th Place: Liz Masakayan and Linda Chisholm
5th Place: Nina Matthies and Rita Crockett Royster
5th Place: Deb Richardson and Lisa Strand Ma'a

TOKYO JAPAN
August 3rd-4th, 1991

The 1991, WPVA $100,000.00 Salem Invitational Women's Open, in Tokyo Japan, was canceled when promoters lost the title sponsor.

LAS VEGAS NEVADA
August 24th-25th, 1991

The 1991, WPVA $75,000.00 Women's World Championship, in Las Vegas Nevada, was staged on the parking lot of the Flamingo Hilton. Liz Masakayan and Linda Chisholm-Carrillo were the winners. They shared $18,000.00 for their efforts. This was Masakayan's first career open championship. In the championship match, Masakayan and Carrillo outlasted Jackie Silva and Deb Richardson by a score of 16-14.

3rd Place: Lori Kotas and Gail Castro
4th Place: Angela Rock and Karolyn Kirby
5th Place: Rita Crockett and Lisa Strand
5th Place: Alison Johnson and Gayle Stammer

JANICE OPALINSKI HARRER
On the 1991 WPVA Tour, Janice Opalinski Harrer finished within the top five 14 times, advancing to the finals five times, finishing in the second spot each time. Above photo, Opalinski attacking the ball.
Photo Courtesy of Frank Goroszko

LORI KOTAS FORSYTHE
On the 1991 WPVA Tour, Lori Kotas Forsythe finished within the top five 13 times, advancing to the finals six times, winning the championship 3 times. Above photo, Kotas reaches high to spike the ball.
Photo Courtesy of Frank Goroszko

TOP PHOTOS: Left: Patty Dodd reaches high for the ball. **Center:** Barbra Fontana ready to make the play. **Right:** Elaine Roque attacking the ball.

MIDDLE PHOTOS: Left: Elaine "EY" Youngs spiking the ball. **Center:** Marie Anderson hits the ball into the block of Lisa Arce. **Right:** Deb Richardson hits the ball away from the block.

1991 WOMEN'S BEACH VOLLEYBALL ACTION

BOTTOM PHOTOS: Left: Gail Stammer reaches high to hit the ball. **Center:** Dennie Schupyt Knoop hitting the ball towards the defense of Nancy Reno. **Right:** Cammy Ciarelli at the net.
Middle Photos courtesy of Frank Goroszko. Top and Bottom Photos Courtesy of the AVP

ADDITIONAL VOLLEYBALL INFORMATION
1991

In addition to the pro-beach volleyball tour's players in 1991, the CBVA listed 103 Men "AAA" rated players, 138 Men "AA" rated, players, 222 Men "A" rated players, 372 Men "B" rated players, 332 Men "Unrated" players, and 257 "Novice" players.

SCARBOROUGH BEACH RHODE ISLAND
The Volleyball Hall of Fame joined forces with Heritage Productions of Rhode Island to host New England "Beach" Invitational at Scarborough Beach, Rhode Island. The semifinals and finals were televised nationally by Prime Sports Network.

Volleyball Hall of Fame Induction Ceremonies were held October 25, 1991. Inductees are: Dr. George Fisher, Rolf Engen, Thomas Haine, and Catalino Ignacio.

CAPISTRANO BEACH CALIFORNIA
May 12th, 1991

Lance Lyons and Brent Gonnerman won the Men's Open Division of the Jose Cuervo amateur beach volleyball tournament at Capistrano Beach.

Krista Atkinson and Renee Rozunko won by default over Shannon Williams and Mary McDowell, to win the Women's Open Division of the Jose Cuervo amateur beach volleyball tournament at Capistrano Beach.

Tom Grindel and Cathy Jones defeated Tim Muret and Wendy Lewis, 15-4, to win the Mixed-Doubles Open Division of the Jose Cuervo amateur beach volleyball tournament at Capistrano Beach. Third place went to the team of Kirt Riedl and Shannon Meixsell.

SAN DIEGO CALIFORNIA
June 8th, 1991

The 1991 Ocean Beach "James Gang" Mixed Open was won by the team of Tom Grindle and Cathy Jones. In the championship match, they defeated Rocky Ciarelli and Cammy Ciarelli. Third place went to Butch Miali and Wendy Potter. Scott Bailey and Linda Johnson took fourth. There were 15 teams entered in this tournament that was directed by George Stepanof.

LAGUNA BEACH CALIFORNIA
July, 13th-14th, 1991

In 1991 the Laguna Beach Men's Open became an amateur "AAA" tournament (a non-AVP event). Andy Klussman and Jeff Williams were the winners. In the championship match, they defeated Jim Menges and Jeff Southcott. Tom Lee and Mike Minier were in the third spot. The fourth place finishers were Dain Blanton and Burt Blanton.

CAMMY CIARELLI
In 1991, Cammy Ciarielli teamed-up with Rocky Ciarelli for a second place finish at the 1991 San Diego Ocean Beach "James-Gang" Mixed-Open. Above photo, Ciarelll challenges the block of Ali Wood.
Photo Courtesy of Frank Goroszko

DAIN BLANTON
Dain Blanton showed-up on the beach, at the 1991 Laguna Beach Men's AAA, paired-up with his brother Burt, for a fourth place finish. Above photo, Dain makes a diving effort to get the ball.
Photo Courtesy of "Couvi"

LOUISVILLE KENTUCKY
September 21st-22nd, 1991

The 1991 Bud Light FOVA North American Sand Volleyball championships were held at Waterfront Park. In the men's "AAA" division, Californians Kevin Waterbury and John Ribarich defeated Rob Long and Jeff Hurst, from Kentucky, for the championship. In the Women's "AAA" division, Californians Diane Ayres and Christine Starczak defeated Texans Mardji Hyde and Shannon Williams for the championship. In the Mixed-Doubles "AAA" division, Californians Mark Knudsen and Alicia Anaker defeated the Canadian team of Keal Prince and Tracy Mills for the championship.

MANHATTAN BEACH CALIFORNIA
August 10th-11th, 1991

The 1991 Marine Street Mixed-Double's Open was won by Todd Schaffer and Lindsey Hahn. In the championship match, they defeated Butch Miali and Liz Masakayan. Tournament director Mike Cook said that they used "pool-play" on Saturday and single elimination on Sunday. This accounts for the tie in third place and the four-way tie in the fifth spot. There were 44 teams entered in this tournament.

3rd Place: Rocky Ciarelli and Cami Ciarelli
3rd Place: Rick Shaw and Danica Djujich
5th Place: Christian Kiernan and Betsy Chaves
5th Place: Paul Cook and Michelle Johnson
5th Place: Mark Anderson and Cindy Helgesen
5th Place: Lars Hazen and Mary Diamond

ADDITIONAL "PRO" BEACH TOURNAMENTS
TERRIGAL AUSTRALIA
January 12th-13th, 1991

The U.S.A. team of Kent Steffes and Adam Johnson won the Terrigal Australian Open over fellow countrymen Mike Safford and George Carey. This event that attracted some U.S.A. teams, as reflected by the results. The winner's shared the $2,200.00 prize.

3rd Place: Jeff West and Brett Gonnerman-USA
4th Place: Fulvio DiPrinzo and Lachlan Granger-Aus
5th Place: Paul Calder and Stuart Jemesen

In the women's division final, the American team of Linda Carrillo and Janice Opalinski defeated the Australian team of Sally Bacon and Susan Carroll, by a score of 15-8. The winner's shared the first place prize of $1,000.00.

3rd Place: Vicki Shea and Marion Taylor-Aus
4th Place: Charisse Cormack and Jane Howard-Aus
5th Place: Sharon Byres and Jill McKinnon

MANLY AUSTRALIA
January 19th-20th, 1991

Australians Stuart Jemessen and Paul Calder won the first 1991 Manly event as they defeated compatriots Fulvio DiPrinzio and Lachain Granger, in the championship match. The winner's shared the $1,100.00 first place prize.

KENT STEFFES & ADAM JOHNSON
Kent Steffes and Adam "AJ" Johnson teamed-up to win a couple of championships on the 1991 Australian Pro-Beach Volleyball Tour. Above photo, "AJ" hits a set from Steffes, into the block of Mike Whitmarsh.
Photo Courtesy of the AVP

BETSY CHAVEZ
Betsy Chaves paried-up with her future husband, Christian Kiernan, to gain a four-way tie for 5th place, at the Marine Street Mixed-Doubles Open. Above photo, Chavez spikes the ball during an event on the WPVA Tour.
Photo Courtesy of Frank Goroszko

The women's division was won by Australians Jane Howard and Julie Ann McMahon. The runner-ups were compatriots Sue Carroll and Marion Taylor. The winner's shared the $600.00 first place prize.

COOLANGATTA AUSTRALIA
January 26th-27th, 1991

The U.S.A. team of Kent Steffes and Adam Johnson won the Terrigal Australian Open over fellow countrymen Mike Safford and George Carey. The winner's shared the $2,200.00 first place prize.

3rd Place: Jeff West and Brett Gonnerman-USA
4th Place: Rick Amon and Edwin Fernandez-Aus
5th Place: Fulvio DiPrinzo and Lachlan Granger-Aus

The Australian team of Jane Howard and Julie-Ann McMahon won the women's division over compatriots Susan Carroll and Marion Taylor. The winner's shared the $1,000.00 first place prize.

3rd Place: Carla Kinross and Vicki Shea-Aus
4th Place: Sharon Byers and Jill McKinnon-Aus
5th Place: Kristen Jones and Debra Marr-Aus

WOLLONGONG AUSTRALIA

February 2nd-3rd, 1991 The Wollongong Circuit men's event was an all Australian final, won by Paul Calder and Stuart Jemessen over Rod Kinross and Matt Donohoe. The winner's shared the $1,100.00 first place prize.

In the women's division championship match was also an all Australian final as Jane Howard and Julie Ann McMahon defeated Sue Carroll and Marion Taylor. The winner's shared the $1,000.00 first place prize.

BONDI BEACH AUSTRALIA
February 9th-10th, 1991

The Bondi Beach men's event was won by Paul Calder and Stuart Jemessen over Rob Wilson and Dave Armstrong. The winner's shared the $6,000.00 first place prize.

In the women's division championship match, Australians Sue Carroll and Marion Taylor defeated compatriots Jane Howard and Julie Ann McMahon. The winner's shared the $1,000.00 first place prize.

3rd Place: Sharon Byers and Jill McKinnon-Aus
4th Place: Charisse Cormack and Colleen Wald-Aus
5th Place: Carla Kinross and Katrina Mardell

JANICE OPALINSKI & LINDA CHISHOLM
Janice Opalinski Harrer teamed-up with Linda Chisholm Carrillo for some great success on the 1991 Australian Pro-Beach Volleyball Tour, winning two events. Above photo, Carrillo (left) and Opalinski take a break.
Photo Courtesy of Dennis G. Steers

JEFF WEST
Jeff "Westy" West teamed-up with Brett Gonnerman for some good results on the 1991 Australian Pro-Beach Volleyball Tour. Above photo, "Westy" hits a set from Gonnerman, past the block of Kent Steffes.
Photo Courtesy of Jeff West

SAINT KILDA AUSTRALIA
February 16th-17th, 1991

The Saint Kilda Festival Open was won by Australians Mike Safford and George Carey. In the championship match, they defeated Americans Jeff West and Brett Gonnermann. The winner's shared the $2,200.00 first place prize.

3rd Place: Paul Calder and Lachlan Granger-Aus
4th Place: Fulvio DiPrinzo and Paul Raudkeep-Aus
5th Place: Stuart Jemesen and Rod Kinross-Aus

In the all Australian women's division final, Jane Howard and Vicki Shea defeated Marion Taylor and Liane Fenwick to capture the $1,000.00 first place prize.

3rd Place: Susan Carroll and Julie-Ann McMahon-Aus
4th Place: Allison Brown and Sally Downes-Aus
5th Place: Roxanne Kitchener and Cathy Norman-Aus

MANLY AUSTRALIA
February 23rd-24th, 1991

At the Manly Men's Open, Americans Mike Safford and George Carey defeated compatriots Dan Vrebalovich and Tim Walmer, 15-8 and 7-5, in the championship double final match. The winner's shared the $1,800.00 first place prize. Earlier, in the finals of the winner's bracket, Walmer and Vrebalovich provided a lesson in the transition game as they ate-up fellow Americans Brent Frohoff and Al Janc 15-7.

In the finals of the loser's bracket Safford and Carey were trailing Frohoff and Janc 8-13 before they managed to win by a score of 15-13.

3rd Place: Brent Frohoff and Al Janc-USA
4th Place: Jeff West and Brett Gonnerman-USA
5th Place: Paul Calder and Stuart Jemessen-Aus

In the women's division final, the American team of Linda Carrillo and Janice Opalinski defeated the Australian team of Jane Howard and Vicki Shea, by a score of 15-8. The winner's shared the first place prize of $1,000.00.

3rd Place: Liane Fenwick and Marion Taylor-Aus
4th Place: Roxanne Kitchener and Cathy Norman-Aus
5th Place: Sally Bacon and Susan Carroll-Aus

HAMILTON ISLAND AUSTRALIA
March 1st-3rd, 1991

The Hamilton Island International Open was won by the U.S.A. team of Dan Vrebalovich and Tim Walmer over compatriots Brent Frohoff and Al Janc.

3rd Place: Stuart Jemesen and Fulvio DiPrinzio -Aus
4th Place: Thomas Harrer Paul Raudkepp-Aus
5th Place: Paul Calder and Lachlan Granger-Aus

In the women's division, The U.S.A. team of Linda Carrillo and Janice Opalinski defeated the Australian team of Sue Carroll and Marion Taylor.

3rd Place: Jane Howard and Julie-Ann McMahon-Aus
4th Place: Sharon Byers and Jil McKinnon-Aus
5th Place: Carla Kinross and Colleen Wald-Aus

JEFF WEST
Jeff "Westy" West had a best finish of second place, on the 1991 Australian Pro-Beach Volleyball Tour, at the Saint Kilda event. Above photo, "Westy" hits a set from Rick Arce.
Photo Courtesy of Jeff West

DAN VREBALOVICH
Dan Vrebalovich paired-up with Tim Walmer to win the Hamilton Island Pro-Beach event in Australia. Above photo, Vrebalovich challenging the block of Tim Hovland.
Photo Courtesy of Dennis G. Steers

FORT WALTON FLORIDA
March 16th-17th, 1991

Frank Hall and Richmond Hall defeated Manny Agant and Matt Sonnichsen to earn first place and a prize of $1,500.00, at the Fort Walton stop of the E.V.A. Tour.

COCOA BEACH FLORIDA
March 23rd-24th, 1991

On the EVA tour Chris Hanneman and Rick Arce won the "Molson" Cocoa Beach Open over Al Janc and Brian Gatzky. Manny Agant and Matt Sonnichsen held on for third place. The winner's shared the $1,200.00 first place prize.

CLEARWATER BEACH FLORIDA
March 30th-31st, 1991

Richmond Hall and Frank Hall were able to knock off Chris Hanneman and Rick Arce in the championship match to take first place at the "Molson" Clearwater Beach Open. Manny Agant and Matt Sonnichsen were in the third spot again. The winner's shared the $3,000.00 first place prize.

AROUND THE U.S.A.

The "Michelob Light" four-man beach volleyball tour was born in 1991, with the use of the numerous good indoor players. Craig Elledge was the man that got it going,. There was a total purse of $200,000.00.

The first tour went to seven sites from June 1st to July 28th, 1991. The stops included: San Diego California, Phoenix Arizona, Cleveland Ohio, Boston Massachusetts, Fort Myers Florida, Clearwater Beach Florida, and Myrtle Beach South Carolina.

Some of the 25 players to first participate included Olympians Jeff Stork, Craig Buck, Doug Partie, Bob Ctvrtlik. Additional players were Steve Salmons, Scott Fortune, Tom Duke, Mike Fitzgerald, Javier Gasper, Eugene LeDuff, Bill Stetson, Rocky Ciarelli, Pono Ma'a, Jon Root, Steve Rottman, Dave Yoder, Bob Yoder, Rod Wilde, Jon Roberts, Mike Blanchard, Don Dendinger, and Jeff Williams along with some familiar beach players: Dane Selznick, Jeff Southcott and Gary Hooper.

Each team had a sponsor. Team Club Sportswear won this first season. Jeff Stork was the MVP. The other team names were: Team Laguna, Team Spikline, Team Speedo, and Team I Dig.

CHRIS HANNEMANN
Chris Hanneman teamed-up with Rick Arce for a championship victory at Floridia's EVA event on Cocoa Beach. Above photo, Hannemann gets up high to block Dan Vrebalovich's spiked ball.
Photo Courtesy of the AVP

JEFF WILLIAMS
In 1991, Jeff Williams was one of the top players on the inaugeral Four-Man Professional Volleyball Tour. Above photo, Williams concentrates while passing the ball.
Photo Courtesy of the AVP

MEN'S BEACH VOLLEYBALL
1992

AVP

In 1992, there were thirty-one recorded "Professional" Beach Volleyball tournaments. twenty-six of these tournaments were staged in the U.S.A. while five were played internationally. Of the twenty-six U.S. tournaments, seven were California events, three were played in Florida. There were seventeen U.S. events staged in thirteen states other than Florida and California. The California tournaments were held in Fresno, Santa Cruz, Santa Barbara, Manhattan Beach, Hermosa Beach, Seal Beach, and San Diego. The tournaments in Florida were in Fort Myers, Clearwater, and Daytona. The remaining U.S. tournaments were held in Honolulu Hawaii (twice), Phoenix Arizona, Dallas/Fort Worth, Austin and San Antonio Texas, Boulder Colorado, Philadelphia Pennsylvania, Cape Cod Massachusetts, Louisville Kentucky, New Orleans Louisiana, Belmar New Jersey, Grand Haven Michigan, Milwaukee Wisconsin, Cleveland Ohio, and Chicago Illinois. The five international events were held in Sydney Australia, Rio de Janeiro Brazil, Enoshima Japan, Almeria Spain, and Lignano Italy.

In addition to the above International events, beach volleyball became a professional sport that was invading the planet. It was played as a demonstration sport in the Olympic Games in Barcelona Spain. Also, the first Swiss Championship in beach volleyball took place in Lucerne. There were more than 3,000 spectators that watched this event. The women's division was won by the team of Annalea Hartman and Silvia Meier. The men's division was won by Martin Walser and Christian Wandeler.

Karch Kiraly and Kent Steffes took over the top spot on the tour as they each won a total of seventeen tournaments, 16 together. First Steffes won at the Fresno event with Adam Johnson, then "K&K" won their 16 together with 4 wins in California, at: Santa Barbara, Manhattan Beach, San Diego, and the U.S. Championships in Hermosa Beach. They had twelve additional U.S. wins, which came in: Boulder Colorado, Dallas/Fort Worth, Austin and San Antonio Texas, Chicago Illinois, Louisville Kentucky, Belmar New Jersey, Grand Haven Michigan, Milwaukee Wisconsin, Cleveland Ohio, Philadelphia Pennsylvania, and Cape Cod Massachusetts. Kiraly added the "King of the Beach" title, in Daytona Beach Florida., to earn his 17th tournament championship.

Sinjin Smith and Randy Stoklos won six tournaments together in 1992. Three of their victories came in the U.S.A. when they won the Hawaiian, Fort Myers and the

KARCH KIRALY & KENT STEFFES
Karch Kiraly and Kent Steffes teamed-up togeter to become the top team on the 1992 AVP Tour. They had 13 tournament championships in a row, tying them with Greg Lee and Jim Menges for the record. Above photo, Kiraly (left) tries to inspire Steffes (right) to another victory.
Photo Courtesy of the AVP

KARCH KIRALY & KENT STEFFES
In 1992, as a team, Karch Kiraly and Kent Steffes advanced to the championship match at 17 AVP events, winning 16 times. Above photo, Kiraly (left) and son (center) accept the 1st place trophy, along with Steffes (right).
Photo Courtesy of the AVP

Phoenix Open's. They added three international wins by winning the FIVB events in Sydney Australia, Almeria Spain and the "World Championships" in Rio de Janeiro Brazil, Additional teams that won in 1992 were Pat Powers winning the Clearwater Beach event with Brian Lewis and the Seal Beach event with Mike Dodd. Brent Frohoff won the New Orleans event with Mike Whitmarsh and the Santa Cruz event with Ricci Luyties.

In 1992 there were five AVP tournaments televised nationally and live by NBC-TV. New sponsors were requesting to get involved. The televised games utilized a nine minute rally clock. Most other AVP tournaments utilized a ten minute rally clock.

Karch declined an offer to join the Olympic indoor team. Instead, Kiraly remained on the beach and teamed-up with Kent Steffes again. In 1992, they went on to prove that they were here to stay. Karch and Kent won 13 tournaments in a row, between May 19th and August 9th, 1992. They also won 16 out of 19 tournaments. The 13 tournament championships tied them with Greg Lee and Jim Menges's record of 13 in a row, set during the 1976 and 1977 beach volleyball tour's. The 13 wins came in order in San Antonio and Fort Worth Texas, San Diego California, Boulder Colorado, Chicago Illinois, Cape Cod Massachusetts, Louisville Kentucky, Manhattan Beach California, Philadelphia Pennsylvania, Belmar Beach New Jersey, Grand Haven Michigan, Milwaukee Wisconsin, and Cleveland Ohio. Karch and Kent won 75 games while they only lost 3 games over the 13 week period.

Kent Steffes was the top 1992 AVP money winner, earning $332,740.00, while winning 17 tournaments that he entered. Karch Kiraly was a close second, earning $327,100.00, while winning 17 tournaments that he entered. Karch Kiraly also won the 1992 "King of the Beach" tournament. This was the second year in a row, taht Kiraly was crowned King of the Beach.

Randy Stoklos became the first beach volleyball player to earn $1 million in prize money on February 1st, 1992. Sinjin Smith joined him two months later. Karch Kiraly, Kent Steffes, and Mike Dodd entered the exclusive million dollar club in 1994. In 2003, Kiraly surpassed the $3 million mark.

1992 marked the fifth anniversary of the AVP Cuervo Gold Crown Series. The 1992 series shelled out over $500,000.00 in prize money. The fifth annual schedule included trips to three of pro-beach volleyball's favorite tour locations. In April there was the $150,000.00 Clearwater Florida event, won by Brian Lewis and Pat Powers. In June there was the $175,000.00 Boulder Colorado event, won by Karch Kiraly and Kent Steffes. Then in August Ricci Luyties and Brent Frohoff won the $200,000.00 Santa Cruz event. First place prize money was $60,000.00, $80,000.00, and $100,000.00 respectively.

MIKE WHITMARSH & BRIAN LEWIS
In 1992, Mike Whitmarsh and Brian Lewis both recorded their first career AVP championships. Whitmarsh won his first tournament with Brent Frohoff, at the 1992 event in New Orleans Louisiana while Lewis teamed-up with Pat Powers to win the 1992 event in Clearwater Florida. Above photo, Whitmarsh passes the ball to Lewis, during a 1992 event, when they were teamed-up together.
Photo Courtesy of the AVP

INDIVIDUAL AVP TOURNAMENT FINISHES
1992

Player	1st	2nd	3rd	4th	5th
Scott Ayakatubby	0	0	0	0	2
Eric Boyles	0	0	0	1	0
Bill Boullianne	0	0	0	0	1
Robert Chavez	0	0	0	0	3
Roger Clark	0	0	0	1	2
Mike Dodd	1	2	12	2	2
Rudy Dvorak	0	0	0	0	2
John Eddo	0	0	0	0	1
Doug Foust	0	0	0	0	3
Scott Friederichsen	0	0	0	1	3
Brent Frohoff	2	1	4	4	4
Brian Gatzke	0	0	0	0	1
John Hanley	0	0	1	1	4
Leif Hanson	0	0	0	1	1
Tim Hovland	0	4	6	2	3
Adam Johnson	1	5	3	4	1
Karch Kiraly	17	1	0	1	1
Brian Lewis	1	4	5	2	6
Ricci Luyties	1	1	1	5	4
Larry Mear	0	3	0	0	1
Craig Moothart	0	0	1	0	2
Pat Powers	2	3	7	3	3
Jeff Rodgers	0	0	0	0	1
Andrew Smith	0	0	0	2	0
Sinjin Smith	3	8	3	3	1
Kent Steffes	17	4	0	2	1
Jon Stevenson	0	0	1	0	2
Randy Stoklos	3	8	3	3	2
Troy Tanner	0	0	0	0	3
Bruk Vandeweghe	0	0	1	3	2
Dan Vrebalovich	0	0	0	0	3
Tim Walmer	0	0	0	0	3
Wes Welch	0	0	0	0	1
Mike Whitmarsh	1	2	3	4	9
Eric Wurts	0	3	0	0	1

1992 AVP AWARDS
MOST IMPROVED PLAYER: BRIAN LEWIS
MOST INSPIRATIONAL: ERIC WURTS
ROOKIE OF THE YEAR: TROY TANNER
BEST OFFENSIVE PLAYER: KARCH KIRALY
SPORTSMANSHIP AWARD: LARRY MEAR
MOST VALUABLE PLAYER: KARCH KIRALY

FIVB

The 1992 FIVB beach volleyball tour included four men's tour sites with the total prize money worth $494,750.00. The women's FIVB Pro-Beach Volleyball Tour would start-up with an additional $100,000.00 in prize money. The 1992 FIVB Men's Tour included stops in five countries, including Sydney Australia, Rio de Janeiro Brazil, Enoshima Japan, Almeria Spain, and Lignano Italy.

Sinjin Smith and Randy Stoklos entered the first three FIVB events and won all three of them. There three international wins came at the FIVB events in Sydney Australia, Almeria Spain and the "World Championships" in Rio de Janeiro Brazil, The Brazilian team of Paulo Roberto DaCosta Moreira and Paulo Emilo Azevedo Silva showed that they could play the game of beach volleyball by winning two FIVB events. The Brazilian team picked-up tournament championships at the Enoshima Japan and Lignano Italy FIVB events.

RANDY STOKLOS
Randy Stoklos teamed-up with Sinjin Smith for 6 tournament championships in 1992. They won 3 AVP and 3 FIVB events. Above photo, Stoklos cuts the ball into the block of Kent Steffes.
Photo Courtesy of the AVP

INDIVIDUAL FIVB TOURNAMENT FINISHES
1992

Player	1st	2nd	3rd	4th	5th
Osvaldo Agustine Archer Abreu	0	0	0	0	1
Claudino Aloizio	0	0	0	1	0
Eduardo Bacil	0	0	1	0	0
Andrew Burdin	0	0	0	2	0
George Carey	0	0	0	0	1
Robert Anthony Curci	0	0	0	0	1
Carlos Eduardo Garrido Dias	0	2	1	0	0
Roberto Duarte Dias	0	2	1	0	0
Mark Eller	0	1	0	0	0
Scott Friederichsen	0	0	1	0	0
Andrea Ghiurghi	0	0	0	0	1
Jean Philippe Jodard	0	0	1	0	3
Hannes Kronthaler	0	0	0	0	1
Jan Kvalheim	0	0	0	1	1
Dionisio Lequaglie	0	0	0	0	1
Andre Perlingeiro Lima	0	1	1	0	1
Jose Loiola	0	0	0	1	0
Roberto Costa Lopes	0	0	1	0	0
Bjorn Maaseide	0	0	0	1	1
Luiz Guilherme Marquez	0	1	1	0	1
Guliberto Chavarry Martins	0	0	1	0	0
Paulo Roberto DaCosta Moreira	2	1	0	0	0
Jose Franco Vieira Neto	0	0	1	0	0
Jose Marco Melo Ferreira Nobrega	0	0	0	0	1
Denny Gomes Paredes	0	0	0	0	1
Christian Penigaud	0	0	1	0	3
Stefan Potyka	0	0	0	0	1
Julien Prosser	0	0	0	2	0
Todd Schaffer	0	1	0	0	0
Paulo Emilo Azevedo Silva	2	1	0	0	0
Sinjin Smith	3	0	0	0	0
Randy Stoklos	3	0	0	0	0
Eugenio Telles	0	0	0	0	1
Tim Walmer	0	0	1	0	0

MEN'S TOURNAMENT RESULTS
1992-AVP

HONOLULU HAWAII
January 30th-February 1st, 1992

The AVP Pro-Beach Volleyball Tour went to Honolulu Hawaii for the $75,000.00 Miller Lite Hawaiian Open. Sinjin Smith and Randy Stoklos won the tournament, after working their way out of the loser's bracket. In the championship match, Smith and Stoklos defeated Adam Johnson and Kent Steffes by scores of 15-5 and 6-4 to earn the $15,000.00 first place check.

3rd Place: Mike Dodd and Tim Hovland
4th Place: Andrew Smith and Bruk Vandeweghe
5th Place: Bill Boullianne and John Eddo
5th Place: Jon Stevenson and Mike Whitmarsh

PENSACOLA FLORIDA
March 21st-22nd, 1992

On the weekend of March 21st-22nd, 1992, the AVP Pro-Beach Tour was scheduled to compete in Pensacola Florida. Due to heavy rain, the tournament was canceled with the four teams remaining in the semi-finals receiving fifth-place money and the eight teams in the loser's bracket pocketed ninth-place money.

FORT MYERS FLORIDA
March 28th-29th, 1992

The AVP Pro-Beach Volleyball Tour's next stop was at Fort Myers Florida. Again, after working their way out of the loser's bracket, the team of Sinjin Smith and Randy Stoklos were defeated by, Adam Johnson and Kent Steffes, by scores of 15-5 and 6-5 in the championship match. The winners collected $15,000.00 for their efforts.

Earlier, Smith and Stoklos had defeated Johnson and Steffes by the lopsided score of 15-3 in the winner's bracket final. After returning the favor with their lopsided victory in the first game of the final, Stoklos and Johnson were behind by a score of 5-2 in the overtime match, but they were able to come back and tie the score at 15-all. Then a rally followed, featuring two digs by Johnson, two by Sinjin and one by Steffes. The rally took 25 seconds off the rally clock and finally ended when Steffes made a tight shot down the line. With 5 and 1/2 seconds left, Johnson served a "skyball" that was passed by Stoklos

SINJIN SMITH
Sinjin Smith enjoyed some success in 1992, advancing to 11 AVP finals and 3 FIVB finals, winning 6 times. Above photo, Smith reaches-up to make the block.
Photo Courtesy of Frank Goroszko

ERIC WURTS
Eric Wurts played well on the 1992 , advancing to the finals of 3 AVP Tour events, finishing in the 2nd spot each time. Above photo, Wurts hits a set from Pono Ma'a past the block of Kent Steffes.
Photo Courtesy of the AVP

and put-away by Sinjin on a second hit, leaving one second on the clock. Smith and Stoklos now had one last serve to try to send the match into sudden death, but Johnson put the ball away off of a Stoklos block attempt.

3rd Place: Mike Dodd and Tim Hovland
4th Place: Andrew Smith and Bruk Vandeweghe
5th Place: John Hanley and Dan Vrebalovich

FRESNO CALIFORNIA
April 4th-5th, 1992

The AVP Pro-Beach Volleyball Tour moved out of Florida to Fresno California. Adam Johnson and Kent Steffes defeated Brent Frohoff and Mike Whitmarsh in an exciting championship match, by a score of 15-12. They earned $15,000.00 for their first place effort.

During this tournament, Powers and Lewis were so disgusted with each other at one point Powers told Lewis that this was going to be their last tournament together, Lewis reacted by throwing sand at Powers. In return, the 6'6" Powers rifled a ball into the chest of Lewis as the pair threatened to come to blows, but they did not, and they remained partners for additional tournaments in 1992.

3rd Place: Mike Dodd and Tim Hovland
4th Place: Eric Boyles and Leif Hanson
5th Place: Pat Powers and Brian Lewis
5th Place: Larry Mear and Eric Wurts

PHOENIX ARIZONA
April 11th-12th, 1992

The AVP Pro-Beach Tour moved onto Phoenix Arizona. The team of Sinjin Smith and Randy Stoklos defeated Adam Johnson and Kent Steffes by a score of 15-11. Stoklos and Smith split the first place prize of $15,000.00.

3rd Place: Mike Dodd and Tim Hovland
4th Place: Brian Lewis and Pat Powers
5th Place: Rudy Dvorak and Craig Moothart
5th Place: Brent Frohoff and Mike Whitmarsh

CLEARWATER BEACH FLORIDA
April 24th-25th, 1992

On the weekend of April 24th-25th, 1992, the AVP Pro-Beach Volleyball Tour was on the beach in Clearwater Florida for the $150,000.00 Jose Cuervo Gold Crown. In the championship match, the fourth seeded team of Brian Lewis and Pat Powers defeated Sinjin Smith and Randy Stoklos by a score of 15-10 to earn the $60,000.00 first place prize. Powers and Lewis started the final by taking a 3-2 lead. Stoklos and Smith went ahead at 7-5. Then Powers took control of the net as he blocked seven balls in the championship match and forced at least two additional hitting errors as he and Lewis rolled to their 15-10 triumph. This was the first career championship for Lewis.

3rd Place: Bruk Vandeweghe and John Hanley
4th Place: Adam Johnson and Kent Steffes
5th Place: Tim Hovland and Mike Dodd

BRIAN LEWIS
In 1992, Brian "Lewey" Lewis played well enough to advance to 5 championship matches, winning once. Above photo, Lewey bangs the ball past the block of Randy Stoklos.
Photo Courtesy of the AVP

CHRIS YOUNG
Chris Young provided some stiff competition on the 1992 AVP Tour. Above photo, Young hits a set from Dan Vrebalovich past the block of Robert Chavez.
Photo Courtesy of the AVP

AUSTIN TEXAS
May 2nd-3rd, 1992

The AVP Pro-Beach Volleyball Tour was in Austin Texas on the weekend of May 2nd-3rd, 1992 for the Miller Lite Austin Open. The team of Karch Kiraly and Kent Steffes showed a preview of what the tour could expect to see in the next few seasons, by winning the championship match. Randy Stoklos and Sinjin Smith were not able to continue due to an injury to Smith, allowing Kiraly and Steffes to take home the $15,000.00 purse.

3rd Place: Brian Lewis and Pat Powers
4th Place: Adam Johnson and Ricci Luyties
5th Place: Mike Dodd and Jon Stevenson
5th Place: Scott Ayakatubby and Tim Walmer

NEW ORLEANS LOUISIANA
May 9th-10th, 1992

The AVP Pro-Beach Volleyball Tour made its way to New Orleans Louisiana for the Miller Lite New Orleans Open. The surprise team of the tournament, Brent Frohoff and Mike Whitmarsh, went through the tournament undefeated as they beat Karch Kiraly and Kent Steffes in the championship match by a score of 15-12. This was the first AVP tournament championship for Whitmarsh.

3rd Place: Mike Dodd and Jon Stevenson
4th Place: Randy Stoklos and Sinjin Smith
5th Place: Scott Ayakatubby and Tim Walmer
5th Place: Rudy Dvorak and Craig Moothart

SAN ANTONIO TEXAS
May 16th-17th, 1992

On this weekend, the AVP Pro-Beach Volleyball Tour was in San Antonio Texas for the Miller Lite San Antonio Open. This tournament would mark the start of an historic string of championship victories for Karch Kiraly and Kent Steffes. Kiraly and Steffes split the $15,000.00 earnings. In the championship match, Kiraly and Steffes defeated Brian Lewis and Pat Powers, by a score of 15-11. This victory was the first of thirteen consecutive AVP Tour championships for them, equaling the mark set by Jim Menges and Greg Lee that began during the 1976 beach volleyball tour and completed during the 1977 beach volleyball tour.

3rd Place: Sinjin Smith and Randy Stoklos
4th Place: Bruk Vandeweghe and John Hanley
5th Place: Robert Chavez and Doug Foust
5th Place: Adam Johnson and Ricci Luyties

FORT WORTH TEXAS
May 16th-17th, 1992

The AVP Pro-Beach Volleyball Tour continued its Texas swing, in Fort Worth Texas for the Miller Lite Fort Worth Open. Larry Mear and Eric Wurts surprised everybody by going undefeated into the championship match, where they lost in an exhilarating double final to Karch Kiraly and Kent Steffes, by scores of 15-10 and 7-3. Mear and Wurts were impressive in the semi-finals with a victory over Mike Whitmarsh and Brent Frohoff 13-10.

KENT STEFFES
Kent Steffes was able to side-out against all of the oposition on the 1992 AVP Tour. Above photo, Steffes hits the ball past the block of Randy Stoklos for another side-out.
Photo Courtesy of the AVP

BRENT FROHOFF
In 1992, Brent "Fro" Frohoff finished within the top five 15 times, advancing to the championship match 3 times, winning one championship. Above photo, "Fro" jump serving.
Photo Courtesy of Frank Goroszko

They were even more impressive in the winner's bracket final with a 15-2 victory over Leif Hanson and Eric Boyles. Hanson and Boyles then lost to Kiraly and Steffes in a fifty-five minute battle. By the time the finals started, Kiraly and Steffes were tired, but not spent, as they went on to collect the $15,000.00 winnings. This was Kiraly's 45th career tournament championship, which put him ahead of Jim Menges on the all-time career open winner's list.

3rd Place: Brian Lewis and Pat Powers
4th Place: Roger Clark and Scott Friederichsen
5th Place: Brent Frohoff and Mike Whitmarsh
5th Place: Bruk Vandeweghe and John Hanley

SAN DIEGO CALIFORNIA
May 30th-31st, 1992

The AVP Pro-Beach Volleyball Tour was back in California, on Mission Beach, in San Diego, for the $75,000.00 Men's Miller Lite San Diego Open. After dropping into the loser's bracket, Karch Kiraly and Kent Steffes came back to claim the title and split the $15,000.00 first prize. In the championship match, Karch and Kent defeated Sinjin Smith and Randy Stoklos, in an arousing double final, by scores of 14-7 and 6-3.

3rd Place: Brian Lewis and Pat Powers
4th Place: Adam Johnson and Ricci Luyties
5th Place: Brian Gatzke and Jeff Rodgers
5th Place: Brent Frohoff and Mike Whitmarsh

BOULDER COLORADO
June 5th-6th, 1992

The AVP Pro-Beach Volleyball Tour was in Boulder Colorado for the $150,000.00 Men's Jose Cuervo Gold Crown event. The team of Karch Kiraly and Kent Steffes were the winner's of the title and claimed the top prize of $80,000.00. In the championship match, Kiraly and Steffes embarrassed Randy Stoklos and Sinjin Smith 15-1. The runners-up collected $16,880.00 for their efforts.

3rd Place: Brent Frohoff and Mike Whitmarsh
4th Place: Pat Powers and Brian Lewis
5th Place: Troy Tanner and Dan Vrebalovich

CHICAGO ILLINOIS
June 13th-14th, 1992

The AVP Pro-Beach Volleyball Tour staged its next event in Chicago Illinois, the $100,000.00 Men's AVP/Miller Lite Chicago Open. Karch Kiraly and Kent Steffes were the winners of the championship match and the $20,000.00 first place prize. In the championship match, Kiraly and Steffes out-pointed Mike Dodd and Tim Hovland, by a score of 15-10. Dodd and Hovland split $12,000.00 as the runners-up.

3rd Place: Adam Johnson and Ricci Luyties
4th Place: Brent Frohoff and Mike Whitmarsh
5th Place: Robert Chavez and Doug Foust
5th Place: Brian Lewis and Pat Powers

ADAM JOHNSON
Adam "AJ" Johnson finished within the top five 14 times, on the 1992 AVP Tour, advancing to the finals 6 times, winning once. Above photo, "AJ" hits the ball past the block of Mike Whitmarsh.
Photo Courtesy of the AVP

BRUK VANDEWEGHE
On the 1992 AVP Tour, Bruk Vandeweghe finished within the top five on six occasions. Above photo, Vandeweghe hits the ball into the block of Randy Stoklos. Sinjin Smith is on defense.
Photo Courtesy of the AVP

CAPE COD MASSACHUSETTS
June 20th-21st, 1992

The 1992 Men's $75,000.00 AVP/Miller Lite Cape Cod Open was won by Karch Kiraly and Kent Steffes. They split the $15,000.00 first place prize money. In the championship match, Kiraly and Steffes defeated Sinjin Smith and Randy Stoklos by a score of 15-7. This victory allowed them to continue their string of championship victories.

3rd Place: Mike Dodd and Tim Hovland
4th Place: Brent Frohoff and Mike Whitmarsh
5th Place: Robert Chavez and Doug Foust
5th Place: Brian Lewis and Pat Powers

LOUISVILLE KENTUCKY
June 27th-28th, 1992

On the weekend of June 27th-28th, 1992, the AVP Pro-Beach Volleyball Tour was in Louisville Kentucky for the $75,000.00 Miller Lite Louisville Open. Karch Kiraly and Kent Steffes were the winner's once again. They added another $15,000.00 check to their 1992 earnings. In the championship match, Kiraly and Steffes easily defeated Adam Johnson and Ricci Luyties by a score of 15-5.

3rd Place: Brent Frohoff and Mike Whitmarsh
4th Place: Mike Dodd and Tim Hovland
5th Place: Roger Clark and Scott Friederichsen
5th Place: Bruk Vandeweghe and Dan Vrebalovich

MANHATTAN BEACH CALIFORNIA
July 3rd-5th, 1992

The 1992 AVP Killer Loop Manhattan Beach Men's Open took place on the south side of the pier, on the sands of Manhattan Beach California. The championship match was another victory for Karch Kiraly and Kent Steffes, but not without a scare provided by the challengers. Sinjin Smith and Randy Stoklos had worked their way through the loser's bracket to get to the championship match. They then went on to win the first game in the finals, by a score of 12-10, ending a 31-game winning streak for Kiraly and Steffes. This set the stage for one of the most unusual Manhattan Championships of all time. Before the tournament, players were informed that in case of a double final the second game would be a one minute or three points because Prime Ticket was televising the event live with a ridged schedule. The first game win forced the one-game, one-minute final. Both teams sensed the pressure of the match. The only score of the game came, forty seconds into the game, on a dig and put-away by Steffes. Kiraly and Steffes eventually posted the first 1-0 victory in the history of the Manhattan Beach Men's Open.

3rd Place: Brian Lewis and Craig Moothart
4th Place: Mike Dodd and Tim Hovland
5th Place: John Hanley and Troy Tanner
5th Place: Mike Whitmarsh and Brent Frohoff

JON STEVENSON
Jon Stevenson was still providing some stiff competition on the AVP Tour in 1992. Above photo, Stevenson slices the ball past the block of Albert Hannemann.
Photo Courtesy of the AVP

SHAWN DAVIS
Shawn Davis made the top teams work for their victories on the 1992 AVP Tour. Above photo, Davis hits the ball over the block of Randy Stoklos. Sinjin Smith is on defense.
Photo Courtesy of the AVP

PHILADELPHIA PENNSYLVANIA
July 11th-12th, 1992

The AVP Pro-Beach Volleyball Tour moved into Philadelphia Pennsylvania for their 17th scheduled tournament of the 1992 season. In the championship match, Karch Kiraly and Kent Steffes were winners again as they earned $15,000.00 for their efforts. They defeated the newly formed team of Tim Hovland and Brian Lewis by a score of 15-6. Hovland and Dodd had "divorced" their very successful and long-standing partnership during the prior week.

3rd Place: Mike Dodd and Pat Powers
4th Place: Sinjin Smith and Randy Stoklos
5th Place: Leif Hanson and Wes Welch

BELMAR BEACH NEW JERSEY
July 18th-19th, 1992

The AVP Pro-Beach Volleyball Tour was on the beach at Belmar Beach New Jersey for the Miller Lite Belmar Open. This time, in the championship match, it was Karch Kiraly and Kent Steffes by a score of 13-6 over Tim Hovland and Brian Lewis. Kiraly and Steffes split the $20,000.00 first place prize money.

3rd Place: Mike Dodd and Pat Powers
4th Place: Sinjin Smith and Randy Stoklos
5th Place: Ricci Luyties and Mike Whitmarsh
5th Place: Roger Clark and Scott Friederichsen

MIKE DODD
Mike Dodd earned 19 top five finishes, on the 1992 AVP Tour, advancing to the finals 3 times, winning once. Above photo, Dodd spikes the ball past the block of Mike Whitmarsh.
Photo Courtesy of the AVP

GRAND HAVEN MICHIGAN
July 25th-26th, 1992

The AVP Pro-Beach Volleyball Tour was in Grand Haven Michigan, for its 19th stop of the season. Mike Dodd and Pat Powers won the semifinal match over Brent Frohoff and Adam Johnson, putting them into the championship match, where they were defeated by Karch Kiraly and Kent Steffes, by a score of 15-9. This time Kiraly and Steffes split $15,000.00 for the win. This win by Karch and Kent, set a single-season AVP record for most consecutive tournament wins at eleven. The old record of ten was established by Sinjin Smith and Randy Stoklos in 1986. The all-time record of 13 straight open tournament titles was established in the 1975 and 1976 seasons by Jim Menges and Greg Lee. Lee and Menges won the last nine tournaments of 1975 and the first four of 1976.

3rd Place: Brent Frohoff and Adam Johnson
4th Place: Ricci Luyties and Mike Whitmarsh
5th Place: John Hanley and Troy Tanner
5th Place: Sinjin Smith and Randy Stoklos

MILWAUKEE WISCONSIN
August 1st-2nd, 1992

The AVP Pro-Beach Volleyball Tour's 20th event of the 1992 season was in Milwaukee Wisconsin for the Miller Lite Milwaukee Men's Open. Karch Kiraly and Kent Steffes continued their winning streak by defeating Larry Mear and Eric Wurts for the title. In the championship match, Kiraly and Steffes won by a score of 15-9. This win put them at twelve championships in a row, setting them up for a chance to tie Jim Menges's and Greg Lee's record of thirteen in a row.

3rd Place: Sinjin Smith and Randy Stoklos
4th Place: Brent Frohoff and Adam Johnson
5th Place: Ricci Luyties and Mike Whitmarsh
5th Place: Tim Hovland and Brian Lewis

DAN VREBALOVICH
On the 1992 AVP Tour, Dan Vrebalovich was still a competitive player. Above photo, Vrebalovich has perfect form while passing the ball during a 1992 AVP Tour event.
Photo Courtesy of the AVP

CLEVELAND OHIO
August 8th-9th, 1992

The AVP Pro-Beach Volleyball Tour was in Cleveland Ohio, where the tournament had an historic finish. At the 1992 AVP Miller Lite Cleveland Open, Karch Kiraly and Kent Steffes moved into the record books by defeating Sinjin Smith and Randy Stoklos in the championship match. Their 15-11 win was the thirteenth tournament championship win in a row, for Kiraly and Steffes, tying them with Greg Lee and Jim Menges's record of thirteen in a row, set during the 1976 and 1977, beach volleyball tours.

3rd Place: Brent Frohoff and Adam Johnson
4th Place: Mike Dodd and Pat Powers
5th Place: Mike Whitmarsh and Ricci Luyties
5th Place: Tim Hovland and Brian Lewis

SEAL BEACH CALIFORNIA
August 14th-16th, 1992

The AVP Pro-Beach Volleyball Tour was on the beach at Seal Beach California, where Kiraly and Steffes finished out of the top four to put a stop to their incredible streak of thirteen championship wins in a row. The 1992 AVP Miller Lite Seal Beach Open was won by Mike Dodd and Pat Powers. In the championship match, the surprise team of the tournament, Larry Mear and Eric Wurts lost to Dodd and Powers by a score of 15-5.

3rd Place: Sinjin Smith and Randy Stoklos
4th Place: Ricci Luyties and Mike Whitmarsh
5th Place: Luyties and Whitmarsh
5th Place: Scott Friederichsen and Tim Walmer

SANTA CRUZ CALIFORNIA
August 21st-22nd, 1992

On the weekend of August 21st-22nd, 1992, the AVP Pro-Beach Volleyball Tour was in Santa Cruz California, for the $225,000.00 Men's Jose Cuervo Gold Crown event. Ricci Luyties and Brent Frohoff moved up for a tournament championship. In the championship match, they defeated Brian Lewis and Mike Whitmarsh, in an arousing, back-and-forth championship match, by a score of 15-13. Luyties and Frohoff split the first place prize of $100,000.00.

3rd Place: Scott Friederichsen and Tim Walmer
4th Place: Karch Kiraly and Kent Steffes
5th Place: Tim Hovland and Adam Johnson

HERMOSA BEACH CALIFORNIA
August 28th-30th, 1992

The 1992 AVP $250,000.00 Men's Miller Lite "U.S. Championship" was held on the north side of the pier, in Hermosa Beach California. Karch Kiraly and Kent Steffes were back with their winning ways. They won their first three matches by scores of 15-1, 15-6, and 15-0. They then outlasted Brent Frohoff and Ricci Luyties by a score of 15-13. Next they put away Sinjin Smith and Randy Stoklos by a score of 15-7. In the championship match, with TV cameras rolling, Kiraly and Steffes squared-off with Tim Hovland and Adam Johnson. The match started as Hovland roofed Kiraly at 1-1, "Hov" then ripped-off his shirt at 3-3. Next he roofed Steffes for a 5-4 lead. At 5-5 Kiraly and Steffes took over, winning

SCOTT AYAKATUBBY
Scott "Ack" Ayakatubby provided some "thunder" on the 1992 AVP Tour. Above photo, "Ack" reaches high for another successful put-away.
Photo Courtesy of "Couvi"

SINJIN SMITH & RANDY STOKLOS
Sinjin Smith and Randy Stoklos played well against all of the top teams, on the 1992 AVP Tour. Above photo, Smith hits a set from Stoklos, past the block of Tim Hovland.
Photo Courtesy of the AVP

seven points in a row and closing out to an easy 15-6 victory. This victory put Karch only one tournament title behind the legendary Ron Von Hagen's 62 career tournament championships.

3rd Place: Sinjin Smith and Randy Stoklos
4th Place Mike Dodd and Pat Powers
5th Place: Ricci Luyties and Brent Frohoff
5th Place: Brian Lewis and Mike Whitmarsh

FORMER U.S. CHAMPIONS

1976	Jim Menges and Greg Lee
1977	Jim Menges and Chris Marlowe
1978	Steve Obradovich and Gary Hooper
1979	Sinjin Smith and Karch Kiraly
1980	Andy Fishburn and Dane Selznick
1981	Sinjin Smith and Karch Kiraly
1982	Sinjin Smith and Randy Stoklos
1983	Mike Dodd and Tim Hovland
1984	Andy Fishburn and Jay Hanseth
1985	Mike Dodd and Tim Hovland
1986	Mike Dodd and Tim Hovland
1987	Mike Dodd and Tim Hovland
1988	Sinjin Smith and Randy Stoklos
1989	Mike Dodd and Tim Hovland
1990	Sinjin Smith and Randy Stoklos
1991	Brent Frohoff and Ricci Luyties

SANTA BARBARA CALIFORNIA
September 10th-12th, 1992

The AVP Pro-Beach Volleyball Tour's next event was the $100,000.00 Men's Miller Lite "Tournament of Champions," in Santa Barbara California. Karch Kiraly and Kent Steffes took the title and the $30,000.00 first place check. In an exciting double final, Kiraly and Steffes defeated Sinjin Smith and Randy Stoklos by scores of 12-7 and 6-5. This victory for Karch tied him with the legendary Ron Von Hagen's 62 career tournament championships.

3rd Place: Brian Lewis and Mike Whitmarsh
4th Place: Mike Dodd and Pat Powers
5th Place: Brent Frohoff and Ricci Luyties
5th Place: Tim Hovland and Adam Johnson

DAYTONA BEACH FLORIDA
September 25th-27th, 1992

The 1992 AVP "King of the Beach" tournament was staged at Daytona Beach Florida. Karch Kiraly was crowned the "King of the Beach." He earned the most points during this "partner switching" round-robin tournament. Kiraly also earned $64,000.00 for his first place finish. This was Kiraly's 63rd victory, which put Karch ahead of the legendary Ron Von Hagen's 62 career tournament championships. Pat Powers was second.

3rd Place: Mike Dodd
4th Place: Tim Hovland
5th Place: Randy Stoklos
6th Place: Adam Johnson
7th Place: Sinjin Smith
8th Place: Kent Steffes

RICCI LUYTIES
Ricci Luyties was up for the competition on the 1992 AVP Tour. Luyties finished within the top five 12 times, advancing to the finals twice, winning once. Above photo, Luyties up for the block.
Photo Courtesy of the AVP

KARCH KIRALY
In 1992, Karch Kiraly had a great season, winning 17 tournament championships, including the 1992 "King of the Beach" title. Above photo, Kiraly hits the ball past the block of Randy Stoklos.
Photo Courtesy of the AVP

MEN'S TOURNAMENT RESULTS
1992-FIVB

SYDNEY, AUSTRALIA
January 15th-19, 1992

In Sydney Australia, the U.S.A. team of Randy Stoklos and Sinjin Smith defeated the Brazilian team of Andre Perlingeiro Lima and Luiz Guilherme Marquez, to win the $50,000.00 FIVB Pro Beach Volleyball event. The final scores were 12-9 and 12-2. The winner's split the first place prize of $12,000.00. Smith and Stoklos came-out number one out of sixty-nine teams from twenty-one countries that participated.

3rd Place: Jose Franco Vieira Neto and Roberto Costa Lopes-Bra
4th Place: Julien Prosser and Andrew Burdin-Aus
5th Place: George Carey and Robert Anthony Curcci-USA
5th Place: Jean Philippe Jodard and Christian Penigaud-Fra

RIO DE JANEIRO, BRAZIL
February 19th-23rd, 1992

The U.S.A. team of Randy Stoklos and Sinjin Smith won the $100,000.00 FIVB World Beach Volleyball Championship at Copacabana Beach in Rio de Janeiro Brazil, where sixty-nine teams from twenty-one countries participated. In the championship match, Smith and Stoklos defeated the Brazilian team of Paulo Roberto Moreira and Paula Emilio Azevedo Silva, by scores of 12-3 and 12-5. They earned $24,000.00 for their winning effort.

3rd Place: Carlos Eduardo Garrido Dias and Roberto Duarte Dias-Bra
3rd Place: Eduardo Bacil and Guliberto Chavarry-Bra
5th Place: Andre Perlingeiro Lima and Guilherme Marquez-Bra
5th Place: Jose Melo Ferreira Nobrega and Denny Gomes Paredes-Bra

ALMERIA, SPAIN
August 12th-15th, 1992

The next FIVB Pro Beach Volleyball event was staged in Almeria Spain. This event had a purse of $200,000.00 and hosted thirty-seven teams from fourteen countries. The U.S.A. team of Stoklos and Smith outclassed Carlos Eduardo Garrido Dias and Roberto Duarte Dias, from Brazil, 12-3 and 12-3, to win the championship match. They also split the $70,000.00 first place check.

3rd Place: Andre Perlingeiro Lima and Guilherme Marquez-Bra
4th Place: Jan Kvalheim and Bjorn Maaseide-Nor
5th Place: Jean Philippe Jodard and Christian Penigaud-France
5th Place: Osvaldo Abreau and Eugenio Ortiz-Cuba

The U.S.A. team of Steve Obradovich and Steve Timmons were in the eighth spot.

LIGNANO, ITALY
August 18th-23rd, 1992

At Lignano Italy, the FIVB Pro Beach Volleyball event was an all Brazilian final, with Paulo Roberto Da Costa Moreira and Paulo Emilo Azevedo Silva winning the event. This event hosted thirty-seven teams from fourteen countries. In the championship match, they defeated Carlos Eduardo Garrido Dias and Roberto Duarte Dias by scores of 9-12, 13-11, and 15-12.

3rd Place: Tim Walmer and Scott Friederichsen-USA
4th Place: Jose Loiola and Claudino Aloizio-Bra
5th Place: Hannes Kronthaler and Stefan Potyka-Austria
5th Place: Jean Philippe Jodard and Christian Penigaud-France

Americans, Al Janc and Craig Moothart finished in ninth place.

ENOSHIMA, JAPAN
August 28th-30th, 1992

The next $100,000.00 FIVB Pro Beach Volleyball event took place at Enoshima Japan., where thirty-seven teams from fourteen countries participated. The Brazilian team of Paulo Roberto Da Costa Moreira and Paulo Emilio Azevedo Silva defeated the U.S.A. team of Mark Eller and Todd Schaffer, 12-6 and 12-4, to win the championship match. The winner's split a $30,000.00 for their winning effort.

3rd Place: Jean Philippe Jodard and Christian Penigaud-Fra
4th Place: Julien Prosser and Andrew Burdin-Aus
5th Place: Andrea Ghiurghi and Dionisio Lequaglie-Italy
5th Place: Jan Kvalheim and Bjorn Maaseide-Nor

JOSE LOIOLA
Jose Loiola began to show-off his extraordindary abilities on the 1992 FIVB Tour. Above photo, Loiola "coils" with the follow-through, after another thundering spike.
Photo Courtesy of "Couvi"

TOP PHOTOS: Left: Leif Hanson takes a good swing. **Center:** Tony Zapata setting the ball while Andrew Smith gets ready on defense. **Right:** Albert Hannemann passing the ball.

MIDDLE PHOTOS: Left: Eric Boyles hits the ball past the block of Ricci Luyties. **Center:** Marvin Hall entertaining the crowd with some dance moves. **Right:** Al Janc passing the ball.

1992 MEN'S BEACH VOLLEYBALL ACTION

BOTTOM PHOTOS: Left: Pat Powers ready to make the play at the net. **Center:** Canadian Brian Gatzke passing the ball. **Right:** Dr. Tim Brown passing the ball to partner Jim Menges.

Photo's Courtesy of the AVP

TOP PHOTOS: Left: Paul Sunderland (left) interviewing Ricci Luyties (center) and Brent Frohoff (right). **Center:** Mark Eller gets the ball past the block. **Right:** Roger Clark hits a set from Scott Friederichsen past the block of Tim Hovland.

MIDDLE PHOTOS: Left: Chris Young Passing the ball. **Center:** John Brajevic passing the ball. **Right:** Brian Lewis demonstrates perfect form, while passing the ball.

1992 MEN'S BEACH VOLLEYBALL ACTION

BOTTOM PHOTOS: Left: Craig Moothart passing the ball. **Center:** The "Primitive-Prince" Scott Ayakatubby reaches high to bump the ball. **Right:** Mike Dodd reaches high to make a dig.

Photo's Courtesy of the AVP

WOMEN'S BEACH VOLLEYBALL
1992

WPVA

In August of 1992, the WPVA announced the loss of their ESPN television contract. They also announced a decrease in prize money. The players were not happy about these events, but were saddened even more when the WPVA founding president, and legendary player Nina Grouwinkel Matthies announced her retirement at the age of 39. Nina's career lasted for twenty-seven years as she was one of the driving forces behind women's professional beach volleyball.

The 1992 WPVA tour had 17 tour stops with a total of $624,300.00 in prize money.

Karolyn Kirby proved to be the top player on the 1992 WPVA Tour. She reached 11 finals and with eight tournament championships she was the top money winner, earning nearly $75,000.00. Kirby, won 5 events with Angela Rock and 3 with Nancy Reno. Angela Rock entered 9 finals as she finished the season with 6 tournament championships, winning 5 with Karolyn Kirby and 1 with Jackie Silva. Liz Masakayan and Linda Chisholm Carrillo, as a team, reached 9 finals, winning 5 times.

1992 WPVA AWARDS
BEST SETTER: JACKIE SILVA
BEST BLOCKER: NANCY RENO
BEST HITTER: KAROLYN KIRBY
MOST IMPROVED PLAYER: NANCY RENO
MOST INSPIRATIONAL: CAMMY CIARELLI
ROOKIE OF THE YEAR: VALINDA HILLEARY
BEST DEFENSIVE PLAYER: LIZ MASAKAYAN
SPORTSWOMANSHIP AWARD: ELAINE ROQUE
MOST VALUABLE PLAYER: LIZ MASAKAYAN

INDIVIDUAL WPVA TOURNAMENT FINISHES
1992

Player	1st	2nd	3rd	4th	5th
Linda Chisholm Carrillo	5	4	1	3	2
Gail Castro	0	1	0	1	7
Cammy Ciareilli	1	1	8	1	2
Patty Dodd	0	1	3	3	3
Barbara Fontana	0	0	1	2	3
Lori Kotas Forsythe	0	1	0	1	6
Heather Hafner	0	0	0	0	1
Janice Opalinski Harrer	1	4	0	3	4
Alison Johnson	0	0	0	1	0
Karolyn Kirby	8	3	2	0	1
Lisa Strand Ma'a	0	1	0	0	0
Liz Masakayan	5	4	1	3	2
Nina Grouwinkel Matthies	0	0	0	0	1
Holly McPeak	0	0	3	2	4
Shannon Miller	0	0	0	0	1
Marla O'Hara	0	0	0	0	3
Nancy Reno	4	3	2	2	2
Deb Richardson	0	0	1	3	3
Angela Rock	6	3	2	0	3
Elaine Roque	0	3	2	4	2
Rita Crockett Royster	0	1	1	0	1
Dennie Schupyt-Knoop	0	0	0	0	3
Jackie Silva	2	2	5	1	3
Gail Stammer	0	0	0	1	4

KAROLYN KIRBY
1992 WPVA "Best-Hitter, Karolyn Kirby was the top winner on the 1992 WPVA Tour with 8 tournament championships. Above photo, Kirby shows good form while passing the ball.
Photo Courtesy of Frank Goroszko

LIZ MASAKAYAN
1992 WPVA "Most Valuable Player" Liz Masakayan was also the WPVA "Best Defensive" player in 1992. Above photo, Masakayan coils to deliver a hard-driven jump serve.
Photo Courtesy of Frank Goroszko

FIVB

The 1992 FIVB women's tour had only one stop, it was in Almeria Spain. The total prize money on the FIVB women's pro beach volleyball tour for 1992 was worth $50,000.00.

ALMERIA, SPAIN
August 12th-15th, 1992

In Almeria, Spain the first $50,000.00 FIVB women's beach volleyball crown was won by the U.S.A. team of Nancy Reno and Karolyn Kirby. They were the winner's over a field of sixteen teams from eight countries. In the championship match, they defeated fellow American's Linda Chisholm Carrillo and Angela Rock, 12-3 and 12-3, to take home the first place prize of $9,500.00. Kirby, went on to win five out of the next eight FIVB tournaments that she participated in.

3rd Place: Ana Roseli Timm and Roseliane Dos Santos-Brazil
4th Place: Jackie Silva and Maria Isabel Salgado Barroso-Brazil
5th Place: Anita Palm and Jacqui Vukosa-Australia

1992 INDIVIDUAL FIVB TOURNAMENT FINISHES

Player	1st	2nd	3rd	4th	5th
Marialsabel Salgado Barroso	0	0	0	1	0
Linda Chisholm	0	1	0	0	0
Karolyn Kirby	**1**	**0**	**0**	**0**	**0**
Anita Palm	0	0	0	0	1
Nancy Reno	**1**	**0**	**0**	**0**	**0**
Angela Rock	0	1	0	0	0
Roseliane Dos Santos	0	0	1	0	0
Jackie Silva	0	0	0	1	0
Ana Roseli Timm	0	0	1	0	0
Jacqui Vukosa	0	0	0	0	1

JACKIE SILVA
In 1992, Brazilian Jackie Silva played successfully on both the WPVA and the FIVB Tours. Above photo, Silva shows her hustle while making another dig
Photo Courtesy of Frank Goroszko

1992 WPVA ACTION
Left-To-Right: Elaine Roque, Patty Dodd, Liz Masakayan and Angelia Rock all give the Manhattan Beach crowd a exciting "losers-final" match during the 1992 WPVA event, staged south of the Manhattan Beach Pier.
Photo Courtesy of Frank Goroszko

WOMEN'S TOURNAMENT RESULTS
1992-WPVA

ISLA VERDE PUERTO RICO
April 11th-12th, 1992

The WPVA Pro-Beach Volleyball Tour started its 1992 season at Isla Verde Puerto Rico. Liz Masakayan and Linda Carrillo defeated Janice Harrer and Elaine Roque, in a thrilling double final, after losing the first game 7-15, Liz and Linda put their game back on track for a 7-2 victory to earn the $11,750.00 first place prize.

3rd Place: Karolyn Kirby and Angela Rock
4th Place: Deb Richardson and Jackie Silva
5th Place: Gail Castro and Lori Kotas
5th Place: Cammy Ciarelli and Nancy Reno

FORT MYERS FLORIDA
April 18th-19th, 1992

The WPVA Pro-Beach Volleyball Tour, was played on the beach of Fort Myers Florida, on the weekend of April 18th-19th, 1992, for the Coors Light Fort Myers Open. After a rain delay, Karolyn Kirby and Angela Rock defeated Janice Harrer and Elaine Roque, 15-6, in the championship match. The match was eventually played in the rain on the puddled sand, under dark skies, as Kirby and Rock had a quick run of points to take a 9-4 advantage. At this point the sun came out from behind the dark skies and Rock and Kirby moved onto a 13-4 advantage and eventual 15-6 win.

3rd Place: Cammy Ciarelli and Nancy Reno
4th Place: Lori Kotas and Gail Castro
5th Place: Nina Matthies and Gayle Stammer
5th Place: Linda Chisholm Carrillo and Liz Masakayan

PHOENIX ARIZONA
May 2nd-3rd, 1992

For their next event, the WPVA Pro-Beach Volleyball Tour went to Phoenix Arizona for the Coors Light Phoenix Open. After going through the loser's bracket, Karolyn Kirby and Angela Rock came back to defeat Lori Kotas and Gail Castro, in an inspiring double final, by scores of 15-12 and 7-0. They earned $9,400.00 for their efforts.

3rd Place: Cammy Ciarelli and Nancy Reno
4th Place: Linda Carrillo and Liz Masakayan
5th Place: Janice Harrer and Elaine Roque
5th Place: Marla O'Hara and Dennie Knoop

LINDA CHISHOLM CARRILLO
Linda Chisholm Carrillo teamed-up with Liz Masakayan, on the 1992 WPVA Tour. They advanced to 9 finals, winning five of them. Above photo Chisholm challenging the block of Elaine Roque.
Photo Courtesy of Dennis G. Steers

KAROLYN KIRBY
Karolyn Kirby was the top player on the 1992 WPVA Tour. She reached 11 finals, winning 8 times. Above photo, Kirby attacks a jump serve.
Photo Courtesy of Frank Goroszko

SANTA CRUZ CALIFORNIA
May 9th-10th, 1992

The WPVA Pro-Beach Volleyball Tour's next event was in Santa Cruz California for the Coors Light Santa Cruz Open. Linda Carrillo and Liz Masakayan defeated Karolyn Kirby and Angela Rock in one of the most thrilling double finals of recent WPVA tradition. After working their way through the loser's bracket Kirby and Rock won the first game of the championship match by a score of 16-14, only to loose the second game by a score of 7-5. Carrillo and Masakayan split $9,400.00 for their effort.

3rd Place: Barbra Fontana and Deb Richardson
4th Place: Holly McPeak and Gayle Stammer
5th Place: Gail Castro and Lori Kotas
5th Place: Patty Dodd and Jackie Silva

FRESNO CALIFORNIA
May 16th-17th, 1992

The WPVA Pro-Beach Volleyball Tour made its next stop in Fresno California for the Coors Light Fresno Open. Karolyn Kirby and Angela Rock were able to defeat Linda Carrillo and Liz Masakayan, in the championship match, by a score of 15-10.

3rd Place: Patty Dodd and Jackie Silva
4th Place: Janice Harrer and Elaine Roque
5th Place: Gail Castro and Lori Kotas
5th Place: Marla O'Hara and Dennie Knoop

SEAL BEACH CALIFORNIA
May 23rd-24th, 1992

The next WPVA Coors Light Open Pro-Beach Volleyball Tour event, was played on the beach in Seal Beach California. Nancy Reno and Janice Harrer won the tournament and the first place prize money of $11,750.00. In the surprise championship match-up, Reno and Harrer defeated Rita Crockett and Lisa Strand Ma'a by a score of 15-10.

3rd Place: Karolyn Kirby and Angela Rock
4th Place: Linda Carrillo and Liz Masakayan
5th Place: Heather Hafner and Shannon Miller
5th Place: Patty Dodd and Jackie Silva

LAS VEGAS NEVADA
May 30th-31st, 1992

On the weekend of May 30th-31st, 1992, Linda Carrillo and Liz Masakayan defeated Karolyn Kirby and Angela Rock 15-9, in the finals at the Flamingo Hilton, in Las Vegas, Nevada, to win the $37,500.00 WPVA "Shootout" tournament.

3rd Place: Cammy Ciarelli and Jackie Silva
4th Place: Janice Harrer and Nancy Reno
5th Place: Holly McPeak and Deb Richardson

FORMER WPVA "SHOOTOUT" CHAMPIONS:
1990   Karolyn Kirby and Jackie Silva
1991   Gail Castro and Lori Kotas

NANCY RENO
Nancy Reno was voted the 1992 WPVA "Most Improved Player" and "Best Blocker" Above photo, during the 1992 WPVA event in Seal Beach California, Reno makes a perfect pass.
Photo Courtesy of Frank Goroszko

VALINDA HILLARY
Valinda Hillary was voted the 1992 WPVA "Rookie of the Year" Above photo, Hillary shows good concentration while passing the ball.
Photo Courtesy of the AVP

SAN DIEGO CALIFORNIA
June 6th-7th, 1992

Karolyn Kirby and Angela Rock won their fourth tournament of the season, with a 15-12, championship match victory, over Linda Carrillo and Liz Masakayan at the WPVA Pro-Beach Volleyball Tour's stop in San Diego California.

3rd Place: Cammy Ciarelli and Jackie Silva
4th Place: Janice Harrer and Nancy Reno
5th Place: Elaine Roque and Patty Dodd
5th Place: Gail Castro and Lori Forsythe

HERMOSA BEACH CALIFORNIA
June 13th-14th, 1992

The WPVA Pro-Beach Volleyball Tour's next event was on the beach, in Hermosa Beach California. After working their way through the loser's bracket, Cammy Ciarelli and Jackie Silva were able to win the tournament. In the championship match, Ciarelli and Silva defeated Janice Opalinski Harrer and Nancy Reno, in an arousing double final, by scores of 15-11 and 7-3.

3rd Place: Linda Chisholm Carrillo and Liz Masakayan
4th Place: Barbara Fontana and Deb Richardson
5th Place: Karolyn Kirby and Angela Rock
5th Place: Holly McPeak and Gayle Stammer

AUSTIN TEXAS
June 20th-21st, 1992

Karolyn Kirby and Angela Rock won the WPVA Pro-Beach Volleyball tournament in Austin Texas. After falling into the loser's bracket, Rock and Kirby came back to defeat Patty Dodd and Elaine Roque, in a spirited double final, by scores of 15-9 and 7-3.

3rd Place: Cammy Ciarelli and Jackie Silva
4th Place: Barbra Fontana and Deb Richardson
5th Place: Holly McPeak and Gayle Stammer
5th Place: Nancy Reno and Janice Harrer

CAPE COD MASSACHUSETTS
June 27th-28th, 1992

Linda Carrillo and Liz Masakayan were back on top at the Coors Light WPVA Pro-Beach Volleyball event held in Cape Cod Massachusetts. Masakayan and Carrillo defeated Janice Harrer and Nancy Reno, in a spirited championship match, by a score of 16-14. The winners split $9,400.00 for their efforts.

3rd Place: Patty Dodd and Elaine Roque
4th Place: Cammy Ciarelli and Holly McPeak
5th Place: Barbra Fontana and Deb Richardson
5th Place: Marla O'Hara and Gayle Stammer

JACKIE SILVA
Jackie Silva was voted the 1992 WPVA "Best Setter" Above photo, Silva reaches high to hit the ball over the block. Silova advanced to 4 finals, winning twice. Action took place at the 1992 WPVA event staged on Venice Beach California. Above photo, Silva spiking.
Photo Courtesy of Frank Goroszko

LIZ MASAKAYAN
Liz Masakayan was voted the 1992 WPVA "Best Defensive Player & "Most Valuable Player" Above photo, later in her career, Masakayan hits a set from Linda Hanley, towards the block of Kerri Walsh. Misty May is on defense..
Photo Courtesy of "Couvi"

ATLANTIC CITY NEW JERSEY
July 4th-5th, 1992

Karolyn Kirby and Nancy Reno teamed-up together to win the Coors Light WPVA Pro-Beach Volleyball event held in Atlantic City New Jersey. Kirby and Reno defeated Cammy Ciarelli and Jackie Silva, in the championship match, by a score of 15-11. Reno and Kirby split the $9,400.00 prize money.

3rd Place: Rita Crockett and Holly McPeak
4th Place: Linda Carrillo and Liz Masakayan
5th Place: Barbra Fontana and Deb Richardson
5th Place: Gail Castro and Lori Kotas

MINNEAPOLIS MINNESOTA
July 18th-19th, 1992

The Coors Light WPVA Pro-Beach Volleyball Tour went to Minneapolis Minnesota, where Karolyn Kirby and Nancy Reno defeated Linda Carrillo and Liz Masakayan, in the championship match, by a score of 15-11. Reno and Kirby took home $9,400.00 for their efforts.

3rd Place: Cammy Ciarelli and Jackie Silva
4th Place: Patty Dodd and Elaine Roque
5th Place: Rita Crockett and Holly McPeak
5th Place: Lori Kotas and Angela Rock

BOULDER COLORADO
July 24th-26th, 1992

The Coors Light WPVA Pro-Beach Volleyball Tour made it's next stop in Boulder Colorado. Linda Carrillo and Liz Masakayan were able to reverse last weeks championship match out-come with a 15-13 victory over Karolyn Kirby and Nancy Reno. The victory, after a 4-1 deficit, spoiled a fourteen game win streak by Reno and Kirby.

3rd Place: Cammy Ciarelli and Holly McPeak
4th Place: Patty Dodd and Elaine Roque
5th Place: Angela Rock and Jackie Silva
5th Place: Gail Castro and Janice Harrer

VENICE BEACH CALIFORNIA
August 1st-2nd, 1992

The WPVA Pro-Beach Volleyball Tour went to Venice Beach California to stage the Coors Light "U.S. Women's Open Championships." The team of Angela Rock and Jackie Silva surprised everyone by coming out of the loser's bracket to to win the tournament. In the championship match, Rock and Silva defeated Linda Carrillo and Liz Masakayan, by scores of 15-11 and 7-0 in a arousing double final. The winner's shared $13,800.00.

3rd Place: Cammy Ciarelli and Holly McPeak
4th Place: Patty Dodd and Elaine Roque
5th Place: Barbra Fontana and Deb Richardson
5th Place: Gail Castro and Janice Harrer

FORMER U.S. CHAMPIONS:
1988   Linda Carrillo and Jackie Silva
1989   Linda Carrillo and Janice Harrer
1990   Karolyn Kirby and Jackie Silva
1991   Gail Castro and Lori Kotas

MANHATTAN BEACH CALIFORNIA
August 22nd-23rd, 1992

The WPVA Pro-Beach Volleyball Tour went to Manhattan Beach California, to stage the Coors Light "World Championships." Karolyn Kirby and Nancy Reno were the winners. In the championship match, Kirby and Reno held on for a 16-14 victory over Angela Rock and Jackie Silva, in the thrilling "World Championship" match. The final was filled with the kind of fireworks worthy of a "World Championship" event. With the score at 3-all, Rock served her 100th "Spader" of the season. There was never a spread of more than one point until the score was at 9-7 in favor of Rock and Silva. The gap grew only as big as three when Rock and Silva went ahead at 14-11, as they threatened to force a double final. But Kirby served an ace to make the score 14-12 and later tied the score at 14-all with another spader. After a couple of side-outs, Reno served a service winner off of Rock's arms to make the score 15-14 in favor of Kirby and Reno. Kirby then "roofed" Rock to win the match at 16-14. The winner's took home $18,400.00 with the victory.

3rd Place: Patty Dodd and Elaine Roque
4th Place: Allison Johnson and Dennie Shupryt-Knoop
5th Place: Cammy Ciarelli and Holly McPeak
5th Place: Linda Carrillo and Liz Masakayan

FORMER WORLD CHAMPION'S:
1987   Linda Carrillo and Jackie Silva
1988   Linda Carrillo and Jackie Silva
1989   Rita Crockett and Jackie Silva
1990   Nina Matthies and Elaine Roque
1991   Linda Carrillo and Liz Masakayan

CAMMY CIAREILLI
Cammy Ciareilli was voted the 1992 WPVA "Most Inspirational Player" Above photo Ciareilli gets above and over the net for the block.

Photo Courtesy of the AVP

TOP PHOTOS: Left: Dennie Schupyt-Knoop hitting the ball over the block of Linda Hanley. **Center:** Angelia Rock jump serving. **Right:** Barbra Fontana spiking the ball.

MIDDLE PHOTOS: Left: Holly McPeak reaching high for the spike. **Center:** Gail Castro gets-up high to hit the ball. **Right:** Elaine Roque attacking the ball.

1992 WOMEN'S BEACH VOLLEYBALL ACTION

BOTTOM PHOTOS: Left: Marla O'Hara ready for action. **Center:** Deb Richardson slices the ball away from the block of Nancy Reno. **Right:** Patty Dodd reaches-up for the pokie.

Photo's Courtesy of the AVP

ADDITIONAL VOLLEYBALL INFORMATION 1992

AROUND THE U.S.A.
The four-man beach volleyball tour continued into it's second season, with ten tournaments. The Ocean Pacific team was the tour champions. Tom Duke was the MVP. There was a partial women's competition inaugurated in 1992.

In 1992 both the American mens and women's indoor National Teams earned Bronze Medals at the Olympics in Barcelona, Spain. The countries of Brazil and Cuba won their first Olympic gold medals, in volleyball, when the Brazilian men's team and the Cuban women's team each won. The men's U.S.A. Olympic Team roster included Fred Sturm (head coach), Doug Partie, Scott Fortune, Brian Ivie, Bob Samuelson, Brent Hillard, Steve Timmons, Carlos Briceno, Dan Greenbaum, Jeff Stork, Bob Ctvrlik, Rick Becker, Eric Sato, and Kevin Ringermanger. The assitant coach's were John Cook and Gary Sato. The women's roster included: Terry Liskevych (head coach), Caren Kremner, Elaina Oden, Kim Oden, Paula Weishoff, Janet Cobbs, Tree Sanders, Tammy Liley, Yoko Zetterland, Ruth Lawanson, Lori Endicott, Tara Cross-Battle, and Liane Sato. The asstant coach's were Greg Giovanazzi and Kent Miller.

HOLYOKE MASSACHUSETTS
The Volleyball Hall of Fame induction ceremonies were held October 23, 1992, at the VBHF in Holyoke Massachusetts. James Coleman, Merton Kennedy, Ron Von Hagen, and Jon Stanley were inducted.

EAST COAST OF U.S.A.
In 1992 there were twelve "East Coast" volleyball tournaments, with Richmond Hall and Frank Hall winning the East Coast Championships.

TOP 1992 EAST COAST TOUR PLAYERS:
1. Jim Nichols
2. Dave Morehouse
3. Chris Hannemann
4. Wally Goodrick
5. Doug Mauro
6. Jeff Williams
7. Frank Hall
8. Richmond Hall
9. Ken Engeis
10. Manny Agnant

FORMER EAST COAST CHAMPIONS:
1988   Richmond Hall and Frank Hall
1989   Richmond Hall and Frank Hall
1990   Kevin Drake and Manny Agnant
1991   Matt Sonnichsen and Manny Agnant

SANTA MONICA CALIFORNIA
March 28th, 1992

The 1992 State Beach Women's Open, a non-WPVA event, was won by Bonnie Fisk and Shannon Williams. In the championship final, they defeated Kathy Hanley and Kathy Gregory.
3rd Place: Ruth Rydberg and Terri Tachovsky
4th Place: Nancy Madrich and Anne Blac

PLAYA DEL REY CALIFORNIA
April 5th, 1992

The 1992 Playa Del Rey Spring Festival Women's Open, a non-WPVA event, was won by Bonnie Fisk and Kathy Hanley. In the championship final, they defeated Lori Rodman and Tiffany Carrillo.
3rd Place: Roxanne McMiller and Karen Barber
4th Place: Amy Prout and Lisle Vaughs

SANTA CRUZ CALIFORNIA
May 24th, 1992

The 1992 Santa Cruz Open was a non-AVP event. The winner's of the tournament were Tim Pappas and Mark Anderson. In the championship match, they defeated Tate Walthan and Mike Nash.
3rd Place: Kent Kitchel and Eric Anderson
4th Place: Brant Lee and Andrew Cavanaugh

SANTA CRUZ CALIFORNIA
May 23rd-24th, 1992

On the same weekend that the WPVA was at Seal Beach, there was a non-WPVA event held in Santa Cruz. The 1992 Santa Cruz Women's Open was won

ERIC SATO
In 1992, Eric Sato was an outstanding setter for USA National Team as well as a star setter on the 4-Man Professional Beach Volleyball circuit. Above photo, Sato showing that he can set from anywhere.
Photo Courtesy of the AVP

by Ilga Clemins and Mary Doerner. In the championship match, they defeated Laureen Eisenberg and Sarah Beyer.
3rd Place: Mary Stevenson and Cathy Davis
4th Place: Julie Pon and Therese Ammiro

VENTURA CALIFORNIA
June 6th-7th, 1992

On the same weekend that the WPVA was in San Diego, there was a non-WPVA event in Ventura. The 1992 Ventura Women's Open was won by the team of Kathy Gregory and Kathy Hanley. In the championship final, they defeated Jen Noonan and Cindy Helgesen.
3rd Place: Marie Salyer and Sandra Fahey
4th Place: Kathy Garfield and Christy Mickey

SANTA MONICA CALIFORNIA
June 13th-14th, 1992

On the same weekend that the WPVA was in Hermosa Beach, there was a non-WPVA event at State Beach in Santa Monica. The 1992 State Beach Women's Open was won by the team of Jen Noonan and Bonnie Fisk. In the championship final, they defeated and Margie Wiher and Dela Kidd.
3rd Place: Misty May and Tracey Hefflin
4th Place: Christine Porsch and Connie Gilbert

CORONA DEL MAR CALIFORNIA
June 20th-21st, 1992

On the same weekend that the WPVA was in Austin Texas, there was a non-WPVA event in Corona Del Mar California. The 1992 Corona Del Mar Women's Open was won by the team of Kristi Atkinson and Corky Watson. Second place went to Keri Pier and Colleen Cassidy.
3rd Place: Jennifer Reinke and Kathy Banks
4th Place: Leigh Cockerill and Claire Stewart

PLAYA DEL REY CALIFORNIA
June 27th-28th, 1992

On the same weekend that the WPVA was in Cape Cod Massachusetts, there was a non-WPVA event in Playa Del Rey California. The 1992 Playa Del Rey Women's Open was won by the team of Diane Ayers and Margie. In the championship match, they defeated Christine Starczak and Marie Gingres.
3rd Place: Anna Proussalis and Karen Barber
4th Place: Dana Quirarte and Dela Kidd

LAGUNA BEACH CALIFORNIA
June 27th-28th, 1992

On the weekend of June 27th-28th, 1992, the AVP Pro-Beach Volleyball Tour was in Louisville Kentucky. On the same weekend, there was a non-AVP "AAA" event staged in Laguna Beach California. The 1992 Laguna Beach Open was won by Canyon Ceman and David Swatik. In the championship final, they defeated Toby Braun and Mike Garcia.
3rd Place: Dan Castillo and Scott Sjoquist
4th Place: Kevin Norman and Mark Paaluhi

OCEANSIDE CALIFORNIA
June 27th-28th, 1992

On the same weekend that the WPVA was in Cape Cod Massachusetts, and the non-WPVA event in Playa Del Rey California. The 1992 Ocean Festival Pro-Am Women's Open, at Oceanside California, was won by the team of Kathy Hanley and Bonnie Fisk. In the championship match, they defeated Karen Barber and Anna Proussalis.
3rd Place: Ruth Rydberg and Diane Ayers
4th Place: Margie Wiher and Dela Kidd

MISTY MAY
In 1992, Misty May began to show her abilities on the beach with a third place finish at the State Beach Women's Open. Above photo, May gives an all-out effort to get the ball up.
Photo Courtesy of "Couvi"

KEVIN NORMAN
In 1992, the heavy hitting Kevin Norman teamed-up with Mark Paaluhi for a fourth place finish at the Laguna Beach Men's Open. Above photo, Norman follows through with his powerful swing.
Photo Courtesy of "Couvi"

LAGUNA BEACH CALIFORNIA
July 18th-19th, 1992

On the same weekend that the WPVA was in Minneapolis Minnesota, there was a non-WPVA event in Laguna Beach California. The 1992 Laguna Beach Women's Open was won by the team of Mary Jane Smith and Mary Bailey. In the championship final, they defeated Renee Rozunko and Wendi Dvorak.

3rd Place: Janice Stimpfig and Melinda Czuleger
4th Place: Dana Bragado and Lisa Wenker

OXNARD CALIFORNIA
July 25th-26th, 1992

On the same weekend that the WPVA was in Boulder Colorado, there was a non-WPVA event in Oxnard California. The 1992 Oxnard Women's Open was won by the team of Lisa Willcocks and Christine Wilson. In the championship match, they defeated Antoinnette White and Sabrina Hernandez.

3rd Place: Anne Black and Alissa Evans
4th Place: Cindy Helgreen and Jeniffer Paredes

MIXED-DOUBLES TOURNAMENT RESULT

PLAYA DEL REY CALIFORNIA
April 5th, 1992

The 1992 Playa Del Rey Spring Festival Mixed-Doubled Open was won by Mark Knudsen and Diane Ayres. In the championship final, they defeated Jeffery Ryberg and Christina Starczak.

3rd Place: Dave Gallenson and Drasan Myatt
4th Place: Mark Tarpley and Shirley Tarpley

PLAYA DEL REY CALIFORNIA
June 27th, 1992

Another 1992 Playa Del Rey Mixed-Doubled Open was won by Sean Keefe and Rita Gingras. In the championship final, they defeated Richard Bailey and Mary Bailey.

3rd Place: Ted Mueller and Meesh Joslyn

SANTA CRUZ CALIFORNIA
July 26th, 1992

The 1992 Santa Cruz Mixed-Doubles Open was won by David King and Shannon King. In the championship match, they defeated Don Jameison and Roxanne McMiller.

3rd Place: Mark McNamara and Stephanie Weber
4th Place: Sam Edwards and Deanna Heller

MANHATTAN BEACH CALIFORNIA
August 15th-16th, 1992

On a hot and sunny day, the 1992 Marine Street Mixed-Doubles Open, the 26th annual, was won by Butch Miali and Liz Masakayan. They staged a comeback victory Sunday to defeated Rick Arce and Christina Gage. Maili and Masakayan found themselves down 14-11 in the final, but were able to eke out a 16-14 win behind some strong serving by Miali. Tournament director Mike Cook utilized pool play on Saturday and single elimination on Sunday.

3rd Place: David Swatik and Debbi Black
4th Place: Dan Sayler and Marie Sayler
5th Place: Steve Napolitano and Lisa Arce
5th Place: Curt Moothart and Jessica Kyle
5th Place: Kevin Cleary and Tracy Tatum
5th Place: Rick Shaw and Amy Baltus

JANICE STIMPFIG
Janice Stimpfig played with some success in some WPVA events as well as non-WPVA tournaments. Above photo, during a Hermosa Beach event, Stimpfig hits a set from Kerri Pier towards the defense of Patti Bright.
Photo Courtesy of the "Commander"

DEBBI BLACK
In 1992, Debbi Black teamed-up with David Swatik for a third place finish at the Marine Street Mixed-Doubles Open. Above photo, Debbi uses her talents to help keep the tournament moving.
Photo Courtesy of George Stepanof

MEN'S BEACH VOLLEYBALL
1993

In 1993, there were twenty-five recorded "Pro" Beach Volleyball tournaments. Twenty-three of these tournaments were staged in the U.S.A. while two were played internationally. Of the twenty-three U.S. tournaments, five were California events. The California events have gradually been diminishing over the past few years. In 1990 there were twelve tournaments in California. In 1993 there were three tournaments played in Florida and three in Texas. There were twelve U.S. events staged in ten states other than Texas, Florida and California. The California tournaments were held in Santa Cruz, Manhattan Beach, Hermosa Beach, Seal Beach, and San Diego. The tournaments in Florida were in Fort Myers, Clearwater, and Daytona. The tournaments in Texas were in Dallas/Fort Worth, Austin, and San Antonio. The remaining U.S. tournaments were held in: Honolulu Hawaii, Phoenix Arizona, Boulder Colorado, Cape Cod Massachusetts, Belmar and Seaside Heights New Jersey, Grand Haven Michigan, Milwaukee Wisconsin, Cleveland and Cincinnati Ohio, Ocean City Maryland, and Chicago Illinois. The two international events were held in Rio de Janeiro Brazil and Enoshima Japan.

In addition to the above International beach events, the first European Championships took place in Almeria Spain. Also, the first Swiss Beach Volleyball Tour was established, with the participation of 480 players. The Swiss Championship finals were again held in Lucerne. The 1993 women's division winner's were Gaby Meili and Kathy Stocker. The men's champions were Marc Gerson and Daniel Stauffer.

As a team, Karch Kiraly and Kent Steffes remained in the top spot on the AVP Tour winning a total of 18 tournaments together. Four of their wins came in California, at Santa Cruz, Manhattan Beach, San Diego, and the U.S. Championships in Hermosa Beach. They had 14 additional U.S. wins, which came in: Honolulu Hawaii, New York City, Boulder Colorado, Dallas/Fort Worth, and Austin Texas, Clearwater Florida, Belmar and Seaside Heights New Jersey, Grand Haven Michigan, Milwaukee Wisconsin, Cleveland and Cincinnati Ohio, Ocean City Maryland, and Cape Cod Massachusetts. Kiraly added the "King of the Beach" title in Daytona Beach Florida, while Steffes also won with Adam Johnson at the FIVB "World Championships" in Rio de Janeiro Brazil.

KARCH KIRALY & KENT STEFFES
In 1993, Karch Kiraly and Kent Steffes remained in the top spot on the AVP Tour, winning a total of 18 AVP tournament championships together. Above photo, Steffes hits a set from Kiraly, past the block of Craig Moothart.
Photo Courtesy of the AVP

Additional teams that won in 1993: Sinjin Smith and Randy Stoklos had only one win together in 1993, winning the Fort Myers event. Stoklos added another victory at the Chicago event with Brian Lewis. Adam Johnson and Bruk Vandeweghe won the event in San Antonio Texas. Tim Hovland and Mike Dodd won in Phoenix Arizona. Dodd won again in Seal Beach with Mike Whitmarsh. The Brazilian team of Franco Neto and Roberto Lopes won the FIVB event in Enoshima Japan.

The AVP and FOVA joined forces in 1993. They each committed to a five-year agreement where FOVA would organize the qualifying tournaments for all of the AVP events. This was the first major expansion of the AVP, which was formed in 1983. The two organizations expected the alliance to appeal to sponsors that wanted exposure in the beach volleyball market.

AVP

NBC broadcast 10 events in 1993. The 1993 AVP tournament schedule awarded $3,700,000.00 to the players. The estimated live attendance was set at 600,000 fans.

1993 started off with the AVP's first U.S.A indoor beach volleyball tournament. Eight teams were invited to compete on 244 tons of relocated sand. In the championship match, Kiraly and Steffes easily handled Smith and Stoklos by a score of 15-4 in front of 10,000 satisfied volleyball fans.

Karch Kiraly moved into the third spot for career wins, by surpassing Ron Von Hagen's career total of 62 Open Tournament wins. Sinjin Smith and Randy Stoklos hold the first and second spots respectively.

In 1993, Smith and Stoklos ended their eleven-year partnership, prior to the San Diego Open, Stoklos broke off his partnership with Smith, after a record-breaking career together. It was the end of an era. It was a tough year for Sinjin Smith. Smith, hooked-up with old time rival Tim Hovland to play on the tour, but it did not last. In 1993, Sinjin went through seven partners and never finished higher than third place without Stoklos.

In 1993, Mike Dodd and Tim Hovland also split-up to match-up with new partners. Dodd teamed-up with Mike Whitmarsh, which started another successful partnership for Dodd, while Hovland struggled to find a successful partner.

Brazilians Eduardo Anjinho and Jose Loiola became the first non-American team to reach the finals of an AVP tour event, placing second in Fort Worth to Kiraly and Steffes.

Scott Ayakatubby returned to the tour after almost a year absence due to illness/injuries. "Ack" started 1993 at number 43 on the computer rankings, finished ninth, appearing in two finals and winning more than $75,000.00.

BRUK VANDEWEGHE
Bruk Vandeweghe paired-up with Adam Johnson for an AVP championship win at the 1993 San Antonio Texas event. Above photo, Vandeweghe spiking past the block of Randy Stoklos.
Photo Courtesy of the AVP

TIM HOVLAND & MIKE DODD
Tim Hovland and Mike Dodd were teamed-up in 1993, long enough, to win the AVP event in Phoenix Arizona. Above photo, Hovland hits a set from Dodd past the block of Eric Boyles.
Photo Courtesy of the AVP

Also, in 1993, the "most expensive throw" in the history of beach volleyball was made by Brian Lewis. While making a gutsy attempt to set a high pass with his hands during a sudden death match against Kiraly and Steffes, in the finals of the $200,000.00 Jose Cuervo Gold Crown in Clearwater Florida, he was called for a setting violation! The setting violation gave Kiraly and Steffes the $100,000.00 payday, while Lewis and Whitmarsh settled for $17,500.00.

In 1993 Kiraly and Steffes entered 23 events together, winning 18. Kiraly earned almost $470,000.00 and Steffes earned nearly $410,000.00. The next approaching earner, Mike Dodd, was just under $150,00.00. Kiraly commented that he had as much confidence in Steffes, on the beach, that he had with Steve Timmons indoors.

In 1993, Kiraly and Steffes became the first team, in a single season, to win the "Triple Crown", as they won all three "Cuervo Gold Crown" events, and then they also won the Manhattan Open, and the U.S. Championship.

Karch Kiraly won his third consecutive "King of the Beach" title. Paul Sunderland, former Olympic volleyball player and current broadcaster, placed Kiraly in the company of other great athletes such as: Michael Jordan, Magic Johnson, Charles Barkley, Sergei Bubka, and Albert Juantarena. Sunderland said: "These Guy's have more ability than the rest... but they work harder and are more competive, Karch is in that group."

In 1993, the AVP team of the future was Eric Fonoimoana teamed with Brian Ivie. They had good success in a few tournaments in 1993 and teamed-up together later in their careers, at the start of the 1997 AVP season, after Ivie finished with his National Indoor Team commitment at the 1996 Olympics in Atlanta Georgia. Fonoimoana and Ivie are close friends, on and off the volleyball court. Ivie and Fonoimoana grew-up together in Hermosa Beach and Manhattan Beach, where they also played together at High School volleyball powerhouse Mira Costa.

The biggest up-set of the 1993 season took place in Chicago, when Chris Hannemann and Daniel Cardenas defeated Karch and Kent, 16-14, in the first round of play. Hannemann and Cardenas had seven spaders on their way to victory.

KARCH KIRALY & KENT STEFFES
Karch Kiraly and Kent Steffes were the top money winner's on the 1993 AVP Tour. Karch won $467,877.00 while Kents took home $409,877.00. Above photo, Karch passing the ball to Kent.
Photo Courtesy of Frank Goroszko

1993 AVP PLAYERS & MONEY EARNED
(men)

1.	**Karch Kiraly**	$467,877
2.	Kent Steffes	$409,877
3.	Mike Dodd	$147,822
4.	Randy Stoklos	$147,674
5.	Adam Johnson	$140,408
6.	Mike Whitmarsh	$129,934
7.	Ricci Luyties	$116,636
8.	Brian Lewis	$112,122
9.	Jose Loiloa	$111,062
10.	Brent Frohoff	$ 98,563
11.	Bruk Vandeweghe	$ 95,544
12.	Sinjin Smith	$ 89.590
13.	Tim Hovland	$ 83,402
14.	Eduardo Bacil	$ 79,817
15.	Scott Ayakatubby	$ 76,518
16.	Dan Vrebalovich	$ 66,631
17.	Troy Tanner	$ 59,024
18.	Eric Wurts	$ 49,588
19.	Al Janc	$ 47,943
20.	Craig Moothart	$ 46,704
21.	Eric Fonoimoana	$ 41,029
22.	Bill Boullianne	$ 40,358
23.	John Hanley	$ 39,252
24.	Tim Walmer	$ 39,247
25.	Leif Hanson	$ 37,998
26.	Steve Timmons	$ 36,298
27.	David Swatik	$ 33,145
28.	Larry Mear	$ 32,746
29.	Scott Friederichsen	$ 32,688
30.	Wes Welch	$ 31,075
31.	Eric Boyles	$ 29,192
32.	Andrew Smith	$ 23,618
33.	Doug Foust	$ 22,621
34.	Chris Young	$ 22,484
35.	Brian Gatzke	$ 20,996
36.	John Brajevic	$ 18,917
37.	Marcelo Duarte	$ 17,234
38.	Robert Chavez	$ 16,803
39.	Matt Sonnichsen	$ 15,261
40.	Jeff Rodgers	$ 15,255
41.	Mark Kerins	$ 13,676
42.	Kevin Martin	$ 12,551
43.	Albert Hannemann	$ 12,187
44.	Matt Unger	$ 12,187
45.	Jim Nichols	$ 11,473
46.	Mike Stafford	$ 11,176
47.	Bill Suwara	$ 10,925
48.	Tony Zapata	$ 8,500
49.	Shawn Davis	$ 6,936
50.	Kevin Waterbury	$ 6,906

1993 INDIVIDUAL AVP TOURNAMENT FINISHES

Player	1st	2nd	3rd	4th	5th
Scott Ayakatubby	0	3	3	1	4
Eduardo Bacil	0	3	1	4	4
Bill Boullianne	0	0	0	0	3
Mike Dodd	2	4	3	2	3
Brent Frohoff	0	3	4	1	8
Eric Fonoimoana	0	0	0	0	1
John Hanley	0	0	0	0	1
Leif Hanson	0	0	0	0	3
Tim Hovland	2	1	4	2	2
Al Janc	0	0	0	0	2
Adam Johnson	1	3	5	5	5
Karch Kiraly	**19**	**3**	**2**	**0**	**0**
Brian Lewis	1	3	4	3	3
Jose Loiola	0	4	1	4	4
Ricci Luyties	1	4	4	3	6
Craig Moothart	0	0	0	0	2
Sinjin Smith	1	2	4	3	2
Kent Steffes	18	3	2	0	0
Randy Stoklos	2	5	4	2	2
David Swatik	0	0	0	0	1
Troy Tanner	0	0	0	2	4
Steve Timmons	0	0	0	1	2
Bruk Vandeweghe	1	1	4	5	3
Dan Vrebalovich	0	0	1	0	6
Tim Walmer	0	0	0	0	2
Mike Whitmarsh	1	5	3	1	5
Eric Wurts	0	0	0	2	0

1993 MEN'S AVP AWARDS:
MOST OUTSTANDING (MVP): Karch Kiraly
MOST UNDERRATED: Bruk Vandeweghe & Troy Tanner
BEST NEWCOMER: Eduardo Bacil
MOST INTENSE PLAYER: Brent Frohoff
MOST EXCITING PLAYER: Jose Loiola
MOST DEPENDABLE PLAYER: Mike Dodd
BEST DEFENSIVE PLAYER: Adam Johnson
BEST OFFENSIVE PLAYER: Kent Steffes
COMEBACK PLAYER OF YEAR: Scott Ayakatubby

FIVB

The 1993 FIVB men's pro-beach volleyball tour included two tour sites with the total prize money worth $198,938.00. The 1993 FIVB Men's Tour made two stops in two different countries: Rio de Janeiro Brazil and Enoshima Japan. In Enoshima, Brazil's Franco Neto and Roberto Lopes were on top while in Rio, American's Kent Steffes and Adam Johnson received top honors as beach volleyball attained global status.

The most successful American team on the 1993 FIVB Tour was Kent Steffes and Adam Johnson, winning the $100,000.00 FIVB Men's World Championships, at Copacabana Beach Stadium, Rio de Janeiro, Brazil. The only other 1993 Men's FIVB Pro-Beach event was in Enoshima, Japan. This $98,938.00 pro-beach event was won by the Brazilian team of Franco Jose Vieira Neto and Roberto Lopes de Costa.

1993 INDIVIDUAL FIVB TOURNAMENT FINISHES

Player	1st	2nd	3rd	4th	5th
Eduardo Bacil	0	1	0	0	0
Andrew Burdin	0	0	0	0	2
Carlos Edwardo Garrido Dias	0	1	0	0	0
Roberto Duarte Dias	0	1	0	0	0
Dionisio	0	0	0	0	1
Andrea Ghiurghi	0	0	0	0	1
Al Janc	0	0	1	0	0
Adam Johnson	**1**	**0**	**0**	**0**	**0**
Jose Loiola	0	1	0	0	0
Roberto Costa Lopes	**1**	**0**	**0**	**1**	**0**
Craig Moothart	0	0	0	1	0
Jose Franco Vieira Neto	**1**	**0**	**0**	**1**	**0**
Jose Marco Melo Ferreira Nobrega	0	0	0	0	1
Denny Gomes Paredes	0	0	0	0	1
Julien Prosser	0	0	0	0	2
Sinjin Smith	0	0	1	0	0
Kent Steffes	**1**	**0**	**0**	**0**	**0**
Randy Stoklos	0	0	1	0	0

SCOTT AYAKATUBBY
After a year of injuries in 1992, Scott "Ack" Ayakatubby returned to the AVP Tour at #43 on the computer, finishing at #9. He was voted the 1993 AVP Tour's "Come-Back" player of the year. Above photo, "Ack" slices the ball past the block of Jose Loiola.
Photo Courtesy of Eric Barnes

JOSE LOIOLA & EDUARDO BACIL
Brazilians, Jose Loiola and Eduardo "Anjinho" Bacil, finished second at the 1993 FIVB World Championship in Rio De Janeiro Brazil. Above photo, Loiola hits a set from "Anjinho" towards the block of Scott Ayakatubby.
Photo Courtesy of Eric Barnes

MEN'S TOURNAMENT RESULTS
1993-AVP

HONOLULU OPEN
February 4th-6th, 1993

The AVP staged it's first outdoor tournament of 1993 in Honolulu Hawaii. The championship match was won by Karch Kiraly and Kent Steffes, as they embarrassed Sinjin Smith and Randy Stoklos by a score of 15-3.

3rd Place: Brian Lewis and Mike Whitmarsh
4th Place: Mike Dodd and Tim Hovland
5th Place: Scott Friederichsen and Tim Walmer
5th Place: Brent Frohoff and Ricci Luyties

MANHATTAN NEW YORK INDOOR
February 20th, 1993

The AVP moved to the "indoor beach," on the coldest day of the year, in Manhattan (New York). Beach volleyball was being played on the floor of New York's Madison Square Garden, covered with 244 tons of sand. This may seem out of place to the beach volleyball enthusiast of Southern California, but not to local players like Tom Gould and Eric Pavels, who both play on Long Island's Atlantic Beach during the hot summers. They have even played in the snow during the winter months. During this event, Tim Hovland began to incite the crowds by taking off his T-shirts during stressful periods of a match. He continued to stimulate the crowds in this manner in future tournaments as well. Karch Kiraly and Kent Steffes went on to win the championship match over Sinjin Smith and Randy Stoklos by a score of 10-4 as the rally clock expired.

3rd Place: Mike Whitmarsh and Brian Lewis
3rd Place: Tim Hovland and Mike Dodd
5th Place: Brent Frohoff and Ricci Luyties
5th Place: Adam Johnson and Steve Timmons
5th Place: John Hanley and Bruk Vandeweghe
5th Place: Larry Mear and Eric Wurts

FORT MYERS FLORIDA
March 27th-28th, 1993

Fort Myers, Florida was the site of the next AVP Tour stop. In the championship match, of the 1993 Miller Lite Fort Myers Open, Sinjin Smith and Randy Stoklos defeated Karch Kiraly and Kent Steffes, to win their first AVP tournament in nearly a year. After Kiraly and Steffes lost the winner's bracket final to Smith and Stoklos, by a score of 14-12, the first game of the championship match was easily won by Kiraly and Steffes as the

BRENT FROHOFF
Brent "Fro" Frohoff was in the top 10 money earners, on the 1993 AVP Tour, with $98,563.00 earned in prize money. Above photo, "Fro" renders his noteable cut shot on the opposition..
Photo Courtesy of Frank Goroszko

TIM HOVLAND
Tim "Hov" Hovland advanced to 3 championship matches on the 1993 AVP Tour, winning once, while earning over $80,000.00. Above photo, "Hov" gets up high for a cut shot.
Photo Courtesy of the AVP

crushed Sinjin and Randy 15-1. But after being down in the second game of the double final, Sinjin and Randy came back to win 7-3. This was Sinjin Smith's 139th and final career title and the 114th for Randy Stoklos.

3rd Place: Brent Frohoff and Ricci Luyties
4th Place: Tim Hovland and Mike Dodd
5th Place: Brian Lewis and Mike Whitmarsh
5th Place: Tim Walmer and Bruk Vandeweghe

This tournament provided the AVP with a taste of foreign competition when the Brazilian team of Jose Loiola and Eduardo "Anjino" Bacil participated as a wild card team. They finished in thirteenth place. This tournament saw some of the lower ranked teams perform skillfully. The twenty-eighth seeded team of Jim Nichols, last years top player on the Molson Pro Beach Tour, and partner Tony Zapata finished in ninth place along with the twenty-second seeded team of George Carey Jr. and Mike Safford. The twenty-ninth seeded team of Lance Lyons and Brett Gonnerman finished in the thirteenth spot, along with the Brazilians.

PENSACOLA FLORIDA
April 3rd-4th, 1993

The AVP Tour went to Pensacola Florida on the weekend of April 3rd-4th, 1993. The 1993 Miller Lite Pensacola Open was canceled due to excessive rain. At the time of the cancellation, the four remaining teams in the winner's bracket were: Karch Kiraly and Kent Steffes, Brent Frohoff and Ricci Luyties, Tim Hovland and Mike Dodd, along with Sinjin Smith and Randy Stoklos. Each team split $4,500.00.

PHOENIX ARIZONA
April 17th-18th, 1993

On the weekend of April 17th-18th, 1993, the AVP Tour went to Phoenix Arizona for the Miller Lite Phoenix Open. In an outstanding championship match, Tim Hovland and Mike Dodd came through the loser's bracket to win this double final by scores of 14-12 and 7-6 over Karch Kiraly and Kent Steffes. Hovland and Dodd turned back the clock as they rose from the dead. They were down 6-1 before going on to win 7-6 in the rubber game of a startling final. When the score reached 6-4 in the final game, the crowd was in a frenzy as they were all on their feet during Hovland and Dodd's startling comeback. Hovland got in a jump serve as he and Dodd won the decisive rally, 7-6. This was Hovland's 60th and last career Open win. The winners split $15,000.00 for the efforts. In this tournament, the Brazilian team of Loiola and Bacil served notice with a seventh, after losing 15-13, in the first round, to Smith and Stoklos.

3rd Place: Sinjin Smith and Randy Stoklos
4th Place: Adam Johnson and Bruk Vandeweghe
5th Place: Brian Lewis and Mike Whitmarsh
5th Place: Troy Tanner and Dan Vrebalovich

CLEARWATER FLORIDA
April 22nd-24th, 1993

The AVP held the first Jose "Cuervo Gold Crown" Beach Volleyball Series, of the 1993 season, at Clearwater, Florida. In an electrifying championship match, as the

DAVID SWATIK
Davit "Swatty" Swatik began to show some beach volleyball ability on the 1993 AVP Tour. Above photo, "Swatty" reaches high to "swat" the ball.
Photo Courtesy of Frank Goroszko

CRAIG MOOTHART
During the 1993 AVP season, Craig Moothart presented the opposition with formidable competion. Above photo, Moothart reaches-up for the "Kong" block.
Photo Courtesy of Frank Goroszko

time clock ran out, Karch Kiraly and Kent Steffes defeated Brian Lewis and Mike Whitmarsh by a score of 14-13. Lewis and Whitmarsh were down by a score of 12-6 when they rallied to tie the score at 13-all in regulation play. In overtime, Lewis was called for the "infamous $80,000.00 throw," giving Kiraly and Steffes the lofty first place prize of $100,000.00. Lewis and Whitmarsh collected $17,960.00 as the runner-ups.

3rd Place: Mike Dodd and Tim Hovland
4th Place: Adam Johnson and Bruk Vandeweghe
5th Place: Brent Frohoff and Ricci Luyties
5th Place: Eduardo "Anjinho" Bacil and Jose Loiola

AUSTIN TEXAS
May 1st-2nd, 1993

Karch Kiraly and Kent Steffes had an easy time as they defeated Brent Frohoff and Ricci Luyties, in the championship match, by a score of 15-7, at the $75,000.00 Miller Lite AVP Austin Texas Open. Kiraly and Steffes took home $15,000.00 with their victory.

3rd Place: Sinjin Smith and Randy Stoklos
4th Place: Eduardo "Anjinho" Bacil and Jose Loiola
5th Place: Tim Hovland and Mike Dodd
5th Place: Adam Johnson and Bruk Vandeweghe

SAN ANTONIO TEXAS
May 8th-9th, 1993

The Miller Lite AVP Tour made another stop in Texas. In San Antonio, Texas, Adam Johnson and Bruk Vandeweghe were the surprise winner's. In the championship match, Johnson and Vandeweghe defeated Brent Frohoff and Ricci Luyties, as the time clock ran out, by a score of 14-10. They shared $15,000.00 for their efforts. This was Bruk Vandeweghe's first (and only) AVP Pro-Beach win, in his fourth pro beach season.

3rd Place: Karch Kiraly and Kent Steffes
4th Place: Sinjin Smith and Randy Stoklos
5th Place: John Hanley and David Swatik
5th Place: Troy Tanner and Dan Vrebalovich

FORT WORTH TEXAS
May 15th-16th, 1993

The Miller Lite AVP Pro-beach Tour continued it's tour in Texas, as they staged their next $75,000.00 event in Fort Worth Texas. Karch Kiraly and Kent Steffes easily defeated Eduardo Bacil and Jose Loiola, in the championship match, by a score of 15-8. This was the first appearance in the finals for the Brazilians. Kiraly and Steffes split the $15,000.00 winnings.

3rd Place: Adam Johnson and Bruk Vandeweghe
4th Place: Brian Lewis and Mike Whitmarsh
5th Place: Brent Frohoff and Ricci Luyties
5th Place: Troy Tanner and Dan Vrebalovich

SAN DIEGO CALIFORNIA
May 22nd-23rd, 1993

The 1993 Miller Lite AVP Pro-beach Tour staged their next $75,000.00 event in San Diego California. Karch Kiraly and Kent Steffes defeated Brian Lewis and Randy Stoklos, with a steady performance during the championship match, by a score of 15-9, to earn the $15,000.00 first place prize. The winner's were virtually flawless during this tournament. They gave-up an average of less than five points a match in their five victories leading up to the final. This tournament marked the weekend of Sinjin Smith and Randy Stoklos' historical breakup.

3rd Place: Adam Johnson and Bruk Vandeweghe
4th Place: Jose Loiola and Eduardo Bacil
5th Place: Brent Frohoff and Ricci Luyties
5th Place: Al Janc and Craig Moothart

BOULDER COLORADO
May 27th-29th, 1993

The AVP Pro-Beach Tour went to Boulder Colorado for the second "Cuervo Gold Crown" series event of 1993. Karch Kiraly and Kent Steffes won an exciting match over Mike Dodd and Mike Whitmarsh by a score of 16-14. Kiraly and Steffes split the $100,000.00 first place winnings.

3rd Place: Brian Lewis and Randy Stoklos
4th Place: Brent Frohoff and Ricci Luyties
5th Place: Adam Johnson and Bruk Vandeweghe

CLEVELAND OHIO
June 5th-6th, 1993

The Miller Lite AVP Pro-Beach Volleyball Tour went to Cleveland Ohio, where Karch Kiraly and Kent Steffes easily defeated Brent Frohoff and Ricci Luyties, 14-8, in the championship match. Kiraly and Steffes split $15,000.00 for their efforts. Earlier, in the winner's bracket final, Scott Ayakatubby and Tim Hovland gave Kiraly and Steffes a scare as they took a 13-6 lead. Karch and Kent came back to win 16-14.

3rd Place: Scott Ayakatubby and Tim Hovland
4th Place: Adam Johnson and Bruk Vandeweghe
5th Place: Troy Tanner and Dan Vrebalovich
5th Place: Bill Boullianne and Leif Hanson

SINJIN SMITH & RANDY STOKLOS
In 1993, just prior to the San Diego event, Sinjin Smith and Randy Stoklos broke-off their eleven year, record breaking, partnership. Above photo, Sinjin hits a set from Stoklos.
Photo Courtesy of the AVP

SEASIDE HEIGHTS NEW JERSEY
June 12th-13th, 1993

The Miller Lite AVP Pro-Beach Volleyball Tour's next stop was in Seaside Heights New Jersey. Karch Kiraly and Kent Steffes won their fifth tournament in a row as they defeated Mike Dodd and Mike Whitmarsh, 7-1, in a double final. In the first game of the final, Whitmarsh was suffering from dehydration forcing him and Dodd to forfeit the first game. Kiraly and Steffes then easily won the overtime game 7-1 to take home the $15,000.00 winnings.

3rd Place: Sinjin Smith teamed with Dan Vrebalovich
4th Place: Adam Johnson and Bruk Vandeweghe
5th Place: Scott Ayakatubby and Steve Timmons
5th Place: Jose Loiola and Eduardo Bacil

CHICAGO ILLINOIS
June 19th-20th, 1993

The Miller Lite AVP Pro-Beach Volleyball Tour made it's next stop in Chicago Illinois. Brian Lewis and Randy Stoklos humiliated Mike Dodd and Mike Whitmarsh by a score of 15-2 in the championship match. Lewis and Stoklos split the $30,000.00 prize money. Earlier in the tournament, the upset of the year took place. The 32nd-seeded team of Chris Hannemann and Daniel Cardenas stunned the number one seeded team in the first round of play. They beat Karch Kiraly and Kent Steffes by a score of 15-14 in sudden death.

3rd Place: Karch Kiraly and Kent Steffes
4th Place: Scott Ayakatubby and Tim Hovland
5th Place: Al Janc and Craig Moothart
5th Place: Brent Frohoff and Ricci Luyties

OCEAN CITY MARYLAND
June 26th-27th, 1993

Karch Kiraly and Kent Steffes soundly defeated Scott Ayakatubby and Tim Hovland, in the championship match, by a score of 15-2, at the $75,000.00 Miller Lite Ocean City AVP Pro-Beach Tournament on June 26th-27th, 1993 in Ocean City Maryland. They split the $15,000.00 prize.

3rd Place: Jose Loiola and Eduardo Bacil
4th Place: Adam Johnson and Bruk Vandeweghe
5th Place: Brent Frohoff and Ricci Luyties
5th Place: Sinjin Smith and Dan Vrebalovich

MANHATTAN BEACH CALIFORNIA
July 2nd-4th, 1993

The 1993 $100,000.00 Killer Loop Manhattan Beach Open took place on the south side of the pier in Manhattan Beach California. Karch Kiraly and Kent Steffes won the tournament and the top prize of $20,000.00. This was the sixth Manhattan Beach Open title for Kiraly. The tournament was televised on NBC. The telecast drew a respectable rating on both days, especially during the championship match. In the championship match, Adam Johnson came out ripping as he knocked Kiraly down with a jump serve, while he and Bruk Vandeweghe stormed to a 10-3 lead, but the top seeded team of Kiraly and Steffes methodically came back to defeat Johnson and Vandeweghe, by a score of 15-10.

3rd Place: Mike Dodd and Mike Whitmarsh
4th Place: Brian Lewis and Steve Timmons
5th Place: Brent Frohoff and Ricci Luyties
5th Place: Eduardo Bacil and Jose Loiola

KENT STEFFES & KARCH KIRALY
Kent Steffes and Karch Kiraly were on top of their game in 1993. As a team they won 18 AVP events together=. Above photo, Steffes lets go with a jump serve, while Karch is ready at the net. Defense is Tim Walmer (left) and Owen McKibbon (right).
Photo Courtesy of the AVP

ANDREW SMITH & STEVE TIMMONS
Andrew Smith and Steve Timmons both demonstrated their abilities on the 1993 AVP Tour. Above photo, Smith hits the ball past the imposing block of Timmons.
Photo Courtesy of the AVP

CAPE COD MASSACHUSETTS
July 17th-18th, 1993

The AVP traveled to Cape Cod, Massachusetts, where Karch Kiraly and Kent Steffes narrowly defeated Scott Ayakatubby and Adam Johnson 16-14, in the championship match of the Miller Lite $75,000.00 Cape Cod Open. Ayakatubby and Johnson teamed-up after Johnson was upset about the loss with Bruk Vandeweghe at Manhattan Beach when they were ahead 10-3. In this week's final, Johnson and Ayakatubby promptly blew a 12-4 lead as they lost to Kiraly and Steffes by the score of 16-14. The winners took home $15,000.00 for their efforts.

3rd Place: Tim Hovland and Vandeweghe
4th Place: Ricci Luyties and Sinjin Smith
5th Place: Brent Frohoff and Mike Whitmarsh
5th Place: Brian Lewis and Randy Stoklos

BELMAR BEACH NEW JERSEY
July 24th-25th, 1993

Karch Kiraly and Kent Steffes methodically defeated Mike Dodd and Mike Whitmarsh, in the championship match of the Miller Lite $100,000.00 Belmar Open, by a score of 11-4, when Whitmarsh had to retire because of dehydration. This AVP event took place on the weekend of July 24th-25th, 1993, on Belmar Beach in New Jersey. Kiraly and Steffes shared the $20,000.00 winnings. This was Kiraly's 75th career tournament championship.

3rd Place: Brian Lewis and Randy Stoklos
4th Place: Troy Tanner and Eric Wurts
5th Place: Tim Walmer and Dan Vrebalovich
5th Place: Leif Hanson and Bill Boullianne

MILWAUKEE WISCONSIN
July 31st-August 1st, 1993

The AVP traveled to Milwaukee Wisconsin for the $150,000.00 Men's Miller Lite Milwaukee Open. Karch Kiraly and Kent Steffes took the title and the first place prize of $30,000.00. In the championship match, Kiraly and Steffes systematically defeated Brian Lewis and Randy Stoklos, by a score of 15-6. This was the fifth title in a row for Kiraly and Steffes, equaling their best streak of the season. The final was televised live on NBC.

3rd Place: Scott Ayakatubby and Adam Johnson
4th Place: Ricci Luyties and Sinjin Smith
5th Place: Mike Dodd and Mike Whitmarsh
5th Place: Eduardo Bacil and Jose Loiola

GRAND HAVEN MICHIGAN
August 7th-9th, 1993

The AVP Pro-Beach Volleyball Tour's next event was in Grand Haven Michigan, for the $100,000.00 Men's Miller Lite Grand Haven Open. Karch Kiraly and Kent Steffes won the tournament and first place check of $20,000.00. In the championship match, Kiraly and Steffes, in a deliberate fashion, defeated Jose Loiola and Eduardo Bacil by a score of 15-11.

3rd Place: Brent Frohoff and Bruk Vandeweghe
4th Place: Brian Lewis and Randy Stoklos
5th Place: Scott Ayakatubby and Adam Johnson
5th Place: Bill Boullianne and Leif Hanson

MIKE WHITMARSH & BRENT FROHOFF
Mike Whitmarsh and Brent Frohoff paired-up for some competition on the 1993 AVP Tour. Above photo, Whitmarsh hits a set from Frohoff past the block of Kent Steffes.
Photo Courtesy of the AVP

ERIC FONOIMOANA
Eric "Foni" Fonoimoana began to show his talents on the 1993 AVP Tour, breaking his way into a top five finish. Above photo, "Foni" gets his hands-up to make a nice dig.
Photo Courtesy of "Couvi"

SEAL BEACH CALIFORNIA
August 13th-15th, 1993

The AVP Pro-Beach Volleyball Tour returned to California, staging an event at Seal Beach California. Mike Dodd and Mike Whitmarsh won the 1993 Men's $150,000.00 Miller Lite Seal Beach Open. They split $30,000.00 along with the championship. In the championship match, Dodd and Whitmarsh subdued Karch Kiraly and Kent Steffes, 14-11, when the time clock expired. Kiraly and Steffes shared the runners-up check of $18,000.00.

3rd Place: Ricci Luyties and Sinjin Smith
4th Place: Eduardo Bacil and Jose Loiola
5th Place: Eric Fonoimoana and Tim Hovland
5th Place: Scott Ayakatubby and Adam Johnson

KARCH KIRALY
Karch Kiraly was crowned "King of the Beach" at the Old Spice "KOB" event, staged in Daytona Beach Florida. Karch took home a check for $58,000.00 along with his "KOB" title. Above photo, Karch puts another ball away.
Photo Courtesy of "Couvi"

SANTA CRUZ CALIFORNIA
August 20th-21st, 1993

The AVP Pro-Beach Volleyball Tour made its next stop, in Santa Cruz California, for the third "Jose Cuervo Gold Crown" series tournament of 1993. Karch Kiraly and Kent Steffes won the $200,000.00 event, splitting $100,000.00 along with the title. In the championship match, Kiraly and Steffes flustered Scott Ayakatubby and Adam Johnson, 15-2. Karch and Kent became the first team, in a single season, to win the "Triple Crown" winning all three "Jose Cuervo Gold Crown" events.

3rd Place: Brent Frohoff and Ricci Luyties
4th Place: Eric Wurts and Troy Tanner
5th Place: Mike Dodd and Mike Whitmarsh

HERMOSA BEACH CALIFORNIA
August 27th-29th, 1993

The AVP Pro-Beach Tour went to Hermosa Beach California for the 1993 Men's $750,000.00 Miller Lite "U.S. Championships." Karch Kiraly and Kent Steffes won the championship and the top prize of $100,000.00. They were also the winner's in 1992.

In the championship match, Kiraly and Steffes easily deposed Randy Stoklos and Ricci Luyties, by a score of 15-5. The match started off with Luyties serving an ace, but his team fell behind almost immediately, when he and Stoklos committed a series of errors, six of which resulted in points for Kiraly and Steffes. The final error came when Stoklos hit the ball into the net, giving Kiraly and Steffes a 13-4 lead and eventual 15-5 victory. Stoklos and Luyties split $22,500.00 for second place.

3rd Place: Mike Dodd and Mike Whitmarsh
4th Place: Eduardo Bacil and Jose Loiola
5th Place: Scott Ayakatubby and Adam Johnson
5th Place: Brent Frohoff and Steve Timmons

CINCINNATI OHIO
September 3rd-4th, 1993

The AVP Pro-Beach Tour went to Cincinnati Ohio for the 1993 Men's $100,000.00 Old Spice "Tournament of Champions." Karch Kiraly and Kent Steffes won the title and the $20,000.00 first place check. In the championship match, Kiraly and Steffes defeated Jose Loiola and Eduardo Bacil, by a score of 15-6.

3rd Place: Scott Ayakatubby and Adam Johnson
3rd Place: Tim Hovland and Brian Lewis
5th Place: Sinjin Smith and Bruk Vandeweghe
5th Place: Ricci Luyties and Randy Stoklos
5th Place: Mike Dodd and Mike Whitmarsh
5th Place: Troy Tanner and Eric Wurts

DAYTONA BEACH FLORIDA
September 23rd-25th, 1993

The AVP Pro Beach Volleyball Tour ended its 1993 season with the $200,000.00 Men's Old Spice "King of the Beach Tournament" in Daytona Beach, Florida. The 1993 "King of the Beach" title went to Karch Kiraly. Kiraly took home a check for $58,000.00 along with his "King of the Beach" title. Jose Loiola was the runner-up. Loiola earned $31,000.00 for his second place effort. The final eight standings were as follows:

1. Karch Kiraly
2. Jose Loiola
3. Adam Johnson
4. Mike Dodd
5. Randy Stoklos
6. Mike Whitmarsh
7. Ricci Luyties
8. Bruk Vandeweghe

MEN'S TOURNAMENT RESULTS
1993-FIVB

RIO DE JANEIRO, BRAZIL
February 9th-14th, 1993

The $100,000.00 FIVB Men's World Championships, at Copacabana Beach Stadium, Rio de Janeiro, Brazil, was won by the American team of Kent Steffes and Adam Johnson. They won the event out of a field of thirty-seven teams from fourteen countries. Johnson and Steffes split the $24,000.00 first place money. In the championship match, Johnson and Steffes outlasted the Brazilian team of Eduardo "Anjinho" Bacil and Jose Loiola.

3rd Place: Sinjin Smith and Randy Stoklos-USA
4th Place: Franco Vieira Neto and Roberto Costa Lopes-Bra
5th Place: Jose Melo Ferreira Nobrega and Denny Gomes Parreira-Bra
5th Place: Julien Prosser and Andrew Burdin-Aus

ENOSHIMA, JAPAN
July 29th-August 1st, 1993

The Men's FIVB Pro-Beach Tour was in Enoshima, Japan, for the $98,938.00 pro-beach event. In the championship match, Franco Jose Vieira Neto and Roberto Lopes de Costa, from Brazil, defeated another Brazilian team, Carlos Eduardo Dias Garrido and Francismar Adriano Dias Garrido. The winners split the $22,000.00 purse.

3rd Place: Troy Tanner and Dan Vrebalovich-USA
4th Place: Al Janc and Craig Moothart-USA
5th Place: Andrea Ghiurghi and Dionisio-Italy
5th Place: Julien Prosser and Andrew Burdin-Aus

JULIEN PROSSER
Australian Julien Prosser teamed-up with compatriot Andrew Burdin for a couple of fifth place finishes on the 1993 FIVB Tour. Above photo, Prosser makes a good effort to get to the ball.
Photo Courtesy of the AVP

STEFFES & JOHNSON vs LOIOLA & BACIL
At the 1993 "World Championship" in Brazil, Kent Steffes teamed-up with Adam "AJ" Johnson to come-out "on-top" of Jose Loiola and Eduardo Bacil. **Top photo:** Steffes passing the ball to "AJ" **Bottom photo:** Loiola, jump-serving, teamed-up with Bacil.
Top Photo Courtesy of the AVP Bottom courtesy of Eric Barnes

TOP PHOTOS: Left: Adam Johnson follows-through after hitting the ball. **Center:** Sinjin Smith gets "pumped-up" on the beach. **Right:** Randy Stoklos takes a look after spiking the ball.

MIDDLE PHOTOS: Left: Andrew Smith challenges the block of Steve Timmons. **Center:** Wess Welch reaches-over for the block attempt. **Right:** Leif Hanson takes a good swing for the "put-away".

MEN'S BEACH VOLLEYBALL ACTION

BOTTOM PHOTOS: Left: Mike Whitmarsh feels good after making the shot. **Center:** Ricci Luyties follows-through after another side-out. **Right:** Steve Timmons reaches-up high for the ball.

Photo's Courtesy of the AVP

TOP PHOTOS: Left: Eric Boyles gets down low to make the pass. **Center:** Matt Unger attacking at the net. **Right:** Scott Friederichsen gets a piece of the ball during the block attempt.

MIDDLE PHOTOS: Left: Bruk Vandeweghe avoids the block of Scott Ayakatubby. **Center:** Canadian Brian Gatzke gets on one knee to make the dig. **Right:** Troy Tanner follows through after attacking the ball.

MEN'S BEACH VOLLEYBALL ACTION

BOTTOM PHOTOS: Left: Chris Young concentrates while making the pass. **Center:** Bill "Beef" Boullianne cuts the ball by the block of Kevin Martin. **Right:** Eric Fonoimoana gets above the net for the block attempt.

Photo's Courtesy of "Couvi"

WOMEN'S BEACH VOLLEYBALL
1993

AVP

In 1993, the AVP began its version of the "Women's Pro-Beach Volleyball Tour." The AVP Women's Tour signed eight former WPVA players in March and staged a series of round-robin tournaments at the men's events. The Women's AVP Tour staged 16 events including four stops in California (San Diego, Manhattan Beach, Seal Beach and Hermosa Beach). There were three stops in Texas (Austin, San Antonio and Fort Worth). The remaining nine events were staged in Phoenix Arizona, Cleveland Ohio, Seaside Heights New Jersey, Chicago Illinois, Ocean City Maryland, Cape Cod Massachusetts, Belmar Beach New Jersey, Milwaukee Wisconsin, and Grand Haven Michigan.

The women that signed-on for the first AVP Women's Tour, included Angela Rock, Holly McPeak, Rita Crockett, Linda Hanley, Cammy Ciarelli, Jackie Silva, and Nancy Reno. There were also two alternates: Dagmara Szyszczak and Lisa Strand Ma'a. The tour saw Holly McPeak win 11 out of 16 tournaments that she entered, earning a total of $65,000.00. Cammy Ciarelli earned $55,000., while winning 8 out of 15 tournaments.

Nancy Reno earned $50,000.00 and Angela Rock earned $40,000.00.

1993 AVP-WOMEN PLAYERS & MONEY EARNED

1.	Holly McPeak	$ 65,000.00
2.	Cammy Ciarelli	$ 55,000.00
3.	Nancy Reno	$ 50,000.00
4.	Angela Rock	$ 40,000.00
5.	Linda Hanley	$ 33,000.00
6.	Linda Carrillo	$ 30,000.00
7.	Jackie Silva	$ 27,000.00
8.	Rita Crockett	$ 25,000.00

1993 INDIVIDUAL AVP TOURNAMENT FINISHES WOMEN

Player	1st	2nd	3rd	4th
Linda Chisholm Carrillo	4	3	1	9
Cammy Ciarelli	8	2	3	3
Linda Robertson Hanley	2	5	7	2
Lisa Strand Ma'a	0	1	0	0
Holly McPeak	**11**	**2**	**0**	**3**
Nancy Reno	3	6	6	1
Angela Rock	2	8	4	2
Rita Crockett Royster	0	2	5	6
Jackie Silva	2	3	5	4
Dagmara Szyszczak	0	0	1	2

HOLLY MC PEAK
In 1993, Holly McPeak was the top player on the inaugural "Women's" AVP Tour. She advanced to 13 championship matches, winning 11 times on her way to a total of $65,000.00 in prize money. Above photo, Holly makes a perfect pass.
Photo Courtesy of Frank Goroszko

CAMMY CIAREILLI
In 1993, Cammy Ciareilli was in the second spot on the inaugural AVP Tour, advancing to 10 finals, winning 8 times, while earning $55,000.00 in prize money. Above photo, Ciareilli reaches above the net to make a nice block.
Photo Courtesy of Frank Goroszko

WPVA

The WPVA was down to 14 events in 1993 and the total prize money was down to $352,000.00. The top WPVA money earner took home a total of $65,025.00.

The WPVA was having difficulties in 1992. Paychecks were bouncing and the organization was in disarray. In 1993 the AVP seized the opportunity to start an AVP women's tour. Six of the top WPVA women players were invited to play on the AVP tour. Of the six originally invited four players went: Linda Chisholm Carrillo, Jackie Silva, Nancy Reno, and Angela Rock. Liz Masakayan and Karolyn Kirby did not accept. They were worried about representation. The AVP was not offering any positions to women on their board.

With Kirby's partner, Nancy Reno off to the AVP, she needed a new partner for the 1993 WPVA season. Kirby selected Masakayan, a menacing combination in speculation that would go on to prove even more overwhelming on the WPVA tour. They won 13 straight open titles and lost only one tournament. Kirby made over $65,000.00, while Masakayan made just short of $60,000.00. Other teams such as Barbara Fontana and Lori Kotas-Forsyth (the only other team to win on the WPVA Tour in 1993) along with Gail Castro and Elaine Roque earned around $25,000. Karolyn Kirby was crowned the winner of the "I Dig Top of the Tour" event. This was the WPVA's version of the "King of the Beach." This win gave Kirby a total of 14 WPVA championships in 1993, which was the highest total for the season.

1993 WPVA AWARDS

MVP:	Karolyn Kirby and Liz Masakayan
BEST SETTER:	Karolyn Kirby
BEST HITTER:	Liz Masakayan
BEST BLOCKER:	Elaine Roque
BEST DEFENSE:	Barbara Fontana
MOST IMPROVED:	Wendy Fletcher
BEST ROOKIE:	Johanna Wright
MOST INSPIRATIONAL:	Dennie Shupryt Knoop
SPORTSWOMANSHIP:	Dennie Shupryt Knoop

1993 WPVA PLAYERS & MONEY EARNED

1.	**Karolyn Kirby**	$ 65,025
2.	Liz Masakayan	$ 59,575
3.	Elaine Roque	$ 24,325
4.	Gail Castro	$ 23,875
5.	Barbara Fontana	$ 23,580
6.	Lori Kotas	$ 23,280
7.	Deb Richardson	$ 19,450
8.	Janice Harrer	$ 14,225
9.	Dennie Schupyt-Knoop	$ 11,880
10.	Alison Johnson	$ 8,430
11.	Maria O'Hara	$ 8,070
12.	Lori Biller	$ 7,910
13.	Wendy Fletcher	$ 7,145
14.	Charlotte Mitchell	$ 6,860
15.	Gayle Stammer	$ 6,785
16.	Shannon Miller	$ 5,038
17.	Marie Anderson	$ 4,273
18.	Jackie Campbell	$ 3,863
19.	Monique Oliver	$ 3,175
20.	Heather Hafner	$ 2,975

KAROLYN KIRBY
Karolyn Kirby was the top player on the 1993 WPVA Tour. She advanced to 13 championship matches, winning all 13 times on her way to a total of $65,025.00 in prize money. Above photo, Kirby makes a nice dig.
Photo Courtesy of Frank Goroszko

LIZ MASAKAYAN
Liz Masakayan was in the second spot on the 1993 WPVA In Tour, advancing to 12 finals, winning all 12 times, while earning $59,575.00 in prize money. Above photo, Masakayan reaches high to deliver a jump serve for partner Karolyn Kirby.
Photo Courtesy of Frank Goroszko

1993 INDIVIDUAL WPVA TOURNAMENT FINISHES

Player	1st	2nd	3rd	4th	5th
Marie Anderson	0	0	0	0	1
Lori Biller	0	0	0	1	2
Krista Blomquist	0	0	0	0	1
Gail Castro	0	6	3	3	2
Wendy Fletcher	0	0	1	0	5
Barbara Fontana.	1	6	3	2	1
Lori Kotas Forsythe	1	6	3	2	1
Heather Hafner	0	0	0	0	2
Janice Opalinski Harrer	0	1	4	2	2
Alison Johnson	0	0	0	4	3
Karolyn Kirby	13	0	1	0	0
Liz Masakayan	12	0	1	0	0
Shannon Miller	0	0	0	0	3
Charlotte Mitchell	0	0	0	1	2
Marla O'Hara	0	0	1	0	7
Deb Richardson	0	2	5	4	1
Elaine Roque	0	7	3	2	2
Dennie Schupyt-Knoop	0	0	1	6	3
Gail Stammer	0	0	0	0	5
Johanna Wright	0	0	0	0	1

FIVB

The 1993 FIVB women's tour included two $50,000.00 stops in. The first in Rio de Janeiro Brazil and the second in Santos Brazil. Total 1993 FIVB prize money available on the women's FIVB tour was $100,000.00.

Karolyn Kirby was the top player, winning both events. She won the $50,000.00 FIVB women's beach volleyball tournament on Copacabana Beach in Rio de Janeiro, Brazil, with Nancy Reno. They were the winner's over a field of sixteen teams from eight countries. Then in the final 1993, FIVB World Series of Beach Volleyball event, on the beach at Santos Brazil, where a field of fifty-five teams from twenty-one countries participated, Kirby won the championship match with Liz Masakayan.

1993 INDIVIDUAL FIVB TOURNAMENT FINISHES

Player	1st	2nd	3rd	4th	5th
Maria Isabel Salgado Barroso	0	1	0	0	1
Adriana Behar Brando	0	0	1	0	0
Natalie Cook	0	0	0	0	1
"Jackie" Louise Silva Cruz	0	0	1	0	0
Karolyn Kirby	2	0	0	0	0
Magda Rejane Falco De Lima	0	0	1	0	0
Liz Masakayan	1	0	0	1	0
Anita Palm	0	0	0	0	2
Adriana Samuel Ramos	0	1	0	0	1
Nancy Reno	1	0	0	0	0
Angela Rock	0	0	0	1	0
Monica Rodriguez	0	1	0	0	1
Karina Silva	0	0	1	1	0
Sandra Pires Tavsares	0	0	0	1	0
Roseli Ana Timm	0	1	0	0	1
Jacqui Vukosa	0	0	0	0	1

LIZ MASAKAYAN
Liz Masakayan was was voted "Co-Most Valuable Player" on the 1993 WPVA Tour, along with Karolyn Kirby. She was also voted the "Best-Hitter" on 1he 1993 WPVA Tour. Above photo, Masakayan hits another hard spike.
Photo Courtesy of Frank Goroszko

NANCY RENO
Nancy Reno paired-up with Karolyn Kirby for a championship victory at the 1993 FIVB Tour event on Copacabana Beach in Rio de Janeiro Brazil. Above photo, Reno prepares to serve the ball to the opposition.
Photo Courtesy of Frank Goroszko

WOMEN'S TOURNAMENT RESULTS
1993-AVP

PHOENIX ARIZONA
April 17th-18th, 1993

The 1993 Women's AVP Tour began in Phoenix, Arizona. Holly McPeak and Angela Rock easily defeated Linda Carrillo and Lisa Strand Ma'a, in the championship match, by a score of 15-5.

3rd Place: Nancy Reno and Jackie Silva
4th Place: Linda Hanley and Cammy Ciarelli

AUSTIN TEXAS
May 1st-2nd, 1993

The Women's AVP Tour moved into Texas for a series of three events. The first took place in Austin Texas, where Linda Chisholm Carrillo and Jackie Silva held on to defeat Cammy Ciarelli and Angela Rock by a score of 15-12.

3rd Place: Linda Hanley and Nancy Reno
4th Place: Holly McPeak and Rita Crockett Royster

SAN ANTONIO TEXAS
May 8th-9th, 1993

The Women's AVP Tour made its second 1993 Texas tour stop in San Antonio Texas. Cammy Ciarelli and Holly McPeak won in "Texas Style" winning the championship match, by a score of 15-12, over Nancy Reno and Angela Rock.

3rd Place: Linda Hanley and Linda Chisholm
4th Place: Rita Crockett Royster and Jackie Silva

FORT WORTH TEXAS
May 15th-16th, 1993

The Women's AVP Tour made its third and final 1993 "Texas Loop" stop in Fort Worth Texas. In the championship match, Linda Chisholm Carrillo and Nancy Reno easily defeated Linda Hanley and Holly McPeak by a score of 15-4.

3rd Place: Rita Crockett Royster and Cammy Ciarelli
4th Place: Angela Rock and Dagmara Szyszczak

NANCY RENO
In 1993, Nancy Reno advanced to 9 Women's AVP Championship matches, winning 3 events. Above photo, Reno reaches high in the sky for another block attempt.
Photo Courtesy of Frank Goroszko

ANGELA ROCK
Angela Rock advanced to 10 WPVA championship matches in, 1993, winning twice. Above photo, Rock hits the ball towards the block of Holly McPeak.
Photo Courtesy of Frank Goroszko

SAN DIEGO CALIFORNIA
May 22nd-23rd, 1993
The Women's AVP Tour moved out of Texas and into California, on the beach in San Diego. In the championship match, Cammy Ciarelli and Nancy Reno held on for a victory, as the time clock expired, by a score of 13-12, over Linda Carrillo and Angela Rock.
3rd Place: Jackie Silva and Linda Hanley
4th Place: Holly McPeak and Dagmara Szyszczak

CLEVELAND OHIO
June 5th-6th, 1993
The Women's AVP tournament in Cleveland Ohio, on the weekend of June 5th-6th, 1993 was won by the team of Linda Carrillo and Holly McPeak. In the championship match, they defeated Linda Hanley and Angela Rock by a score of 15-11.
3rd Place: Cammy Ciarelli and Dagmara Szyszczak
4th Place: Rita Crockett Royster and Nancy Reno

SEASIDE HEIGHTS NEW JERSEY
June 12th-13th, 1993
The Women's AVP Tour traveled to Seaside Heights New Jersey, where they staged an electrifying championship match. In the final game, Nancy Reno and Holly McPeak captured a 16-14 victory over Jackie Silva and Linda Hanley.
3rd Place: Rita Crockett Royster and Angela Rock
4th Place: Linda Chisholm and Cammy Ciarelli

CHICAGO ILLINOIS
June 19th-20th, 1993
The Women's AVP Tour traveled to Chicago Illinois, where in the championship match, Linda Chisholm Carrillo and Holly McPeak snatched a thrilling 15-13 victory over Nancy Reno and Angela Rock.
3rd Place: Rita Crockett Royster and Linda Hanley
4th Place: Jackie Silva and Cammy Ciarelli

OCEAN CITY MARYLAND
June 26th-27th, 1993
On the weekend of June 26th-27th, 1993, the Women's AVP Tour went to Ocean City, Maryland. In the championship match, Angela Rock and Linda Hanley systematically gained a 15-7 victory over Nancy Reno and Rita Crockett.
3rd Place: Jackie Silva and Cammy Ciarelli
4th Place: Holly McPeak and Linda Chisholm

MANHATTAN BEACH CALIFORNIA
July 2nd-4th, 1993
The Women's AVP Tour was in the lime-light at Manhattan Beach California, where in the championship match, Cammy Ciarelli and Holly McPeak earned a 15-11 victory over Nancy Reno and Angela Rock.
3rd Place: Rita Crockett Royster and Linda Hanley
th Place: Jackie Silva and Linda Chisholm Carrillo

LINDA ROBERTSON HANLEY
Linda Robertson Hanley advanced to 7 WPVA championship matches in 1993, winning twice. Above photo, Hanley shows the hustle that has helped her succeed during her career.
Photo Courtesy of the AVP

RITA CROCKETT ROYSTER
In 1993, Rita Crockett Royster played well enough to finish within the top three places on 7 occasions to earn $25,000.00 in prize money.
Photo Courtesy of the AVP

CAPE COD MASSACHUSETTS
July 17t--18th, 1993
For it's next event, the Women's AVP Tour traveled to Cape Cod Massachusetts. In the championship match, Cammy Ciarelli and Holly McPeak outscored Rita Crockett and Linda Hanley 15-10.
3rd Place: Nancy Reno and Angela Rock
4th Place: Jackie Cruz Silva and Linda Chisholm Carrillo

BELMAR BEACH NEW JERSEY
July 24th-25th, 1993
The Women's AVP Tour went to New Jersey's Belmar Beach, for their next event. In the championship match, Cammy Ciarelli and Holly McPeak put together a respectable performance to take a 13-9 win over Linda Carrillo and Jackie Silva.
3rd Place: Nancy Reno and Angela Rock
4th Place: Linda Hanley and Linda Chisholm

MILWAUKEE WISCONSIN
July 31st-August 1st, 1993
The next Women's AVP Tour took place in Milwaukee Wisconsin, where Cammy Ciarelli and Holly McPeak put together another masterful match to gain a 15-6 victory over Nancy Reno and Angela Rock, in the championship final.
3rd Place: Linda Hanley and Jackie Silva
4th Place: Linda Chisholm and Rita Crockett Royster

GRAND HAVEN MICHIGAN
August 7th-8th, 1993
The Women's AVP Tour traveled to Grand Haven Michigan for an exhilarating tournament. In the championship match, Linda Hanley and Jackie Silva held on for a 15-14 victory over Cammy Ciarelli and Holly McPeak, when the time clock expired.
3rd Place: Reno and Angela Rock
4th Place: Linda Chisholm and Rita Crockett Royster

SEAL BEACH CALIFORNIA
August 13th-15th, 1993
In Seal Beach California, the Women's AVP Tour's event was won by Cammy Ciarelli and Holly McPeak. In the championship match, Ciarelli and McPeak played an inspiring 14-11 game, for the victory over Nancy Reno and Angela Rock. Ciarelli and McPeak started off by taking a two-point lead. They maintained that lead until they pulled away at 11-9. The score went to 13-9 and finally to the 14-11 winning margin.
3rd Place: Jackie Silva and Linda Hanley
4th Place: Linda Chisholm and Rita Crockett Royster

HERMOSA BEACH CALIFORNIA
August 27th-29th, 1993
The Women's AVP Tour was on the beach in Hermosa Beach California, where in the championship match, Cammy Ciarelli and Holly McPeak held on for a 11-10 victory over Linda Hanley and Jackie Silva, as time expired on the nine-minute clock.
3rd Place: Rita Crockett and Nancy Ren
4th Place: Linda Chisholm and Angela Rock

GRAND HAVEN MICHIGAN
The Women's AVP Tour was staged in-front of large crowds, from coast-to-coast. In the above photo, the Women's AVP Tour enjoyed a large crowd at the Grand Haven Michigan event. The 1993 event was won by the team of Linda Robertson Hanley and Jackie Silva, in an exciting championship match, over Cammy Ciareilli and Holly McPeak, by a score of 15-14.

Photo Courtesy of the AVP

WOMEN'S TOURNAMENT RESULTS
1993-WPVA

ISLE VERDE PUERTO RICO
April 17th-18th, 1993

The first 1993 WPVA event took place in Isle Verde, Puerto Rico. In the championship match, of the Coors Light Puerto Rico Open, the team of Karolyn Kirby and Liz Masakayan defeated Gail Castro and Elaine Roque by the score of 15-8. Kirby and Masakayan played well as they showed that they were the team to beat in 1993. The winners bagged $13,250.00 with their first place finish. Kirby, became the first women's player to go over the $200,000.00 mark in career earnings. This win also marked Kirby's 30th title in the 85 events held in the seven-year history of the WPVA. Earlier, Castro and Roque had lost in the quarter-finals and had to win 5 consecutive matches to reach the final.

3rd Place: Janice Harrer and Deb Richardson
4th Place: Lori Biller and Charlotte Mitchell
5th Place: Dennie Shupryt Knoop and Gayle Stammer
5th Place: Barbra Fontana and Lori Kotas

SAN DIEGO CALIFORNIA
April 24th-25th, 1993

Karolyn Kirby and Liz Masakayan were the champions of the WPVA event in San Diego California. They were easy 15-4 winners over Barbara Fontana and Lori Kotas-Forsythe, in the championship match of the 1993 Coors Light San Diego Open. Kirby and Masakayan rolled through the field for the second week in a row. The duo upped their season record to 10 wins without a loss, as they outscored their opponents 150-38. Kirby and Masakayan earned $5,300.00 for their endeavor.

3rd Place: Gail Castro and Elaine Roque
4th Place: Janice Harrer and Deb Richardson
5th Place: Lori Biller and Charlotte Mitchell
5th Place: Alison Johnson and Marla O'Hara

FRESNO CALIFORNIA
May 1st-2nd, 1993

At the WPVA Coors Light Women's Open in Fresno California, Karolyn Kirby and Liz Masakayan were 15-6 and 7-6 winners over Gail Castro and Elaine Roque, in the championship double final match. Kirby and Masakayan went through the loser's bracket after losing their first match of the season 15-12 to Barbra Fontana and Lori Kotas. They earned $5,300.00 for the first place finish.

3rd Place: Barbra Fontana and Lori Kotas
4th Place: Janice Harrer and Deb Richardson
5th Place: Dennie Shupryt Knoop and Gayle Stammer
5th Place: Marie Anderson and Shannon Miller

ELAINE ROQUE
In 1993, Elaine Roque advanced to the championship match at 7 WPVA Tour events, finishing in second place each time. Above photo, Roque reaches up fo make the serve.
Photo Courtesy of Frank Goroszko

DENNIE SCHUPYT-KNOOP
In 1993, Dennie Schupyt-Knoop was awarded the "Sportswomanship" and voted the "Most Inspirational Player" on the WPVA Tour.
Photo Courtesy of the AVP

AUSTIN TEXAS
May 15th-16th, 1993

In the championship match, Barbara Fontana and Lori Kotas-Forsythe were 15-12 and 7-2 double final winners over Deb Richardson and Janice Harrer, at the WPVA Coors Light Women's Open, in Austin Texas. The winners took home $5,300.00 for their efforts. This was Fontana's first pro beach tournament championship.

3rd Place: Liz Masakayan and Karolyn Kirby
4th Place: Gail Castro and Elaine Roque
5th Place: Alison Johnson and Dennie Shupryt Knoop
5th Place: Marla O'Hara and Gayle Stammer

NEW ORLEANS LOUISIANA
May 22nd-23rd, 1993

The WPVA was in New Orleans Louisiana for the Coors Light New Orleans Women's Open. In the championship match, Karolyn Kirby and Liz Masakayan defeated Barbara Fontana and Lori Kotas-Forsythe, in a double final, 15-9 and 7-3. Kirby and Masakayan came out of the looser's-bracket to win the $5,300.00 first place prize. Earlier in the tournament, Kirby and Masakayan had lost to Fontana and Kotas by a score of 15-2, the worst defeat in Kirby's beach career.

3rd Place: Janice Harrer and Deb Richardson
4th Place: Alison Johnson and Dennie Shupryt Knoop
5th Place: Heather Hafner and Gayle Stammer
5th Place: Gail Castro and Elaine Roque

JACKSONVILLE OPEN
May 29th-30th, 1993

The 1993 WPVA Coors Light Women's Open at Jacksonville, Florida was won by Karolyn Kirby and Liz Masakayan. In the championship match, Kirby and Masakayan continued their sound play, with a 15-9 victory over Barbara Fontana and Lori Kotas-Forsythe. The winner's took home the $5,300.00 top prize.

3rd Place: Janice Harrer and Deb Richardson
4th Place: Alison Johnson and Dennie Shupryt Knoop
5th Place: Wendy Fletcher and Marla O'Hara
5th Place: Gail Castro and Elaine Roque

HERMOSA BEACH CALIFORNIA
June 12th-13th, 1993

The sand of Hermosa Beach, California, was packed with a boisterous crowd of beach volleyball fans. They were on hand for the WPVA Hermosa Beach Women's Open. This tournament was taped and later shown on CBS, making the first women's pro beach volleyball tournament to be televised on national network television. The CBS telecast drew a respectable rating in major metropolitan areas. In the championship match, Karolyn Kirby and Liz Masakayan continued their dominance, on the WPVA Tour, with a 15-7 victory over Barbara Fontana and Lori Kotas-Forsythe, earning $5,300.00 for their efforts.

3rd Place: Janice Harrer and Deb Richardson
4th Place: Gail Castro and Elaine Roque
5th Place: Heather Hafner and Shannon Miller
5th Place: Wendy Fletcher and Marla O'Hara

SANTA CRUZ OPEN
June 19th-20th, 1993

The WPVA Tour went to Santa Cruz, California, where once again Karolyn Kirby and Liz Masakayan won the championship match. They were 15-7 winners over Barbara Fontana and Lori Kotas-Forsythe. This was the fourth consecutive tournament that these two teams had met in the finals. Kirby and Masakayan took home the $5,300.00 winnings.

3rd Place: Gail Castro and Elaine Roque
4th Place: Alison Johnson and Dennie Shupryt Knoop
5th Place: Janice Harrer and Deb Richardson
5th Place: Wendy Fletcher and Marla O'Hara

JACKIE CAMPBELL
Jackie Campbell provided some competitive play on the 1993 WPVA Tour. Above photo, Campbell positions herself to make another perfect bump-set.
Photo Courtesy of the AVP

GAIL CASTRO
In 1993, Gail Castro advanced to the championship match at 6 WPVA Tour events, finishing in second place each time. Above photo, Castro hits a set from Elaine Roque.
Photo Courtesy of Frank Goroszko

BOSTON MASSACHUSETTS
July 3rd-4th, 1993

The WPVA staged the Coors Light "Boston Shootout" on the weekend of July 3rd-4th, 1993 in Boston, Massachusetts. In the championship match, Liz Masakayan and Karolyn Kirby defeated Gail Castro and Elaine Roque by the score of 15-9. Kirby and Masakayan took home the top prize of $5,600.00 for their efforts. Final standings/records:

1. Karolyn Kirby and Liz Masakayan - 8-1
2. Gail Castro and Elaine Roque - 6-2
3. Wendy Fletcher and Marla O'Hara- 5-3
4. Barbra Fontana and Lori Kotas-Forsythe- 3-4

FAIRBORN OHIO
July 10th-11th, 1993

In Fairborn Ohio, the WPVA Coors Light Ohio Open event was won by 1993's dominant team Karolyn Kirby and Liz Masakayan. In the championship match, they defeated Gail Castro and Elaine Roque by a score of 15-10. Kirby and Masakayan took home the top prize of $5,300.00 for their efforts.

3rd Place: Barbra Fontana and Lori Kotas
4th Place: Alison Johnson and Dennie Shupryt Knoop
5th Place: Krista Blomquist and Johanna Wright
5th Place: Wendy Fletcher and Marla O'Hara

PISMO BEACH CALIFORNIA
July 24th-25th, 1993

At the WPVA Coors Light Pismo Beach Open, in the championship match Karolyn Kirby and Liz Masakayan flustered Gail Castro and Elaine Roque, by a score of 15-5. The winners earned $5,300.00 as they won their tenth event in eleven 1993 tournaments efforts.

3rd Place: Deb Richardson and Dennie Shupryt Knoop
4th Place: Barbra Fontana and Lori Kotas
5th Place: Lori Biller and Alison Johnson

LONG BEACH CALIFORNIA
August 7th-8th, 1993

The WPVA's U.S. Open was held in Long Beach, California. In the championship match, Karolyn Kirby and Liz Masakayan defeated Barbara Fontana and Lori Kotas-Forsythe, by a score of 15-9.

3rd Place: Elaine Roque and Gail Castro
4th Place: Deb Richardson and Dennie Shupryt Knoop
5th Place: Shannon Miller and Janice Harrer

MANHATTAN BEACH CALIFORNIA
August 21st-22nd, 1993

The 1993 WPVA "WORLD CHAMPIONSHIPS", were staged on the south side of the pier in Manhattan Beach, California. Karolyn Kirby and Liz Masakayan, prevailed, in the championship match, with a 15-9 victory over Gail Castro and Elaine Roque.

3rd Place: Lori Forsythe and Barbara Fontana
4th Place: Deb Richardson and Dennie Schupyt Knoop
5th Place: Wendy Fletcher and Marla O'Hara

POWELL OHIO
August 28th-29th, 1993

The 1993 WPVA "Top of the Tour" tournament, on the weekend of August 28th-29th, 1993, was staged in Powell, Ohio. The final resultsrecords were:

1. Karolyn Kirby 5-1   2. Deb Richardson 4-2
3. Elaine Roque 3-3   4. Gail Castro 2-4

PISMO BEACH CALIFORNIA
The Women's WPVA Tour was staged in-front of large crowds, from coast-to-coast. In the above photo, the Women's WPVA Tour enjoyed a large crowd at the Pismo Beach California event. The 1993 event was won by the team of Karolyn Kirby and Liz Masakayan, in the championship match, they over-powered the team of Gail Castro and Elaine Roque, by a score of 15-5.

Photo Courtesy of Frank Goroszko

WOMEN'S TOURNAMENT RESULTS
1993-FIVB

RIO DE JANEIRO, BRAZIL
February 9th-14th, 1993

On Copacabana Beach, Rio de Janeiro, Brazil, the $50,000.00 FIVB women's beach volleyball tournament was won by Karolyn Kirby and Nancy Reno. They were the winner's over a field of sixteen teams from eight countries. In the championship match, they beat the Brazilian team of Monica Rodriguez and Adriana Samuel Ramos, by scores of 12-3 and 12-10. The winner's picked-up a check for $10,000.00 each, along with their victory. There were sixteen teams from eight countries that participated in this tournament.

3rd Place: Karina Silva and Jacqueline Louise Silva Cruz-Bra
4th Place: Angela Rock and Liz Masakayan-USA
5th Place: Ana Roseli Timm and Maria Isabel Salgado Barroso-Bra
5th Place: Anita Palm and Jacqui Vukosa-Aus

SANTOS, BRAZIL
November 11th-14th, 1993

The final 1993, FIVB World Series of Beach Volleyball event was worth $50,000.00. This FIVB women's volleyball tournament took place on the beach at Santos Brazil, where a field of fifty-five teams from twenty-one countries participated. In the championship match, the U.S.A. team of Karolyn Kirby and Liz Masakayan defeated the Brazilian team of Isabel Timm and Roseli Salgado, 12-7 and 13-11. The winner's earned $5,500.00 for their efforts. There were sixteen teams from eight countries that participated in this tournament.

3rd Place: Magda Falcao and Adriana Behar-Bra
4th Place: Karina Silva and Sandra Pires-Bra
5th Place: Monica Rodriguez and Adriana Samuel Ramos-Bra
5th Place: Anita Palm and Natalie Cook-Aus

The U.S.A. team of Lori Kotas Forsythe and Barbra Fontana-Harris finished in seventh place.

NANCY RENO
Nancy Reno teamed-up with Karolyn Kirby to win the 1993 FIVB Tour event staged in Rio de Janeiro Brazil. Above photo, Reno gets up high for the spike.
Photo Courtesy of the AVP

KAROLYN KIRBY
In 1993, Karolyn Kirby paired-up with Nancy Reno to win the FIVB event in Rio de Janeiro Brazil and then with Liz Masakayan to win in Santos Brazil. Above photo, Kirby passing the ball
Photo Courtesy of the AVP

TOP PHOTOS: Left: Deb Richardson reaches over the net for a joust. **Center:** Brazilian Sandra Pires hits the ball past the block of Barbra Fontana. **Right:** Karolyn Kirby attacking the ball.

MIDDLE PHOTOS: Left: Linda Robertson Hanley go's "all-out" to make a block. **Center:** Holly McPeak attacking the ball at the net. **Right:** Barbra Fontana hits the ball over the net.

WOMEN'S BEACH VOLLEYBALL ACTION

BOTTOM PHOTOS: Left: Angela Rock attacking with the jump serve. **Center:** Janice Opalinski Harrer attacks the ball at the net. **Right:** Elaine Roque reaching for the ball.

Photo's Courtesy of the AVP

ADDITIONAL VOLLEYBALL INFORMATION
1993

1993
In addition to the players on the 1993 pro-beach volleyball tour's there were a total of 176 "AAA" rated male players and over 500 male players rated "AA", "A", "B", "Unrated", and "Novice" on the CBVA Sand Tour.

SANTA BARBARA CALIFORNIA
September, 1993
The FOVA National Sand Championship's "AAA" Women's-Doubles championship was played on Santa Barbara's East Beach. In the championship match, Kathy Hanley and Stephanie Cox defeated Margie Wiher and Anna Proussallis by a score of 15-7.

MONTE CARLO
On September 21, 1993, the 101st International Olympic Committee (IOC) granted beach volleyball Olympic medal status. FIVB President Ruben Acosta felt that it would strengthen the international governing body's position in the beach game. The political cooperation of the International Olympic Committee, the FIVB, NBC Television, and the Atlanta Organizing Committee, along with the games popularity, made it all happen.

LAGUNA BEACH CALIFORNIA
1993
The 1993 Laguna Beach Men's Open was an amateur "AAA" tournament. Dain Blanton and Dave Smith were the winners. In the championship match, they defeated Rick Ownbey and Mike Minier. The third spot went to Rudy Dvorak and Tom Duke. Scott Sjoquist and Dan Castillo finished in fourth place.

SANTA BARBARA CALIFORNIA
September, 1993
Although not an AVP event, the FOVA National Sand Championships "AAA" Men's-Doubles championship was played on Santa Barbara's East Beach. In the championship match, Todd Rogers and Dax Holdren defeated Steve Rottman and Andrew Cavanaugh by a score of 15-6. Early in the match, Holdren and Rogers were trailing 5-4, when they went on an 11-1 scoring spree to win the championship.

AROUND THE U.S.A.
In 1993, Mike Bright and Al Scates were inducted into the Volleyball Hall of Fame. The Federation Internationale de Volleyball (FIVB) was selected to the "VBHF Court of Honor."

Also, in 1993, the four-man Bud Light Pro Beach Volleyball League was going strong. There was a national tour for both men and women. Five teams participated in various cities almost every weekend of the summer. ESPN televised the matches.

TODD ROGERS & DAX HOLDREN
Todd Rogers and Dax Holdren won the 1993 FOVA National Sand "AAA" Championship, staged in Santa Barbara California. Above photo, later in their careers, Dax hits a set from Rogers towards the block of Mike Whitmarsh, during an AVP Tour event.
Photo Courtesy of "Couvi"

MIKE BRIGHT
In 1993, Mike Bright was inducted into the Volleyball Hall of fame. Above photo, Bright hitting the ball infront of a large crowd on Santa Monica's State Beach during the 1970's.
Photo Courtesy of Kevin Goff

1993 TOP 4-PERSON "BEACH" PLAYERS

(men)	(women)
Bob Ctvrtlik	Gabrielle Reece
Scott Fortune	Paula Weishoff
Tom Duke	Kristen Klein
Steve Salmons	Kim Oden
Doug Partie	Keba Phipps
Dan Hanan	Lisa Strand Ma'a
Jeff Williams	Lianne Sato
Wally Goodrick	Stephanie Cox
Dusty Dvorak	Antoinette White
Craig Buck	Lisa Hudak
Roger Clark	Tammy Liley
Jeff Stork	Natalie Williams

In 1993, the four-man Bud Light Pro Beach Volleyball League men's division Champion was "Team Champion." The second place team was "Team Club Sportswear." Bob Ctvrtlik was the "Most Valuable Player." The women's division team champion was also "Team Champion," while "Lady Footlocker" was the runner-up. Paula Weishoff was the "Most Valuable Player."

1993 MIXED-DOUBLES BEACH TOURNAMENTS

SAN DIEGO CALIFORNIA
1993

The West Coast Beach Volleyball Mixed-Doubles tournament was won by the team of Bob Bruce and Caron Janc. In the championship match, they defeated Brian Passman and Sherry Boyer.

SCOTT FORTUNE
Scott Fortune was a fixture on the 1993 Men's "Four-Person" Beach Volleyball Tour. Above photo, Fortune exhibits good form while passing the ball.
Photo Courtesy of the AVP

SAN DIEGO CALIFORNIA
June 12th, 1993

The 1993 Ocean Beach Mixed-Open was won by Scott Criswell and Carol Lipson. In the championship match, they defeated Butch Miali and Cristina Gage. Tournament director George Stepanof recorded that there were only four teams entered this tournament.
3rd Place: Paul Rion and Simone Ferreira
4th Place: Dismas Abelman and Sheri Snow Powers

MANHATTAN BEACH CALIFORNIA
August 14th-15th, 1993

The 1993 Marine Street Mixed-Doubles was won by the team of Steve Anderson and Lucy Hahn. In the championship match, they defeated David Swatik and Chrissy Boehle. Tournament director Mike Cook reported that the weather was cool in the AM, then warm and sunny in the afternoon. There were 19 teams entered in this tournament.
3rd Place: Dan Slayer and Marie Salyer
3rd Place: Christian Kiernan and Elizabeth Chavez
5th Place: Tim Muret and Mary Ann Wagner
5th Place: John Stalder and Danica Djujich
5th Place: Bob Trapnel and Katie Henderson
5th Place: Dave Gallenson and Donna Janulitis

SANTA BARBARA CALIFORNIA
September, 1993

The FOVA National Sand Championship's "AAA" Mixed-Doubles championship was played on Santa Barbara's East Beach. In the championship match, David Gallenson and Donna Janulatis defeated Bob Trapnell and Carrie Sutton

GABRIELLE REECE
Gabrielle "Gabby" Reece was a big hit on the 1993 Women's "Four-Person" Beach Volleyball Tour. Above photo, "Gabby" gets above the net for the spike.
Photo Courtesy of "Couvi"

MEN'S BEACH VOLLEYBALL
1994

In 1994, there were thirty-three recorded "Pro" Beach Volleyball tournaments. Twenty-eight of these tournaments were staged on U.S. soil, while five were played outside of the U.S. Of the twenty-eight U.S. tournaments, California and Florida each hosted seven events. There were fifteen U.S. events staged in ten states/regions other than, Florida and California. The California tournaments were held in Santa Cruz, San Francisco, San Jose, Manhattan Beach, Hermosa Beach, Seal Beach, and San Diego. The tournaments in Florida were in Fort Myers, Clearwater, Jacksonville, Orlando, and Miami (twice: AVP & FIVB). The remaining U.S. tournaments were held in Kauai Hawaii, Phoenix Arizona, Boulder Colorado, Belmar New Jersey, Grand Haven Michigan, Milwaukee Wisconsin, Cincinnati Ohio, Baltimore Maryland, Atlanta Georgia, Dallas Texas, Chicago Illinois, and Puerto Rico (twice, AVP & FIVB). The five events held outside of the U.S.A. were hosted by:

1. Copacabana Beach, in Rio de Janeiro, Brazil
2. Marseille France
3. Enoshima Japan
4. Fortaleza Brazil
5. Saint Petersburg, Russia (Goodwill Games)

In addition to the proceeding International events, the Swiss Beach Volleyball Tour became larger, with the participation of 1,000 players. The Swiss Championship finals were again held in Lucerne. The 1994 women's division winner's were Barbara Bossi and Cornelia Gerson. The men's champions were Martin Laciga and Paul Laciga.

In the summer of 1994, Volleyball Magazine conducted a nationwide search that confirmed that demographics of a relatively young market group (aged 25-34) made up equally of male and female. The majority, 75%, were active volleyball players, and close to 90% enjoyed watching volleyball on TV.

In 1994, Karch Kiraly and Kent Steffes remained in the top spot on the tour, this time with seventeen tournament championships together. Four of their wins came in California, at: Santa Cruz, San Francisco, San Diego, and the U.S. Championships in Hermosa Beach. An additional four of their wins came in Florida: Boca Raton, Miami, Clearwater, and Jacksonville. Their nine additional wins came in: New York City (indoor's at

RANDY STOKLOS & ADAM JOHNSON
Randy Stoklos and Adam Johnson were teamed-up together on the 1994 AVP Tour. They advanced to the championship match of 8 events, winning 3 times. Above photo, Stoklos passing the ball to Johnson. Action took place at the 1994 Manhattan Beach Men's Open.
Photo Courtesy of Frank Goroszko

Madison Square Garden), Kauai Hawaii, Phoenix Arizona, Boulder Colorado, Dallas Texas, Grand Haven Michigan, Atlanta Georgia, Chicago Illinois, and at the Tournament of Champions in Cincinnati Ohio.

Additional teams that won in 1994, included Adam Johnson and Randy Stoklos winning together at three events, Belmar Beach, San Francisco and Manhattan Beach. Johnson added the "King of the Beach" title in Orlando Florida. The "Twin Towers" Mike Dodd and Mike Whitmarsh won three tournaments together in 1994. They won the Fort Myers and Seal Beach events along with the AVP event in Isle Verde Puerto Rico. Brent Frohoff and Ricci Luyties won the event at Bradford Beach in Milwaukee Wisconsin, while Scott Ayakatubby and Eric Fonoimoana won the Baltimore Maryland tournament. Jan Kvalhelm and Bjoern Maaseide from Norway won three events together. They won the FIVB World Series events in Miami Beach and Marseille France. They added a win in Saint Petersburg, Russia by winning the Goodwill Games. The Brazilian team of Roberto Lopes and Paulo Roberto "Paulao" Moreira de Costa won the FIVB World Series events at Carolina Beach Puerto Rico and Enoshima Japan. Lopes also won the FIVB "World Championships" at Copacabana Beach, in Rio de Janeiro, Brazil.

AVP

In 1994, the AVP season included a schedule of 27 events with $4,000,000.00 dollars awarded to the players. NBC televised 10 events with a total coverage time of 21 hours.

Miller Brewing Company signed a four-year deal to continue as the AVP's umbrella sponsor. The deal called for Miller Lite to be the title sponsor for 10 AVP events. Evian sponsored the indoor event at Madison Square Garden, in New York City.

In 1994 Karch Kiraly and Kent Steffes won 17 of 20 tournaments that they competed in. Kent Steffes made $460,000.00 Karch made $30,000.00 less than Kent due to injuries, but he subsidized his earnings with another $500,000.00 in endorsements.

At the end of the AVP season, Kiraly and Steffes won in Santa Cruz, San Diego, and Hermosa Beach. The season ending run included their sixth straight Jose Cuervo Gold Crown title, third consecutive U.S. Championship and third straight win, at the grand finale in Hermosa Beach. Along with the Miller Lite Cup money awarded in Hermosa, the monthly earning for Steffes in August 1994 was $215,700.00, Kiraly collected $170,000.00 in the same time span.

MIKE DODD & MIKE WHITMARSH
Mike Dodd and Mike Whitmarsh were paired-up together for much of the 1994 AVP Tour. They were able to win 3 tournament championships together. **Left Photo:** Mike Dodd concentrates while passing the ball. **Right Photo:** Mike Whitmarsh gets to the ball to make a nice pass.

Photos Courtesy of Frank Goroszko

The Santa Cruz win was the sixth straight Jose Cuervo Gold Crown victory for Kiraly and Steffes. They collected $600,000.00 in six "Gold Crown" tournaments! In 1994, Kiraly and Steffes won more money at the "Gold Crowns" than all but eight other players on the entire tour. They were 22-3 in games, over the 1993 and 1994 "Gold Crown" events.

In 1994, NBC televised two of the most exciting tournaments on back-to-back weekends, when the Seal Beach event and the U.S. Championships both went down to sudden death. Dodd and Whitmarsh came back for a victory in Seal Beach, which arguably may have been the most exciting final of all time. Kiraly and Steffes did the honors the following week at the U.S. Championships, in San Diego, winning on the first serve of the sudden death contest.

There was over $98,000.00 difference in winnings from first place to 48th place in the Miller Lite Cup, but number 48 was not whining. Kent Steffes was the big winner at $100,000.00 (thanks to Kiraly injuring his kidney earlier in the season) Mike Schlegel edged out Bill Suwara to earn an extra $1,125.00 for finishing in the 48th spot.

The AVP made plans for their first "International" stops on the tour. The AVP scheduled stops in Italy and Spain. Because of scheduling complications, they had to cancel the tournaments before they could take place.

KARCH KIRALY
Karch Kiraly teamed-up with Kent Steffes to win 17 events in 1994. Kiraly won over $400,000.00 on the 1994 AVP Tour. Above photo, Kiraly gets low to make the pass.
Photo Courtesy of Frank Goroszko

1994 MEN's AVP AWARDS

Karch Kiraly was again the big winner at the AVP post-season banquet. In the annual voting by the tour players, Kiraly was selected the tour MVP for the third season in a row and for the fourth time in five years. Kiraly also was named the "Best Offensive Player.

Most Valuable Player: Karch Kiraly
Most Improved: Bill Boullianne
Top Rookie: Rob Heidger
Sportmanship: Larry Mear
Sportsmanship: Mike Dodd
Defensive Player: Mike Dodd
Offensive Player: Karch Kiraly
Comeback Player: Wes Welch
Ace Award: Brian Lewis
Ron Von Hagen Award: Scott Friederichsen

1994 AVP MEN'S TOUR EARNINGS

1.	Kent Steffes	$459,106
2.	Karch Kiraly	$430,636
3.	Adam Johnson	$211,286
4.	Mike Dodd	$204,253
5.	Mike Whitmarsh	$202,253
6.	Randy Stoklos	$163,286
7.	Jose Loiloa	$156,571
8.	Ricci Luyties	$131,169
9.	Eduardo Bacil	$124,571
10.	Brent Frohoff	$109,620
11.	Brian Lewis	$ 92,778
12.	Eric Fonoimoana	$ 82,953
13.	Troy Tanner	$ 82,358
14.	Bill Boullianne	$ 81,346
15.	Tim Hovland	$ 80,989
16.	Wes Welch	$ 72,021
17.	Leif Hanson	$ 65,963
18.	Scott Ayakatubby	$ 61,340
19.	Dan Vrebalovich	$ 57,869
20.	Scott Friederichsen	$ 54,048
21.	Al Janc	$ 48,619
22.	Pat Powers	$ 46,328
23.	Jeff Rodgers	$ 44,520
24.	Chris Young	$ 41,056
25.	Kevin Martin	$ 39,014
26.	Brian Gatzke	$ 37,041
27.	Andrew Smith	$ 36,966
28.	Doug Foust	$ 35,614
29.	Eric Wurts	$ 35,460
30.	John Brajevic	$ 32,211
31.	Rob Heidger	$ 31,360
32.	Tim Walmer	$ 30,903
33.	Matt Unger	$ 30,630
34.	Jim Nichols	$ 28,513
35.	Mark Kerins	$ 27,955
36.	Bruk Vandeweghe	$ 27,869
37.	Albert Hannemann	$ 25,565
38.	Canyon Ceman	$ 22,620
39.	David Swatik	$ 20,688
40.	Steve Timmons	$ 20,410
41.	Matt Sonnichsen	$ 19,113
42.	Marcelo Duarte	$ 18,930
43.	Mike Stafford	$ 18,869
44.	Eric Boyles	$ 18,325
45.	Daniel Cardenas	$ 17,756
46.	Mike Schlegel	$ 17,318
47.	Craig Moothart	$ 16,205
48.	Bill Suwara	$ 14,285
49.	Dain Blanton	$ 13,521
50.	Doug Mauro	$ 10,060

1994 AVP TOUR INDIVIDUAL MEN

Player	1st	2nd	3rd	4th	5th
Scott Ayakatubby	1	0	2	1	5
Eduardo Bacil	0	2	5	5	7
Bill Boullianne	0	2	1	0	5
Eric Boyles	0	0	0	0	1
Canyon Ceman	0	0	0	1	0
Mike Dodd	3	9	3	5	3
Brent Frohoff	1	2	4	1	6
Eric Fonoimoana	1	0	0	1	7
Scott Friederichsen	0	0	1	0	3
Brian Gatzke	0	0	0	0	3
Leif Hanson	0	0	1	1	3
Rob Heidger	0	0	1	0	0
Tim Hovland	0	0	0	1	7
Al Janc	0	0	0	1	1
Adam Johnson	4	5	3	5	3
Karch Kiraly	17	2	2	0	1
Marc Kerins	0	0	0	1	0
Brian Lewis	0	4	0	1	6
Jose Loiola	0	3	5	5	7
Ricci Luyties	1	3	2	2	7
Jim Nichols	0	0	0	1	0
Pat Powers	0	0	0	1	0
Jeff Rogers	0	0	1	0	4
Kent Steffes	17	2	1	1	1
Randy Stoklos	3	5	3	5	3
David Swatik	0	0	0	1	0
Troy Tanner	0	2	3	2	1
Steve Timmons	0	0	0	0	1
Matt Unger	0	0	0	0	1
Bruk Vandeweghe	0	0	1	1	0
Dan Vrebalovich	0	0	1	2	2
Tim Walmer	0	0	0	1	0
Wes Welch	0	2	2	1	1
Mike Whitmarsh	3	4	5	3	4
Eric Wurts	0	0	1	0	0

FIVB

The FIVB scheduled seven men's beach volleyball tournaments (including the Goodwill Games in Saint Petersburg, Russia) in 6 countries as well as 6 women's beach volleyball tournaments in 6 countries. The total FIVB prize money available was set at $1,000,000.00, with $700,000.00 going to the men and $300,000.00 to the women.

The 1994 Men's FIVB World Series of Volleyball Tour went to Saint Petersburg Russia, Marseille France, Enoshima Japan, San Juan Puerto Rico, Fortaleza Brazil, Miami Florida U.S.A., along with their World Championship in Rio de Janeiro Brazil. Beach volleyball truly attained global status in 1994 when Norway's Jan Kvalheim and Bjorn Maaseide, contrary to the stereotyped image of cold men from the icy North, dominated the scene on the warm sands of Miami.

The founder of the FIVB, Paul Libaud, from France, died at the age of 89 in March of 1994. Libaud formed the Federation International de Volleyball in 1945, uniting the 14 national federations. He also founded the World Championships in 1947, the first major international competition for volleyball.

KENT STEFFES
In 1994, Kent Steffes was teamed-up, on the AVP Tour, with Karch Kiraly. They were the top team, winning 17 events. Steffes was the top money winner, collecting $459,106.00. Above photo, Steffes hits the ball past the block of Mike Whitmarsh.
Photo Courtesy of the AVP

1994 FIVB TOUR INDIVIDUAL MEN

Player	1st	2nd	3rd	4th	5th
Vince Ahmann	0	0	0	1	0
Claudino Aloizio	0	0	0	1	3
Carlos Briceno	0	3	2	0	0
Andrew Burdin	0	0	0	1	1
Roberto Lopes da Costa	1	1	0	0	0
Roberto Duarte Dias	0	0	0	2	0
Carlos Eduard Garrido Dias	0	0	0	2	0
Eddie Drakich	0	0	0	1	1
Andre Faria Gomes	0	0	0	0	2
Axel Hager	0	0	0	1	0
Reid Hamilton	0	0	0	0	1
Glen Hamilton	0	0	0	0	1
Jean Philippe Jodard	0	1	1	0	2
Jan Kvalheim	3	1	1	0	1
Roberto Costa Lopes	3	0	0	0	0
Carlos Frederico "Alemao" Loss	0	0	0	0	2
Bjorn Maaseide	3	1	1	0	1
Luiz Guilherme Marquez	0	0	1	0	0
Paulo Roberto Da Costa Moreira	2	0	0	0	0
Jose Franco Vieira Neto	2	1	0	0	0
Jose Marco Melo Ferreira Nobrega	0	0	1	0	1
Marco "Pako" Pakosta	0	0	0	0	1
Michal "Palda" Palinek	0	0	0	0	1
Christian Penigaud	0	1	1	0	2
Julien Prosser	0	0	0	1	1
Emanuel Rego Scheffer	0	0	0	1	3
Paulo Emilo Azevedo Silva	0	0	1	0	1
Sinjin Smith	0	1	1	1	0
Rogrio "Para" Ferrirsde Souza	0	0	1	0	0
Bruk Vandeweghe	0	1	1	1	0
Jeff Williams	0	3	2	0	0

MEN'S TOURNAMENT RESULTS
1994-AVP

NEW YORK, NEW YORK
February 26 1994.

After the AVP qualifier, the first AVP tournament of 1994 was the $100,000.00 "Evian Indoor" tournament, in front of 12,000 fans, at Madison Square Garden, in New York City. In the championship match, Karch Kiraly and Kent Steffes prevailed, 15-13 over Adam Johnson and Randy Stoklos. The winners earned $25,000.00. Earlier, in the semi-finals, Kiraly and Steffes edged-out Scott Ayakatubby and Brent Frohoff by a score of 12-11. In the other semi-final match, Johnson and Stoklos edged-out Mike Dodd and Mike Whitmarsh by the score of 14-13.

3rd Place: Mike Dodd and Mike Whitmarsh
3rd Place: Scott Ayakatubby and Brent Frohoff

BOCA RATON FLORIDA
March 19th-20th, 1994

On the beach of Boca Raton, Florida, the AVP Tour put on the $100,000.00 "Old Spice Open". In the championship match, Karch Kiraly and Kent Steffes won 15-13 over Mike Dodd and Mike Whitmarsh to earn the $20,500.00 first place prize money. During the final Dodd and Whitmarsh had leads of 4-1, 10-3 and 13-8 before they fell apart and lost 15-13.

3rd Place: Adam Johnson and Randy Stoklos
4th Place: Troy Tanner and Dan Vrebalovich
5th Place: Tim Hovland and Eric Fonoimoana
5th Place: Scott Ayakatubby and Brent Frohoff

FORT MYERS FLORIDA
March 26th-27th, 1994

On the weekend of March 26th-27th, 1994, in Fort Myers, Florida, the $100,000.00 "Miller Lite Open" was won by Mike Dodd and Mike Whitmarsh. They won as the time clock expired in the championship match, 14-13 over Karch Kiraly and Kent Steffes. During this final, Dodd and Whitmarsh were ahead by the score of 13-7, when the self destructed as Kiraly and Steffes tied the score at 13, as the rally clock expired, sending the game into overtime. After a side-out, in the one-point tiebreaker, Dodd ended the match with a dig off Kiraly, followed by a cross-court dink shot, for the win. This was Mike Dodd's sixty-first career title, moving him ahead of Tim Hovland and one behind the legendary Ron Von Hagen. The winners each took home a check for $10,000.00.

3rd Place: Jose Loiola and Eduardo Bacil
4th Place: Tim Walmer and Bruk Vandeweghe
5th Place: Randy Stoklos and Adam Johnson
5th Place: Scott Ayakatubby and Brent Frohoff

MIAMI FLORIDA
April 9th-10th, 1994

The AVP Pro-Beach Volleyball Tour was in Miami Beach Florida for the $100,000.000 Miller Lite Miami Beach Open. Karch Kiraly and Kent Steffes, after losing

DODD-WHITMARSH-KIRALY-STEFFES
Mike Dodd and Mike Whitmarsh, along with, Karch Kiraly and Kent Steffes spent a lot of time on the winner's podium in 1994. Above photo, left-to-right: Dodd, Whitmarsh, Kiraly and Steffes are on the podium for their awards.
Photo Courtesy of the AVP

KARCH KIRALY & KENT STEFFES
With 17 AVP tournament championships, Karch Kiraly and Kent Steffes were the top team on the AVP Tour in 1994. Above photo, Kiraly hits a set from Steffes. Scott Ayakatubby gets up high in the block attempt.
Photo Courtesy of the AVP

a second round match to Bill Boullianne and Pat Powers 15-10, came through the looser's bracket, to outlast Brian Lewis and Ricci Luyties 15-9 and 7-6, in the exciting double-final championship match. The winners took home $20,000.00 for their efforts.

3rd Place: Adam Johnson and Randy Stoklos
4th Place: Mike Dodd and Mike Whitmarsh
5th Place: Eric Fonoimoana and Tim Hovland
5th Place: Scott Friederichsen and Leif Hanson

CLEARWATER BEACH FLORIDA
April 14th-16th, 1994

The 1994 seasons first AVP $250,000.00 "Cuervo Gold Crown" event was staged at Clearwater Beach, Florida. In the championship match, Karch Kiraly and Kent Steffes baffled Brian Lewis and Ricci Luyties 15-5. Kiraly and Steffes pocketed the $100,000.00 first prize.

3rd Place: Mike Dodd and Mike Whitmarsh
4th Place: Adam Johnson and Randy Stoklos
5th Place: Eric Fonoimoana and Tim Hovland

JACKSONVILLE FLORIDA
April 23rd-24th, 1994

In Jacksonville Florida, after high winds canceled Saturday's matches, Karch Kiraly and Kent Steffes overpowered Adam Johnson and Randy Stoklos 15-4, in the championship match, of the $100,000.00 Miller Lite Jacksonville Open. This was the fifth title out of six events for Kiraly and Steffes, as they only gave-up an average of about five points a match as they dominated the event. The winners split the $20,000.00 first place prize money. Johnson was fighting cramps in the final, after rallying from 9-0 and 11-1 deficits against Troy Tanner and Dan Vrebalovich in the semi-finals.

3rd Place: Troy Tanner and Dan Vrebalovich
4th Place: Brian Lewis and Ricci Luyties
5th Place: Al Janc and Steve Timmons
5th Place: Eduardo Bacil and Jose Loiola

ATLANTA GEORGIA
April 29th-May 1st, 1994

The AVP'S $75,000.00"Nestea Atlanta Open" took place on the weekend of April 29th-May 1st, 1994 in Atlanta, Georgia. In the championship match, Karch Kiraly and Kent Steffes were victorious again with a 15-9 victory over Mike Dodd and Mike Whitmarsh. This was Kiraly's 83rd career tournament championship and it was the 60th for Steffes, which tied him with Tim Hovland for sixth on the list, one behind Mike Dodd. The $15,000.00 first place prize money was split by Karch and Kent.

3rd Place: Brent Frohoff and Bruk Vandeweghe
4th Place: Adam Johnson and Randy Stoklos
5th Place: Ricci Luyties and Brian Lewis
5th Place: Eduardo Bacil and Jose Loiola.

TIM HOVLAND
Tim Hovland did not win any AVP Tour events in 1994, but he still managed to earn over $80,000.00 in prize money. Above photo, Hovland slices the ball past the block of Eric Boyles.
Photo Courtesy of the AVP

BRIAN LEWIS & RICCI LUYTIES
Brian Lewis and Ricci Luyties teamed-up for a couple of events on the 1994 AVP Tour. Above photo, Lewis hits a set from Luyties, past the block.
Photo Courtesy of the AVP

DALLAS TEXAS
May 6th-7th, 1994

The AVP Pro-Beach volleyball Tour went to Dallas Texas, to stage the $75,000.00 Nestea Dallas Open. Troy Tanner and Wes Welch played outstanding volleyball to earn their way into the championship match. They had defeated Adam Johnson and Randy Stoklos 15-12, in the loser's bracket semi-final. They then defeated Mike Dodd and Mike Whitmarsh 16-14, in the loser's bracket final, to reach the championship match where they were embarrassed by Karch Kiraly and Kent Steffes 15-0. Kiraly and Steffes took home $15,000.00 for their victory.

3rd Place: Mike Dodd and Mike Whitmarsh
4th Place: Eric Fonoimoana and Dan Vrebalovich
5th Place: Adam Johnson and Randy Stoklos
5th Place: Brian Lewis and Ricci Luyties

PHOENIX ARIZONA
May 13th-15th, 1994

The AVP then traveled to Phoenix Arizona, for the $100,000.00 Miller Lite Phoenix Open. At the Gateway Center, Karch Kiraly and Kent Steffes defeated Adam Johnson and Randy Stoklos, in the championship match. They did it the hard way, coming out of the loser's bracket to win the overtime double final, by scores of 15-7 and 7-5. Kiraly and Steffes each took home a check for $10,000.00 with their victory.

3rd Place: Troy Tanner and Wes Welch
4th Place: Eduardo Bacil and Jose Loiola
5th Place: Eric Fonoimoana and Dan Vrebalovich
5th Place: Mike Dodd and Mike Whitmarsh

SAN JOSE CALIFORNIA
May 21st-22nd, 1994

The AVP staged a tournament on a man-made beach at Guadalupe River Park in San Jose California, the $100,000.00 Miller Lite San Jose Open. After dropping into the loser's bracket, Karch Kiraly and Kent Steffes came back to outlast Adam Johnson and Randy Stoklos by scores of 12-10 and 7-4 in a thrilling double final match. This was the seventh title in a row for Kiraly and Steffes. With this his 63rd career tournament title, Kent Steffes passed the great Ron Von Hagen's mark of 62.

3rd Place: Ricci Luyties and Brent Frohoff
4th Place: Canyon Ceman and David Swatik
5th Place: Eduardo Bacil and Jose Loiola
5th Place: Eric Boyles and Jeff Rogers

SAN FRANCISCO CALIFORNIA
May 27th-29th, 1994

The AVP staged its next event at the Embarcadero Center in San Francisco California. The 1994 $75,000.00 Nestea San Francisco Open was won by Adam Johnson and Randy Stoklos, as they prevailed, 15-8 and 7-6 over Troy Tanner and Wes Welch, in the double-final match. Johnson and Stoklos split the $15,000.00 first place prize.

3rd Place: Karch Kiraly and Kent Steffes
4th Place: Mike Dodd and Mike Whitmarsh
5th Place: Eduardo "Anjinho" Bacil and Jose Loiola
5th Place: Tim Hovland and Bill Boullianne

ALBERT HANNEMANN & SCOTT FRIEDERICHSEN
Albert Hannemann and Scott "Freddy" Friederichsen both participated on the 1994 AVP Tour. Above photo, Hannemann challenges the block of Friederichsen.
Photo Courtesy of the AVP

CANYON CEMAN
Canyon Ceman began to show some beach volleyball promise on the 1994 AVP Tour. Above photo, Ceman shows his powerful hitting form.
Photo Courtesy of "Couvi"

GRAND HAVEN MICHIGAN
June 3rd-5th, 1994

The State Beach, in Grand Haven, Michigan was the site for the next AVP Pro-Beach volleyball Tour event. The 1994 $100,000.00 Grand Haven Open was won by Karch Kiraly and Kent Steffes, as they easily defeated Mike Dodd and Mike Whitmarsh. In the championship match, Kiraly and Steffes prevailed, by a score of 15-5, as they earned $20,000.00 for their efforts.

3rd Place: Eduardo Bacil and Jose Loiola
4th Place: Pat Powers and Al Janc
5th Place: Brent Frohoff and Ricci Luyties
5th Place: Adam Johnson and Randy Stoklos

BOULDER COLORADO
June 9th-11th, 1994

The 1994 seasons second AVP $250,000 "Cuervo Gold Crown" took place at the Boulder Reservoir in Boulder Colorado. Karch Kiraly and Kent Steffes were the "big money" winners as they took home $100,000.00. In the championship match, they defeated Brent Frohoff and Ricci Luyties by a score of 15-9. During the final, Kiraly dove for a ball, and when he landed on the sideline barriers, he bruised a kidney. The injury sidelined him from the next four tournaments.

3rd Place: Mike Dodd and Mike Whitmarsh
4th Place: Eduardo Bacil and Jose Loiola
5th Place: Dan Vrebalovich and Bill Boullianne

MILWAUKEE WISCONSIN
June 18th-19th, 1994

On the weekend of June 18th-19th, 1994, on Bradford Beach in Milwaukee Wisconsin, the 1994 $100,000.00 Miller Lite Milwaukee Open was staged. Brent Frohoff and Ricci Luyties had a great tournament as they earned a 15-9 victory over Adam Johnson and Randy Stoklos, in the championship match. Johnson and Stoklos played well after losing in the first round to Daniel Cardenas and Eric Wurts. The match that got them into the final was amazing. In the loser's bracket final, they were losing to Scott Friederichsen and Leif Hanson, by a score of 9-11, with one second left on the rally clock. It was made possible when Johnson served a "spader" that hit just inside the back line. Then there was a discussion among the players, ref's and the Tour Director Matt Gage, as to whether the match was over or if there was a fraction of a second left on the clock. Even though the clock read 00, Gage ruled that there was some time left. After another "spader" by "AJ", tying the score at 11-all, the match went into sudden-death overtime. Stoklos and Johnson then won the first point in sudden-death. The winners split $20,000.00 for their efforts. It should be mentioned, that later, Matt Gage sent a letter to all of the players stating that he'd erred and that time would not be added to the clock in the future.

3rd Place: Scott Friederichsen and Leif Hanson
4th Place: Troy Tanner and Wes Welch
5th Place: Eduardo Bacil and Jose Loiola
5th Place: Mike Dodd and Mike Whitmarsh

WES WELCH & TROY TANNER
Wes Welch and Troy Tanner advanced to the finals of 2 AVP Tour events in 1994, only to come-up short both times, with second place finishes. Abve photo, Brian Lewis hits the ball past the block of Tanner towards the defense of Welch.
Photo Courtesy of the AVP

BILL BOULLIANNE
Bill "Beef" Boullianne was a force to contend with on the 1994 AVP Tour. "Beef" advanced to 2 finals, finishing second both times. Boullianne was voted "Most Improved" player by his peers. Above photo, "Beef" attacking the ball.
Photo Courtesy of "Couvi"

BALTIMORE MARYLAND
June 24th-26th, 1994

The AVP'S Pro-Beach Volleyball Tour traveled to Baltimore Maryland to stage the $75,000.00 Nestea Baltimore Open. Scott Ayakatubby returned to the tour in style, after a two-month interruption, because of a severe groin injury. Ayakatubby and Eric Fonoimoana played flawless volleyball during the whole weekend. They were 15-10 winners over Mike Dodd and Mike Whitmarsh in the championship match. This was Fonoimoana's first AVP Pro-Beach Volleyball title as he and "Ack" split the $15,000.00 prize money.

3rd Place: Bill Boullianne and Jeff Rogers
4th Place: Mark Kerins and Jim Nichols
5th Place: Eduardo Bacil and Jose Loiola
5th Place: Brent Frohoff and Ricci Luyties

MANHATTAN BEACH CALIFORNIA
July 1st-3rd, 1994

The "renowned" Manhattan Beach Open, played on the sands of Manhattan Beach California, was the next tour site for the AVP. The 1994 $100,000.00 Old Spice Manhattan Beach Open was won by Adam Johnson and Randy Stoklos. In the championship match, Johnson and Stoklos defeated Bill Boullianne and Brian Lewis by a score of 14-7, as the rally clock ran out. This was the fourth Manhattan Open win for Stoklos. He has won with three different partners. Besides this win with Johnson, he won in 1981 with Jim Menges, then in 1986 and 1989 with Sinjin Smith. This was also "Stokie's" 118 career title. Johnson and Stoklos each took home a $10,000.00 check along with their victory.

3rd Place: Eduardo Bacil and Jose Loiola
4th Place: Brent Frohoff and Ricci Luyties
5th Place: Mike Dodd and Mike Whitmarsh
5th Place: Tim Hovland and and Eric Fonoimoana

PUERTO RICO
July 8th-10th, 1994

The AVP Pro-Beach Volleyball Tour made an historic stop in Puerto Rico, for the $75,000.00 Miller Genuine Draft Puerto Rico Open. In the championship match, Mike Dodd and Mike Whitmarsh easily defeated Brian Lewis and Bill Boullianne by a score of 15-5. Dodd tied the legendary Ron Von Hagen with his 62nd career title.

3rd Place: "Anjino" Bacil and Jose Loiola
4th Place: Scott Ayakatubby and Kent Steffes
5th Place: Troy Tanner and Wes Welch
5th Place: Scott Friederichsen and Leif Hanson

ERIC FONOIMOANA & SCOTT AYAKATUBBY
Eric "Foni" Fonoimoana teamed-up with Scott Ayakatubby, to earn his first AVP Tour career championship, in Baltimore Maryland. Above photo, Ayakatubby, playing against Fonoimoana, hits the ball into "Foni's" block.
Photo Courtesy of "Couvi"

ROB HEIDGER
Rob Heidger provided some stiff competition on the 1994 AVP Tour. Heidger was voted the AVP Tour's "Rookie of the Year" by his AVP Tour peers. Above photo, Heidger (left) challenges Karch Kiraly (right) to a "joust" at the net.
Photo Courtesy of "Couvi"

CHICAGO ILLINOIS
July 23rd-24th, 1994

The AVP'S Pro Beach Volleyball Tour moved to North Avenue Beach in Chicago Illinois, for the $100,000.00 Miller Lite Chicago Open. In the championship match, Karch Kiraly and Kent Steffes prevailed, 15-11 over Mike Dodd and Mike Whitmarsh, to win the tournament as well as $20,000.00. This was their 12th tournament title of the season.

3rd Place: Troy Tanner and Wes Welch
4th Place: Eduardo Bacil and Jose Loiola
5th Place: Brian Lewis and Bill Boullianne
5th Place: Scott Ayakatubby and Eric Fonoimoana

BELMAR NEW JERSEY
July 30th-31st, 1994

On Belmar Beach in New Jersey, the 1994 $100,000.00 Nestea Belmar Open, AVP Pro-Beach Volleyball event, was won by Adam Johnson and Randy Stoklos. In the championship match, they defeated Mike Dodd and Mike Whitmarsh by a score of 15-8 to take home the $20,000.00 for first place.

3rd Place: Brent Frohoff and Ricci Luyties
4th Place: Tim Hovland and Leif Hanson
5th Place: Karch Kiraly and Kent Steffes
5th Place: Bill Boullianne and Brian Lewis

SANTA CRUZ CALIFORNIA
August 4th-6th, 1994

The 1994 seasons third AVP $250,000.00 "Cuervo Gold Crown" took place on Main Beach in Santa Cruz California. Karch Kiraly and Kent Steffes were the "big money" winners of the championship match. They defeated Jose Loiola and Eduardo Bacil by a score of 15-9 to earn the $100,000.00 first place check. This completed a sweep of the "Cuervo Gold" series for Kiraly and Steffes.

3rd Place: Mike Dodd and Mike Whitmarsh
4th Place: Randy Stoklos and Adam Johnson
5th Place: Brent Frohoff and Ricci Luyties

KAUAI HAWAII
August 8th-9th, 1994

The AVP'S Pro Beach Volleyball Tour was on Poipu Beach in Kauai, Hawaii for the $100,000.00 Men's "Jose Cuervo Gold Crown" series tournament. Karch Kiraly and Kent Steffes were the winner's. They shared the $20,000.00 first place prize. In the championship match, Kiraly and Steffes defeated Mike Dodd and Mike Whitmarsh, by scores of 10-7, 8-9, and 6-0. This was Karch Kiraly's 100th career championship title. Kiraly and Steffes made it into the final with their 9-10, 10-5, and 6-0 semi-final match victory over Eric Wurts and Rob Heidger. Dodd and Whitmarsh had an easier time in the semi-finals, with their 10-5 and 10-2 match victory over Brian Lewis and Ricci Luyties.

3rd Place: Brian Lewis and Ricci Luyties
3rd Place: Eric Wurts and Rob Heidger
5h Place: Brian Gatzke and Jeff Rogers
5th Place: Eduardo Bacil and Jose Loiola
5th Place: Scott Ayakatubby and Brent Frohoff
5th Place: Bill Boullianne and Tim Hovland

SEAL BEACH CALIFORNIA
August 12th-14th, 1994

The AVP moved its Pro-Beach Volleyball Tour to the north side of the Seal Beach Pier, on the sands of Seal Beach California, for the 1994 $100,000.00 Seal Beach Men's Open. Mike Dodd and Mike Whitmarsh won the tournament and the first place prize of $20,000.00. In an exceptionally exciting, overtime championship match, Dodd and Whitmarsh defeated Karch Kiraly and Kent Steffes by a score of 15-14.

3rd Place: Randy Stoklos and Adam Johnson
4th Place: Jose Loiola and Eduardo Bacil
5th Place: Scott Friederichsen and Matt Unger
5th Place: Brian Gatzke and Jeff Rogers

MIKE WHITMARSH & KENT STEFFES
Mike Whitmarsh and Kent Steffes were two of the top players on the 1994 AVP Tour. They battled it out all season long. Above photo, Steffes spikes the ball past the huge block of Whitmarsh.
Photo Courtesy of the AVP

LEIF HANSON
Leif Hanson played competitively on the 1994 AVP Tour, earning nearly $70,000.00 in prize money. Above photo, Hanson makes a nice dig.
Photo Courtesy of the AVP

SAN DIEGO CALIFORNIA
August 19th-21st, 1994
The AVP Pro-Beach Volleyball Tour was at Mariner's Point in San Diego California, for the $100,000.00 Old Spice U.S. Championships. Karch Kiraly and Kent Steffes were 11-10 winners over Mike Dodd and Mike Whitmarsh, in another overtime championship match. Karch and Kent split the $20,000.00 first place prize.

3rd Place: Jose Loiola and Eduardo Bacil
4th Place: Adam Johnson and Randy Stoklos
5th Place: Brian Lewis and Ricci Luyties
5th Place: Brian Gatzke and Jeff Rogers

HERMOSA BEACH CALIFORNIA
August 26th-28th, 1994
The AVP'S Pro Beach Volleyball Tour was in Hermosa Beach California for the $250,000.00 Miller Lite Championship. Karch Kiraly and Kent Steffes won the tournament and split the $100,000.00 first place prize money for their efforts. In the championship match, Kiraly and Steffes were 11-7 winners over Jose Loiola and Eduardo Bacil.

3rd Place: Scott Ayakatubby and Brent Frohoff
4th Place: Mike Dodd and Mike Whitmarsh
5th Place: Leif Hanson and Tim Hovland
5th Place: Brian Lewis and Ricci Luyties

CINCINNATI OHIO
September 9th-10th, 1994
The AVP'S Pro Beach Volleyball Tour was at Sawyer Point in Cincinnati, Ohio for the Old Spice "Tournament of Champions." In the championship match, Karch Kiraly and Kent Steffes defended their title as they were 15-4 winners over Mike Dodd and Mike Whitmarsh. Kiraly and Steffes split $37,500.00 with the win. The final was played in front of 5,140 "paid" beach volleyball enthusiast, the largest "paid" crowd in AVP history.

3rd Place: Jose Loiola and Eduardo Bacil
4th Place: Adam Johnson and Randy Stoklos
5th Place: Scott Ayakatubby and Eric Fonoimoana

ORLANDO FLORIDA
September 23rd-25th, 1994
The AVP Pro Beach Volleyball Tour staged the $200,000.00 Old Spice "King of the Beach" tournament, in Orlando, Florida. At Disney World, Adam Johnson put an end to Karch Kiraly's dominance of this tournament by being the first player other than Karch to win this event.

FINAL STANDINGS:
1. Adam Johnson
2. Jose Loiola
3. Karch Kiraly
4. Mike Dodd
5. Mike Whitmarsh
6. Tim Hovland
7. Randy Stoklos
8. Brian Lewis.

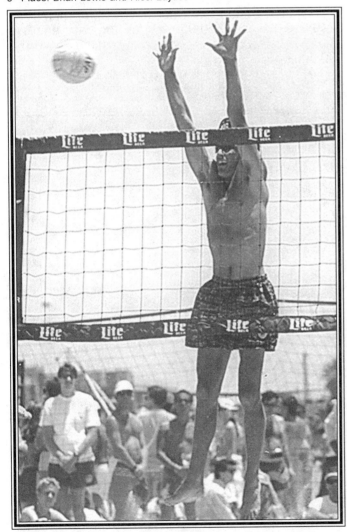

AL JANC
Al Janc broke into the top five at a couple of 1994 AVP Tour events, on his way to earning nearly $50,000.00 in prize money. Above photo, Janc gets up high for the block attempt.
Photo Courtesy of the AVP

ADAM JOHNSON
Adam "AJ" Johnson was the big winner at the 1994 AVP $200,000.00 Old Spice "King of the Beach" tournament. Above photo, "AJ" braces himself for the dig of a hard driven ball.
Photo Courtesy of Frank Goroszko

MEN'S TOURNAMENT RESULTS
1994-FIVB

MIAMI, FLORIDA, U.S.A.
January 15th-22nd, 1994

Miami Florida U.S.A. was the site for the first $100,000.00 FIVB Men's World Series event of 1994. The championship match, was won by the team of Jan Kvalheim and Bjorn Maaseide, from Norway. They outscored the Brazilian team of Roberto Lopes da Costa and Franco Jose Vieira Neto 12-3 and 12-8. The winners took home $22,000.00 for their efforts. There were teams from 16 countries participating in this event.

3rd Place: Carlos Briceno and Jeff Williams-USA
4th Place: John Child and Eddie Drakich-Canada
5th Place: Glenn Hamilton and Reid Hamilton-New Zeland
5th Place: Andy Burdin and Julien Prosser-Aus
Additional U.S.A. finishers: Roger Clark and Rudy Dvorak in seventh, Marc Jones and Wally Goodrick along with Ken Engels and Manny Agnant in ninth, Thomas Duke and Dan Greenbaum finished in thirteenth place.

RIO DE JANEIRO, BRAZIL
February 1st-6th, 1994

The $200,000.00 FIVB Men's World Series event at Copacabana Beach, in Rio de Janeiro, Brazil was played in front of a capacity crowd in the "Beach Volleyball Stadium." The 10,000 Brazilian fans were thrilled by the victory of the home team Roberto Lopes da Costa and Franco Jose Vieira Neto, 12-7 and 12-8 winner's over the team of Carlos Briceno and Jeff Williams, from the U.S.A. Lopes and Neto each pocketed $22,000.00 for their efforts. The championship match was played under the hot Brazilian sun, about 110 degrees with 95% humidity.

3rd Place: Z-Marco Nobrega and Barbosa da Silva-Bra
4th Place: Aloizio Claudino and Emanuel Rego-Bra
5th Place: Carlos "Alemao" Galletti Loss and Andre Gomes-Bra
5th Place: John Child and Edward Drakich-Canada
Americans Roger Clark and Rudy Dvorak finished in 17th place..

1994 GOODWILL GAMES
SAINT PETERSBURG, RUSSIA
July 23rd-28th, 1994

Saint Petersburg Russia, was the site for the first appearance of beach volleyball in a multi-sport international event. The event was the fourth convening of the **Goodwill Games**. These 1994 Goodwill Games, an FIVB event, were considered the precursor to the 1996 Olympic Games in Atlanta. The championship match was won by Jan Kvalhelm and Bjorn Maaseide, from Norway. Kvalhelm and Maaseide captured the Gold Medal while two American teams finished in second and third place. Jeff Williams and Carlos Briceno won a Silver Medal, while Bruk Vandeweghe and Sinjin Smith won the Bronze Medal. In the championship match, the Norwegian team took two straight games from the Americans with scores of 12-8 and 12-6. The winners earned $30,000.00 for this international win. Prize money for the men was $100,000.00 and $50,000.00 for the women. The television viewing audience was estimated to be 600,000,000.

3rd Place: Bruk Vandeweghe and Sinjin Smith-USA
4th Place: Andrew Burdin and Julien Allen Prosser-Aus
5th Place: Emanuel Rego and Alozio Claudino-Bra

BJORN MAASEIDE & JAN KVALHEIM
The Norwegian team of Bjorn Maaseide (left) and Jan Kvalheim (right) were the top team on the 1994 FIVB Tour, winning 3 events, including the Goodwill Games.
Photo Courtesy of the FIVB

CARLOS BRICENO
Carlos Briceno teamed-up with Jeff Williams for a silver medal, at the 1994 Goodwill Games, staged in Saint Petersburg Russia. Above photo, Briceno gets down low to pass the ball.
Photo Courtesy of the AVP

MARSEILLE, FRANCE
July 25th-31st, 1994

In a three set championship final, the team of Jan Kvalheim and Bjorn Maaseide, from Norway defeated Christian Penigaud and Jean Phillipe Jodard, from France. The enthusiastic French volleyball crowd was treated to a very exciting championship match, as the Norwegians outlasted the French team by scores of 12-8, 7-12, and 15-10. This FIVB Men's World Series event had a total purse of $100,000.00, with the winners collecting $11,000.00 each.

3rd Place: Carlos Briceno and Jeff Williams-USA
4th Place: Vince Ahmann and Axel Hager-Ger
5th Place: Marco "Pako" Pakosta and Michal "Palda" Palinek-Czk
5th Place: Carlos Frederico Galletti Loss and Andre Gomes-Bra
Additional U.S.A. finishers: Sinjin Smith and Bruk Vandeweghe in seventh, John Eddo and Sean Fallowfield in thirteenth.

ENOSHIMA JAPAN
August 4th-7th, 1994

In Enoshima Japan, the Brazilian team of Roberto Lopes and Paulao Moreira defeated the U.S.A. team of Carlos Briceno and Jeff Williams, to win the first place prize of $22,000.00, at the $100,000.00 FIVB Men's World Series event. The championship match was another thrilling three game final as the Brazilians topped the American's by scores of 12-9, 10-12, and 15-11.

3rd Place: Jan Kvalheim and Bjorn Maaseide
4th Place: Roberto Duarte Dias and Carlos Garrido Dias-Bra
5th Place: Christian Penigaud and Jean Phillipe Jodard-Fra
5th Place: Emanuel Rego Scheffer and Claudino Aloizio-Bra
Americans Sinjin Smith and Bruk Vandeweghe finished in ninth.

CAROLINA BEACH, PUERTO RICO
August 17th-21st, 1994

The Brazilian team of Roberto Lopes and Paulao Moreira defeated the U.S.A. team of Sinjin Smith and Bruk Vandeweghe, by a score of 15-10, in the championship match, to win the $100,000.00 FIVB Men's World Series event at Carolina Beach Puerto Rico. The winners shared $22,000.00 for their efforts.

3rd Place: Christian Penigaud and Jean Phillipe-Fra
4th Place: Roberto Moreira Duarte Dias and Carlos Garrido Dias-Bra
5th Place: Emanuel Rego Scheffer and Claudino Aloizio-Bra
5th Place: Jan Kvalhein and Bjorn Maaseide-Nor
Manny Agnant and James Mears from the U.S.A. finished in a distant 21st.

FORTALEZA, BRAZIL
August 28th-September 4th, 1994

The Brazilian team of Franco Jose Vieira Neto and Roberto Costa Lopes defeated the team from Norway, Jan Kvalheim and Bjorn Maaseide, 12-7 and 12-2, to win the $100,000.00 FIVB World Series event at Fortaleza Brazil. Neto and Lopes split the $22,000.00 first place check.

3rd Place: Luiz Marquez and Rogrio "Para" Ferrirs de Souza-Bra
4th Place: Sinjin Smith and Bruk Vandeweghe-USA
5th Place: Christian Penigaud and Jean Phillipe Jodard-Fra
5th Place: Jose Marco Melo Nobrega and Paulo Azevedo-Bra
Americans Teams, Mark Andesen and Gary Gysin along with Sean Fallowfield and Anthony Curci, finished in 13th and 17th place, respectively

BRUK VANDEWEGHE
Bruk Vandeweghe paired-up with Sinjin Smith for several top-five finishes on the 1994 FIVB Tour, including a second in Puerto Rico. Above photo, Vandeweghe passing the ball.
Photo Courtesy of the AVP

JEFF WILLIAMS
Jeff Williams teamed-up with Carlos Briceno for several top five finishes on the 1994 FIVB Tour, including 2nd place finishes in Brazil, Japan and Russia. Above photo Williams passing the ball.
Photo Courtesy of the AVP

TOP PHOTOS: Left: Ricci Luyties makes a difficult pass. **Center:** Albert Hannemann spikes the ball over the net. **Right:** Mike Miner (left) jousting with Doug Foust (right).

MIDDLE PHOTOS: Left: Brent Frohoff hits the ball over the block of Mike Dodd. **Center:** Jim Nichoils gets low to dig the ball. **Right:** Scott Ayakatubby consentrates while passing the ball.

 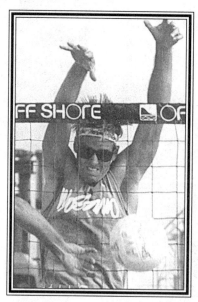 

1994 MEN'S BEACH VOLLEYBALL ACTION

BOTTOM PHOTOS: Left: Mike Dodd attacking the ball. **Center:** Andrew Smith with the huge block. **Right:** Adam Johnson follows-through after attacking the ball.

Photo's Courtesy of the AVP

TOP PHOTOS: Left: Jose Loiola hits the ball past the block of Andrew Smith. **Center:** Wes Welch gets into position to make the pass. **Right:** Chris Young tries to avoid the block of Shawn Davis.

MIDDLE PHOTOS: Left: Brian Lewis attacking the ball. **Center:** Marvin Hall smiles while refereeing an AVP Tour match. **Right:** Karch Kiraly accommodates the crowd with another perfect pass.

1994 MEN'S BEACH VOLLEYBALL ACTION

BOTTOM PHOTOS: Left: Eric Fonimoana watches the ball close while making a pass. **Center:** Eduardo Bacil challenges the block of Ricci Luyties. **Right:** Bill Boullianne watches the ball "all-the-way-in" as he makes the pass.

Photo's Courtesy of the AVP

WOMEN'S BEACH VOLLEYBALL
1994

AVP

The women's AVP tour was worth $600,000.00 in 1994, with the number one team at the end of the season, earning the $50,000.00 Miller Lite Cup. The prize money was cut in half prior to the end of the season, due to sponsorship problems. By 1994 seasons end Holly McPeak and Cammy Ciarelli had earned $41,000.00 each. Nancy Reno and Angela Rock were next at $38,000.00. Then there was Linda Chisholm and Linda Hanley along with Jackie Silva and Sandra Pires at almost $30,000.00, whith the rest of the field far behind.

There was not a dominant team on the 1994 AVP Tour as the top three teams were all within 2 titles. The top team of McPeak and Ciarelli reached 9 finals, winning 5 times. The second best team of Reno and Rock also reached 9 finals, winning 4 times. Silva and Pires reached 4 finals, winning 3 times. Hanley and Carrillo reached 7 finals, winning twice.

The women's AVP Tour tried to increase 1993's eight-woman show to a full sixteen-team, 32 player tour. But when the target of sixteen-teams was not met, the number fell down to twelve-teams.

The 1994 women's AVP schedule included fourteen events in nine different states. Six of the events were staged in California: San Jose, San Francisco, Manhattan Beach, Seal Beach, along with the U.S. Championship in San Diego and the World Championship in Hermosa Beach. The additional events were staged in Atlanta Georgia, Dallas Texas, Phoenix Arizona, Grand Haven Michigan, Milwaukee Wisconsin, Baltimore Maryland, Chicago Illinois, and Belmar Beach New Jersey.

1994 WOMEN's AVP AWARDS
Most Valuable Player: Jackie Silva
Top Rookie: Sandra Pires
Sportswomanship: Rita Crockett

HOLLY McPEAK
Holly McPeak was teamed-up with Cammy Ciarelli as the top Women's AVP team in 1994. They advanced to 9 finals, winning 5 times. Above photo, McPeak gets ready to serve the ball.
Photo Courtesy of Tim Andexler

CAMMY CIARELLI
Cammy Ciarelli was on top of the AVP Tour's list for prize money earned. She was tied with her partner Holly McPeak at $41,307.00. Above photo, Ciarelli gets ready to serve the ball.
Photo Courtesy of the AVP

1994 AVP-WOMEN EARNINGS

1.	Cammy Ciarelli	$ 41,307
1.	Holly McPeak	$ 41,307
3.	Nancy Reno	$ 38,015
3.	Angela Rock	$ 38,015
5.	Linda Chisholm	$ 29,491
5.	Linda Hanley	$ 29,491
7.	Sandra Pires	$ 28,970
7.	Jackie Silva	$ 28,970

1994 AVP TOUR INDIVIDUAL WOMEN

Player	1st	2nd	3rd	4th	5th
Linda Chisholm Carrillo	2	5	2	4	1
Cammy Ciarelli	5	4	2	2	1
Patti Dodd	0	0	2	1	5
Linda Robertson Hanley	2	5	2	4	1
Valinda Hilleary	0	0	1	2	9
Pat Keller	0	0	1	2	9
Holly McPeak	**5**	**4**	**2**	**2**	**1**
Sandra Pires	3	1	4	2	4
Karrie Trieschmann Poppinga	0	0	0	0	8
Nancy Reno	4	5	2	3	0
Angela Rock	4	5	2	3	0
Rita Crockett Royster	0	0	2	1	9
Jackie Silva	3	1	4	2	4

WPVA

The WPVA players were not getting rich but they seemed to be happier than their counterparts of the AVP. Some of the AVP players would reveal that if they had it to do over again they would have remained in the WPVA.

The fans of women's beach volleyball saw the WPVA survive the loss of big name players and the rough times of 1993 to make a comeback in 1994. The eighth WPVA tour was worth $639,600.00 in 1994, with the help of sponsors: Coors and Reebok. CBS helped out by televising four separate one hour broadcast.

The WPVA tour stopped at 16 tour sites. Schedule was as follows, 1: April 16th-17, Carolina Beach, Isla Verde, Puerto Rico. 2: April 23rd-24th, Fort Lauderdale, Florida. 3: April 30th-May 1st, Austin, Texas. 4: May 13th-15th, New Orleans, Louisiana. 5: May 28th-29th, Myrtle Beach, South Carolina. 6: June 4th-5th, San Diego, California. 7: June 18th-19th, Hermosa Beach, California. 8: June 24th-26th, Sacramento, California. 9:

SANDRA PIRES
Brazilian Sandra Pires was voted ther "Top-Rookie" on the 1994 Women's AVP Tour. Pires was teamed-up with compatriot Silva, who was voted the 1994 AVP Tour's "MVP" Above photo, Pires attacking the ball.
Photo Courtesy of Frank Goroszko

KAROLYN KIRBY
Karolyn Kirby teamed-up with Liz Masakayan as the top team on the 1994 WPVA Tour. They advanced to 12 finals, winning 11 while they each earned $82,850.00 in prize money. Above photo, Kirby lets loose with her "high-Powered" jump serve.
Photo Courtesy of Frank Goroszko

July 1st-3rd, Newport, Rhode Island. 10: July 9th-10th, Santa Cruz, California. 11:July 23rd-24th, Pismo Beach, California. 12: July 29th-31st, Long Beach, California. 13: August 13th-14th, Santa Monica, California. 14: August 19th-21st, Manhattan Beach, California. 15: September 3rd-4th, Powell, Ohio. 16: September 30th-October 2nd, Las Vegas, Nevada.

On the 1994 WPVA tour Kirby and Masakayan advanced to 12 finals and won 11 out of 13 tournaments, that they played in together. Kirby and Masakayan also won the Gold Medal in beach volleyball at the Goodwill Games in Saint Petersburg, Russia. This event was considered the precursor to the 1996 Olympic Games in Atlanta.

1994 WPVA TOUR EARNINGS

1.	Karolyn Kirby	$ 82,850
1.	Liz Masakayan	$ 82,850
3.	Barbra Fontana	$ 52,425
4.	Lori Kotas-Forsythe	$ 44,925
5.	Elaine Roque	$ 36,400
6.	Gail Castro	$ 24,900
7.	Deb Richardson	$ 28,825
8.	Dennie Schupyt-Knoop	$ 28,625
9.	Monique Oliver	$ 21,550
10.	Gayle Stammer	$ 21,450
11.	Maria O'Hara	$ 15,650
12.	Wendy Fletcher	$ 12,250
13.	Christine Schaefer	$ 12,200
14.	Kengelin Gardiner	$ 11,850
15.	Janice Harrer	$ 11,150
16.	Lisa Arce	$ 10,900
17.	Jackie Campbell	$ 9,700
18.	Charlotte Roach	$ 9,150
19.	Johanna Wright	$ 8,575
20.	Krista Blomquist	$ 7,575

1994 WPVA TOUR INDIVIDUAL WOMEN

Player	1st	2nd	3rd	4th	5th
Marie Anderson	0	0	0	1	0
Tiffany Anderson	0	0	0	0	2
Lisa Arce	0	0	0	2	2
Krista Atkinson	0	0	0	0	1
Krista Blomquist	0	0	0	1	1
Danalee Bragado	0	0	0	0	1
Jackie Campbell	0	0	0	0	2
Gail Castro	0	4	4	2	3
Wendy Fletcher	0	0	1	1	4
Barbara Fontana	3	6	4	0	1
Lori Kotas Forsythe	2	6	4	1	1
Kengelin Gardiner	0	0	0	0	2
Heather Hafner	0	0	0	0	1
Janice Opalinski Harrer	0	0	1	1	1
Karolyn Kirby	**11**	**1**	**1**	**0**	**0**
Liz Masakayan	**11**	**1**	**1**	**0**	**0**
Shannon Miller	0	0	0	0	1
Marla O'Hara	0	0	2	1	5
Monique Oliver	1	0	1	4	5
Deb Richardson	0	2	4	3	3
Charlotte Roach	0	0	0	0	2
Elaine Roque	0	5	3	2	3
Christine Schaefer	0	0	0	0	2
Dennie Schupyt-Knoop	0	2	4	3	3
Gail Stammer	1	0	1	4	4
Johanna Wright	0	0	0	1	1

1994 WPVA ACTION

Action on the 1994 WPVA Tour was "fast-and-Furious" In the above photo, Liz Masakayan gets-up high for a jump-serve towrds the team of Deb Richardson (left) and Dennie Schupyt-Knoop (right). Karolyn Kirby is Masyakayan's partner. Action took place at the championship match of the 1994 WPVA Tour stop in Santa Cruz California. The event was won by Kirby and Masakayan, by a score of 15-7 over Richardson and Knoop.

Photo Courtesy of Frank Goroszko

FIVB

The FIVB women's tour included 6 stops in five countries: U.S.A., Chile, Russia (Goodwill Games), France, Japan, Puerto Rico, and 2 stops in Brazil. The six tour sites offered a total of $300,000.00 in prize money.

The 1994 Women's FIVB World Series of Beach Volleyball Tour went to Saint Petersburg Russia, Osaka Japan, Santos Brazil, Miami Florida U.S.A., La Serena Chile, along with their World Championship in Rio de Janeiro Brazil.

The top American team on the FIVB Tour was Liz Masakayan and Karolyn Kirby. They were also the top team of the tour, reaching 3 finals, winning 2 of them. They won at La Serena Chile and at the 1994 **Goodwill Games**. Masakayan and Kirby almost had their third title, in front of a sell-out Brazilian crowd of Beach volleyball fans, at the $50,000.00 FIVB Women's beach volleyball tournament, held at Santos Brazil, but in the championship match, after winning the first game 12-10 and leading the second game 7-0, Masakayan hurt her right knee. The Americans used all of their time-outs, in addition to their five minute injury time-out, to see if the pain in Masakayan's knee would subside. The pain continued and it clearly hampered her performance as the Brazilians, Monica Rodriquez and Adriana Samuel Ramos, who had lost the previous eight meetings against Kirby and Masakayan, won the second and third games 12-8, and 5-3, earning the top prize of $11,000.00.

1994 FIVB TOUR INDIVIDUAL WOMEN

Player	1st	2nd	3rd	4th	5th
Maria Isabel Salgado Barroso	1	2	2	1	0
Adriana Behar Brando	0	0	0	1	1
Gail Castro	1	0	0	1	2
Natalie Cook	0	0	0	0	4
Lori Kotas Forsythe	1	1	2	1	0
Sachika Fujita	0	0	0	1	0
Barbra Fontana	1	1	2	1	0
Karolyn Kirby	2	1	2	0	0
Magda Rejane Falco De Lima	0	0	0	0	1
Liz Masakayan	2	1	2	0	0
Anita Palm	0	0	0	0	4
Renata Costa Palmier	0	0	0	0	1
Kerri Ann Pottharst	0	0	0	0	2
Adriana Samuel Ramos	1	2	0	1	1
Deb Richardson	0	0	0	0	1
Monica Rodriguez	1	2	0	1	1
Elaine Roque	1	0	0	1	1
Karina Silva	0	0	0	0	1
Yukiko Takashi	0	0	0	1	0
Annette Huygens Tholen	0	0	0	0	2
Roseli Ana Timm	1	2	2	2	0

LIZ MASAKAYAN
In 1994, Liz Masakayan was teamed-up with Karolyn Kirby on the WPVA and FIVB Tour's. They were the top team on both tours, winning 11 WPVA events and 2 FIVB events. Above photo, Masakayan cuts the ball past the block of Deb Richardson.
Photo Courtesy of Frank Goroszko

ADRIANA SAMUEL RAMOS
Brazilian Adriana Sanuel Ramos Paried-up with Compatriot Monica Rodriguez to win the 1994 FIVB Tour event in Santos Brazil, over the American team of Liz Masakayan and Karolyn Kirby. Above photo, Adriana focuses on a successful spike.
Photo Courtesy of the FIVB

WOMEN'S TOURNAMENT RESULTS
1994-AVP

ATLANTA GEORGIA
April 29th -May 1st, 1994

1994's season opener for the AVP'S Women's Pro-Beach Volleyball Tour was in Atlanta Georgia, for the $20,000.00 Nestea Atlanta Open. In the championship match at "Dancing Waters," Nancy Reno and Angela Rock were 14-12 winners over Cammy Ciarelli and Holly McPeak. Reno and Rock started out fast as they were up by a score of 12-6, but McPeak and Ciarelli got close when they pulled to within one point at 13-12. The winners were then able to put the match away by scoring on the bad side.

3rd Place: Sandra Pires and Jackie Silva
4th Place: Linda Chisholm and Linda Hanley
5th Place: Valinda Hilleary and Pat Keller
5th Place: Rita Crockett and Karrie Trieschmann-Poppinga

DALLAS TEXAS
May 6th-7th, 1994

The AVP'S Women's Pro-Beach Volleyball Tour was in Dallas Texas for the $20,000.00 Nestea Dallas Open. Nancy Reno and Angela Rock won the championship match, in front of the Crescent Hotel, by a score of 11-8 over Linda Chisholm and Linda Hanley. The first place team of Reno and Rock split $5,714.00 for their efforts.

3rd Place: Sandra Pires and Jackie Silva
4th Place: Holly McPeak and Cammy Ciarelli
5th Place: Karrie Trieschman Poppinga and Rita Crockett
5th Place: Valinda Hilleary and Pat Keller

PHOENIX ARIZONA
May 13th-15th, 1994

The AVP'S Women's Pro-Beach Volleyball Tour staged their next event at the Gateway Center in Phoenix Arizona, the $20,000.00 Nestea Phoenix Open. Nancy Reno and Angela Rock, repeated last week's championship match results with a thrilling 17-15 victory over Linda Chisholm and Linda Hanley. The first place team of Reno and Rock again split $5,714.00.

3rd Place: Rita Crockett and Patti Dodd
4th Place: Sandra Pires and Jackie Silva
5th Place: Karrie Trieschman Poppinga and Holly McPeak
5th Place: Pat Keller and Cammy Ciarelli

NANCY RENO
In 1994, Nancy Reno teamed-up with Angela Rock on the AVP Women's Tour and they ranked as the number two team. They advanced to 9 finals, winning 4 times. Above photo, Reno reaches up to spike the ball.
Photo Courtesy of the AVP

ANGELA ROCK
Angela Rock was paired-up with Nancy Reno, on the 1994 AVP Women's Tour. They were the number two team on the tour, winning nearly $40,000.00 in prize money. Above photo, Rock attacks the ball.
Photo Courtesy of Frank Goroszko

SAN JOSE CALIFORNIA
May 20th-21st, 1994

The AVP'S Women's Pro-Beach Volleyball Tour went to San Jose California for the $20,000.00 Miller Lite San Jose Open. Cammy Ciarelli and Holly McPeak defeated Linda Chisholm and Linda Hanley, in the championship match, by a score of 15-7. The tournament was staged at Guadalupe River Park. McPeak and Ciarelli split $5,714.00.

3rd Place: Nancy Reno and Angela Rock
4th Place: Jackie Silva and Sandra Pires
5th Place: Valinda Hilleary and Kerri Poppinga
5th Place: Rita Crockett and Patty Dodd

SAN FRANCISCO CALIFORNIA
May 27th-28th, 1994

The AVP'S Women's Pro-Beach Volleyball Tour made its fourth tour stop of the 1994 season at the Embarcadero Center in San Francisco California, for the $20,000.00 Nestea San Francisco Open. In the championship match, Cammy Ciarelli and Holly McPeak held on for a 5-15 and 7-4 double final victory over Nancy Reno and Angela Rock. Ciarelli and McPeak split a check in the amount of $5,714.00.

3rd Place: Linda Chisholm and Linda Hanley
4th Place: Valinda Hileary and Karrie Trieschmann Poppinga
5th Place: Sandra Pires and Jackie Silva
5th Place: Rita Crockett and Patty Dodd

GRAND HAVEN CONNECTICUT
June 3rd-4th, 1994

The AVP'S Women's Pro-Beach Volleyball Tour moved onto Grand Haven Connecticut, for the $20,000.00 Miller Lite Grand Haven Open. In the championship match, played on the State Beach, Nancy Reno and Angela Rock were 15-11 winners over Cammy Ciarelli and Holly McPeak. The winners took home $5,714.00.

3rd Place: Rita Crockett and Patti Dodd
4th Place: Linda Chisholm and Linda Hanley
5th Place: Valinda Hileary and Karrie Trieschmann Poppinga
5th Place: Sandra Pires and Jackie Silva

MILLWAUKEE WISCONSIN
June 17th-19th, 1994

The next stop for the AVP'S Women's Pro-Beach Volleyball Tour was on Bradford Beach in Milwaukee Wisconsin, for the $20,000.00 Miller Lite Milwaukee Open. In the championship match, the Brazilian team of Sandra Pires and Jackie Silva put on an awesome display of defense in their 11-10 win over Linda Chisholm and Linda Hanley. The first place prize of $5,714.00 went to the winners.

3rd Place: Cammy Ciarelli and Holly McPeak
4th Place: Nancy Reno and Angela Rock
5th Place: Valinda Hilleary and Pat Keller
5th Place: Rita Crockett and Patti Dodd

BALTIMORE MARYLAND
June 24th-26th, 1994

On the weekend of June 24th-26th, 1994, the AVP'S

LINDA HANLEY
Linda Hanley had a successful year on the 1994 AVP Women's Tour. She advanced to 7 finals, winning the championship match twice, earning nearly $30,000.00 in prize money. Above photo, later in her career, Hanley attacks the block of Misty May.
Photo Courtesy of "Couvi"

VALINDA HILLEARY
Valinda Hilleary had some success on the 1994 AVP Women's Tour. She finished in the top five on 12 occasions with a third place at the Belmar Beach NJ event. Above photo, Hilleary makes a perfect pass.
Photo Courtesy of the AVP

Women's Pro-Beach Volleyball Tour was at Harbor View, in Baltimore Maryland, for the 1994 Nestea $20,000.00 Baltimore Open. In an exciting double final Linda Chisholm and Linda Hanley were 15-12 and 7-1 winners over Nancy Reno and Angela Rock. The first place prize of $5,714.00 went to Hanley and Chisholm.
3rd Place: Cammy Ciarelli and Holly McPeak
4th Place: Rita Crockett and Patti Dodd
5th Place: Valinda Hilleary and Pat Keller
5th Place: Sandra Pires and Jackie Silva

MANHATTAN BEACH CALIFORNIA
July 1st-3rd, 1994

The AVP'S Women's Pro-Beach Volleyball Tour was, at the Manhattan Pier, on the beach in Manhattan Beach California, for the $20,000.00 Old Spice Manhattan Beach Women's Open. In the championship match, Linda Chisholm and Linda Hanley defeated Cammy Ciarelli and Holly McPeak by a score of 15-9 to earn a prize of $5,714.00.
3rd Place: Sandra Pires and Jackie Silva
4th Place: Nancy Reno and Angela Rock
5th Place: Rita Crockett and Patty Dodd
5th Place: Pat Keller and Valinda Hilleary

CHICAGO ILLINOIS
July 22nd-24th, 1994

The AVP'S Women's Pro-Beach Volleyball Tour made the 10th tour stop of the season, at North Avenue Beach, in Chicago Illinois, for the $20,000.00 Chicago Open. In an arousing championship match, as the time clock expired, Cammy Ciarelli and Holly McPeak were slim 13-12 winners over Nancy Reno and Angela Rock. McPeak and Reno were happy to split $5,714.00.
3rd Place: Sandra Pires and Jackie Silva
4th Place: Linda Chisholm and Linda Hanley
5th Place: Rita Crockett and Karrie Trieschmann
5th Place: Pat Keller and Valinda Hilleary

BELMAR BEACH NEW JERSEY
July 29th-31st, 1994

On the weekend of July 29th-31st, 1994, the AVP'S Women's Pro-Beach Volleyball Tour was at Belmar Beach New Jersey, for the $20,000.00 Nestea Open. In an exciting double final, the Brazilian team of Sandra Pires and Jackie Silva held on for a 5-12, 7-5 win over Nancy Reno and Angela Rock. Silva and Pires split the $5,714.00 first place prize check.
3rd Place: Valinda Hilleary and Pat Keller
4th Place: Cammy Ciarelli and Holly McPeak
5th Place: Ritta Crockett and Karrie Poppinga
5th Place: Linda Chisholm and Linda Hanley

SEAL BEACH CALIFORNIA
August 12th-14th, 1994

The AVP'S Women's Pro-Beach Volleyball Tour was north of the Seal Beach Pier, on the beach in Seal Beach California, for the 12th tournament of the season. In the championship match, of the 1994 $20,000.00 Miller Lite Seal Beach Open, Cammy Ciarelli and Holly McPeak were 15-9 winners over Sandra Pires and Jackie Silva. Ciarelli and McPeak split $5,714.00 for their efforts.
3rd Place: Nancy Reno and Angela Rock
4th Place: Linda Chisholm and Linda Hanley
5th Place: Rita Crockett and Patty Dodd
5th Place: Valinda Hilleary and Pat Keller

SAN DIEGO CALIFORNIA
August 19th-21st, 1994

The AVP'S Women's Pro-Beach Volleyball Tour staged the $40,000.00 Old Spice U.S. Championship, at Mariner's Point in San Diego California. This week Sandra Pires and Jackie Silva took home a first place prize of $11,428.00, as they reversed last weeks championship match out-come. They defeated Cammy Ciarelli and Holly McPeak by a score of 12-10.
3rd Place: Linda Chisholm and Linda Hanley
4th Place: Nancy Reno and Angela Rock
5th Place: Rita Crockett and Karrie Poppinga
5th Place: Valinda Hilleary and Pat Keller

HERMOSA BEACH CALIFORNIA
August 25th-28th, 1994

The AVP'S Women's Pro-Beach Volleyball Tour made the 14th and final tour stop of the season, next to the pier, in Hermosa Beach California for the $50,000.00 Miller Lite "World Championship." The championship match was won by Cammy Ciarelli and Holly McPeak. They defeated Nancy Reno and Angela Rock by a score of 15-6, to earn the $14,285.00 first place check.
3rd Place: Linda Chisholm and Linda Hanley
4th Place: Valinda Hilleary and Pat Keller
5th Place: Sandra Pires and Jackie Silva
5th Place: Patty Dodd and Karrie Poppinga

KARRIE TRIESCHMANN-POPPINGA
In 1994, Karrie Trieschmann-Poppinga began to play some competitive beach volleyball, on the Women's AVP Tour, earning 8 fifth place finishes. Above photo, Poppinga hits the ball towards the block of her opponent.
Photo Courtesy of Tim Andexler

WOMEN'S TOURNAMENT RESULTS
1994-WPVA

ISLA VERDE PUERTO RICO
April 16th-17th, 1994

Staging their season tournament opener, the WPVA Pro-Beach Volleyball Tour was on Carolina Beach, at Isla Verde, Puerto Rico, for the $40,000.00 Coors Light Puerto Rico Open. In the championship match, first seed's Karolyn Kirby and Liz Masakayan were easy winners over third seeds Gail Castro and Elaine Roque. The final score was 15-4. This victory gave the 32 year old Kirby 42 career titles, surpassing Brazilian Jackie Silva's 41, making her the winningest player in WPVA history. Kirby and Masakayan split the $9,400.00 first place prize money. There were twenty-five teams entered in this tournament.

3rd Place: Barbra Fontana and Lori Kotas-Forsythe
4th Place: Wendy Fletcher and Maria O'Hara
5th Place: Krista Blomquist and Johanna Wright
5th Place: Jackie Campbell and Charlotte Roach

FORT LAUDERDALE FLORIDA
April 23rd-25th, 1994

The WPVA Pro-Beach Volleyball Tour made its second tour stop of 1994 in Fort Lauderdale Florida, for the $40,000.00 Reebok Fort Lauderdale Open. The championship match was a thriller. After trailing by the score of 13-9, Karolyn Kirby and Liz Masakayan won it by a score of 15-13 over Gail Castro and Elaine Roque. They snatched the $9,400.00 first place check with the comeback victory. Because of the continual rain, the final match was not played until Monday, and the third place match was canceled. This was the first rain-out in a total of 98 WPVA events. The finals were supposed to be televised by CBS, so the Monday final was taped for "Eye on Sports."

3rd Place: Barbra Fontana and Lori Kotas-Forsythe,
3rd Place: Wendy Fletcher and Maria O'Hara
5th Place: Deb Richardson and Dennie Shupryt Knoop
5th Place: Monique Oliver and Gayle Stammer

KAROLYN KIRBY

Karolyn Kirby paired-up with Liz Masakayan to dominate the 1994 WPVA Tour. As a team they won 11 WPVA events together, while earning over $80,000.00 each. Above photo, Kirby challenges the block of Elaine Roque.

Photo Courtesy of Frank Goroszko

LIZ MASAKAYAN

Liz Masakayan entered 13 WPVA Tour events in 1994, all with Karolyn Kirby. They won 11 championship matches added 1 second and 1 third place finish. Above photo, Masakayan attacking her jump-serve.

Photo Courtesy of "Couvi"

AUSTIN TEXAS
April 30th-May 1st, 1994

The next WPVA Pro-Beach Volleyball event was in Austin Texas. The $40,000.00 Reebok Austin Open was won by Karolyn Kirby and Liz Masakayan. In the championship match, they were easy 15-5 winners over Deb Richardson and Dennie Shupryt-Knoop.

3rd Place: Barbra Fontana and Lori Kotas-Forsythe
4th Place: Gail Castro and Elaine Roque
5th Place: Heather Hafner and Shannon Miller
5th Place: Wendy Fletcher and Marla O'Hara

NEW ORLEANS LOUISIANA
May 13-15th, 1994

The WPVA Pro-Beach Volleyball Tour made its fourth tour stop of 1994 at Coconut Beach in New Orleans Louisiana, for the $40,000.00 New Orleans Open. In a rousing championship match, Karolyn Kirby and Liz Masakayan were 15-13 winners over Barbra Fontana and Lori Kotas-Forsythe. This was the thirteenth consecutive tournament championship for Liz and Karolyn, which ties them with beach volleyball's all-time streak held by Karch Kiraly and Kent Steffes (1992) along with Jim Menges and Greg Lee (1975-76). Kirby and Masakayan also stretched their consecutive match streak to 53. The duo hadn't lost since July 1993. Kirby and Masakayan split the $9,400.00 check that they received for their victory.

3rd Place: Gail Castro and Elaine Roque
4th Place: Deb Richardson and Dennie Shupryt-Knoop
5th Place: Kengelin Gardner and Christine Schaefer
5th Place: Monique Oliver and Gayle Stammer

MYRTLE BEACH SOUTH CAROLINA
May 28th-29th, 1994

The WPVA Pro-Beach Volleyball Tour staged its next event at the Kingston Plantation in Myrtle Beach South Carolina. In the championship match, of the 1994 Reebok Myrtle $40,000.00 Beach Open, Barbra Fontana and Lori Kotas-Forsythe defeated Karolyn Kirby and Liz Masakayan by a score of 15-12. Fontana and Forsythe split $9,400.00 with the title. Earlier, in the semifinals, Deb Richardson and Dennie Shupryt-Knoop snapped Masakayan and Kirby's 55-game winning streak with a 15-13 victory. The final was televised live on CBS.

3rd Place: Deb Richardson and Dennie Shupryt Knoop
4th Place: Monique Oliver and Gayle Stammer
5th Place: Gail Castro and Elaine Roque
5th Place: Wendy Fletcher and Marla O'Hara

LORI FORSYTHE-KOTAS
Lori Forsythe-Kotas provided some stiff competition on the 1994 WPVA Tour. Kotas advanced to the championship match at 8 events, winning twice. Above photo, Kotas tips the ball over the block of Christine Podraza Schaefer.

Photo Courtesy of Frank Goroszko

BARBRA FONTANA
Barbra Fontan was a top contender on the 1994 WPVA Tour. She advanced to the final of 9 events, winning 3 times, earning over $50,000.00. Above photo, Fontana hits a set from Elaine Youngs into the block of Lisa Arce. Holly McPeak is on defense.

Photo Courtesy of "Couvi"

SAN DIEGO CALIFORNIA
June 4th-5th, 1994

The WPVA Pro-Beach Volleyball Tour staged the U.S. Open at Mariner's Point in San Diego California. In the championship match, Karolyn Kirby and Liz Masakayan rebounded from their first loss of the season the previous week in Myrtle Beach, as they easily won their fifth WPVA tournament of the season with a 15-10 win over Barbra Fontana and Lori Kotas-Forsythe. Kirby and Masakayan split the $9,400.00 first place check.

3rd Place: Gail Castro and Elaine Roque
4th Place: Monique Oliver and Gayle Stammer
5th Place: Deb Richardson and Dennie Shupryt-Knoop
5th Place: Kengelin Gardiner and Christine Schaefer

HERMOSA BEACH CALIFORNIA
June 18th-19th, 1994

The WPVA Pro-Beach Volleyball Tour made its seventh tour stop of 1994 in Hermosa Beach California, for the $40,000.00 Hermosa Beach Open. First seeds, Karolyn Kirby and Liz Masakayan easily won their sixth tournament of the season. In the championship match, by a score of 15-5, they won over third seed's Gail Castro and Elaine Roque. Kirby and Masakayan went undefeated through the entire tournament. This title gave Kirby and Masakayan 18 career title together, surpassing Kirby's record of 17 with Angela Rock, making them the winningest team in women's pro-beach volleyball history. The record includes a streak of 69 game wins with only two losses, over a period from July of 1993 to this date. Prior to the final, Castro and Roque played a 90-minute semifinal match, in scorching 95 degree heat, against Deb Richardson and Dennie Shupryt-Knoop. The match included 106 sideouts, a WPVA record. Kirby and Masakayan split another $9,400.00 check for their victory.

3rd Place: Deb Richardson and Dennie Shupryt-Knoop
4th Place: Lisa Arce and Marie Anderson
5th Place: Barbra Fontana and Lori Kotas-Forsythe
5th Place: Wendy Fletcher and Marla O'Hara

SACRAMENTO CALIFORNIA
June 25th-26th, 1994

Next, the WPVA Pro-Beach Volleyball Tour was in Sacramento California, for the $40,000.00 Reebok Sacramento Open. In an electrifying championship match Karolyn Kirby and Liz Masakayan defeated Barbra Fontana and Lori Kotas-Forsythe by a score of 16-14. Kirby and Masakayan won $9,400.00.

3rd Place: Deb Richardson and Dennie Shupryt-Knoop
4th Place: Monique Oliver and Gayle Stammer
5th Place: Gail Castro and Elaine Roque
5th Place: Wendy Fletcher and Marla O'Hara

NEWPORT RHODE ISLAND
July 4th-5th, 1994

The 1994 WPVA $40,000.00 "Reebok Shootout" was held at Newport, Rhode Island. In the championship match, Karolyn Kirby and Liz Masakayan were once

CHRISTINE SCHAEFER & KENGELIN GARDINER
In 1994, Christine Podraza Schaefer and Kengelin Gardiner played well on the 1994 WPVA Tour. Both players finished within the top ten on several occasions. Above photo, Schaefer hits a set from Gardiner, over the block of Gail Stammer.
Photo Courtesy of the AVP

GAIL CASTRO
Gail Castro presented some stiff competition on the 1994 WPVA Tour. Castro finished within the top five at 13 events, advancing to 4 finals, finishing in second place 4 times. Above photo, Castro hits the ball towards the block of Linda Hanley.
Photo Courtesy of the AVP

again easy winners over Barbra Fontana and Lori Kotas-Forsythe by a score of 15-4. Kirby and Masakayan dominated the eight-team, round-robin event going 7-0, while winning their $12,300.00 check.
3rd Place: Gail Castro and Elaine Roque
4th Place: Lisa Arce and Janice Opalinski Harrer
5th Place: Monique Oliver and Gayle Stammer

SANTA CRUZ CALIFORNIA
July 9th-10th, 1994

The WPVA Pro-Beach Volleyball Tour was in Santa Cruz, California, for the $40,000.00 Santa Cruz Open. This was the tenth WPVA Tour stop of the season. In the championship match, Karolyn Kirby and Liz Masakayan defeated Deb Richardson and Dennie Shupryt-Knoop by a score of 15-7. This was the fifth consecutive tournament title and nine of ten this season for Kirby and Masakayan. The winners collected $9,400.00.
3rd Place: Barbra Fontana and Lori Kotas-Forsythe
4th Place: Gail Castro and Elaine Roque
5th Place: Lisa Arce and Tiffany Anderson

PISMO BEACH CALIFORNIA
July 23rd-24th, 1994

The WPVA Pro-Beach Volleyball Tour, remained in California, staging their next event in front of the Sea Venture Hotel in Pismo Beach. The $30,000.00 Pismo Beach Open was won by Monique Oliver and Gail Stammer. They became the new faces on the victory stand with a 16-14 championship match victory over Gail Castro and Elaine Roque for their first career title.
3rd Place: Janice Harrer and Marla O'Hara
4th Place: Krista Blomquist and Johanna Wright
5th Place: Deb Richardson and Dennie Shupryt-Knoop
5th Place: Kristi Atkinson and Danalee Bragado

LONG BEACH CALIFORNIA
July 30th-31st, 1994

The WPVA Pro-Beach Volleyball Tour was at the Promenade in Long Beach California for their 12th event of the season. Karolyn Kirby and Liz Masakayan won their tenth tournament of the WPVA season, to collect another $9,400.00. In the championship match, of the $40,000.00 Long Beach "Volley-fest," Kirby and Masakayan scored a 15-9 triumph over Barbra Fontana and Lori Kotas-Forsythe.
3rd Place: Monique Oliver and Gayle Stammer
4th Place: Deb Richardson and Dennie Shupryt-Knoop
5th Place: Gail Castro and Elaine Roque
5th Place: Marla O'Hara and Tiffany Anderson

MANHATTAN BEACH CALIFORNIA
August 19th-21st, 1994

On the weekend of August 19th-21st, 1994 the WPVA Pro-Beach Volleyball Tour was in Manhattan Beach California for the "Nationals." Karolyn Kirby and Liz Masakayan won their eleventh tournament of the WPVA season by winning this $40,000.00 Reebok event. In the championship match, Kirby and Masakayan skillfully worked their way to a 15-4 win over Barbra Fontana and Lori Kotas-Forsythe, winning $9,400.00.
3rd Place: Deb Richardson and Dennie Shupryt-Knoop
4th Place: Monique Oliver and Gayle Stammer
5th Place: Jackie Campbell and Charlotte Roach
5th Place: Lisa Arce and Janice Harrer

POWELL OHIO
September 3rd-4th, 1994

The WPVA Pro-Beach Volleyball Tour was in Powell Ohio for the second annual "Top of the Tour" event. The winner was Barbra Fontana, as she took home the largest individual pay day in WPVA history, when she earned $9,750.00. The WPVA's top two players, Liz Masakayan and Karolyn Kirby did not participate. Both players expressed a dislike for this event. Barbra Fontana finished with a 5-1 record to win the "Top of the Tour" title. Final standings:

1. Barbra Fontana
2. Elaine Roque
3. Gail Castro
4. Lori Kotas
5. Monique Oliver
6. Gayle Stammer
7. Deb Richardson
8. Dennie Shupryt-Knoop

LAS VEGAS NEVADA
September 30th-October 1st, 1994

The WPVA's final tournament of the season, the "Best of the Beach" tournament, was held in Las Vegas, Nevada. In the championship match, Barbra Fontana and Lori Kotas-Forsythe embarrassed Gail Castro and Elaine Roque with a 15-2 thrashing. Fontana and Kotas-Forsythe split $10,000.00 with the win. Karolyn Kirby and Liz Masakayan lost, 15-8, in the semi-finals to Fontana and Forsythe. The loss snapped Kirby and Masakayan's 44-match winning-streak.
3rd Place: Karolyn Kirby and Liz Masakayan
4th Place: Deb Richardson and Dennie Shupryt-Knoop
5th Place: Monique Oliver and Gayle Stammer

GAIL STAMMER & MONIQUE OLIVER
Gail Stammer and Monique Oliver won the championship match at the 1994 WPVA Tour event in Pismo Beach California. Above photo, Stammer hits a set from Oliver, towards the block of Elaine Roque.
Photo Courtesy of the AVP

WOMEN'S TOURNAMENT RESULTS
1994-FIVB

MIAMI, FLORIDA, U.S.A.
January 15th-22nd, 1994

On the beach of Lummus Park in Miami, Florida, U.S.A., the $50,000.00 FIVB Women's World Series of Beach Volleyball event was won by the Brazilian team of Ana Roseli Timm and Maria Salgado Barroso over the U.S.A. team of Barbara Fontana and Lori Kotas Forsythe. The winner's came-out on top of a field of fifty-five teams from twenty-one countries to earn a first place check of $7,500.00 each. The championship match was a thrilling three game match, with the winners taking the first game 12-3. They then were outplayed by the Americans as they lost 12-14. The third and final game saw the lead change several times as the Brazilians held on for the victory by the score of 16-14.

3rd Place: Karolyn Kirby and Liz Masakayan-USA
4th Place: Monica Rodriguez and Adriana Samuel Ramos-Bra
5th Place: Natalie Cook and Anita Palm-Aus
5th Place: Gayle Castro and Elaine Roque-USA

Additional U.S.A. finishers: Deb Richardson and Gayle Stammer along with Nancy Cothron and Barbara Bierman finished in 13th place.

LA SERENA, CHILE
February 8th-11th, 1994

At La Serena Chile, the $50,000.00 FIVB Women's beach volleyball tournament was won by the U.S.A. team of Karolyn Kirby and Liz Masakayan, 9-12, 12-10, and 15-13, over the Brazilian team of Ana Roseli Timm and Maria Salgado Barroso. Kirby and Masakayan came-out on top of a field of fifty-five teams from twenty-one countries, to earn a first place check, sharing the prize of $11,000.00.

3rd Place: Barbra Fontana and Lori Kotas Forsythe-USA
4th Place: Elaine Roque and Gail Castro
5th Place: Monica Rodriguez and Adriana Samuel Ramos-Bra
5th Place: Annette Huygens Tholen and Kerri Ann Pottharst-Aus

1994 GOODWILL GAMES
SAINT PETERSBURG, RUSSIA
July 23rd-28th, 1994

In the women's division, at the 1994 **Goodwill Games**, Karolyn Kirby and Liz Masakayan from the U.S.A. won the gold medal. The Brazilian team of Monica Rodriguez and Adriana Samuel Ramos took the silver medal. In the championship match, the Americans easily handled the Brazilians with scores of 12-9 and 12-1. Masakayan and Kirby received $15,000.00 for the win. These 1994 Goodwill Games, an FIVB event, were considered the precursor to the 1996 Olympic Games in Atlanta GA. Prize money for the men was $100,000.00 and $50,000.00 for the women. The estimated television viewing audience was estimated to be 600,000,000.

3rd Place: Barbara Fontana and Lori Kotas-Forsythe=USA
4th Place: Maria Salgado and Roseli Timm-Bra
5th Place: Natalie Cook and Anita Palm-Aus

LIZ MASAKAYAN
Liz Masakayan and compatriot Karolyn Kirby were the most successful team on the 1994 FIVB Tour, winning 2 of the 6 events. Above photo, Masakayan attacks the block of Brazilian Jackie Silva.
Photo Courtesy of the FIVB

KAROLYN KIRBY
In 1991, Karolyn Kirby played on the FIVB Tour with Liz Masakayan, where they were the most successful team on the Tour, winning 2 of the 6 events. They also nearly won the Goodwill Games, but Liz got injured. Above photo, Kirby makes a nice dig.
Photo Courtesy of Frank Goroszko

OSAKA, JAPAN
August 4th-7th, 1994

At Osaka Japan, the $50,000.00 FIVB Women's beach volleyball tournament was won by the U.S.A. team of Barbra Fontana and Lori Kotas Forsythe, 15-2 over the Brazilian team of Ana Roseli Timm and Maria Salgado Barroso. Fontana and Forsythe each earned $5,500.00 for their efforts. In the championship match, the Americans easily defeated the Brazilians, by a score of 15-2.

3rd Place: Karolyn Kirby and Liz Masakayan-USA
4th Place: Sachiko Fujita and Yukiko Takahashi-Jpn
5th Place: Falcao De Lima and Adriana Behar Brandao-Bra
5th Place: Natalie Cook and Anita Palm-Aus

CAROLINA, PUERTO RICO
August 19th-21st, 1994

On Carolina Beach, in Puerto Rico, Elaine Roque and Gail Castro, from the U.S.A., defeated Brazilians Monica Rodriquez and Adriana Samuel Ramos, to win the $50,000.00 FIVB women's beach volleyball tournament. The winner's split the $11,000.00 first place prize money. In the stirring three game championship match, the Americans outlasted the Brazilians with scores of 12-4, 12-14, and 15-12. The winners share of the prize money was $11,000.00.

3rd Place: Ana Roseli Timm and Maria Salgado Barroso-Bra
4th Place: Magda Falcao De Lima and Adriana Behar Brandao-Bra
5th Place: Natalie Cook and Anita Palm-Aus
5th Place: Kerrie Ann Pottharst and Annette "HT" Huygens Tholen-Aus

SANTOS, BRAZIL
November 17th-20th, 1994

In front of the sell-out Brazilian crowd of Beach volleyball fans, at the $50,000.00 FIVB Women's beach volleyball tournament, held at Santos Brazil, was won by the Brazilian team of Monica Rodriquez and Adriana Samuel Ramos. In the championship match, the American team of Liz Masakayan and Karolyn Kirby, won the first game 12-10 and were leading the second game 7-0 when Masakayan hurt her right knee. The Americans used all of their time-outs, in addition to their five minute injury time-out, to see if the pain in Masakayan's knee would subside. The pain continued and it clearly hampered her performance. The Brazilians, who had lost the previous eight meetings against Kirby and Masakayan, won the second and third games 12-8, and 5-3, earning the top prize of $11,000.00.

3rd Place: Ana Roseli Timm and Maria Salgado Barroso-Bra
4th Place: Barbra Fontana and Lori Kotas Forsythe-USA
5th Place: Gail Castro and Deb Richardson-USA
5th Place: Karina Silva and Renata Costa Palmier-Bra

NATALIE COOK

Australian Natalie Cook began to show some beach volleyball promise on the 1994 FIVB Tour, finishing within the top five on four occasions. Above Cook reaches above the net to attack the ball during an international event.

Photo Courtesy of "Couvi"

ELAINE ROQUE

Elaine Roque was a top contender on the 1994 FIVB Tour, finishing within the top five on 3 occasions, including a championship match victory on Carolina Beach in Puerto Rico. Above photo, Roque gives a nice effort to dig the ball.

Photo Courtesy of Frank Goroszko

  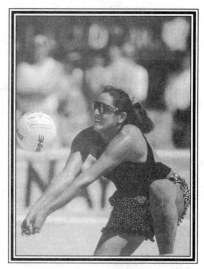

TOP PHOTOS: Left: Gayle Stammer reaches high for the "Pokie" shot. **Center:** Elaine Roque is braced to make the pass. **Right:** Lisa Arce gets down low to pass the ball.

MIDDLE PHOTOS: Left: Wendy Fletcher reaches for the sky to make an effective jump serve. **Center:** Jackie Campbell stretches to poke the ball over the block. **Right:** Charlotte Roach attacking a jump serve.

1994 WOMEN'S BEACH VOLLEYBALL ACTION

BOTTOM PHOTOS: Left: Danalee Bragado gets high above the net in the block attempt. **Center:** Deb Richardson clears the net to make a successful "Pokie" against the opposition. **Right:** Dennie Schupyt-Knoop slices the ball over the net.
Top photo's courtesy of Frank Goroszko. Center and Bottom Photo's Courtesy of the AVP

ADDITIONAL VOLLEYBALL INFORMATION
1994

1994 FOUR-PERSON BEACH TOUR
In 1994 the four-man "Bud Light Pro Beach Volleyball League was won by "Team Paul Mitchell" in the men's division. They split $110,00.00. The women's winner was the "Sony Autosound" team. They split $75,000.00. The MVP for the men for the second time was Jeff Stork. Women's winner was Kim Oden.

1994 4-PERSON "BEACH" PLAYERS

(men)	(women)
Bob Ctvrtik	Gabrielle Reece
Carlos Briceno	Wendy Stammer
Mike Diehl	Elaine Youngs
Steve Salmons	Kim Oden
Doug Partie	Keba Phipps
Dan Hanan	Marissa Hatchett
Jeff Williams	Lianne Sato
Matt Rigg	Stephanie Cox
Dusty Dvorak	Katy Eldridge
Craig Buck	Christa Cook
Jon Wallace	Tammy Liley
Jeff Stork	Bev Oden

ASPEN COLORADO
The 22nd Annual Motherload Volleyball Classic was staged over Labor Day Weekend, in Aspen Colorado. There were over 575 teams entered in the twelve divisions. The 1994 event included players from the pros of the AVP and WPVA, along with participants from the 4-Person Tours, as well as the best amateur players. There were more teams from the state of California than all other states combined. The best match of the tournament was the winner's bracket final in the men's division. In that one-hour and 45-minute all AVP marathon match, Craig and Curt Moothart were pitted against Leif Hanson and Rob Heidger. The Moothart's, dazzling in their trademark outlandish hats were in the lead at 14-10 when Hanson and Heidger took over and won 17-15 in an endurance match. In the championship match Hanson and Heidger went on to win the men's open division and the $2,000.00, by defeating Coloradans Curtis Griffin and Dane Hansen.

There were four California pros in the women's open division final. In the championship double final, WPVA players Christine Bailey and Chris Schaeffer defeated WPVA player Danalee Bragado teamed with Bud Light 4-Woman Tour player Missy Curt. The final scores were 15-9 and 7-2. Bailey and Schaeffer split $2,000.00.

LEIF HANSON
Leif Hanson paired-up with Rob Heidger to defeat the Moothart brothers, Curt & Craig, at the 1994 Motherload Volleyball Classic, in Aspen Colorado. Above, Hanson makes a diving effort.
Photo Courtesy of the AVP

MATT RIGG
In 1994, Matt Rigg was a steady competitor on the Bud-Light Four-Person Pro-Beach Volleyball Tour. Above photo, Rigg uses perfect form while passing the ball.
Photo Courtesy of the AVP

MANHATTAN BEACH CALIFORNIA
August 13th-14th, 1994

The WPVA held a "National Qualifier" on the south side of the Manhattan Beach Pier. In the championship match, Colleen Harp and Missy Kurt defeated Evelyn Conley and Stephanie Cox by the score of 15-8.

3rd Place: Sara Straton and Melanie Sullivan
4th Place: Mindy Rich and Terry Schroeder.

LAGUNA BEACH CALIFORNIA
1994

The 1994 Laguna Beach Men's Open was an amateur "AAA" tournament. Dan Castillo and Scott Sjoquist were the winners. In the championship match, they defeated Kevin Cleary and Dana McFarland.

3rd Place: Brett Gunnermann and Aaron Guimaraes
4th Place: Rick Ownbey and Dave Morehouse

FORT LAUDERDALE FLORIDA
1994

The 1994 Jose Cuervo Beach Championship were staged on the beach in Fort Lauderdale Florida. In the championship match, John Child and Mark Heese, from Canada, defeated Americans Manny Agant and Jay Mears by a score of 15-11. During the final, the large crowd was treated to a rousing match, as Childs and Heese took quick advantage of 21 year old Mears' inexperience for a 10-3 lead. Agant steadied his young teammate and they scored six unanswered points, to get close at 10-9. The Canadians then went on top 11-9, and Agant and Mears scored twice more, before losing 15-11.

In the women's division, it was an all-California final. WPVA pros Michal Clingman and Ali Wood against Lynda Johnson and Dianna Evans. Johnson and Evans won the final by a score of 15-11.

AROUND THE U.S.A.

In September of 1994, Adam Johnson ended Karch Kiraly's domination of the "King of the Beach" tournament by taking the title and $54,500.00 in prize money. Johnson still felt that Karch remained the greatest beach volleyball player in the world!

After a total of 135 victories, at age 37, Sinjin Smith finished off his last season with the AVP. Sinjin was instrumental in forming the organization. Sinjin was leaving the AVP in 1994 to play on the FIVB tour. Smith didn't think that the AVP should restrict the players from having the opportunity of playing internationally and having the opportunity to play in the Olympics. At the time he left the AVP, there was only one way to participate in the Olympics, and that was to participate in the FIVB World Series events.

The U.S.A. women's National Team coach, Terry Liskevych, did not allow team members to participate in any beach competition until the conclusion of the 1996 Olympics.

The USVBA turned its attention to the beach game. The USVBA hosted a "World Series" of Beach Volleyball event in Miami Beach, Florida. The organization also recognized the WPVA as the national women's beach volleyball league and granted it the right to select participants for international pro-beach events, although the FIVB World Series events still determined the U.S.A. number one selection for the Olympics in Atlanta Georgia. The AVP was out of the international and Olympic selection process, until later, when an agreement was made to allow the second and third U.S.A. Olympic Beach Volleyball Teams to be selected with an "Olympic Trials".

In 1994 the "USVBA", after 66 years of effort, took on a new name: "USA Volleyball."

The Federation of Outdoor Volleyball Association (FOVA) was disbanded and replaced by the Armature Volleyball Association (AVA).

On Octovber 21, 1994, the Volleyball Hall of Fame inducted Patty Dowdell, Marv Dunphy, John Kock, and Larry Rundle into the Volleyball Hall of Fame. The American Volleyball Coaches Association (AVCA) was selected as "VBHF Court of Honor" recipient and ASICS Tiger Corporation was selected as the first recipient of "VBHF William G. Morgan Award," to honor organizations for their efforts to promote volleyball.

LARRY RUNDLE
1964 Olympic National Team member and beach volleyball "Legend" Larry Rundle was inducted into the Holyoke Volleyball Hall of Fame in 1994. Above photo, Rundle spikes the ball during his successful beach volleyball career.
Photo Courtesy of Dewey Schurman

ATHENS GREECE

The United States men's National Team shocked the field at the 13th World Volleyball Championships in Athens Greece. The U.S.A. won the bronze medal with a 3-1 match victory over the Cuban team. The Americans lost only one match in the tournament, a 3-2 decision to the Netherlands in the semi-finals. The team from Italy won the gold medal. Also, the World Congress in Athens approved new rules:
1. OK to contact the ball with any part of the body.
2. Service zone extended to the entire back line.
3. Elimination of the "double-hit" error on the first touch of a ball coming over the net.
4. OK to touch the net when not playing the ball.

SAO PAULO BRAZIL

At the Women's World Indoor Championship in Brazil, 26,000 fans crowded into Belo Horizonte, to view the matches. This set a new record for the women's division. In the championship match, the team from Cuba defeated the team from Brazil.

ADDITIONAL 1994 BEACH RESULTS

MANHATTAN BEACH CALIFORNIA
February 12th, 1994

The AVP began the 1994 season with an AVP qualifier in Manhattan Beach. First place was occupied by two teams. Eric Fonoimoana and Brian Ivie along with Bill Boullianne and Dan Vrebalovich. These two teams qualified for the $100,000.00 Evian Indoor tournament.
3rd Place: Albert Hannemann and Matt Unger
3rd Place: Scott Friederichsen and Lief Hanson

BRIAN IVIE
Brian Ivie teamed-up with Eric Fonoimoana to win the AVP Qualifier, along with the team of Bill Boullianne and Dan Vrebalovich, allowing both teams to qualify for an AVP event. Above photo, Ivie gets "way-above" the net for a block.
Photo Courtesy of "Couvi"

SAN DIEGO CALIFORNIA
June 4th, 1994

The 1995 San Diego-Ocean Beach "Jose Cuervo" Men's Open was won by Matt Winterburn and James Fellows. In the championship match, they defeated Mike Mattarocci and Dave Smith. Tournament director George Stepanof said that there were 32 "AAA" teams in this open. The tournament was played with 4-Team Pools and 16 teams made it to a single elimination tournament.
3rd Place: Brett Gonnerman and Mike Garcia
3rd Place: Christian "K-9" Kiernan and Rick Ownbey

1994 MIXED-DOUBLE'S RESULT

MANHATTAN BEACH CALIFORNIA
August 14th-15th, 1994

The 1994 Marine Street Mixed-Doubles was won by the team of Rick Arce and Lisa Arce. In the championship match, they defeated Jeff Southcott and Christina Gage. Tournament Director Mike Cook reported that the weather was "unbelievably hot!" There were 17 teams entered in this tournament.
3rd Place: Noble Smith and Jan Kyle
3rd Place: Brent Frohoff and Christian Romero
5th Place: Tim Muret and Mary Ann Wagner
5th Place: Mark Williams and Christy Cramer
5th Place: Dan Jamieson and Roxanne McMiller
5th Place: Butch Miali and Chris Starczak

LISA ARCE
Pro-Beach competitor Lisa Arce teamed-up, with her brother Rick, to win the 1994 Marine Street Mixed-Doubles Open. Rick was a successful player on the Eastern Volleyball Tour. Above photo, Lisa gets low to make the dig on a hard-driven ball.
Photo Courtesy of "Couvi"

MEN'S BEACH VOLLEYBALL
1995

In 1995, "The Centennial of Volleyball," there were forty-five recorded "Open-Professional" Beach Volleyball tournaments. Thirty of these tournaments were staged on U.S.A soil, while fifteen were played outside of the U.S.A. Of the thirty U.S. tournaments, California hosted eight events. There were twenty-one U.S. events staged in ten states/regions other than California. The California tournaments were held in Santa Cruz, San Francisco, Manhattan Beach, Hermosa Beach (twice, AVP & FIVB), Seal Beach, Long Beach, and San Diego. Florida hosted five tournaments in Fort Myers, Pensacola, Singer Island, and Clearwater Beach (twice: AVP & FIVB). The remaining U.S. tournaments were in: were held in Phoenix Arizona, Boulder Colorado, Belmar and Seaside Heights New Jersey, Milwaukee Wisconsin, Baltimore Maryland, Atlanta Georgia, Dallas Texas, Chicago Illinois, Newport Rhode Island, Washington D.C. (indoor), New York City (indoor), Minneapolis Minnesota (twice: indoor & outdoor), Boston Massachusetts (twice: indoor & outdoor), and Carolina Beach Puerto Rico (FIVB). The fifteen events held outside of the U.S.A. were hosted by:

1. Copacabana Beach, in Rio de Janeiro, Brazil
2. Marbella Spain
3. Marseille France
4. Berlin Germany
5. Kwang An Ri Beach in Pusan, Korea
6. Enoshima Japan
7. Lignano, Sabbiadoro Italy
8. Espinho Portugal
9. LaBaule France
10. Tenerife Spain
11. Fortaleza Brazil
12. Ostende Belgium
13. Kuta Beach Bali Indonesia
14. Capetown, South Africa
15. Venzuela

In addition to the above International events, the third Swiss Beach Volleyball Tour moved into the heart of the Swiss towns. The Swiss Championship moved to Buochs. The 1995 women's division winner's were

SCOTT AYAKATUBBY
In 1995, Scott "Ack" Ayakatubby completed his most successful season on the AVP Tour. "Ack" advanced to 11 championship matches, winning 8 times. Above photo, "Ack" hits the ball past the block of Jose Loiola.
Photo Courtesy of Eric Barnes

KARCH KIRALY & SCOTT AYAKATUBBY
Karch "KK" Kiraly was the top player on the 1995 AVP Tour, advancing to 17 finals, winning 12 times (KK also won an FIVB event). Kiraly teamed-up with Scott "Ack" Ayakatubby for 8 titles. Above photo, Ayakatubby passing the ball to Kiraly.
Photo Courtesy of "Couvi"

Gaby Meili and Margot Schlafli. The men's champions were Patrick Egger and Sascha Heyer.

Karch Kiraly and Scott Ayakatubby narrowly took the top spot on the AVP tour as they won eight tournament championships together. Their wins came in San Diego, Newport Rhode Island, Boulder Colorado, Boston Massachusetts, Chicago Illinois, Atlanta Georgia, Dallas Texas, and Mesa Arizona. Kiraly also won five tournaments with Kent Steffes. They won together at: Minneapolis Minnesota (indoor), Santa Cruz California, Singer Island and Fort Myers Florida. K&K also won an invitational event in Venezuela. Right behind Ayakatubby and Kiraly, with seven tournament championships, was the team of Mike Dodd and Mike Whitmarsh. Their wins came in: Baltimore Maryland, Milwaukee Wisconsin, Pensacola and Clearwater Florida, and in California at San Francisco, Seal Beach and the FIVB event in Hermosa Beach. Whitmarsh also won the Long Beach California tournament with Canyon Ceman, Al Janc, and James Fellows (this was a two-man tournament that had squads of four players, allowing substitution).

Additional AVP teams that won in 1995: Adam Johnson and Jose Loiola won four tournaments together. They won at: Seaside Heights New Jersey, Minneapolis Minnesota, Hermosa Beach, and Manhattan Beach. Johnson also won two tournaments with Randy Stoklos. They won the Boston Massachusetts (indoor) and New York City (indoor events together. Eduardo Bacil and Jose Loiola won the Washington D.C. (indoor) event. Bill Boullianne and Brian Lewis won the Belmar New Jersey event.

On the 1995 California Beach Sand Volleyball Tour there were 339 events scheduled. The 1995 CBVA State Championships, the Bud Light California Cup, started on September 2nd, 1995 at the Manhattan Beach Pier. Working in cooperation with USA Volleyball, the CBVA event was also the US Open Beach Championships, drawing regional qualifying teams from around the country to the Mecca of beach volleyball to compete against the best amateurs along with some WPVA and AVP players, in the country. The 1995 Bud Light California Cup was the largest rated event in CBVA history with 269 teams competing over the two day period on 52 courts. Competition in the Men's "AAA" and Women's Open divisions was especially intense with $2,000.00 up for grabs in each division. In the men's "AAA" division, Leland Quinn and Dan Castillo were the winners. In the Women's Open, Heather Hafner and Evelyn Conley took home the first place prize. Paul Boyd and Michelle Morse won the Mixed-Doubles Open.

MIKE DODD
Mike Dodd paired-up with Mike Whitmarsh on the 1995 AVP Tour. They were the second most successful team on the tour, advancing to 13 finals, winning 6 times. Above photo, Dodd attacking the ball.
Photo Courtesy of the AVP

MIKE WHITMARSH
In 1995, Mike Whitmarsh was paired-up with Mike Dodd. As a team, they won 1 FIVB Tour and 6 AVP Tour events. Above photo, Whitmarsh utilizes his best attribute, a huge block, while Adam Johnson tries to poke the ball onto the court.
Photo Courtesy of the AVP

AVP

In 1995 there were 27 men's AVP events, including Evian's expanding the indoor tour to four sites: Washington DC, Boston Massachusetts, Minneapolis Minnesota, and New York City.

On February 4th, 1995, The team of Eduardo Bacil and Jose Loiola, both from Brazil, became the first non-U.S.A. team to win an AVP event. They defeated Adam Johnson and Randy Stoklos 15-9 at the $50,000.00 Evian Indoor, "beach tournament". This tournament was played on 240 tons of sand inside the Patriot Center in Washington D.C.. Loiola would go on to win four more tournaments in 1995 with Adam Johnson.

After winning the $100,000.00 Miller Lite Fort Myers Open, on April 2nd with Kiraly, Kent Steffes shoulder required surgery that kept him off the tour until the $100,000.00 Miller Lite Milwaukee Open, July 22-23, 1995.

Because of Steffes injury, Karch Kiraly needed a new partner! He would try to get Adam Johnson to leave his partnership with Randy Stoklos, but he was not ready to do so. Karch would also be unsuccessful in trying to get Jose Loiola to break-up with Eduardo Bacil. He was also unsuccessful in connecting with Scott Ayakatubby. He finally would team with Rob Heidger for a 5th place finish at the $100,000.00 Miller Lite Pensacola Beach Open. The following week he finally connected with Scott Ayakatubby. They took a third place over Johnson and Stoklos, at the $250,000.00 Jose Cuervo Gold Crown Series at Clearwater Florida. The tournament was won by Dodd and Whitmarsh over Loiola and Bacil 15-13. Karch went on to win six out of eleven tournaments with Ayakatubby before teaming up with Steffes again. Karch went back to Steffes after playing at the FIVB International tournament, in Hermosa Beach, with Ayakatubby, when Ayakatubby injured his back.

Soon after Kiraly had teamed up with Ayakatubby, Johnson teamed-up with Loiola, and Bacil teamed-up with Stoklos. Johnson and Loiola would be successful, Stoklos and Bacil would not be successful.

After Ayakatubby's injury, Kiraly went back to Steffes, and Stoklos teamed-up with Ayakatubby. Stoklos and Ayakatubby had some minor success, including a second at the Manhattan Open, behind Loiola and Johnson.

Kiraly stayed with Steffes for four tournaments, winning the $250,000.00 Cuervo Gold Crown at Santa Cruz, but only reaching one other final was not good enough for Kiraly and he went back with Ayakatubby. Ack and Karch would win the $250,000.00 Cuervo Gold Crown at

ADAM JOHNSON
During the 1995 season, on the AVP Tour, Adam "AJ" Johnson teamed-up with Brazilian Jose Loiola for a successful year of beach volleyball. They advanced to 11 finals, winning 5 times. Above photo, "AJ" challenges the block of Chris Young.
Photo Courtesy of the AVP

JOSE LOIOLA
Brazilian Jose Loiola had a succesful season on the 1995 AVP Tour. Teramed-up with Adam Johnson, Loiola advanced to 11 finals, gaining 6 titles. Above photo, Loiola reaches high in the block attempt of Scott Ayakatubby's spike.
Photo Courtesy of Eric Barnes

Boulder Colorado over Frohoff and Luyties. They would also win the $100,000.00 Nestea Player's Championship at Newport Rhode Island. They would then lose in the finals of the Hermosa Beach championship to Johnson and Loiola.

Jose Loiola and Adam Johnson became the force to reckon with, when they won the $100,000.00 Miller Lite Open in Manhattan Beach over Ayakatubby and Stoklos 15-7. They then finished the season with the 15-5 win, in convincing fashion, over Kiraly and Ayakatubby at the $250,000.00 Miller Lite Championships in Hermosa Beach.

Kiraly finished the season with 12 tournament titles, after reaching the finals on 17 occasions. The 1995 AVP final prize money standings had Kiraly on the top of the list with winnings of $392,610.00. Mike Whitmarsh was in the second spot with $278,512.00, after reaching 13 finals, winning 6 times with Mike Dodd. Adam Johnson also reached 13 finals with 6 wins.. As far as tournament titles were concerned, Scott Ayakatubby was in the second spot, behind Kiraly with eight. Ayakatubby advanced to the finals 11 times. Jose Loiola also reached 11 finals, winning 5 times.

Television coverage for the 1995 AVP tour was provided by NBC, ESPN, Prime Network, and Syndication.

TOP 50 PLAYERS ON 1995 AVP TOUR

1. Karch Kiraly
2. Scott Ayakatubby
3. Mike Dodd
3. Mike Whitmarsh
5. Adam Johnson
6. Jose Loiola
7. Brian Lewis
8. Bill Boullianne
9. Randy Stoklos
10. Eric Fonoimoana
11. Rob Heidger
12. Kent Steffes
13. Ricci Luyties
14. Brent Frohoff
15. Eduardo Bacil
16. Wes Welch
17. Canyon Ceman
18. Troy Tanner
19. Tim Hovland
20. Chris Young
21. Leif Hanson
22. Jeff Rodgers
23. Kevin Martin
24. David Swatik
25. Mark Kerins
26. Andrew Smith
27. Brian Gatzke
28. Bill Suwara
29. Dain Blanton
30. Ian Clark
31. Eric Wurts
32. Pat Powers
33. Matt Sonnichsen
34. Doug Foust
35. Dan Vrebalovich
36. Al Janc
37. Craig Moothart
38. Matt Unger
39. John Brajevic
40. Daniel Cardenas
41. Jim Nichols
42. Albert Hannemann
43. Mike Schiegel
44. Mark Paaluhi
45. Scott Friederichsen
46. James Fellows
47. Marcelo Duarte
48. Burke Stefko
49. Nick Hannemann
50. Lee LeGrand

KENT STEFFES
Kent Steffes also had some success when paired-up with Karch Kiraly, winning 4 finals after 7 appearances. Above photo, Steffes passing the ball to Kiraly, infront of a large crowd.
Photo Courtesy of the AVP

BRIAN LEWIS
Brian Lewis played well on nthe 1995 AVP Tour with 11 top five finishes, including 2 finals with 1 tournament championship. Above photo, Lewis pounds the ball past the block of Jose Loiola.
Photo Courtesy of the AVP

1995 INDIVIDUAL AVP TOURNAMENT FINISHES

Player	1st	2nd	3rd	4th	5th
Scott Ayakatubby	8	3	2	3	1
Eduardo Bacil	1	2	2	3	5
Dain Blanton	0	0	0	0	2
Bill Boullianne	1	1	5	4	6
John Brajevic	0	0	0	0	1
Daniel Cardenas	0	0	0	0	1
Canyon Ceman	0	1	0	0	1
Ian Clark	0	0	0	0	1
Roger Clark	0	0	0	0	1
Mike Dodd	6	7	6	1	2
James Fellows	0	1	0	0	0
Brent Frohoff	0	1	3	0	3
Eric Fonoimoana	0	0	3	4	7
Doug Foust	0	0	0	0	2
Scott Friederichsen	0	0	0	0	1
Brian Gatzke	0	0	0	0	2
Albert Hannemann	0	0	0	0	1
Leif Hanson	0	1	0	0	3
Rob Heidger	0	0	4	0	5
Tim Hovland	0	0	0	1	2
Brian Ivie	0	0	0	0	1
Al Janc	0	0	0	0	2
Adam Johnson	6	7	4	2	3
Karch Kiraly	**12**	**5**	**4**	**2**	**1**
Marc Kerins	0	0	0	1	0
Lee LeGrand	0	0	0	0	2
Brian Lewis	1	1	5	4	5
Jose Loiola	5	6	3	3	4
Ricci Luyties	0	1	2	4	5
Kevin Martin	0	0	0	0	4
Craig Moothart	0	0	0	0	1
Pat Powers	0	0	0	0	2
Jeff Rogers	0	1	0	0	1
Andrew Smith	0	0	0	1	1
Matt Sonnichsen	0	0	0	1	1
Kent Steffes	4	3	2	2	0
Randy Stoklos	2	4	3	4	3
Bill Suwara	0	0	0	0	1
David Swatik	0	0	0	0	2
Troy Tanner	0	0	2	0	2
Matt Unger	0	0	0	0	2
Dan Vrebalovich	0	0	1	0	1
Tim Walmer	0	0	0	0	1
Wes Welch	0	0	2	1	4
Mike Whitmarsh	6	7	6	1	2
Eric Wurts	0	0	1	0	1
Chris Young	0	1	0	0	1

EDUARDO BACIL
In 1995, Brazilian Eduardo Bacil teamed-up with compatriot Jose Loiola to becom the first "Non-USA" team to win an AVP Tour event. Above photo, Bacil gets low to make the pass.
Photo Courtesy of the AVP

RANDY STOKLOS
On the 1995 AVP Tour, Randy Stoklos still had some moments to celebrate. He advanced to 6 finals winning twice. Above photo, Stoklos celebrates a winnig moment at the 1995 MB Open.
Photo Courtesy of Frank Goroszko

FIVB

With the FIVB International Tour being the basis for men and women qualifying to participate in beach volleyball at the 1996 Atlanta Olympics, 1995 saw the FIVB grow into another stronghold for the beach volleyball circuit. With beach volleyball's growth all over the world, the FIVB expanded to twenty-nine international events on five continents. There were more than 800,000 spectators attending the events and over 50 million viewers on television.

The FIVB men's tour included 17 stops in thirteen countries: Spain (twice), France (twice), Germany, Korea, Japan, Italy, Portugal, Brazil (twice), Belgium, Indonesia, Puerto Rico, South Africa, and including 2 stops in the U.S.A. (Hermosa Beach California and Clearwater, Florida). The total FIVB prize money was worth $2,650,000. The men to got $2,000,000.00 and the women $650,000.00.

The 1995 FIVB World Tour was dominated by teams from Brazil. Brazilian teams won all but three of the seventeen FIVB events. The top team on the FIVB World Tour in 1995 was the Brazilian team Franco Jose Vieira Neto and Roberto Costa Lopes. They won seven FIVB World Series events in 1995. They won at: Clearwater Beach Beach Florida, Marbella Spain, Kwang An Ri Beach in Pusan Korea, Enoshima Japan, Espinho Portugal, LaBaule France, and Fortaleza Brazil. The Brazilian team of of Z-Marco Nobrega Ferreira de Melo and Emanuel Fernando Scheffer Rego won five FIVB World Series events. They won at: Marseille France, Tenerife Spain, Ostende Belgium, Kuta Beach Bali Indonesia, and Capetown south Africa. The Brazilian team of Carlos Frederico Galletti Loss and Andre Faria Gomes won the FIVB "World Championships" at Copacabana Beach, in Rio de Janeiro, Brazil. The Brazilian team of Luiz Antonio "Lula" Barbosa da Silva and Paulo Roberto "Paulao" Moreira da Costa won the FIVB event at Lignano Sabbiadoro Italy. Jan Kvalheim and Bjorn Maaseide, from Norway won the FIVB event in Berlin Germany. The Cuban team of Juan Miguel Rosell Milanes and Francisco "Francis" Alvarez Cutio won the FIVB event at Carolina Beach in Puerto Rico. As mentioned before, Mike Dodd and Mike Whitmarsh won the FIVB event in Hermosa Beach California.

American player's Mike Dodd and Mike Whitmarsh won the $100,000.00 Bud Light World Beach Invitational FIVB event, in Hermosa Beach California, while Karch Kiraly and Kent Steffes won an invitational event staged in Curacao Venezuela. This was Kiraly's 99th official career tournament championship.

1995 INDIVIDUAL FIVB TOURNAMENT FINISHES

Player	1st	2nd	3rd	4th	5th
Vince Ahmann	0	0	0	0	4
Francisco Alverez	1	1	0	1	1
Jose Carlos Pereira Brenha Alves	0	0	0	1	0
Carlos Briceno	0	0	0	2	1
John Child	0	0	3	0	3
Martin Alejo Conde	0	2	0	1	5
Roberto Lopes da Costa	**7**	**2**	**3**	**0**	**3**
Mike Dodd	1	0	0	0	0
Tom Englen	0	0	0	0	1
Eric Fonoimoana	0	1	0	0	0
Scott Friederichsen	0	1	0	0	0
Andre Faria Gomes	1	1	1	1	1
Andrea Ghiurghi	0	0	0	0	2
Nicola Grigolo	0	0	0	0	2
Axel Hager	0	0	0	0	4
Mark Heese	0	0	3	0	3
Carl Henkel	0	1	1	3	4
Sixto Jiminez	0	1	1	0	2
Jean Philippe Jodard	0	0	0	2	0
Adam Johnson	0	0	1	0	0
Karch Kiraly	1	0	0	0	0
Jan Kvalheim	1	1	2	2	0
CarlosFrederico Galletti Loss	1	1	1	1	1
Bjorn Maaseide	1	1	2	2	0
Luis Miguel Babosa Maia	0	0	0	1	0
Luiz Guilherme Marquez	0	2	1	0	1
Eduardo Esteban "Mono" Martinez	0	2	0	1	6
Juan Miguel Rosell Milanes	0	0	0	1	0
Javier Bosma Minguez	0	1	1	0	2
Paulo Roberto Da Costa Moreira	1	0	0	3	0
Javier Yuste Muniz	0	0	0	0	2
Jose Franco Vieira Neto	**7**	**2**	**3**	**0**	**3**
Jose Z-Marco Melo Ferreira Nobrega	5	3	3	1	1
Christian Penigaud	0	0	0	2	0
Fredrik "Figge" Peterson	0	0	0	0	1
Miguel Angel Martin Prieto	0	0	0	2	2
Julien Prosser	0	0	0	0	1
Wilfredo "Sombra Garcia Rizo	0	0	0	0	1
Emanuel Rego Scheffer	5	3	3	1	1
Luiz Antonio Silva	1	0	0	3	0
Sinjin Smith	0	1	1	3	4
Federico "Fred" Doria de Souza	0	0	0	0	1
Rogrio "Para" Ferrirs de Souza	0	2	1	0	0
Kent Steffes	1	1	0	0	0
Gonzalo Manuel Torres	0	0	0	0	1
Bruk Vandeweghe	0	0	1	0	0
Mike Whitmarsh	1	1	0	0	0
Jeff Williams	0	0	1	2	1
Eric Wurts	0	2	0	0	0
Lee Zahner	0	0	0	0	1

MARTIN ALEJO CONDE
Martin Alejo Conde, from Argentina, began to play some competitive beach volleyball on the 1995 FIVB Tour. He advanced to the finals twice, finishing second both times. Above photo, Conde makes a great effort to get the ball up.
Photo Courtesy of the FIVB

MEN'S TOURNAMENT RESULTS
1995-AVP

WASHINGTON DC
February 4th, 1995

The 1995 AVP Men's Pro-Beach Volleyball Tour started in Washington DC on the "beach" indoors. Eduardo Bacil and Jose Loiola became the first foreign team to win an AVP event with a 15-9 win over Adam Johnson and Randy Stoklos, in the championship match. They collected $15,000.00 for their efforts. In the semi-finals, Karch Kiraly and Kent Steffes were upset, 14-13, by Loiola and Bacil. This was was the first career championship for both Jose Loiola and Eduardo Bacil.

3rd Place: Karch Kiraly and Kent Steffes
3rd Place: Mike Dodd and Mike Whitmarsh
5th Place: Andrew Smith and Doug Foust
5th Place: Brian Lewis and Ricci Luyties
5th Place: Al Janc and Pat Powers
5th Place: Scott Friederichsen and Matt Unger

BOSTON MASSACHUSETTS
February 12th, 1995

In Boston Massachusetts, the second AVP Men's Pro-Beach Volleyball Tour stop was also indoors on the beach. In the championship match, with the lead changing numerous times, Adam Johnson and Randy Stoklos were 16-14 winners over Karch Kiraly and Kent Steffes. The winners shared a check for $15,000.00.

3rd Place: Eduardo Bacil and Jose Loiola
3rd Place: Rob Heidger and Eric Wurts
5th Place: Mike Dodd and Mike Whitmarsh
5th Place: Brian Gatzke and Jeff Rodgers
5th Place: Bill Boullianne and Tim Hovland
5th Place: Tim Walmer and John Brajevic

MINNEAPOLIS MINNESOTA
February 18th, 1995

In Minneapolis Minnesota, the third AVP Men's Tour stop was also indoors on the beach. As the clock ran out in the championship match, Karch Kiraly and Kent Steffes held on for a 13-11 victory over Mike Dodd and Mike Whitmarsh.

3rd Place: Adam Johnson and Randy Stoklos
3rd Place: Brent Frohoff and Dan Vrebalovich
5th Place: Eric Fonoimoana and Brian Ivie
5th Place: Eduardo Bacil and Jose Loiola
5th Place: Leif Hanson and Wes Welch
5th Place: Kevin Martin and Chris Young

EDUARDO BACIL & JOSE LOIOLA
Eduardo Bacil and Jose Loiola became the first foreign team to win an AVP event when they won the 1995 Washington DC event. Above photo, Bacil hits a set from Loiola, over the block of Eric Fonoimoana.
Photo Courtesy of "Couvi"

KARCH KIRALY
In 1995, Karfch Kiraly continued his beach volleyball mastery, advancing to 17 AVP Tour championship matches, winning 8 events with Scott Ayakatubby and 4 events with Kent Steffes. Above photo, Kiraly stays in control with a perfect pass.
Photo Courtesy of Frank Goroszko

NEW YORK NEW YORK
February 25th, 1995
On the "beach" in Madison Square Garden, New York City, New York, the fourth AVP Men's Pro-Beach Volleyball Tour stop was the final indoor "beach" tournament of the season. Nearly 12,000 "beach" volleyball fans were on hand in Madison Square Garden for the conclusion of the $250,000.00 Evian Indoor Series. In the championship match, Adam Johnson and Randy Stoklos, easily handled, Karch Kiraly and Kent Steffes, with a 15-7 win. The winners collected $30,000.00 for their efforts.
3rd Place: Eduardo Bacil and Jose Loiola
3rd Place: Mike Dodd and Mike Whitmarsh

SINGER ISLAND FLORIDA
March 25th-26th, 1995
The AVP's fifth pro-beach volleyball tournament of the 1995 season (first outdoor) was staged at Singer Island Florida. The $100,000.00 Men's Nestea Singer Island Open was won by the team of Kent Steffes and Karch Kiraly. They split $20,000.00 for their efforts. In the championship match Kiraly and Steffes easily defeated Mike Dodd and Mike Whitmarsh by a score of 15-4. With this win, Kiraly became only the third player in beach volleyball history to win more than 100 open beach tournaments. They did not give-up more than eight points in any game.
3rd Place: Adam Johnson and Randy Stoklos
4th Place: Eduardo Bacil and Jose Loiola
5th Place: Daniel Cardenas and Albert Hannemann
5th Place: Canyon Ceman and Lee LeGrand

FORT MYERS FLORIDA
April 1st-2nd, 1995
At the Holiday Inn, the 1995 $100,000.00 Miller Lite Fort Myers Open was won by Karch Kiraly and Kent Steffes. In the championship match, they defeated Jose Loiola and Eduardo Bacil, as the rally clock expired, 13-12, to collect the $20,000.00 first place prize.
3rd Place: Adam Johnson and Randy Stoklos
4th Place: Eric Fonoimoana and Ricci Luyties
5th Place: Mike Dodd and Mike Whitmarsh
5th Place: Scott Ayakatubby and Brent Frohoff

PENSACOLA FLORIDA
April 8th-9th, 1995
The AVP Men's Pro-Beach Volleyball tour went to the Pier in Pensacola Florida, for the second outdoor tournament of the season, The $100,000.00 Pensacola Miller Lite Open. In the championship match, Mike Dodd and Mike Whitmarsh were 15-9 winners over Adam Johnson and Randy Stoklos. This was Dodd's 64th career title. The winners split the $20,000.00 first place check.
3rd Place: Bill Boullianne and Brian Lewis
4th Place: Eduardo Bacil and Jose Loiola
5th Place: Kevin Martin and Chris Young
5th Place: Karch Kiraly and Rob Heidger

CLEARWATER FLORIDA
April 20th-22nd, 1995
The AVP Men's Pro-Beach Volleyball Tour went to Clearwater Beach in Clearwater Florida, for the $250,000.00 "Cuervo Gold Crown" tournament. In the championship match Mike Dodd and Mike Whitmarsh were 15-9 winners over Eduardo Bacil and Jose Loiola. The winners split the $100,000.00 first prize.
3rd Place: Karch Kiraly and Scott Ayakatubby
4th Place: Adam Johnson and Randy Stoklos
5th Place: Eric Fonoimoana and Ricci Luyties

BRIAN LEWIS
Brian "Lewey" Lewis played well on the 1995 AVP Tour, finishing within the top five on 16 occasions, with two championship matches to his credit, winning the event in Belmar New Jersey with Bill Boullianne. Above photo, "Lewey" makes a nice pass.
Photo Courtesy of Frank Goroszko

PAT POWERS
Pat "PP" Powers was still a force to contend with on the 1995 AVP Tour, usually because of his blocking ability. In the above photo, Powers shows that he has additional abilities when he makes this nice diving-dig, during the 1995 AVP event in Long Beach, CA.
Photo Courtesy of Frank Goroszko

MESA ARIZONA
April 29th-30th, 1995

On the weekend of April 29th-30th, 1995 the AVP Men's Pro-Beach Volleyball tour went to the Mesa Amphitheater in Mesa Arizona, for the $100,000.00 Men's Miller Lite Mesa Open. Scott Ayakatubby and Karch Kiraly won the tournament and first place prize of $20,000.00. In the championship match, Kiraly and Ayakatubby teamed-up together to earn their first victory together. They were winners by default over Adam Johnson and Randy Stoklos after Stoklos became ill.

3rd Place: Brent Frohoff and Rob Heidger
4th Place: Mike Dodd and Mike Whitmarsh
5th Place: Dan Vrebalovich and Wes Welch
5th Place: Eric Fonoimoana and Ricci Luyties

SAN DIEGO CALIFORNIA
May 13th-14th, 1995

The AVP Men's Pro-Beach Volleyball tour made its first 1995 California stop at Mariner's Point in San Diego California, for the $100,000.00 Men's "1-800-COLLECT" San Diego Open. Karch Kiraly and Scott Ayakatubby took the title and the first place check of $20,000.00. In the championship match Kiraly and Ayakatubby earned a 15-7 win over Mike Dodd and Mike Whitmarsh. Dodd and Whitmarsh split $11,400.00 as the runners-up.

3rd Place: Eric Fonoimoana and Ricci Luyties
4th Place: Bill Boullianne and Brian Lewis
5th Place: Dain Blanton and Ian Clark
5th Place: Brian Gatzke and Eric Wurts

DALLAS TEXAS
May 20th-21st, 1995

The next AVP Men's Pro-Beach Volleyball event was staged at the Crescent Court Hotel in Dallas Texas. The $100,000.00 Men's Nestea Dallas Open was won by Scott Ayakatubby and Karch Kiraly. They split the $20,000.00 first place check. In the championship match, Kiraly and Ayakatubby effortlessly defeated Canyon Ceman and Jeff Rodgers by a score of 15-3, as Ayakatubby consistantly "Bomed" power spikes into the Texas sand.

3rd Place: Mike Dodd and Mike Whitmarsh
4th Place: Eric Fonoimoana and Ricci Luyties
5th Place: Troy Tanner and Wes Welch
5th Place: Bill Boullianne and Brian Lewis

SAN FRANCISCO CALIFORNIA
May 27th-28th, 1995

The AVP Men's Pro-Beach Volleyball tour was back in California, when they staged the next event at the Embarcadero Center in San Francisco California. The $100,000.00 Men's "1-800-COLLECT" San Francisco Open was won by Mike Whitmarsh and Mike Dodd. They earned $20,000.00 for their efforts. In the championship match Dodd and Whitmarsh were 15-9 winners over Karch Kiraly and Scott Ayakatubby.

3rd Place: Bill Boullianne and Brian Lewis
4th Place: Adam Johnson and Jose Loiola
5th Place: Troy Tanner and Wes Welch
5th Place: Eduardo Bacil and Randy Stoklos

RANDY STOKLOS & ADAM JOHNSON
At the start of the 1995 AVP Tour, Randy Stoklos and Adam Johnson paired-up for some success. They advanced to five finals, winning twice. Above photo, Johnson challenges the block of Stoklos.
Photo Courtesy of the AVP

SCOTT AYAKATUBBY
During the 1995 AVP Tour, Scott Ayakatubby faced-off against Mike Whitmarsh on numerous occasions. In the above photo, Whitmarsh looks-on as Ayakatubby gets low to pass the ball at the 1995 AVP event in San Francisco California.
Photo Courtesy of Frank Goroszko

ATLANTA GEORGIA
June 3rd-4th, 1995

At the AVP Men's Pro-Beach Volleyball event staged on Atlantic Beach Park, in Atlanta Georgia. The $100,000.00 Men's Nestea Atlanta Open was won by the team of Karch Kiraly and Scott Ayakatubby. They split a prize of $20,000.00. In the championship match, as the time clock expired, Kiraly and Ayakatubby earned a 14-6 win over Mike Dodd and Mike Whitmarsh.

3rd Place: Eric Fonoimoana and Ricci Luyties
4th Place: Bill Boullianne and Brian Lewis
5th Place: Adam Johnson and Jose Loiola
5th Place: Eduardo Bacil and Randy Stoklos

BALTIMORE MARYLAND
June 10th-11th, 1995

At the AVP Men's Pro-Beach Volleyball event staged in Baltimore Maryland. The $100,000.00 Men's Nestea Baltimore Open was won by Mike Whitmarsh and Mike Dodd. They shared the $20,000.00 first place check. In the championship match, Adam Johnson and Jose Loiola defaulted to Dodd and Whitmarsh.

3rd Place: Eric Fonoimoana and Ricci Luyties
4th Place: Karch Kiraly and Scott Ayakatubby
5th Place: Eduardo Bacil and Randy Stoklos
5th Place: Bill Boullianne and Brian Lewis

SEASIDE HEIGHTS NEW JERSEY
June 17th-18th, 1995

The AVP Men's Pro-Beach Volleyball tour went to Seaside Heights New Jersey, for the $100,000.00 Men's Miller Lite Seaside Heights Open. Jose Loiola and Adam Johnson were the winners. They split the top prize of $20,000.00. In the exciting double final, Johnson and Loiola defeated Mike Dodd and Mike Whitmarsh, 8-11 and 7-3.

3rd Place: Bill Boullianne and Brian Lewis
4th Place: Eric Fonoimoana and Ricci Luyties
5th Place: Lee LeGrand and Matt Unger
5th Place: Matt Sonnichsen and Bill Suwara

CHICAGO ILLINOIS
June 24th-25th, 1995

The AVP Men's Pro-Beach Volleyball tour went to North Avenue Beach, in Chicago Illinois, where in the championship match Karch Kiraly and Scott Ayakatubby were 11-8 winners over Adam Johnson and Jose Loiola. Ayakatubby and Kiraly split their $10,000.00 share of the $100,000.00 Miller Lite Chicago Open.

3rd Place: Brent Frohoff and Rob Heidger
4th Place: Tim Hovland and Eduardo Bacil
5th Place: Dain Blanton and Roger Clark
5th Place: Bill Boullianne and Brian Lewis

BRENT FROHOFF
Brent "Fro" Frohoff played competitively on the 1995 AVP Tour. "Fro" finished within the top five at seven AVP events. He advanced to the championship match of the Boulder Collorado event. Above photo, "Fro" on the offensive attack.
Photo Courtesy of Frank Goroszko

ROGER CLARK
Roger Clark played some competitive beach volleyball on the 1995 AVP Professional Beach Volleyball Tour. Clark broke into the top five at the 1995 AVP event in Chicago Illinois. Above photo, Clark cuts the ball past the block of Ricci Luyties.
Photo Courtesy of the AVP

MINNEAPOLIS MINNESOTA
July 1st-2nd, 1995

The following week, the AVP Men's Pro-Beach Volleyball tour went to The Mall of America, in Minneapolis Minnesota, for the $100,000.00 Miller Lite Open. In the championship match, Adam Johnson and Jose Loiola defeated Mike Dodd and Mike Whitmarsh 15-7, to earn the right to split the $20,000.00 first prize.

3rd Place: Karch Kiraly and Scott Ayakatubby
4th Place: Eric Fonoimoana and Ricci Luyties
5th Place: Brent Frohoff and Rob Heidger
5th Place: Kevin Martin and David Swatik

BOSTON MASSACHUSETTS
July 8th-9th, 1995

The AVP Men's Pro-Beach Volleyball tour went to "The Tent", in Boston Massachusetts, for the $100,000.00 Miller Lite Open. In the championship match, Karch Kiraly and Scott Ayakatubby skillfully defeated Bill Boullianne and Brian Lewis, by a score of 15-5. Karch dumped Ack two weeks later when Kent Steffes returned from shoulder surgery.

3rd Place: Mike Dodd and Mike Whitmarsh
4th Place: Matt Sonnichsen and Bill Suwara
5th Place: Leif Hanson and Chris Young
5th Place: Adam Johnson and Jose Loiola

BELMAR BEACH NEW JERSEY
July 15th-16th, 1995

The AVP Tour was on the beach at Belmar Beach New Jersey, for the $100,000.00 Nestea Open. Most of the top AVP teams were on the beach in Hermosa Beach California, taking part in an FIVB event, so that they could earn the necessary points to qualify for the "U.S.A. Olympic Trials." In the championship match, the team of Bill Boullianne and Brian Lewis were able to skate to a 15-2 victory over Leif Hanson and Chris Young. They took home the $20,000.00 first place prize.

3rd Place: Adam Johnson and Jose Loiola
4th Place: Andrew Smith and Mark Kerins
5th Place: Ricci Luyties and Eric Fonoimoana
5th Place: Doug Foust and Craig Moothart

MILWAUKEE WISCONSIN
July 22nd-23rd, 1995

The AVP Tour was at Bradford Beach, in Milwaukee Wisconsin, for the $100,000.00 Miller Lite Open. In the championship match, Mike Dodd and Mike Whitmarsh were 15-7 winners over Adam Johnson and Jose Loiola. They took home $20,000.00 for the win.

3rd Place: Karch Kiraly and Kent Steffes
4th Place: Scott Ayakatubby and Randy Stoklos
5th Place: Tim Hovland and Eduardo Bacil
5th Place: Al Janc and Pat Powers

BILL BOULLIANNE
Bill "Beef" Boullianne played well on the 1995 AVP Tour. "Beef advanced to 2 finals, winning the Belmar NJ event with Brian Lewis. Beef finished within the top 5 at 17 events. Above photo, "Beef" is in the right spot to make the dig.
Photo Courtesy of the AVP

CHRIS YOUNG
Chris Young provided some stiff competition on the 1995 AVP Tour. Young advanced to the championship match of one AVP Tour event where he finished in the second spot. Above photo, Young challenges the block of Kent Steffes.
Photo Courtesy of the AVP

SEAL BEACH CALIFORNIA
July 28th-30th, 1995

The AVP Tour was back in California, with a stop north of the Pier, in Seal Beach California, for the $100,000.00 Miller Lite Open. Mike Dodd and Mike Whitmarsh won the tournament and the $20,000.00 first prize. In the championship match, Dodd and Whitmarsh skillfully defeated Karch Kiraly and Kent Steffes 15-2, as Whitmarsh put on a blocking clinic.

3rd Place: Adam Johnson and Jose Loiola
4th Place: Bill Boullianne and Brian Lewis
5th Place: Leif Hanson and Chris Young
5th Place: Kevin Martin and David Swatik

SANTA CRUZ CALIFORNIA
August 3rd-5th, 1995

The next AVP California event was on Main Beach, in Santa Cruz California. This was a $250,000.00 "Cuervo Gold Crown" series event. Karch Kiraly and Kent Steffes earned $100,000.00 with a 15-11 championship match victory over Adam Johnson and Jose Loiola.

3rd Place: Mike Dodd and Mike Whitmarsh
4th Place: Scott Ayakatubby and Randy Stoklos
5th Place: Eric Fonoimoana and Rob Heidger

MANHATTAN BEACH CALIFORNIA
August 11th-13th, 1995

For the third weekend in a row the AVP Men's Pro-Beach Volleyball tour was in California. They were south of the pier, on the beach, in Manhattan Beach California. The renowned "Manhattan Open," was part of the 1995 $100,000.00 Miller Lite Beach Volleyball Series. Adam Johnson and Jose Loiola won the title and the $20,000.00 first place check. In the championship match, Johnson and Loiola were in control, defeating Scott Ayakatubby and Randy Stoklos 15-7.

3rd Place: Mike Dodd and Mike Whitmarsh
4th Place: Karch Kiraly and Kent Steffes
5th Place: Eric Fonoimoana and Rob Heidger
5th Place: Bill Boullianne and Brian Lewis

BOULDER COLORADO
August 17th-19th, 1995

The AVP Tour was at the Boulder Reservoir, in Boulder Colorado, for a $250,000.00 "Cuervo Gold Crown" series event. In the championship match, Karch Kiraly and Scott Ayakatubby held on for a thrilling 12-11 win over Brent Frohoff Ricci Luyties. The win earned Kiraly and Ayakatubby $50,000.00 each.

3rd Place: Eric Fonoimoana and Rob Heidger
4th Place: Bill Boullianne and Brian Lewis
5th Place: Adam Johnson and Jose Loiola

HERMOSA BEACH CALIFORNIA
August 25th-27th, 1995

The AVP Tour was north of the pier, in Hermosa Beach California, for the $250,000.00 "Miller Lite Men's Open." Adam Johnson and Jose Loiola were the winners. They celebrated their victory along with the $100,000.00 prize money that they split for their efforts. In the championship match, Johnson and Loiola were in control from the start, winning 15-5 over Karch Kiraly and Scott Ayakatubby. This match was never close. First it was 1-0, then 7-0, then 8-1, then all of a sudden it was 14-1. Johnson and Loiola were serving Karch and Ack off the court. The losers managed to score four more points before it was over. Kiraly and Ayakatubby settled for the $21,500.00 second place check.

3rd Place: Bill Boullianne and Brian Lewis
4th Place: Kent Steffes and Randy Stoklos
5th Place: Mike Dodd and Mike Whitmarsh
5th Place: Eric Fonoimoana and Rob Heidger

NEWPORT RHODE ISLAND
September 1st-2nd, 1995

The AVP Tour went to Newport Rhode Island for the $100,000.00 "Nestea Players' Championship". In the championship match, Karch Kiraly and Scott Ayakatubby were 15-11 winners over Mike Dodd and Mike Whitmarsh. Kiraly and Ack split $21,000.00.

3rd Place: Bill Boullianne and Brian Lewis
4th Place: Adam Johnson and Jose Loiola
5th Place: Eric Fonoimoana and Rob Heidger
5th Place: Brent Frohoff and Ricci Luyties

LONG BEACH CALIFORNIA
September 7th-9th, 1995

The final event, of the 1995 AVP Men's Pro-Beach Volleyball Tour was on the Beach, in Long Beach California. It was a $100,000.00 "Cuervo Gold Crown" series event. This was a two-man tournament, but the format of this tournament was different than others. The teams were comprised of a four-man roster, with two players playing in the game with substitutions allowed. In the championship match, the team of Mike Whitmarsh, Canyon Ceman, Al Janc, and James Fellows defeated Brian Lewis, Brian Gatzke, Scott Friederichsen, and Lee LeGrand by a score of 15-5. The winners split the check of $20,000.00 four ways.

3rd Place: Mike Dodd, Pat Powers, Jeff Rogers, and Burke Stefko
3rd Place: Adam Johnson, Ian Clark, David Swatik, and Mark Paaluhi
This tournament was not counted towards total career wins.

MARK PAALUHI

In 1995, Mark Paaluhi began to play professional beach volleyball on the AVP Tour. Paaluhi was one of the "Top-50" players on the circuit in 1995. Above photo, Paaluhi gives an "all-out" effort to make a dig.

Photo Courtesy of "Couvi"

MEN'S TOURNAMENT RESULTS
1995-FIVB

RIO DE JANEIRO, BRAZIL
February 16th-19th, 1995

On Copacabana Beach, in Rio de Janeiro Brazil, the $200,000.00 FIVB Men's World Series event was a Brazilian sweep of the first three places. In front of 15,000 screaming Brazilian fans, Carlos Frederico "Alemao" Galletti Loss and Andre Faria Gomes defeated Jose Marco Melo Ferreira Nobrega and Emanuel Rego Scheffer to win the championship. "Alemao" and Gomes split the $40,000.00 first place check. The championship match was played in pleasant, rain cooled, 90 degree weather. Gomes and "Alemao" lost the first game 12-6 in the best of three match. The rain delayed the second game before Rego and Z-Marco went on to win 12-4. "Alemao" and Gomes then won the third game, a rally-point tiebreaker, 15-13.

3rd Place: Franco Jose Vieira Neto and Roberto Costa Lopes-Bra
4th Place: Carlos Briceno and Jeff Williams-USA
5th Place: "Sombra" Garcia Rizo and Gonzalo Manuel Torres-Cuba
5th Place: Guilherme Luiz Marquez and Esteban "Mono" Martinez-Bra
Americans, Sinjin Smith and Bruk Vandeweghe, finished a distant twenty-fifth, as they went "Uno-Dos" on the first day of the competition.

CURACAO VENEZUELA
March, 1995

Karch Kiraly and Kent Steffes won an invitational event staged in Curacao Venezuela. This was Kiraly's 99th official career tournament championship.

MARBELLA, SPAIN
April 14th-16th, 1995

It was another Brazilian sweep, at the $100,000.00 FIVB Men's 1995 World Beach Volleyball Championship Series, in Marbella Spain. Roberto Lopes da Costa and Franco Jose Vieira Neto defeated Carlos Frederico "Alemao" Galetti Loss and Andre Faria Gomes, 12-4 and 12-9, to win the championship match and the $20,000.00 first prize.

3rd Place: Jose Z-Marco Nobrega and Emanuel Scheffer Rego-Bra
4th Place: Juan Miguel Rosell Milanes and Francisco Alverez-Cuba
5th Place: Axel "Hagar" Hager and Jorg "Vince" Ahmann-Ger
5th Place: Javier Bosma Minguez and Sixto Jiminez.-Spain
The top U.S.A. finishers were Carlos Briceno and Jeff Williams with a ninth place finish. Other U.S.A. finishers: Sinjin Smith and Carl Henkel along with Sean Fallowfield and Bruk Vandeweghe in ninth. The U.S.A. team of Terry Stevens and Stephen Miller were in a distant thirty-seventh place.

AXEL HAGER & JORG AHMANN
During the 1995 FIVB season, German's, Axel "Hagar" Hager and Jorg "Vince" Ahmann played some respectabel beach volleyball. Above photo, "Hagar" hits a set from "Vince" away from the block of Karch Kiraly.
Photo Courtesy of "Couvi"

CARLOS LOSS
Brazilian Carlos Frederico Galletti Loss was one of the top competitors on the 1995 FIVB Tour. He finished within the top 5 on five occasions, advancing to the finals twice while winning one event. Above photo, Loss gets above the net for the block attempt.
Photo Courtesy of "Couvi"

CLEARWATER, FLORIDA, U.S.A.
May 5th-7th, 1995

The large crowd, at the $100,000.00 FIVB Men's World Series event, on the beach in Clearwater, Florida, U.S.A., saw another exciting final. In the championship match, the Brazilian team of Roberto Lopes da Costa and Franco Jose Vieira Neto defeated Jose Z-Marco Nobrega Ferreira de Melo and Emanuel Fernando Scheffer Rego, also from Brazil, 12-6 and 12-6, to win the gold medal and first place prize of $20,000.00.

3rd Place: Jeff Williams and Bruk Vandeweghe-USA
4th Place: Carlos "Alemao" Galetti Loss and Andre Faria Gomes-Bra
5th Place: Sinjin Smith and Carl Henkel-USA
5th Place: Javier Yuste Muniz and Miguel Angel Martin Prieto-Spain
Americans Kevin Waterbury and Roger Clark along with Todd Schaefer and Mike Diehl finished in the twenty-fifth spot.

MARSEILLE, FRANCE
June 22nd-25th, 1995

The excited crowd, at the $100,000.00 FIVB Men's World Series beach volleyball tournament in Marseille France, saw the Brazilian team of Jose Z-Marco Nobrega Ferreira de Melo and Emanuel Fernando Scheffer Rego defeat Bjorn Maaseide and Jan Kvalheim, from Norway, 11-12, 12-10, and 12-8, to win the championship match. The winner's shared the first place prize of $20,000.00.

3rd Place: Carlos Frederico Galetti Loss and Andre Faria Gomes-Bra
4th Place: Roberto "Paulao" Moreira da Costa and Barbosa da Silva-Bra
5th Place: Carl Henkel and Sinjin Smith-USA
5th Place: Franco Jose Vieira Neto and Roberto Costa Lopes-Bra
Americans, Roger Clark and Bruk Vandeweghe along with Jeff Williams and Carlos Briceno, finished in seventeenth place. The U.S.A. team of Terry Stevens and Stephen Miller were again in a distant thirty-seventh place.

BERLIN, GERMANY
June 30th-July 2nd, 1995

The FIVB Men's Pro-Beach Volleyball Tour made its next stop in Berlin Germany for another $100,000.00 event. The team of Jan Kvalheim and Bjorn Maaseide, from Norway defeated the Brazilian team of Roberto Lopes da Costa and Franco Jose Vieira Neto, 12-6 and 12-8, to win the championship match and a check for $20,000.00.

3rd Place: Z-Marco Ferreira de Melo and Emanuel Scheffer Rego-Bra
4th Place: Carlos Briceno and Jeff Williams-USA
5th Place: Axel Hager and Vince Ahmann
5th Place: Eduardo Esteban "Mono" Martinez and Martin Alejo Conde-Arg
Americans, Roger Clark and Bruk Vandeweghe along with Sinjin Smith and Carl Henkel finished in the seventh spot, while Chris Young and Leif Hanson picked up a thirteenth place finish.

HERMOSA BEACH, CALIFORNIA, U.S.A.
July 14th-16th, 1995

The large and boisterous crowds, at the $100,000.00 Bud Light World Beach Invitational FIVB event, in Hermosa Beach California, witnessed some of the most exciting beach volleyball ever played. The U.S.A. team of Karch Kiraly and Scott "Ack" Ayakatubby breezed their way through a long stretch of qualifying matches, only to drop out of the tournament during the quarter finals due to "Ack" experiencing back spasms. It was a all U.S.A. (and AVP) final with Mike Dodd and Mike Whitmarsh winning the tournament and first place prize of $20,000.00. In the two game championship match, they beat up on Eric Wurts and Scott Friederichsen by a score of 12-3, twice in a row. Wurts and Friederichsen had made an incredible ascent out of the qualifier, to get into the finals. During this tournament, many other AVP teams "played" in order to receive qualifying points for the 1996 Olympics. Many of the teams lost, while just going through the motions during the qualifying games. These players then rushed off to the AVP tournament at Belmar Beach in New Jersey, which was won by Brian Lewis and Bill Boullianne over Leif Hansen and Chris Young, 15-2.

3rd Place: Z-Marco Ferreira de Melo and Emanuel Scheffer Rego-Bra
4th Place: Christian Penigaud and Jean-Philippe "JP" Jodard-Fra
5th Place: Sinjin Smith and Carl Henkel-USA
5th Place: Franco Jose Vieira Neto and Roberto Costa Lopes-Bra
Additional U.S.A. finishes: Mike Schlegel and Jim Nichols 7th, Carlos Briceno and Jeff Williams along with Kiraly and Ayakatubby 9th. Also, Randy Stoklos and Bruk Vandeweghe, Lee LeGrande and Sean Fallowfield, Kevin Martin and Roger Clark, Mike Stafford and Daniel Hannemann, Brent Frohoff and Rob Heidger, Terry Stevens and Stephen Miller, Kevin Waterbury and Tony Zapata, Kevin Wong and John Anselmo.

KARCH KIRALY
During the 1995 FIVB event in Hermosa Beach, Karch Kiraly was flying-high with partner Scott Ayakatubby until "Ack" injured his back and had to retire from the competition. Above photo, Kiraly gets-up high for the jump serve.
Photo Courtesy of the FIVB

MEN'S FIVB ACTION-HERMOSA BEACH CALIFORNIA

TOP LEFT PHOTO: An "All-American" championship match hand-shake. Left-to-Right: Mike Dodd, Mike Whitmarsh, Scott Friederichsen and Eric Wurts. **TOP RIGHT PHOTO:** Mike Dodd (left:) is ready for action while his parner, Mike Whitmarsh completes a serve. Dodd and Whitmarsh won the gold medal when they defeated Scott Friederichsen and Eric Wurts in the championship match, by scores of 12-3 and 12-3. **BOTTOM PHOTO:** The "Volliseum" is ready for some beach volleyball action.

Photo's Courtesy of "Couvi"

PUSAN, KOREA
July 22nd-26th, 1995

The next $100,000.00 FIVB Men's World Series beach volleyball tournament was staged at Kwang An Ri Beach in Pusan, Korea. The championship match was an all Brazilian, dramatic three-game final. The team of Roberto Lopes da Costa and Franco Jose Vieira Neto defeated Luiz Marquez and Rogrio De Souza, 6-12, 12-10, and 12-10, to capture the title and first place check of $20,000.00.

3rd Place: Bjorn Maaseide and Jan Kvalheim-Nor
4th Place: Carl Henkel and Sinjin Smith-USA
5th Place: Carlos Frederico Galetti Loss and Dennys Paredes Gomes-Bra
5th Place: Axel "Hagar" Hager and Jorg "Vince" Ahmann-Ger
The American team of Carlos Briceno and Jeff Williams finished in a distant seventeenth.

ENOSHIMA, JAPAN
July 29th-31st, 1995

At Enoshima Japan, the $100,000.00 FIVB Men's World Series of beach volleyball tournament was won by Roberto Lopes da Costa and Franco Jose Vieira Neto, from Brazil. In the championship match, they defeated the U.S.A. team of Carl Henkel and Sinjin Smith to win the championship and a check for $20,000.00. In the rousing three game final, Lopes and Neto outlasted the Americans by scores of 11-12, 12-3, and 13-11.

3rd Place: Jan Kvalheim and Bjorn Maaseide-Nor
4th Place: Christian Penigaud and Jean-Philippe "JP" Jodard-Fra
5th Place: John Child and Mark Heese-Canada
5th Place: Julien Prosser and Lee Zahner-Aus
The American teams of Jeff Williams and Carlos Briceno along with Mark Eller and Todd Schaefer ended up in the ninth position.

LIGNANO, ITALY
August 4th-6th, 1995

The $100,000.00 FIVB Men's World Series event at Lignano, Sabbiadoro Italy, was won by the Brazilian team of Paulo Roberto "Paulao" Moreira da Costa and Luiz Antonio "lula" Barbosa da Silva. The champions earned $20,000.00 for their efforts. In the championship match, they defeated the team of Esteban Eduardo Martinez and Alejo Martin Conde, from Argentina The scores of the two game final were 12-9 and 12-3.

3rd Place: Roberto Lopes da Costa and Franco Jose Vieira Neto-Bra
4th Place: Bjorn Maaseide and Jan Kvalheim-Nor
5th Place: Sinjin Smith and Carl Henkel-USA
5th Place: Jose Z-Marco Nobrega and Emanuel Scheffer Rego-Bra
Additional U.S.A. finishers: Carlos Briceno and Jeff Williams seventh, Bruk Vandeweghe and Jeff Southcott seventeenth.

ESPINHO, PORTUGAL
August 11th-13th, 1995

At Espinho Portugal, the $100,000.00 FIVB Men's World Series event was won by Roberto Lopes da Costa and Franco Jose Vieira Neto, 12-8, 10-12, 12-7, over Jose Z-Marco Nobrega Ferreira de Melo and Emanuel Fernando Scheffer Rego, in an all Brazilian final. The winner's split first place prize of $20,000.00.

3rd Place: Javier Bosma Minguez and Sixto Jimenez-Spain
4th Place: Paulo Moreira da Costa and Luiz Barbosa da Silva-Bra
5th Place: Esteban Eduardo Martinez and Alejo Martin Conde-Arg
5th Place: Tom Englen and Fredrik "Figge" Peterson-Sweden
Additional U.S.A. finishers: Jon Stevenson and Scott Friederichsen along with Carlos Briceno and Jeff Williams in ninth, Carl Henkel and Sinjin Smith finished in the thirteenth spot while Jeff Southcott and Bruk Vandeweghe were a distant thirty-ninth.

OSTENDE, BELGIUM
August 17th-19th, 1995

Another all Brazilian final took place, in Ostende Belgium. Jose Z-Marco Nobrega Ferreira de Melo and Emanuel Fernando Scheffer Rego defeated Guilherme Luiz Marquez and Rogrio "Para" Ferreira De Souza, to win this $100,000.00 FIVB Men's World Series beach volleyball tournament. In the arousing, back-and-forth, three game championship match, Z-Marco and Rego won by scores of 10-12, 12-1, and 14-12. They earned $20,000.00 for their efforts.

3rd Place: John Child and Mark Heese-Canada
4th Place: Bjorn Maaseide and Jan Kvalheim-Nor
5th Place: Eduardo Esteban "Mono" Martinez and Martin Alejo Conde-Arg
5th Place: Roberto Lopes da Costa and Franco Jose Vieira Neto-Bra
Additional U.S.A. finishers: Jeff Southcott and Bruk Vandeweghe finished in ninth place, while Sinjin Smith and Carl Henkel along with Jeff Williams and Carl Briceno settled for thirteenth place finishes.

LA BAULE, FRANCE
August 24th-26th, 1995

At Pornichet-LaBaule France, the $200,000.00 FIVB World Series beach volleyball tournament was won by Roberto Lopes da Costa and Franco Jose Vieira Neto over Jose Z-Marco Nobrega Ferreira de Melo and Emanuel Fernando Scheffer Rego, in another all Brazilian final. Neto and Lopes earned a check for $40,000.00. In the thrilling three game championship match, the scores were 12-9, 9-12, and 14-12.

3rd Place: John Child and Mark Heese-Canada
4th Place: Carl Henkel and Sinjin Smith
5th Place: Eduardo Esteban "Mono" Martinez and Martin Alejo Conde-Arg
5th Place: Jose Javier "Javi" Muniz and Miguel Angel Martin Prieto-Spain
Additional U.S.A. finishers: Carlos Briceno and Jeff Williams were in seventh place, while Jeff Southcott and Bruk Vandeweghe were in seventeenth place.

TENERIFE, SPAIN
August 31st-September 3rd, 1995

The $100,000.00 FIVB Men's World Series event at Tenerife Spain was played in front of an excited Spanish crowd. In the thrilling three game championship match, the Spanish team of Sixto Jimenez and Javier Bosma Minguez was outlasted by Jose Z-Marco Nobrega Ferreira de Melo and Emanuel Fernando Scheffer Rego, from Brazil, The Brazilians won by scores of 10-12, 12-10, and 12-8, to earn a first place check in the amount of $20,000.00.

3rd Place: Roberto Lopes da Costa and Franco Jose Vieira Neto-Bra
4th Place: Eduardo Esteban "Mono" Martinez and Martin Alejo Conde-Arg
5th Place: Francisco Alvarez Cutio and Juan Miguel Rosell Milanes-Cuba
5th Place: Jorg "Vince" Ahmann and Axel "Hagar" Hager-Ger
Additional U.S.A. finishers: Sinjin Smith and Carl Henkel ninth, Jeff Williams and Carlos Briceno seventeenth, Bruk Vandeweghe and Jeff Southcott a distant thirty-fourth.

FORTALEZA, BRAZIL
September 14th-17th, 1995

In front of a sellout Brazilian crowd, at Fortaleza Brazil, the Brazilian team of Roberto Lopes da Costa and Franco Jose Vieira Neto, from Brazil defeated Juan Miguel Rosell Milanes and Francisco Alvarez, from Cuba, to win this 1995 FIVB Men's World Series event. In the championship match, the Brazilians won in two straight games with identical scores of 12-9, earning $20,000.00 for their efforts.

3rd Place: Rogrio Ferrirs de Souza and Guilherme Luiz Marquez-Bra
4th Place: Z-Marco Nobrega Ferreira de Melo and Emanuel Rego-Bra

5th Place: Jose Eduardo "Duda" Macedo and "Fred" Doria de Souza
5th Place: Mark Child and John Heese-Canada
Additional U.S.A. finishers: Carlos Briceno and Jeff Williams were in seventh place, while Sinjin Smith and Carl Henkel finished ninth. Tim Hovland and Canyon Ceman showed up for a twenty-fifth place finish.

BALI, INDONESIA
September 22nd-24th, 1995

Two Brazilian teams took over the finals again, at Kuta Beach Bali Indonesia. The team of Jose Z-Marco Nobrega Ferreira de Melo and Emanuel Fernando Scheffer Rego defeated Roberto Lopes da Costa and Franco Jose Vieira Neto to win this $100,000.00 FIVB Men's World Series event. In the championship match, Nobrega and Scheffer won in three games, by scores of 6-12, 12-9, and 12-6. The winners split a check in the amount of $20,000.00.
3rd Place: Adam Johnson and Kent Steffes-USA
4th Place: Sinjin Smith and Carl Henkel-USA
5th Place: Jeff Williams and Carlos Briceno-USA
5th Place: Andrea Ghiurghi and Nicola Grigolo-Italy
Bill Boulianne and Kevin Martin, also from the U.S.A. finished in thirteenth place.

CAROLINA, PUERTO RICO
November 10th-12th, 1995

The Cuban team of Juan Miguel Rosell Milanes and Francisco "Francis" Alvarez Cutio, won the $100,000.00 FIVB Men's World Series beach volleyball tournament, at Carolina Beach in Puerto Rico. In the rousing, three game Championship match, they beat the U.S.A. team of Mike Whitmarsh and Eric Fonoimoana, by scores of 12-6, 6-12, and 18-16. Milanes and Alvarez split the $20,000.00 first place purse, while Whitmarsh and Fonoimoana split $15,000.00.
3rd Place: Carl Henkel and Sinjin Smith-USA
4th Place: Luis Babosa Maia and Jose Carlos Brenha Alves-Portugal
5th Place: Eduardo "Mono" Martinez and Martin Alejo Conde-Arg
5th Place: Mark Child and John Heese-Canada
Additional U.S.A. finishers: Carlos Briceno and Bruk Vandeweghe were in ninth place, Randy Stoklos and Mike Dodd were in thirteenth place, Brian Lewis and Ricci Luyties finished in thirty-third place, Dain Blanton and Eric Wurts were in thirty-fourth.

CAPETOWN, SOUTH AFRICA
December 21st-23rd, 1995

On the beach in Capetown, South Africa, the Brazilian team of Jose Z-Marco Nobrega Ferreira de Melo and Emanuel Rego Scheffer defeated the team of Eduardo Esteban "Mono" Martinez and Martin Alejo Conde, from Argentina, 12-8 and 12-11, to win the championship match, at the $100,000.00 FIVB Men's World Series beach volleyball tournament.
3rd Place: John Child and Mark Heese-Canada
4th Place: Luiz Antonio Barbosa de Silva and Pailo Moreira da Costa-Bra
5th Place: Andrea Ghiurghi and Nicola Grigolo-Italy
5th Place: Sixto Jimenez and Javier Bosma Minguez-Spain
U.S.A. finishers: Sinjin Smith and Carl Henkel along with Matt Unger and Carlos Briceno finished in seventeenth place.

CARL HENKEL
Carl Henkel teamed-up with Sinjin Smith for some success on the 1995 FIVB Tour. They had 9 top five finnishes, including a second place finish. Above photo, Henkel challenges the block of Mike Whitmarsh, during the 1995 Hermosa Beach FIVB event.
Photo Courtesy of Frank Goroszko

SINJIN SMITH
Sinjin Smith was paired-up with Carl Henkel, on the 1995 FIVB Tour. Their best finish was a second at the 1995 Enoshima Japan FIVB event. Above photo, Smith makes a nice dig, during action at the 1995 Hermosa Beach FIVB event.
Photo Courtesy of Frank Goroszko

TOP PHOTOS: Left: Ricci Luyties gets the ball past the block of Mike Whitmarsh. **Center:** Chris Young gets down on one knee to make the pass. **Right:** Doug Foust leans-over to make the pass.

MIDDLE PHOTOS: Left: Randy Stoklos lets gravity bring him down after the block attempt. **Center:** Sinjin Smith takes a good swing at the ball. **Right:** Eduardo Esteban "Mono" Martinez, from Argentina, gets braced to make the pass.

1995 MEN'S BEACH VOLLEYBALL ACTION

BOTTOM PHOTOS: Left: Andrew Smith hits the ball away from the block of Jose Loiola. **Center:** Albert Hannemann hits the ball off the block of Scott Friederichsen. **Right:** Carl Henkel challenges the block of Mike Whitmarsh.

Photo's Courtesy of the AVP

WOMEN'S BEACH VOLLEYBALL
1995

AVP

The 1994 AVP Women's Tour was the final year of its existence. Whether the APV-WPVA split was good or bad for beach volleyball it is hard to tell, but it does not matter, the AVP announced in March, 1995 that it was not going to continue it's tour. It lasted only two seasons. In 1996 all of the best U.S. players were playing on the same WPVA tour. (Note: The AVP Women's Tour came back to life in 1999 with five events. In 2000 there was only one event, but was back up to five in 2001. By 2002, the AVP Women's Tour was a fixture, along with the men's tour with seven events. In 2003 They staged nine events. By 2004 there were twelve AVP Women's Tour events on the schedule).

WPVA

In 1995 there were 15 WPVA Tour events, worth $576,000.00. Evian expanded the indoor tour with four additional sites, including Washington DC, Boston Massachusetts, Minneapolis Minnesota, New York City.

On the WPVA 15 tournament schedule of 1995, including the WPVA "Best of the Beach II", Holly McPeak and Nancy Reno won nine tournaments out of the fifteen scheduled WPVA events. They capped the season with a 15-11 victory over Linda Hanley and Karolyn Kirby, at the $40,000.00 Bally Total Fitness National Championships, in Huntington Beach. They also had a 15-7 win over Cammy Ciarelli and Barbra Fontana at the Nationally televised finals of the Evian Best of the Beach, staged at Nawiliwili Park near Kalapaki Beach, in Lihue, Kauai, Hawaii. The win in Hawaii marked their 10th straight event title, on the WPVA Tour and in International FIVB tournament play. McPeak topped the list of 1994 money winners with $57,900.00. She was followed closely by her teammate Nancy Reno at $57,540.00.

Holly McPeak was voted the WPVA's "MVP" by the players on the tour. She also earned "Best Defensive Player" honors. Nancy Reno, the only other player to receive MVP votes, was named "Best Hitter" and "Best Blocker." The "Best Setter" award went to Karolyn Kirby for the third straight year. The "most Improved Player" went to last years "Rookie of the Year," Lisa Arce. This years "Rookie of the Year" honors went to Jenny Griffith. Liz Masakayan was honored with the WPVA's 1995 "Most Inspirational" award.

TOP 20 WPVA PLAYERS of 1995

1. Nancy Reno
1. Holly Mc Peak
3. Linda Hanley
4. Karolyn Kirby
5. Angela Rock
6. Liz Masakayan
7. Lori Forsythe
8. Gail Castro
8. Elaine Roque
10. Barbara Fontana
11. Patty Dodd
12. Deb Richardson
13. Dennie Shupryt-Knoop
14. Lisa Arce
15. Christine Schaefer
16. Cammy Ciarelli
17. Maria O'Hara
18. Ali Wood
19. Krista Blomquist
20. Karrie Poppinga

LIZ MASAKAYAN & KAROLYN KIRBY
On the 1995 WPVA Tour, Liz Masakayan and Karolyn Kirby were teamed-up again, but the tour's competition was at full strength with the addition of teams from the dissolved AVP Women's Tour. After winning 11 WPVA events in 1994, Masakayan and Kirby were only able to win 3 events in 1995. Above photo, Masakayan passes the ball to Kirby, during the 1995 Hermosa Beach WPVA event.
Photo Courtesy of Frank Goroszko

1905 WPVA TOURNAMENT FINISHES

Player	1st	2nd	3rd	4th	5th
Marie Anderson	1	0	0	0	1
Lisa Arce	0	1	3	2	1
Krista Atkinson	0	0	0	0	1
Krista Blomquist	0	0	0	0	1
Danalee Bragado	0	0	0	0	1
Jackie Campbell	0	0	0	0	1
Gail Castro	0	2	2	2	2
Cammy Ciarelli	0	1	1	2	0
Patti Dodd	0	0	2	3	1
Wendy Fletcher	0	0	0	1	2
Lori Kotas Forsythe	1	0	3	2	1
Linda Robertson Hanley	2	6	0	4	1
Janice Opalinski Harrer	0	0	0	0	1
Barbara Fontana Harris	1	1	2	0	0
Karolyn Kirby	3	2	2	2	0
Dennie Schupyt Knoop	0	1	2	1	5
Liz Masakayan	3	0	1	2	0
Holly McPeak	**8**	**5**	**1**	**0**	**0**
Marla O'Hara	0	0	1	0	2
Monique Oliver	0	0	0	0	1
Karrie Poppinga	0	0	0	1	4
Nancy Reno	**8**	**5**	**1**	**0**	**0**
Deb Richardson	0	1	2	1	4
Charlotte Roach	0	0	0	0	1
Angela Rock	2	5	2	4	1
Elaine Roque	1	2	1	1	3
Christine Schaefer	0	0	1	3	0
Gail Stammer	0	0	0	0	2
Ali Wood	0	0	1	0	1

FIVB

The 1995 FIVB women's tour included 11 stops in nine countries: Korea, Japan, Portugal, Indonesia, Australia, Puerto Rico, Brazil, Chili, and including 2 stops in the U.S.A. (Hermosa Beach CA and Clearwater, Florida). The Tour offered over a million dollars in prize money. There were nearly 200 participants from 26 countries competing on the 1995 FIVB Tour, for the 16 openings at the 1996 Atlanta Olympiad. It seemed that each country was searching for the optimum duo to compete at the Olympics. Partnerships, form almost every country, seemed to be changing at a very high rate. The most successful duo on the 1995 FIVB Tour was Holly McPeak and Nancy Reno, winning 6 events together. Reno won an additional event with Karolyn Kirby. The Brazilian team of Sandra Pires and Jackie Silva finished the season with 3 tournament championships, after reaching the finals 7 times. Linda Robertson Hanley and Barbara Fontana also won a tournament, winning the Santo Brazil event.

1995 INDIVIDUAL FIVB TOURNAMENT FINISHES

Player	1st	2nd	3rd	4th	5th
Lisa Arce	0	0	0	1	0
Beate Buhler	0	0	1	1	1
Adriana Behar Brando	0	0	0	1	2
Gail Castro	0	0	0	0	3
Natalie Cook	0	0	0	2	4
Jacqueline Louise Silva Cruz	3	4	4	0	0
Liane Fenwick	0	0	0	0	2
Lori Kotas Forsythe	0	0	1	4	2
Sachika Fujita	0	0	0	0	1
Linda Robertson Hanley	1	2	0	0	0
Barbra Fontana Harris	1	0	1	4	2
Yukikio Ishizaka	0	0	0	0	1
Karolyn Kirby	1	3	3	0	0
Dennie Schupyt Knoop	0	0	0	1	0
Magda Rejane Falco De Lima	0	0	0	1	2
Liz Masakayan	0	2	1	0	0
Holly McPeak	6	1	1	0	0
Danja Musch	0	0	1	1	1
Teruko "Peko" Nakano	0	0	0	0	1
Anita Palm	0	0	0	0	2
Kerri Ann Pottharst	0	0	0	2	4
Adriana Samuel Ramos	0	1	1	1	2
Nancy Reno	**7**	**0**	**1**	**0**	**0**
Deb Richardson	0	1	1	1	0
Angela Rock	0	3	1	1	0
Monica Rodriguez	0	1	1	1	2
Elaine Roque	0	0	0	0	2
Christine Schaefer	0	0	0	1	0
Sara Stratton	0	0	0	0	1
Yukiko Takashi	0	0	0	0	2
Sandra Pires Tavares	3	4	4	0	0
Christine Wilson	0	0	0	0	1

NANCY RENO
Nancy Reno paired-up with Holly McPeak for a successful season on the 1995 WPVA Tour. They advanced to 13 finals, winning 8 events. Reno was voted "Best-Hitter" and "Best-Blocker" by her peers on the WPVA Tour. Above photo, Reno reaches over the net to make a block during the 1995 San Diego event.

Photo Courtesy of Frank Goroszko

ANGELA ROCK
Angela Rock played well in 1995, on both the WPVA and FIVB Tours, advancing to 10 finals, winning 2 events. Above photo, Rock makes an all-out effort to dig the ball.

Photo Courtesy of Frank Goroszko

WOMEN'S TOURNAMENT RESULTS
1995-WPVA

DEERFIELD BEACH FLORIDA
April 8th-9th, 1995

The first 1995 WPVA Pro-Beach Volleyball event was next to the International Pier, at Deerfield Beach Florida. The event was the $40,000.00 "Coors Light Women's Open." In the championship match, Barbara Fontana and Lori Forsythe held on for a 15-13 win over Linda Hanley and Angela Rock.

3rd Place: Holly Mc Peak and Nancy Reno
4th Place: Cammy Ciarelli and Patti Dodd
5th Place: Marla O'Hara and Dennie Shupryt Knoop
5th Place: Monique Oliver and Gayle Stammer

AUSTIN TEXAS
April 22nd-23rd, 1995

The second outdoor WPVA Pro-Beach Volleyball event was at Lake Travis, in Austin Texas, for the $40,000.00 Austin Open. In the championship match, Holly McPeak played superb defense as she and Nancy Reno defeated Gail Castro and Elaine Roque by a score of 15-8, to collect the first place prize of $9,400.00.

3rd Place: Barbara Fontana and Lori Forsythe
4th Place: Karolyn Kirby and Liz Masakayan
5th Place: Linda Hanley and Angela Rock
5th Place: Deb Richardson and Dennie Shupryt Knoop

CAROLINA BEACH, PUERTO RICO
April 29th-30th, 1995

The WPVA Pro-Beach Volleyball Tour traveled to Carolina Beach, in San Juan Puerto Rico, to stage its third outdoor event of the season. In the championship match, Linda Hanley and Angela Rock played outstanding volleyball as they were 15-12 winners over Holly McPeak and Nancy Reno.

3rd Place: Deb Richardson and Dennie Shupryt-Knoop
4th Place: Lisa Arce and Christine Schaefer

NEW ORLEANS LOUISIANA
May 13th-14t, 1995

The following week the WPVA Pro-Beach Volleyball Tour was on Coconut Beach in New Orleans, Louisiana. In the championship match Holly McPeak and Nancy Reno played classic side-out volleyball as they defeated Linda Hanley and Angela Rock, 15-8.

3rd Place: Gail Castro and Elaine Roque
4th Place: Deb Richardson and Dennie Shupryt-Knoop

DALLAS TEXAS
May 27th-28th, 1995

The WPVA Pro-Beach Volleyball Tour was back in Texas as the next tournament was held in Dallas Texas. In an exciting championship match, Karolyn Kirby and Liz Masakayan defeated Holly McPeak and Nancy Reno, 15-13.

3rd Place: Deb Richardson and Dennie Shupryt-Knoop
4th Place: Linda Hanley and Angela Rock

NANCY RENO & HOLLY McPEAK
The team of Nancy Reno and Holly McPeak were the top team on both the WPVA and FIVB Tours, winning 8 WPVA events and 6 FIVB Women's Tour events. Above photo, Reno and McPeak disscuss their winning strategy
Photo Courtesy of the AVP

HOLLY McPEAK
In 1995, Holly McPeak, teamed with Nancy Reno for 8 WPVA Tour championships. Mcpeak was voted the WPVA's "MVP" as well as the "Best-Defensive" player by her peers. Above photo, McPeak shows the kind of defensive effort that brought her success.
Photo Courtesy of "Couvi"

SAN DIEGO CALIFORNIA
June 3rd-4th, 1995
The WPVA Pro-Beach Volleyball Tour was in California for the next two weekends. The first was held at Mariner's Point in San Diego, California. In the championship match, Holly McPeak, again played superb defense as she and Nancy Reno defeated Linda Hanley and Angela Rock, 15-10.

3rd Place: Karolyn Kirby and Liz Masakayan
4th Place: Gail Castro and Elaine Roque

HERMOSA BEACH CALIFORNIA
June 9th-11th, 1995
This weekend, the WPVA Pro-Beach Volleyball tour was on the beach for the U.S. Championship, in Hermosa Beach California. Karolyn Kirby and Liz Masakayan won the tournament. In the championship match, Kirby and Masakayan, played well to defeat Holly McPeak and Nancy Reno by a score of 15-10.

3rd Place: Barbara Fontana and Lori Forsythe
4th Place: Linda Hanley and Angela Rock
5th Place: Gail Castro and Elaine Roque
5th Place: Deb Richardson and Dennie Shupryt Knoop

GRAND HAVEN MICHIGAN
June 17th-18th, 1995
The WPVA Pro-Beach Volleyball tour went to City Beach in Grand Haven, Michigan to stage the next tournament. In the championship match, Linda Hanley and Angela Rock outplayed Holly McPeak and Nancy Reno, winning by a score of 15-6.

3rd Place: Gail Castro and Elaine Roque
4th Place: Patti Dodd and Christine Schaefer

NEWPORT RHODE ISLAND
June 30th-July 2nd, 1995
The WPVA Pro-Beach Volleyball Tour was on Easton's Beach in Newport Rhode Island, for the $50,000.00 Bally's Total Fitness "Shootout." In the championship match, Karolyn Kirby and Liz Masakayan played superior side-out volleyball as they defeated Holly McPeak and Nancy Reno 15-11.

3rd Place: Cammy Ciarelli and Lisa Arce
4th Place: Linda Hanley and Angela Rock
5th Place: Deb Richardson and Dennie Shupryt Knoop

OLD ORCHARD BEACH MAINE
July 8th-9th, 1995
On the weekend of July 8th-9th, 1995 the WPVA Pro-Beach Volleyball tour was on Old Orchard Beach in Maine. Top-seeded Holly McPeak and Nancy Reno captured their fourth event title of the season by defeating second-seeded Linda Hanley and Angela Rock in the championship finals by a score of 15-10. The $40,000.00 Coors Light Old Orchard Beach Open was played on five newly-constructed sand courts. Mc Peak and Reno split $9,400.00 along with the tournament championship

3rd Place: Patti Dodd and Christine Schaefer
4th Place: Cammy Ciarelli and Lisa Arce
5th Place: Marla O'Hara and Ali Wood
5th Place: Jackie Campbell and Charlotte Roach

KARRIE POPPINGA
Karrie Poppinga was a steady player on the 1995 WPVA Tour. She finished within the top five at five tournaments. Her best finish was a fourth place with Wendy Fletcher at the Pismo Beach event. Above photo, Poppinga concentrates to make a perfect pass.
Photo Courtesy of the AVP

GAIL CASTRO
Gail Castro provided some worthy competition on the 1995 WPVA Tour. She finished within the top five 8 times, including 2 finals, finishing second twice. Above photo, Castro, paired with Barbra Fontana, attempts to block a spike from Karolyn Kirby.
Photo Courtesy of the AVP

PISMO BEACH CALIFORNIA
July 22nd-23rd, 1995

The WPVA was back in California, on the beach in Pismo Beach California, for the $10,000.00 Coors Light Open. The second-seeded team of Marie Anderson and Elaine Roque played exceptional volleyball, in front of the Sea Venture Hotel, as they went 6-0 to capture this WPVA Pro-Beach Volleyball event. They earned a check for $2,000.00. In the championship match, they beat the first-seeded team of Deb Richardson and Dennie Shupryt-Knoop by a score of 15-10. Anderson and Roque were playing in their first WPVA event together. Eight of the WPVA Tour's top players missed this event in order to take part in the FIVB tournament at Pusan, Korea.

3rd Place: Marla O'Hara and Ali Wood
4th Place: Wendy Fletcher and Karrie Poppinga
5th Place: Kristi Atkinson and Janice Opalinski Harrer
5th Place: Krista Blomquist and Gayle Stammer

PORTLAND OREGON
August 5th-6th, 1995

On the weekend of August 5th-6th, 1995 the WPVA Pro-Beach Volleyball Tour was in Portland Oregon, for the $40,000.00 Jantzen Pro Volleyball Tournament. In the championship match, Holly McPeak and Nancy Reno were unstoppable as they defeated Linda Hanley and Karolyn Kirby 15-4. The winners earned $9,400.00 for their efforts.

3rd Place: Lisa Arce and Angela Rock
4th Place: Patti Dodd and Christine Schaefer were
5th Place: Gail Castro and Lori Kotas Forsythe
5th Place: Karrie Poppinga and Wendy Fletcher

LONG BEACH CALIFORNIA
August 11th-13th, 1995

The WPVA Pro-Beach Volleyball tour went to Long Beach, California for 125th event in the history of the WPVA. The $40,000.00 Evian Long Beach Women's Invitational was the first ever single elimination tournament for the WPVA. The top-seeded team of Holly McPeak and Nancy Reno continued to play extraordinary beach volleyball as they captured their sixth straight event win. This win netted Reno and McPeak a check for $8,200.00. In the Championship match, Reno and McPeak out-pointed the third-seeded team of Lisa Arce and Angela Rock 15-3. This marked the 35th game win for Reno and McPeak in their last 36 games, 25 straight for the 1995 season.

3rd Place: Gail Castro and Lori Forsythe
4th Place: Linda Hanley and Karolyn Kirby
5th Place: Elaine Roque and Marie Anderson
5th Place: Wendy Fletcher and Karrie Poppinga

DENNIE SCHUPYT-KNOOP & DEB RICHARDSON
Dennie Schupyt-Knoop and Deb Richardson paired-up for some success on the 1995 WPVA Tour. They finished within the top five 8 times. Above photo, Knoop hits a set from Richardson, past the block of Nancy Reno, towards the defense of Holly McPeak.
Photo Courtesy of the AVP

BARBRA FONTANA & LORI FORSYTHE KOTAS
Barbra Fontana and Lori Forsythe Kotas teamed-up for some success on the 1995 WPVA Tour, including a championship victory at the Deerfield Beach Florida event. Above photo, Fontana is down low after the play, while Kotas looks on.
Photo Courtesy of the AVP

HUNTINGTON BEACH CALIFORNIA
August 18th-20th, 1995

Huntington Beach, California, was the site for the next WPVA event, the $40,000.00 Bally Total Fitness Nationals. Top-seeded Holly McPeak and Nancy Reno won the tournament and collected the first place prize of $9,400.00, for their efforts. In the championship match, McPeak and Reno used a four-point spurt at the end of the match to capture their first "major" domestic title. They used the point spurt to break an 11-11 tie and defeated the second-seeded team of Linda Hanley and Karolyn Kirby, 15-11. This match was tied on eight separate occasions, during the live telecast on CBS. This win was the 28th consecutive for McPeak and Reno.

3rd Place: Lisa Arce and Patti Dodd
4th Place: Angela Rock and Liz Masakayan
5th Place: Elaine Roque and Dennie Shupryt-Knoop
5th Place: Karrie Poppinga and Deb Richardson

LIHUE KAUAI HAWAII
September 21st-23rd, 1995

In front of the Kauai Marriott, in Lihue Kauai Hawaii, was the site for the WPVA $40,000.00 "Best of the Beach II". Top-seeded Holly McPeak and Nancy Reno played well through the entire tournament. In the championship match, of the final WPVA event of the season, they defeated sixth seeded Barbra Fontana and Cammy Ciarelli 15-7, to earn the $10,000.00 prize. Reno and McPeak parted ways after this tournament, even though they had won 10 titles in a row. Reno wanted to pair-up with Karolyn Kirby.

3rd Place: Angela Rock and Karolyn Kirby
4th Place: Gail Castro and Lori Forsythe
5th Place: Danalee Bragado and Karrie Poppinga
5th Place: Lisa Arce and Patty Dodd

1995 WOMEN'S BEACH VOLLEYBALL ACTION

Top Right Photo: Linda Hanley played well enough to win 3 WPVA events in 1995. Above photo, Hanley reacting to the play. **Bottom Left Photo:** In 1995, Lisa Arce finished within the top five 7 times, including a second place finish at the Long Beach CA event with Angela Rock. Above photo Arce attacking the block of Liz Masakayan. **Bottom Right Photo:** Marie Anderson stepped-up for a championship victory at the 1995 WPVA event in Pismo Beach California, Above photo. Anderson rejects a hit by Tiffany Anderson.

Photo's Courtesy of "Couvi"

WOMEN'S TOURNAMENT RESULTS
1995-FIVB

LA SERENA, CHILE
February 9th-12th, 1995

In La Serena Chile, the Women's $50,000.00 FIVB beach volleyball tournament was won by the Brazilian team of Jacqueline Louise Silva Cruz and Sandra Pires Tavares. In the sensational, three game championship match, they defeated Americans Karolyn Kirby and Deb Richardson, by scores of 12-7, 9-12, and 13-11. Silva and Pires won $11,000.00 for their efforts.

3rd Place: Barbra Fontana and Lori Kotas Forsythe=USA
4th Place: Lisa Arce and Christine Schaefer-USA
5th Place: Elaine Roque and Gail Castro-USA
5th Place: Kerri-Ann Pottharst and Natalie Cook-Aus
Additional U.S.A. finishers: Krista Blomquist and Marla O'Hara twenty-fifth, Ali Wood and Krissy Middler twenty-eighth.

RIO DE JANEIRO, BRAZIL
March 2nd-5th, 1995

The stadium on Copacabana Beach, in Rio de Janeiro, Brazil was jumping with excitement, for the $50,000.00 FIVB Women's Pro-Beach Volleyball final. The championship match was an all Brazilian affair. The team of Jackie Silva and Sandra Pires defeated Monica Rodriguez and Adriana Ramos Samuel, to take the championship and first place prize of $22,000.00, by scores of 12-6 and 12-9.

3rd Place: Karolyn Kirby and Deb Richardson-USA
4th Place: Adriana Brando Magda Behar and Adriana Falcao Lima-Bra
5th Place: Gail Castro and Elaine Roque-USA
5th Place: Barbra Fontanas and Lori Kotas Forsythe-USA

CLEARWATER, FLORIDA, U.S.A.
May 5th-7th, 1995

The beach at Clearwater, Florida, U.S.A., was the site for the $50,000.00 FIVB Women's beach volleyball tournament. The Brazilian team of Jackie Silva and Sandra Pires snatched the championship with a victory over the U.S.A. team of Karolyn Kirby and Liz Masakayan, in the finals. The final scores were 12-3 and 12-8. The Brazilians shared $10,000.00 for their winning effort.

3rd Place: Nancy Reno and Holly McPeak-USA
4th Place: Barbra Fontana and Lori Kotas Forsythe-USA
5th Place: Kerri-Ann Pottharst and Natalie Cook-Aus
5th Place: Magda Falco De Lima and Adriana Behar Brandao-Bra
Additional U.S.A. finishers: Elaine Roque and Gail Castro along with Lisa Arce and Christine Schaefer in ninth place, Angela Rock and Gayle Stammer along with Linda Hanley and Monique Oliver in twenty-fifth place, Wendy Fletcher and Krista Blomquist in twenty-seventh place, Danalee Bragado and Marie Andersson twenty-eighth place.

SANDRA PIRES
Brazilian Sandra Pires Tavares teamed-up with compatriot Jackie Silva for some success on the 1995 FIVB Women's Tour. They advanced to 7 finals, winning 3 times. Above photo Pires reaches above the net for a block attempt.
Photo Courtesy of Frank Goroszko

NANCY RENO
Nancy Reno was the top player on the 1995 FIVB Women's Tour. She advanced to 7 championship matches, winning all 7 times. She won 6 events with Holly McPeak and 1 event with Karolyn Kirby. Above photo, Reno attacks a jump serve.
Photo Courtesy of the AVP

HERMOSA BEACH, CALIFORNIA, U.S.A.
July 11th-16th, 1995

The U.S.A. team of Holly McPeak and Nancy Reno moved up to win the $50,000.00 Bud Light World Beach Invitational FIVB women's beach volleyball "World Series" event at Hermosa Beach California, U.S.A. In the championship match, McPeak and Reno defeated the Brazilian team of Sandra Pires and Jackie Silva, 12-4 and 12-9. The winner's shared a check for $10,000.00.

3rd Place: Karolyn Kirby and Liz Masakayan-USA
4th Place: Deb Richardson and Dennie Shupryt-Knoop-USA
5th Place: Barbra Fontana and Lori Kotas Forsythe-USA
5th Place: Monica Rodriguez and Adriana Brandao Samuel-Bra

Additional U.S.A. finishers: Angela Rock and Linda Hanley along with Lisa Arce and Christine Schaefer in 9th place. Elaine Roque and Gail Castro in 25th place. Gayle Stammer and Wendy Fletcher, Krista Blomquist and Karrie Poppinga, Atkinson and Gathright, along with Keller and Griffith, all finished in the 27th position. Janice Harrer and Danalee Bragado along with Andersson and Nelson finished in the 35th spot.

PUSAN, KOREA
July 20th-22nd, 1995

There was an all U.S.A. final in the $50,000.00 FIVB World Series women's beach volleyball final on Xwang An Ri Beach, in Pusan Korea. In the All-American final, the team of Nancy Reno and Holly McPeak defeated Karolyn Kirby and Liz Masakayan, to win the championship match by scores of 12-11 and 12-9. They earned a $10,000.00 check for their efforts.

3rd Place: Jackie Silva and Sandra Pires-Bra
4th Place: Monica Rodriguez and Adriana Brandao Samuel-Bra
5th Place: Angela Rock and Gail Castro-USA
5th Place: Adriana Brandao Behar and Adriana Falcao Lima-Bra

The USA team of Lori Kotas Forsythe and Barbra Fontana ended up in 9th.

OSAKA, JAPAN
July 27th-29th, 1995

Another all U.S.A. final took place at Osaka, Japan, at the $50,000.00 FIVB World Series of women's beach volleyball tournament. Nancy Reno and Holly McPeak defeated Angela Rock and Linda Hanley, by scores of 12-10 and 12-7, to win the championship match. The winners earned $10,000.00.

3rd Place: Jackie Silva and Sandra Pires-Bra
4th Place: Lori Kotas Forsythe and Barbra Fontana-USA
5th Place: Beate Buhler and Danja Musch-Ger
5th Place: Christine Wilson and Sara Stratton-Aus

The U.S.A. team of Liz Masakayan and Karolyn Kirby finished in seventh place.

ESPINHO, PORTUGAL
August 25th-27, 1995

The $50,000.00 FIVB Women's World Series volleyball event, in Espinho Portugal was another all U.S.A. final. This was the third consecutive FIVB tournament in a row that two American teams made it to the championship match. Nancy Reno and Holly McPeak defeated Angela Rock and Linda Hanley, in a three game final. In the championship match, they scored a 6-12, 12-8, and 12-10 victory, to earn the top prize of $10,000.00.

3rd Place: Jackie Silva and Sandra Pires-Bra
4th Place: Natalie "Nat" Cook and Kerri Ann Pottharst-Aus
5th Place: Yukiko Takahashi and Sachiko Fujita-Japan
5th Place: Anita Palm and Liane Fenwick-Aus

The U.S.A. teams of Karolyn Kirby and Liz Masakayan along with Lori Kotas Forsythe and Barbra Fontana finished in seventeenth place. During the early rounds, Masakayan, already recovering from major knee surgery, broke the patella (kneecap) on her right knee.

JACKIE SILVA & SANDRA PIRES
Brazilians, Jackie Silva and Sandra Pires advanced to championship match of the 1995 FIVB Women's event that was staged in the "Volliseum" on the sands of Hermosa Beach CA. Above photo Silva (left) chases-down the ball for partner Pires.
Photo Courtesy of "Couvi"

HOLLY McPEAK
Holly McPeak teamed-up with Nancy Reno to advance to 6 finals on the 1995 FIVB Women's Tour, winning all 6 events, including the "World-Series" event in Hermosa Beach CA. Above photo, McPeak is ready to serve the ball in the "Volliseum" in Hermosa.
Photo Courtesy of "Couvi"

BALI, INDONESIA
September 15th-17th, 1995

The American team of Holly McPeak and Nancy Reno won their fourth consecutive $50,000,000 FIVB World Series tournament on Kuta Beach, Bali, Indonesia. McPeak and Reno defeated the Brazilian team of Sandra Pires and Jackie Silva, 12-5 and 12-7, to win the championship match and the $10,000.00 first place check.

3rd Place: Karolyn Kirby and Angela Rock-USA
4th Place: Lori Kotas Forsythe and Barbra Fontana-USA
5th Place: Linda Hanley and Deb Richardson Additional U.S.A. finishers: Gail Castro and Marla O'Hara along with Janice Harrer and Deiters in twenty-fifth place.

BRISBANE, AUSTRALIA
October 6th-8th, 1995

In Brisbane Australia, the U.S.A. team of Holly McPeak and Nancy Reno made it five consecutive $50,000.00 FIVB World Series women's beach volleyball tournament wins. In the championship match, they defeated Jackie Silva and Sandra Pires, from Brazil, 12-10 and 12-8, The winners split the $10,000.00 purse.

3rd Place: Danja Muesch and Beate Buehler-Ger
4th Place: Barbra Fontana-Harris and Lori Kotas Forsythe-USA
5th Place: Anita Palm and Liane Fenwick-Aus
5th Place: Natalie "Nat" Cook and Kerri Ann Pottharst-Aus
Other U.S.A. finishes: Angela Rock and Karolyn Kirby in seventh place. Gail Castro and Marla O'Hara along with Desire Leipham and Kathy Luciano in twenty-fifth place.

CAROLINA, PUERTO RICO
November 9th-11th, 1995

The U.S.A. team of Nancy Reno and Holly McPeak terminated their partnership prior to the $50,000.00 FIVB women's beach volleyball tournament on Carolina Beach in Puerto Rico. This break-up nullified their chance to win a sixth consecutive 1995 FIVB tournament together. Reno did win her sixth in a row with new partner Karolyn Kirby. They defeated the Brazilian team of Jackie Silva and Sandra Pires to win the championship match, by scores of 12-4 and 12-8. Kirby and Reno split the $10,000.00 purse.

3rd Place: Monica Rodriguez and Adriana Brandao Samuel-Bra
4th Place: Danja Muesch and Beate Buehler-Ger
5th Place: Natalie Cook and Kerri Ann Pottharst-Aus
5th Place: Teruko "Peko" Nakano and Yukikio Ishizaka-Japan
Additional U.S.A. finishes: Deb Richardson and Linda Hanley in seventh, Angela Rock and Holly McPeak in ninth, Lori Kotas Forsythe and Barbra Fontana Harris in seventeenth, Christine Schaefer and Karrie Poppinga along with Gail Castro and Lisa Arce in twenty-fifth place.

SANTOS, BRAZIL
November 16th-19th, 1995

The $50,000.00 FIVB women's beach volleyball tournament, at Santos Brazil, saw Nancy Reno's winning streak end at six. In the championship match, Americans Linda Hanley and Barbra Fontana defeated another U.S.A. team, Holly McPeak and Angela Rock, by scores of 12-4 and 12-7. This was the first tournament together for Hanley and Fontana. Hanley and Fontana won $10,000.00.

3rd Place: Jackie Silva and Sandra Pires-Bra
4th Place: Natalie Cook and Kerri-Ann Pottharst-Aus
5th Place: Sachiko Fujita and Yukiko Takahashi-Japan
5th Place: Monica Rodriguez and Adriana Brandao Samuel-Bra
Additional U.S.A. finishers: Ali Wood and Marla O'Hara along with Kathy Luciano and Rhonda Kottke were in a distant 31st place.

ADRIANA BEHAR
Brazilian Adriana Behar began to show some promise on the 1995 FIVB Women's Tour. Behar "broke-in" to the top five at 3 FIVB Women's events in 1995. Above photo, Behar gets ready to serve the ball.
Photo Courtesy of the FIVB

BEATE BUHLER & DANJA MUSCH
The German Team of Beate Buhler and Danja Musch provided some competition on the 1995 FIVB Women's Tour. Above photo, Buhler tries to poke a set from Musch past the huge block of Nancy Reno.
Photo Courtesy of "Couvi"

TOP PHOTOS: Left: Krista Bloomquist reaches high to make the shot. **Center:** Ali Wood braces herself for the dig. **Right:** Gail Castro gets-up to spike the ball.

  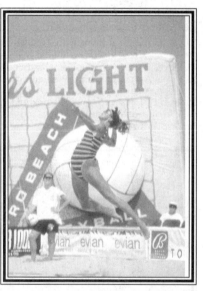

MIDDLE PHOTOS: Left: Gayle Stammer attacking the ball. **Center:** Marla O'Hara gets down in the sand to pass the ball. **Right:** Christine Schaefer gets-up high for the jump serve.

1995 WOMEN'S BEACH VOLLEYBALL ACTION

BOTTOM PHOTOS: Left: Cammy Ciarelli gets above the net to make the shot. **Center:** LeAnn Schuster McSorely concentrates while passing the ball. **Right:** Janice Opalinski Harrer gets ready to pass the ball.

Photo's Courtesy of the AVP

ADDITIONAL VOLLEYBALL INFORMATION
1995

CALIFORNIA
In addition to the players on the 1995 pro-beach volleyball tour's there were nearly 1,500 - "AAA", "AA", "A", "B", "Unrated", and "Novice" rated male and female players on the CBVA Sand Tour.

MANHATTAN BEACH CALIFORNIA
September 2nd-3rd, 1995

The 1995 CBVA U.S. Open Beach Championships were won by Dan Castillo and Leland Quinn. In the championship final, they defeated Todd Rogers and Dax Holdren in a double final, losing 5-15 and then winning the exciting double final by the score of 15-13. The victory, which also earned Castillo and Quinn the California Beach Volleyball Association title, was the pair's fourth open win in four years. As the third seed, they went undefeated in the double elimination tournament, defeating Rogers and Holdren 15-11 in the winners' bracket final. Rogers and Holdren defeated Greg Shankle and Cameron Green in the loser's bracket final for a rematch with Castillo and Quinn. Rogers and Holdren pushed the match to the double final with their 15-5 win over the champions. It was the only game loss in four tournaments for Quinn and Castillo. Castillo and Quinn started out fast in the second game and at 13-9 it looked like they had the title. But Rogers and Holdren chipped away, tying the match at 13-13. Then the 6'-8" Quinn blasted an ace for a 14-13 lead and then blocked Holdren for match point. This was a non-AVP event.

In the women's division WPVA veterans, Heather Hafner and Evelyn Conley were the winners. In the championship match, they defeated Caroline McDonald and Deanna Johnson by a score of 15-8, earning both the California and U.S. National title.

LAGUNA BEACH CALIFORNIA
1995

The 1995 Laguna Beach Men's Open was an amateur "AAA" tournament. Dan Castillo and Leland Quinn were the winners. In the championship match, they defeated Chad Jones and Brent Doble.
3rd Place: Todd Ahmadi and Stacie Lougeay
4th Place: Richard Bolt and Kenny Lentin

PLAYA DEL REY CALIFORNIA
April 1st-2nd, 1995

The 1995 Bud Light Spring Festival Women's Open was won by Beth Meade and Carla Kerker. In the championship final, they defeated Darlene Hurd and Jan Kyle. This tournament was not a WPVA event.
3rd Place: Karen Barber and Roxanne McMiller

SAN DIEGO CALIFORNIA
June 3rd, 1995

The 1995 San Diego-Ocean Beach Jose Cuervo Men's Open was won by Chad Jones and George Carey Jr. In the championship match, they defeated Brian Passman and Mark Jones Tournament director George Stepanof said that there were 32 teams that participated in the event and that during the finals there was a crowd of about 2,000 spectators watching the match.
3rd Place: Dismas Abelman and Nick Pabarcus
3rd Place: Tone Pekich and John Braunstein

SAN DIEGO CALIFORNIA
June 4th, 1995

The 1995 Ocean Beach Mixed-Open was won by Eric Holman and Caron Janc. In the championship match, they defeated Jim Nichols and Michelle Kobhshi. Tournament director George Stepanof said that even though there were only 12 teams entered the tournament there was a crowd of about 17,000 that watched or walked by during the event.
3rd Place: Todd Ahmddi and Suzanne Hitt

SAN DIEGO CALIFORNIA
June 8th, 1995

The 1995 Mission Beach Mixed-Open was won by Sean Burke and Sheri Powers. In the championship match, they defeated Brian Passman and Margo Malowney. Tournament director George Stepanof said that even though there were only six teams entered the tournament there was a crowd of about 8,200 that watched or walked by during the event.

DAN CASTILLO
Dan Castillo teamed-up with LeLand Quinn to win the 1995 CBVA U.S. Beach Championships. Above photo, Castillo gets down low to make the pass.
Photo Courtesy of Tim Andexler

MANHATTAN BEACH CALIFORNIA
September 2nd-3rd, 1995

The 1995 CBVA U.S. Women's Beach Championships were won by Heather Hafner and Evelyn Conley. These WPVA veterans defeated Caroline McDonald and Deanna Johnson, 15-8, for both the US National and California State title. It was the first tournament title ever for Hafner, 33, who, at the time, had been playing beach volleyball for 20 years. In the last 10 years, on the Pro-Beach Volleyball Tour, she had great finishes within the top five, but never quite broken through to win a tournament. The title was doubly important for the right-handed Hafner because she was playing with a shoulder injury that forced her to retire from the WPVA tour and learn to play left handed.

FLORIDA

The 1995 Florida State Championships were won by James Fellows and Matt Winterburn. In the championship final, they defeated Tony Cothron and Arthur Brown.

3rd Place: Henry Russell and Burke Stefko
4th Place: Ronnie Jenkins and Jimmy Overton

FORT LAUDERDALE FLORIDA

California AVP pros Jim Nichols and Mike Schlegel rallied from a 14-9 deficit to defeat Ronnie Jenkins and Jimmy Overton of Florida, 17-15, in the final of the men's division at the Jose Cuervo National Beach Volleyball Championship in Fort Lauderdale Florida. They Split $6,000.00 for their efforts. Nichols and Schlegel fought-off nine match-points before they were able to tie the score at 15. They then won the match when Schlegel blocked Overton at championship point. Dave Smith and Aaron Smith finished in third place.

In the women's division, Wendy Stammer and Lisa Westlake, both from Oregon, defeated Californian's Jennifer Wrightson and Beth Engman, 15-8. The winners split the $6,000.00 first place purse.

AROUND THE U.S.A.

Team Sony Autosound defeated Team Sideout for the championship of the "Bud-Light 4-Man tour. In the women's division Team Sony Autosound beat Team Nike for the championship.

TOP 4-MAN - WOMAN PLAYERS 1995

MEN	WOMEN
Craig Buck	Gabrielle Reece
Steve Salmons	Stephanie Cox
Doug Partie	Kim Oden
Dan Hanan	Wendy Stammer
Eric Sato	Alyson Randick
Roger Clark	Annett Buckner
Dan Greenbaum	Liane Sato
Matt Lyles	Missy Kurt

HOLYOKE MASSACHUSETTS

After the first 100 years, since it's 1895 invention in the United States, by William G. Morgan, the sport of volleyball had finally achieved the type of popularity in the United States that it had received on a global basis. 1995 was the 100 year anniversary of volleyball and volleyball ranked behind only soccer among participation sports. Today there are more than 46 million Americans who play the game of volleyball. There are 800 million players worldwide who play volleyball at least once a week.

The 1995 "Spectacular Volleyball Centennial" year began in Western Massachusetts, where the game of volleyball began 100 years ago. The Volleyball Hall of Fame (VBHF), was the hosts, as they staged an outstanding series of events commencing with Volley "Ball" party at City Hall Auditorium in January. Other action included, sellout crowds at the annual Hall of Fame Indoor Volleyball Classic, featuring Penn State, Ball State, UCLA, and Springfield College. The "Men's NCAA Collegiate Championship" in early May; a record setting 297 teams at the U.S. Open Volleyball Championships, held at the Westover Air Reserve Base, in late May; and first annual Mayor's Challange Cup, and celebrate Holyoke Sand Tournament held during "Celebrate Holyoke Festival" in August. Holyoke College hosted the NCAA Division III Women's Tournament. NCAA Division I Women's Volleyball Championship was contested at University of Massachusetts in December with the AVCA Coaches Convention held in Springfield.

VBHF enshrined Debbie Green, "Bob" Miller, Robert Lindsey, Arie Selinger, and honors Special Olympics International, with "VBHF Court of Honor Award." Spalding Sports Worldwide was honored with the "Morgan Award," during the October 20, 1995 Volleyball Hall of Fame induction ceremonies. Also during this weekend, plaque ceremonies take place to commemorate site of original YMCA, and Reebok Gold Medal Clinic takes place at University of Massachusetts.

VBHF planning committee developed plans for a new, two building, interactive Volleyball Hall of Fame Complex for next century of volleyball.

AROUND THE WORLD

The 1995 World Cup of Volleyball men's division champion was won by Italy for the first time. In the women's division, Cuba won it for the third time in a row.

MIXED-DOUBLES RESULTS

MANHATTAN BEACH CALIFORNIA
August 12th, 1995

The 1995 Marine Street Mixed-Doubles Open was won by the team of Mark Knudsen and Chris Starczak. In the championship final, they defeated Butch Miali and Kerry House. Tournament director Mike Cook noted that the weather was warm and sunny for this tournament with 13 teams entered.

3rd Place: Dave Gallenson and Donna Janulitis
3rd Place: Sean Keefe and Barbara Belding
5th Place: Jeff West and Debbie Black
5th Place: Cody Cowell and Christina Gage

MEN'S BEACH VOLLEYBALL
1996

The big news in beach volleyball for 1996 was the staging of the sports first inclusion in the Olympics.

In 1996, there were forty-one recorded "Pro" Beach Volleyball tournaments. Twenty-seven of these tournaments were staged on U.S.A soil, while fourteen were played outside of the U.S.A. Of the twenty-seven U.S.A. tournaments, California hosted six events. There were twenty-one U.S. events staged in seventeen states/regions other than California. The California tournaments were held in Santa Cruz, San Francisco, Manhattan Beach, Hermosa Beach (twice: AVP & FIVB), and San Diego. Florida hosted three tournaments in Fort Myers, Clearwater, and Rivera Beach. The remaining U.S. tournaments were held in: Fairfax Virginia (indoor), New York City (indoor), Phoenix Arizona, Boulder Colorado, Belmar New Jersey, Milwaukee Wisconsin, Baltimore Maryland (Olympic Trials), Atlanta Georgia (twice: AVP & FIVB/Olympics), Orchard Beach Maine, Austin Texas, Chicago Illinois, Minneapolis Minnesota, and Carolina Beach Puerto Rico (FIVB). The fourteen events held outside of the U.S.A. were hosted by:

1. Copacabana Beach, in Rio de Janeiro, Brazil
2. "El Fuerte" Marbella Spain
3. Joao Pessoa, Brazil
4. Damlatas Kleopatra International Blue Flag Beach, in Alanya Turkey
5. "Golfe du Lion" shore, at the "Plages du Prado" in Marseille France
6. On the "Platz an der Jannowitzbruske," close to the world famous "Brandeburg" door and to the German "Reichstag" in downtown Berlin
7. Pornichet, France
8. Espinho Portugal, on Baia Beach
9. Grote Shand Beach, at Ostend Belgium
10. Lignano Italy
11. On Las Teresitas Beach in Tenerife, Canary Islands, Spain
12. Outdoor Beach Volley Center, within the city of Jakarta in Indonesia
13. Fortaleza, Brazil
14. Durban, South Africa

1996 - "PRO" BEACH VOLLEYBALL ACTION - HERMOSA BEACH CALIFORNIA
In 1996, there were forty-one recorded "Pro" Beach Volleyball tournaments. Twenty-seven of these tournaments were staged on U.S. soil, while fourteen were played outside of the U.S.A. Above photo, Karch Kiraly hits a set from Kent Steffes, over the block of Mike Whitmarsh, towards the defense of Mike Dodd. Action took place at the 1996 "Miller-Lite" U.S. Championship in Hermosa Beach, CA.
Photo Courtesy of Frank Goroszko

Karch Kiraly and Kent Steffes took the top spot on the 1996 AVP tour as they won thirteen tournament championships together. They had three wins in Florida at Rivera Beach, Clearwater Beach, and Fort Myers. They also had wins at: Fairfax Virginia (indoor), Indianapolis Indiana, Cleveland Ohio, Belmar New Jersey, Boulder Colorado, Atlanta Georgia (twice: AVP & Olympics), Austin Texas, Hermosa and Manhattan Beach California. Kiraly also won the "King of the Beach" tournament in Las Vegas Nevada. Jose Loiola and Adam Johnson were the second highest winning team in 1996 with seven tournament championships. Their wins came in: New York City (indoor), Phoenix Arizona, Minneapolis Minnesota, Orchard Beach Maine, Milwaukee Wisconsin, Chicago Illinois, and in California at Santa Cruz.

Additional AVP teams that won in 1996: Mike Dodd and Mike Whitmarsh won four tournaments together. They won in San Francisco California, Espinho Portugal on Baia Beach, Fortaleza Brazil, and the Olympic Trials in Baltimore Maryland. Scott Ayakatubby and Brian Lewis won two tournaments together. They won at: Grand Haven Michigan and San Diego California.

Again in 1996, the FIVB World Tour was dominated by teams from Brazil. Brazilian teams won ten of the seventeen FIVB events. The top team on the FIVB World Tour in 1996 was the Brazilian team of Z-Marco Nobrega Ferreira de Melo and Emanuel Fernando Scheffer Rego. They won five FIVB World Series events. They won at Pornichet France, on Las Teresitas Beach in Tenerife Canary Islands Spain, "El Fuerte" Beach in Marbella Spain, Ligano Italy, and Isla Verde's Carolina Beach in Puerto Rico.

The Brazilian team Franco Jose Vieira Neto and Roberto Costa Lopes. won three FIVB World Series events in 1996. They won at: Copacabana Beach in Rio de Janeiro Brazil, on the "Golfe du Lion shore at the "Plages du Prado" in Marseille France, and at the outdoor volley center in the city of Jakarta in Indonesia. Additional winners on the FIVB Tour: The Brazilian team of Luiz Antonio "Lula" Barbosa da Silva and Paulo Roberto "Paulao" Moreira da Costa won the FIVB event at Joao Pessoa Brazil. Jan Kvalheim and Bjorn Maaseide, from Norway won the FIVB event in Hermosa Beach California. The Cuban team of Juan Miguel Rosell Milanes and Francisco "Francis" Alvarez Cutio won the FIVB event at Carolina Beach in Puerto Rico. As mentioned before, Mike Dodd and Mike Whitmarsh won the FIVB event in Hermosa Beach California. The Argentine team of Eduardo Esteban "Mono" Martinez and Martin Alejo Conde won at Damlatas Kleopatra International Blue Flag Beach, in Alanya Turkey. The Canadian team of John Child and Mark Heese won on the "Platz an der Jannowitzbruske," close to the world famous "Brandeburg" door and to the German "Reichstag" in downtown Berlin. The U.S.A. Team of Mike Whitmarsh and Mike Dodd won two FIVB events first on Baia Beach in Espinho Portugal, and then at at Fortaleza, Brazil. The FIVB event at Grote Shand Beach, at Ostend Belgium was won by Rogerio Dias de Assis Lopes and Mario Luiz Rodrigues Schmidt Nogueira from Portugal. The FIVB event that took place on the beautiful coastline of Durban, South Africa was won by the Brazilian team of Ferreira De Souza Para' and Guilherme Luiz Marquez. The 1996 Olympic Beach Volleyball event, in Atlanta Georgia, was won by the U.S.A. team of Karch Kiraly and Kent Steffes.

KARCH KIRALY
In 1996, Karch Kiraly paired-up with Kent Steffes to win 13 events, including the "Gold-Medal" at the Atlanta Olympics. Kiraly also was the winner of the 1996 King of the Beach event, staged in Las Vegas, NV. Above photo, Kiraly makes a perfect pass.
Photo Courtesy of Tim Andexler

KENT STEFFES
Kent Steffes teamed-up with Karch Kiraly on the 1996 AVP Tour. They advanced to 16 finals winning 12 times. They also won an Olympic "Gold-Medal" in Atlanta GA. Above photo, Steffes grovels in the sand to make the dig.
Photo Courtesy of the AVP

AVP

The 1996 AVP season started "Under New Management." The new Chief Executive Officer was Jerry Solomon, Senior Vice President of Tour Operations was Jon Stevenson, and The Chief Operating Officer was Lon Monk.

With the greatest, most notable season of changes in the history of beach volleyball. The big intention was to distribute tournaments out to private promoters. In the past the AVP had tried to promote all of the tournaments from their office in Los Angeles California, regardless of the location that the tournament was to take place in. The AVP decided to put geographically desirable tournaments in the hands of promoters that could promote them year-round. Five such tournaments in 1996 and ten tournaments in 1997. And hopefully more in the future. The new AVP boss, Jerry Solomon came up with this strategy to localize fan support, increase prize money and move the AVP out of a two-year "decline" and back into America's fastest growing sport. This concept was not new to sports, Golf and Tennis have been doing this, with great success, for years.

An additional change that Solomon made for the 1996 season, much to the disappointment of most fans, was to break-up the Prime Ticket TV announcing team of Chris Marlowe and Paul Sunderland. The team was missed by everyone that followed the beach volleyball telecast. Marlowe and Sunderland were the Saenz and Holtzman, Holtzman and Selznick, Selznick and Lang, O'Hara and Bright, Von Hagen and Lang, Menges and Lee, Obradovich and Hooper, Smith and Stoklos, Hovland and Dodd, Kiraly and Steffes of beach volleyball, "broadcasting." Marlowe was replaced by Tim Hovland, well-established on the volleyball court, but not ready for the "prime-time" of beach volleyball on TV.

Karch Kiraly and Kent Steffes proved to be the "Cream of the Crop" in 1996. They advanced to 16 AVP championship matches, winning 12 titles. Kiraly added the "King of the Beach" to his list, giving him the top spot, with 13 event titles in 1996. Adam Johnson and Jose Loiola were the next best team of 1996, advancing to the finals on 14 occasions, winning 7 times.

TOP TEN ALL-TIME CAREER OPEN WINNERS

At the end of the **1996** beach volleyball season, the top ten all-time career open beach volleyball tournament winners were:

1.	Sinjin Smith	139
2.	Karch Kiraly	122
3.	Randy Stoklos	122
4.	Kent Steffes	88
5.	Mike Dodd	71
6.	Ron Von Hagen	62
7.	Tim Hovland	60
8.	Jim Menges	43
9.	Ron Lang	41
10.	Gene Selznick	27
10.	Greg Lee	27

1996 U.S.A. AVP PRO-BEACH MEN PLAYERS

Scott Ayakatubby	Lance Lyons
Eduardo Anjinho Bacil	Kevin Martin
Dain Blanton	Mike Mattarocci
Bill Boullianne	Doug Mauro
Eric Boyles	Dana McFarland
John Brajevic	Owen McKibbin
Daniel Cardenas	Larry Mear
George Carey	Craig Moothart
Canyon Ceman	Curt Moothart
Robert Chavez	Jim Nichols
Roger Clark	Steve O'Bradovich
Kevin Cleary	Justin Perlstrom
Mike Dodd	Pat Powers
Chuck Donlon	Jeff Rodgers
Marcelo Duarte	Dave Rottman
Rudy Dvorak	Todd Schaefer
Mark Eller	Mike Schlegel
Sean Fallowfield	Wayne Seligson
Eric Fonoimoana	Dane Selznick
Doug Foust	Andrew smith
Craig Freeburg	Sinjin Smith
Scott Friedrichsen	Matt Sonnichsen
Brent Frohoff	Jeff Southcott
Brian Gatzke	Mike Stafford
Brett Gonnerman	Kent Steffes
Wally Goodrick	Jon Stevenson
John Hanley	Randy Stoklos
Albert Hannemann	Bill Suwara
Chris Hannemann	Dave Swatick
Leif Hanson	Troy Tanner
Rob Heidger	Steve Timmons
Carl henke	Matt Unger
Tim Hovland	Bruk Vandeweghe
Al Janc	Dan Vrebalovich
Adam Johnson	Tim Walmer
Karch Kiraly	Kevin Waterbury
Mark Kerins	Wes Welch
Lee LeGrande	Mike Whitmarsh
Brian Lewis	Eric Wurts
Jose Loiola	Chris Young
Ricci Luyties	Tony Zapata

INDIVIDUAL AVP TOURNAMENT FINISHES
1996

Player	1st	2nd	3rd	4th	5th
Scott Ayakatubby	2	2	7	4	3
Eduardo Bacil	0	1	0	1	4
Dain Blanton	0	1	2	1	4
Bill Boullianne	0	0	3	4	4
Canyon Ceman	0	1	0	1	4
Ian Clark	0	0	0	0	5
Mike Dodd	1	6	4	1	5
Brent Frohoff	0	0	1	2	1
Eric Fonoimoana	0	0	1	5	5
Scott Friederichsen	0	0	0	1	0
Brian Gatzke	0	0	0	0	1
Leif Hanson	0	0	0	0	1
Rob Heidger	0	2	3	1	2
Adam Johnson	7	7	1	2	4
Karch Kiraly	**13**	**4**	**2**	**1**	**2**
Brian Lewis	2	2	6	3	3
Jose Loiola	7	8	1	2	4
Ricci Luyties	0	0	1	2	1
Kevin Martin	0	0	0	1	0
Jim Nichols	0	0	0	1	0
Mike Schlegel	0	0	0	0	1
Kent Steffes	12	4	2	1	2
Randy Stoklos	0	1	4	1	4
David Swatik	0	0	0	1	0
Troy Tanner	0	2	2	0	3
Wes Welch	0	0	0	1	2
Mike Whitmarsh	1	6	5	1	5
Eric Wurts	0	0	0	1	1

FIVB

The 1996 FIVB beach volleyball tour includes 17 mens and 12 women's tour sites (includes 1996 Olympics in Atlanta) with the total prize money worth $4,250,000. The men to get $2,660,000.00 and the women $1,590,000.00.

The FIVB mens tour included 17 stops in twelve countries: Spain (twice), Brazil (three times), Turkey, France (twice), Germany, Portugal, Belgium, Italy (twice), Indonesia, Puerto Rico, South Africa, and including 2 stops in the U.S.A. (Hermosa Beach California and the Atlanta Olympics).

The top duo of the 1996 FIVB World Tour was the Brazilian team of Emanuel Fernando Scheffer Rego and Jose Z-Marco Nobrega Ferreira de Melo. This team advanced to the "Gold-Medal" match on 7 occasions, winning 5 times. Another Brazilian team, Roberto Lopes da Costa and Jose Franco Vieira Neto, were the second most successful team on the FIVB World Tour in 1996. Neto and Lopes advanced to the finals on 5 occasions, winning 3 times.

The most successful American team was Mike Dodd and Mike Whitmarsh. Dodd and Whitmarsh entered 5 events, advancing to the finals 4 times, winning the "Gold Medal" twice.

INTERNATIONAL 1996 FIVB MEN'S PRO-BEACH VOLLEYBALL PLAYERS

As of 1-28-96 the top 25 men playing beach volleyball on the FIVB tour were from 9 different countries, four of the men were from the USA. These rankings are determined by points earned on the FIVB tour, therefore most AVP and WPVA players are not ranked on this list because of conflicting schedules.

TOP 25 FIVB MEN BEACH PLAYERS
1996 MEN'S FIVB INDIVIDUAL WORLD RANKINGS
(beginning of 1996 season)

The following list of international players are in the order of their rankings according to the amount of points that they had at the beginning of the 1996 FIVB Tour.

Rank	Name	Country
1.	Franco Jos Vieira Neto	Brazil
1.	Roberto Costa Lopes	Brazil
3.	Emanuel Rego Scheffer	Brazil
3.	Jose Z-Marco Melo Ferreira Nobrega	Brazil
5.	Bjrn Maaseide	Norway
5.	Jan Kvalheim	Norway
7.	Cristopher St. John Sinjin Smith	USA
7.	Carl J. Henkel	USA
9.	Mark Heese	Canada
9.	John Child	Canada
11.	Eduardo Esteban Mono Martinez	Argentina
11.	Martin Alejo Conde	Argentina
13.	Jeff Williams	USA
13.	Carlos Frederico Galletti Loss	Brazil
13.	Andre Faria Gomes	Brazil
16.	Juan Miguel Rosell Milanes	Cuba
16.	Francisco Alvarez	Cuba
18.	Javier Bosma Minguez	Spain
19.	Christian Penigaud	France
19.	Jean-Philippe Jodard	France
21.	Sixto Jimenez	Spain
21.	Carlos Briceno	USA
23.	Axel Hager	Germany
23.	Jurg Ahmann	Germany
25.	Paulo Roberto da Coata Moreira	Brazil

"PAULAO" DA COSTA MOREIRA
Brazilian, "Paulao" Roberto da Costa Moeira was a tough competitor on the 1996 FIVB Tour, winning the $100,000.00 World Series event in Joao Pessoa Brazil. Above photo, "Paulao" hits the ball past the block of Martine Alejo Conde from Argentina.
Photo Courtesy of the FIVB

JOSE Z-MARCO NOBREGA
Brazilian, Jose Z-Marco Nobrega teamed-up with compatriot Emanuel Rego for the best record on the 1996 FIVB Tour, advancing to 7 finals, winning 5 gold-medals. Above photo, Z-Marco gets ready to make a dig.
Photo Courtesy of the FIVB

1996 TOP 25 FIVB MEN PLAYERS
MEN'S FINAL FIVB INDIVIDUAL WORLD RANKINGS

The following list of international players are in the order of their rankings according to the amount of points that they earned by the end of the 1996 FIVB Tour.

1.	Emanuel Fernando Scheffer Rego	Brazil
2.	Jose Z-Marco Nobrega Ferreira de Melo	Brazil
3.	Martin Alejo Conde	Argentina
4.	Rodrgio "Paro" Ferreira de Souza	Brazil
4.	Guilherme Luiz Marquez	Brazil
6.	Eduardo Esteban "Mono" Martinez	Argentina
7.	Jan Kvalheim	Norway
7.	Bjorn Maaseide	Norway
9.	John Child	Canada
9.	Mark Heese	Canada
11.	Franco Jose Vieira Neto	Brazil
12.	Roberto Lopes da Costa	Brazil
13.	Paulo Emilio Silva Azevedo	Brazil
13.	Paulo Roberto "Paulao" Moreira da Costa	Brazil
15.	Carl Henkel	USA
16.	Sinjin Smith	USA
17.	Julien Prosser	Australia
18.	Lee Zahner	Australia
19.	Francisco Alvarez	Cuba
19.	Juan Miguel Rosell Milanes	Cuba
21.	Mike Dodd	USA
23.	Luis Miguel Barbosa Maia	Portugal

1996 INDIVIDUAL FIVB TOURNAMENT FINISHES

Player	1st	2nd	3rd	4th	5th
Eduardo "Duda" Pinto de Abreau	0	0	1	0	0
Francisco Alverez	0	0	1	1	3
Jogo Pereira Brenha Alves	0	0	0	1	0
Paulo Emilo Silva Azevedo	1	0	0	2	2
Bill Boullianne	0	0	0	0	1
Canyon Ceman	0	0	0	0	1
John Child	1	2	1	1	2
Ian Clark	0	0	0	0	1
Martin Alejo Conde	1	1	4	0	2
Roberto Lopes da Costa	3	2	0	2	0
Mike Dodd	2	2	0	0	1
Eric Fonoimoana	0	0	0	0	1
Carlos Eduardo Garrido	0	0	0	0	1
Andre Faria Gomes	0	0	1	0	1
Mark Heese	1	2	1	1	2
Carl Henkel	0	3	0	0	2
Sixto Jiminez	0	0	0	0	1
Jean Philippe Jodard	0	0	0	1	1
Dmitri Karasev	0	0	0	0	1
Karch Kiraly	1	0	0	0	0
Jan Kvalheim	1	0	3	3	2
Martin Laciga	0	0	0	1	1
Paul Laciga	0	0	0	1	1
CarlosFrederico"Alemao"Galletti Loss	0	0	1	0	1
Bjorn Maaseide	1	0	3	3	2
Luis Barblsa Maia	0	0	0	1	0
LuizGuilherme Marquez	1	4	0	0	4
Eduardo Esteban "Mono" Martinez	1	1	4	0	2
Juan Miguel Rosell Milanes	0	0	1	1	3
Javier Bosma Minguez	0	0	0	0	1
Paulo Roberto Da Costa Moreira	1	0	1	2	1
Jose Franco Vieira Neto	3	2	0	2	0
Jose Z-Marco Melo Ferreira Nobrega	5	2	3	1	0
Marek Pakosta	0	0	0	0	1
Michal Palinek	0	0	0	0	1
Christian Penigaud	0	0	0	1	1
Maxim Popelov	0	0	0	0	1
Julien Prosser	0	0	1	1	1
Emanuel Rego Scheffer	5	2	4	1	0
Sinjin Smith	0	3	0	0	2
Kent Steffes	1	0	0	0	0
Rogrio "Para" Ferrirs de Souza	1	4	0	1	4
Mike Whitmarsh	2	2	0	0	1
Lee Zahner	0	0	1	1	2

CBVA

While beach volleyball made its debut in the Olympics in Atlanta GA, the California Beach Volleyball Association (CBVA) continued its decades (over 30 years) long tradition of offering the best on the beach in 1996 with over 275 sand tournaments.

Many international players competed in events to prepare for the Olympics. This brought a new level of excitement to the tournaments as well as allowing those competing to see just how good they were when measured against top international players.

The CBVA continued to expand their events in 1996, adding a new Cuervo tournament and two "Spike-It-Up" events as part of their national tour. The CBVA also added four new members to the California Beach Volleyball hall of fame. Mary Jo Peppler, Jon Stevenson, Bob Vogelsang, and Butch May were the 1996 inductees.

Also, in 1996 the CBVA was still attempting to organize coaches for the beach game. In 1996 the CBVA was working with the newly-formed Association of Beach Volleyball Coaches in an effort to provide quality coaching to athletes and coaches interested in developing their skills.

BOB VOGELSANG
In 1996, Bob "Vogie" Vogelsang, along with Jon Stevenson, Butch May and Mary Jo Peppler, was inducted into the California Beach Volleyball Hall of Fame. Above photo, "Vogie" hits a set from Gene Selznick, during a 1959 tournament, on Santa Monica's State Beach, in California.

Photo Courtesy of Kevin Goff

MEN'S TOURNAMENT RESULTS
1996-AVP

FAIRFAX VIRGINIA
February 3rd, 1996

Karch Kiraly and Kent Steffes won the first AVP tournament of 1996, the "Evian Indoor", on the "beach" at Fairfax Virginia's Patriot Center. This indoor beach tournament was played on February 3rd, 1996. Kiraly and Steffes won the championship match with a 15-7 victory over Adam Johnson and Jose Loiola.
3rd Place: Scott Ayakatubby and Randy Stoklos
3rd Place: Mike Dodd and Mike Whitmarsh

NEW YORK NEW YORK
February 24th, 1996

Adam Johnson and Jose Loiola reversed the outcome on February 24th, 1996, on the "beach" in New York's Madison Square Garden with a 10-9, come from behind victory over Karch Kiraly and Kent Steffes, as the clock ran out in the championship match.
3rd Place: Scott Ayakatubby and Brian Lewis
3rd Place: Mike Dodd and Mike Whitmarsh

LAS VEGAS NEVADA
March 8th-10th, 1996

The first "outdoor" stop of the 1996 AVP outdoor tour was in Las Vegas, Nevada. The $175,000.00 Men's Swatch "King of the Beach Invitational Tournament" was won by Karch Kiraly. In this, the fifth King of the Beach Tournament, Kiraly earned $54,000.00. This was Karch's fourth title as "King of the Beach." At the time, the only other player to ever win this title is Adam Johnson in 1994. Jose Loiola earned $34,000.00 as the runner-up. Mike Whitmarsh took home $26,500.00 for his third place finish. Scott Ayakatubby took home $15,000.00 for his fourth place finish. Randy Stoklos was in fifth place. Adam Johnson was the sixth place finisher, while Rob Heidger was in seventh and Mike Dodd was in the eighth spot.

PHOENIX ARIZONA
March 16th-17th, 1996

On Saint Patrick's Day, March 17th, 1996, the $100,000.00 Miller Lite Phoenix Arizona Men's Open, was won by the second seeds Adam Johnson and Jose Loiola. They collected $20,000.00 for their efforts. In the championship match, with the help of 11 serving aces (8 by Johnson) against the first seeds, Karch Kiraly and Kent Steffes. Johnson and Loiola won by a final score of 15 to 10. Johnson and Loiola advanced straight to the final by edging third place Randy Stoklos and Bill Boullianne, 15-14 in the winners' bracket final. Kiraly and Steffes had to fight their way through the consolation

ADAM JOHNSON
Adam "AJ" Johnson was paired-up with Jose Loiola, on the 1996 AVP Tour. They advanced to 14 championship matches, winning 7 times. Above photo, "AJ" attacking the ball. Action took place at the 1996 AVP Tour event in Santa Cruz California.
Photo Courtesy of Frank Goroszko

JOSE LOIOLA
Jose Loiola teamed-up with Adam Johnson for the second best record on the 1996 AVP Tour. Loiola and Johnson finished within the top five at 21 events. Above photo, Loiola hits the ball away from the block of Brian Lewis.
Photo Courtesy of the AVP

bracket by beating fourth place finishers, Mike Dodd and Mike Whitmarsh, 15-4. Kiraly and Steffes fell into the consolation bracket after losing 15-6 to Stoklos and Boullianne in the winners' bracket quarterfinal. The tournament took place at the Arizona Gateway Center. The first Arizona open was staged in 1984. Prime Sports Networks' provided same day TV coverage of the championship match, with Paul Sunderland calling play-by-play and pro beach volleyball legend Tim Hovland stepped off the beach to handle the "mike" for his season debut as color commentator.

3rd Place: Randy Stoklos and Bill Boullianne
4th Place: Mike Dodd and Mike Whitmarsh
5th Place: Eduardo Bacil and Ian Clark
5th Place: Scott Ayakatubby and Brian Lewis

RIVIERA BEACH FLORIDA
March 23rd-24th, 1996

Karch Kiraly and Kent Steffes disregarded their status as the number four seeded team as they won their second straight $100,000.00 Miller Lite Men's Open at Riviera Beach, (Singer Island) Florida. In the championship final, against Adam Johnson and Jose Loiola, the tournament's number two seeded team, and the Miller Lite/AVP Tour's hottest team, 12-15 and 7-3 in the first AVP Pro-Beach Volleyball double final of the 1996 season. The teams had split matches to force the extra play. Kiraly, the 1996 Miller Lite/AVP Tour's top ranked player, and Steffes, playing together for the 99th time, had beaten Johnson and Loiola in the morning in the tournament's winner's bracket final, 15-11. But Johnson and Loiola came through the consolation bracket to beat Kiraly and Steffes, 15-12, setting up the first double final of the season. The win revenged a loss by Kiraly and Steffes to Johnson and Loiola in the final's of last week's Miller Lite Phoenix Open, and was worth $20,000.00. Kiraly and Steffes seemed headed for an easy victory over Johnson and Loiola, racing out to a 5-0 lead in their second game of the day, but Johnson and Loiola battled back to take an 8-7 lead, and were never caught. The double final was all Kiraly and Steffes, with the latter leading the way with four service aces.

3rd Place: Scott Ayakatubby and Brian Lewis
4th Place: Eric Fonoimoana and Rob Heidger
5th Place: Mike Dodd and Mike Whitmarsh
5th Place: Eduardo Bacil and Ian Clark

FORT MYERS FLORIDA
March 29th - 30th, 1996

The 1996 Men's $100,000.00 Miller Lite/Footaction USA/Fila Fort Myers Open was won by Karch Kiraly and Kent Steffes. Their share of the prize money was $20,000.00. In the semifinals, Dain Blanton and Canyon Ceman surprised everybody by making it to the winner's bracket finals, where they lost to Kiraly and Steffes. Then in the losers bracket final Blanton and Ceman defeated Bill Boullianne and Randy Stoklos, to set up a rematch in the tournament final against Kiraly and Steffes. In the championship match, Blanton and Ceman went out to a 13-8 lead. Kiraly and Steffes showed what they are made of by coming back to win 15-13.

3rd Place: Bill Boullianne and Randy Stoklos
4th Place: Adam Johnson and Jose Loiola
5th Place: Mike Dodd and Mike Whitmarsh
5th Place: Brent Frohoff and Ricci Luyties

DAIN BLANTON
Dain Blanton provided some worthy competition on the 1996 AVP Tour, finishing within the top five 8 times, including a second place finish at the Fort Myers Florida event. Above photo, Blanton slices the ball past the block of Karch Kiraly.
Photo Courtesy of Tim Andexler

CANYON CEMAN
Canyon Ceman began to show some promise on the 1996 AVP Tour, finishing within the top five on 6 occasions. Ceman paired-up with Dain Blanton for a second place finish at the Fort Myers event. Above photo, Ceman digs a hard driven ball.
Photo Courtesy of "Couvi"

CLEARWATER FLORIDA
April 11th-13th, 1996

The first place prize of $100,000.00, at the 1993 Clearwater Men's "Jose Cuervo Gold Crown" event, was seized by Karch Kiraly and Kent Steffes. In the championship match, Kiraly and Steffes scored a 15-12 victory over Mike Dodd and Mike Whitmarsh at the first $200,000.00 Jose Cuervo Open Tournament of 1996. In the last 10 Cuervo events in which Kiraly and Steffes had teamed, they won nine of them. This was the first final for Dodd and Whitmarsh on the 1996 AVP Tour, earning them $16,000.00, for their second place finish.

3rd Place: Scott Ayakatubby and Brian Lewis
4th Place: Jose Loiola and Adam Johnson
5th Place: Bill Boullianne and Randy Stoklos

SAN DIEGO CALIFORNIA
April 20th 1996

Scott Ayakatubby and Brian Lewis won their first AVP Pro-Beach Volleyball tournament together at the San Diego Open. They defeated Adam Johnson and Jose Loiola 15-6 after breaking out to leads of 5-0 and 12-1. This was the first team to win a tournament besides the teams of Karch Kiraly with Kent Steffes or Johnson with Loiola, after the first six tournaments of the year. Ayakatubby and Lewis did not loose a game during the tournament. This was the first tournament in five that Karch and Kent failed to reach the final in 1996.

3rd Place: Eric Fonoimoana and Rob Heidger
4th Place: Dain Blanton and Canyon Ceman
5th Place: Karch Kiraly with Kent Steffes
5th Place: Mike Dodd and Mike

SCOTT AYAKATUBBY & BRIAN LEWIS
Scott "Ack" Ayakatubby and Brian "Lewey" Lewis paired-up for a couple of 1996 AVP Tour championships. "Ack" and "Lewy" advanced to four finals on their way to their way to the wins. Above photo, Lewy makes a dig as "Ack" gets ready to help-out.
Photo Courtesy of "Couvi"

SAN FRANCISCO CALIFORNIA
May 3rd-5th, 1996

Mike Dodd and Mike Whitmarsh won their first tournament of the season at the $115,000.00 "1-800-COLLECT" San Francisco Open. Their share of the prize money was $23,000.00. In the championship match, Dodd and Whitmarsh outlasted Karch Kiraly and Kent Steffes, 15-11. With this victory, Dodd, at the age of 38, tied Ron Von Hagen as the oldest player to win an open beach volleyball tournament (Note: in 2004, Karch Kiraly was still winning at age 43). This tournament was played at "Crissy Field" in the Prisido at the base of the Golden Gate Bridge. The winds, that came off the San Francisco Bay, made the team starting out on the good side (serving into the wind) almost automatic winners. As an example as to how much the winds affected the matches, the winds here turned many of Mike Whitmarsh's jump serves into service aces. Not even Karch Kiraly was able to get to the "awesome" display of serving power!

3rd Place: Scott Ayakatubby and Brian Lewis
4th Place: Kevin Martin and David Swatik
5th Place: Troy Tanner and Wes Welch
5th Place: Adam Johnson and Jose Loiola

INDIANAPOLIS INDIANA
May 17th-19th, 1996

The 1996 Men's $125,000.00 Kodak Fun Saver Camera Indianapolis Open was played on the floor of the Indianapolis Tennis Stadium. Kent Steffes and Karch Kiraly won the tournament and the $25,000.00 first place check. In the championship match, "K & K" defeated Randy Stoklos and Eduardo Bacil, 15-7 to win the $125,000.00 Indianapolis Indiana Open. Kiraly and Steffes had leads of 7-1 and 12-4 on their way to the easy 15-7 victory over Bacil and Stoklos, who were playing together for the first time since last year.

3rd Place: Bill "Beef" Boullianne and Dain Blanton
4th Place: Scott Ayakatubby and Brian Lewis
5th Place: Eric Fonoimoana and Rob Heidger
5th Place: Adam Johnson and Jose Loiola

The above team changes were brought about when Stoklos decided to go to the Olympic trials in Baltimore with Johnson instead of Boullianne. "Beef" was very upset and said if he was not good enough to go to the "trials" with, then the partnership with Stoklos was finished!

ATLANTA GEORGIA
May 15th-29th, 1996

The 1996 Men's $125,000.00 AVP Atlanta Open was staged in the Olympic Beach Volleyball Stadium, Atlanta (Jonesboro) Georgia. Kent Steffes and Karch Kiraly won the championship and the $25,000.00 first place prize. In the championship match, Kiraly and Steffes defeated, by default, Adam Johnson and Jose Loiola as they were unable to participate due to Johnson's dehydration. This was Kiraly and Steffes sixth tournament victory of the 1996 season and the 70th of their partnership.

3rd Place: Randy Stoklos and Eduardo Bacil
4th Place: Jim Nichols and Scott Friederichsen,
5th Place: Mike Dodd and Mike Whitmarsh
5th Place: Eric Fonoimoana and Ian Clark

DALLAS TEXAS
May 31st-June 2nd, 1996

The tournament in Dallas Texas, scheduled for the weekend of May 31st-June 2nd, 1996, was canceled due to a "Twister" with thunderstorms and 70 mile an-hour winds. After playing the tournament to the point of ninth place, the stands had to be evacuated with fans seeking refuge in the AVP trucks. The "Twister" was flinging the concession and player's tents in all direction, while the stands were shaking in a frightening manner. There was an eight-way tie for ninth place. The teams ending-up in ninth place were: Kiraly and Steffes, Dodd and Whitmarsh, Ayakatubby and Lewis, Tanner and welch, Johnson and Loiola, Stoklos and Bacil, Fonoimoana and Heidger, Frohoff and Luyties.

BOULDER COLORADO
June 13th-15th, 1996

The 1996 Men's $200,000.00 Jose Cuervo Gold Crown, at Boulder Colorado was taken by Karch Kiraly and Kent Steffes. Their share of the prize money was $100,000.00. In the championship match, they scored a 15-11 win over Scott Ayakatubby and Brian Lewis. This was the best finish by "Ack" and "Lewy" since their victory in San Diego, late in April. They split $16,000.00 for their efforts. This win put Kiraly and Steffes in position to sweep the Cuervo Gold Crown Series. They had already won the Cuervo in Clearwater Florida. The pair swept the Cuervo series in 1994. Sinjin Smith and Randy Stoklos are the only other team to win all three Cuervo Tournaments in a single season.

3rd Place: Mike Dodd and Mike Whitmarsh
4th Place: Brent Frohoff and Ricci Luyties
5th Place: Adam Johnson and Jose Loiola

CLEVELAND OHIO
June 21st-23rd, 1996

The Miller Lite AVP tour went to Cleveland Ohio on the weekend of June 21st-23rd, 1996. This event was the $100,000.00 Men's Miller Lite Cleveland Open. The tournament was won by Karch Kiraly and Kent Steffes. They split $20,000.00 for the victory. In the championship match, Kiraly and Steffes scored a 15-8 victory over Mike Dodd and Mike Whitmarsh. This was their third consecutive tournament win.

3rd Place: Adam Johnson and Jose Loiola
4th Place: Wes Welch and Eric Wurts
5th Place: Scott Ayakatubby and Brian Lewis
5th Place: Ian Clark and Troy Tanner

GRAND HAVEN MICHIGAN
June 28th-30th, 1996

Fourth-ranked Scott Ayakatubby and Brian Lewis captured the Association of Volleyball Professionals' $125,000.00 West Michigan Open in Grand Haven. This was the second title, of 1996, for "Ack" and "Lewey." They split $25,000.00 for their efforts. In the championship match, "Ack" and "Lewey" out-pointed Adam Johnson and Jose Loiola 15-10. Johnson and Loiola shared $14,250.00 as the runners-up.

3rd Place: Mike Dodd and Mike Whitmarsh
4th Place: Karch Kiraly and Kent Steffes
5th Place: Eric Fonoimoana and Bill Boullianne
5th Place: Dain Blanton and Canyon Ceman

MINNEAPOLIS MINNESOTA
July 5th-7th, 1996

In the Twin Cities, Minneapolis Minnesota, the 1996 Men's $125,000.00 Miller Lite "Twin Cities" Open was won by Adam Johnson and Jose Loiola. They broke a three and a half month period without winning a tournament. In the championship match, they defeated Karch Kiraly and Kent Steffes 15-11, to collect the $25,000.00 first place check.

3rd Place: Scott Ayakatubby and Brian Lewis
4th Place: Bill Boullianne and Eric Fonoimoana
5th Place: Rob Heidger and Troy Tanner
5th Place: Wes Welch and Eric Wurts

ORCHARD BEACH MAINE
July 12th-14th, 1996

The $125,000.00 Miller Lite Championship of New England, at Old Orchard Beach, Maine was won by Adam Johnson and Jose Loiola 15-10 over Mike Dodd and Mike Whitmarsh. This was the second straight tournament victory for Johnson and Loiola. The second place finish for Dodd and Whitmarsh was an improvement for them after their ninth place finish the week before. Dodd and Whitmarsh eliminated Kiraly and Steffes 15-11 in this tournament. This was the first time that Kiraly and Steffes had gone three straight tournaments, without winning the tournament, while playing together. This was the last tournament, before the Olympics were scheduled to take place in Atlanta GA, that the Olympic qualifiers of Kiraly and Steffes along with Dodd and Whitmarsh could participate in.

3rd Place: Karch Kiraly and Kent Steffes
4th Place: Scott Ayakatubby and Brian Lewis
5th Place: Bill Boullianne and Eric Fonoimoana
5th Place: Canyon Ceman and Dain Blanton

MILWAUKEE WISCONSIN
July 19th-21st, 1996

The 1996 Men's $125,000.00 Miller Lite Milwaukee Open was played on Bradford Beach. The event was won by Adam Johnson and Jose Loiola. This was their third straight tournament championship. In the championship match, Loiola and Johnson defeated Troy Tanner and Rob Heidger 15-11. Along with the victory, they collected the $25,000.00 first place check. Karch Kiraly and Kent Steffes along with Mike Dodd and Mike Whitmarsh, skipped the Milwaukee event, in order to participate in the Atlanta Olympics Games Opening Ceremonies.

3rd Place: Brent Frohoff and Ricci Luyties
4th Place: Eric Fonoimoana and Bill Boullianne
5th Place: Scott Ayakatubby and Brian Lewis
5th Place: Eduardo Bacil and Randy Stoklos

SANTA CRUZ CALIFORNIA
August 1st-3rd, 1996

The $200,000.00 "Cuervo Gold Crown" in Santa Cruz, California was won by Jose Loiola and Adam Johnson. They collected the first place prize of $100,000.00 along with the title. In the championship match, Johnson and Loiola made it four straight with a win over Rob Heidger and Troy Tanner. Tanner and Heidger were the top team in the round-robin play, but they were trounced in the final 15-0.

3rd Place: Karch Kiraly and Kent Steffes
4th Place: Brent Frohoff and Ricci Luyties
5th Place: Mike Dodd and Mike Whitmarsh

MANHATTAN BEACH OPEN
August 9th-11th, 1996

Olympic Gold Medalists Karch Kiraly and Kent Steffes regained their winning ways with a win at the renowned $150,000.00 Miller Lite Manhattan Beach Men's Open. Karch and Kent ended Adam Johnson and Jose Loiola's Win Streak as they jumped to an early 8-1 lead and went on to defeat Johnson and Loiola 15-10 denying the tandem their fifth consecutive Miller Lite/AVP Tour victory. This was Kiraly's seven Manhattan Beach Open title. He and Steffes have shared the title four times as a team. Kiraly and Steffes split $30,000.00 for their first place finish while Johnson and Loiola share $17,100.00 for second. This was the twenty-first stop on the 1996 Miller Lite/AVP Tour, which traveled to 24 cities and 17 states during the eight month 1996 season. There were, a total of 64 teams entered in the competition.

Earlier in the tournament, Olympic Silver medalists, Mike Dodd and Mike Whitmarsh jumped to leads of 5-1 and 13-3 and upset Kiraly and Steffes 15-6 in the quarter-finals on Saturday to advance to Sunday's winner bracket final.

In the highly anticipated Olympic "Gold Medal" round rematch, Dodd's eleven kills and Whitmarsh's two stuffed blocks, dismantled the top seeds' offensive attack. Kiraly and Steffes drew first blood with an early one point advantage. Dodd and Whitmarsh quickly responded as they scored 5 straight points to take a 5-1 advantage. the two teams exchanged sideouts until Steffes rattled off a jump serve ace to cut the lead to 5-2. However, Whitmarsh's defensive threats at the net and Dodd's play behind his partner's stifling block, were too much for Kiraly and Steffes to overcome. Led by Dodd's 17 kills, Dodd and Whitmarsh were able to rally off seven more straight points that pushed the lead to 13-3. Kiraly and Steffes combined for 2 quick service aces for a 14-6 side change. However, it was not enough, as Dodd and Whitmarsh were able to sideout and put the game away off Dodd's cut shot beyond an outstretched Kiraly for the surprising 15-6 victory. Kiraly and Steffes went on to defeat Dodd and Whitmarsh in the finals of the loser's bracket.

In the championship match, against Jose Loiola and Adam Johnson, Kiraly and Steffes came out on fire with

MIKE WHITMARSH
Mike "Whitty" Whitmarsh played well on the 1996 AVP Tour. He advanced to 7 championship matches, winning the AVP event on "Crissy-Field" in San Francisco California, with Mike Dodd. Above photo, "Whitty" gets-up high for the shot.
Photo Courtesy of Frank Goroszko

MIKE DODD
Mike Dodd was competitive on the 1996 AVP Tour, finishing within the top five 17 time, advancing to the finals 7 times, winning in San Francisco with Mike Whitmarsh. Above photo, Dodd spikes the ball past the block of Karch Kiraly.
Photo Courtesy of the AVP

a Steffes jump serve ace to take a quick one point advantage. Kiraly and Steffes added two more quick points with a Kiraly touch shot down the left line and a Steffes spike off a Loiola block attempt that turned the score to 3-0. All Johnson and Loiola could do, was sideout to keep Kiraly and Steffes from scoring. Kiraly and Steffes then sided out and Steffes responded with his second jump serve ace of the match to push the lead to 4-0. Johnson and Loiola scored their first point of the match off a Loiola poke shot at the net that hit the back line for point and a 4-1 side change. Combining for 19 kills and 6 service aces in the match, Kiraly and Steffes built an 8-1 lead. The momentum shifted slightly after Johnson and Loiola rallied with 4 straight points to cut the lead to 8-6. After a 9-6 side change, Kiraly and Steffes never looked back as they capitalized on 7 Johnson and Loiola service errors to build a 14-9 lead. After a cross court spike by Steffes for sideout, Kiraly sealed the victory with a stuffed block against Johnson for the 15-10 victory.

3rd Place: Mike Dodd and Mike Whitmarsh
4th Place: Scott Ayakatubby and Brian Lewis
5th Place: Bill Boullianne and Eric Fonoimoana
5th Place: Brian Gatzke and Mike Schlegel

BRIAN LEWIS
Brian Lewis, paired with Scott Ayakatubby, extend the top team on the AVP Tour (Karch Kiraly and Kent Steffes) to a tie-breaker at the 1996 AVP event on the beach in Belmar New Jersey. Above photo, Lewis hits the ball past the block of Steffes.
Photo Courtesy of Frank Goroszko

BELMAR BEACH NEW JERSEY
August 16th-18th, 1996

The 1996 Men's $100,000.00 Kodak Fun Saver Pocket Camera Belmar Open was won by Karch Kiraly and Kent Steffes. They collected $20,000.00 along with the title. In the championship match, after trailing 9-6 and 13-12, Kiraly and Steffes won the first game 15-13, forcing a tie breaker against the team of Scott Ayakatubby and Brian Lewis, which they won by a score of 7-2. This was the second straight tournament win for Kiraly and Steffes. Steffes joined Kiraly as only the second player to surpass $2 million in career prize money.

3rd Place: Troy Tanner and Rob Heidger
4th Place: Bill Boullianne and Eric Fonoimoana
5th Place: Dain Blanton and Canyon Ceman
5th Place: Ian Clark and Leif Hanson
Note: Adam Johnson broke his finger during this tournament. Johnson and Jose Loiola finished ninth in this competition.

HERMOSA BEACH CALIFORNIA
August 23rd-25th, 1996

On the weekend of August 23rd-25th, 1996 the $175,000.00 Miller Lite Men's "U.S. Championships," in Hermosa Beach, California took place. Karch Kiraly and Kent Steffes were the champions as they collected the first place check for $35,000.00. In the championship match, Kiraly and Steffes defeated Mike Dodd and Mike Whitmarsh 11-8. This was Kiraly's 122nd tournament victory, tying him with Randy Stoklos for second place on the "all-time" list. Sinjin Smith was still in the first spot with 139 tournament victories. This was the first time that this tournament charged for all seating during the event. Despite the fact that there were a few people boycotting the paid event, the crowds were large and the tournament was a great success! especially for Kiraly and Steffes

3rd Place: Troy Tanner and Rob Heidger
4th Place: Bill Boullianne and Eric Fonoimoana
5th Place: Eduardo Bacil and Randy Stoklos
5th Place: Adam Johnson and Jose Loiola

CHICAGO ILLINOIS
August 29th-September 1st, 1996

The 1996 Men's $175,000.00 Miller Lite/AVP Tour Championship at Chicago, Illinois, was won by Adam Johnson and Jose Loiola. In the championship match, Johnson and Loiola accepted the win in a double final 5-4 (forfeit) when Mike Dodd and Mike Whitmarsh were forced to retire. This was the seventh tournament win of the season for Johnson and Loiola. They collected $30,000.00 for the victory.

3rd Place: Scott Ayakatubby and Brian Lewis
4th Place: Randy Stoklos and Eduardo "Anjino" Bacil
5th Place: Karch Kiraly and Kent Steffes
5th Place: Dain Blanton and Canyon Ceman

AUSTIN TEXAS
September 15th, 1996

The "Great Texas Shoot-out" was won by Karch Kiraly and Kent Steffes over Jose Loiola and Adam Johnson. In this best two out of three format "K&K" won in two straight by scores of 12-8 and 12-6. This tournament was a competition of the top two teams of the 1996 AVP Pro-Beach Volleyball Tour.

MEN'S TOURNAMENT RESULTS 1996-FIVB

RIO de JANEIRO BRAZIL
February 8th-11th, 1996

The $200,000.00 FIVB Beach Volleyball Championship on Copacabana Beach, at Rio de Janeiro, Brazil (this tournament was for the championship for the 1995 season), was an all Brazilian final. In the championship match, Franco Vieira Neto and Roberto Costa Lopes from Brazil defeated Jose ZeMarco Melo Ferreira Nobrega and Emanuel Rego Scheffer, also from Brazil. The final scores were 12-8 and 12-3. The winner's split the $40,000.00 first place prize.

3rd Place: John Child and Mark Heese-Canada
4th Place: Jan Kvalheim and Bjorn Maaseide-Nor
5th Place: Carlos "Alemao" Galletti Loss and Andre Gomes-Bra
5th Place: Francisco Alveraz and Juan Miguel Rosell Milanes-Cuba

The U.S.A. teams of Carl Henkel and Sinjin Smith, along with Bruk Vandeweghe and Brent Frohoff, finished in 9th place. Jeff Williams and Carlos Briceno finished in 13th place.

MARBELLA SPAIN
April 5th-7th, 1996

The Men's $100,000.00 FIVB World Series event, staged at "El Fuerte" Beach, Marbella, Spain, had 22 teams, including 6 from Spain, compete for the first place prize of $20,000.00. The championship match was an all Brazilian celebration, in what started out as a cold and rainy day, turned into a bright sunny Easter Sunday. The championship final was won by Ze Marco Melo and Emanuel Rego. They held on to win over the duo of Franco Vieira Neto and Roberto Lopes Costa 12-7, 7-12, and 16-14, in an exhilarating 71 minute match.

3rd Place: Eduardo Esteban "Mono" Martinez and Martin Alejo Conde-Arg
4th Place: Mark Heese and John Child-Canada
5th Place: Marek Pakosta and Michael Palinek-Czk
5th Place: Maxim Popelov and Dmitri Karasev-Rus

The U.S. team of Bruk Vandeweghe and Jeff Williams finished a respectable ninth, while Sinjin Smith and Carl Henkel settled for a 13th place finish.

JOAO PESSOA BRAZIL
May 10th-12th, 1996

The 1996 Men's FIVB $100,000.00 World Series event, held at Joao Pessoa, Brazil, was won by the Brazilian team of Paulao daCosta and Paulo Emillo Azvedo. The winner's shared the $20,000.00 first place check. In the championship match, they defeated Eduardo Esteban "Mono" Martinez and Martin Alejo Conde from Argintina, 12-10 and 12-0. There were 32 teams from 21 countries that participated on the hot white sands of Tambau Beach, in the Brazilian city of Joao Pessoa, where there were four courts set up for the second leg of this 1996 FIVB Beach Volleyball Men's World Series event.

3rd Place: Ze Marco Melo and Emanuel Rego-Bra
4th Place: Julien Prosser and Lee Zahner-Aus
5th Place: Luiz Marquez and Rogrio Ferreira de Souza-Bra
5th Place: Bjorn Maaseide and Jan Kvalheim-Nor

FRANCO JOS VIERA NETO
Brazilian, Franco Jos Viera Neto, began the 1996 FIVB season rated as the number-one player. He enjoyed a successful season, advancing to 5 championship matches, winning 3 times. Above photo, Neto gets above the net for the block attempt.
Photo Courtesy of "Couvi"

EMANUEL REGO SCHEFFER
Brazilian Emanuel Rego Scheffer paired-up with Jose Z-Marco Nobrega for the best record on the 1996 FIVB Tour. They advanced to 7 gold-medal matches, winning 5 times. Above photo, Rego grovels in the sand to make a dig.
Photo Courtesy of "Couvi"

ALANYA TURKEY
May 31st-June 2nd, 1996

The Men's FIVB $100,000.00 tournament at, Damlatas Kleopatra International Blue Flag Beach, in Alanya Turkey, was won by the team from Argentina, Eduardo Esteban "Mono" Martinez and Martin Alejo Conde. The winner's split the $20,000.00 first place prize. In the championship match, they defeated the Brazilian team of Ze Marco Melo and Emanuel Rego, by scores of 12-4 and 12-7. The final match started at 3:30pm and was telecast live on Star TV (one of the biggest TV channels in Turkey), with a crowd of over 5,000 electrified spectators in the magnificent 70-minute performance from the finalist. The Turkish volleyball fans were treated to a surprise as one Turkish team, Cengizan and Gskhan, made it to the second day of the tournament. There was a closing ceremony following the play in which the players got their medals from the FIVB, their cups from the Turkish National Federation and the promoter "All Sports Organization" along with their special prizes from "Alanya Municipality" and the sponsors.

3rd Place: Jan Kvalheim and Bjorn Maaseide-Nor
4th Place: Franco Vieira Neto and Roberto Costa Lopes-Bra
5th Place: Mark Heese and John Child-Canada
5th Place: Paulo Azevedo and Roberto "Paulao" Moreira da Costa-Bra
The U.S. team of Sinjin Smith and Carl Henkel finished in the ninth spot.

JAN KVALHEIM
Norwegian Jan Kvalheim teamed-up with compatriot Bjorn Maaseide to win the 1996 FIVB event in Hermosa Beach California. Above photo, Kvalheim hits a set from Maaseide, towards the block of Brazilian Franco Jos Vieira Neto.
Photo Courtesy of "Couvi"

HERMOSA BEACH CALIFORNIA U.S.A.
June 19th-23rd, 1996

The $140,000.00 FIVB World Series event, on the beach in Hermosa Beach, California, U.S.A. was the FIVB's 1996 final U.S. based international volleyball tournament. The tournament was promoted as an Olympic preview and it was a good thing for the U.S.A. teams that it was not the actual Olympics. The best finish by an American team was a third place finish in the women's division by Holly McPeak and Nancy Reno. The best that the American men could do was a seventh by U.S.A. Olympic qualifier's Sinjin Smith and Carl Henkel. The other USA Olympic qualifiers, Karch Kiraly, Kent Steffes, Mike Dodd and Mike Whitmarsh were in Cleveland Ohio playing in an AVP tournament that also included the remainder of the best American teams. The only other U.S.A. men's team to participate in the tournament was Mark Eller and Todd Schaffer, they were unable to win a match. All of the best American women teams participated in the tournament. This FIVB "Bud Light World Beach Volleyball Invitational" event provided somewhat of an Olympic preview, with a total of 38 out of a possible 42 men's and women's Olympic bound teams competing.

The men's division was won by Jan Kvalheim and Bjorn Maaseide of Norway. They Defeated Franco Vieira Neto and Roberto Lopes Costa of Brazil, 12-8 and 12-5, in the best two out of three final. First place finishers earned $10,000 each, second $6,500 each, third $4,000 each and fourth place finishers earned $3,000 each.

3rd Place: Esteban Martinez and Martin Conde-Arg
4th Place: Ze Marco Melo and Emanuel Rego-Bra
5th Place: Francisco Cutio and Juan Miguel Rosell Milanes-Cuba
5th Place: Bosma Minquez and Sixto Jimenez-Spain

MARTIN LACIGA & PAUL LACIGA
The Swiss team of brothers, Martin Laciga (left) and Paul Laciga (right) paired-up in 1996 to provide some stiff competition on the FIVB Tour. Above photo, Paul passing the ball to his brother Martin.
Photo Courtesy of the FIVB

MARSILLE FRANCE
On June 27th-30th, 1996

The next FIVB Men's Pro-Beach Volleyball event, took place on the "Golfe du Lion" shore, at the "Plages du Prado" in Marseille France. The final was won by the Brazilian team of Franco Neto and Roberto Lopes over the U.S.A. team of Sinjin Smith and Carl Henkel, by scores of 12-6, 6-12, and 12-10. Neto and Lopes each took home a check for $10,000.00 for their efforts. This tournament produced new and interesting results which could help experts to forecast the final rankings for the Olympics, that were scheduled to take place in three weeks. The stadium was packed with over 4,000 cheering fans. They were treated to an exciting 70 minute championship match that ended with a gasping tie breaking game. Smith and Henkel were in their first final in almost a year. During this event in Marseille, the FIVB staged the drawing of lots to determine the seedings of the men's and women's Olympic touirnament.

3rd Place: Esteban Martinez and Martin Conde-Arg
4th Place: Christian Peniguad and Jean-Phillip Jodard-Fra
5th Place: Martin Laciga and Paul Laciga-Swiss
5th Place: Luiz Marquez and "Para" de Souza-Bra

BERLIN GERMANY
uly 5th-7th, 1996

On the "Platz an der Jannowitzbruske," close to the world famous "Brandeburg" door and to the German "Reichstag" in downtown Berlin, sandy beach volleyball courts were set-up. The Canadian team of John Child and Mark Heese won the $150,000.00 FIVB final over Brazil's Rogerio deSouza and Guilherme Luiz Marquez, for the second straight year. The Canadians split the $20,000.00 first place prize. Under the sun filled skies of Berlin, the over-crowded stadium was filled with excitement during the rousing final. If it could have been possible, both teams deserved to win this tournament that started with 63 teams. The championship match was a thrilling performance, that lasted one and one half hours, with the Canadian's taking the match in three sets 7-2, 12-10, and 12-10.

3rd Place: Julien Prosser and Lee Zahner-Aus
4th Place: Francisco Alvarez and Juan Rosell Milanes-Cuba
5th Place: Esteban Martinez and Martin Conde-Arg
5th Place: Christian Peniguad and Jean-Phillip Jodard-Fra
The U.S. team of Jeff Williams and Mike Diehl finished in the 25th spot.

PORNICHET FRANCE
August 9th-11th, 1996

The Men's FIVB $200,000.00 tournament at Pornichet, France, was an all Brazilian final. The team of Ze Marco Melo and Emanuel Rego defeated Guiherme Luiz Marquez and Rogrio "Para" Ferreira de Souza, after being down 7-1 in the first set. They came back to win by scores of 12-10 and 12-9, in front of a full, 4,000 seat stadium. There were also numerous spectators looking through any and all openings, crevices, holes, etc. in the stadium to try and get a look at the final match. The winner's were happy to split the $40,000.00 first place prize money.

3rd Place: Bjorn Maaseide and Jan Kvalheim-Nor
4th Place: Paulo Azevedo and "Paulao" Moreira da Costa-Bra
5th Place: Mark Heese and John Child-Canada
5th Place: Esteban Martinez and Martin Conde-Arg
The U.S.A. team of Carl Henkel and Sinjin Smith finished in the 13th spot.

ESPINHO PORTUGAL
August 16th-18th, 1996

The $200,000.00 Men's, FIVB tournament, at Espinho Portugal, on Baia Beach, was won by the American team of Mike Dodd and Mike Whitmarsh. In the championship match, they outlasted the Canadian team of John Child and Mark Heese. It was an electrifying final, ending in scores of 10-12, 12-11, and 15-13. By winning the one hour and 55 minute match, Dodd and Whitmarsh collected over $40,000.00 with the win. The final match show-cased the proficiency of both teams on numerous occasions. Dodd and Whitmarsh took a 10-7 lead in the first set, but the Canadians then scored five points in a row to win the first set 12-10. In the second set, the Canadians were down again 10-7, and again they came back to take the lead 11-10, but this time after four unsuccessful match point tries they fell to the U.S.A. team by a score of 12-11. In the emotional third and deciding set, the points were very hard to gain. At a score of 5-5, Whitmarsh needed the assistance of water and salt tablets. When he returned to the court he had just enough resolve to finish the match, going on to win the last three points and the match, after the Canadians had got to another match point at 13-12.

3rd Place: Esteban Martinez and Martin Conde-Arg
4th Place: Jan Kvalheim and Bjorn Maaseide-Nor
5th Place: Julien Prosser and Lee Zahner-Aus
5th Place: Luiz Marquez and Rogrio "Para" Ferreira de Souza-Bra
The U.S. team of Carl Henkel and Sinjin Smith finished in the 7th position.

OSTEND BELGIUM
August 17th-18th, 1996

There was a $30,000.00 Men's FIVB "Qualifier" tournament on Grote Shand Beach, at Ostend Belgium. The final was won by Rogerio Dias de Assis Lopes and Mario Luiz Rodrigues Schmidt Nogueira, from Portugal. They defeated Stefan Potyka and Robertt Nowotny, from Austria. The scores of the championship match were 12-9 and 12-5.

3rd Place: Frank Blasi and David Holmes-Canada
4th Place: Groos and Voos-Ger
5th Place: Gernot Leitner and Stamm-Austria
5th Place: Pascal Delfosse and Van Hoyweghen-Bel
No Americans participated in this European qualifier.

LIGNANO ITALY
August 23rd-25th, 1996

The Men's $150,000.00 FIVB tournament, at Lignano Italy, was won by the Brazilian team of Ze-Marco Melo and Emanuel Rego. In a thrilling championship match, they defeated the U.S.A. team of Sinjin Smith and Carl Henkel, by scores of 3-12, 12-11, and 16-14. The Brazilians were happy to split the $40,000.00 first place check, while the Americans shared $26,000.00. The "Beach Volleyball Stadium" errected on Lignano Sabbiadoroos Beach, by the organising committee was filled with fans that vigorously supported the teams from Italy.

3rd Place: Bjorn Maaseide and Jan Kvalheim-Nor
4th Place: Paulao da Costa and Paulo Azevedo-Bra
5th Place: Francisco Alvarez and Juan Rosell-Cuba
5th Place: Julien Prosser and Lee Zahner-Aus

ARIGENTO ITALY
August 26th-28th, 1996

There was a $30,000.00 Men's FIVB qualifier tournament held in the seaside community of San Leone, Arigento, Italy, August 26th-28th, 1996. The results were not available.

TENERIFE CANARY ISLANDS SPAIN
September 5th-8th, 1996.

On Las Teresitas Beach in Tenerife, Canary Islands, Spain, the $150,000.00 FIVB Tournament was won by the Brazilian team of Ze Marco Melo and Emanuel Rego. They defeated the Canadian team of Mark Heese and John Child 12-11 and 12-4. The winner's shared the check of $20,000.00 for their efforts.

3rd Place: Francisco Alvarez and Juan Rosell-Cuba
4th Place: Martin Laciga and Paul Laciga-Swiss
5th Place: Carl Henkel and Sinjin Smith-USA
5th Place: Luiz Marquez and Ferreira de Souza-Bra

JAKRATA INDONESIA
October 4th-6th, 1996

The $150,000.00 Men's FIVB tournament was held within the city of Jakarta in Indonesia at the brand new National Tennis Stadium and Outdoor Beach Volley Center. There were 24 teams in the main draw. In the championship match, the team of Franco Neto and Roberto Lopes, from Brazil, defeated Sinjin Smith and Carl Henkel, from the U.S. The winning scores were 12-7 and 12-8. The winner's shared a check for $20,000.00.

3rd Place: Andre' Faria Gomes and Emanuel Rego-Bra
4th Place: Guiherme Luiz Marquez and Rogrio Ferreira de Souza-Bra
5th Place: Eric Fonoimoana and Bill Boullianne-USA

Americans, Mike Dodd and Mike Whitmarsh also participated in this tournament. They finished in 17th place.

CAROLINA, PUERTO RICO
October 18th-20th, 1996

The next $150,000.00 Men's FIVB tournament took place on Isla Verde Beach, Carolina, just outside of San Juan, Puerto Rico. There were 24 teams that participated in this event. Four Brazilian teams captured the top four positions. In the championship match, Ze-Marco Melo and Emanuel Rego won over Guiherme Luiz Marquez and Rogrio "Para" Ferreira de Souza, 12-9 and 12-9.

3rd Place: "Duda" Pinto de Abreau and Carlos "Alemao" Loss-Bra
4th Place: Franco Vieira Neto and Roberto Costa Lopes-Bra
5th Place: Mike Dodd and Mike Whitmarsh-USA
5th Place: Canyon Ceman and Ian Clark-USA

Carl Henkel and Sinjin Smith finished in the seventh spot.

FORTALEZA BRAZIL
October 24th-27th, 1996

The $150,000 Men's FIVB tournament was contested at Fortaleza, Brazil, by 32 teams from fifteen different countries. Brazil was represented with 10 teams entered to participate. The U.S.A. team of Mike Dodd and Mike Whitmarsh had a difficult time capturing the championship against the young and improved Brazilian teams. They first beat the team of Andrea Raffaelli and Antonio Babini form Italy, 15-11. They then went on to play five straight matches against five different teams from Brazil. First a win over Araujo and Castro, 15-10, then Franco Neto and Roberto Lopes, 15-8, followed by a win over Carlos Eduardo Garrido and Andre Gomes 15-4. Then, in the semifinals, Dodd and Whitmarsh outlasted Ze Marco Nobrega and Emmanuel Rego 15-10. In the championship match, Dodd and Whitmarsh took over an hour to defeat Guiherme Luiz Marquez and Rogrio "Para" Ferreira de Souza, also from Brazil, by scores of 12-8 and 12-4. Dodd and Whitmarsh split the $20,000.00 first place money.

3rd Place: Ze Marco Nobrega and Emmanuel Rego-Bra
4th Place: Eduardo Garrido and Andre Gomes-Bra
5th Place: Paulo Emilo Azevedo and Paulao Moreira-Bra
5th Place: Jan Kvalheim and Bjorn Maaseide-Nor

Canyon Ceman and Ian Clark from the U.S.A. worked their way into a ninth place finish. Carl Henkel and Sinjin Smith, from the U.S.A., slipped to a 17th place finish.

DURBAN SOUTH AFRICA
December 13th-15th, 1996

The final 1996 FIVB $150,000.00 tournament took place on the beautiful coastline of Durban, South Africa. Forty-four teams from sixteen different countries participated. South Africa was represented with 11 teams entered in the tournament. The tournament was won by the Brazilian team of Ferreira De Souza Para' and Guilherme Luiz Marquez. This was the first tour win for them and they were happy to collect the $20,000.00 first place money. Guilherme and Para' have had a good season with a 2nd in Berlin, Pornichet, Carolina, and Fortaleza. They took a 4th in Jakarta and 5th's in Joao Pessoa, Marseille, Espinho, and Tenerife. They also grabbed a 7th in Lignano and a 13th in Hermosa Beach. This final victory allowed Para' and Guilherme to finish second to Ze Marco Nobrega and Emanuel Rego in the 1996 FIVB World Rankings. Mike Dodd and Mike Whitmarsh, from the U.S.A. finished in second place. In the best two out of three Championship match, against the Brazilian team of Ferreira De Souza and Guilherme Luiz Marquez, they won the first set 12-7. The long road through the losers bracket finally caught up with them as they ran out of gas and lost the next two sets 9-12 and 8-12, settling on their second place finish.

3rd Place: Ze Marco Mello and Emanuel Scheffer Rego-Bra
4th Place: Jan Kvalheim and Bjorn Maaseide-Nor
5th Place: Esteban Martinez and Martin Conde-Arg
5th Place: Eduardo Garrido and Franco Neto-Bra

The U.S.A. team of Canyon Ceman and Eric Fonoimoana finished in ninth place. The U.S.A. team of Carl Henkel and Adam Johnson finished in a disappointing 17th place.

TOP PHOTOS: Left: Eric Fonoimoana executing a bump-set. **Center:** Wally Goodrick attacking the block of Brik Vandeweghe. **Right:** Brian Lewis jumps to the task of passing the ball.

  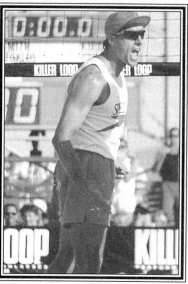

MIDDLE PHOTOS: Left: Mark Eller hits the ball past the block of Chris Young. **Center:** Brent Frohoff attacks the block of Doug Foust. **Right:** Karch Kiraly displays some emotion during a match.

1996 MEN'S BEACH VOLLEYBALL ACTION

BOTTOM PHOTOS: Left: Brian Lewis slices the ball past the block mof Kent Steffes. **Center:** Rob Heidger "hones-in" on the ball to make the block. **Right:** David Swatik braces himself for the pass.

Top and Middle Photo's Courtesy of the AVP. Bottom Photos courtesy of Frank Goroszko

WOMEN'S BEACH VOLLEYBALL
1996

BALTIMORE MARYLAND
June 4th-9th, 1996

The "OLYMPIC TRIALS", took place from June 4th-9th, 1996, at the Harbor View Complex on Baltimore's Inner Harbor, in Baltimore, Maryland. The top players from the FIVB, AVP, WPVA, and the Bud-Four-Person Tours, that had earned at least five points on the FIVB World Series Tour were eligible to compete in the Olympic Trials. Holly McPeak and Nancy Reno were the first team to qualify for the U.S.A. Olympic Team, based having the highest FIVB point total for teams representing the U.S.A.

WPVA

Nancy Reno, the number two money earner on the 1996 Evian Women's Pro Beach Volleyball Tour, missed the final five WPVA events of the 1996 season due to shoulder surgery. She returned to the tour in 1997. For the second straight season, Holly McPeak was honored as the 1996 Evian Women's Pro Beach Volleyball Tour's top player and defender. The post season honors were announced at the $75,000.00 "Best of the Beach III," in LIhue, Kauai, Hawaii, on the weekend of September 14th-15th. This was the final event of the 1996 WPVA Tour. In the final championship of the season, Holly and partner Lisa Arce won the tournament over the top-seeded team of Barbra Fontana and Linda Hanley, by a score of 15-7.

In all, there were nine awards presented: MVP: Holly McPeak, Best Setter: Karolyn Kirby (5th time), Best Hitter/Offensive Player: Linda Hanley, Best Blocker: Nancy Reno (3rd time), Top Sportswomen: Elaine Roque (4th time), Most Inspirational: Dennie Shupryt-Knoop (3rd time), Rookie of the Year: Lynda Johnson. Angela Rock won the "Silver Bullet" ace competition with a total of 103 "Spaders" (Aces), Lisa Arce was in the second spot with 73, and Holly McPeak had 71 for the third spot. This was the only season-ending award that was won on the courts. All of the previous awards mentioned were voted on by the active members of the WPVA.

Rookie of the Year, Lynda Johnson's point total (114.4) was the 10th best ever for a rookie. Her three, ninth place finishes, helped her earn a 30th over-all finish and helped her earn over $5,000.00 on the tour. Lynda was a four-time NCAA Division II All-American at Portland State. She is an inductee in the Oregon Sports Hall of Fame.

Holly McPeak, the 1991 "Rookie of the Year," set a single season earnings record by earning a total of $88,025.00, beating the old mark of $83,010.00 set in 1994 by Karolyn Kirby. McPeak now ranked 10th in career earnings at $177,194.00 with 16 career Evian Tour wins. She was the only player to finish in the top three of each of her domestic starts. By the end of the 1996 season, McPeak had won 39 pro-beach titles.

On the 1996 WPVA Tour, McPeak advanced to the finals on 9 occasions, winning 8 times. McPeak won 4 titles with Lisa Arce and 4 titles with Nancy Reno. Reno had a total of 5 titles, the 4 with McPeak and an additional 1 with Karolyn Kirby. Arce advanced to 7 finals, winning 4 times. Arce and McPeak's 4 titles, as a team, were matched by the team of Linda Robertson Hanley and Barbra Fontana. Fontana and Hanley had advanced to the finals on 9 occasions. McPeak and Arce became the youngest team (54 years combined) to win a pro-beach title when they won in Puerto Rico on the weekend of April 27th-28th. Together they had a 48-6 match record for the season.

1996 WPVA TOUR ACTION
The top two teams on the 1996 WPVA Tour were Lisa Arce and Holly McPeak, along with Barbra Fontana and Linda Hanley. Both teams earned four 1996 WPVA championship wins. Above photo McPeak is ready at the net, while her partner, Arce serves the ball to Hanley (left) and Fontana (right). Action took place at the 1996 WPVA event in Huntington Beach California.
Photo Courtesy of Frank Goroszko

WPVA AWARDS
1990-1996

MOST VALUABLE PLAYER
1996	Holly McPeak
1995	Holly McPeak
1994	Karolyn Kirby
1993	Karolyn Kirby
	Liz Masakayan
1992	Liz Masakayan
1991	Karolyn Kirby
1990	Karolyn Kirby

ROOKIE OF THE YEAR
1996	Lynda Johnson
1995	Jenny Griffith
1994	Lisa Arce
1993	Johanna Wright
1992	Valinda Hilleary
1991	Holly McPeak
1990	Alison Johnson

BEST HITTER - OFFENSIVE PLAYER
1996	Linda Hanley
1995	Nancy Reno
1994	Liz Masakayan
1993	Liz Masakayan
1992	Karolyn Kirby
1991	Angela Rock
1990	Karolyn Kirby

BEST SETTER
1996	Karolyn Kirby
1995	Karolyn Kirby
1994	Karolyn Kirby
1993	Karolyn Kirby
1992	Jackie Silva
1991	Karolyn Kirby

BEST DEFENSIVE PLAYER
1996	Holly McPeak
1995	Holly McPeak
1994	Barbra Fontana-Fontana
1993	Barbra Fontana-Fontana
1992	Liz Masakayan
1991	Liz Masakayan
1990	Janice Harrer

BEST BLOCKER
1996	Nancy Reno
1995	Nancy Reno
1994	Deb Richardson
1993	Elaine Roque
1992	Nancy reno
1991	Elaine Roque

MOST IMPROVED
1996	Krista Blomquist
1995	Lisa Arce
1994	Monique Oliver
1993	Wendy Fletcher
1992	Nancy Reno
1991	Marla O'Hara
1990	Gayle Stammer

SPORTSWOMANSHIP AWARD
1996	Elaine Roque
1995	Elaine Roque
1994	Dennie Shupryt-Knoop
1993	Dennie Shupryt-Knoop
1992	Elaine Roque
1991	Elaine Roque
1990	Dennie Shupryt-Knoop

MOST INSPIRATIONAL PLAYER
1996	Dennie Shupryt-Knoop
1995	Liz Kasakayan
1994	Dennie Shupryt-Knoop
1993	Dennie Shupryt-Knoop
1992	Cammy Ciarelli
1991	Nina Matthies
1990	Nina Matthies

BEST SERVER - "SILVER BULLET ACE AWARD"
1996	Angela Rock
1995	Angela Rock
1994	Deb Richardson
1993	Gail Castro
1992	Angela Rock

HOLLY McPEAK

Holly McPeak was the top player on the 1996 WPVA Tour. She advanced to 9 finals, winning 8 of them, with 2 different partners. McPeak was voted the 1996 WPVA "Most Valuable Player" Above photo, Mcpeak shows the hustle that helped her earn the WPVA's MVP award.

Photo Courtesy of "Couvi"

1996 U.S.A. PRO-BEACH WOMEN PLAYERS

Melissa Allen
Tiffany Rochelle-Anderson
Marie Andersson
Lisa Arce
Kristi Atkinson
Jackie Auzias de Turenne
Kristine Bailey
Amy Baltus
Barbara Belding
Lisa Bettio
Barbara Bierman
Krista Blomquist
Danalee Bragado
Bonnie Bright
Nancy Brookhart
Jackie Campbell
Gail Castro
Julia Celotto
Elizabeth Chavez
Nancy Christian
Michelle Chryst
Cammy Ciarelli
Michal Clingman
Evelyn Conley
Mindy Czuleger
Erin Deiters
Patty Dodd
Alissa Evans-Lund
Wendy Fletcher
Barbra Fontana
Lori Forsythe
Kengy Gardiner
Lisa Gathright
Kathy Gedney
Connie Gibbon
Jeanne Goldsmith
Jenny Griffith
Heather Hafner
Lucy Han
Colleen Harp
Janice Harrer
Katie Henderson
Valinda Hilleary
Mary Holland
Alison Johnson
Lynda Johnson
Patricia Keller
Karolyn Kirby
Jeanette Kollasch
Rhonda Kottke
Desiree Leipham
Bonnie Levin
Bev Lidyoff
Kathleen Luciano
Laura Martin
Liz Masakayan
Nancy Mason
Holly McPeak
Kristine middeler
Marsha Miller
Shelly Miller
Michelle Morse
Stephanie Nelson
Marla O'Hara
Monique Oliver
Liz Pagano
Amy Matthews
Lael Perlstrom
Maggie Philgence
Gina Pillitiere
Karrie Poppinga
Helen reale
Nancy Reno
Melinda Rich
Deb Richardson
Charlotte Roach
Angela Rock
Elaine Roque
Veronica Sanchez
Christine Schaefer
Ann Schirman
Teri Schroeder
Beth Schuler
Leanne Schuster
Garciela Schutt
Dennie-Schupryt-Knoop
Mary Jane Smith
Gayle Stammer
Melanie Sullivan
Shannon Vessup-Miller
Stephanie Weber
Ali Wood

The 1996 WPVA tour presented a total of 15 events, 13 outdoor and 2 indoor tournaments.

INDIVIDUAL WPVA TOURNAMENT FINISHES

Player	1st	2nd	3rd	4th	5th
Marie Anderson	0	0	0	1	0
Lisa Arce	4	3	3	0	2
Krista Blomquist	0	0	0	2	2
Danalee Bragado	0	0	0	2	2
Gail Castro	0	0	0	0	5
Cammy Ciarelli	0	0	0	1	1
Patti Dodd	0	2	2	4	3
Linda Robertson Hanley	4	5	4	0	1
Janice Opalinski Harrer	0	1	0	0	1
Barbra Fontana	4	5	4	0	1
Pat Keller	0	0	0	1	0
Karolyn Kirby	3	3	3	3	2
Dennie Schupyt Knoop	0	0	2	3	3
Liz Masakayan	0	3	0	0	4
Holly McPeak	**8**	**1**	**5**	**0**	**0**
Karrie Poppinga	0	0	1	0	4
Nancy Reno	5	1	4	1	1
Deb Richardson	0	0	0	0	3
Angela Rock	1	5	1	4	2
Elaine Roque	0	0	2	3	3
Christine Schaefer	1	0	3	1	5
Gail Stammer	0	1	0	0	3

FIVB

The women's 12 event 1996 FIVB tour went to nine different countries: Brazil, Italy, Japan, Portugal, Belgium, Korea, Indonesia, Puerto Rico, and including 2 stops in the U.S.A. (Hermosa Beach, California and the Atlanta Olympic Games in Georgia). Total prize money for the women's 1996 FIVB tour was $1,590,000.00. The Brazilian team of Sandra Tavares Pires and Jacqueline Louise "Jackie" Cruz Silva compiled the best winning record of the 1996 FIVB Women's World Tour. Pires and Silva advanced to the "Gold-Medal" match at 8 events, winning 6 times. The next best record was also recorded by a Brazilian team. The team of Shelda Kelly Bruno Bede and Adriana Brandao Behar advanced to the "Gold-Medal" match twice, winning both times. The only American team to win on this years tour was Lisa Arce and Holly McPeak. Arce and McPeak won the World Series event, Pusan Haewoondae Beach Korea.

1996 FIVB BEACH VOLLEYBALL SCHEDULE

Date	Location	Prize
February 2-4	La Serena, Chili	$ 50,000
Feb 28 - March 3	Rio de Janeiro, Brazil	$150,000
April 12-14	Macelo, Brazil	$ 80,000
April 19-20	Recife, Brazil	$ 80,000
June 21-23	Hermosa Beach, USA	$ 80,000
July 23-27	Atlanta, GA, USA	Olympics
August 9-11	Osaka, Japan	$ 80,000
August 9-11	Espinho, Portugal	$ 80,000
August 16-18	Ostend, Belgium	$ 80,000
October 11-13	Carolina Beach, PR	$150,000
November 7-10	Lombok, Indonesia	$ 80,000
November 22-24	Korea	$ 80,000

SANDRA TAVARES PIRES
Brazilian Sandra Tavares Pires teamed-up with compatriot Jackie Silva as the top team on the 1996 FIVB Women's Tour. They advanced to the "Gold-Medal" match of 8 events, winning 6 times. Above photo, Pires makes an offensive attack.
Photo Courtesy of "Couvi"

TOP 25 FIVB WOMEN PLAYERS
(start of 1996)

1.	Jackie" Silva Cruz	Brazil
1.	Sandra Pires Tavares	Brazil
3.	Nancy Reno	USA
4.	Holly McPeak	USA
5.	Karolyn Kirby	USA
6.	Barbra Fontana	USA
7.	Angela Rock	USA
8.	Adriana Samuel Ramos	Brazil
8.	Monica Rodriguez	Brazil
10.	Kerri-Ann Pottharst	Australia
10.	Natalie Cook	Australia
12.	Lori Forsythe	USA
13.	Linda Hanley	USA
14.	Liz Masakayan	USA
15.	Yukiko o Yukko Takahashi	Japan
15.	Sachiko Fujita	Japan
17.	Danja Muesch	Germany
17.	Beate Buehler	Germany
19.	Adriana Behar Brandao	Brazil
20.	Anita Palm	Australia
21.	Liane Fenwick	Australia
22.	Magda Rejane Falco de Lima	Brazil
23.	Christine Eleanor Wilson	Australia
23.	Sarah Straton	Australia
23.	Beate Paetow	Germany
23.	Cordula Borger	Germany

INDIVIDUAL FIVB TOURNAMENT FINISHES
1996

Player	1st	2nd	3rd	4th	5th
Lisa Arce	1	0	1	1	0
Shelda Kelly Bruno Bede	2	0	6	0	0
Adriana Brandao Behar	2	0	6	0	0
Donalee Bragado	0	1	0	0	0
Laura Bruschini	0	0	0	0	2
Beate Buhler	1	1	0	1	1
Gayle Castro	0	0	0	0	1
Natalie Cook	1	1	0	3	3
Berta Kaize Engel	0	0	0	0	1
Liane Fenwick	0	0	1	0	0
Maike Friedrichsen	0	2	0	1	1
Camilla Funck	0	0	0	0	1
Barbra Fontana	0	0	0	0	2
Maya Hashimoto	0	0	0	0	1
Yukikio Ishizaka	0	1	0	0	0
Gerusa Ferreirde Jesus	0	0	0	0	1
Pernille Jorgensen	0	0	0	0	1
Debora Schoon Kadijk	0	0	0	0	1
Pat Keller	0	1	0	0	0
Eri Kinugasa	0	0	0	0	1
Karolyn Kirby	0	0	0	0	2
Chikako Kumamae	0	0	0	0	1
Liz Masakayan	0	0	0	1	2
Holly McPeak	1	0	2	3	1
Silke Meyer	0	1	0	0	1
Junko Moriyama	0	0	0	0	1
Danja Musch	1	2	0	2	1
Sandra Tavares Pires	6	2	1	0	0
AnnaKarrie Poppinga	0	0	1	1	1
KerriAnn Pottharst	1	1	0	3	3
NiPutuTim Rahayu Yudhani	0	0	0	0	1
Deb Richardson	0	0	0	0	1
Nancy Reno	0	0	1	1	1
Angela Rock	0	0	0	1	3
AdrianaBento Rodrigues	0	0	0	0	3
Monica Rodrigues	1	4	2	0	1
MariaIsabelBarroso Salgado	0	0	0	0	1
AdrianaRamos Samuel	1	4	1	1	1
Christine Schaefer	0	0	1	0	0
JacquelineLouise"Jackie"Cruz Silva	6	2	1	0	0
Karina Lins de Silva	0	0	0	0	3
Annamaria Solazzi	0	0	0	1	2
Sarah Straton	0	0	1	0	0
Yukiko Takahashi	0	1	0	1	0
Consuelo Tureita	0	0	0	1	0
Kaori Tsuchiya	0	0	0	1	0
LisetteVanDe Ven	0	0	0	0	1

TOP 50 FIVB WOMEN PLAYERS
(end of 1996)

1.	Sandra Tavares Pires	Brazil
1.	Jacqueline Louise "Jackie" Cruz Silva	Brazil
3.	Shelda Kelly Bruno Bede	Brazil
3.	Adriana Brandao Behar	Brazil
5.	Monica Rodrigues	Brazil
5.	Adriana Ramos Samuel	Brazil
7.	Holly McPeak	USA
7.	Natalie Cook	Australia
8.	Kerri-Ann Pottharst	Australia
10.	Danja Musch	Germany
11.	Angela Rock	USA
12.	Adriana Rodrigues Bento	Brazil
12.	Karina Lins e Silva	Brazil
14.	Lisa Arce	USA
15.	Yukiko Takahashi	Japan
16.	Anna Karrie Poppinga	USA)
17.	Barbra Fontana	USA
18.	Maike Friedrichsen	Germany
19.	Annamaria Solazzi	Italy
20.	Beate Buhler	Germany
21.	Liz Masakayan	USA
21.	Monica Rodrigues	Brazil
23.	Angela Clarke	Australia
23.	Laura Bruschini	Italy
27.	Gerusa Ferreira de Jesus da C	Brazil
27.	Maria Isabel Barroso Salgado	Brazil
27.	Karolyn Kirby	USA
30.	Barb Broen Ouellette	Canada
30.	Camilla Funck	Denmark
31.	Pernille Jorgensen	Denmark
33.	Sarah Straton	Australia
34.	Donalee Bragado	USA
35.	Berta Kaize Engel	Indonesia
35.	Ni Putu Timy Rahayu Yudhani	Indonesia
37.	Christine Schaefer	USA
38.	Merita Berntsen	Norway
38.	Ragni Hestad	Norway
40.	Linda Hanley	USA
41.	Nancy Reno	USA
42.	Kristine Drakich	Canada
43.	Renata de Castro Palmier Costa	Brazil
43.	Roseli Ana Timm	Brazil
45.	Audrey Cooper	England
45.	Amanda Jane Glover	England
47.	Krista Blomquist	USA
48.	Guylaine Dumont	Canada
49.	Dez Leipham	USA
50.	Maya Hashimoto	Japan
51.	Monique Oliver	USA

After two events of 1996, Brazil had claimed 31 medals in 22 FIVB Women's events since the start of the series in August 1992. Brazil had won seven events while placing second 12 times and third 12 times. The U.S.A. had earned 33 medals, with 15 first place finishes, nine second place finishes, and nine third place finishes.

ADRIANA BEHAR & SHELDA BEDE
The Brazilian team of Adriana Behar and Shelda Bede had the second best record, on the 1996 FIVB Tour, advancing to the "Gold-Medal" match twice, winning both times. Above photo, Behar (left) and Bede (right) enjoy the flavor of their "Gold-Medals"
Photo Courtesy of the FIVB

WOMEN'S TOURNAMENT RESULTS
1996-WPVA

FAIRFAX VIRGINIA
February 3rd, 1996

The 1996 WPVA Tour began on an indoor "beach" on February 3rd, 1996. The site was George Mason University's, Patriot Center, in Fairfax, Virginia. Karolyn Kirby and Christine Schaefer defeated Liz Masakayan and Angela Rock 15-4, to capture the championship match.

3rd Place: Holly McPeak and Nancy Reno
3rd Place: Barbra Fontana and Linda Hanley

NEW YORK NEW YORK
February 24th, 1996

Madison Square Garden was the site for the second WPVA Tour indoor "beach" event. Holly McPeak and Nancy Reno defeated Liz Masakayan and Angela Rock 15-13 in a thrilling final.

3rd Place: Karolyn Kirby and Christine Schaefer
3rd Place: Barbra Fontana and Linda Hanley

DEERFIELD BEACH FLORIDA
April 5th-7th, 1996

The top-seeded team of Holly McPeak and Nancy Reno, after trailing 5-2, scored seven un-answered points to take a 9-5 lead over Liz Masakayan and Angela Rock. Rock and Masakayan would make it close again at 10-8, but McPeak and Reno would score five straight points to win the final 15-8, over the second-seeded team, at Deerfield Beach, Florida.

3rd Place: Lisa Arce and Patty Dodd
4th Place: Elaine Roque and Dennie Shupryt-Knoop
5th Place: Barbra Fontana and Linda Hanley
5th Place: Karolyn Kirby and Christine Schaefer

CAROLINA BEACH PUERTO RICO
April 27th-28th, 1996

The $50,000.00 WPVA Evian Beach Volleyball tour's second outdoor stop was on Carolina Beach in Puerto Rico. Second-seeded Lisa Arce won her first WPVA Pro-Beach Volleyball Tour final. She was teamed with Holly McPeak. They won over the third seeded team of Patty Dodd and Angela Rock 15-10. While Arce was claiming her first Evian Tour title, McPeak was winning her 11th WPVA title, after posting her first 10 championships with Nancy Reno. Dodd was playing in her first final since June 21, 1991 when she and Elaine Roque lost a double final to Karolyn Kirby and Angela Rock. Arce and McPeak advanced to the finals with a 15-6 win over the fourth seeded team of Barbra Fontana and Linda Hanley. There were 29 teams competing in the tournament. There were four partnership changes among the top eight seeded teams in this tournament. This was only the third time, in the 10-year history of the WPVA, that a number one-seeded team, McPeak and Reno, had changed during the season.

3rd Place: Barbra Fontana and Linda Robertson Hanley
4th Place: Karolyn Kirby and Nancy Reno
5th Place: Karrie Poppinga and Christine Schaefer
5th Place: Gail Castro and Deb Richardson

NANCY RENO & HOLLY McPEAK
Nancy Reno and Holly McPeak had a lot to talk about, with their various partner changes during the 1996 beach volleyball season. Above photo, McPeak (right) points-out an idea to partner Reno (left).
Photo Courtesy of the AVP

KAROLYN KIRBY & NANCY RENO
When they were paired-up, Karolyn Kirby and Nancy Reno were all smiles as well as successful. In 1996, they advanced to 2 finals winning the WPVA event in San Diego California. Above photo, Kirby (left) and Reno (right) are happy to be together.
Photo Courtesy of the AVP

HERMOSA BEACH CALIFORNIA
May 3rd-5th, 1996

In Hermosa Beach, California, Barbra Fontana and Linda Hanley defeated Karolyn Kirby and Nancy Reno 12-11 to win this "Evian" Pro tournament. Fontana and Hanley scored two upset wins on Sunday to claim the $50,000.00 Evian Hermosa Beach Open. Fontana, playing in front of a hometown crowd of 4,500 fans and Hanley downed the top seeded team of Kirby and Reno 12-11 to claim the $11,000 first place earnings in a final that was televised nationally by ABC Sports. They advanced to the final with an upset victory over third seeded Arce and McPeak 14-9. The victory in the final was great retaliation for Fontana and Hanley, after losing 18-16, in an 80-minute and 86-sideout, decision to Kirby and Reno in an earlier match.

3rd Place: Lisa Arce and Holly McPeak
4th Place: Cammy Ciarelli and Patty Dodd
5th Place: Liz Masakayan and Angela Rock
5th Place: Gail Castro and Deb Richardson

SAN DIEGO CALIFORNIA
May 17th-19th, 1996

The number one-seeded team, of Karolyn Kirby and Nancy Reno, scored six straight match wins over the weekend, to win the Evian Women's Pro Beach Volleyball Tour event. The tournament was staged at Mariner's Point, in San Diego, California. They defeated the fourth-seeded team of Barbara Fontana and Linda Hanley 15-4 in the finals. This was the fourth Evian Tour title together for Kirby and Reno. Kirby, at this event, reached a record 57 Evian Tour titles. She also captured her fifth San Diego Open title. Kirby, has won 38 of 42 matches in San Diego, including 26 straight from 1991 through three matches in 1995.

3rd Place: Lisa Arce and Holly McPeak
4th Place: Elaine Roque and Dennie Shupryt Knoop
5th Place: Karrie Poppinga and Christine Schaefer
5th Place: Liz Masakayan and Angela Rock

ANGELA ROCK
Angela Rock had a good year on the 1996 WPVA Tour. She advanced to 6 finals, winning once. She was also voted the "Best-Server" on the WPVA Tour. Above photo, Rock hits a set from Linda Hanley, towards the block of Nancy Reno.
Photo Courtesy of the AVP

AUSTIN TEXAS
May 31st-June 2nd, 1996

The reunited Olympians, Holly McPeak and Nancy Reno, the USA number one Olympic beach volleyball team, captured the Evian Open, at Emerald Point on Lake Travis in Austin, Texas. This was their first event together since their breakup in mid-April. The number one-seeded team, of McPeak and Reno defeated the third-seeded team of Lisa Arce and Karolyn Kirby by a score of 15-7. McPeak and Reno moved into the finals with a 15-6 win over the fourth seeded team of Patty Dodd and Angela Rock. Arce and Kirby squeezed out a 16-14 victory over the second-seeded team of Barbra Fontana and Linda Hanley.

3rd Place: Barbra Fontana and Linda Hanley
4th Place: Patty Dodd and Angela Rock
5th Place: Janice Harrer and Gayle Stammer
5th Place: Elaine Roque and Dennie Shupryt-Knoop

BALTIMORE MARYLAND
June 4th-9th, 1996

The "OLYMPIC TRIALS", took place from June 4th-9th, 1996, at the Harbor View Complex on Baltimore's Inner Harbor, in Baltimore, Maryland. The top players from the FIVB, AVP, WPVA, and the Bud-Four-Person Tours, that had earned at least five points on the FIVB World Series Tour were eligible to compete in the Olympic

DENNIE SCHUPYT KNOOP
Dennie Schupyt Knoop played well on the 1996 WPVA Tour, finishing within the top five 8 times. She was also voted the WPVA's "Most Inspirational" player. Above photo, Knoop hits a set from Elaine Roque.
Photo Courtesy of the AVP

Trials. Holly McPeak and Nancy Reno were the first team to qualify for the U.S.A. Olympic Team, based on having the highest FIVB point total for teams representing the U.S.A. The second U.S.A. team to qualify was Barbra Fontana and Linda Hanley with a 16-14 victory over Elaine Roque and Dennie Shupryt-Knoop in the first Olympic qualification match. Gail Castro and Deb Richardson became the third and final U.S.A. team to qualify for the Olympics with a 15-13 win over Roque and Knoop, in a 53 minute match that featured five ties and three lead changes. Castro and Richardson rallied from an 8-4 deficit to tie the score at 8-8 when Richardson rejected Knoop at the net. Roque and Knoop scored the next three points to take an 11-8 lead. Castro and Richardson scored the next five points to take a 13-11 lead Roque and Knoop pulled within one at 14-13, but Richardson's block off Roque at the net ended the match on the fifth match point.

OCEAN CITY MARYLAND
June 14th-16th, 1996

Olympians Barbra Fontana and Linda Robertson Hanley, seeded second, won their second event of the season in Ocean City Maryland, on Dorchester Beach. They defeated the eighth-seeded team of Harrer and Stammer by a score of 15-11 to win the final of this $100,000.00 Evian United States Open. The $100,000.00 prize money for this U.S. Open was the highest total purse in WPVA women's domestic beach volleyball history. This was the seventh Evian tour win for Fontana and the sixth for Hanley. Fontana and Hanley moved into the final with a 15-10 win over the top-seeded team of McPeak and Reno. Harrer and Stammer were the first eighth-seeded team in the History of the WPVA Pro-Beach Volleyball Tour to reach a tournament final.

3rd Place: Holly McPeak and Nancy Reno
4th Place: Dennie Knoop Shupryt and Elaine Roque
5th Place: Gail Castro and Deb Richardson
5th Place: Karrie Poppinga and Christine Podraza

NEWPORT RHODE ISLAND
June 29-30, 1996

On the weekend of June 29-30, 1996, the longest and highest scoring game in WPVA history took place. In a thrilling, marathon championship match, the second-seeded team of Barbra Fontana and Linda Hanley defeated the third-seeded team of Karolyn Kirby and Angela Rock 22-20. They won in one hour and twenty-seven minutes, to win their second consecutive Women's Pro Beach Volleyball Association tournament. The tournament was staged on Easton's Beach in Newport Rhode Island. The match was tied 12 times as Hanley was able to break a 20-20 tie with an ace serve for the fourth lead change of the match. After the 76th and 77th sideout's of the match, Kirby hit a shot that was just long to end the second longest match in terms of time in WPVA history. This was the third tournament win this year for Fontana and Hanley. The 22-20 score in the final was the highest-scoring championship match in

LINDA HANLEY
Linda Hanley was successful on the 1996 WPVA Tour. She advanced to the finals 9 times, winning 4 times. She was voted the "Best-Hitter" on the WPVA Tour. Above photo, Hanley is in position to pass the ball.
Photo Courtesy of Dennis G. Steers

KRISTA BLOMQUIST
Krista Blomquist provided some creditable competition on the 1996 WPVA Tour. She was voted the "Most-Improved" player, on the tour, by her peers. Above photo, Blomquist shows excellent form while passing the ball.
Photo Courtesy of the AVP

the 10-year history of the WPVA and tied the record for the highest-scoring match in women's pro beach volleyball history. Holly McPeak and Nancy Reno lost a heart-breaker 16-14 earlier in the tournament to Rock and Kirby.

3rd Place: Holly McPeak and Nancy Reno
4th Place: Krista Blomquist and Danalee Bragado
5th Place: Karrie Poppinga and Christine Schaefer
5th Place: Patty Dodd and Lisa Arce

CHICAGO ILLINOIS
July 13th-14th, 1996

The Chicago Illinois Evian Women's Pro Beach Volleyball Tour event, on North Avenue Beach, featured two Olympic-bound teams. Top-seeded Holly McPeak and Nancy Reno defeated second-seeded Barbra Fontana and Linda Hanley 15-11. McPeak and Reno, who were seeded second in the 1996 Atlanta Olympic Games beach volleyball competition that began July 23rd, 1996, rebounded from an opening loss on Sunday morning They lost, 15-10 to fifth-seeded Elaine Roque and Dennie Shupryt-Knoop. They then went on to defeat Angela Rock and Karolyn Kirby 15-11 in a semi-final match. After trailing in the match 9-4, they then went on to win the tournament. This was their fourth championship of the season and twelfth championship since April of 1995.

3rd Place: Elaine Roque and Dennie Knoop
4th Place: Angela Rock and Karolyn Kirby
5th Place: Lisa Arce and Patty Dodd
5th Place: Krista Blomquist and Danalee Bragado

LONG BEACH CALIFORNIA
July 20th-21st, 1996

The WPVA's 11th Open of the 1996 season took place on Belmont Shore's in Long Beach, California. The tournament was won by the top-seeded team of Karolyn Kirby and Angela Rock. This was their 18th tournament win together. They defeated the second-seeded team of Lisa Arce and Patty Dodd 15-11 in the final. The teams of Nancy Reno and Holly McPeak, Linda Hanley and Barbra Fontana, Deb Richardson and Gail Castro were all out of the tournament to participate at the 1996 Atlanta Olympic Games. With these teams out, Kirby and Rock scored six-straight wins this weekend en route to the title. They gave up only 35 points in the six matches. The WPVA's all-time tournament winner, Kirby seized her 58th domestic tournament win and her 64th in her 10 season pro beach volleyball career. Kirby and Rock

NANCY RENO
Nancy Reno was number two on the 1996 WPVA Tour's win list. Reno advanced to 6 finals, winning 5 times. She was voted the "Best-Blocker" on the 1996 WPVA Tour. Above photo, Reno, the "Best-Blocker" on the tour shows her winning form.
Photo Courtesy of the AVP

ELAINE ROQUE
Elaine Roque was still competitive in 1996, on the WPVA Tour. She finised within the top five places at 8 tournaments. Roque was votes the 1996 WPVA Tour's "Sportswomanship-Award" by her peers. Above photo, Roque serving the ball.
Photo Courtesy of Dennis G. Steers

earned their way into the finals by defeating the eight-seeded team of Marie Anderson and Pat Keller. Arce and Dodd beat the fourth-seeded team of Karrie Poppinga and Christine Schaefer by a score of 15-4.

3rd Place: Karrie Poppinga and Christine Schaefer
4th Place: Marie Andersson and Pat Keller
5th Place: Elaine Roque and Dennie Shupryt-Knoop
5th Place: Cammy Ciarelli and Liz Masakayan

NEW YORK CITY NEW YORK
August 8th-11th, 1996

With the Olympics over, the WPVA continued it's season with a tournament at Rumsey Play-Field in Central Park, New York City, New York, The third seeded team of Lisa Arce and Holly McPeak, after losing 15-12 to the second seeded team of Karolyn Kirby and Nancy Reno, earned a spot in the finals by recording the best round-robin record of 6-1. In the finals they defeated the top-seeded team of Barbra Fontana and Linda Hanley by a score of 15-6. ABC TV provided "same-day" coverage of the finals.

3rd Place: Karolyn Kirby and Nancy Reno
4th Place: Patty Dodd and Angela Rock
5th Place: Elaine Roque and Dennie Shupryt-Knoop

HUNTINGTON BEACH CALIFORNIA
August 16th-18th, 1996

Third-seeded Holly McPeak and Lisa Arce captured their second-straight Evian WPVA event at the $100,000.00 National Championship, in Huntington Beach, California. Arce and McPeak fought back to win over Barbra Fontana and Linda Hanley, after Fontana and Hanley tied the match at 6-6 and 7-7 before taking leads of 9-7 and 11-9. Arce and McPeak then tied the match at 11-11 and 12-12 as the time clock ran out following 19-successive sideouts. On the first, 1996 serve in overtime, Arce connected on a spike that ended the match with only six seconds of the 30 second sudden-death session expired. Arce and McPeak earlier advanced to the finals with a 15-10 win over 5th seeded Patty Dodd and Christine Schaefer. ABC TV provided "same-day" coverage of the finals.

3rd Place: Patty Dodd and Christine Schaefer
4th Place: Krista Blomquist and Danalee Bragado
5th Place: Karolyn Kirby and Nancy Reno
5th Place: Gail Castro and Gayle Stammer

PORTLAND OREGON
August 31st-September 1st, 1996

The $50,000.00 WPVA "Jantzen Pro Beach Volleyball" event, took place in River Place Square, Portland, Oregon. The top seeded team of Barbra Fontana and Linda Hanley regained their winning ways with a 15-12 victory over the 2nd-seeded team of Lisa Arce and Holly McPeak. This was their fourth WPVA tour win of the season. Fontana and Hanley gained the finals with a 15-10 win over Kirby and Rock. Arce and McPeak made the finals by defeating Elaine Roque and Dennie Shupryt Knoop by a score of 15-5.

3rd Place: Elaine Roque and Dennie Shupryt Knoop
4th Place: Karoly Kirby and Angela Rock
5th Place: Krista Blomquist and Danalee Bragado
5th Place: Patty Dodd and Christine Schaefer

KAUAI HAWAII
September 13th-15th, 1996

Lisa Arce and Holly McPeak won their third "major" tournament, of the 1996 WPVA season. They were the winners oft "The Best of the Beach III" in Lihuee Kauai, Hawaii, at Nawiliwili Park, near Kalapaki Beach. This was the final WPVA Evian Tour event, of the fifteen held in 1996. Arce and McPeak up-ended the top seeded team of Barbra Fontana and Linda Hanley by a score of 15-7. Arce and Mc Peak earned their way into the final match by defeating the fourth-seeded team of Dodd and Schaefer. Fontana and Hanley earned their spot in the finals with a victory over the third-seeded team of Karolyn Kirby and Angela Rock, by a score of 15-8.

3rd Place: Karoly Kirby and Angela Rock
4th Place: Patty Dodd and Christine Schaefer
5th Place: Gail Castro and Gayle Stammer
5th Place: Liz Masakayan and Karrie Poppinga

LISA ARCE
Lisa Arce experienced an excellent year on the 1996 WPVA Tour. She advanced to 7 finals, winning 4 times. Above photo, Arce is in position to dig the ball.
Photo Courtesy of "Couvi"

KAROLYN KIRBY
Karolyn Kirby also experienced an excellent year on the 1996 WPVA Tour. She advanced to the finals 6 times, winning 3 times. Above photo, Kirby grouvels in the sand for the ball.
Photo Courtesy of the AVP

WOMEN'S TOURNAMENT RESULTS 1996-FIVB

RIO DE JANERIO BRAZIL
February 28th-March 3rd, 1996

The $150,000.00 Women's FIVB Pro-Beach Volleyball event, in Rio de Janeiro Brazil, was won by the Brazilian team of Jackie Silva and Sandra Pires. In the championship match, they defeated the Australian team of Natalie Cook and Kerri Pottharst, 12-8 and 12-9, to earn a paycheck for $30,000.00.

3rd Place: Adriana Behar and Shelda Bruno Bede-Bra
4th Place: Nancy Reno and Holly McPeak-USA
5th Place: Monica Rodriguez and Adriana Samuel Ramos-Bra
5th Place: Danja Muesch and Beate Buehler-Ger
Additional U.S.A. finishers: Barbra Fontana-Fontana and Linda Hanley in the seventh spot, Karolyn Kirby and Liz Masakayan, along with Angela Rock and Christine Schaefer in the ninth spot.

MACEIO BRAZIL
April 10th-14th, 1996

The $140,000.00 Women's FIVB tournament at Maceio Brazil, was a Brazilian sweep. The top three finishes by the Brazilian teams was the first time in FIVB Women's Pro Beach Volleyball World Championship-Series events history that one country was able to do this. This also was the first time in the last 22 FIVB Beach Volleyball World Championship-Series international events that a WPVA player from the U.S.A. did not finish in the top four. In the championship match, the second-seeded team of Sandra Pires and Jackie Silva scored a 12-6 and 12-11 win over compatriots Monica Rodrigues and Adriana Samuel. Pires and Silva advanced to the finals with a 15-10 win over Shelda Bede and Adriana Behar. Rodrigues and Samuel advanced to the finals with a 15-12 win over the seventh-seeded German team of Beate Buhler and Danja Musch.

3rd Place: Shelda Bede and Adriana Behar-Bra
4th Place: Beate Buhler and Danja Musch-Ger
5th Place: Holly McPeak and Nancy Reno-USA
5th Place: Kerri Pottharst and Natalie Cook-Aus
Additional U.S.A. finishes: Karolyn Kirby and Angela Rock finished seventh. Linda Hanley and Barbra Fontana finished thirteenth. Karrie Poppinga and Christine Schaefer finished 17th.

ADRIANA BEHAR & SANDRA PIRES
On the 1996 FIVB Women's Tour, Adriana Behar teamed-up with Shelda Bede for 2 "Gold-Medals" while Sandra Pires paired-up with Jackie Silva for 6 "Gold-Medals" Above photo, Behar challenges the block of Pires.
Photo Courtesy of the FIVB

NATALIE COOK
Australian, Natalie Cook stepped-up to win a "Gold-Medal" at the 1996 Fivb Women's event in Osaka Japan, with compatriot Kerrie Ann Pottharst. Cook also finished second at the "World Championships in Brazil. Above photo, Cook spiking the ball.
Photo Courtesy of "Couvi"

RECIFE BRAZIL
April 17th-21st, 1996

The $140,000.00 Women's FIVB tournament at Pina Beach in Revife Brazil was another Brazilian sweep. In the championship match, the top-seeded team of Sandra Pires and Jackie Silva scored a 12-9, 7-12 and 12-10 win over compatriots, fifth-seeded Monica Rodrigues and Adriana Samuel. In front of over 5,000 screaming fans. Silva and Pires gained entry into the finals with a 15-8 win over Adriana Behar and Shelda Bede. Rodrigues and Samuel moved into the finals via the loser's bracket and then with a win over Kerri Pottharst and Natalie Cook by a score of 16-14.

3rd Place: Shelda Bede and Adriana Behar-Bra
4th Place: Natalie Cook and Kerri-Ann Pottharst-Aus
5th Place: Angela Rock and Liz Masakayan-USA

Finishes by U.S.A. teams: Angela Rock and Liz Masakayan along with Karolyn Kirby and Barbra Fontana-Fontana took fifth place, Kerrie Poppinga and Christine Schaefer finished in seventh place, Nancy Reno and Holly McPeak dropped to a ninth place finish. Desirae Leipham and Luciano were in 25th place.

HERMOSA BEACH CALIFORNIA, U.S.A.
June 19th-23rd, 1996

The Women's $140,000.00 FIVB, Bud Light World Beach Volleyball Invitational, at Hermosa Beach, California, U.S.A. was won by the number one women's beach volleyball team in the world, Brazilians Sandra Pires and Jackie Silva. In the best of three championship match, Pires and Silva defeated fellow Brazilians, Adriana Samuel and Monica Rodrigues, 12-9 and 12-8. Silva and Pires, the number one seeded team, in the 1996 Olympic debut of beach volleyball, advanced to the finals without a loss in six games. This was their seventh career FIVB tournament win together. This FIVB "Bud Light World Beach Volleyball Invitational" provided somewhat of an Olympic preview, with a total of 38 out of a possible 42 men's and women's Olympic bound teams competing here.

3rd Place: Holly McPeak and Nancy Reno-USA
4th Place: Kerrie-Ann Pottharst and Natalie Cook-Aus
5th Place: Angela Rock and Liz Masakayan-USA
5th Place: Gail Castro and Deb Richardson-USA

Additional U.S.A. finishes: Barbra Fontana and Linda Hanley along with Christine Schaefer and Karrie Poppinga in seventh place, Krista Blomquist and Wendy Fletcher along with Karolyn Kirby and Lisa Arce in ninth place, Janice Harrer and Gayle Stammer were in thirteenth place.

VASTO ITALY
July 5th-7th, 1996

The next Women's FIVB tournament took place on the Baiocco's Beach in Vasto, Italy. Eight of the nineteen teams, entered in the women's $30,000.00 challenger event, were participating in their first ever FIVB World Championship-Series event. It was an all German final, Beate Buhler and Danja Musch defeated Maike Friedrichsen and Silke Meyer, 12-8 and 12-8, in the 55 minute, best of three match. The winner's were happy to take home the $3,000.00 first place prize. Earlier in the tournament, the U.S.A. team of Kerrie Poppinga and Christine Schaefer beat the team of Annamaria Solazzi and Consuelo Turetta, from Italy by a score of 15-13 in

DANJA MUSCH & BEATE BUHLER
German's Danja Musch and Beate Buhler played well as a team on the 1996 FIVB Women's Tour. They advanced to the finals of 2 events, winning the "Gold-Medal" at the Vasto Italy event. Above photo, Buhler hits a set from Musch, over the block of Nancy Reno and away from the defense of Holly McPeak.
Photo Courtesy of "Couvi"

MONICA RODRIGUES
Brazilian Monica Rodrigues played well on the 1996 FIVB Women's Tour. Rodrigues advanced to 5 finals with compatriot Adriana Samuel, winning the "Gold-Medal" at the Salvador Bahia Brazil event. Above photo, Rodrigues pokes the ball over the block of Linda Hanley, towards the defense of Barbra Fontana.
Photo Courtesy of "Couvi"

a crowd pleasing 60 minute match. The team of Friedrichsen and Meyer made it to the finals with a 16-14 win over Anna Maria Solazzi and Turetta. The team of Buhler and Musch made it to the finals with a 15-8 win over Poppinga and Schaefer.
3rd Place: Christine Schaefer and Karrie Poppinga-USA
4th Place: Annamaria Solazzi and Consuelo Turetta-Italy
5th Place: Lisette Van de Ven and Debora Schoon Kadijk-NED
5th Place: Maria Barroso Salgado and Gerusa de Jesus-Bra

OSAKA JAPAN
August 9th-11th, 1996

Tannowa Beach on the coast of Osaka, Japan, was the site of the next $80,000.00 Women's FIVB tournament. In the championship match, the team of Kerrie-Ann Pottharst and Natalie Cook, from Australia, defeated the U.S.A. team of Pat Keller and Donalee Bragado by a score of 12-6.
3rd Place: Liane Fenwick and Sarah Straton-Aus
4th Place: Ykiko Takahashi and Kaori Tsuchiya=Japan
5th Place: Maya Hashimoto and Eri Kinugasa=Japan
5th Place: Chikako Kumamae and Junko Moriyama-Japan

ESPINHO PORTUGAL
August 9th-11th, 1996

On the same weekend that there was a women's FIVB event in Japan, the FIVB promoted an $80,000.00 competition at Perrier Beach, in Espinho, Portugal. While the Australian team of Kerrie-Ann Potthart and Natalie Cook took care of business in Japan, it was a Brazilian, 1-2-3 sweep in Portugal. In the championship match, Jackie Silva and Sandra Pires defeated compatriots Adriana Samuel and Monica Rodrigues by scores of 12-3 and 12-7.
3rd Place: Adriana Behar and Shelda Bede-Bra
4th Place: Maike Friedrichsen and Danja Musch-Ger
5th Place: Anna Maria Solazzi and Laura Bruschini-Italy
5th Place: Karina Lins e Silva and Adriana Bento Rodrigues-Bra
Marla O'Hara and Monique Oliver were the top U.S.A. finishers, with a seventh place finish. Other U.S.A. finishers: Ali Wood and Wendy Fletcher, along with Dez Leipham and Jen Murrell finished in ninth place.

OSTEND BELGIUM
August 16th-18th, 1996

Grote Shand Beach, in Ostend, Belgium, was the location for the next FIVB Women's World Series event. There were a total of 32 women's teams participating. In the championship match, with the weather hot and sunny, the packed stadium of 5,000 plus fans enjoyed watching the German team of Beate Buhler and Danja Musch battle the Brazilian team of Sandra Pires and Jackie Silva. The Germans went down in defeat by scores of 12-6 and 12-8.
3rd Place: Adriana Behar and Shelda Bede-Bra
4th Place: Adriana Samuel and Monica Rodrigues-Bra
5th Place: Maike Friedrichsen and Silke Meyer-Ger
5th Place: Annamaria Solazzi and Laura Bruschini-Italy
The best U.S.A. finish was by Dez Leipham and Jen Murrell, in 17th place.

PUSAN KOREA
August 23rd-25th, 1996

The next FIVB Women's World Series event took place on Pusan Haewoondae Beach, in Pusan, Korea. The large Asian crowd of volleyball fans were thrilled to have the new Japanese team of Yukiko Takahashi and Yukiko Ishizaka participating in the championship match. In the championship match, the Japanese were paired off against the U.S.A. team of Holly McPeak and Lisa Arce.

The Japanese duo started off splendidly, but still lost the first match 12-10. In the second match of the final McPeak and Arce dominated 12-2, earning $16,000.00 for their first place effort. Arce and McPeak had made it into the final by defeating compatriots Rock and Masakayan 15-8 in the semi-finals. Takahashi and Ishizaka won their semifinal match, 15-8, against Brazilians Samuel and Monica.
3rd Place: Adriana Samuel and Monica Rodrigues-Bra
4th Place: Liz Masakayan and Angela Rock-USA
5th Place: Ni PutuTimy Rahayu Yudhani and Berta "Etta" Kaize Engel-Indo
5th Place: Pernille Jorgensen and Camilla Funck-Den

CAROLINA PUERTO RICO
September 6th-8th, 1996

The first ever women's $300,000.00 Grand Slam event took place on Isla Verde Beach, in Carolina, Puerto Rico. This $300,000.00 event was honored with the presence of the FIVB President Rubin Acosta and his wife. The President and his wife were able to observe some of the best matches, since the 1996 Olympics, in Atlanta. There were 32 participating teams from 12 countries. It was an all Brazilian final with Adriana Behar and Shelda Bede defeating Sandra Pires and Jackie Silva, 12-4 and 12-9, to snatch the championship match. Bede and Behar's share of the purse was $15,000.00 each.
3rd Place: Lisa Arce and Holly McPeak-USA
4th Place: Kerrie-Ann Pottharst and Natalie Cook-Aus
5th Place: Karolyn Kirby and Kerrie Poppinga-USA
5th Place: Karina Lins Silva and Adriana Rodrigues Bento-Bra
Additional U.S.A. finishes: Angela Rock and Liz Masakayan along with Barbra Fontana and Linda Hanley in 7th. Donalee Bragado and Krista Blomquist in 9th, Dez Leipham and Gayle Stammer in 13th, Gail Castro and Deb Richardson along with Marla O'Hara and Monique Oliver in 17th.

SALVADOR BAHIA, BRAZIL
November 7th-10th, 1996

There were 19 teams, from 12 countries that participated in the $140,000.00 FIVB women's event in Salvador, Bahia, Brazil. The Brazilian crowd was enthusiastic because it was an all Brazilian final. In the championship match Monica Rodriguez and Adriana Samuel outlasted Sandra Pires and Jackie Silva 12-10 and 12-8 to win the first place prize of $16,000.00.
3rd Place: Adriana Behar and Shelda Bede-Bra
4th Place: Holly McPeak and Lisa Arce-USA
5th Place: Karina Lins Silva and Adriana Rodrigues Bento-Bra
5th Place: Australians Kerrie-Ann Potthart and Natalie Cook-Bra
Additional U.S.A. finishers: Angela Rock and Barbra Fontana in 7th place. Kerrie Poppinga and Christine Schaefer, along with Donalee Bragado and Ali Wood finished in the 13th spot.

JAKARTA INDONESIA
November 22nd-24th, 1996

At Jakarta Indonesia the $140,000.00 FIVB Women's World series event was won by the Brazilian team of Adriana Behar and Shelda Bede. In the championship match, Behar and Bede defeated the German team of Maike Friedrichsen and Danja Muesch, 12-4 and 12-8. Shelda and Behar earned $8,000.00 each for their winning effort. They went undefeated in this tournament.
3rd Place: Jackie Silva and Sandra Pires–Bra
4th Place: Holly McPeak and Kerrie Poppinga-USA
5th Place: Angela Rock and Barbra Fontana-USA
5th Place: Kerrie-Ann Pottharst and Natalie Cook-Aus
Additional U.S.A. finishers: Monique Oliver and Jennifer Meredith, Christine Schaefer and Leanne Schuster, Ali Wood and Wendy Fletcher all in 9th place. Donalee Bragado and Krista Blomquist were in the 13th spot.

TOP PHOTOS: Left: Angela Rock gets above the net for the hit. **Center:** Chris Podraza gets ready for action. **Right:** Michelle Morse gets above the net to make a cut shot.

MIDDLE PHOTOS: Left: Liz Masakayan attacking the ball. **Center:** Pat Keller jumps high to attack the ball. **Right:** Kerrie Poppinga attacking a jump serve.

1996 WOMEN'S BEACH VOLLEYBALL ACTION

BOTTOM PHOTOS: Left: Gail Castro celebrates a victory. **Center:** Evelyn Conley reaches high to hit the ball. **Right:** Jackie Campbell concentrates on making a good cut shot.

Photo's Courtesy of the AVP

OLYMPIC BEACH VOLLEYBALL 1996

USOC QUALIFYING RULES
OLYMPIC BEACH VOLLEYBALL

The rules for men and women qualifying for the 1996 "Olympic Beach Volleyball" in Atlanta, Georgia, U.S.A. started out by stating that the highest-ranked team of each of the first eight countries including the organizing country appearing in the FIVB world ranking, total eight teams. This first rule meant that the top AVP men's teams from the U.S.A. would not automatically qualify for the Olympics.

The men's team, from the U.S.A., that qualifed from the above rule would be a team that did/could not compete in the AVP that year because of the conflicting schedules. The other two U.S.A. teams (U.S.A. will have a total of 3 teams since it is the host country) was determined at a qualifying tournament that was open to 32 teams of players that had accumulated a minimum of 5 FIVB points or they had participated in the tournaments at Clearwater Florida or Hermosa Beach California in 1995. There were several AVP players that had enough points to participate in this qualifying tournament.

The qualifying rules continued for another 3000+ words of rhetoric.

U.S.A. QUALIFYING PARTICIPANTS
MEN:

Mike Dodd and Mike Whitmarsh*
Karch Kiraly and Kent Steffes*
Randy Stoklos and Adam Johnson
Scott Ayakatuby and Brian Lewis
Eric Fonoimoana and Rob Heidger
Brent Frohoff and Ricci Luyties
Bill Boullianne and Dain Blanton
Mike Schlegel and Jim Nichols
Leif Hanson and Chris Young
Jeff Rodgers and Bruk Vandeweghe
Mark Eller and Todd Schaefer
Scott Friederichsen and Eric Wurts
Sean Fallowfield and Kevin Martin
Canyon Ceman and Lee LeGrands
Tim Hovland and Jon Stevenson
Jeff Williams and Carlos Briceno

WOMEN:

Linda Hanley and Barbara Fontana*
Deb Richardson and Gail Castro*
Lisa Arce and Karolyn Kirby
Liz Masakayan and Angela Rock
Dennie Shupryt-Knoop and Elaine Roque
Karrie Poppinga and Christine Schaefer
Janice Harrer and Gayle Stammer
Danalee Bragado and Maria O'Hara
Krista Blomquist and Wendy Fletcher
Erin Deiters and Desiree Lelpham
Marie Anderson and Monique Oliver
*=qualified

1996 OLYMPICS
The 1996 Atlanta Olympics became the inaugural site for the inclusion of beach volleyball. In front of a capacity crowd of more than 80,000, inside the Olympic Stadium, Muhammad Ali, the world's best-known sports figure, ignited the Olympic cauldron. The beach volleyball venue on "Olympic Beach" in Jonesboro Georgia, a suburb of Atlanta. was also filled to capacity for each and every session. The photo above shows the Olympic cauldron surrounded by the Olympic audience.
Photo Courtesy of "Couvi"

OLYMPIC TRIALS: MEN & WOMEN
June 4th-9th, 1996

The first U.S.A. teams to qualify for the beach competition in the 1996 Atlanta Olympics, by earning the most FIVB points, were: Sinjin Smith with Carl Henkel for men and Nancy Reno with Holly McPeak for the women. Prior to the Olympics, Nancy Reno and Holly McPeak separated (twice), because Reno "needed a change." At the time this impacted their Olympic status that would not be rectified until about a month prior to the Olympics actually taking place. They would get back together and play in the remaining, pre-Olympic tournaments together. In the men's event Carlos Briceno and Jeff Williams, from the U.S.A., earned the second most FIVB points to give them an automatic spot in the final four of the Olympic trials in Baltimore Maryland, held June 4th-9th, 1996

History was made in Baltimore Maryland during the period of June 4th through June 9th 1996. The first ever Beach Volleyball Olympic Trials took place at the Inner Harbor Complex. The team of Mike Whitmarsh and Mike Dodd was the first men's team to qualify, at the Olympic trials, for an Olympic birth after experiencing a bumpy road in the losers bracket, squeaking out a 16 to 14 victory over Brent Frohoff and Ricci Luyties. They had lost to them earlier 15 to 13. They then went on to beat up Karch Kiraly and Kent Steffes 15 to 8 as Whitmarsh was in the "Zone", he blocked or touched almost every ball that came his way! Kiraly and Steffes went on to play Jeff Williams and Carlos Briceno in the losers bracket, thrashing them 15-3. Briceno and Williams were in the loser's bracket after being seeded in the final four by way of FIVB points. They were quickly ousted from there by Randy Stoklos and Adam Johnson by a score of 15 to 4. Stoklos and Johnson met Kiraly and Steffes for the final Olympic birth. K&K won 15-3 as Stoklos put forth a valiant effort after injuring his ankle in warm-ups. Dodd and Whitmarsh along with Kiraly and Steffes joined Sinjin Smith and Carl Henkel, who qualified via FIVB points, on the 1996 Olympic team to compete in the first ever Men's Olympic "Beach Volleyball" competition.

At the women's qualifier, the team of Linda Hanley and Barbara Fontana was the first women's team to qualify for an Olympic birth. They were seeded into the final four via their FIVB point total. They then went on to defeat Elaine Roque and Dennie Shupryt-Knoop in a thrilling comeback victory 16 to 14. Then they defeated Gail Castro and Deb Richardson 15 to 6 in the winners final, thus qualifying for the Olympics. Castro and Richardson defeated Scupryt-Knoop and Roque for the last remaining Olympic birth with another come from behind victory by a score of 15-13. Hanley and Fontana along with Castro and Richardson joined Nancy Reno and Holly McPeak, who qualified via FIVB points, on the 1996 Olympic team to compete in the first ever Women's Olympic "Beach Volleyball" competition. Joining the teams from the USA, in the Olympics were 21 teams from different countries in the men's division and 13 teams in the women's division for a total of 24 men's teams and a total of 16 women's teams competing.

CARL HENKEL & SINJIN SMITH
Carl Henkel and Sinjin Smith were the first men's USA team to qualify for the 1996 Atlanta Olympiad, via FIVB points. Above photo, Smith hits a set from Henkel towards the defense of Kent Steffes (left) and Karch Kiraly (right), during 1996 Olympics.
Photo Courtesy of "Couvi"

HOLLY McPEAK & NANCY RENO
Holly McPeak and Nancy Reno were the first women's USA team to qualify for the 1996 Atlanta Olympiad, via FIVB points. Above photo, McPeak hits a set from Reno, over the block of Linda Hanley, away from the defense of Barbra Fontana.
Photo Courtesy of "Couvi"

1996 OLYMPICS ATLANTA, GEORGIA
July 23rd-28th, 1996

The 1996 Olympics in Atlanta Georgia U.S.A. began with the opening ceremonies on July 19, 1996. The indoor volleyball took place for 16 days: July 20, 1996 thru August 4, 1996. Beach Volleyball made its debut in the Olympics on July 23rd, 1996 at Atlanta Beach. The "Olympic Beach" was located in Jonesboro, a suburb of Atlanta, Georgia. The Olympic venue was a splendid, permanent beach-volleyball stadium. The stadium was specifically designed for beach volleyball. During each of the double sessions, held from July 23rd, 1996 to July 26th, 1996, the stadium was filled to capacity with 8,000 screaming fans on the "main court," and another 3,000 fans on the "outside court." The main court was overflowing on July 27-28, 1996 for the medal matches.

A double elimination tournament was played for both men and women until a total of four teams qualified for the semifinals (The two final teams from the winners bracket and the two final teams from the elimination bracket). Semifinal winners played for the first and second places; semi-final losers played for third and fourth places.

Prior and during the Olympics, the U.S.A. players let it be known that they did not like the Mikasa ball that was used for the Olympics. The players criticized the ball. The Mikasa ball is considered harder to control than the Wilson ball, used on the 1996 AVP tour. The Mikasa ball is smoother, like an indoor ball. Since the seams of the ball are smaller the ball has a tendency to sail more.

Because of their Olympic participation, the USA player's were hot items on the talk show circuit and they also made appearances at Major League baseball games to throw out the first pitch.

The U.S. players utilized technical advisors. Smith and Henkel utilized the original "King of the Beach", Gene Selznick. Kiraly and Steffes brought in a flexibility and movement coach, named Adrian Crook. Dodd and Whitmarsh employed Whitmarsh's brother, Rusty as a technical advisor. Linda Hanley and Barbra Fontana utilized the talents of Linda's Husband, John Hanley for detailed advice. The players were disappointed with the limited role that the advisors were allowed to play. The advisors had no access to the players. Also, the advisor's were not even allowed to talk to the players during the matches.

The Olympic Beach Volleyball event consisted of 24 men's teams and 16 women's teams from all over the world (two person teams). Following is a list of the beach volleyball teams participating in the 1996 Atlanta Georgia Olympic

1996 OLYMPIC BEACH VOLLEYBALL - ATLANTA GEORGIA
The 1996 Atlanta Olympiad was packed full of excitement, as was the beach volleyball venue. The 8,000 seat "Main-Court" stadium, as well as the 3,000 seat "Out-Side" court was sold-out for every session, usually twice-a-day! The "Main-Court" was overflowing for the medal-matches. Above photo, In front of a packed 1996 Olympic beach volleyball stadium, Mike Dodd and Mike Whitmarsh get ready to receive serve from the Australian team of Julian Prosser and Lee Zahner!
Photo Courtesy of "Couvi"

MEN'S OLYMPIC BEACH VOLLEYBALL PARTICIPATING TEAMS

UNITED STATES OF AMERICA:
- #1 Carl Henkel and Sinjin Smith
- #2 Mike Dodd and Mike Whitmarsh
- #3 Karch Kiraly and Kent Steffes

BRAZIL:
- #1 Roberto Lopes and Franco Vieira Neto
- #2 Melo Ferreira Nobrega and Emanual Rego

NORWAY
- #1 Jan Kvalheim and Bjoern Maaseide

CANADA:
- #1 John Child and Mark Heese
- #2 Ed Drakich and Marc Dunn

ARGENTINA:
- #1 Martin Conde and Esteban Martinez

CUBA:
- #1 Francisco Alvarez and Rosell Milanes

SPAIN:
- #1 Bosma Minguez and Sixto Jimenez Galan
- #2 Miguel Martin Prieto and Javier Yuste

FRANCE:
- #1 Philippe Jodard and Christian Penigaud

GERMANY:
- #1 Jorg Ahmann and Axel Hager

ITALY:
- #1 Andrea Gihurghi and Nicola Grigolo

AUSTRALIA:
- #1 Julien Prosser and Lee Zahner

NETHERLANDS:
- #1 Michael Everaet and Sander Mulder
- #2 Marko Kiok and Michell Vander Kulp

PORTUGAL:
- #1 Luis Maia and Jogo Pereira Brenha Alves

JAPAN:
- #1 Shoji Setoyama and Kazuyuki Takao

NEW ZEALAND:
- #1 Glenn Hamilton and Reid Hamilton

INDONESIA:
- #1 Mohammed Nurmifid and Markojl Markojl

SWEDEN:
- #1 Tom Englen and Fredrick Petersson

CZECH REPUBLIC:
- #1 Marek Pakosta and Michal Palinek

LUIS MAIA & JOGO BRENHA ALVES
The Portugese team of Luis Maia and Jogo Brenha Alves finished in 4th place, as they gave USA teams fits as well as eliminating Sinjin Smith and Carl Henkel from the competition. Above photo Brenha hits a set from Maia, towards the block of Mike Whitmarsh.
Photo Courtesy of "Couvi"

JOHN CHILD & MARK HEESE
At the 1996 Olympics, Canadian's John Child and Mark Heese played outstanding volleyball, on their way to winning the "Bronze-Medal" Above photo, Child hits a set from Heese, away from the block of Kent Steffes, towards the defense of Karch Kiraly.
Photo Courtesy of "Couvi"

MEN'S BEACH VOLLEYBALL RESULTS
1996-OLYMPICS

ATLANTA, GEORGIA
July 23rd-28th, 1996

The men's Olympic matches were filled with excitement and surprises. The number one seeded team from Brazil, Roberto Costa Lopes and Roberto/Franco Vieira Neto was eliminated early prior to the medal matches. The team of Jan Kvalheim and Bjoern Maaseide from Norway, another team that had potential for a medal was eliminated before they could get to the medal round.

The most exciting matches, of the inaugural beach volleyball Olympics, all included teams from the USA In a winner's bracket game between the USA's Carl "Carlton" Henkel and Sinjin Smith against Cuba's Francisco Alvarez and Juan Miguel Rosell Milanes, the lead changed on numerous occasions until the Cuban's took the lead at 14-13 and were serving match point, when the main referee made a call against the Cuban's. The Cuban's argued so intensely that they received a red card, this gave the Americans a point, tying the match at 14-14. Smith and Henkel then took the lead 15-14, and on match-point the referee made another call against the Cuban's giving the U.S.A. the victory.

After Smith and Henkel beat the Cuban's one of the most electrifying matches in the history of beach volleyball was setup, it took place between Sinjin Smith and Carl Henkel against Karch Kiraly and Kent Steffes in the semifinals of the winners bracket. This match was really set up, prior to the Olympics, by all of the verbal jousting that had taken place between the F.I.V.B. and the A.V.P. Smith and Henkel on one side defending their right to be in the Olympics and Kiraly pointing out has to why they did not belong there. Prior to the Olympics Henkel was looking forward to a showdown with Kiraly and Steffes in the Olympics. Henkel said "I don't mind playing that team at all. I would be happy to have both American teams in my bracket. They are the enemy I know and would like to take them down myself after all the smack they've been talking."

In the end it came down to the match on center court at Atlanta Beach, during the 1996 Olympics. Henkel and Smith came into the match as heavy "under-dogs." They played the game as if they had nothing to lose, their intensity and preparation showed as the scoring went back and forth as both teams took turns with the lead.

1996 MEN'S OLYMPIC BEACH VOLLEYBALL - ATLANTA GEORGIA
The most exciting beach volleyball match, of the 1996 Atlanta Olympiad, was the long-awaited match-up between the USA teams of Carl Henkel and Sinjin Smith against Karch Kiraly and Kent Steffes. The lead in this match changed hands on several occasions, with Henkel and Smith advancing to match-point first, but Kiraly and Steffes prevailed, winning the match 17-15, after four tries at match-point. Above photo, In-front of a huge crowd, Sinjin hits a set from Henkel towards the defense of Steffes (left) and Kiraly (right).
Photo Courtesy of "Couvi"

Midway through the match Henkel took charge, blocking Kiraly on several occasions. Henkel and Smith went ahead 12-8 and looked as if the momentum was in their favor. Kiraly and Steffes, as they have on so many prior occasions, began to come back. They tied the score at 13-13. Henkel and Smith would then get to match point on four occasions, but were unable to get the winning point. Kiraly and Steffes came back to tie the scorer at 15-15 and then take the lead 16-15. After their fourth try at match point Kiraly and Steffes won the match 17-15, putting Smith and Henkel into the losers bracket. Kiraly and Steffes moved on to the medal round.

The other U.S.A. team of Mike Dodd and Mike Whitmarsh also moved on to the medal round with a win over the Canadian team of John Child and Mark Heese. This match was a surprisingly competitive match with Dodd and Whitmarsh taking the win.

The U.S.A. now had two teams set for the medal round. Henkel and Smith had a chance to make it three U.S.A. teams in the medal round. All they had to do was beat the team of Luis Barblsa Maia and Jogo Pereira Brenha Alves, from Portugal. Smith and Henkel had beat this team earlier in the competition 15-7, and had never lost to this team in four previous tries. Of course this would turn out to be a "barn-burner." The team from Portugal played magnificently, especially the defense of Maia, he made dig after dig on balls that nobody in the stadium thought would ever come up. This was an authentic " in the zone" performance by Maia. The team from Portugal would go on to beat the U.S.A. 15-13 in another truly sensational match. This took Smith and Henkel out of the competition. Sinjin Smith had shown that he still has a few top notch games left in him, and Carl Henkel showed that he can play beach volleyball with the best of them!

In the first medal match Dodd and Whitmarsh were paired against the team from Portugal, Luis Barblsa Maia and Jogo Pereira Brenha Alves. The team from Portugal showed that their previous match against Smith and Henkel was not a fluke. They would trade the lead with Dodd and Whitmarsh until they would forge ahead 11-9, Dodd and Whitmarsh battled back and win the match 15-13 qualifying for the "Gold-Medal" match.

The other team to play in the gold medal match was to be determined in the match between Karch Kiraly and Kent Steffes against the team from Canada, John Child

KARCH KIRALY & KENT STEFFES
Karch Kiraly showed the world that they were the best team on the planet as they won the "Gold-Medal" at the 1996 Atlanta Olympics. Above photo, Kiraly hits a set from Steffes, away from the block of Mike Whitmarsh..
Photo Courtesy of "Couvi"

MIKE WHITMARSH & MIKE DODD
Mike Whitmarsh and Mike Dodd played excellent volleyball on their way to winning the "Silver-Medal" at the 1996 Atlanta Olympics. Above photo, Whitmarsh hits a set from Dodd, towards the block of Kent Steffes.
Photo Courtesy of "Couvi"

and Mark Heese. The Canadian team made it to the medal round by defeating the favored team of Jan Kvalheim and Bjoern Maaseide from Norway.

As in most of the matches of the inaugural Olympic beach volleyball, this match turned out to be an exciting one to watch. Kiraly and Steffes came as if there was no tomorrow, taking the lead 4-0. On the next play they went ahead 5-0, but after the Canadians discussed the play with the referee, the point was taken off the board and the serve was awarded to the Canadians. They went on to tie the score at 5-5. In typical Karch and Kent fashion the Americans would go on to win 15-11.

The "Gold-Medal" match was set, U.S.A. against the U.S.A., the A.V.P. against the A.V.P. Out of 24 teams only two were from the A.V.P., and as the A.V.P. had proclaimed the cream did flow to the top, although it was a tougher road than most thought that it would be.

The gold medal match was anticlimactic as Kiraly and Steffes came out unstoppable. They finished of Dodd and Whitmarsh with scores of 12-8 and 12-5 in the best two-out-of-three, final to take the gold medal, Dodd and Whitmarsh settling for the silver medal. Kiraly and Steffes were the clear aggressors, scoring the first six points on the way to winning the opening set. The second set was started with an ace serve by Steffes, and the best that Dodd and Whitmarsh could do the rest of the match was tie it three times.

Kiraly, who had led the United States to two Olympic volleyball titles indoors, this time won on the sand.

In the bronze medal match, Child and Heese, from Canada, handled the team from Portugal, Luis Barbosa Maia and Jogo Pereira Brenha Alves, in another anticlimactic match 12-5 and 12-8. The Portuguese, seeded 18th in the 24-team field couldn't come up with another defensive effort like those that helped them oust the Smith-Henkel duo and nearly upset Dodd and Whitmarsh.

1st Place: Karch Kiraly and Kent Steffes-USA
2nd Place: Mike Dodd and Mike Whitmarsh-USA
3rd Place: John Child and Mark Heese- Canada
4th Place: Joao Brenha Alves and Luis Maia-Portugal
5th Place: Sinjin Smith and Carl Henkel-USA
5th Place: Javier Bosma and Sixto Jimenez- Spain

1996 MEN'S OLYMPIC BEACH VOLLEYBALL - ATLANTA GEORGIA
The 1996 Olympic beach volleyball venue provided non-stop action, with virtually every match that was contested. Above photo, against the team from Cuba, Sinjin Smith slices a set from Carl Henkel, past the block of Juan Miguel Rosell Milanes, towards the defense of Francisco Alverez, during 1996 Olympic action. Smith and Henkel defeated Milanes and Alverez by a score of 15-13.
Photo Courtesy of "Couvi"

U.S.A. MEN'S TEAM RECORDS 1996 - OLYMPICS
July 23rd-28th, 1996

Karch Kiraly and Kent Steffes USA, defeated Italians Andrea Ghiurghi and Nicola Grigolo, by a score of 15-7.

Mike Dodd and Mike Whitmarsh USA, defeated Julien Prosser and Lee Zahner, from Australia with a game score of 15-10.

Sinjin Smith and Carl Henkel USA, defeated Joao Carlos Pereira Brenha Alves and Luis Barbose Maia from Portugal with a game score of 15-7.

Karch Kiraly and Kent Steffes USA, defeated Axel Hager and Jorge Ahmann from Germany with a score of 15-5.

Mike Dodd and Mike Whitmarsh USA, defeated Emanuel Rego and Josi Marco De Melo Ferrira Nobrega from Brazil with a game score of 15-9.

Sinjin Smith and Carl Henkel USA, defeated Francisco Alverez and Juan Miguel Rosell Milanes from Cuba with a game score of 15-13.

Karch Kiraly and Kent Steffes USA, defeated Sinjin Smith and Carl Henkel USA with a game score of 17-15.

Mike Dodd and Mike Whitmarsh USA, defeated Javier Bosma Minguez and Sixto Jimenez Galan from Spain with a game score of 15-6.

Sinjin Smith and Carl Henkel USA were eliminated by Joao Carlos Pereira Brenha Alves and Luis Miguel Barbosa Maia from Portugal with a game scores of 15-13.

Karch Kiraly and Kent steffes USA, defeated John Child and Mark Heese with a game score of 15-11.

Mike Dodd and Mike Whitmarsh USA defeated Joao Carlos Pereira Brenha Alves and Luis Miguel Barbosa Maia from Portugal deferating them with a game score of 15-13.

Karch Kiraly and Kent Steffes USA defeated Mike Dodd and Mike Whitmarsh USA with game scores of 12-8 and 12-5.

Karch Kiraly and Kent Steffes, USA won the "Gold Medal" while Mike Dodd and Mike Whitmarsh, USA won the "Silver Medal."

MIKE DODD & MIKE WHITMARSH
Americans Mike Dodd and Mike Whitmarsh provided a lot of excitement on their way to winning the "Silver-Medal" at the 1996 Atlanta Olympics. Above photo, During the "Gold-Medal" match of the 1996 Olympiad, Dodd hits a set from Whitmarsh towards the block of Karch Kiraly.
Photo Courtesy of "Couvi"

KARCH KIRALY & KENT STEFFES
During the 1996 Olympiad, Karch Kiraly and Kent Steffes were involved in possibly the most exciting beach volleyball match ever contested, against Sinjin Smith and Carl Henkel, on their way to winning the "Gold-Medal" Above photo, Kiraly hits a set from Steffes, towards the block of Henkel.
Photo Courtesy of "Couvi"

1996 MEN'S OLYMPIC BEACH VOLLEYBALL - ATLANTA GEORGIA
Top Left Photo: Canadian John Child attacks a set from compatriot Mark Heese. **Top Right Photo:** Brazilian Franco Neto attempting to poke the ball over the block of Bjorn Maaseide, from Norway. **Bottom Photo:** Italy's Andrea Gihurghi hits a set from compatriot Nicola Grigolo into the block of Karch Kiraly, while Kent Steffes is set for action. All of the above action took place during the 1996 Olympics, on "Olympic Beach" in Jonesboro Georgia, a suburb of Atlanta.

Photos Courtesy of "Couvi"

1996 MEN'S OLYMPIC BEACH VOLLEYBALL - ATLANTA GEORGIA
Top Left Photo: Portuguese player, Jogo Brenha Alves hits a set from compatriot Luis Maia, towards the block of Jan Kvalheim, from Norway. **Top Right Photo:** Karch Kiraly and Carl Henkel battle above the net for the ball. **Bottom Photo:** Australian Julien Prosser hits a set from fellow countryman Lee Zahner, past the block of Mike Whitmarsh, towards the defense of Mike Dodd. All of the above action took place during the 1996 Olympics, on "Olympic Beach" in Jonesboro Georgia.
Photos Courtesy of "Couvi"

1996 MEN'S OLYMPIC BEACH VOLLEYBALL - ATLANTA GEORGIA
Top Photo: Karch Kiraly slices a set from Kent Steffes, past the block of Mike Whitmarsh. Mike Dodd is on defense. **Bottom Photo:** The large crowd enjoying the Olympic beach volleyball action, inside the jam-packed lakeside, beach volleyball stadium. All of the above action took place during the 1996 Olympics, on "Olympic Beach" in Jonesboro Georgia, a suburb of Atlanta.
Photos Courtesy of "Couvi"

TOP PHOTOS: Left: Bill Walton interviewing Leonard Armato. **Center:** USA Olympic Gold Medalist Karch Kiraly Top Left) and Kent Steffes (Top Right) and Silver Medal winners Mike Dodd (Bottom Lef) and Mike Whitmarsh (Bottom Right) acknowledge the crowd support. **Right:** The beach volleyball venue scoreboard was capable of doing more than keep score!

MIDDLE PHOTOS: Left: A Portugese fan shows his collors. **Center:** The numer-one Brazilian fan and cheerleader, "Eight-Ball". **Right:** A Canadian fan looks for some crowd support.

1996 OLYMPIC BEACH VOLLEYBALL - ATLANTA GEORGIA

BOTTOM PHOTOS: Left: The scoreboard shows how the scoring went in the very exciting match between the two American teams of Kent Steffes and Karch Kiraly against Sinjin Smith and Carl Henkel. **Center:** A USA fan gets his head into volleyball. **Right:** Another USA fan cheers-on his favorite team. All of the above activities took place during the 1996 Olympics, at "Olympic Beach" venue in Jonesboro Georgia.

Photos Courtesy of "Couvi"

TOP PHOTOS: Left: Jogo Perira Brenha Alves, from Portugal, gets above the net for the block attempt. **Center:** Portugals Luis Maia attempts to poke the ball over the block of John Child, from Canada. **Right:** Mike Dodd maneuvers into position to pass the ball.

MIDDLE PHOTOS: Left: Norway's Jan Kvalheim challenges the block of Brazilian Franco Vieira Neto. **Center:** Karch Kiraly acknowledging the crowd with the wave of his familiar pink hat. **Right:** Spain's Sixto Jimenez Galen hits a set from compatriot Bosma Minguez, towards the block of Mike Whitmarsh.

1996 OLYMPIC BEACH VOLLEYBALL - ATLANTA GEORGIA

BOTTOM PHOTOS: Left: Jogo Pereira Brenha Alves, from Portugal, "joust" with Carl Henkel. **Center:** Canadian Mark Heese reaches high for the ball. **Right:** Kent Steffes reaches high for the block attempt. All of the above action took place during the 1996 Olympics, at "Olympic Beach" venue in Jonesboro Georgia, a suburb of Atlanta.

Photos Courtesy of "Couvi"

WOMEN'S BEACH VOLLEYBALL RESULTS 1996-OLYMPICS

ATLANTA, GEORGIA
July 23rd-28th, 1996

The 1996 Olympics at Atlanta, Georgia, on Atlanta Beach, in Jonesboro, took place from July 23rd-28th, 1996. Located in Clayton County International Park, which is operated by Clayton County, Atlanta Beach features a man-made lake with large beach areas. The area's 5,000 seat permanent beach volleyball stadium was adapted to seat 8,000 spectators during the 1996 Olympic Games and remained intact after the Games. The adjacent, grandstand court had an additional 3,000 seats available for preliminary matches. The women's bracket was an all Brazilian final with the top-seeded team of Jacqui Silva and Sandra Pires defeating Monica Rodrigues and Adriana Samuel 12-11 and 12-6 in the best-of-three "Gold-Medal" match. After the women's final, all four Brazilian players took enormous Brazilian flags and waved them as they raced around the fringe of the stadium court. In the "Bronze-Medal" match, Linda Hanley and Barbra Fontana of the U.S.A. took an 11-9 first set lead against Australia's Natalie Cook and Kerri Pottharst, only to lose 12-11. The Australians built a 7-1 lead in the second set and went on to win the "Bronze Medal" 12-7. Earlier, Hanley and Fontana scored eight of the final nine points for a 15-10 victory to eliminate fellow Americans Holly McPeak and Nancy Reno, the second-seeded team. After this match, McPeak announced that her sometimes stormy partnership with Reno was over. They lost earlier to the Australian team of Cook and Pottharst by a score of 15-1. The third American Olympic team of Deb Richardson and Gail Castro won their first match over the team of Debora Kadjik and Lisette Van de Ven, from the Netherlands, 15-8. They then lost to Cook and Pottharst from Australia, 15-7 and were then soundly eliminated by a the Japanese team of Fujita and Takahashi, 15-1. All of the matches, over the entire tournament were watched by a full capacity "Olympic Spirited" crowd of fans in the main stadium. The Brazilian fans were especially animated.

1996 WOMEN'S OLYMPIC BEACH VOLLEYBALL - ATLANTA GEORGIA

The Women's bracket of the 1996 Olympic beach volleyball on "Olympic Beach" in Jonesboro Georgia, was every-bit as entertaining as the Men's division. Above photo, in an All-American match, Nancy Reno hits a set from Holly McPeak, past the block of Barbra Fontana, towards the defense of Linda Hanley. Fontana and Hanley won this match by a score of 15-10, thus eliminating McPeak and Reno from the Olympic competition.

Photo Courtesy of "Couvi"

U.S.A. WOMEN'S TEAM RECORDS 1996 - OLYMPICS
July 23rd-28th, 1996

Holly McPeak and Nancy Reno defeated Annabelle Prawerman and Brigitte Lesage from France with a score of 15-4.

Gail Castro and Deb Richardson defeated Debora Schoon Kafijk and Lisette Van de Ven from the Netherlands with a score of 15-8.

Barbra Fontana and Linda Hanley defeated Merita Bernsten and Ragni Hestad from Norway with a score of 15-4.

Holly Mc Peak and Nancy Reno defeated Beate Buhler and Danja Musch from Germany with a score of 15-6.

Barbra Fontana and Linda Hanley were defeated by Monica Rodrigues and Adriana Samuel from Brazil with a score of 15-10.

Gail Castro and Deb Richardson were defeated by Natalie Cook and Keri Pottharst from Australia with a score of 15-7.

Holly Mc PeakMc Peak and Nancy Reno were defeated by Natalie Cook and Keri Pottharst from Australia with a score of 15-3.

Gail Castro and Deb Richardson were eliminated by Sachiko Fujita and Yukiko Takahashi from Japan with a score of 15-7.

Barbra Fontana and Linda Hanley defeated Liane Fenwick and Anita Spring Palm from Australia with a score of 15-6.

Barbra Fontana and Linda Hanley eliminated Holly McPeak and Nancy Reno with a score of 15-10.

Barbra Fontana and Linda Hanley were defeated by Jackie Silva and Sandra Pires from Brazil with a score of 15-8.

Barbra Fontana and Linda Hanley were eliminated by Natalie Cook and Keri Pottharst from Australia with a scores of 12-11 and 12-6.

Linda Hanley and Barbra Fontana finished with 4 wins 2 losses.

Nancy Reno and Holly McPeak finished with 2 wins and 2 losses.

Deb Richardson and Gail Castro finished with 1 win and 2 losses.

1996 WOMEN'S OLYMPIC BEACH VOLLEYBALL - ATLANTA GEORGIA
The American team of Holly McPeak and Nancy Reno did not live-up to expectations at the 1996 Atlanta Olympics. Above photo, German Danja Musch hits a set from her compatriot Beate Buhler towards the block of Nancy Reno as Holly McPeak is ready if the ball comes her way. McPeak and Reno won this match by a score of 15-6.

Photo Courtesy of "Couvi"

WOMEN'S OLYMPIC BEACH VOLLEYBALL PARTICIPATING TEAMS

UNITED STATES OF AMERICA:
#1 Holly McPeak and Nancy Reno
#2 Barbra Fontana and Linda Hanley
#3 Deb Richardson and Gail Castro

BRAZIL:
#1 Sandra Pires and Jackie Silva
#2 Monica Rodrigues and Andriana Samuel

AUSTRALIA:
#1 Natalie Cook and Keri Pottharst
#2 Liane Fenwick and Anita Palm

JAPAN
#1 Sachiko Fujita and Yukiko Takahashi
#2 Yukiko Ishizaka and Teruko Nakano

GERMANY
#1 Beate Buhler and Danja Musch

ITALY:
#1 Maria Solazzi and Consuelo Turetta

ENGLAND:
#1 Audrey Cooper and Amanda Glover

NORWAY:
#1 Merita Bernsten and Ragni Hestad

NETHERLANDS:
#1 Debora-Kadjik and Lisette Van de Ven

INDONESIA:
#1 Eta Berta Kaize and Timy Yudhani

CANADA:
#1 Margo Malowney and Barb Oullette

SANDRA PIRES & JACKIE SILVA
Brazilians Sandra Pires and Jackie Silva were the winners at the 1996 Atlanta Olympics, winning the All-Brazilian "Gold-Medal" match against Adriana Samuel and Monica Rodrigues. Above photo, Silva (right) prepares to set the ball for Pires (left).
Photo Courtesy of "Couvi"

BEATE BUHLER
Beate Buhler, from Germany, paired-up with compatriot Danja Musch to compete in the 1996 Olympics in Atlanta Georgia. Above photo, on "Olympic Beach" Buhler challenges the block of the USA's Nancy Reno.
Photo Courtesy of "Couvi"

1996 WOMEN'S OLYMPIC BEACH VOLLEYBALL - ATLANTA GEORGIA

Top Left Photo: Brazilian Sandra Pires digs the ball for her compatriot, Jackie Silva. **Middle Photo:** Holly McPeak digging the ball for partner Nancy Reno. **Top Right Photo:** Gail Castro hits a set from Deb Richardson, towards the defense of Australia's Natalie Cook (right) and Keri Pottharst (left). **Bottom Photo:** Team Japan, Yukiko Ishizaka hits a set from Teruko Nakano over the block of Barbra Fontana away from the defense of Linda Hanley. Action took place on the outside court. All of the above action took place during the 1996 Olympics, on "Olympic Beach" in Jonesboro Georgia, a suburb of Atlanta.

Photos Courtesy of "Couvi"

1996 WOMEN'S OLYMPIC BEACH VOLLEYBALL - ATLANTA GEORGIA

Top Left Photo: In an All-American match, Linda Hanley looks-on as Barbra Fontana (left) and Nancy Reno (right) "joust" for the ball. **Top Right Photo:** Holly McPeak setting the ball. **Bottom Photo:** Barbra Fontana is ready as Linda Hanley serves the ball to the Brazilian team of Adriana Samuel (left) and Monica Rodrigues (right). All of the above action took place during the 1996 Olympics, on "Olympic Beach" in Jonesboro Georgia.

Photos Courtesy of "Couvi"

1996 WOMEN'S OLYMPIC BEACH VOLLEYBALL - ATLANTA GEORGIA

Top Left Photo: Japan's Yukiko Ishizaka hits a set from compatriot Teruko Nakano, past the block of Barbra Fontana and away from the defense of Linda Hanley. **Top Right Photo:** Nancy Reno hitting a set from Holly McPeak, past the block of Barbra Fontana, towards the defense of Linda Hanley. **Bottom Photo:** The large crowd enjoying the Olympic beach volleyball action, inside the jam-packed lakeside, beach volleyball stadium. All of the above action took place during the 1996 Olympics, on "Olympic Beach" in Jonesboro Georgia.

Photos Courtesy of "Couvi"

TOP PHOTOS: Left: Germany's Beate Buhler pokes the ball over the block of Nancy Reno, while Holly McPeak gets ready to cover the shot. **Center:** Gail Castro follows through after attacking with a jump-serve. **Right:** Barbra Fontana (left) and Linda Hanley (right) celebrate a victory.

MIDDLE PHOTOS: Left: Deb Richardson watches the ball, after serving to the opposition. **Center:** Barbra Fontana hits the ball past the block of Australia's Keri Pottharst. **Right:** Linda Hanley follows through after spiking the ball.

1996 WOMEN'S OLYMPIC BEACH VOLLEYBALL ACTION

BOTTOM PHOTOS: Left: Brazilian Jackie Silva is ready for Olympic action. **Center:** Linda Hanley slices the ball past the block of Japan's Teruko Nakano. **Right:** Nancy Reno stretches-out in an effort to reach the ball. All of the above action took place during the 1996 Olympics, on "Olympic Beach" in Jonesboro Georgia.

Photo's Courtesy of "Couvi"

ADDITIONAL VOLLEYBALL INFORMATION 1996

In addition to the players on the 1996 pro-beach volleyball tour's there were over 3,600 - "AAA", "AA", "A", "B", "Unrated", and "Novice" rated male and female players on the CBVA Tour.

U.S. BEACH VOLLEYBALL DEMOGRAPHICS

In 1996, 14,331,000 Americans, over the age of six, played Beach Volleyball at least once. The male population of Beach players outnumber women participants 58% to 42%. Beach Volleyball players had an average household income of $46,700 versus $39,500 for court players. Beach Volleyball's highest incident of play was in the North-Central Region and the sport was being played on sand courts in virtually every land-locked state in the union. The total indoor and outdoor participation was at 41.3 million. The participation of beach volleyball, by U.S. region was 14.6% in the Northeast, 33.8% in North Central, 36.4% in the South, and 15.2% in the West.

SAN DIEGO CALIFORNIA
May 18th-19th, 1996

The 1996 San Diego-Ocean Beach "Bud Light Volleyball Festival" Women's Open was won by Australians Anita "Palm" Springs and Liane Fenwick. In the championship match, they defeated Susie Turner and Vickie Bohino. Tournament director, George Stepanof recorded that there were 7 teams entered in the tournament

3rd Place: Caroline Krattli and Karen Helyer
3rd Place: Jan Lighter and Rene Richey

SAN DIEGO CALIFORNIA
June 1st-2nd, 1996

The 1996 San Diego-Ocean Beach "Redsand" Men's "AAA" was won by Jason Stimpfig and Duncan Blackman. In the championship match, they defeated Aaron Smith and David Withrington. Tournament director, George Stepanof recorded that there were 20 teams entered in the tournament.

3rd Place: Dave Pearson and Bill Brown
4th Place: Chad Convis and John Hribar

SAN DIEGO CALIFORNIA
June 1st-2nd, 1996

The 1996 San Diego-Ocean Beach "Redsand" Women's Open was won by Kamila Pavlakosva and J.B. In the championship match, they defeated Kristine Scheitter and Veronica Sanchez. Tournament director, George Stepanof recorded that there were 18 teams entered in the tournament.

3rd Place: Jennifer Murrell and Sara Straton
4th Place: Monica Stewart and Linda Burton

SAN DIEGO CALIFORNIA
July 13th, 1996

The 1996 San Diego-Ocean Beach "Jose Cuervo" Men's Open was won by Andy Aguiar and Sean Burke. In the championship match, they defeated Tyson Kerr and Tom Black. Tournament director, George Stepanof recorded that there were about 15,000 "Walk-Bys" and 1,200 spectators at this event that had 20 teams entered.

3rd Place: Mike Garcia and Toby Braun
3rd Place: Brad Hayward and Chris Lippincott

LAGUNA BEACH CALIFORNIA
1996

The 1996 Laguna Beach Men's Open was an amateur "AAA" tournament. Mike Garcia and Brian Wisely were the winners. In the championship match, they defeated Dismas Abelman and Nick Pabareus.

3rd Place: Danny Lane and Matt Perry

SAN DIEGO CALIFORNIA
July 14th, 1996

The 1996 San Diego-Ocean Beach "Jose Cuervo" Women's Open was won by Julie Sprague and Elizabeth Chavez. In the championship match, they defeated Carolyn McDonald and Caron Janc. Tournament director, George Stepanof recordedhat there were 28 teams entered in the tournament.

3rd Place: Channon Nembach and Deanna Johnson
3rd Place: Laura Martin and Dianna Evans

MIXED-DOUBLES BEACH TOURNAMENT'S

MANHATTAN BEACH CALIFORNIA
July 6th, 1996

The 1996 Marine Street Mixed-Doubles Open was won by the team of Butch Miali and Christina Gage. In the championship final, they defeated Sean Icaza and Lisa Hoven. Tournament director Mike Cook noted that the weather was warm and sunny for this tournament with only 6 teams entered.

3rd Place: Brett Coordt and Lee Hoven
4th Place: Wayne Kresin and Wendy Fletcher
5th Place: Jeremy Cornwell and Tracy Tatum.

SAN DIEGO CALIFORNIA
July 14th, 1996

The 1996 San Diego-Ocean Beach "Jose Cuervo" Mixed-Double's Open was won by Bob Bruce and Caron Janc. In the championship match, they defeated Sean Burke and Robin Enciso. Tournament director, George Stepanof recorded that there were 6 teams entered in the event.

3rd Place: Eric Holman and Karen Helyer
3rd Place: Paul Kotas and Deanna Johnson

SAN DIEGO CALIFORNIA
June 1st-2nd, 1996

The 1996 San Diego-Ocean Beach "Redsand" Mixed-Double's Open was won by Tim Muret and Mary Ann Muret. In the championship match, they defeated Jack Quinn and Susie Turner.

MEN'S BEACH VOLLEYBALL
1997

In 1997, for the first time in the history of beach volleyball, California did not have the most "Pro" tournaments scheduled. Florida led all states with five. California had it's lowest total, since the "early days" of beach volleyball, with only four of the "Major" events scheduled.

In 1997, there were thirty-six recorded "Major" Beach Volleyball tournaments. Twenty-four of these tournaments were staged on U.S.A soil, while thirteen were played outside of the U.S.A. As mentioned above, of the twenty-four U.S. tournaments, Florida hosted five events while California hosted four. There were fifteen U.S. events staged in twelve states other than Florida and California. The California tournaments were held in Sacramento, Hermosa Beach (twice), and Westwood. Florida hosted tournaments in Fort Myers, Clearwater, Riveria Beach, Miami, and Orlando. The remaining U.S. tournaments were were held in: Phoenix Arizona, Las Vegas and Lake Tahoe Nevada, Vail Colorado, Belmar New Jersey, Milwaukee Wisconsin, Chicago Illinois, Minneapolis Minnesota, Indianapolis Indiana, Cleveland Ohio, Cape Cod Massachusetts, Grand Haven Michigan, along with three events in Texas San Antonio, Dallas, and Corpus Christi. The thirteen events held outside of the U.S.A. were hosted by:

1. Copacabana Beach, in Rio de Janeiro, Brazil
2. Czech Republic, at Spa Karlovy Vary Spa
3. Berlin, Germany
4. Ligano Italy, Lignano Sabbiadoro
5. "Golfe du Lion" shore, at the "Plages du Prado" in Marseille France
6. Klagenfurt, Austria
7. Espinho Portugal, on Baia Beach
8. Grote Shand Beach, at Ostend Belgium
9. Albena Bulgaria, at Balkan Beach
10. Mediterranean Coast of Turkey at Alanya, Turkey
11. On Las Teresitas Beach in Tenerife, Canary Islands, Spain
12. Fortaleza, Brazil
13. "Independence Cup" in Guaruja Sao Paulo Brazil

GRAND SLAM SERIES

The 1997 Miller Lite Grand Slam Series consisted of four prestigious events on the AVP Pro-Beach Tour: The Manhattan Open (replaced by the Hermosa Grand Slam), Chicago Open, Hermosa Open, and the Walt Disney World AVP Tour Championships at Orlando, Florida. The Grand Slam series featured a combined $1.25 million in prize money. The Grand Slam events also played a major role in determining which 16 AVP players participated at the World Championships, September 10th-14th, 1997, at the Los Angeles Tennis Center on the Campus of UCLA, with each individual player receiving points for their respective finishes. The top 14 ranked AVP players from the Grand Slam tournaments formed seven teams, while the eighth team consisted of the 15th and 16th ranked player's.

The top eight WPVA Pro-Beach teams also competed in the women's division of these "World Championships". Also participating at these "World Championships" were several of the top international, mens and women's teams that were competing on the FIVB Pro-Beach Tour. There was also a Four-Person Pro-Beach Division.

BEACH VOLLEYBALL EXPOSURE

In 1997, Professional Beach Volleyball was being exposed all over the world. Along with the twenty-four domestic events that were staged in the USA, there were thirteen events hosted by countries outside of the USA. Above photo, a large crowd enjoys a professional beach volleyball event in Klagenfurt Austria.

Photo Courtesy of the FIVB

AVP

The 1997 AVP Schedule included 24 events over 6 months in 14 states with over $4 million in total prize money.

Jose Loiola and Kent Steffes took the top spot on the 1997 AVP tour as they won 12 tournament championships together. They had four wins in Florida at Rivera Beach, Clearwater Beach, Miami and the "AVP Tour Championships" in Orlando. They also had wins at Cleveland Ohio, Corpus Christi and San Antonio Texas, Lake Tahoe Nevada, Chicago Illinois, Grand Haven Michigan, Milwaukee Wisconsin, and Phoenix Arizona. Loiola also won the "King of the Beach" tournament in Las Vegas Nevada. Karch Kiraly and Adam Johnson were the distant second highest winning record in 1997 with 4 tournament championships. Their wins came in Minneapolis Minnesota, Vail Colorado, and in California at Sacramento and Hermosa Beach.

Additional AVP teams that won in 1997, included: Mike Dodd and Mike Whitmarsh won two tournaments together. They won at Fort Myers Florida and Dallas Texas. Whitmarsh also won in Belmar New Jersey with Canyon Ceman. Ceman also won the Hermosa Beach Grand Slam event with Dain Blanton. Mark Kerins and Henry Russell won the tournament in Cape Cod Massachusetts. The tournament in Indianapolis Indiana was stopped because of rain, causing an eight-team tie for fifth place.

BEACH VOLLEYBALL POLITICS

In 1997, the political hot-button for Manhattan Beach was professional beach volleyball. The AVP was at the center of the dispute. The AVP's pursuit to charge for the tournament was challenged by a group of activists. The AVP was raised in Manhattan Beach, and has been a "local institution", since its inception in August of 1960. It has grown into the sports most prestigious beach volleyball event. To the disdain of the activists, the Manhattan Open's popularity had reached it's present stage of popularity with it's major sponsors, huge crowds, and live TV coverage. In 1996, the AVP informed the City of Manhattan Beach that the tournament cost more to produce than it was taking in. This is when the AVP asked for permission to charge for viewing the event. But instead the City Council voted to subsidize the event. This subsidy came back to create difficulty for the council, because it served as a tool for the activists when they accused the council of poor judgement. The council had even disregarded their own Department of Recreation Commission's recommendation and went ahead and announced the sale of tickets for the Manhattan Open. The group of activists filed legal action against the City. At least for 1997, they were successful in moving the event out of Manhattan Beach. It was moved to Hermosa Beach, and called the "Hermosa Grand Slam." This was the first time, since its inception in 1960, that the Manhattan Open was not staged in Manhattan Beach.

AVP BEACH VOLLEYBALL ACTION
In 1997, the AVP Tour provided monumental beach volleyball controversy when they proposed charging for events, especially in Manhattan Beach California. There was also plenty of beach volleyball action at all of the tour venues. Above photo, In front of a large, non-paying crowd, Brian Lewis challenges the block of Kent Steffes during last years Manhattan Beach Open.
Photo Courtesy of Frank Goroszko

1997 AVP MEN'S SCHEDULE

When	Where	TV
March 14-16	Las Vegas, Nevada	NBC
	King of the Beach Invitational	
March 28-30	Phoenix, Arizona	Fox Sports
April 4-6	Riviera Beach, Florida	Fox Sports
April 11-13	Clearwater Beach, Florida	Fox Sports
April 18-20	Ft. Myers Beach, Florida	Fox Sports
April 25-27	Miami Beach, Florida	Fox Sports
May 9-11	Dallas, Texas	Fox Sports
May 17-18	Corpus Christi, Texas	Fox Sports
May 23-25	San Antonio, Texas	Fox Sports
May 30	Indianapolis, Indiana	Fox Sports
June 6-8'	Lake Tahoe, California	Syndicated
June 13-15	Manhattan Beach, California	NBC
	(changed to the Hermosa Grand Slam)	
June 20-22	Chicago, Illinois	NBC
June 27-29	Cleveland, Ohio	Fox Sports
July 4-6	Cape Cod, Massachusetts	Fox Sports
July 11-13	Grand Haven, Michigan	Fox Sports
July 18-20	Milwaukee, Wisconsin	Fox Sports
July 25-27	Hermosa Beach, California	NBC
August 1-3	Sacramento, California	Fox Sprts
August 8-10	Vail, Colorado	Fox Sports
August 15-17	Minneapolis, Minnesota	Fox Sports
August 22-24	Belmar, New Jersey	Fox Sports
August 29-31	Orlando, Florida	NBC
	Walt Disney World - AVP Tour Championships	
Sept. 10-13	World Championships	NBC
	(FIVB and AVP)	
Sept. 14	Seattle, Washington	Fox Sports
	"Shootout"	

1997 AVP TOUR PLAYERS
End of Season - August 31, 1997

Scott Ayakatubby	Eduardo Anjinho Bacil
Dain Blanton	Aaron Boss
Bill Boulliane	Daniel Cardenas
Dan Castillo	Canyon Ceman
Ian Clark	Brent Doble
Mike Dodd	Eric Fonoimoana
Scott Friedrichsen	Brent Frohoff
Mike Garcia	Brian Gatzke
Albert Hannemann	Rob Heidger
Dax Holdren	Bryan Ivie
Adam Johnson	Mark Kerins
Wong, Kevin	Karch Kiraly
Lee LeGrande	Brian Lewis
Jose Loiola	Carlos Loss
Ricci Luyties	Matt Lyles
Jim Nichols	Raul Papaleo
Justin Perlstrom	Jason Pursley
Jeff Rodgers	Todd Rogers
Henry Russell	Wayne Seligson
Andrew Smith	Kent Steffes
Randy Stoklos	David Swatik
Troy Tanner	Matt Unger
Bruk Vandeweghe	Mike Whitmarsh
Eric Wurts	Chris Young

INDIVIDUAL AVP TOURNAMENT FINISHES
1997

Player	1st	2nd	3rd	4th	5th
Scott Ayakatubby	0	4	1	0	0
Eduardo Anjinho Bacil	0	0	1	0	1
Dain Blanton	1	1	4	3	4
Aaron Boss	0	0	0	0	2
Bill Boulliane	0	1	3	0	5
John Brajevic	0	0	0	0	1
Dan Castillo	0	0	0	1	3
Canyon Ceman	2	1	6	3	3
Ian Clark	0	0	1	2	3
Mike Dodd	2	1	2	2	7
Eric Fonoimoana	0	1	3	3	6
Scott Friedrichsen	0	0	0	0	1
Mike Garcia	0	0	0	0	1
Brian Gatzke	0	0	1	0	2
Nick Hannemann	0	0	0	0	1
Rob Heidger	0	0	1	1	5
Leif Hanson	0	0	0	0	1
Dax Holdren	0	1	0	2	3
Bryan Ivie	0	0	1	1	2
Adam Johnson	4	2	3	2	1
Mark Kerins	1	1	0	1	1
Karch Kiraly	4	2	3	2	1
Lee LeGrande	0	0	0	0	1
Brian Lewis	0	5	2	1	3
Jose Loiola	**13**	**2**	**2**	**0**	**1**
Matt Lyles	0	0	0	0	1
Guilherme Marques	0	0	0	1	1
Raul Papaleo	0	0	0	0	4
Justin Perlstrom	0	0	0	0	1
Jason Pursley	0	0	0	1	1
Todd Rogers	0	1	0	2	3
Henry Russell	1	1	0	1	1
Wayne Seligson	0	0	0	0	1
Andrew Smith	0	1	0	0	2
Rogerio Para de Souza	0	0	0	1	1
Kent Steffes	12	2	3	0	1
Randy Stoklos	0	6	2	0	3
David Swatik	0	0	2	0	4
Troy Tanner	0	6	3	1	5
Matt Unger	0	0	0	0	1
Mike Whitmarsh	3	2	5	2	6
Kevin Wong	0	0	0	0	4
Eric Wurts	0	1	0	0	1

JOSE LOIOLA
Jose Loiola was on top of the 1997 AVP Tour's win list. Loiola won 12 events with Kent Steffes as well as the "KOB" event in Las Vegas NV. Above photo, Loiola attacking the ball.
Photo Courtesy of "Couvi"

FIVB

Total prize money for 1997 FIVB Men's beach violleyball events was $2,400,000.00.

Again in 1997 the FIVB World Tour was dominated by teams from Brazil. Brazilian teams won nine of the fourteen FIVB events. The top team on the FIVB World Tour in 1997 was the Brazilian team of of Z-Marco Nobrega Ferreira de Melo and Emanuel Fernando Scheffer Rego. They won four FIVB World Series events. They won at: Berlin, Germany, Klagenfurt Austria, Grote Shand Beach at Ostend Belgium, and Fortaleza Brazil.

Additional Brazilian wins came when the Brazilian teams of: Emanuel Rego Scheffer and Jose Marco Melo Ferreira Nobrega won at Copacabana Beach in Rio de Janeiro Brazil. Paulo Emilio Silva Azevedo and Paulo Roberto "Paulao" Moreira da Costa, won the FIVB event on the Mediterrenean Coast of Turkey at Alanya Turkey. The FIVB event played at Marseille, France on the "Golfe du Lion" shore, on the "Plages du Prado" was won by Rogrio "Para" Ferreira de Souza and Guilherme Luiz Marquez. The team of Para Ferreira De Souza and Guilherme Luiz Marques won the FIVB "World Championship of Beach Volleyball" in Los Angeles, California (U.S.A.) on the UCLA campus in Westwood. The "Brazilian Team" topped-off their string of victories by winning the "Independence Cup" in Guaruja Sao Paulo Brazil.

Additional winning teams on the FIVB Tour: Jan Kvalheim and Bjorn Maaseide, from Norway won the FIVB events in Espinho Portugal on Baia Beach and on Las Teresitas Beach in Tenerife Canary Islands Spain. The Argentine team of Eduardo Esteban "Mono" Martinez and Martin Alejo Conde won at Ligano Italy, Lignano Sabbiadoro. The Russian team of Dmitri Areshkin and Senin won in Albena Bulgaria, at Balkan Beach.

EMANUEL REGO SCHEFFER
Brazilian Emanuel Rego Schaffer teamed-up with compatriot Z-Marco Nobrega on the 1997 FIVB Tour. They advanced to 7 "Gold-Medal" matches, winning 5 times. Above photo, Rego reaches over the net to make a nice block.
Photo Courtesy of "Couvi"

MARTIN CONDE & EDUARDO MARTINEZ
Martin Conde and Eduardo Martinez, from Argentina, were the number four team on the 1997 FIVB Tour. They advanced to 3 "Gold-Medal" matches winning once. Above photo, Conde hits a set fromMartinez, towards the block of a Brazil's Ricardo Santos.
Photo Courtesy of "Couvi"

FIVB BEACH VOLLEYBALL SCHEDULE
1997-MEN

When	Where	Prize Money
Feb 18-23	Rio Brazil	$150,000.00
Jun 28-29	Czech Republic Spa Karlovy Vary Spa	$ 30,000.00
Jul 4-6	Berlin Germany	$150,000.00
Jul 11-13	Carolina Puerto Rico	$150,000.00
Jul 18-20	Lignano Italy	$150,000.00
Jul 24-27	Marseille France	$150,000.00
Aug 1-3	Klagenfurt Austria	$150,000.00
Aug 8-10	Espinho Portugal	$300,000.00
Aug 15-17	Ostend Belgium	$150,000.00
Aug 29-31	Alanya Turkey	$150,000.00
Sep 4-7	Tenerife Spain Canary Islands	$150,000.00
Sep 10-13	Los Angeles, CA-USA	$300,000.00
Nov 28-30	Durban South Africa	$150,000.00

TOP 50 FIVB MEN's TEAMS
(fall of 1997)

1. Z-Marco and Emanuel-Brazil
2. Paro and Guilherme-Brazil
3. Kvalheim and Maaseide-Norway
4. Paulo and Paulo Emilio-Brazil
5. Martinez and Conde-Argintina
6. Child and Heese-Canada
6. M.Laciga and P.Laciga-Switzerland
8. Holden and Leinemann-Canada
9. Roberto Lopes and Franco-Brazil
10. Prosser and Zahner-Australia
11. Salema and Baracetti-Argintina
12. Kubala and Palinek-Czech Republic
13. Duda and Fred-Brazil
14. Bosma and Diez-Spain
15. Ahmann and Hager-Germany
16. Maia and Brenha-Portugal
17. Ghiurghi and Lione-Italy
18. Hoidalen and Kjemperud-Norway
19. Sinjin Smith and Carl Henkel-USA
20. Pakosta and Dzavoronok-Czech Republic
20. Karasev and Pospelov-Russia
22. Englen and Petersson-Sweden
23. Deulofeu and Guissart-France
24. Grigolo and Raffaelli-Italy
25. Anjinho and Loiola-Brazil&USA
26. Whitmarsh and Ceman-USA
27. Leitner and Stamm-Austria
28. Steffes and Blanton-USA
29. Perez-Conte-Argintina
30. Krank and Oetke-Germany
30. Sayfulin and Kouchnerev-Russia
30. Kiraly and Johnson-USA
30. Tanner- and Ian Clark-USA
34. Seuseu and Eade-New Zealand
35. Anton and Pomerenke-Germany
36. Ceman and Fonoimoana-USA
37. Canet and Hamel-France
38. Stejskal and Chromy-Czech Republic
39. Dodd and Whitmarsh-USA
40. Penigaud and Glowacz-France
41. De Jesus and Velasco-Portugal
42. Penigaud and Jodard-France
43. Yoyi Rodriguez and Carrasco-Spain
44. Lula and Adriano-Brazil
44. Dodd and Heidger-USA
44. Fonoimoana and Lewis-USA
44. Holdren and Rogers-USA
48. Dekker and Van der Hoek-Netherlands
49. Franco and Garrido-Brazil
50. Schroffenegger/Schroffenegger-Austria

INDIVIDUAL FIVB TOURNAMENT FINISHES
1997

Player	1st	2nd	3rd	4th	5th
Jose Luis Salema Abrantes	0	0	0	0	2
Eduardo "Duda" Pinto de Abreau	0	0	0	0	2
Jorge Ahmann	0	1	0	0	0
Dain Blanton	0	0	1	0	0
Joao Carlos Pereira Brenha Alves	0	0	0	1	0
Paulo Emilo Silva Azevedo	0	3	1	2	?
Eduardo "Anjinho" Bacil	0	1	0	0	1
Marino Baracetti	0	0	0	0	2
Canyon Ceman	0	1	0	0	1
John Child	0	0	1	1	1
Ian Clark	0	0	0	0	1
Martin Alejo Conde	1	2	1	1	0
Roberto Lopes da Costa	0	1	0	2	1
Fabio Diez	0	0	0	0	1
Eric Fonoimoana	0	0	0	0	1
Adriano Dias Garrido	0	1	0	0	0
Axel Hager	0	1	0	0	0
Mark Heese	0	0	1	1	1
Carl Henkel	0	0	0	1	0
Jody Holden	0	0	1	0	2
Adam Johnson	0	0	0	0	1
Karch Kiraly	0	0	0	0	1
Jan Kvalheim	2	0	2	1	0
Martin Laciga	0	0	0	1	2
Paul Laciga	0	0	0	1	2
Conrad Leinemann	0	0	1	0	2
Jose Loiola	0	1	0	0	1
Bjorn Maaseide	2	0	2	1	0
Luis Miguel Barbosa Maia	0	0	0	1	0
LuizGuilherme Marquez	2	3	0	0	2
Eduardo Esteban "Mono" Martinez	1	2	1	1	0
Javier Bosma Minguez	0	0	0	0	1
Paulo Roberto Da Costa Moreira	1	0	3	1	2
Jose Franco Vieira Neto	0	1	0	2	1
Jose Z-Marco Melo Ferreira Nobrega	5	2	2	0	1
Julien Prosser	0	0	1	1	1
Emanuel Rego Scheffer	5	2	2	0	1
Sinjin Smith	0	0	0	1	0
Federico "Fred" Doria de Souza	0	0	0	0	2
Rogrio "Para" Ferrirs de Souza	2	2	0	0	2
Kent Steffes	0	0	1	0	0
Troy Tanner	0	0	0	0	1
Mike Whitmarsh	0	1	0	0	0
Lee Zahner	0	0	1	1	1

JAN KVALHEIM & BJORN MAASEIDE
Jan Kvalheim and Bjorn Maaseide, from Norway, were the number three team on the 1997 FIVB Tour, advancing to the "Gold-Medal" match at 2 events, winning both times. Above photo, Kvalheim looks-on as partner Maaseide makes a diving dig.
Photo Courtesy of the FIVB

MEN'S TOURNAMENT RESULTS
1997-AVP

LAS VEGAS NEVADA
March 14th-16th 1997

The first AVP tournament of the season was an "outdoor" event. (there were no indoor beach events scheduled in 1997) The tournament was in Las Vegas, Nevada, at the Hard Rock Hotel and Casino (4,500 seat parking lot beach stadium). Brazilian, Jose Loiola earned $78,000 and the $250,000.00 "King of the Beach" title, by dethroning the defending champion Karch Kiraly. After finishing as runner-up for the last three years, Jose went undefeated on Sunday. He recorded a pair of 15-7 victories while playing with partner's Eric Fonoimoana and Olympic gold medalist Kent Steffes. Next he notched a 15-13 overtime win with Olympic silver medalist Mike Dodd, to become only the third player to be named King of the Beach, in the six-year history of the event.

Dodd, who who had just turned 40-years old in August, earned a career-high second-place finish while Steffes placed third. The four-time King of the Beach Kiraly, along with 1994 King of the Beach Adam Johnson, each posted 1-2 records on Saturday and failed to advance to Sunday's action. This event invited the top 14 players from the AVP Tour. The players change partners each match, while accumulating points to determine the best individual player on the tour.

1997 "KING OF THE BEACH" RESULTS/EARNINGS:

1st	Jose Loiola	$78,000
2nd	Mike Dodd	$42,000
3rd	Kent Steffes	$33,000
4th	Eric Fonoimoana	$32,000
5th	Mike Whitmarsh	$18,000
6th	Karch Kiraly	$11,000
	Adam Johnson	$11,000
8th	Brian Lewis	$ 8,000
9th	Eduardo Bacil	$ 4,000
10th	Troy Tanner	$ 4,000
11th	Canyon Ceman	$ 2,000
12th	Dain Blanton	$ 2,000
13th	Scott Ayakatubby	$ 2,000
14th	Randy Stoklos	$ 0
	Bill Bouillane	$ 0

"KING OF THE BEACH" CHAMPIONS

Player	Year
Karch Kiraly	1991
Karch Kiraly	1992
Karch Kiraly	1993
Adam Johnson	1994
Karch Kiraly	1996
Jose Loiola	1997

(Note: 1995 tournament was moved from September 1995 to March 1996)

MIKE DODD

Mike Dodd, at 40 years of age, was the runner-up as he finished second behind Jose Loiola at the 1997 "King of the Beach" Above photo, Dodd makes a diving effort to dig the ball at the 1997 "KOB" event at the Hard-Rock Hotel and Casino, in Las Vegas Nevada.
Photo Courtesy of "Couvi"

JOSE LOIOLA

Jose Loiola earned a pay-daqy of $78,000.00 along with his 1997 "KOB" title, when he outdistanced all the competition, to win the event at the parking lot beach stadium that was constructed at the Hard-Rock Hotel and Casino in Las Vegas Nevada.
Photo Courtesy of "Couvi"

PHOENIX ARIZONA
March 28th-30th, 1997

The AVP Miller Lite Open at Phoenix, was won by the No. 1 seeded team of Kent Steffes and Jose Loiola. They captured their first tournament victory together as a team. In the championship match, they defeated the third seeded team of Scott Ayakatubby and Brian Lewis, 15-8, to win the $100,000 tournament. Kent Steffes' earned his 89th career victory as he won his first tournament without longtime partner Karch Kiraly since he won with Tim Hovland to win the "Hard Rock Café Challenge Cup" at Santa Monica in 1992. Kent teamed-up with Jose when it was determined that Kiraly would miss the event due to a nerve injury in his right shoulder. This victory was Loiola's 14th career win on the AVP.

3rd Place: Dain Blanton and Canyon Ceman
4th Place: Mike Dodd and Mike Whitmarsh
5th Place: Dan Castillo and Jason Pursley
5th Place: Troy Tanner and Ian Clark

Rookie sensations Dan Castillo and Jason Pursley, the #29 seeds, playing together in their first AVP tournament, after qualifying for the AVP Tour last season, upset Dain Blanton and Canyon Ceman, the #4 seeds, 15-13 on Saturday. Their fifth place marks the best finish by a rookie team playing together in their first tournament on the AVP Tour.

RIVIERA BEACH FLORIDA
April 5th-6th, 1997

The $100,000.00 AVP Event at Riviera Beach, Florida, was won by Kent Steffes and Jose Loiola. They were the number one seeded team on the AVP Tour. They defeated Scott Ayakatubby and Brian Lewis (#2 seeds) 15-11. Steffes and Loiola, playing in only their second AVP tournament together, finished the weekend undefeated. They had not lost a match in the first two tournaments of 1997. It was a rematch of last week's contest as the two teams battled it out on the beach at Riviera Beach, Florida. Steffes had won all three events held at Riviera Beach, the first two with Karch Kiraly.

3rd Place: Randy Stoklos and David Swatik
4th Place: Mike Dodd and Mike Whitmarsh
5th Place: Bill Boullianne and Eric Fonoimoana
5th Place: Nick Hannemann and Henry Russell

CLEARWATER FLORIDA
April 11th-13th, 1997

The $100,000.00 AVP Clearwater Open, in Florida, was won by Kent Steffes and Jose Loiola (#1 seeds). They defeated Scott Ayakatubby and Brian Lewis (#3 seeds) for the third straight tournament. The score was 15-11. Kent Steffes registered two blocks and one ace in route to his 90th career win, while his partner Loiola had two blocks to record his 16th career victory on the AVP Tour.

3rd Place: Mike Dodd and Mike Whitmarsh
4th Place: Dan Castillo and Jason Pursley
5th Place: Ian Clark and Troy Tanner
5th Place: Mike Dodd and Mike Whitmarsh

DAN CASTILLO
In 1997, rookie sensation Dan Castillo teamed-up with Jason Pursley for the best finish by a rookie team playing together in their first tournament on the AVP Tour. Above photo, Castillo positions himself for the pass.
Photo Courtesy of Tim Andexler

JASON PURSLEY
Jason Pursely paired-up with Dan Castillo on the 1997 AVP Tour. Their best finish was a fouth place at the 1997 Clearwater Beach Florida event. Above photo, Pursley utilizes a conventional hit rather than his patented "reverse-no-look" backhand spike.
Photo Courtesy of "Couvi"

FORT MEYERS FLORIDA
April 18th-20th, 1997

The first ever scheduled AVP "Single Elimination" Tournament at Fort Myers, Florida, was won by Mike Dodd and Mike Whitmarsh (#2 seeds). Playing in their first tournament final of the season, they defeated Brian Lewis and Scott Ayakatubby (#3 seeds) by scores of 10-8 and 14-12 to win the $100,000.00 Miller Lite Open at Fort Myers. In this tournament teams played best two-out-of-three matches with the first two games played to 11 and if a third games was necessary they played to 6. Whitmarsh registered three blocks and four aces to earn his 15th career win, while Dodd recorded on hi 73rd career victory at this the first single elimination tournament of the season on the AVP Tour.

3rd Place: Kent Steffes and Jose Loiola
3rd Place: Dain Blanton and Canyon Ceman
5th Place: Rob Heidger and Troy Tanner
5th Place: Bill Boullianne and Eric Fonoimoana
5th Place: Randy Stoklos and David Swatik
5th Place: Mark Kerins and Andrew Smith

MIAMI BEACH FLORIDA
April 25th-27th, 1997

The $100,000.00 AVP Miami Beach Open, in Florida, was won by Jose Loiola and Kent Steffes (#1 seeds), as they defeated Mark Kerins and Andrew Smith (#10 seeds) 15-7. Steffes and Loiola had won four out of the five tournaments that had taken place so far this year. The surprise team of the weekend was Kerins and Smith. They upset two of the top seeded teams on the tour this weekend including Loiola and Steffes in the winner's bracket final. It was Kerins first final appearance and it was Smith's first final since 1991.

3rd Place: Scott Ayakatubby and Brian Lewis
4th Place: Canyon Ceman and Dain Blanton
5th Place: Bill Boullianne and Eric Fonoimoana
5th Place: Rob Heidger and Troy Tanner

DALLAS TEXAS
May 10th-11th, 1997

The AVP's second "Single Elimination" tournament in history was the Dallas Texas Open. The final was won by the second seeded team of Mike Whitmarsh and Mike Dodd. This was their second tournament championship victory of the 1997 AVP Tour. They defeated the 6th-seeded team of Randy Stoklos and Troy Tanner, 11-6, 11-13, 7-5. Dodd and Whitmarsh, advanced to their second tournament final of the season after defeating Bill Boullianne and Brian Lewis, 11-4, 11-6 in the semifinals. Stoklos and Tanner earned their first tournament final together after a 11-6, 11-1 win over Eric Fonoimoana and Bryan Ivie. The top ranked team of Kent Steffes and Jose Loiola finished fifth after a loss to Fonoimoana and Ivie by a score of 4-11, 11-9, 6-3 in the quarterfinal round.

3rd Place: Bill Boullianne and Brian Lewis
3rd Place: Eric Fonoimoana and Bryan Ivie
5th Place: Kent Steffes and Jose Loiola
5th Place: Dain Blanton and Canyon Ceman
5th Place: Scott Friederichsen and Leif Hanson
5th Place: Lee LeGrand and Matt Unger

BRIAN LEWIS

Brian Lewis teamed-up with Scott Ayakatubby to advance to 4 finals on the 1997 AVP Tour. They finished in the second spot each time. Lewis added another second place finish with Randy Stoklos. Above photo, Lewis braces himself for the pass.
Photo Courtesy of the AVP

MARK KERINS

In 1997, Mark Kerins won his first AVP Tour event with Henry Russell. They won the Cape Cod Massachusetts event. Above photo, Kerins hits a set from Andrew Smith towards the block of Scott Ayakatubby.
Photo Courtesy of the AVP

CORPUS CHRISTI TEXAS
May 17th-18th, 1997

The Corpus Christi, Texas Open, was won by Kent Steffes and Jose Loiola. They won their fifth tournament of the season on the AVP Pro-Beach Tour. They won the championship match by a score of 5-0 as the fifth-seeded team of Randy Stoklos and Troy Tanner withdrew because of medical reasons. In their second consecutive tournament final, Stoklos and Tanner fell behind 5-0 to Steffes and Loiola, and did not retake the court after the first side change as Tanner could not continue play due to severe cramping. Steffes and Loiola, advanced to the championship match after edging the 6th seeded team of Dain Blanton and Canyon Ceman, 15-13, in the winner's bracket final. Stoklos and Tanner defeated Blanton and Ceman in the losers-bracket final, 15-10, to advance to the championship.

3rd Place: Dain Blanton and Canyon Ceman
4th Place: Guilherme Marques and Rogerio Para-Brazil
5th Place: Brian Lewis and Bill Boullianne,
5th Place: Mike Dodd and Mike Whitmarsh

SAN ANTONIO TEXAS
May 24th-25th, 1997

The 1997 AVP $100,000.00 San Antonio Texas Men's Open was won by the top seeded team of Kent Steffes and Jose Loiola. This was their sixth tournament championship on the 1997 tour. In the championship match, they pounded-out a 15-4 victory over the 14th seeded team of Eric Wurts and Henry Russell. The winners collected $20,000.00, while the runners-up shared $11,400.00. Earlier, Loiola and Steffes advanced to the championship match after defeating Wurts and Russell 15-7, in the winner's bracket final match. Wurts, was appearing in an AVP championship final for the first time since recording two second-place finishes in 1992, at the Fort Wort Open and the Milwaukee Open. Henry Russell was in his first career final, after upsetting the 2nd seeded team of Karch Kiraly and Adam Johnson, 15-7.

3rd Place: Karch Kiraly and Adam Johnson
4th Place: Eric Fonoimoana and Bryan Ivie
5th Place: Troy Tanner and Randy Stoklos
5th Place: Rogerio Para de Souza and Guilherme Marques-Brazil

INDIANAPOLIS INDIANA
May 31st-June 1st, 1997

The AVP Indianapolis, Indiana Open, (single-elimination tournament) was stopped due to rain during Sunday's Quarterfinal round. The top-ranked team of Kent Steffes and Jose Loiola, along with seven other teams reaching Sunday's quarterfinal round, all shared a fifth-place finish. After two of the top three teams were eliminated in the constant rain and chilling winds during play on Saturday, the inclement weather continued Sunday, forcing play to be canceled. All those at the facility did their best to keep the courts playable, however ultimately they had to give into the weather conditions. Steffes, and partner Loiola, reached Sunday's quarter-finals after recording an 11-7,11-4 victory over Aaron Boss and Nick Hannemann, and later defeating Lee LeGrand and Matt Unger 11-2, 11-1 on Saturday. The eight quarter-finalists, all in the fifth spot were Kent Steffes ands Jose Loiola, Bill Boullianne and Brian Lewis, Randy Stoklos and Troy Tanner, Dain Blanton and Canyon Ceman, Eric Fonoimoana and Bryan Ivie, Mark Kerins and Andrew Smith, Ian Clark and David Swatik, Brent Doble and Albert Hannemann.

LAKE TAHOE NEVADA
June 6th-8th, 1997

The AVP Pro-Beach Lake Tahoe Open, in Nevada, was won by Kent Steffes and Jose Loiola. This was their seventh tournament championship, out of the first ten tournaments of the 1997 Pro-Beach Tour. Steffes and Loiola defeated, AVP seasoned veteran Randy Stoklos and his partner Troy Tanner 11-4, 11-9 in the finals of this single elimination tournament. The tournament was held at the base of Heavenly Ski Area in South Lake Tahoe. This three-day tournament was the last of the four single-elimination tournaments being held this season. Earlier in the day, Steffes and Loiola faced off against their former partners Karch Kiraly and Adam Johnson, in the most anticipated match-up so far during the 1997 AVP Pro-Beach Tour season. The first game was won by Loiola and Steffes 11-9 in overtime, after the lead had changed on several occasions. Then after a twenty-five minute rain delay, Steffes and Loiola took charge with an 11-2 victory, allowing them to move onto the championship match.

3rd Place: Karch Kiraly and Adam Johnson
3rd Place: Bill Boullianne and Rob Heidger
5th Place: Dain Blanton with Canyon Ceman
5th Place: Mike Garcia with Justin Perlstrom
5th Place: Eric Fonoimoana with Brian Ivie
5th Place: Mike Dodd and Mike Whitmarsh

HENRY RUSSELL
Henry Russell rejected balls at the net, all tournament long, on his way to his first AVP Tour championship at the 1997 Cape Cod event with Mark Kerins. Above photo, Russell rejects an attack from Scott Friedrichsen.
Photo Courtesy of "Couvi"

MANHATTAN BEACH CALIFORNIA
June 4th, 1997

The 1997 Manhattan Beach Open was moved to Hermosa Beach and called the "Hermosa Beach Grand Slam" (for results, see the June 13th-15th, 1997 Hermosa Beach tournament listing). The tournament was moved because of the California State Coastal Commission's decision to not allow paid events on the beach along with a court injunction, that was pursued and obtained by a small vocal minority, against the Manhattan Open, being staged on the beach of Manhattan Beach. On June 4, 1997, the AVP and Manhattan Beach City officials collectively announced that the annual Manhattan Beach open was to be moved to a new site due to legal issues having nothing to do with the sport of beach volleyball. The scheduled June 13-15 event was renamed the Miller Lite/AVP Hermosa Beach Grand Slam, and was held on the south side of Hermosa Beach Pier. AVP CEO Jerry Solomon was quick to say that "The AVP is not abandoning Manhattan Beach as a tournament site!" he went on to say: "We are enraged that because of a law suit brought against the City of Manhattan Beach, Los Angeles County, and the AVP by a small local interest group, we are forced to make a decision today to move the tournament, interrupting 38 years of tradition."

CHRIS BROWN
The 1997 Manhattan Beach Grand Slam event was moved to Hermosa Beach, where the competition included qualifiers such as Chris "CB" Brown. In the photo above, during the 1997 Hermosa Beach Grand Slam, "CB" attacking his jump serve.
Photo Courtesy of Chris Brown

HERMOSA BEACH CALIFORNIA
June 13th-15th, 1997

On the weekend of June 13th-15th, 1997 the $300,000.00 Men's Miller Lite/AVP Hermosa Beach "Grand Slam" event was won by Dain Blanton and Canyon Ceman. Blanton became the first African-American pro-beach volleyball player, in history, to win a tournament on the AVP Tour. In the championship match, Blanton and Ceman scored a 15-13, overtime win, against the first seeded team of Kent Steffes and Jose Loiola. Blanton's record-setting victory was also the first tournament title of his three-year career. After Blanton and Ceman charged out to a 11-7 lead, Loiola and Steffes roared back to force the match into overtime before the underdogs posted their first tournament win of the season. The winners split $60,000.00 for their efforts, while the runners-up collected $34,200.00. Blanton and Ceman, making their first appearance in a tournament final this season, advanced to the championship match after beating the 5th-seeded team of Troy Tanner and Randy Stoklos in the looser's bracket final with a 10-8 victory in overtime. The 1997 Miller Lite/AVP Hermosa Beach Grand Slam offered the most prize money for a single tournament in the history of beach volleyball. The weekend tourney also marked the debut of the Miller Lite Grand Slam, a four-event series featuring a combined $1.2 million in prize money.

3rd Place: Troy Tanner and Randy Stoklos
4th Place: Karch Kiraly and Adam Johnson
5th Place: Mike Whitmarsh and Mike Dodd
5th Place: John Brajevic and Brian Gatzke

DAIN BLANTON & CANYON CEMAN
Dain Blanton and Canyon Ceman teamed-up to win the 1997 AVP Grand Slam Tour stop in Hermosa Beach CA. Blanton became the first African American to win an AVP Championship match. Above photo, Ceman passing the ball to Blanton.
Photo Courtesy of the AVP

CHICAGO ILLINOIS
June 20th-22nd, 1997

The $300,000.00 Men's Miller Lite/AVP "Grand Slam" event at Chicago, Illinois was won by Kent Steffes and Jose Loiola. Loiola became the first, Non--U.S.A., player to reach the $1 million mark in career earnings. This was Steffes and Loiola's first Miller Lite Grand Slam event win of the season. Steffes and Loiola had won 8 out of the 11 completed tournaments so far this season. In the championship match, Loiola and Steffes out-pointed Troy Tanner and Randy Stoklos, to win the $60,000.00 first place prize. With this championship match victory, Loiola kept his crown as defending champion of the Windy City tourney. He also won last season with former partner Adam Johnson. Loiola and Steffes advanced to the final after defeating Troy Tanner and Randy Stoklos 15-8, earlier in the day in the winner's bracket final. Tanner and Stoklos advanced to the championship final after defeating Mike Dodd and Mike Whitmarsh, 15-3, in the looser's bracket final.

3rd Place: Mike Dodd and Mike Whitmarsh
4th Place: Dain Blanton and Canyon Ceman
5th Place: Rob Heidger and Brian Lewis
5th Place: David Swatik and Ian Clark

CLEVELAND OHIO
June 27th-29th, 1997

The next AVP event was the Cleveland Open, in Cleveland Ohio. For the fourth time this season, the first seeded team of Jose Loiola and Kent Steffes were too strong for the second seeded team of Randy Stoklos and Troy Tanner. In the championship match, Steffes and Loiola pounded-out a 10-6 victory as time expired in front of a sold-out crowd. Stoklos and Tanner, who finished second to Steffes and Loiola at last week's AVP Pro-Beach Grand Slam event in Chicago, advanced to their fifth final of the season after earning a victory over the fifth seeded team of Karch Kiraly and Adam Johnson 15-12.

3rd Place: Karch Kiraly and Adam Johnson
4th Place: Rob Heidger and Brian Lewis
5th Place: Dain Blanton and Canyon Ceman
5th Place: Dax Holdren and Todd Rogers

CAPE COD MASSACHUSETTS
July 4th-6th, 1997

There was an upset win at the AVP Championships of New England, in Hyannis, Massachusetts. It was won by the underdog team of Mark Kerins and Henry Russell, playing in their first tournament together. They upset Mike Dodd and Mike Whitmarsh 15-5 to win the final. The AVP tournament win was the first Pro-Beach Tour victory of their careers. The tournament, held on the man-made beach at Cape Cod Mall in Hyannis, marked the first time the AVP Tour had been on the Cape since 1993. Kerins and Russell, who teamed up for the first time earlier this week, were the second team to break into the win column this year. Dain Blanton and Canyon Ceman also became first time winners as they won the AVP Hermosa Beach Grand Slam back in June. Russell and Kerins were making only their second appearance in an AVP final. Kerins, a former member of the U.S. National Volleyball Team, made the final at the Coppertone Championships of Florida and Russell, who won the 1996 Most Improved Player award, made the final at the AVP San Antonio Open.

3rd Place: Dain Blanton and Canyon Ceman
4th Place: Karch Kiraly and Adam Johnson
5th Place: Eric Fonoimoana and Bryan Ivie
5th Place: Raul Papaleo and Kevin Wong

GRAND HAVEN MICHIGAN
July 11th-13th, 1997

The tenth AVP Grand Haven Open, in Michigan, took place this season. The first seeded team of Jose Loiola and Kent Steffes established their top billing on the beach as they beat the third seeded team of Randy Stoklos and Brian Lewis 15-8, earning the title. The championship match was played in front of a near sold-out crowd at the AVP Midwest Championships. Stoklos and his partner Lewis, who had teamed with Scott Ayakatubby to win the AVP West Michigan Open in 1996, advanced to the finals after defeating the second seeded team of Troy Tanner and Mike Whitmarsh 15-7, in the looser's bracket final-match. This was the first time that Lewis and Stoklos had teamed-up together since playing nine tournaments in the 1993 season.

3rd Place: Troy Tanner and Mike Whitmarsh
4th Place: Ian Clark and Canyon Ceman
5th Place: Dax Holdren and Todd Rogers
5th Place: Ian Clark and Canyon Ceman

KENT STEFFES
In 1997, Kent Steffes teamed-up with Jose Loiola to advance to 14 AVP Tour championship matches. They won 12 times together as a team. Above photo, Steffes attacking the ball at the net, while Adam Johnson braces himself on defense.
Photo Courtesy of the AVP

MILWAUKEE WISCONSIN
July 19th-20th, 1997

The next AVP tournament was the Milwaukee Open, in Wisconsin. Kent Steffes and Jose Loiola won their eleventh tournament of the season, while Steffes claimed his 100th career victory on the Pro-Beach Tour. In the championship match, Loiola and Steffes teamed-up together to gain a 10-8 decision over Bill Boullianne and Troy Tanner. Boullianne and Tanner playing in their first tournament together, advanced to the final undefeated in the winner's bracket. They defeated Steffes and Loiola earlier in the day, 15-13, to place them in the contender's bracket. On their way to the final they also defeated Karch Kiraly and Adam Johnson 15-12. They then beat-up on the fourteenth, twelfth and twenty-eighth seeded teams of Brian Gatzke and Eduardo Bacil, 15-5, Kevin Wong and Raul Papaleo 15-4, Aaron Smith and David Smith 15-3. Steffes' victory marked the third time he had won in Milwaukee, the home of Tour sponsor Miller Brewing Company, and at the time ranked fourth all-time with 100 career tournament wins. Loiola, who teamed with Adam Johnson to win last year's Milwaukee tourney, and Steffes advanced to the finals after beating-up on the 14th-seeded team of Eduardo Bacil and Brian Gatzke 10-5 in the looser's bracket final-match.

3rd Place: Eduardo Bacil and Brian Gatzke
4th Place: Dax Holdren and Todd Rogers
5th Place: Mike Dodd and Mike Whitmarsh
5th Place: Andrew Smith and Eric Wurts

HERMOSA BEACH CALIFORNIA
July 25th-27th, 1997

Amongst continuing controversy, the AVP staged the $300,000.00 Men's Miller Lite "U.S. Championships," on the beach of Hermosa Beach California. The winners of this 1997 event were Karch Kiraly and Adam Johnson. Their share of the purse was $60,000.00. Because of the California State Coastal Commission's decision on commercialization of the State's beaches, this tournament was not allowed to charge for admission. The commission would allow volleyball tournaments on the beach, but it would not allow paid events on the beach. At this time, it was thought if the AVP and the commission did not come to some sort of agreement that would allow an admission fee, this may have been the last "beach" pro-volleyball tournament to be held on a California beach. As to the tournament itself, in a championship match between veterans and rookies from the AVP Pro-Beach Tour, Kiraly and Johnson defeated the rookie team of Dax Holdren and Todd Rogers, 15-4, to win the U.S. Championships. The victory was the first of 1997 for the sixth-seeded Kiraly and Johnson. It was Kiraly's 127th career Pro-Beach Tour win, and the 28th for Johnson. Kiraly and Johnson reached the final by defeating the 5th-seeded team of Dain Blanton and Canyon Ceman, 15-8, in the winner's bracket final. With their second place finish, the 10th-seeded team of Holdren and Rogers set an AVP Pro-Beach Tour record for best finish by a rookie team.

TROY TANNER & BILL BOULLIANNE
Troy Tanner and Bill Boullianne paried-up together to advance to the championship match of the 1997 AVP Tour stop in Milwaukee WI. They finished in second place. Above photo, Boullianne is ready at the net while Tanner serves the ball towards Jose Loiola.
Photo Courtesy of the AVP

DAX HOLDREN & TODD ROGERS
In 1997, Dax Holdren and Todd Rogers set an AVP record by advancing to the finals of the Hermosa Beach CA event. This was the best finish by a "Rookie" team on the AVP Tour. Above photo, Holdren slices a set from Rogers, past the block of Matt Lyles.
Photo Courtesy of "Couvi"

Holdren and Rogers reached the final by defeating the 13th-seeded team of Brian Gatzke and Eduardo Bacil, 15-12, along with wins over the number 3 seeds Mike Dodd and Mike Whitmarsh, 11-8 when time expired. They added a victory over Dain Blanton and Canyon Ceman 13-11, also as time ran out.
3rd Place: Dain Blanton and Canyon Ceman
4th Place: Mike Dodd and Mike Whitmarsh
5th Place: Rob Heidger and David Swatik
5th Place: Brian Gatzke and Eduardo Bacil

SACRAMENTO CALIFORNIA
August 2nd-3rd, 1997

Without controversy the next AVP event was the Golden State Open, at Folsom Lake's Granite Bay in Sacramento California. Karch Kiraly and Adam Johnson made it two tournaments in a row by winning over Jose Loiola and Kent Steffes. It was an emotional final that featured four of beach volleyball's greatest players, Johnson and Kiraly defeated top-seeded Loiola and Steffes, 15-8. Johnson and Kiraly won their second straight AVP Tour event, taking the Miller Lite U.S. Championships last week at Hermosa Beach. In this tournament, they had to work their way to the finals via the loser's bracket. They lost to the seventh-seeded team of Eric Fonoimoana and David Swatik, 14-10, in the winner's semifinals. Johnson and Kiraly then beat-up on the fourteenth-seeded team of Aaron Boss and Dan Castillo, 15-1, and the sixth seeded team of Dax Holdren and Todd Rogers, 15-3. Johnson and Kiraly then got revenge against Fonoimoana and Swatik with a 15-10 victory in the loser's bracket final. The number one team on the beach Steffes and Loiola began Sunday's competition with a 15-8 win over Raul Papaleo and Kevin Wong and then blasted Fonoimoana and Swatik in the winner's bracket final, 15-5.
3rd Place: Eric Fonoimoana and David Swatik
4th Place: Dax Holdren and Todd Rogers
5th Place: Raul Papaleo and Kevin Wong
5th Place: Aaron Boss and Dan Castillo

VAIL COLORADO
August 8th-10th, 1997

Next, the AVP traveled to Vail Colorado. The tournament was showcased amongst the beautiful setting of the Rocky Mountains. The championship match pitted Eric Fonoimoana and Dain Blanton against Karch Kiraly and Adam Johnson. Kiraly and Johnson, going for their third championship in a row, went out to a 5-0 lead, but Eric and Dain fought back to make a match out of it. Karch and Adam went on to win as time expired by a score of 13-8. Kiraly and Johnson reached the final with a 15-7 victory over Mike Whitmarsh and Canyon Ceman. This tournament marked the first time that Fonoimoana and Blanton played together after Ceman broke off the partnership with Blanton, so that he could pair-up with Whitmarsh. Whitmarsh asked Ceman to team-up with him because of Mike Dodd's injuries and unwillingness to compete in all of the tournaments. Fonoimoana was willing to pair-up with Blanton because Brian Ivie, his former partner, wanted to play professionally on the indoor circuit in Europe.
3rd Place: Mike Whitmarsh and Canyon Ceman.
4th Place: Mark Kerins and Henry Russell
5th Place: Bill Boullianne and Brian Lewis
5th Place: Matt Lyles and Wayne Seligson

MINNEAPOLIS MINNESOTA
August 16th-17th, 1997

On the weekend of August 16th-17th, 1997, the AVP went to Minneapolis, Minnesota for the 21st tournament of the season. The excitement of the final was at the highest level of the season as Karch Kiraly and Adam Johnson won their fourth consecutive tournament title as they defeated Kent Steffes and Jose Loiola 14-12 in overtime to win the championship match. This was the third time Johnson had won at Minneapolis in as many tries. Kiraly and Johnson, lost the winner's bracket final earlier in the day to Steffes and Loiola 13-11 in another overtime match. This win was the sixth time the former partners had matched up, and the second time in an AVP Tour final. Earlier Kiraly and Johnson defeated Mike Whitmarsh and Canyon Ceman 15-11 and 15-4 to get to the final.
3rd Place: Mike Whitmarsh and Canyon Ceman
4th Place: Ian Clark and Troy Tanner
5th Place: Dax Holdren and Todd Rogers
5th Place: Raul Papaleo and Kevin Wong

BELMAR NEW JERSEY
August 22nd-24th, 1997

In Belmar New Jersey, Canyon Ceman and Mike Whitmarsh, teaming-up in only their third tournament together, defeated Karch Kiraly and Adam Johnson 15-7, to win the championship match. This was the first tournament win for Whitmarsh since splitting with long-

KARCH KIRALY & ADAM JOHNSON
In 1997, Karch Kiraly and Adam "AJ" Johnson teamed-up for 4 AVP Tour championships, after advancing to 6 finals. Above photo, Johnson hits a set from Kiraly away from the block of Kent Steffes.
Photo Courtesy of the AVP

time partner and fellow Olympic silver medalist Mike Dodd just three weeks ago. The Belmar victory was only the second career win for Canyon Ceman. Whitmarsh and Ceman faced Kiraly and Johnson earlier in the day, in the winner's bracket semi-final round, with Ceman and Whitmarsh advancing to the winner's bracket after a 15-8 decision. For Kiraly and Johnson, their second place finish ended a four-week winning streak.

3rd Place: Kent Steffes and Jose Loiola
4th Place: Dain Blanton and Eric Fonoimoana
5th Place: Ian Clark and Troy Tanner
5th Place: Aaron Boss and Dan Castillo

ORLANDO FLORIDA
August 29th-31st, 1997

The 1997 Miller Lite/AVP Tour's $325,000.00 Championships took place at the Wide World of Sports Complex in Orlando, Florida. Top-seeded Jose Loiola and Kent Steffes, the winningest team on this year's AVP Pro-Beach Tour, completed their partnership's successful season with a 15-6 championship victory over Canyon Ceman and Mike Whitmarsh, at the "Walt Disney World AVP Tour Championships". Playing for the largest prize in the history of beach volleyball, Loiola and Steffes, won their 12th tournament of the 1997 season. Loiola and Steffes defeated Randy Stoklos and David Swatik in the quarter-finals (best two out of three games) 9-4, 11-7, Then pitted against Kiraly and Johnson in the semifinals, Loiola and Steffes played extremely well for a 15-4 victory to reach the championship match. Ceman and Whitmarsh reached the finals by defeating Mike Dodd and Rob Heidger in the quarter-finals, 11-4, 11-9, and then subduing Ian Clark and Troy Tanner in the semi-final match, 15-10. In the other quarterfinal matches, Johnson and Kiraly defeated Raul Papaleo and Kevin Wong, 6-11, 11-3, 6-1 while Clark and Tanner outlasted Dain Blanton and Eric Fonoimoana, 5-11, 11-8, 7-5.

3rd Place: Karch Kiraly and Adam Johnson
3rd Place: Ian Clark and Troy Tanner
5th Place: Dain Blanton and Eric Fonoimoana
5th Place: Randy Stoklos and David Swatik
5th Place: Mike Dodd and Rob Heidger
5th Place: Raul Papaleo and Kevin Wong

LOS ANGELES CALIFORNIA
September 10th-15tht, 1997

See results and information of the AVP & FIVB "World Championships" under the FIVB heading.

SEATTLE WASHINGTON

The 1997 "Seattle Shootout" was canceled.

GUARUJA SAO PAULO BRAZIL
December 11th-14th, 1997

The first "Independence Cup" was held in Guaruja Sao Paulo Brazil. This was the first time that pro-beach volleyball staged a tournament that pitted one country against another, much like the Davis Cup in tennis and the Ryder Cup in golf. There were five teams that represented the U.S.A. and five from Brazil. The teams were as follows:

U.S.A.
Troy Tanner and Ian Clark
Brian Lewis and Rob Heidger
Kent Steffes and Bill Boullianne
Karch Kiraly and Adam Johnson
Canyon Ceaman and Eric Fonoimoana

BRAZIL
Tande and Giovane
Guilherme and Para
Paulo and Para Emilo
Emanuel and Z-Marco
Jose Loiola and Anjinho Bacil

They were not only playing for National glory, there was a purse of $100,000.00, with $60,000.00 going to the winning team, $40,000.00 to the losers. It was an all AVP championship match, with the Brazilian team of Loiola and Bacil defeating the U.S.A. team of Kiraly and Johnson by a scores of 12-10 and 12-8. The final result in the head-to-head AVP vs FIVB confrontation was 14 wins for the AVP and 14 wins for the FIVB. It should be mentioned that Canyon Ceman, of the U.S.A. and the AVP, forfeited three matches because of an injury. The final result of the head-to-head Brazil vs U.S.A. was 22 wins for Brazil and 8 wins for the U.S.A.

MIKE WHITMARSH & CANYON CEMAN
Mike Whitmarsh and Canyon Ceman advanced to the finals of the 1997 Walt Disney World AVP Tour Championship, where they finished in 2nd place. Above photo, Whitmarsh hits a set from Ceman over Scott Ayakatubby and away from Brian Lewis.
Photo Courtesy of "Couvi"

MEN'S TOURNAMENT RESULTS
1997-FIVB

RIO DE JANEIRO BRAZIL
February 18th-23rd, 1997

The 1997 "Men's" FIVB Pro-Beach volleyball season began with the $150,000.00 Men's World Championship Series on Copacabana Beach, in Rio de Janeiro Brazil. The championship match was won by the Brazilian team of Emanuel Rego Scheffer and Jose Z-Marco Melo Ferreira Nobrega, 12-9, 8-12 and 12-8 over Eduardo "Anjinho" Bacil and Jose Loiola also from Brazil. The first place team shared the $20,000.00 first place prize.

3rd Place: Conrad Leinemann and Jody Holden-Canada
4th Place: Julien Prosser and Lee Zahner-Aus
5th Place: Canyon Ceman and Eric Fonoimoana-USA
5th Place: Jose Eduardo "Duda" de Abreu and "Fred" Doria de Souza-Bra
Additional USA finishes included a 13th by Mike Dodd and Dain Blanton while Matt Unger and Carl Henkel ended up in 17th place.

SPA KARLOVY VARY CZECH REPUBLIC
June 28th-29th, 1997

This FIVB Men's Pro-Beach Volleyball event was the $30,000.00 "Challenger" tournament in the Czech Republic, at Spa Karlovy Vary. In the championship match, the Swiss team of Paul Laciga and Martin Laciga defeated Jorre Andre' Kjemperud and Vegard Hoidalen from Norway, by scores od 8-12, 12-2, 12-9. The Swiss team earned $3,000.00 for their winning effort.

3rd Place: Ricardo Lione and Andrea Ghiurghi-Italy
4th Place: Edgar Krank and Oliver Oetke-Ger
5th Place: Gernot Leitner and Oliver Stamm-Austria
5th Place: Petr Chromy and Igor Stejskal-Czech

BERLIN GERMANY
July 4th-6th, 1997

The $150,000.00 FIVB Men's World Tour stopped at Berlin, Germany, where the Norwegian team of Jan Kvalheim and Bjorn Maaseide were the only team able to challenge the Brazilian dominance in downtown Berlin. The Norwegians lost to the number one seeded Brazilian team of Z-Marco Nobrega and Emanuel Rego in the semi's. They then played for third place against Paulo "Paulao" Roberto Moreira da Costa and Paulo Emilio Silva Azevedo, also from Brazil. Paulao and Emilo could not overcome Rogrio "Para" Ferreira de Souza and Guilherme Luiz Marquez, another Brazilian team, in the other semi. First place Z-Marco and Rego, Brazil, while second place went to "Para" and Guilherme, BrazilThe tournament was played in front of 15,000 fans that included Dr. Rubin Acosta, President of the FIVB. This tournament drew a total of 84 teams, with the very first participation of new players from Belarus, Denmark, England, Latvia, Lithuania, Ukraine, Venezuela and Yugoslavia. Z-Marco and Rego won $10,000.00.

3rd Place: Jan Kvalheim and Bjorn Maaseide-Nor
4th Place: Paulo "Paulao" Moreira da Costa and Paulo Emilio Silva Azevedo
5th Place: Paul Laciga and Martin Laciga -Swiss
5th Place: Conrad Leinemann and Jody Holden-Aus.

LIGANO SABBIADORO ITALY
July 18th-20th, 1997

The next $150,000.00 Men's Pro-Beach FIVB World Tour was held in Ligano Italy. Ligano is located in the Friuli north Italian region, between Venice and Trieste, Lignano Sabbiadoro. This area is known for it's over 14 hours of sun on several miles of "Golden Sand Beaches." The location was golden for the Argentine team of Eduardo Esteban "Mono"Martinez and Martin Alejo Conde. They won the championship match over the Brazilian team of Emanuel Rego Scheffer and Jose Z-Marco Melo Ferreira Nobrega. Martinez and Conde won in two sets by scores of 12-9 and 12-5. Conde and Martinez each collected $10,000.00 along with the "Gold-Medal." Martinez and Conde earned their way into the championship match with a 15-11 victory over Lopes and Neto, in the semifinal round. Kvalheim and Maaseide earned their way into the championship match with a 15-11 victory over the Brazilian team of Z-Marco and Emanuel. The FIVB reported that the TV coverage for the Men's Open Championship match, in Lignano, was watched by 996,000 spectators and the semifinals on Saturday was watched by 672,000.

3rd Place: Jan Kvalheim and Bjorn Maaseide-Nor
4th Place: Roberto Lopes and Franco Neto-Bra
5th Place: Julien Prosser and Lee Zahner-Aus
5th Place: Jose Luis Salema Abrantes and Marino Baracetti-Arg

The only U.S.A. team competing was Carl Henkel and Sinjin Smith. They lost their first match to Fabio Diez and Javier Bosma Minguez from Spain by a score of 16-14. They then went on to win their next four matches: 15-12 over the French team of Stephane Canet and Mathieu Hamel, 15-8 over the Swedish team of Tom Englen and Fredrik Petersson, and a 15-7 victory over the Brazilian team of Jose Eduardo "Duda" Macedo Pinto de Abreu and Federico "Fred" Doria de Souza, before losing to the Brazilian team of "Para" Ferreira de Souza and Guilherme Luiz Marquez.

PAULO EMILO SILVA AZEVEDO
Brazilian Paulo Emilo Silva Azevedo played well on the 1997 FIVB Tour, advancing to 3 "Gold-Medal" matches, finishing in second place each time. Above photo, Azevedo gets up above the net to block the attack by Canyon Ceman of the USA.
Photo Courtesy of Kevin Goff

MARSEILLE FRANCE
July 25th-27th, 1997

The next $150.000.00 Men's Beach FIVB World Tour was held in Marseille, France. The tournament took place just south of the Parisian capital, on the "Golfe du Lion" shore, on the "Plages du Prado." This tournament used the single elimination format and the rally scoring system (2 out of 3 sets to 21 points, win by two, no cap). This format was used all through the competition. Because of very strong winds on Saturday the tournament was postponed, moving the 12 remaining matches to Sunday's competition. Luckily Sunday brought ideal weather conditions. FIVB President Ruben Acosta attended the competition, along with over 5000 spectators. The championship match was won by the Brazilian team of Rogrio "Para" Ferreira de Souza and Guilherme Luiz Marquez. The scores were 19-21, 23-21, and 21-17 over compatriots Z-Marco and Emanuel. The winner's split the $20,000.00 prize for first place. The Australian team of Julien Prosser and Lee Zahner tried hard to reach the final, losing against Para and Guilherme 21-19, 21-23, 17-21, on Sunday morning. The Aussies then had to face the Portuguese team Joao Carlos Pereira Brenha Alves and Luis Miguel Barbosa Maia. They defeated the Portuguese by scores of 23-21 and 21-16, for the third place.

3rd Place: Julien Prosser and Lee Zahner-Aus
4th Place: Joao Carlos Pereira Brenha Alves and Luis Barbosa Maia-Port
5th Place: Mark Heese and John Child-Canada
5th Place: Conrad Leinemann and Jody Holden-Canada
5th Place: Roberto Lopes and Franco Neto-Bra
5th Place: avier Bosma Minguez and Fabio Diez-Spain

The only U.S.A. team in the competition, Carl Henkel and Sinjin Smith, were eliminated in the first round, as they lost to the Russian team of Dmitri Karasev and Maxim Pospelov, 21-17 and 21-17.

KLAGENFURT AUSTRIA
August 1st-3rd, 1997

The next $150,000.00 FIVB Men's World Beach Volleyball Tour stopped in Klagenfurt, Austria. This was the first ever Men's Beach Volleyball World Tour event ever promoted by Acts Innovative and the Austrian National Federation. The organizers built a excellent stadium on the edge of the "Wortersee", a gorgeous alpine lake in the heart of the culturally-rich city of Klagenfurt. There were a record number of accredited journalists (110) for a World Tour event, and some 5,000 spectators enjoyed the thoroughly organized Austrian Open. As luck would have it for the German fans, the German team of Jorge Ahmann and Axel Hager reached the championship match, their first FIVB final ever. In the, over one hour, championship match, the German team was defeated by the Brazilian team of Z-Marco Nobrega and Emanuel Rego. The two set final scores were 12-6 and 12-4. The winners each took home a check for $10,000.00 while the second place Germans shared a check in the amount of $13,000.00. The Brazilian team made it to the finals via the losers' bracket. In the, over one hour, match for third place, the Brazilian team of Paulo "Paulao" Roberto Moreira da Costa and Paulo Emilio Silva Azevedo edged the Canadian team of John Child and Mark Heese by a score of 17-15.

3rd Place: Paulo Roberto Moreira da Costa and Paulo Silva Azevedo-Bra
4th Place: John Child and Mark Heese-Canada
5th Place: Paul Laciga and Martin Laciga-Swiss
5th Place: Conrad Leinemann and Jody Holden-Canada

The U.S.A. team of Sinjin Smith and Carl Henkel finished in the 7th spot.

ESPINHO PORTUGAL
August 8th-10th, 1997

The next Men's FIVB World Pro-Beach Volleyball event took place on Espinho Baia Beach, in Portugal. The total prize money was $300,000.00. Jan Kvalheim and Bjorn Maaseide, from Norway, defeated the Brazilizn team of Lopes and Franco, in the one and half hour championship match, by scores of 12-7, 4-12, and 12-10. The winner's split the $40,000.00 first place prize money. The crowd of over 5,000 spectators in Espinho were treated to over four hours of Pro-Beach Volleyball, that not only included the battle in the championship match, but also a close semifinal match between the Brazilian team of Roberto Lopes and Franco Neto. They were pitted against the Canadian team of John Child and Mark Heese, with the Brazilians winning the match, that took over one hour, by a score of 15-13. Following that match, in the other semifinal match, between the Norwegians, Kvalheim and Maaseide against Eduardo Estaban Martinez and Martine Alejo Conde, from Argentina, there were several lead changes, with the Norwegians prevailing by a score of 15-8. In the match for third place Child and Heese easily defeated Martinez and Conde by a score of 15-6.

3rd Place: ohn Child and Mark Heese-Canada
4th Place: Estaban Martinez and Martine Alejo Conde-Arg
5th Place: Jose luis Salema Abrantes and Mariano Baracetti-Arg
5th Place: Jose Eduardo "Duda" Macedo Pinto de Abreu and Federico "Fred" Doria de Souza-Bra

The U.S.A. team of Carl Henkel and Sinjin Smith won their first match against the Russian team of Dmitri Karasev and Maxim Pospelov by a score of 15-13. They lost their next match to the Canadian team of Jody Holden and Conrad Leinemann by a score of 15-8. Against their next opponents, the French team of Stephane Canet and Matieu Hamel, they regained their winning ways by a score of 15-9. Smith and Henkel were then eliminated from the tournament with a loss to the Argentine team of Jose luis Salema Abrantes and Mariano Baracetti, by a score of 15-10, placing them in thirteenth.

OSTEND BELGIUM
August 15th-17th, 1997

On the weekend of August 15th-17th, 1997 the next FIVB Men's $150,000.00 Beach Volleyball event was contested at Ostend, Belgium. The courts were set-up on the magnificent beach of the Thermae Palace Hotel. The 1997 "SPA BEACH VOLLEY was played under the hot bright sunshine that contributed to both the participants and the spectators nearly reaching their boiling points. The most exciting match was, without a doubt, a first round match between the German team of Jorg Ahmann and Axel Hager, against the French team of Guilherm Deulofeu and Eric Guissart. The German team was the heavy favorite, but the French team played excellent defense to pull off the upset by a score of 17-15. The sizzling match took over an hour to complete. Another "Hot Match," that excited the fans, was the first round match between the Spanish team of Fabio Diez and Javier Bosma Minguez against the Russian team of Sergey Safyulin and Dmitroi Kouchnerev. This match was also won by splended defense, on the part of the Spanish team, in just under one hour, by a score of 15-13. The Belgian teams had a tough time in this tournament after drawing some very strong opponents, although the Belgian team of Ceyfs and Kristof Waelkens played a strong match in losing to the team of Andrea Ghiurgi and Ricardo Lione, from Italy by a score of 14-16. The match took forty-five minutes to complete. Another Belgian team, Pascal Delfosse and Jacky Kempenaers, the two F.I.V.B. highest - ranked Belgian players, defeated Gernot Leitner and Oliver Stamm, from Austria, by a score of 15-13, in front of an excited home-town crowd. The tournament came down to a final that saw the Brazilian team of Z-Marco and Emanuel defeat the Argentine team of Eduardo Esteban Martinez and Martine Alejo Conde by scores of 12-3, 2-12, and 12-9. The championship match employed almost one and one-half hours of dazzling play. Each of the winner's took home $10,000.00 for their effort. In the match for third place, Paulo "Paulao" Roberto Moreira da Costa and Paulo Emilio Silva Azevedo, from Brazil, edged Jan Kvalheim and Bjorn Maaseide, from Norway by a score of 16-14.

3rd Place: Paulo "Paulao" Moreira da Costa and Paulo Silva Azevedo-Bra
4th Place: Jan Kvalheim and Bjorn Maaseide-Nor
5th Place: Rogrio "Para" de Souza and Guilherme Luiz Marquez-Bra
5th Place: Guilherme Luiz Marquez along with Bosma and Diez-Spain

The only team from the U.S.A. to participate was Carl Henkel and Sinjin Smith. They won their match against the Argentine team of Martinez and Conde by a score of 15-12. They then lost to the Brazilian team of Paulo Emilio and Paulao by a score of 15-9. They won their next two matches, a 15-13 win over the Canadian team of Jody Holden and Conrad Leinemann and a 15-8 win over the Czech Republic team of Michal Palinek and Premsyl Kubala. Smith and Henkel were eventually eliminated by the Spanish team of Bosma and Diez by a score of 15-10 to finish in seventh place.

ALBENA BULGARIA
August 23rd- 24th, 1997

The Men's FIVB World Pro-Beach Volleyball Tour, made a stop in Albena Bulgaria, at Balkan Beach, on the weekend of August 23rd- 24th, 1997. The event was a $30,000.00 "Challenger" tournament. On this pretty bay, on Black Sea's north coast the over 4,500 fans were treated to a high degree of technical play. Teams fought hard, to obtain one of the four spots available in the main draw. The spectators enjoyed the hard fought early matches, but the over two-hour championship match between the Russian team of Dmitri Areshkin and Sergey Senin against Willie De Jesus Torras and Amaury Velasco from Puerto Rico, who made it to the semifinals through the losers' bracket, was indisputably the best match of the tournament. The Russian's prevailed in this exciting championship match by scores of 12-10, 10-12, and 12-10. Areshkin and Senin each earned $3,000.00 for the win. In the match for third place, Ernesto Vogado and Murilo Toscano from Brazil managed to overtake the Italian team of Nicola Grigolo and Andrea Raffaelli by the score of 15-9.

3rd Place: Murilo Toscano and Ernesto Vogada-Bra
4th Place: Nicola Grigolo and Andrea Raffaelli-Italy
5th Place: Gernot Leitner and Oliver Stamm-Austria
5th Place: Ondrej Koudelka and Vojtech Koudelka-Czech

The U.S.A. team of Morgan Chapman and Greg Ryan won their first match, 15-4 over the Puerto Rican team of DeJesus and Velasco. They lost their next match to the Italian team of Grigolo and Raffaelli by a score of 15-10. They were then eliminated by losing their next match to the Bulgarian team of Stoychev and Stefanov by a score of 15-12.

ALANYA TURKEY
August 29th-31st, 1997

The FIVB Men's World Pro-Beach Volleyball Tour went to the Mediterranean Coast of Turkey at Alanya, Turkey on the weekend of August 29th-31st, 1997. The $150,000.00 tournament took place on Kleopatra Beach, in one of the largest beach volleyball stadiums in Europe. The stadium had the capacity to seat 5,500 spectators. In the championship match, the Brazilian team of Paulo "Paulao" Roberto Moreira da Costa and Paulo Emilio Silva Azevedo, outlasted compatriots Rogrio "Para" Ferreira de Souza and Guilherme Luiz Marquez by scores of 8-12, 12-9, 12-10, in their one hour and forty minute match. Paulao and Emilo split the $20,000.00 prize for first place. In the semifinals, Paulo Emilio and Paulao, easily defeated compatriots Emanuel Rego Scheffer and Jose Marco Melo Ferreira Nobregal by a score of 15-6 to gain entry into the championship match. Paro and Guilherme outlasted Roberto Lopes and Franco Neto, also from Brazil, 17-15 to earn their way into the final. In the match for third place, Z-Marco and Emanuel went on to defeat Lopes and Franco to earn a third place finish. The Brazilian team of Paro and Guilherme had to drop out of the tournament because of injury.

3rd Place: Emanuel Rego Scheffer and Jose Marco Ferreira Nobregal-Bra
4th Place: Roberto Lopes and Franco Neto-Bra
5th Place: Nicola Grigolo and Ricardo Lione
5th Place: John Child and Mark Heese

The American team of Morgan Chapman and Greg Ryan, lost early in the tournament to Z-Marco and Emanuel, 5-15. They then won by injury default to the Russian team of Maxim Pospelov and Dmitroi Kouchnerev. Chapman and Ryan were then eliminated from the tournament after losing to the Portugese team of Jose Carlos Pereira Brenha Alves and Luis Miguel Barbosa Maia 9-15.

CANARY ISLANDS TENERIFE SPAIN
September 4th-7th, 1997

The next Men's $150,000.00 FIVB World Tour event was held at Tenerife, Canary Islands Spain, on Norwegiaach Beach. For six hours, the fans celebrated at Tenerife. As in previous years at Tenerife, the Promoter "Special Events" not only organized an FIVB World Beach Volleyball tournament, but a complete and vivacious show, superbly entertained by the "Winston Fun Girls." The stadium was filled to capacity by the first match of the semifinals and the fans stayed for more than 2 hours, dancing on the bleachers during the break between the semifinals and the bronze and gold medal matches. In the fifty-five minute championship match, Norway's Jan Kvalheim and Bjorn Maaseide easily defeated Argentina's Eduardo Estaban Martinez and Martine Alejo Conde for their second World Tour title this season. The scores were 12-3 and 12-5. The third place match was intense as Paul Laciga and Martin Laciga, from Switzerland, were effortlessly defeated, by the Brazilian team and current leaders of the FIVB World Ranking, Emanuel Rego Scheffer and Jose Z-Marco Melo Ferreira Nobregal, by a score of 15-7.

3rd Place: Emanuel Rego Scheffer and Jose Z-Marco Ferreira Nobrega-Bra
4th Place: Paul Laciga and Martin Laciga-Swiss
5th Place: "Para" Ferreira de Souza and Guilherme Luiz Marquez-Bra
5th Place: "Paulao" Roberto Moreira da Costa and Paulo Silva Azevedo-Bra

LOS ANGELES CALIFORNIA-USA

September 10th-13th, 1997, the FIVB **World Championship of Beach Volleyball** took place at the UCLA Tennis Center, in Los Angeles, California (U.S.A.). This historical tournament was able to take place because of the August 15th, 1997 announcement that the Federation International de Volleyball (the FIVB) and the Association of Volleyball Professionals (the AVP) had reached a "Historical Agreement" for the FIVB Beach Volleyball World Championships. The FIVB, the world international governing body of Volleyball and the AVP, the top governing association of the men's two-person pro Beach Volleyball, as recognized by USA Volleyball in the United States, announced that they had reached an agreement which allowed players to participate in both the FIVB World Tour and the AVP Tour. Nike Sports (and their money) showed an interest in the event, but only if the AVP players were involved along with the the FIVB players. The agreement came about because Leonard Armato (mega-sports agent and co-founder of the AVP) had been frustrated by the feud between the FIVB and the AVP that prevented some of the best players in the world from competing at the 1996 Olympic Games in Atlanta. Armato broke down the political walls and served as liaison between Ruben Acosta of the FIVB and Jerry Solomon of the AVP, along with representatives from the WPVA and the "Four-Person" League to establish the first "World Championship of Beach Volleyball." The result of this historic pact was that it allowed the world's best male and female two-person Beach Volleyball players to compete in the World Beach Volleyball Championship. The "land-locked" beach tournament was held on 2700 tons of rented sand trucked in from Simi Valley and dumped all over the UCLA Tennis Center courts. This World Championships was the most competitive event in the history of Beach Volleyball since the 1996 Atlanta Olympic Games.

The growth of beach volleyball had been remarkable and it was very interesting to see the outcome with such a talented field of male and female players from all over the world playing for the largest prize money in history of beach volleyball. This was a momentous stage for the sport of Beach Volleyball. The Beach Volleyball World Championships presented by Ericsson and Nike brought together the various categories of Beach Volleyball in the richest event in the history of the sport ($600,000). It also marked the first time that the men and women played for equal prize money and the four-person version of Beach Volleyball was demonstrated in such a major event. There were fifty-seven men's teams from 22 countries entered into the tournament along with forty-seven women's teams from 21 countries (including teams that were trying to qualify). The tournament format was 2 out of 3 side-out scoring to 12 with rally-scoring to 12 for the third game. The Brazilian team of Para Ferreira De Souza and Guilherme Luiz Marques defeated the U.S.A. team of Mike Whitmarsh and Canyon Ceman in the mistake-ridden championship match. In the first game, of the hour and half, championship match, Whitmarsh and Ceman were in total control, winning 12-5. In the second game, Ceman seemed to loose his confidence, hitting numerous balls out and missing digs that he would normally execute, as they lost 12-8. In the third and final game (rally scoring), Ceman continued to miscue as he and Whitmarsh were defeated 12-10, by the fired-up Brazilians. The Brazilians split the $40,000.00 first place check. Para and Guilherme reached the championship match, by defeating fellow Brazilians Paulo "Paulao" Roberto Moreira da Costa and Paulo Emilio Silva Azevedo, in an exciting three game, two and on quarter hour, semifinal set. The scores were 10-12, 12-9, and 15-13. Whitmarsh and Ceman gained entry into the championship match by defeating fellow Americans Kent Steffes and Dain Blanton, in their semifinal set, by scores of 12-5 and 12-8. By winning the championship match, the FIVB demonstrated that they are ready to compete on a level with the AVP, although in the 15 matches of head-to-head competition between AVP and FIVB teams the AVP enjoyed an 11-4 advantage winning 26 games to 10 for the FIVB (counting Brazilians Jose Loiola and Eduardo "Anjinho" Bacil as an AVP team).

JOSE LOIOLA
Jose Loiola teamed-up with Eduardo Bacil to represent Brazil at the 1997 FIVB World Championship of Beach Volleyball in Los Angeles CA. Above photo, Loiola (center) celebrates a win over the Swiss team of Paul and Martin Laciga.
Photo Courtesy of Kevin Goff

SEEDINGS:	FINISH:
1. Jose Loiola and Anjinho Bacil (Brazil)	5TH
2. Kent Steffes and Dain Blanton (U.S.A.)	3RD
3. Mike Whitmarsh and Canyon Ceman (U.S.A.)	2ND
4. Paulo Emilio and Paulao (Brazil)	3RD
5. Karch Kiraly and Adam Johnson (U.S.A.)	5TH
6. Z-Marco and Emanuel (Brazil)	5TH
7. Mike Dodd and Rob Heidger (U.S.A.)	9TH
8. Kvalheim and Maaseide (Norway)	17TH
9. Para and Guilherme (Brazil)	1ST
10. Troy Tanner and Ian Clark (U.S.A.)	5TH

MEN'S MAIN DRAW RESULTS:
(ROUND-ONE THE LOSERS FINISH IN 17TH PLACE)

Jose Loiola and Anjinho Bacil (Brazil) defeated Krank and Oetke (Germany) 12-1, 12-8.
P. Laciga and M. Laciga (Switzerland) defeated Palinek and Kubala (Czech Republic) 12-9, 10-12, 12-10.
Para and Guilherme (Brazil) defeated Ahmann and Hager (Germany) 12-11, 12-3.
Duda and Fred (Brazil) defeated Kvalheim and Maaseide (Norway) 12-11, 12-5.
Karch Kiraly and Adam Johnson (U.S.A.) defeated Maia and Brenha (Portugal) 12-10, 12-2.
Dax Holdren and Todd Rogers (U.S.A.) defeated Holden and Leinemann (Canada) 6-12, 12-5, 12-7.
Roberto Lopes and Franco (Brazil) defeated Martinez and Conde (Argentina) 12-11, 12-8.
Paulo Emilio and Paulao (Brazil) defeated Penigaud and Jodard (France) 12-5, 12-4.
Mike Whitmarsh and Canyon Ceman (U.S.A.) defeated Guissart and Deulofeu (France) 12-9, 12-2.
Eric Fonoimoana and Brian Lewis (U.S.A.) defeated Salema-Baracetti (Argentina) 12-3, 12-9.
Child and Heese (Canada) defeated Sinjin Smith and Carl Henke (U.S.A.) 4-12, 12-9, 13-11.

Z-Marco and Emanuel (Brazil) defeated Kjemperud and Hoidalen (Norway) 12-11, 7-12, 12-7.
Mike Dodd and Rob Heidger (U.S.A.) defeated Karasev and Pospelov (Russia) 12-11, 12-7.
Troy Tanner and Ian Clark (U.S.A.) defeated Bosma and Diez (Spain) 12-5, 12-6.
Prosser and Zahner (Australia) defeated Bill Boullianne and David Swatik (U.S.A.) 12-6, 12-5.
Kent Steffes and Dain Blanton (U.S.A.) defeated Pomerenke and Anton (Germany) 12-9, 12-3.

ROUND TWO, THE LOSERS FINISH IN 9TH PLACE

Jose Loiola and Anjinho Bacil (Brazil) defeated P. Laciga and M. Laciga (Switzerland) 12-10, 9-12, 16-14.
Para and Guilherme (Brazil) defeated Duda and Fred (Brazil) 12-8, 12-4.
Karch Kiraly and Adam Johnson (U.S.A.) defeated Dax Holdren and Todd Rogers (U.S.A.) 5-12, 12-6, 12-10.
Paulo Emilio and Paulao (Brazil) defeated Roberto Lopes and Franco (Brazil) 12-9, 12-10.
Mike Whitmarsh and Canyon Ceman (U.S.A.) defeated Eric Fonoimoana and Brian Lewis (U.S.A.) 12-6, 12-3.
Z-Marco and Emanuel (Brazil) defeated Child and Heese (Canada) 12-9, 12-9.
Troy Tanner and Ian Clark (U.S.A.) defeated Mike Dodd and Rob Heidge 7-12, 12-9, 12-9.
Kent Steffes and Dain Blanton (U.S.A.) defeated Prosser and Zahner (Australia) 12-9, 12-8.

ROUND-THREE
(THE LOSERS FINISH IN 5TH PLACE)

Para and Guilherme (Brazil) defeated Jose Loiola and Anjinho (Brazil) 12-7, 12-6.
Paulo Emilio and Paulao (Brazil) defeated Karch Kiraly and Adam Johnson (U.S.A.) 12-6, 5-12, 12-8.
Mike Whitmarsh and Canyon Ceman (U.S.A.) defeated Z-Marco and Emanuel (Brazil) 12-5, 12-4.
Kent Steffes and Dain Blanton (U.S.A.) defeated Troy Tanner and Ian Clark (U.S.A.) 12-4, 12-3.

SEMI-FINALS
(LOSERS FINISH IN 3RD PLACE)

Para and Guilherme (Brazil) defeated Paulo Emilio and Paulao (Brazil) 10-12, 12-9, 15-13.
Whitmarsh and Ceman (U.S.A.) defeated Steffes and Blanton (U.S.A.) 12-5, 12-8.

CHAMPIONSHIP MATCH:

Para Ferreira De Souza and Guilherme Luiz Marques (Brazil) defeated Mike Whitmarsh and Canyon Ceman (U.S.A.) 5-12, 12-8, 12-10.

DURBAN SOUTH AFRICA

The November 28th-30th, 1997 FIVB Men's World Beach Volleyball tournament in Durban South Africa was canceled.

FORTALEZA BRAZIL

On the weekend of December 4th-6th, 1997, the Men's FIVB World Pro-Beach Volleyball Tour stopped in Fortaleza Brazil for the final tournament of the 1997 season. Fortaleza is the hometown of the Brazilian team of Roberto Lopes and Franco Neto. Fortaleza, now a regular stop of the FIVB Pro-Beach Volleyball World Tour, is 500 miles northwest of Recife, and is the capital of the state of Cearç, on the eastern Brazilian coast. The Fortaleza Open was played on a beautiful beach lined with spectacularly tall coconut palms. In the all Brazilian championship match, Z-Marco Norbrega and Emanuel Rego defeated Francismar Adriano Dias Garrido and Guilherme Luiz Marquez by scores of 12-5 and 12-8. They split $20,000.00 for their effort.

3rd Place: Eduardo Estaban Martinez and Martine Alejo Conde-Arg
4th Place: Sinjin Smith and Carl Henkel-USA
5th Place: Franco Neto Roberto Lopes-Bra
5th Place: Paulo "Paulao" Moreira da Costa and Paulo Emilio Azevedo-Bra

MIKE WHITMARSH
Mike Whitmarsh advanced to the finals of the 1997 FIVB World Championship of Beach Volleyball, in Los Angeles CA, with partner Canyon Ceman, finishing in 2nd place. Above photo, Whitmarsh goes-up to block the attack of Brazilian Paulo Emilo.
Photo Courtesy of Kevin Goff

TOP PHOTOS: Left: Brian Ivie slices the ball past the block of Kent Steffes. **Center:** Mark Kerins attacking the ball. **Right:** Troy Tanner smashes the ball towards the defense of Kent Steffes.

MIDDLE PHOTOS: Left: Canadian Brian Gatske sneaks the ball past the block of Andrew Smith. **Center:** Erick Wurts attacking the ball. **Right:** Eric Fonoimoana challenges the block of Adam Johnson.

1997 MEN'S BEACH VOLLEYBALL ACTION

BOTTOM PHOTOS: Left: Jim Nichols cuts the ball past the block of Ricci Luyties. **Center:** Scott Ayakatubby is in position to pass the ball. **Right:** Karch Kiraly aggresively attacks the ball.

Photo's Courtesy of the AVP

WOMEN'S BEACH VOLLEYBALL
1997

WPVA

The 1997 WPVA Schedule included 14 events over 6 months in 8 states. California and Florida lead the way, staging three events each. Texas hosted two events. New Jersey, Illinois, Rhode Island, New York, Colorado and Hawaii each hosted one tournament.

Holly McPeak teamed with Lisa Arce to outdistance the competition by advancing to 9 championship matches, winning 7 titles. Karolyn Kirby and Nancy Reno finished the season with 3 titles after reaching 6 finals. Liz Masakayan and Elaine Youngs were the only other team to capture at least 2 WPVA 1997 titles, winning the Chicago and Hawaiian events.

1997 WPVA SCHEDULE

When	Where
April 5-6	Miami Beach, Florida
April 18-20	Deerfield Beach, Florida
May 9-11	Orlando, Florida
May 16-18	Austin, Texas
May 31-June 1	San Diego, California
June 14-15	Dallas, Texas
June 21-22	Atlantic City, New Jersey
June 28-29	Huntington Beach, Califotnia
July 12-13	Chicago, Illinois
July 26-27	Newport, Rhode Island
August 2-3	New York, New York
August 9-10	Hermosa Beach, California
August 30-31	Aspen, Colorado
September 20-21	Kaua'i, Hawai'i

INDIVIDUAL WPVA TOURNAMENT FINISHES
1997

Player	1st	2nd	3rd	4th	5th
Lisa Arce	7	2	1	1	2
SheldaKellyBruno Bede	0	0	0	0	1
AdrianaBrandao Behar	0	0	0	0	1
Krista Blomquist	0	0	3	0	1
Danalee Bragado	0	0	1	0	1
Gail Castro	0	1	0	1	0
Linda Chisholm	0	0	1	2	2
Cammy Ciarelli	0	0	1	0	0
Natalie Cook	0	0	0	0	1
Annette Davis	0	1	0	0	0
Linda Robertson Hanley	0	4	2	2	2
Barbara Fontana	0	4	2	2	2
Jenny Johnson	0	1	0	0	0
Pat Keller	0	0	0	0	1
Karolyn Kirby	3	3	1	0	5
Dennie Schupyt Knoop	0	0	0	3	1
Liz Masakayan	2	0	1	1	2
Holly McPeak	7	2	0	1	2
Jennifer Meredith	0	0	0	0	2
Marla O'Hara	0	0	0	1	1
Karrie Poppinga	0	1	3	1	3
Nancy Reno	3	3	1	0	4
Deb Richardson	0	0	1	2	2
Angela Rock	0	1	3	1	3
Elaine Roque	0	0	0	3	1
Christine Schaefer	0	0	3	0	2
Leanne Schuster	0	0	0	0	2
Gail Stammer	0	1	0	1	0
Ali Wood	0	0	0	1	0
Elaine Youngs	2	0	1	1	0

HOLLY McPEAK & LISA ARCE
Holly McPeak teamed with Lisa Arce to outdistance the competition, on the 1997 WPVA Tour, by advancing to 9 championship matches, winning 7 titles. Above photo, McPeak and Arce show-off their first place trophies.
Photo Courtesy of the AVP

HOLLY McPEAK & LISA ARCE
Holly McPeak and Lisa Arce played stron defesne to help them become the top team, on the 1997 WPVA Tour. Above photo, McPeak makes a spectacular diving effort to get the ball up for her partner, Lisa Arce.
Photo Courtesy of "Couvi"

1997 WPVA PLAYERS
End of 1997

Melissa Allen
Marie Andersson
Kristi Atkinson
Kristine Bailey
Amy Baltus
Barbara Bierman
Krista Blomquist
Bonnie Bright
Jackie Campbell
Julia Celotto
Linda Chisholm
Michelle Chryst
Michal Clingman
Mindy Czuleger
Jackie deTurenne
Alissa Evans-Lund
Barbra Fontana
Kengy Gardiner
Kathy Gedney
Jeanne Goldsmith
Heather Hafner
Linda Hanley
Janice Harrer
Valinda Hilleary
Tiffany Rochelle-Anderson
Lisa Arce
Jackie Auzias de Turenne
Mary Baily
Lisa Bettio
Barbara (Belding) Birnbaum
Danalee Bragado
Nancy Brookhart
Gail Castro
Elizabeth Chavez
Nancy Christian
Cammy Ciarelli
Evelyn Conley
Erin Deiters
Patty Dodd
Wendy Fletcher
Lori Forsythe
Lisa Gathright
Connie Gibbon
Jenny Griffith
Lucy Han
Colleen Harp
Katie Henderson
Mary Holland
Alison Johnson
Patricia Keller
Jeanette Kollasch
Desiree Leipham
Bev Lidyoff
Laura Martin
Nancy Mason
Jennifer Meredith
Marsha Miller
Michelle Morse
Marla O'Hara
Liz Pagano
Lael Perlstrom
Gina Pillitiere
Helen Reale
Nancy Reno
Deb Richardson
Angela Rock
Veronica Sanchez
Ann Schirman
Beth Schuler
Graciela Schutt
Mary Jane Smith
Melanie Sullivan
Stephanie Weber
Johanna Wright
Lynda Johnson
Karolyn Kirby
Rhonda Kottke
Bonnie Levin
Kathleen Luciano
Liz Masakayan
Holly McPeak
Kristine Middeler
Shelly Miller
Stephanie Nelson
Monique Oliver
Amy Peistrup-Matthews
Maggie Philgence
Karrie Poppinga
Jeanne Reeves
Melinda Rich
Charlotte Roach
Elaine Roque
Christine Schaefer
Teri Schroeder
Leanne Schuster
Dennie Shupryt-Knoop
Gayle Stammer
Shannon Vessup-Miller
Ali Wood
Elaine Youngs

NANCY RENO & LINDA HANLEY
Nancy Reno and Linda Hanley both had a successful season on the 1997 WPVA Tour, with different partners. Reno advanced to 6 finals with Karolyn Kirby and Hanley advanced to four with Barbra Fontana. Above photo, Hanley attacks the block of Reno.
Photo Courtesy of Frank Goroszko

KAROLYN KIRBY
Karolyn Kirby was paired-up with Nancy Reno, on the 1997 WPVA Tour, as the number-two team on the tour. They advanced to 6 championship matches, winning 3 evnts. Above photo, Kirby reaches to make the pass.
Photo Courtesy of Frank Goroszko

FIVB

Total prize money for the Women's 1997 FIVB Beach Volleyball Events reached $1,710,000.00. The Tour staged 11 events in 11 different countries.

The Brazilian team of Monica Rodrigues and Adriana Ramos Samuel edged the field by winning 3 tournament championships. They advanced to 4 finals while gaining their titles. Two other Brazilian teams, Shelda Kelly Bruno Bede and Adriana Brandao Behar along with Jacqueline Louise "Jackie" Cruz Silva and Sandra Tavares Pires finished the season with 2 event titles. Bede and Behar advanced to the finals on 5 occasions, while Pires and Silva accomplished it twice. Americans Lisa Arce and Holly McPeak also finished the season with 2 tournament titles, after advancing to 6 finals.

1997 FIVB BEACH VOLLEYBALL SCHEDULE WOMEN

When	Where	Prize Money
Feb 13-16	Rio Brazil	$120,000.00
Mar 13-16	Melbourne Australia	$120,000.00
Jul 4-6	Pescara Italy	$120,000.00
Jul 19-20	Carolina Puerto Rico	$250,000.00
Jul 23-26	Marseille France	$120,000.00
Aug 1-3	Espinho Portugal	$120,000.00
Aug 8-10	Osaka Japan	$120,000.00
Aug 15-17	Pusan Korea	$120,000.00
Aug 22-24	Qingdao China	$120,000.00
Sep 10-13	Los Angeles, CA-USA	$300,000.00
Nov 21-23	Kuah Mas (Langkawi)	$120,000.00

SANDRA PIRES
Brazilian Sandra Pires, paired-up with compatriot Jackie Silva for the 1997 FIVB Tour. They earned "Medals" on 6 occasions, winning 2 "Gold-Medals" and 4 "Bronze-Medals" Above photo, Pires gets above the net for the block attempt.
Photo Courtesy of Frank Goroszko

TOP 40 FIVB WOMEN's TEAMS
(fall of 1997)

1. Adriana Behar and Shelda-Brazil
2. Adriana Samuel and Monica-Brazil
3. Arce and McPeak-USA
4. Jackie Silva and SandraPires-Brazil
5. Cook and Pottharst-Australia
6. Friedrichsen and Musch-Germany
7. Bruschini and Solazzi-Italy
8. Dosoudilova and Celbova-CZE
9. Fontana and Hanley-USA
10. Masakayan and Youngs-USA
11. Rock and Poppinga-USA
12. Fenwick and Manser-Australia
13. Magda and Siomara-Brazil
14. Kirby and Reno-USA
15. Drakich and Dumont-Canada
16. Ana Richa and Adriana Bento-Brazil
17. Perrotta and Gattelli-Italy
18. Schoon Kadijk and Kadijk R.-Netherlands
19. Straton and Wilson-Australia
20. Hudcova and Tobiasova-CZE
21. Takahashi and Ishizaka-Japan
22. Clarke and Huygens Tholen-Australia
22. De Marinis and Nascimento-Italy
24. Z- Maria and Sarmento-Portugal
25. Schaefer and Bragado-USA
26. Broen Ouellette and Tough-Canada
27. Fontana and Reno-USA
29. Jorgensen and Sommer-Denmark
30. Bragado and O'Hara-USA
31. Schmidt and Staub-Germany
32. Takahashi and Teru Saiki-Japan
33. Cepeliauskas and Barry-Canada
33. Magda and Siomara-Brazil
33. Blomquist and Schaefer-USA
36. Glover and Malone-England
37. Laura Arco and Mayra-Mexico
38. Berjonneau and Gros-France
39. Gougeon-Storch-Canada
40. Clarke and Goole-Australia
40. Isabel and Minello-Brazil
40. Karina and Adriana Bento-Brazil
40. Keller and O'Hara-USA

INDIVIDUAL FIVB TOURNAMENT FINISHES
1997

Player	1st	2nd	3rd	4th	5th
Lisa Arce	2	4	1	0	0
SheldaKellyBruno Bede	2	3	2	2	0
AdrianaBrandao Behar	2	3	2	2	0
Eva Celbova	0	0	0	0	1
Natalie Cook	0	0	1	1	2
Sona Dosoudilvoa	0	0	0	0	2
Liane Fenwick	0	0	0	0	1
Maike Friedrichsen	0	1	0	0	3
Linda Robertson Hanley	0	0	0	0	2
BarbraFontana Harris	0	0	0	1	2
Karolyn Kirby	0	0	1	0	0
Pauline Manser	0	0	0	0	1
Liz Masakayan	0	0	0	1	1
Holly McPeak	2	4	1	0	0
Maria Richa Medeiros	0	0	0	0	1
Danja Musch	0	1	0	0	3
SandraTavares Pires	2	0	4	1	0
AnnaKarrie Poppinga	0	0	0	1	1
KerriAnn Pottharst	0	0	1	1	2
Lima Falcãão De Magda Rejane	0	0	0	0	2
Nancy Reno	0	0	1	1	0
Angela Rock	0	0	0	2	1
AdrianaBento Rodrigues	0	0	0	0	1
Monica Rodrigues	**3**	**1**	**1**	**1**	**2**
Teru Saiki	0	0	0	0	1
AdrianaRamos Samuel	**3**	**1**	**1**	**1**	**2**
JacquelineLouise"Jackie"Cruz Silva	2	0	4	1	0
Siomara Marcia de Souza	0	0	0	0	2
Yukiko Takahashi	0	0	0	0	1
Elaine Youngs	0	0	0	1	1

WOMEN'S TOURNAMENT RESULTS
1997-WPVA

MIAMI BEACH FLORIDA
April 5th-6th, 1997

The WPVA Tour stop at Miami Beach, Florida was won by Lisa Arce and Holly Mc Peak (#4 seeds). McPeak and Arce rallied, from a pair of four-point deficits, to down Karolyn Kirby and Nancy Reno (#5 seeds) 15-12, to capture the $60,000.00 WPVA Miami Beach Open. In the championship match, Arce and McPeak were down 7-3 and 12-8, but went on to win their fourth WPVA event in the last five starts. The win was the 40th in McPeak's career. Arce earned her sixth pro-beach volleyball title, all with McPeak. Kirby and Reno, both playing in their first event together since having off-season shoulder surgery last fall, had to battle back from a loss in the second round of the championship bracket, in order to salvage the second place finish. This was the first of three consecutive 1997 Florida WPVA Tour events. The other two events were the WPVA Deerfield Beach Open April 19-20 and the "Cybergenics" Open in Orlando May 9-11. This 1997 WPVA opening tournament attracted the second largest number of players (45 teams) in the 11-season history of the WPVA.

3rd Place: Krista Blomquist and Cammy Ciarelli
4th Place: Linda Chisholm and Deb Richardson
5th Place: Barbra Fontana and Linda Hanley
5th Place: Shelda Bede and Adriana Behar-Bra

DEERFIELD BEACH FLORIDA
April 18th-20th, 1997

The $50,000.00 WPVA Open, on Deerfield Beach in Florida, was won by Lisa Arce and Holly McPeak (#1 seeds) for their third-straight WPVA Tour event win. Arce and McPeak, won the last WPVA Tour event in 1996, along with the 1997 season opener April 5th-6th, 1997 in Miami Beach Florida. They were the only team from the top four seeds to survive the "upset" minded teams in this tournament. The double-elimination tournament featured 17 seed break-troughs. Arce and McPeak, winners of five of the last six WPVA Tour events, defeated Gail Castro and Gayle Stammer (#17 seeds) 15-8 in the championship match. Castro and Stammer, earned three upset wins this tournament. The championship was the 41st in McPeak's career. In the third-place match, Danalee Bragado and Christine Schaefer (#6 seeds) scored a 15-3 win over Elaine Roque and Dennie Shupryt-Knoop (#6 seeds). Arce and McPeak advanced to the finals with a 15-5 win over Bragado and Schaefer while Castro and Stammer outlasted Roque and Shupryt-Knoop 15-11.

3rd Place: Danalee Bragado and Christine Schaefer
4th Place: Elaine Roque and Dennie Shupryt-Knoop
5th Place: Linda Chisholm and Deb Richardson
5th Place: Karolyn Kirby and Nancy Reno

WPVA rookies Annette Davis and Jenny Johnson, had to qualify for this weekend's event as the 36th-seeded team.

LISA ARCE
Lisa Arce had a successful 1997 WPVA Tour. Paired-up wih Holly McPeak, Arce advanced to 9 finals while winning 7 events for the best record on the 1997 WPVA Tour. Above photo, Arce reaches above the net for the spike.
Photo Courtesy of "Couvi"

CHRISTINE SCHAEFER
Christine Schaefer provided some worthy competition on the 1997 WPVA Tour, finishing within the top five on 5 occasions. Above photo, Schaefer hits a set from Danalee Bragado towards the block of Deb Richardson.
Photo Courtesy of the AVP

ORLANDO FLORIDA
May 9th-11th, 1997

The third tournament of fourteen scheduled WPVA tournaments took place at Disney World's Lake Buena Vista in Orlando Florida. Nancy Reno and Karolyn Kirby won, the inaugural of this professional beach volleyball event, at Disney's Wide World of Sports complex. The finals were televised the same day by ABC Sports. Kirby and Reno won first-place by downing the 31st-seeded team of Annett Davis and Jenny Johnson 15-11 in the championship match. The weekend was filled with upset victories on both days. There were 23 upsets in 63 matches. The number one-seeded team of Lisa Arce and Holly McPeak were ousted early Sunday when they lost to Kirby and Reno, 16-14, in the contender's bracket. Kirby and Reno scored a 15-6 win over fifth-seeded Karrie Poppinga and Angela Rock to advance to their second WPVA Tour final in 1997. This victory was the eighth pro-beach title for the team of Kirby and Reno. Annett Davis and Jenny Johnson (the daughter of Rafer Johnson, the 1960 Olympic Gold Medalist in the decathlon), earned seven-straight upsets wins to earn the best finish by a qualifying team in WPVA Tour history. They were also the first African-American and at the age of 23 years the youngest team ever to play for a pro beach volleyball title. Davis and Johnson advanced to the championship match with a 15-13 win over 1996 Olympians Barbra Fontana and Linda Hanley. In the third-place match, Poppinga and Rock downed Fontana and Hanley 16-14.

3rd Place: Kerrie Poppinga and Angela Rock
4th Place: Linda Hanley and Barbra Fontana
5th Place: Natalie Cook Liz Masakayan
5th Place: Lisa Arce and Holly McPeak

AUSTIN TEXAS
May 16th-18th, 1997

In Austin, Texas Lisa Arce and Holly McPeak won the seventh annual Austin $50,000.00 WPVA Open, at the Emerald Point Pro Volleyball Club, on Lake Travi. Arce and McPeak, the top seeds, rebounded from their worst finish last week in Florida to capture their third WPVA Women's Pro Beach Volleyball Tour of 1997. They shared the $11,000.00 first-place prize money. Arce and McPeak, who finished fifth at the Orlando Open last tournament, downed third-seeded Barbra Fontana and Linda Hanley 18-16, in a 1 hour and 14-minute championship final, that included 84 side-outs. The championship win was Arce and McPeak's sixth-straight game victory of the tournament as the they gained their eighth pro beach volleyball win as a team.

BARBRA FONTANA
Barbra Fontan was paired-up with Linda Hanley, on the 1997 WPVA Tour. They advanced to the championship match at 4 events, finishing as the runners-up on all four occasions. Above photo, Fontana slices the ball away from Marla O'Hara.
Photo Courtesy of Frank Goroszko

ALI WOOD & ELAINE ROQUE
Ali Wood and Elaine Roque both provided some stiff competition on the 1997 WPVA Tour. Wood broke into the top five one time and Roque was able to gain 3 fourth place finishes and 1 fifth. Above photo Wood attacks the block of Roque.
Photo Courtesy of the AVP

The WPVA's top-ranked team of Arce and McPeak had won six of the last eight Evian Tour events, including three out of four tournaments this season. Arce and McPeak, with a 23-3 match mark, made it to the finals with a 15-7 win over fifth-seeded Karrie Poppinga and Angela Rock. The third seeded team Fontana and Hanley earned a spot in the finals with a 15-13 win over the fourth-seeded team of Elaine Roque and Dennie Shupryt-Knoop. This was the fifth time that these teams had met in a championship finale. Arce and McPeak had won four out of the five meetings. This win was McPeak's third-straight in Austin. Holly had now won 42 pro beach volleyball tournaments and Lisa had won 8.

3rd Place: Karrie Poppinga and Angela Rock
4th Place: Elaine Roque and Dennie Shupryt-Knoop
5th Place: Karolyn Kirby and Nancy Reno
5th Place: Danalee Bragado and Christine Schaefer

SAN DIEGO CALIFORNIA
May 31st-June 1st, 1997

The number one seeded team of Lisa Arce and Holly McPeak won their second-straight Evian Women's Pro Beach Volleyball Tournament by capturing the $50,000.00 WPVA San Diego Open, at Mariner's Point. This was the 5th of 14 scheduled tournaments on the 1997 WPVA Pro-Beach Volleyball Tour. The tournament was played on five sand courts at Mariner's Point on Mission Bay, as the WPVA returned to San Diego for the eighth-straight season. Arce and McPeak, who had now won six of the last nine WPVA Tournaments, beat-up the second-seeded team of Barbra Fontana and Linda Hanley 15-4 to share the $11,000 first-place. This win was the second-straight by Arce and McPeak over Fontana and Hanley in 1997 WPVA Tour Championship matches. Arce and McPeak had now won 7 of 10 matches against Fontana and Hanley. This was their eighth Evian Tour title together and ninth pro-beach championship. Arce and McPeak gained their spot in the finals with a 15-5 win over eighth-seeded Gail Castro and Gayle Stammer. This win was McPeak's 20th on the WPVA Tour and her 43rd in pro career victory. Arce had eight WPVA wins and one FIVB for nine overall as a pro. Fontana and Hanley advanced to the finals with a 15-8 win over third-seeded Karrie Poppinga and Angela Rock. Poppinga and Rock earned their 3rd-straight 3rd-place finish by downing Castro and Stammer 15-6.

3rd Place: Karrie Poppinga and Angela Rock
4th Place: Gail Castro and Gayle Stammer
5th Place: Karolyn Kirby and Liz Masakayan
5th Place: Pat Keller and Marla O'Hara

DALLAS TEXAS
June 13th-15th, 1997

The WPVA Tour was in Irving, Texas, on Mustang Beach in Las Colinas, for the Dallas Open. Top-seeded Lisa Arce and Holly McPeak captured their third-straight WPVA Tour title, of the season, with a victory over the second-seeded team of Karolyn Kirby and Nancy Reno. The score was 15-13 in the championship final. Arce and McPeak extended their winning streak to 18-straight matches. They were now winners of eight of the last 10 events on the WPVA Tour, Arce and McPeak had now won 10 professional beach volleyball titles together. The win over Kirby and Reno was the second in a title match this season as Arce and McPeak posted a 15-12 win over Kirby and Reno at Miami Beach, Florida, April 6, 1997. The one hour championship match had 59 side-outs, eight ties and five lead changes as Arce and McPeak won the title on their fifth match point when Reno's attempt to hit over the net on two failed. The biggest lead by either team was three in the match at 12-9 for Arce and McPeak as Reno and Kirby tied the match at 12-12. With Arce and McPeak leading 13-12, Reno's dink attempt on two went into the net to make it 14-12 in favor of Arce and McPeak, who went on to win 15-13. Arce and McPeak advanced to the finals with a 15-4 win over Barbra Fontana and Linda Hanley. Reno and Kirby advanced to the championship match with a 15-8 win over Liz Masakayan and Elaine Youngs. Youngs, a member of the 1996 United States National Team, that competed in the Atlanta Olympic Games, was playing in her first pro beach doubles event.

3rd Place: Liz Masakayan and Elaine Youngs
4th Place: Barbra Fontana and Linda Hanley
5th Place: Karrie Poppinga and Angela Rock
5th Place: Krista Blomquist and Chriatine Podraza

ELAINE YOUNGS & KRISTA BLOMQUIST
Elaine "EY" Youngs and Krista Blomquist both had 4 top five finishes on the 1997 WPVA Tour. In fact 2 of "EY's" were championship victories while Blomquist had 3 thirds. Above photo, "EY" tries to avoid the block of Blomquist.
Photo Courtesy of the AVP

ATLANTIC CITY NEW JERSEY
June 21st-22nd, 1997

The WPVA Atlantic City Open, in New Jersey was won by the second-seeded team of Karolyn Kirby and Nancy Reno. In the championship match, they took an early 9-3 lead in route to a 15-11 win over top-seeded Lisa Arce and Holly McPeak. The win was the sixth WPVA Tour title, for the team of Kirby and Reno, as Arce and McPeak, saw their three-tournament 22-match winning streak end on the beachfront at the Atlantic City Hilton. These two teams were now tied at 3-3 in head-to-head competition. The win also marked Kirby and Reno's second Atlantic City title as the pair won here in 1992 in their first event together. Kirby, had now won 60 Evian Tour titles and 66 overall as a professional while Reno earned her 34th pro-beach title with 19 coming in the WPVA. This year's championship match lasted over 45 minutes and included 44 side-outs, two ties and two lead changes as Kirby and Reno won the title on their fifth-match point on a Kirby dig and kill. Kirby and Reno advanced to the championship match with a 15-11 win over Linda Chisholm and Deb Richardson. Arce and McPeak advanced to the finals with a 15-9 win over Barbra Fontana and Linda Hanley. ABC Sports, which covered six WPVA Tournaments in 1997, taped the championship match for TV.

3rd Place: Barbra Fontana and Linda Hanley
4th Place: Linda Chisholm and Deb Richardson
5th Place: Karrie Poppinga and Angela Rock
5th Place: Elaine Roque and Dennie Schupyt Knoop

HUNTINGTON BEACH CALIFORNIA
June 28th-29th, 1997

The WPVA made its next tour stop in Huntington Beach California. Top-seeded Lisa Arce and Holly McPeak won their fourth-straight WPVA Tour "Grand-Slam" tournament, by winning this U. S. Open, staged at the Huntington Beach Pier. Arce and McPeak, who had won nine of their last 12 WPVA Tour events, handled Barbra Fontana and Linda Hanley 15-9, to take the championship. This was the first of four "Grand-Slam" tournaments on the 1997 WPVA Tour. This win was the third-straight by Arce and McPeak over Fontana and Hanley in a 1997 Evian Tour title match. Arce and McPeak had now won 10 of 13 career meetings against Fontana and Hanley as the pair captured their 10th Evian Tour title together and 11th overall pro-beach title. Arce and McPeak moved into the finals with a 15-1 trouncing over the twelfth-seeded team of Marla O'Hara and Ali Wood. The title was McPeak's 22nd on the WPVA Tour and 45th in her pro career. Arce had 10 WPVA titles and 11 overall as a pro-beach volleyball player. The U. S. Open final was taped by ABC Sports for TV.

3rd Place: Linda Chisholm and Deb Richardson
4th Place: Marla O'Hara and Ali Wood
5th Place: Karolyn Kirby and Nancy Reno
5th Place: Karrie Poppinga and Angela Rock

CHICAGO ILLINOIS
July 12th-13th, 1997

Chicago, Illinois was the site of the next WPVA Tournament. Liz Masakayan and Elaine Youngs became the lowest seeded team to win an Evian Women's Pro Beach Volleyball Tour event. As the 12th-seeded team, they held on to edge the top-seeded team of Lisa Arce and Holly McPeak 16-14, in the championship match. After falling behind 10-2 and 14-9, Masakayan and Youngs held off five championship points by Arce and McPeak to win their first pro beach volleyball title together. Masakayan and Youngs tied the match at 14-14 on an Arce hitting error. They snatched the lead on a Masakayan kill and then won the match when Youngs served a "spader" on Arce. The championship was Masakayan's 36th pro-beach tournament victory, as she won her first WPVA Tour tournament since 1995. Youngs, recorded her first title in only her fourth WPVA Tournament. Arce and McPeak, lost a 15-7 match earlier in the tournament to Masakayan and Youngs. Arce and McPeak had won six of the previous nine WPVA Tournaments this season while Masakayan and Youngs become just the third team to win a WPVA final this season. After losing to Masakayan and Youngs, Arce and McPeak re-grouped with wins over Kirby and Reno, 15-8 then 15-9 over Krista Blomquist and Christine Schaefer, to reach the finals. Masakayan and Youngs won over Poppinga and Rock 15-12 to reach the championship match. ABC taped the championship match for TV.

3rd Place: Krista Blomquist and Christine Schaefer
4th Place: Kerrie Poppinga and Angela Rock
5th Place: Jennifer Meredith and Leanne Schuster
5th Place: Karolyn Kirby and Nancy Reno

NEWPORT RHODE ISLAND
July 26th-27th, 1997

The WPVA Tournament scheduled for Newport Rhode Island on the weekend of July 26th-27th, 1997 was canceled.

LONG ISLAND NEW YORK
August 2nd-3rd, 1997

The WPVA stopped on Long Island, at East Quogue New York, on Tiana Beach, for the 1997 Evian WPVA Invitational. This two-day, 16-match event featured the top eight teams on the WPVA Tour. Top-seeded Lisa Arce and Holly McPeak captured their fifth-straight "Grand-Slam" title by defeating second-seeded Karolyn Kirby and Nancy Reno 15-9 in the championship match. This was Kirby and Reno's third loss, out of four championship meetings, this season, with Arce and McPeak. Arce and McPeak, had won seven of 10 WPVA Tour events this season. The Evian Invitational title was the 13th for the Arce and McPeak tandem in their pro-beach volleyball career together, including 11 on the WPVA Tour. Arce and McPeak, who had now won 25-straight matches in WPVA Tour grand slam events, advanced to the finals with a 15-12 win over Barbra Fontana and Linda Hanley. Kirby and Reno scored a 15-4 win over Elaine Roque and Dennie Shupryt-Knoop to move on to their fifth final this season.

Participants-Summary:
1st	Lisa Arce/Holly McPeak	5-0
2nd	Karolyn Kirby/Nancy Reno	3-2
3rd	Barbra Fontana/Linda Hanley	3-2
4th	Elaine Roque/Dennie Shupryt-Knoop	2-3
5th	Linda Chisholm/Deb Richardson	1-2
6th	Krista Blomquist/Christine Schaefer	0-3
7th	Gail Castro/Gayle Stammer	0-3
8th	Karrie Poppinga/Angela Rock	2-1 (Withdrew)

HERMOSA BEACH CALIFORNIA
August 8th-10th, 1997

The WPVA Tour went to Hermosa Beach California, where Karolyn Kirby and Nancy Reno won their second Evian "National" Championships title. In the championship match, Kirby and Reno defeated Barbra Fontana and Linda Hanley, 15-13. The win was the 10th for Kirby and Reno, as pro beach volleyball partners. They finished the tournament with a perfect 6-0 record. The win was Kirby's 67th in her 11-year pro beach career, including a record 61 titles on the WPVA. Reno, who had teamed to win three WPVA titles this season, posted her 35th pro beach career championship victory. Reno had won 20 WPVA championships. Kirby and Reno advanced to the championship match with a 15-9 win over Krista Blomquist and Christine Schaefer Podraza. Fontana and Hanley, who dropped a 15-8 decision to Kirby and Reno, earlier in the tournament, made it to the finals with 15-13 win over Liz Masakayan and Elaine Youngs.

3rd Place: Krista Blomquist and Christine Podraza
4th Place: Liz Masakayan and Elaine Youngs
5th Place: Jennifer Meredith and Leanne Schuster
5th Place: Lisa Arce and Holly McPeak

LOS ANGELES CALIFORNIA
September 10th-15th, 1997

See results and information of the WPVA & FIVB "World Championships" under the FIVB heading.

DENNIE SCHUPYT KNOOP
In 1997, Dennie Schupyt Knoop showed that she was still capable of provideing worthy competition on the WPVA Tour. Knoop finished within the top five of 4 occasions. Above photo, Knoop challenges the block of Linda Hanley.
Photo Courtesy of the AVP

LIHUE KAUA'I HAWAII
September 26th-28th 1997

The Women's Pro Beach Volleyball Tour's final tournament of the 1997 season took place September 26th-28th 1997. The 12 best WPVA teams competed in the $50,000.00 Best of the Beach at Lihue, Kaua'i, Hawaii. The fourth and final "Grand-Slam" stop on the WPVA Tour was played at the Marriott Resort and Beach Club in Nawiliwili Park near Kalapaki Beach in Lihue. The Best of the Beach featured both pool and bracket play. There were two pools, each pool featuring four teams while the opening day of play featured 12 matches. The top four-seeded teams received byes into bracket play. They then joined the top two teams from each pool in the "Elite Eight." The tournament was taped by The FOX Sports Network. Liz Masakayan and Elaine Youngs overcame a 7-0 deficit before tying the Best of the Beach final at 7-7 and went ahead 8-7 before falling behind again at 13-10, they then scored the last five points of the match to score a 15-13 decision over fourth-seeded Karrie Poppinga and Angela Rock to capture the "Best of the Beach," title in the one hour championship match. The win was the second tournament championship this season for Masakayan and Youngs. The winning pair had to qualify for the final two days of competition by winning three-straight pool play matches. Masakayan and Youngs, who won a record seven of eight matches in the Best of the Beach, advanced to the finals with a 15-13 come-from-behind win over top-seeded Lisa Arce and Holly McPeak in a one hour and twenty-minute match that featured over 100 side-outs. Poppinga, a former University of Hawaii All-American from Mililani, and Rock were playing in their first championship match this season after finishing third three times early this year. Poppinga and Rock, upset second-seeded Karolyn Kirby and Nancy Reno 15-9 to advance to the finals. During that marth, Poppinga and Rock led from the start, as the pair evened their season series at 2-2.

3rd Place: Karolyn Kirby and Nancy Reno
4th Place: Lisa Arce and Holly McPeak
5th Place: Barbra Fontana Linda Hanley
5th Place: Linda Chisholm and Deb Richardson

ANGELA ROCK
Angela Rock "hustled" her way into the top five, eight times on the 1997 WPVA Tour, including a 2nd place finish at the Austin Texas event. Above photo, Rock shows some "hustle" while making a diving dig.
Photo Courtesy of the AVP

WOMEN'S TOURNAMENT RESULTS
1997- FIVB

RIO DE JANEIRO BRAZIL
February 13th-16th, 1997

The 1997 FIVB Women's beach volleyball season began with the $120,000.00 FIVB Women's World Tour at Copacabana Beach, in Rio de Janeiro, Brazil. There were over 7,000 howling Brazilian fans in the Copacabana Beach arena for the first leg of the 1997 FIVB Beach Volleyball Tour, "The Brazilian Open". There were twenty-nine teams from twelve countries that participated in this tournament. The three top teams in the international rankings along with the gold, silver, and bronze medal winners from the 1996 Atlanta Olympics all participated. In the over one hour championship match the Brazilian team of Monica Rodrigues and Adriana Ramos Samuel, the Olympic silver medalist in Atlanta, fought hard in the three-match final to defeat the U.S.A. team of Holly McPeak and Lisa Arce by scores of 12-5, 4-12, and 12-7. The scores showed how balanced these two teams were. In the first set the Brazilians winning 12-5 and in the second set the Americans winning 12-4. The Brazilian fans were loud and boisterous, but were not able to boost Adriana and Monica to a second set victory. The Americans helped themselves, in the second set, by producing a strong service game. In the third tie-breaking set the Americans started off with a 2-0 lead, as they had in the two previous sets, but the Brazilians began to battle back and when the score was 4-4 they took charge and went on to a 9-4 lead and finally winning 12-7. The winner's each took home $8,000.00 for their effort. Both teams, in the finals, had to go through the contender's bracket to get there. First, in their semifinal match, Arce and McPeak outlasted Brazilians Jackie Silva and Sandra Pires by a score of 17-15. Then, Monica and Adriana came out of their semifinal by way of a forfeit by compatriots Adriana Brandao Behar and Shelda Kelly Bruno Bede.

3rd Place: Jackie Silva and Sandra Pires-Bra
4th Place: Adriana Brandao Behar and Shelda Kelly Bruno Bede-Bra
5th Place: Angela Rock and Kerri Poppinga-USA
5th Place: Maike Friedrichsen and Danja Musch-Ger

There were three other U.S.A. teams in the tournament. Barbra Fontana and Linda Hanley along with Christine Schaefer and Danalee Bragado both finished in 9th place. Pat Keller and Marla O'Hara took a seventeenth.

MELBOURNE AUSTRALIA

The Women's FIVB World Tour took place at Melbourne, Australia, March 13th - 16th, 1997. In the all Brazilian final, the team of Jackie Silva and Sandra Pires defeated Adriana Behar and Shelda Bede, by scores of 12-9 and 12-5, each collecting $8,000.00 for their winner's share of this $120,000.00 event. Silva and Pires made it into the championship match by winning their semifinal match against McPeak and Arce 15-11, while Behar and Bede defeated Rock and Poppinga in their semifinal 15-3.

3rd Place: Holly McPeak and Lisa Arce-USA
4th Place: Angela Rock and Kerrie Poppinga-USA
5th Place: Linda Hanley and Barbra Fontana-USA
5th Place: Monica Rodrigues and Adriana Ramos Samuel-Bra

Other USA finishes include: Christine Schaefer and Danalee Bragado in seventh place, Pat Keller and Marla O'Hara in thirteenth place, Jennifer Meredith and Monique Oliver in seventeenth place.

BARBRA FONTANA & KERRI ANN POTTHARST
The USA's Barbra Fontana and Australia's Kerri Ann Pottharst both competed successfully on the 1997 FIVB Women's Tour, finishing within the top five 3 and 4 times respectively. Above photo, Fontana taps the ball past the block of Pottharst.
Photo Courtesy of the FIVB

ADRIANA RAMOS SAMUEL
Brazilian Adriana Ramos Samuel paired-up with compatriot Monica Rodrigues to advance to 4 "Gold-Medal" matches, on the 1997 FIVB Women's Tour, winning 3 times. Above photo Samuel gives an all-out effort to dig the ball.
Photo Courtesy of the FIVB

PESCARA ITALY
July 4th-6th, 1997

The FIVB Women's Pro-Beach Tour went to Pescara Italy, where the U.S.A. team of Holly McPeak and Lisa Arce won the first place prize of $16,000.00 at this $120,000.00 event. In the one hour championship match, they defeated the Brazilian team of Adriana Behar and Shelda Bede by scores of 12-10 and 12-4. McPeak and Arce earned their way into the championship match by way of their 15-7 victory in the semifinals over Jackie Silva and Sandra Pires. Behar and Bede gained entry into the finals with a 15-10 victory in the semifinals over Barbra Fontana and Nancy Reno.

3rd Place: Jackie Silva and Sandra Pires-Bra
4th Place: Barbra Fontana and Nancy Reno-USA
5th Place: SonaDosoudilova and Eva Celbova-Czech
5th Place: Kerri-Ann Pottharst and Natalie Cook-Aus

Additional U.S.A. contestants were in 7th place, Christine Schaefer and Danalee Bragado. In 9th place, Krista Blomquist and Ali Wood. In 13th place Angela Rock and Karri Poppinga. In a distant 33rd place was the team of Desirae Leipham and Kristal Attwood.

MARSEILLE FRANCE
July 24th-26th, 1997

The FIVB Women's Beach Pro Tour went to Marseille, France, where the Brazilian team of Adriana Behar and Shelda Bede won the first place share of $16,000.00 at this $120,000.00 event. In the championship match, Behar and Bede defeated the U.S.A. team of Holly McPeak and Lisa Arce by rally-scores of 25-23 and 21-15. McPeak and Arce advanced to the finals by defeating Adriana Samuel and Monica Rodriguez, in the semifinals, by rally-scores of 21-16, 19-21, and 21-18. Behar and Shelda advanced to the finals by defeating Australians Natalie Cook and Kerri-Ann Pottharst 21-19, 18-21, and 21-18 in their semi-final match.

3rd Place: Adriana Samuel and Monica Rodriguez-Bra
4th Place: Natalie Cook and Kerri-Ann Pottharst-Aus
5th Place: Liane Fenwick and Pauline Manser-Aus
5th Place: Maike Friedrichsen and Danja Musch-Ger

Additional U.S.A. finishes included a seventh for the teams of Donalee Bragado and Marla O'Hara and Barbra Fontana and Linda Hanley. Bragado and O'Hara lost earlier to McPeak and Arce 10-21 and 19-21. While Fontana and Hanley lost to Cook and Pottharst 20-22, and 17-21. Liz Masakayan and Elaine Youngs finished in 13th after losing earlier in the tournament to McPeak and Arce by scores of 21-23 and 18-21.

ESPINHO PORTUGAL
August 1st-3rd, 1997

The FIVB Women's Pro-Beach Tour went to Espinho Portugal, where it was an all Brazilian final. The events total prize money was at $120,000.00. Monica Rodrigues and Adriana Ramos Samuel defeated Adriana Behar and Shelda Bede by a scores of 12-3 and 12-9. The winners each received $8,000.00 for their winning effort. Monica and Adriana Samuel earned their spot in the championship match by way of a 15-9 semi-final victory over the U.S.A. team of Liz Masakayan and Elaine Youngs. Adriana Behar and Shelda earned their spot by defeating comptriots Jackie Silva and Sandra Pires 15-4, in the other semi-final.

3rd Place: Jackie Silva and Sandra Pires-Bra
4th Place: Liz Masakayan and Elaine Youngs-USA
5th Place: Maike Friedrichsen and Danja Musch-Ger
5th Place: Yukiko Takahashi and Teru Saiki-Japan

Additional U.S.A. participants: Christine Schuster and Jennifer Meredith finished 13th. Pat Keller and Ali Wood gained a 17th. Donalee Bragado and Marla O'Hara ended-up in the 25th spot.

NATALIE COOK & DANJA MUSCH
Australian Natalie Cook and German Danja Musch each had four top five finishes on the 1997 FIVB Women's Tour. In fact Musch advanced to the "Gold-Medal" match for a 2nd place finish in Osaka Japan. Above photo, Cook chalanges the block of Musch.
Photo Courtesy of the AVP

SHELDA BRUNO BEDE
Brazilian Shelda Bruno Bede teamed-up with compatriot Adriana Brandao Behar on the 1997 FIVB Women's Tour. They advanced to 5 "Gold-Medal" matches, winning twice. Above photo, Bede gets down in the sand to make a dig.
Photo Courtesy of the FIVB

OSAKA JAPAN
August 8th-10th 1997

The Women's FIVB World Pro-Beach Tour went to Osaka Japan, where they staged a $120,000.00 event in the recently inaugurated permanent stadium on Tannowa Beach. In the championship match, the Brazilian team of Monica Rodrigues and Adriana Ramos Samuel outlasted the German team of Maike Friedrichsen and Danja Musch by scores of 12-5, 3-12, and 12-8. The winner's split the first place prize of $16,000.00. Prior to the finals, and for more than one hour, the beach volleyball fans were treated to an all-Brazilian semifinal match between Adriana Behar and Shelda Bede against Monica and Samuel. Monica and Samuel outlasted their compatriots 17-15. To get to the championship match. Friedrichsen and Musch eliminated the Australian team of Natalie Cook and Kerri-Ann Pottharst in the losers' bracket final 15-8. They then won, by injury forfeit, their semifinal match against Brazilians Jackie Silva and Sandra Pires.

3rd Place: Adriana Behar and Shelda Bede-Bra
4th Place: Jackie Silva and Sandra Pires-Bra
5th Place: Natalie Cook and Kerri-Ann Pottharst-Aus
5th Place: Sona Dosoudilvoa and Eva Celbova-Czech
The American team of Desirae Leipham and Tonya Williams finished in seventeenth place.

PUSAN KOREA
August 15th-17th, 1997

The Women's FIVB World Pro-Beach Tour was in Pusan, Korea, where there were typhoon threats at the beginning of the week. The $120,000.00 event in Pusan was finally played under perfect weather conditions along with brilliant sunshine on the final day. In front of more than 3,000 volleyball fans, in a packed stadium (the weekend was an official holiday in Korea), Holly McPeak and Lisa Arce won their second title of the 1997 season. In the championship match, they started very quickly, winning the first set 12-4, but had to struggle for one hour and thirty minutes to outlast the Brazilian team of Monica Rodrigues and Adriana Ramos Samuel, who fought back to win the second set 12-10, only to lose the third set 12-7. Arce and McPeak split the $16,000.00 first place check. Arce and McPeak earned their way into the championship final with a win over Australia's Keri Ann Pottharst and Natalie Cook by a score of 15-6. Monica and Adriana Samuel earned their spot by defeating fellow Brazilian's, Adrians Behar and Shelda Bede by, a score of 15-9.

3rd Place: Kerri-Ann Pottharst and Natalie Cook-Aus
4th Place: Adriana Behar and Shelda Bede-Bra
5th Place: Ana Maria Richa Medeiros and Adriana Benito Rodrigues-Bra
5th Place: Lima Falcãão De Magda Rejane and Marcia de Souza -Bra
Other U.S.A. teams competing included: In 9th place were Barbra Fontana and Krista Blomquist, along with Nancy Reno and Karolyn Kirby. In 13th place was the team of Donalee Bragado and Marla O'Hara.

LOS ANGELES CALIFORNIA-USA
September 10th-13th, 1997

The FIVB **World Championship of Beach Volleyball** took place at the UCLA Tennis Center, in Los Angeles, California (U.S.A.). The top FIVB and WPVA women pro-beach volleyball players were all together competing for the title of "World Champion." The total prize money was set at $300,000.00. In the championship match, the Brazilian team of Jackie Silva and Sandra Pires staged a heroic comeback to defeat Lisa Arce and Holly McPeak of the U.S.A. to earn the title by scores of 12-11, 1-12, and 12-10. Silva and Pires each took home $20,000.00 for their effort. Arce and McPeak each settled for a $13,000.00 check. Arce and McPeak earned their way into the championship match with a semifinal victory over compatriots Nancy Reno and Karolyn Kirby, by scores of 12-4 and 12-9. Kirby and Reno finished in third place after being seeded #12. Also, in third place, was the Brazilian team of Adriana Behar and Shelda Bede. Jackie Silva and Sandra Pires earned their way into the finals with a victory over fellow Brazilians, Adriana Behar and Shelda Bede, by scores of 12-11, 4-12, and 12-3.

SEEDINGS:	FINISH:
1. Lisa Arce and Holly McPeak (U.S.A.)	2nd
2. Adriana Behar and Shelda (Brazil)	3rd
3. Jackie Silva and Sandra Pires (Brazil)	1st
4. Monica Rodrigues and Adriana Samuel (Brazil)	5th
5. Pottharst and Cook (Australia)	9th
6. Friedrichsen and Musch (Germany)	9th
7. Barbra Fontana and Linda Hanley (U.S.A.)	5th
8. Liz Masakayan and Elaine Youngs (U.S.A.)	5th
9. Ana Richa and Adriana Rodr (Brazil)	9th
10. Karrie Poppinga and Angela Rock (U.S.A.)	9th

SANDRA PIRES
Brazilian Sandra Pires teamed-up with compatriot Jackie Silva, to win the "Gold-Medal" at the 1997 World Championship of beach volleyball, in Los Angeles CA. Above photo, Pires attacking the block of Elaine Youngs, during the 1997 World Chanpionship.
Photo Courtesy of Kevin Goff

WOMEN'S MAIN DRAW RESULTS
(losers finish in 17th place)

Lisa Arce and Holly McPeak (U.S.A.) defeated Elaine Roque and Dennie Shupryt-Knoop (U.S.A.) 12-9, 12-6.
Solazzi and Bruschini (Italy) defeated Manser and Fenwick (Australia) 12-6, 11-12, 12-9.
Ana Richa and Adriana Rodr (Brazil) defeated Eta and Timy (INA) 12-4, 12-4.
Liz Masakayan and Elaine Youngs (U.S.A.) defeated De Marinis and Nascimento (Italy) 12-6, 12-1.
Pottharst and Cook (Australia) defeated Broen Ouellette and Tough (Canada) 12-2, 12-1.
Karolyn Kirby and Nancy Reno (U.S.A.) defeated Schmidt and Staub (Germany) 12-7, 12-8.
Schoon Kadijk and Kadijk R. (Netherlands) defeated Takahashi and Ishizaka (Japan) 4-12, 12-11, 12-10.
Monica Rodrigues and Adriana Samuel (Brazil) defeated Z- Maria and Sarmento (Portugal) 12-10, 12-0.
Jackie Silva and Sandra Pires (Brazil) defeated Linda Chisholm and Deb Richardson (U.S.A.) 12-5, 12-6.
Krista Blomquist and Christine Schaefer (U.S.A.) defeated Perrotta and Gattelli (Italy) 12-8, 9-12, 13-11.
Magda and Siomara (Brazil) defeated Wilson and Straton (Australia) 11-12, 12-5, 12-8.
Friedrichsen and Musch (Germany) defeated Hashimoto and Teru Saiki (Japan) 12-4, 12-7.
Barbra Fontana and Linda Hanley (U.S.A.) defeated Huygens Tholen and Clarke (Australia) 12-1, 12-3.
Angela Rock and Karrie Poppinga (U.S.A.) defeated Hudcova and Tobiasova (Czech Republic) 12-9, 12-11.
Dumont and Drakich (Canada) defeated Dosoudilova and -Celbova (Czech Republic) 12-6, 12-5.
Adriana Behar and Shelda (Brazil) defeated Gail Castro and Gayle Stammer (U.S.A.)12-3, 12-0.

Round Two- losers finished in 9th place:
Lisa Arce and Holly McPeak (U.S.A.) defeated Solazzi and Bruschini (Italy)12-6, 12-3.
Liz Masakayan and Elaine Youngs (U.S.A.) defeated Ana Richa and Adriana Rodr (Brazil) 12-8, 12-8.
Karolyn Kirby and Nancy Reno (U.S.A.) defeated Pottharst and Cook (Australia) 12-4, 12-2.
Monica Rodrigues and Adriana Samuel (Brazil) defeated Schoon Kadijk and Kadijk R. (Netherlands) 12-7, 12-5.
Jackie Silva and Sandra Pires (Brazil) defeated Krista Blomquist and Christine Schaefer (U.S.A.) 12-2, 12-4.
Magda and Siomara (Brazil) defeated Friedrichsen and Musch (Germany) 12-8, 6-12, 12-8.
Barbra Fontana and Linda Hanley (U.S.A.) defeated Angela Rock and Karrie Poppinga (U.S.A.) 12-9, 9-12, 12-7.
Adriana Behar and Shelda (Brazil) defeated Dumont and Drakich (Canada) 12-9, 12-9.

Round Three losers finished in 5th place:
Lisa Arce and Holly McPeak (U.S.A.) defeated Liz Masakayan and Elaine Youngs (U.S.A.) 12-6, 12-5.
Karolyn Kirby and Nancy Reno (U.S.A.) defeated Monica Rodrigues and Adriana Samuel (Brazil) 12-10, 12-4.
Jackie Silva and Sandra Pires (Brazil) defeated Magda and Siomara (Brazil) 12-6, 12-6.
Adriana Behar and Shelda (Brazil) defeated Barbra Fontana and Linda Hanley (U.S.A.) 12-9, 5-12, 12-9.

KUAH MAS (LANGKAWI MALAYSIA)
November 21st-23rd, 1997

The FIVB Pro-Beach volleyball tournament scheduled for November 21st-23rd, 1997 at Kuah Mas (Langkawi) was canceled.

SALVADOR BRAZIL
October 30th-November 2nd, 1997

The last tournament of the Woman's 1997 FIVB Beach Volleyball World Tour was the $80,000.00 "Brazil Salvador de Bahia Open". The tournament was held in the Stella Mares Arena. The championship match was won by the Brazilian team of Adriana Behar and Shelda Bede. They beat the American team of Holly McPeak and Lisa Arce in three sets, by scores of 9-12, 12-10, and 12-8. The match took nearly two hours to complete. The match was very competitive as the U.S.A. team, utilizing a better service attack and controlling the net with more blocks than the Brazilians, won the first set in 41 minutes. The second set started in the same way, with a lot of mistakes by the Brazilian team, allowing the U.S.A. team to forge ahead by a score of 10-7. Behar and Shelda, showed a lot of patience, by fighting for important points that seemed to be lost. The Brazilian team then started serving and passing better, and along with some timely blocks, they went on to win, in the almost one hour game, by a score of 12-10. In the decisive tie-breaking set, the Brazilian team, supported by the crowd, beat the U.S.A. team, 12-8 in only 15 minutes. Behar and Bede each took home a check for $8,000.00 for their winning effort. The Brazilian team of Behar and Shelda had already captured the title of the 1997 World Circuit, before the beginning of the Salvador Tournament, since none of the other teams could catch their point total. This was the first FIVB World Tour win for Behar and Shelda in Brazl. The crowd celebrated wildly in the Stella Mares Arena with two Brazilian teams at the podium, including the third place finishers Jackie Silva and Sandra Pires.

3rd Place: Jackie Silva and Sandra Pires-Bra
4th Place: Monica Rodrigues and Adriana Samuel-Bra
5th Place: Liz Masakayan and Elaine Youngs-USA
5th Place: Rejane Maria da Graca Cannes and Ferreira de Juses-Bra
Additional U.S.A. team finishes: Barbra Fontana and Nancy Reno in seventh place, Angeliua Rock and Kerrie Poppinga in ninth place, and, Desirae Leipham and Deb Richardson in thirteenth place.

LISA ARCE & HOLLY McPEAK
Lisa Arce teamed-up with Holly McPeak to advance to the "Gold-Medal" match of the 1997 FIVB World Championship in Los Angeles CA. finishing 2nd. Above photo, during a "Queen of the Beach" event, McPeak hits the ball past the block of Arce.
Photo Courtesy of the AVP

TOP PHOTOS: Left: Krista Blomquist gets above the net to spike the ball. **Center:** Danalee Bragado gets above the net in an attempt to block an attack by Nancy Reno. **Right:** Australian Kerri Ann Pottharst attacking the ball.

MIDDLE PHOTOS: Left: Annette Davis delivers an aggressive attack at the net. **Center:** Ali Wood attacking the ball. **Right:** Australian Natalie Cook gets into position to make the pass.

1997 WOMEN'S BEACH VOLLEYBALL ACTION

BOTTOM PHOTOS: Left: Liz Masakayan takes advantage of the open net. **Center:** Holly McPeak aggressively spiking the ball. **Right:** Gail Castro follows-through while attacking with a jump serve.

Photo's Courtesy of the AVP

ADDITIONAL VOLLEYBALL INFORMATION
1997

FOUR-PERSON PRO-BEACH TEAMS
4-MEN

Following is a list of the players in the 1997 Men's 4-Man Bud Light Professional Beach Volleyball League. Note some rosters are larger than others because of player changes made during the season.

Team Inglenook
Scott Fortune - Team Captain
Carlos Briceno   Duane Cameron
Tom Hoff   Eric Sato

Team Outdoor Products
Dan Hanan - Team Captain
Erik Sullivan   Matt Rigg
Doug Partie   Mike Sealy

Team Discus Athletic (Team ABVL)
Bob Ctvrtlik - Team Captain
Allen Allen   Jeff Nygaard
Dusty Dvorak

Team Paul Mitchell
Jeff Williams - Team Captain
Chip McCaw   Brent Hillard
Mike Lambert   Matt Rigg
Bob Samuelson   Mark Presho
Mike Diehl   Craig Buck
Tom Duke   Dan Greenbaum
John Wallace

4-WOMEN

Following is a list of the players in the 1997 Women's 4-Woman Bud Light Professional Beach Volleyball League. Note some rosters are larger than others because of player changes made during the season.

Team Nike
Gabrielle Reece - Team Captain
Katy Eldridge   Jenny Johnson
Stephanie Cox

Team Paul Mitchell
Annett Davis - Team Captain
Kristin Klein   Diane Shoemaker
Missy Kurt

Team Norelco
Samantha Shaver - Team Captain
Tammy Liley   Danielle Scott
Marissa Hatchett   Liane Sato
Sabrina Hernandez   Julie Romias

SAN DIEGO CALIFORNIA
May 17th-18th, 1997

The 1997 San Diego-Ocean Beach "Volleyball Festival" Men's "AAA" was won by Norwegians Andre Kjemperud and Vegard Hoidalen. In the championship match, they defeated Sahwn Garus and Jon Cummings. Tournament director, George Stepanof recorded that the weather conditions were overcast. There were about 15,000 "Walk-Bys" and 1,000 mainstay spectators at this event that had 25 teams entered.
3rd Place: Mike Winier and Jason Scott
3rd Place: Dan Ortega and Adam Jewell

SAN DIEGO CALIFORNIA
May 17th-18th, 1997

The 1997 San Diego-Ocean Beach "Volleyball Festival" Women's "AAA" was won by Kelley Spink and Lisa Westlake. In the championship match, they defeated Vickie Bonino and Judy Hissong. Tournament director, George Stepanof recorded that there were 15 teams.
3rd Place: Carolyne Krattli and Karen Helyer
3rd Place: Monica Stewart and Linda Burton

SAN DIEGO CALIFORNIA
May 31st-June 1st, 1997

The 1997 San Diego-Ocean Beach "Redsand" Men's "AAA" was won by Dave Smith and Scott Murdock. In the championship match, they defeated Mike Mattarocci and Larry Richards. George Stepanof recorded that the conditions were great with just a mild wind on this sunny day. There were about 20,000 "Walk-Bys" and 800 mainstay spectators at this event that had 23 teams.
3rd Place: Pepe De La Hoz and Humberto Gonzalez
4th Place: Eric Holman and Brett Hollingshead

SAN DIEGO CALIFORNIA
May 31st-June 1st, 1997

The 1997 San Diego-Ocean Beach "Redsand" Women's "AAA" was won by Christine Wilson and Sara Straton. In the championship match, they defeated Linda Burton and Monica Stewart. George Stepanof recorded that there were 13 teams entered.
3rd Place: Susie Turner and Barbara Nyland
3rd Place: Ulrike Schmidt and Gudula Staub

LAGUNA BEACH CALIFORNIA
1997

The 1997 Laguna Beach Men's Open was an amateur "AAA" tournament. Scott Lane and Casey Jennings were the winners. In the championship match, they defeated George Carey and Mike Safford.
3rd Place: Nichilas Pabareus and Chris Walmer
4th Place: Shawn Garus and Jon Cummings

ASPEN COLORADO
August 28th-September 1st, 1997

At the 25th annual "Motherload Classic" the championship match was won by Curtis Griffin and Eric Moore. They defeated Rob Baily and Jason Robertson. Dane Hansen and Ryan Post finished in 3rd place. In the women's championship match, Valinda Hilleary and Pat Keller defeated Carrie Busch and Nancy Mason. Liz Pagano and Lynda Street finished in third place.

MIXED-DOUBLES BEACH TOURNAMENT'S

MANHATTAN BEACH CALIFORNIA
July 5th, 1997

The 1997 Marine Street Mixed-Doubles Open was won by the team of John Paul Calderon playing with Misty May, the daughter of all time mixed-double champions Butch and Barbara May. In the championship final, they defeated Butch Miali and Michelle Kobashi.
3rd Place: Jeff West and Tracy Tatum
3rd Place: John Stalder and Danica Djujich
5th Place: John Ward and Tamra Blair
5th Place: Sean Icaza and Lisa Hoven

MEN'S BEACH VOLLEYBALL
1998

In 1998 the Pro-Beach Volleyball tournament schedule included twenty-two AVP events, twenty-six FIVB events (fifteen men's events and eleven women's events).

On the domestic "Non-professional" scene of beach volleyball there were thousands of tournaments held virtually in every State of the Union. The CBVA staged well over one-hundred beach events in California, while the AVA staged well over three-hundred events Nationally along with events in Canada and Mexico. Every State in the U.S.A. staged "beach" volleyball tournaments of various classifications. In addition to all of the tournaments staged in the U.S.A. there were beach volleyball tournaments staged in countries all over the world. Many Non-U.S.A. countries now have their own beach volleyball federations, associations, etc., all of which are growing in size and number of events that they schedule each year.

In 1998, California was back on top with most "Pro" tournaments scheduled, with five. Florida had four tournaments scheduled, while Texas had three. In 1998, the Brazilians were winning most of the FIVB tournaments and they were beginning to make their mark, on U.S. soil, in the AVP tournaments.

In 1998, of the thirty-seven recorded "Pro" Men's Beach Volleyball tournaments, twenty-three of the tournaments were staged on U.S. soil, while fourteen were played outside of the U.S. As mentioned above, of the twenty-three U.S. tournaments, California hosted five events while Florida and Texas hosted four and three respectively. There were eleven U.S. events staged in ten states other than Florida, Texas and California. The California tournaments were held in Sacramento, Hermosa Beach, Manhattan Beach, Seal Beach, and San Diego. Florida hosted tournaments in Fort Myers, Clearwater, Jacksonville, and Daytona. The texas tournaments were in Dallas, San Antonio, and Corpus Christi. The remaining U.S. tournaments were were held in Phoenix Arizona, Las Vegas Nevada, Belmar New Jersey, Milwaukee Wisconsin, Chicago Illinois, Minneapolis Minnesota, Cincinnati and Cleveland Ohio, Muskegon Michigan, Atlanta Georgia, and the Goodwill Games in New York.

1998 AVP TOUR
At the start of the 1998 Association of Volleyball Professionals Tour, things were "looking-up" with new management to start off the AVP's fifteenth season. But all of a sudden, the worlds premier domestic beach volleyball tour was in trouble and the players began to scramble to try and save the tour. Above photo, Eric "Foni" Fonoimoana (left) and Karch Kiraly (right) began the season looking-up for both the AVP Tour as well as for the ball, as "Foni" won the opening "KOB" event in Las Veagas Nevada.
Photo Courtesy of "Couvi"

The fourteen events held outside of the U.S.A. were hosted by:

1. Mar del Plata Argentina
2. Vina del Mar Chili
3. Copacabana, Rio de Janeiro, Brazil
4. Toronto Canada
5. Berlin's "Schloplatz" in Berlin Germany
6. Lignano Sabbiadora Italy
7. Marseille France
8. Klagenfurt Beach Volleyball Area at Wurther Lake in Klagenfurt Austria
9. Espinho Portugal
10. Ostend Belgium
11. Albena Bulgaria Italy Satellite tournament
12. Canary Islands Tenerife Spain in Las Teresitas
13. Alanya Turkey
14. Camburi Beach Vitoria Brazil

Jose Loiola took the top spot on the 1998 Pro-Beach Volleyball Tour. He won a total of eleven tournament championships (AVP & FIVB) with two different partners. Five of his wins came with Kent Steffes, all on the AVP Tour. They won together at Daytona Beach, Clearwater Beach, Jacksonville, and Fort Myers Florida. They also won the tournament in Dallas Texas. Loiola won six tournaments with Emanuel Rego. They won the Seal Beach and Cleveland events on the AVP Tour. On the FIVB Tour they won at Klagenfurt Beach Volleyball Area at Wurther Lake in Klagenfurt Austria, Espinho Portugal, Canary Islands Tenerife Spain in Las Teresitas, and Alanya Turkey. Rego also won twice in Texas San Antonio with Andre Gomes and in Corpus Christi with Kent Steffes.

AVP
1998 AVP SCHEDULE

March 13-15	King of the Beach Invitational	Las Vegas, Nevada
April 3-5	Miller Lite Open	Tucson, Arizona
April 17-19	Players Championships	Clearwater, Florida
April 25-26	Miller Lite Open	Ft. Myers, Florida
May 2-3	Sunkist Open	Dallas, Texas
May 9-10	Miller Lite Open	San Antonio, Texas
May 15-17	AVP Open	Jacksonville, Florida
May 22-24	Copertone Championships	Orlando, Florida
May 30-31	Miller Lite South Texas Open	Corpus Christi, Texas
June 5-7	AVP Golden State Open	Sacramento, Calif.
June 12-14	AVP Open	Seal Beach, Calif.
June 19-21	AVP Open	Cincinnati, Ohio
June 27-28	Miller Lite Open	Cleveland, Ohio
July 3-5	Miller Lite Open	Chicago, Illinois
July 10-12	Miller Lite Open	Vail, Colorado
July 17-19	Sunkist Open	Belmar, New Jersey
July 25-26	Miller Lite Open	Minneapolis, MN
August 1-2	Miller Lite Open	Milwaukee, Wisconsin
August 7-9	Miller Lite Beach Challenge	Atlanta, Georgia
August 14-16	Miller Lite U.S. Championships	Hermosa Beach, Calif.
August 21-23	Sunkist Open	San Diego, Calif.
August 28-30	AVP Tour Championships	Muskegon, Michigan

The AVP started off 1998 by cleaning house. They had a change in management. The Executive Director Jerry Soloman and the Chief Operating Officer Lon Monk were out. In was Harry Usher, a respected sports consultant who gained prominence with his work on the Los Angeles 1984 Olympics, signed on as the interim Executive Director of the AVP. Usher was Peter Ueberroth's right-hand man during the very successful 1984 Olympics. Solomon had been in the AVP's top spot since August of 1995.

The world's premier domestic volleyball tour, the AVP, began the season in trouble. A plan to cut tournament prize money was developed by the players to help save the tour. The tour was in debt, reportedly around $2.5 million. The players unanimously agreed to cut the prize money, at 20 tournaments, starting with the Clearwater event. The prize money at each event was reduced to $50,000.00. It wasn't that many seasons ago that tournaments were drawing as many as 40,000 fans, now there was some doubt as to whether the tour can make it through the season. The AVP players and management were trying to appraise the situation as to where the blame exists. Was it last years management, the backlash form charging for events in California, lack of commitment from sponsors, or just decreasing interest in the sport. Many felt that the biggest culprit might be the purses themselves, which had stayed the same despite the decline of revenue and sponsorship.

LOS ANGELES CALIFORNIA

Despite all of the problems that the AVP was experiencing, the 1998 AVP season was the 15th anniversary year of the Association of Volleyball Professionals. The Association of Volleyball Professionals was the recognized leader in professional beach volleyball worldwide. The AVP was founded in 1983, to preserve the integrity of the sport and to look after the players' interests through a representative board of directors elected by the players. The 1998 schedule for the Miller Lite/AVP Tour began in Las Vegas Nevada on the weekend of, March 13th-15th, 1998, with the seventh annual Swatch King of the Beach Invitational. The 1998 AVP season culminated in Grand Haven Michigan, August 28th-30th, 1998, with the Miller Lite/AVP Tour Championship. The sport's greatest stars were back on the beach, Jose Loiola, the 1997 Miller Lite/AVP Tour MVP; Kent Steffes, the youngest player in AVP history to win 100 titles; Karch Kiraly, the all-time leading AVP money winner; Dax Holdren and Todd Rogers, 1997 AVP Rookies of the Year; and Adam Johnson, the 1997 AVP Defensive Player of the Year. Scott Ayakatubby was also back on the tour, after 1997 season ending knee surgery, but an early season back injury put him out again. After a full season off, from knee surgery, Brent Frohoff was back on the tour in 1998.

The 1998 Miller Lite/AVP Tour, highlighted by the crown jewels of the sport, the Miller Lite Grand Slam, a collection of the most prestigious tournaments of the year. These traditional tournaments, the Miller Lite Players Championship in Clearwater, Florida; the Miller Lite Chicago Open; the Miller Lite U.S. Championship in Hermosa Beach, California; and the Miller Lite/AVP Tour Championships in Grand Haven, Michigan are among the longest standing events on the Miller Lite/AVP Tour.

Further accenting the 1998 season was the addition of new cities to the tour. Beach volleyball history was being made as the tour was scheduled to travel north for a stop in Toronto, Canada, July 25th-26th 1998, but plans fell through and it did not happen. This summer marked the first time the AVP went to Tucson, Arizona. The Miller

Lite/AVP Tour also visited some of its old stomping grounds in 1998. San Diego, California staged an event on the weekend of August 21st-23rd, 1998, after a one year absence while Cincinnati, Ohio and Jacksonville, Florida also returned to the schedule. The AVP also made a triumphant return to Atlanta, site of the 1996 Summer Olympics, where beach volleyball made its highly successful debut as a medal sport.

The 1998 Miller Lite/AVP "Tour Championship" was awarded to Muskegon, Michigan. Muskegon hosted only the top 24 AVP teams for the season-ending event. This tournament had become unique by traveling to a different Miller Lite/AVP Tour site each year. A four-day festival surrounded the 1998 tournament, which included a charity golf tournament, awards banquet, finals of the Speedo/AVP Youth Tour events, and the Wilson Qualifying Series.

In 1998, the Miller Lite Open Celebrity Volleyball Bar Tour was inaugurated. Many of the top AVP players teamed-up to play exhibitions at local "Bars" to help promote the sport of beach volleyball.

Karch Kiraly and Adam Johnson won the most tournament championships, as a team, on the 1998 AVP Tour. They won six AVP tournaments: Tucson Arizona, Cincinnati Ohio, Milwaukee Wisconsin, Atlanta Georgia, and in California at the events in Sacramento and Hermosa Beach.

Additional AVP teams that won in 1998: Mike Whitmarsh and Kent Steffes won three tournaments together. They won in Belmar New Jersey, Chicago Illinois, and San Diego California. Along with these wins and the five that he had with Loiola, and the one with Rego, Steffes had a good year with a total of nine tournament championships.

Additional winners on the 1998 AVP Tour: Canyon Ceman and Mark Kerins won the tournament in Muskegon Michigan. Pepe De La Hoz and Sean Scott won the "watered-down" Manhattan Beach Open. Eric Fonoimoana started the season off by winning the "King of the Beach" tournament in Las Vegas Nevada.

AVP TEAM DRAW PLACEMENT
SINGLE ELIMINATION TOURNAMENTS

In response to player input and in an effort to address the static and somewhat unforgiving nature of the single elimination format, the AVP Board instituted the following policy for single elimination tournaments:

Only the top eight seeds were divided into groups of two (i.e. 1&2, 3&4, 5&6, 7&8) for the purpose of determining where each team will be placed in the draw. A coin flip was conducted for each of these respective pairings, the possibility being that a team would be accorded either its traditional place in the draw or that normally accorded the other team in the pairing. For example, the number one seed would be placed in either the traditional number one seed or number two seed spots in a draw.

The remaining teams were divided into four groups by seed as follows: 9 thru 12, 13 thru 16, 17 thru 24, 25 thru 32. A separate random draw was conducted for each group, the first team drawn accorded the highest seeded position in the draw for that respective group, the second team drawn accorded the second highest seeded position in the draw for that respective group and so on.

1998 AVP TOUR PARTICIPANTS

Mark Addy	Rifat Agi
Todd Ahmadi	Eduardo Anjinho Bacil
John Anselmo	Scott Ayakatubby
Derek Bakarich	Paul Baxter
Jeff Belandi	Dain Blanton
Aaron Boss	Bill Boulliane
Paul Boyd	Eric Boyles
Brett Bumgardner	John Brajevic
Dana Camaco	Daniel Cardenas
Dan Castillo	Carlos Cartaya
Canyon Ceman	Ian Clark
Mike Connaughton	Chad Convis
Jon Cummings	Scott Davenport
Mike Diehl	Brent Doble
James Fellows	Dave Fisher
Mike Folstein	Eric Fonoimoana
Scott Friederichsen	Brent Frohoff
Mike Garcia	Eduardo Garrido
Brian Gatzke	Craig Geibel
Andre Gomes	Jerry Graham
Pete Gray	Albert Hannemann
Nick Hannemann	Nathan Heidger
Rob Heidger	Carl Henkel
Dax Holdren	John Hribar
Bryan Ivie	Tim Jaymes+
Ron Jenkins	Adam Jewell
Adam Johnson	Matt Johnson
Karch Kiraly	Mark Kerins
Eric Lazowski	Lee LeGrande
Brian Lewis	Jose Loiola
Roberto Lopes	Stace Lougeay
Ricci Luyties	Matt Lyles
Lance Lyons	Marcos Macau
Carlos Andre Machado	Chris Magill
Chris Makos	Kevin Martin
Brian McDonald	Lou Messier
Stein Metzger	Mike Minier
Erik Moore	Franco Neto
Jim Nichols	Dan Ortega
Jim Overton	Mark Paaluhi
Raul Papaleo	Justin Perlstrom
Randall Petersen	Julien Prosser
Jason Pursley	Leland Quinn
Adam Roberts	Emmanuel Rego
Dave Robertson	Juan Rodriquez
Todd Rogers	Curtis Rollins
Henry Russell	Greg Ryan
J.B. Saunders	Brett Schroeder
Mike Schroeder	Wayne Seligson
Steve Simpson	Aaron Smith
Andrew Smith	David Smith
Sinjin Smith	Matt Sonnichsen
Kent Steffes	Jason Stimpfig
Randy Stoklos	David Swatick
Troy Tanner	Brad Torsone
Matt Unger	Bruk Vandeweghe
Jim Van Zwieten	Andrew Vasquez
Mike Whitmarsh	Kevin Wong
Eric Wurts	Chris Young
Lee Zahner	

THE TOP 50 AVP PLAYERS
AT THE END OF THE 1998 SEASON
(players are listed with points in order of ranking)

#	Player	Points
1	Jose Loiola	86.68
2	Adam Johnson	81.11
3	Karch Kiraly	77.55
4	Kent Steffes	75.51
5	Emanuel Rego	74.70
6	Mike Whitmarsh	65.84
7	Brian Lewis	65.13
8	David Swatik	62.16
9	Roberto Lopes	59.65
10	Eric Fonoimoana	59.11
11	Franco Neto	58.39
12	Dain Blanton	57.68
13	Dax Holdren	56.55
13	Todd Rogers	56.55
15	Canyon Ceman	50.65
16	Mark Kerins	45.92
17	Bill Boullianne	45.16
18	Rob Heidger	44.21
19	Andre Gomes	43.18
20	Ian Clark	42.10
21	Eduardo Garrido	39.72
22	Brent Frohoff	36.74
23	Henry Russell	35.86
24	Troy Tanner	34.55
25	Kevin Martin	34.47
26	A. Hannemann	32.22
27	Stein Metzger	31.14
28	Eduardo Bacil	30.74
29	Nick Hannemann	30.41
30	Kevin Wong	29.38
31	Aaron Boss	27.40
32	Matt Lyles	26.80
33	Eric Wurts	26.25
34	Lee LeGrande	25.38
35	Adam Jewell	24.82
36	Brent Doble	24.46
37	Matt Unger	23.60
38	Wayne Seligson	21.51
39	Dan Castillo	20.78
40	Brian Gatzke	20.70
41	Bryan Ivie	20.25
42	Leland Quinn	19.91
43	Mike Diehl	18.76
44	Ricci Luyties	17.90
45	S Friederichsen	17.67
46	Mark Paaluhi	16.98
47	Scott Davenport	15.59
48	David Smith	13.55
49	Aaron Smith	13.46
50	Sinjin Smith	13.31

1998 INDIVIDUAL AVP TOURNAMENT FINISHES

Player	1st	2nd	3rd	4th	5th
Eduardo Bacil	0	1	0	0	1
Dain Blanton	0	2	7	0	2
Aaron Boss	0	0	0	1	1
Bill Boullianne	0	0	2	1	7
Dan Castillo	0	0	0	0	1
Canyon Ceman	1	0	2	2	6
Ian Clark	0	0	1	0	8
Mike Diehl	0	0	0	0	1
Brent Doble	0	0	0	0	2
Eric Fonoimoana	1	2	7	0	2
Brent Frohoff	0	1	0	0	2
Eduardo Garrido	0	0	2	0	3
Brian Gatzke	0	0	0	0	1
Andre Gomes	1	0	3	0	1
Albert Hannemann	0	1	0	1	2
Nick Hannemann	0	0	1	0	1
Rob Heidger	0	1	2	0	3
Dax Holdren	1	1	1	1	12
Adam Jewell	0	0	0	0	1
Adam Johnson	6	4	2	0	3
Mark Kerins	1	0	1	1	4
Karch Kiraly	6	5	2	0	3
Brian Lewis	0	3	3	3	7
Jose Loiola	7	4	1	1	0
Roberto Lopes	0	3	4	1	2
Kevin Martin	0	0	1	0	5
Stein Metzger	0	1	0	0	1
Franco Neto	0	3	4	1	2
Leland Quinn	0	0	0	0	1
Emanuel Rego	4	4	1	0	1
Todd Rogers	1	1	1	1	12
Henry Russell	0	0	3	0	2
Kent Steffes	**9**	**0**	**1**	**2**	**2**
David Swatik	0	2	3	3	6
Troy Tanner	0	0	2	0	2
Matt Unger	0	0	0	0	1
Mike Whitmarsh	1	1	4	4	0
Kevin Wong	0	1	0	0	1
Eric Wurts	0	0	1	0	1

JIM MENGES & JOSE LOIOLA
Beach Volleyball "Legend" Jim Menges (left) coached Brazilian Jose Loiola to the top of the list on the 1998 AVP Tour's ranking list.
Photo Courtesy of "Couvi"

KENT STEFFES
With nine 1998 AVP Tour championships, Kent Steffes was on top of ther win list. Above photo, Steffes (right) gets ready to set the pass from Canyon Ceman, during 1998 "KOB" in Las Vegas NV.
Photo Courtesy of "Couvi"

FIVB

The 1998 FIVB Pro-Beach Volleyball Season included six new events on the World Tour Calendar. Players from more than 50 countries competed for more than $4 million in prize money. There were 14 men's events carrying a total jackpot of $2,490,000.00. The $300,000.00 Portugal Grand Slam staged at Espinho from August 7th through August 9th, 1998 was the biggest money earner, while the other tournaments offered $170,000.00, which was up $20,000.00 from 1997's $150,000.00 prize money. The Canadian Open, which was staged in Toronto June 19th-21st, 1998 appeared on the men's calendar for the first time. The other new men's events were the Argentinea, Czech Republic and Russian Opens. Additional negations were in progress for a U.S. women's open and two men's events in South Africa and Bahrain. Beach Volleyball tournaments were included in the Goodwill Games and offered $100,000.00 prize money each to the 8 best nations in the World Ranking from July 22nd-26th, 1998 in Central Park (New York).

Also in 1998, the FIVB announced the appointment of Prisma Sports & Media to handle all television sales and broadcaster co-ordination for Beach Volleyball. The agreement followed the success of 1997's World Championships in Los Angeles which was televised in more than 120 countries and was part of the FIVB's long-term strategy to expand the development of the game. There would be a regular Beach Volleyball television highlights program through the season, with ranking updates and player features in addition to coverage of the yearly World Tour events and World Championships (1999 & 2001) running from 1998 to 2001 inclusive.

Again in 1998, the FIVB World Tour was dominated by teams from Brazil. Brazilian teams won eleven of the sixteen FIVB events. The top team on the FIVB World Tour in 1998, with four tournament championships, was the Brazilian team of Jose Loiola and Emanuel Rego as they won at Klagenfurt Beach Volleyball Area on Wurther Lake in Klagenfurt Austria, Espinho Portugal, Canary Islands Tenerife Spain in Las Teresitas, and Alanya Turkey.

Additional Brazilian wins came when the Brazilian team of Z-Marco Nobrega Ferreira de Melo and Ricardo Santos won two events, Copacabana Beach in Rio de Janeiro Brazil and Marseille, France on the "Golfe du Lion" shore, on the "Plages du Prado." The team of Para Ferreira De Souza and Guilherme Luiz Marques also won two FIVB events. They won at Lignano Sabbiadora Italy and the Goodwill Games at Wollman Rink Stadium, located in South Central Park in the heart of Manhattan New York City U.S.A. The event in Vina del Mar Chili was won by the Brazilian team of Luiz Antonio "Lula" Barbosa da Silva and Francismar Adriano Dias Garrido.

Additional winning teams on the FIVB Tour: Jorre Andre' Kjemperud and Vegard Hoidalen from Norway won the FIVB event at Berlin's "Schloplatz" in Berlin Germany. The Argentine team of Eduardo Esteban "Mono" Martinez and Martin Alejo Conde won in Toronto Canada. In Ostend Belgium, Luis Miguel Barbosa Maia and Jose Carlos Pereira Brenha Alves, from Portugal, were the champions. In Mar del Plata Argentina, the brothers Martin Laciga and Paul Laciga from Switzerland, won the FIVB Tour's opening event. The "Satellite" tournament, hosted in Albena Bulgaria, was won by the Italian team of Tigo and Marino. There were no teams from the U.S.A. that were able to earn a tournament championship on the 1998 FIVB World Tour.

MIKE DODD & CHRIS MARLOWE
Beach volleyball "Legends" Mike Dodd (left) and Chris Marlowe (right) were still very active on the 1998 AVP Tour. Dodd and Marlowe were the beach volleyball TV announcers on ESPN 2.
Photo Courtesy of "Couvi"

1998 FIVB BEACH VOLLEYBALL SCHEDULE MEN

When	Where	Prize Money
Jan 16-18	Mar del Plata Argentina	$100,000.00
Feb 12-15	Rio de Janerio Brazil	$100,000.00
June 19-21	Toronto Canada	$100,000.00
June 26-28	Praha Czech Republic	$100,000.00
July 3-5	Berlin Germany	$100,000.00
July 17-19	Lignano Italy	$100,000.00
July 22-26	New York U.S.A Goodwill Games	$100,000.00
Jul 23-26	Marseille France	$100,000.00
July 31-Aug 2	Klagenfurt Austria	$100,000.00
Aug 7-9	Espinho Portugal	$200,000.00
Aug 14-16	Ostend Belgium	$100,000.00
Aug 22-23	Albena Bulgaria Challenger Series	$ 30,000.00
Sep 3-6	Tenerife Spain Canary Islands	$100,000.00
Sep 11-13	Alanya Turkey	$100,000.00
Nov 27-29	Durban South Africa	$100,000.00
Dec 3-6	Fortaleza Brazil	$100,000.00

1998 INDIVIDUAL FIVB TOURNAMENT FINISHES

Player	1st	2nd	3rd	4th	5th
Jose Luis Salema Abrantes	0	0	1	0	0
Eduardo "Duda" Pinto de Abreau	0	0	0	0	1
Jorge Ahmann	0	1	1	0	2
Dain Blanton	0	1	0	0	0
Joao Carlos Pereira Brenha Alves	1	0	0	0	4
Paulo Emilo Silva Azevedo	0	1	0	2	2
Marino Baracetti	0	0	1	0	0
Bill Boullianne	0	0	2	1	0
John Child	0	1	2	0	0
Ian Clark	0	0	2	1	0
Martin Alejo Conde	1	1	0	2	3
Roberto Lopes da Costa	0	1	1	0	0
Charles Dieckmann	0	0	0	0	1
Markus Dieckmann	0	0	0	0	1
Fabio Diez	0	0	1	1	0
Markus Egger.	0	0	0	0	1
Eric Fonoimoana	0	1	0	0	0
Adriano Dias Garrido	1	0	0	0	1
Giovane Gavio	0	0	0	0	1
Andrea Ghiurghi	0	0	0	0	1
Axel Hager	0	1	1	0	2
Mark Heese	0	1	2	0	0
Carl Henkel	0	0	0	0	2
Vegard Hoidalen	1	0	0	0	0
Karch Kiraly	0	1	0	0	0
Jorre Andre' Kjemperud	1	0	0	0	0
Premysl Kubala	0	0	0	1	0
Jan Kvalheim	0	0	1	2	2
Martin Laciga	1	1	0	3	2
Paul Laciga	1	1	0	3	2
Ricardo "Riccardino" Lione	0	0	0	0	1
Jose Loiola	4	2	2	0	1
Ricci Luyties	0	1	0	0	0
Bjorn Maaseide	0	0	1	2	3
Luis Miguel Barbosa Maia	1	0	0	0	3
Luiz Guilherme Marquez	3	1	1	2	0
Eduardo Esteban "Mono" Martinez	1	1	0	2	3
Javier Bosma Minguez	0	0	1	1	0
Paulo Roberto Da Costa Moreira	0	1	0	2	1
Jose Franco Vieira Neto	0	1	1	0	0
Jose Z-Marco Melo Ferreira Nobrega	2	1	2	0	2
Michal Palinek	0	0	0	1	0
Maurizio Pimponi	0	0	0	0	1
Julien Prosser	0	0	0	0	3
Andrea Raffaell	0	0	0	0	1
Ricardo Alex Costa Santos	2	1	2	0	2
Emanuel Rego Scheffer	4	2	2	0	1
Luiz Antonio "Lula" Barbosa da Silva	1	0	0	0	0
Sinjin Smith	0	1	0	0	0
Federico "Fred" Doria de Souza	0	0	0	0	1
Rogrio "Para" Ferrirs de Souza	3	1	1	2	0
Kent Steffes	0	1	0	0	0
Alexandre Tande	0	0	0	0	1
Bernhard Vesti	0	0	0	0	1
Mike Whitmarsh	0	2	0	0	0
Kevin Wong	0	0	0	0	2
Lee Zahner	0	0	0	0	3

TOP 50 MEN'S FIVB PLAYERS AT THE
(START OF 1998)

Emanuel-Brazil	Ze Marco-Brazil
Guilherme-Brazil	Para-Brazil
Kvalheim-Norway	Maaseide-Norway
Paul o-Brazil	Paulo Emilio-Brazil
Conde-Argintina	Martinez-Argintina
Franco-Brazil	John Child-Canada
Mark Heese-Canada	M.Laciga-Switzerland
P.Laciga-Switzerland	Holden-Canada
Leinemann-Canada	Roberto Lopes-Brazil
Prosser-Australia	Zahner-Australia
Baracetti-Argintina	Salema-Argintina
Kubala-CZE	Palinek-CZE
Duda-Brazil	Fred-Brazil
Bosma-Spain	Diez-Spain
Ahmann-Germany	Hager-Germany
Ghiurghi-Italy	Brenha-Portugal
Maia-Portugal	Carl Henkel-USA
Lione-Italy	Hoidalen-Norway
Kjemperud-Norway	Canyon Ceman-USA
Whitmarsh-USA	Sinjin Smith-USA
Dzavoronok-CZE	Pakosta-CZE
Karasev-Russia	Pospelov-Russia
Raffaelli-Italy	Englen-Sweden
Petersson-Sweden	Deulofeu-France
Guissart-France	Grigolo-Italy
Anjinho -Brazil	Loiola-Brazil
Mike Dodd-USA	Dain Blanton-USA
Leitner-Austria	Stamm-Austria

ALBERT HANNEMANN

Albert Hannemann hustled his way to the finals of the 1998 AVP Tour event in Corpus Christi Texas. Paired-up with Kevin Wong, he finished in 2nd place. Above photo, Hanneman makes a nice diving dig.

Photo Courtesy of the AVP

JOSE LOIOLA

Jose Loiola took the top spot on the 1998 "Pro" beach volleyball tour winning 11 events (AVP&FIVB) with two different partners. Above photo, Loiola hits the ball past the block of Eric Fonoimoana and away from the defense of Dain Blanton.

Photo Courtesy of Frank Goroszko

MEN'S TOURNAMENT RESULTS
1998-AVP

LAS VEGAS NEVADA
March 13th-15th, 1998

The format for the "Swatch King of the Beach Invitational" tournament was a three-day round robin event. Each player switched partners, compiled points, and earned prize money based on the number of games they won. The player with the most points at the end of the event determined the King of the Beach. The teams consisted of two players and all matches were played to 15 points. All matches were played on one center court. The AVP Tour utilized Samuel Hamilton's Dallas-based company "All Volleyball" to build the "sand-pits" for this AVP Tour event and other sites where natural beach courts were not available. This years tour included stops at outdoor sites such as the fairgrounds in San Diego, the San Antonio Mall, Granite Bay Beach on Folsom Lake for the Sacramento event, along with this King of the Beach event staged on the parking lot next to the Hard Rock Hotel/Casino.

FRIDAY MARCH 13th, 1998
(two players advance)

The First Round was played on Friday March 13th, 1998. The AVP players ranked from number 7-14 on the AVP computer ranking system competed for the two qualifying spots joining the top six players in the second round of the Miller Lite King of the Beach Invitational on Saturday and Sunday. The players were divided into two groups of four players each. Each player played three matches during the day with a different partner. For each match won, a player in each group earned one point and split $3,000.00 per team. At the end of the day, the player in each group who had compiled the most points earned a spot in the second round. All of the games used the traditional beach volleyball scoring system. The first team to 15 points wins with side-out scoring. An eight minute time clock was used for each match. The first round results were as follows:

Fonoimoana and Clark defeated Tanner and Rogers (pool #1)
Heidger and Holdren defeated Blanton and Lewis (pool #2)
Fonoimoana and Rogers defeated Tanner and Clark (pool #1)
Heidger and Lewis defeated Blanton and Holdren (pool #2)
Rogers and Clark defeated Tanner and Fonoimoana (pool #1)
Heidger and Blanton defeated Holdren and Lewis (pool #2)
Eric Fonoimoana and Rob Heidger, an alternate filling in for Randy Stoklos, who did not show, advanced to second day.

The second day of competition was held on Saturday March 14th, 1998. The top six players from the AVP computer ranking system plus Eric Fonoimoana and Rob Heidger, first round winners, fought it out to advance to the final round on Sunday. The players were

1998 AVP KING OF THE BEACH EVENT-LAS VEGAS NEVADA
The 1998 King of the Beach Invitational tournament was staged on the parking lot of the Hard Rock Hotel and Casino in Las Vegas Nevada. The event was won by Eric "Foni" Fonoimoana as he edged-out Karch Kiraly for the top honor. "Foni" collected a total of $72,000.00 along with his "Crowning" as the King of the Beach. Above photo, in front of an excited crowd, Mike Whitmarsh hits a set from the "King" towards the block of Canyon Ceman.

Photo Courtesy of "Couvi"

divided into two groups of four as described above. Each player again played three matches with a different partner within their group. Each player earned two points for each win and each team earned $6,000.00. The two players in each group with the most points at the end of the day moved into the final on Sunday. The second round results were as follows:

Loiola and Fonoimoana defeated Johnson and Whitmarsh:16-14
Kiraly and Ceman defeated Steffes and Heidger: 15-5
Johnson and Fonoimoana defeated Whitmarsh and Loiola:15-11
Steffes and Ceman defeated Kiraly and Heidger: 15-8
Whitmarsh and Fonoimoana defeated Loiola and Johnson:15-6
Steffes and Kiraly defeated Ceman and Heidger:15-7

THE FINALS
SUNDAY, MARCH 15

The final round was held on Sunday March 15th, 1998. The top four players from the second round each played three matches with each player earning 3 points and each team earning $20,000.00 for a win. The player with the most points at the end of the tournament was determined the King of the Beach. The final round results were as follows:

Kiraly and Ceman defeated Whitmarsh and Fonoimoana:15-6
Ceman and Fonoimoana defeated Kiraly and Whitmarsh:15-9
Kiraly and Fonoimoana defeated Steffes and Ceman: 15-3

The 1998 AVP Swatch King of the Beach Invitational, at the Hard Rock Hotel and Casino, was won by Eric Fonoimoana. Karch Kiraly was the second place finisher. Canyon Ceman made a strong bid for King of the Beach with a third place finish. The championship went down to the final match between Canyon Ceman and Eric Fonoimoana, with the winner of the match winning the crown. Because of point differential, Karch Kiraly edged-out Canyon Ceman for second place. Randy Stoklos did not show-up and Mike Dodd not playing due to injury. Rob Heidger was the alternate that played in Stoklos' place. There was additional prize money along with the prize money mentioned above, each player earned the following amounts:

First Place	$40,000.00
Second Place	$20,000.00
Third Place	$15,000.00
Fourth Place	$12,000.00
Fifth Place	$10,000.00
Sixth Place	$ 8,000.00
Seventh Place	$ 6,000.00
Eighth Place	$ 4,000.00

FINAL RESULTS
1998 King of the Beach - ERIC FONOIMOANA

1st -	Eric Fonoimoana	$72,000.00
2nd -	Karch Kiraly	$46,000.00
3rd -	Canyon Ceman	$41,000.00
4th -	Mike Whitmarsh	$13,000.00
5th -	Kent Steffes	$15,000.00
6th -	Adam Johnson	$ 9,000.00
7th -	Jose Loiola	$ 8,000.00
8th -	Rob Heidger	$ 8,500.00
9th -	Ian Clark	$ 3,000.00
10th-	Todd Rogers	$ 4,000.00
11th-	Brian Lewis	$ 1,500.00
12th-	Dax Holdren	$ 1,500.00
13th-	Dain Blanton	$ 1,500.00
14th-	Troy Tanner	$ 1,000.00
15th-	Bill Boullianne	$ 1,000.00
	TOTAL PRIZE MONEY =	$226,000.00

PAST CHAMPIONS

1997:	Jose Loiola
1996:	Karch Kiraly
1995:	switched from September 1995 to March of 1996.
1994:	Adam Johnson
1993:	Karch Kiraly
1992:	Karch Kiraly
1991:	Karch Kiraly

JOSE LOIOLA
The defending "KOB" champion, Jose Loiola, was unable to repeat. Above photo, Loiola's attack gets rejected by Whitmarsh.
Photo Courtesy of "Couvi"

ERIC FONOIMOANA
The 1998 "KOB" Champion was Eric Fonoimoana. Above photo, The "King" wears his crown.
Photo Courtesy of "Couvi"

TUCSON ARIZONA
April 3rd-5th, 1998 The 1998 AVP $100,000.00 Miller Lite Tucson Open was played at Tucson Sports Park of America in Tucson Arizona. The second seeded team of Karch Kiraly and Adam Johnson won the tournament after defeating the Brazilian wildcard entry team of Emmanuel Rego and Andre Gomes, by the score of 16-14 in an exciting overtime match during the finals of the loser's bracket. Rego and Gomes were seeded 25th. Kiraly and Johnson went on to easily defeat the fourth seeded team of Eric Fonoimoana and Dain Blanton in the championship match, earning the $20,832.00 first place prize money. Fonoimoana and Blanton won the winner's bracket final to earn their way into the finals. Fox Sports Net televised the tournament on a same day tape-delay basis.

3rd Place: Emmanuel Rego and Andre Gomes
4th Place: Kent Steffes and Jose Loiola
5th Place: Mike Whitmarsh and Canyon Ceman
5th Place: Dax Holdren and Todd Rogers

There were three teams that qualified into this AVP Tucson event. The "Qualifier" was held Thursday, April 2nd, 1998 in Tucson. The teams of Scott Davenport and Doug Smith, Pepe Delahoz and Juan Rodriquez, along with Dave Counts and Brian McDonald all qualified to play in the tournament.

CLEARWATER FLORIDA
April 17th-19th, 1998

The 1998 AVP $50,000.00 Miller Lite Players Championship was staged at the Double Tree Resort Surfside in Clearwater Florida. The 50% ($100,000.00 to $50,000.00) cut in prize money was due to money management problems within the AVP. The players voted to take a cut in tournament prize money to help alleviate the problem. On center court, in front of 4,000 fans, the number one-seeded team and winners of 12 events last season, Kent Steffes and Jose Loiola easily defeated the second seeded team of Karch Kiraly and Adam Johnson, in the championship match, by a score of 15-2. They rushed to a 6-1 lead, and extended it to 12-1 as Kiraly uncharacteristically hit two spikes into the net. In the final, Johnson had his worst match of the tournament. The strong winds dominated the match as it unsettled the AVP Tour's number two team. The wind was directing the ball wherever it wanted, contributing to the most lopsided and action starved final in the last several years at Clearwater. The wind was so forceful that the crowd had to turn away and wince from its force when it "whipped-up" the sand into the air. Steffes and Loiola were never threatened all weekend. The closest anyone came to them was 3 points. The championship match win was their second of the day over Kiraly and Johnson. In the semifinals of the double elimination tournament, Steffes and Loiola cruised 15-8 to move to the final with a 5 win no loss record. Kiraly and Johnson made it into the final by defeating Eric Fonoimoana and Dain Blanton 15-11, in the loser's bracket final. Prior to that, they were in two tough matches, a 15-13 win over David Swatik and Brian Lewis and an 18-16 victory over Canyon Ceman and Mike Whitmarsh. Steffes and Loiola split $10,416.00 in prize money for the first place finish.

3rd Place: Eric Fonoimoana and Dain Blanton
4th Place: Mike Whitmarsh and Canyon Ceman
5th Place: Dax Holdren and Todd Rogers
5th Place: Bill Boullianne and Ian Clark

FORT MYERS FLORIDA
April 25th-26th, 1998

The 1998 Fort Meyers AVP Open was played on Fort Meyers Beach, next to the Fishing Pier. The world's best professional beach volleyball players showcased their talents at the Miller Lite Men's AVP Players Championship as part of the 22-city AVP Tour. Fort Myers Beach, was the host for the 32 two-man teams as they spiked and dug their way for a piece of the $50,000.00 purse. The top-ranked AVP players, including Olympic gold medalists Karch Kiraly and Kent Steffes, Olympic silver medalist Mike Whitmarsh, the 1997 number-one ranked player Jose Loiola, 1998 King of the Beach champion Eric Fonoimoana, as well as rising stars Dain Blanton, and Todd Rodgers were among the world's best professional beach volleyball players that competed. The event was broadcast on the FOX Sports Network. The format for this tournament was single elimination and was subject to single elimination re-seeding. In the championship match, the number one-seeded team of Kent Steffes and Loiola won the first place prize of $9,000.00 by defeating the number two-seeded team of Karch Kiraly and Adam Johnson 11-8 and 10-8 as the time clock ran out. Kiraly and Johnson split $5,000.00 for their efforts.

3rd Place: Mike Whitmarsh and Canyon Ceman
3rd Place: Eric Fonoimoana and Dain Blanton
5th Place: Dax Holdren and Todd Rogers
5th Place: Brian Lewis and David Swatik
5th Place: Bill Boullianne and Ian Clark
5th Place: Kevin Martin and Eduardo Garrido

DALLAS TEXAS
May 2nd-3rd, 1998

he 1998 AVP Sunkist Dallas Open, presented by Nokia was played on a court erected across the street from the Crescent Court Hotel. Upsets marked the first day of the tournament as Adam Jewell and Paul Boyd defeated Canyon Ceman and Mike Whitmarsh 11-8 and 11-6, in the first round of this 32 team single elimination tournament. Whitmarsh was the defending champion, as he and Mike Dodd won the 1997 event in Dallas. In the championship match, the number one-seeded team of Jose Loiola and Kent Steffes defeated the sixth-seeded team of Dax Holdren and Todd Rogers, 7-10, 11-3, and 5-2, to win their third consecutive tournament of the season on the Miller Lite AVP Tour. Steffes and Jose Loiola earned $9,000.00 for their first place finish. The second place team of Holdren and Rogers received $5,000.00 for their efforts.

3rd Place: Eric Fonoimoana and Dain Blanton
3rd Place: Brian Lewis and David Swatik
5th Place: Rob Heidger and Troy Tanner
5th Place: Bill Boullianne and Ian Clark
5th Place: Brian Gatzke and Kevin Martin
5th Place: Emmanuel Rego and Andre Gomes

SAN ANTONIO TEXAS
May 9th-10th, 1998

The Association of Volleyball Professionals Tour made its sixth tour stop at Crossroads Mall for the two-day, $50,000.00 Miller Lite Men's Open. The 1998 AVP Miller Lite San Antonio Men's Open was a 32-team, single-elimination tournament played on approximately 1,300 tons of sand that was used to construct the special sand courts for the event. This tournament was one of the

AVP's single-elimination events with a two-out-of-three game format. The first two games, in each match, were to 11 points. If needed, the third games were to six points. Total purse was $50,000.00, with the champions splitting $10,000.00 and the runner-ups share was set at $5,700.00. In the championship final, the seventeenth-seeded team from Brazil, Emanuel Rego and Andre Gomes easily handled the fifth-seeded team of Mike Whitmarsh and Brian Lewis 14-9. After tying the match at six apiece, the unseeded Brazilians seemed to will themselves to victory in the 92-degree temperature. Gomes and Rego had a defensive answer to every Lewis and Whitmarsh attack. They both seemed to see the court very well and they had great vision on offense and defense. A Rego ace made the score 8-6. Lewis and Whitmarsh then cut the margin to 9-8 but seemed to wear down from the heat and the toll of five matches. During the tournament, the heat was taking a lot out of the players, as most of the matches went to three games. Even though Gomes cramped during the end of the match, the Brazilians, appeared to be the fresher of the teams, as they are used to playing a lot of volleyball on the beaches of Brazil where the summers there are very hot. When the score reached 12-9 with one minute remaining, Rego blocked a Lewis spike to make it 13-9. Then Gomes slammed down two deep hits as time ran out. Lewis and Whitmarsh were playing together for the first time this season. Both teams qualified for the championship after marathon semifinal matches. Gomes and Rego came back from one game down and defeated the fourth seeded team of Eric Fonoimoana and Dain Blanton, 8-11, 8-7, 4-2. Gomes and Rego trailed 2-1 in the third game with just 14 seconds remaining. But Rego's slam into Fonoimoana's chest tied it at 2-2. Gomes served, and another Rego spike gave the duo a 3-2 lead with four seconds left. One more hard hit for good measure as time expired provided the final score. Whitmarsh and Lewis also were extended to three games against the first seeded team of Jose Loiola and Kent Steffes, 11-2, 4-11, 8-6. Whitmarsh and Lewis stormed the defending champions in the first game and forced the number-one ranked team on the tour to play catch-up. Leading 7-6 in the third game, Lewis dug a Loiola spike and then, after a set from Whitmarsh, angled a slam for the victory.

3rd Place: Eric Fonoimoana and Dain Blanton
3rd Place: Jose Loiola and Kent Steffes
5th Place: Canyon Ceman and Ian Clark
5th Place: Bill Boullianne and David Swatik
5th Place: Dax Holdren and Todd Rogers
5th Place: Albert Hannemann and Kevin Wong

Because of the single elimination format, the third spot was occupied by both semi final losers.

BRIAN LEWIS
Brian "Lewey" Lewis played well on the 1998 AVP Tour. "Lewey" placed within the top five 16 times, advancing to 3 championship matches, finishing second each time. Above photo, "Lewey" attacking the ball at the net.
Photo Courtesy of Frank Goroszko

TODD ROGERS
In 1998, Todd Rogers teamed-up with Dax Holdren to finish within the top five 16 times, advancing to 2 championship matches, winning the AVP Tour event in Minneapolis Minnesota. Above photo, Rogers gets low to make the pass.
Photo Courtesy of Frank Goroszko

JACKSONVILLE FLORIDA
May 15th-17th, 1998

Beach volleyball fans packed center court, on Jacksonville Beach, for the $50,000.00 1998 "Modis" Jacksonville AVP Men's Open, to witness the four highest-ranked professional beach volleyball players in the world display their skills. In the championship match, the team of Jose Loiola and Kent Steffes defeated Karch Kiraly and Adam Johnson 15-6 to capture the $10,416.00 first-place check, giving the tandem its fourth win in six tournaments this year. Loiola and Steffes appeared to be in better shape than Kiraly and Johnson, as the court temperature at game time was 105 degrees, but the Loiola and Steffes team hardly broke a sweat. Johnson had to have fluids, via an "IV" prior to the match. Steffes opened the scoring with an ace, and his team jumped to a 7-1 lead. After earning a sideout, the 6' 3" Johnson responded with a powerful kill through Loiola's block. Kiraly made a couple of good defensive plays and Johnson followed with a couple of sharp angle shots around Loiola, instead of attempting to go straight at him. This was suitable strategy considering Loiola is 3 inches taller than Johnson and is regarded by players as having the best vertical leap on the AVP Tour. After Johnson and Kiraly won another point to make the score 7-3, Steffes and Loiola answered with a stuff block on "AJ". Johnson was then aced, then he hit the next ball into the net for a 10-3 score, in favor of Steffes and Loiola. After trading eleven sideouts, Loiola and Steffes then built their lead to 14-6, despite some great plays by Kiraly, Loiola served two aces in a row ending the scoring at 15-6, giving him and Steffes the title. Steffes and Loiola made it to the final by defeating Henry Russell and Mark Kerins 15-11, as Russell and Kerins ran out of gas, in the winner's bracket final. At one point during that match, Loiola missed five serves in a row! Kiraly and Johnson made it to the final, in the sunny 99-degree F heat, by defeating Henry Russell and Mark Kerins in the loser's bracket final. They started fast with 4-1 and 7-3 leads as Russell was twice called for "bad-hands", as the ball slipped through his hands while setting. Russell ran out of gas as the lead went to 12-3 and finally to 15-3.

3rd Place: Henry Russell and Mark Kerins
4th Place: Franco Neto and Roberto Lopes
5th Place: Brian Lewis and Mike Whitmarsh
5th Place: Dax Holdren and Todd Rogers

DAYTONA BEACH FLORIDA
May 22nd-24th, 1998

The 1998 Men's AVP $50,000.00 Coppertone Championships of Florida, presented by "Publix" was won by the top seeded team of Jose Loiola and Kent Steffes. In the championship match, they defeated the 18th-seeded team of Roberto Lopes and Franco Neto,

MARK KERINS
In 1998, Mark Kerins stepped-up for a championship victory with partner Canyon Ceman. They won the AVP Tour event in Muskegon Michigan. Above photo, Kerins aggressively attacking the ball.
Photo Courtesy of "Couvi"

RONNY JENKINS
Ronny "RJ" Jenkins teamed-up with Mike Connaughton to qualify as the 32nd seed at the Cleveland Ohio AVP Tour event. The played well against the nummber #1 team of Karch Kiraly and Adam Johnson. Above photo, "RJ" jump serving.
Photo Courtesy of "RJ"

15-6. For the championship win Loiola and Steffes split $10,416.00 while Lopes and Neto split $5,937.00. This was the fifth tournament win, out of seven tournaments, for Loiola and Steffes on the 1998 Miller Lite Men's AVP Tour. This win brought Steffes all-time career wins to 106 while Loiola was at 30 tournament championships. Lopes and Neto advanced to the final match by defeating the second seeded team of Adam Johnson and Karch Kiraly 15-8 in the Loser bracket final.

3rd Place: Adam Johnson and Karch Kiraly
4th Place: Bill Boullianne and David Swatik
5th Place: Dax Holdren and Todd Rogers
5th Place: Mike Whitmarsh and Brian Lewis

CORPUS CHRISTI TEXAS
May 30th-31st, 1998

The 1998 AVP $50,000.00 Miller Lite South Texas Men's Open was played under the hot Texan sun, at Cole Park. The temperature was in the mid-90's. Kent Steffes and his new partner, Brazilian Emanuel Rego, defeated, the freshly "IV-fluid" saturated team, of Kevin Wong and Albert Hannemann 15-7, to win the championship match. The 7 points were the most scored against Steffes and Rego during the entire tournament. This tournament marked the first time that Steffes had paired with Rego. Steffes made the move after his regular Miller Lite Men's AVP Tour partner and co-number-one ranked player Jose Loiola withdrew from the tournament due to tendinitis in his right knee. This was Steffes' sixth tournament win on the 1998 Miller Lite Men's AVP Tour and the second for Rego. Rego had won the 1998 Miller Lite Open at San Antonio with Gomes before pairing with Steffes this weekend. Steffes and Rego split $10,000.00. Steffes and Rego defeated Bill Boullianne and Andre Gomes 11-7, 11-3 to advance to the final match. Wong and Hannemann advanced to their first ever Miller Lite Men's AVP Tour final by defeating the team of Rob Heidger and Troy Tanner 9-7, 10-7. This is the second AVP season for Wong. Earlier in this single elimination tournament, Wong and Hannemann disposed of Karch Kiraly and Adam Johnson as they both made several key blocks. Hannemann excited the crowd with great defense while he also interjected some "show-time" on the court with pose-downs and stares directed towards his opponents. Wong and Hannemann split $5,700.00 for their second place finish. This was the fifth tournament that Wong and Hannemann had entered together.

3rd Place: Rob Heidger and Troy Tanner
3rd Place: Bill Boullianne and Andre Gomes
5th Place: Eric Fonoimoana and Dain Blanton
5th Place: Canyon Ceman and Ian Clark
5th Place: Karch Kiraly and Adam Johnson
5th Place: Eduardo Garrido and Kevin Martin

SACRAMENTO CALIFORNIA
June 5th-7th, 1998

The 1998 $50,000.00 Men's AVP Golden State Open was staged at Sacramento's Granite Bay. There were threatening gray skies and a cold breeze blowing off Folsom Lake. The crowd was covered in jackets and sweats rather than the usual tank tops and bikinis. Activity was slower than normal at the booth handing out free sun-screen. The number one seeded team and last years winner's, Karch Kiraly and Adam "AJ" Johnson defended their title, beating the third seeded Brazilian team of Jose Loiola and Emanuel Rego 14-5. The win was the 132nd of Kiraly's beach volleyball career. The three-time Olympic gold medalist now trailed Sinjin Smith by seven on the all-time tour victory list. With the victory, Kiraly and Johnson each earned $5,208.00 and a 40-ounce beer from a tournament sponsor. Loiola and Rego shared the runner-up prize of $5,937.00.

In the championship match, AJ started off serving a spader, "drawing first blood". After a side-out, Rego served a point, to put a couple of "french fries" on the board at 1 to 1. Kiraly and Johnson earned a side-out on a great dig by Johnson. Karch and "AJ" went ahead with another point for a 3-2 lead and side change. After a lot of long but awesome rallies and sideout's, AJ served a spader for another point, followed by a stuff block from Kiraly. A spader from Karch strengthened the lead by 4 points. Then another spader from AJ as Rego and Loiola were victims of the husband and wife position, making a score of 7-2. On the next play Loiola touched the net to make the score 8-2. Following another point, Karch "roofed" a Rego hit for another point, making it 10-2. After a side-out, Rego hit a clean shot down the line for a point, making the score 10-3. A heater from AJ brought the next sideout and Karch with a hammer scored at 11-3. AJ improvised with a flipper (fake set) to deliver another point and the side change at 12-3. AJ served another ace from to make the score 13-3. After siding-out, with a hit on the back line, Rego scored a point for the Brazilians, followed by a net violation, giving the ball to Karch and AJ. Loiola spanked the ball for the side-out then scored a point 13-4. Kiraly and Johnson won the Sacramento Open for the second time in a row with a score of 14-5 as AJ launched a sky ball that fell into the corner, giving his team the 14-5 lead just as time expired off the rally clock. Kiraly and Johnson won nearly all the extended rallies in the final match. They also won plenty of short ones. Johnson had four aces, including the final serve, and Kiraly had one. Playing together in a tournament for the first time, Loiola and Rego reached the championship by knocking off Dain Blanton and Eric Fonoimoana 13-7 in the losers' bracket final. Loiola, the 1997 tour MVP, also finished second in last year's tournament with then-partner Kent Steffes. Loiola split with Steffes to team with countryman Rego in preparation for the 2000 Olympics.

3rd Place: Dain Blanton and Eric Fonoimoana
4th Place: Mike Whitmarsh and Brian Lewis
5th Place: Nick Hannemann and Matt Unger
5th Place: Dax Holdren and Todd Rogers

CINCINNATI OHIO
June 19th-21st, 1998

On the weekend of June 19th-21st, 1998, the worlds best beach volleyball players from the Association of Volleyball Professionals (AVP) participated in the 12th stop of the 1998 Miller Lite AVP Pro-Beach Volleyball Tour. There was a 32-team field that competed over three days in a single elimination format. The #2 seeded team of Karch Kiraly and Adam Johnson took home their third victory of the season on the Miller Lite AVP Pro-Beach Tour as they defeated the #12 seeded tandem of Eduardo Bacil and Stein Metzger 10-7, 10-2 to win the

$50,000.00 Cincinnati Men's Open presented by Cincinnati Bell Wireless. Johnson and Kiraly took home $10,000.00 for the win. Bacil and Metzger split $5,700.00 for their elevated effort. Kiraly and Johnson dominated the competition in Cincinnati losing only one game over the weekend during a breathtaking semi-final match against the #9 seeded Brazilian team of Franco Neto and Roberto Lopes. The match lasted nearly an hour and 20 minutes. With the score tied at 6-all as the time clock expired, Kiraly and Johnson lost the dramatic first game 9-11, but came back to win the semi-final match by defeating Neto and Lopes in the next two games 11-1, 6-1 giving them their fourth final appearance of the season. In the other semi-final, Eduardo Bacil and Stein Metzger advanced to their first ever appearance in a Miller Lite AVP Pro-Beach Tour final by edging out the #7 seeded team of Andre Gomes and Eduardo Garrido 11-4, 6-9, 9-7. In their first tournament playing together, the Brazilians, Gomes and Garrido took home a third place finish, giving Garrido his best finish of the season on the Miller Lite AVP Pro-Beach Tour. The top seeded team of Kent Steffes and Mike Whitmarsh, playing together for the first time, made an early exit as they lost 10-8, 10-8 to the #14 seeded team of Brent Doble and Dan Castillo in the second round. The semi-final and final were televised on Fox Sports Net.

3rd Place: Andre Gomes and Eduardo Garrido
3rd Place: Franco Neto and Roberto Lopes
5th Place: Dax Holdren and Todd Rogers
5th Place: Brian Lewis and David Swatik
5th Place: Mark Kerins and Kevin Martin
5th Place: Dan Castillo and Brent Doble

CLEVELAND OHIO
June 27th-28th, 1998

The 1998 Cleveland AVP $50,000.00 Miller Lite Men's Open was played at Chicago's Nautica Entertainment Complex. The opening rounds were rain-shortened. After winning the last two AVP Pro-Beach Volleyball tournaments, Karch Kiraly, the 13-year tour veteran who had 133 tournament titles, and Adam Johnson had to struggle to win in the first round against the 32nd seeded team of Ron Jenkins and Mike Connaughton. Kiraly and Johnson defeated Jenkins and Connaughton, 11-6, 8-5. Jenkins and Connaughton had to play five matches on Friday to qualify for one of the final two openings. They jumped ahead, 4-0, in the first game before Kiraly and Johnson could get untracked. Kiraly and Johnson also had to struggle in their second match against Aaron Boss and Albert Hannemann 13-11. Neither team held more than a one-point lead in the second game until the end. A Hannemann ace-serve gave his team an 11-10 lead. But Kiraly and Johnson grabbed a side-out on a Kiraly tip-kill and finished the match with two Johnson kills and a hitting error on match-point. All of this after winning the first game 11-2, in a match that finished in a downpour. Play was delayed three times, including three hours at the start, and was halted midway through the second round. Kiraly and Johnson, the top seeds, were one of four teams to advance to the quarter-finals. Roberto Lopes and Franco Neto, Bill Boullianne and Ian Clark, and #4-seeded Dax Holdren and Todd Rogers also scored two victories. Kiraly and Johnson's second-round match was the highlight in Nautica's stadium court. Jose Loiola and Emmanuel Rego had just started their second match when play was halted by lightning and heavy rain. Loiola teamed with Kent Steffes to win the Cleveland title last season. He was playing his second AVP tournament with fellow Brazilian Rego, in preparation for the Olympics. Loiola and Rego breezed to a first-round victory, 11-8, 11-1, over Craig Geibel and Dan Ortega. Steffes and his new partner, Mike Whitmarsh, also dominated their opponents in the opening round, scoring an 11-1, 11-3 victory over Jeff Bellandi and Pete Gray. Steffes and Whitmarsh, the second-seeded team, were playing in their second AVP tournament. Steffes, 30, the youngest player on the AVP tour to win 100 tournaments, was going for his sixth Cleveland title.

In the all-Brazilian championship match, defending Cleveland champion Jose Loiola and his new partner, Emanuel Rego, defeated Franco Neto and Roberto Lopes, 10-8. It was Loiola's first win with Rego but his seventh of the season. His first six were with Kent Steffes. Last season, Loiola and Steffes were the dominant team on the AVP Pro-Beach Tour, with 12 tournament championships, including the Cleveland Open. Loiola and Rego recently joined forces to prepare for the 2000 Olympics in Sydney, Australia. Lopes and Neto held a 4-0 lead at the outset, but a spike by Rego after a diving save by Loiola got the team rolling. A long rally, which ended with a net violation by Neto, drew a standing ovation from the excited crowd. Neto and Lopes held a 7-6 lead after several side-outs. Loiola followed with a spader to tie the match, at 7-all, and Rego's block-kill gave them their first lead at 8-7, on the next serve. Rego then served a spader that was good for a 9-7 lead. With time running out on the match clock, Loiola's hard hit launched Neto's white baseball cap flying into the air for a 10-8 lead. Lopes last-ditch effort for a spader was long as the time clock expired. Under AVP rules, the first team to take a two-point lead after the eight-minute clock expires is the winner. Earlier, Lopes and Neto, the 9th-seeded team, reached the finals by upsetting top-seeded Karch Kiraly and Adam Johnson in the quarter-finals, 11-8, 7-4, and 6th-seeded team of Bill Boullianne and Ian Clark, 15-6, in the semifinals. Neto and Lopes were playing in their second AVP tour event although they played together on the Brazilian and FIVB World Tour for 11 seasons.

3rd Place: Bill Boullianne and Ian Clark
3rd Place: Henry Russell and Eric Wurts
5th Place: Karch Kiraly and Adam Johnson
5th Place: Brian Lewis and David Swatik
5th Place: Dax Holdren and Todd Rogers
5th Place: Mike Diehl and Leland Quinn

CHICAGO ILLINOIS
July 3rd-5th, 1998

The 1998 Miller Lite Chicago Men's Open was played on North Avenue Beach. This was the sixteenth annual open in Chicago, the first Chicago Men's Open took place in 1983, which makes it the third longest standing tournament on the AVP Pro-Beach Tour. Hermosa Beach California holds the top spot with Clearwater Florida in the runner-up position. Kent Steffes and Mike

Whitmarsh finally lived up to their top billing by winning their first AVP Miller Lite beach volleyball tournament together at this year's Chicago event. Whitmarsh and Steffes announced to the world that the highly-ranked duo was over its growing pains. Last weekend in Cleveland, the Steffes and Whitmarsh duo appeared not only vulnerable, but downright ugly, not even making it into play on the final day. Rumors circulated that the two stars would not last long as teammates. But on a sunny, 92-degree day on North Avenue Beach, the #2-seeded team of Steffes and Whitmarsh punctuated a perfect weekend of play, beating the #4 seeded team of Dain Blanton and Eric Fonoimoana for the second time on the day, 13-8 as the time clock expired.

In that championship match, Steffes and Whitmarsh were down 3-2 early, but they surged into the lead behind Whitmarsh's hustle and Steffes' well-placed shots into corners and down the sidelines. Steffes and Whitmarsh controlled the tempo throughout the match by maintaining a sizable lead toward the latter stages of the match. With the score at 9-6 in his team's favor but the momentum with his opponents, Whitmarsh came up with two huge blocks for consecutive points. This is when the main point of futility in Blanton and Fonoimoana's play came with just over 2 minutes left. A routine serve by Steffes turned into an ace when Blanton and Fonoimoana ran into each other while contesting for the bump. Shortly afterward, Fonoimoana kicked the ball away in disgust after Steffes blocked away a spike, resulting in a loss of service and the potential for a comeback. The lead held at five as time expired with the score at 13-8. Steffes and Whitmarsh won $10,000.00 for their first place efforts. For Steffes, ranked second on the AVP leader board before the tournament, this victory was his fifth in Chicago. Fonoimoana and Blanton have finished seven times in the top three spots without a championship. Earlier in the day, playing in front of large crowds that could have been mistaken for Wrigley Field bleacher bums, Steffes and Whitmarsh defeated Blanton and Fonoimoana in the semifinals, 13-10. With the double-elimination format, Blanton and Fonoimoana had to beat eighth-seeds Rob Heidger and Troy Tanner 15-9 to earn the rematch in the final. The sight of runner-up trophies and third-place finishes has been a recurring nuisance this season for partner's Dain Blanton and Eric Fonoimoana. Association of Volleyball Professionals officials estimated that 8,200 attended the weekend tournament.

3rd Place: Rob Heidger and Troy Tanner
4th Place: Brian Lewis and David Swatik
5th Place: Adam Johnson and Karch Kiraly
5th Place: Henry Russell and Eric Wurts

SEAL BEACH CALIFORNIA
July 10th-12th, 1998

After a two-year absence, the AVP was back on the beach in Seal Beach for the 1998, $50,000.00 Orange County AVP Men's Open. This was the 13th year that the AVP Tour stopped in Seal Beach, an annual tournament site from 1984 to 1995. In the championship match, the 4th-seeded Brazilian team, of Jose Loiola and Emanuel Rego outlasted the 6th seeded U.S.A. team of David Swatik and Brian Lewis 18-16. Because of strong winds and the set-up location of the court, (the stadium court was set-up with one end facing directly into the wind coming off the ocean) there was a definite good-side-bad-side for all matches played on the stadium court. Rego and Loiola started off on the good-side taking a 4-1 lead. After the side switch, Swatik and Lewis scored four points to one making the score 5-all on the next side change. Lewis and Swatik scored two quick points on the bad-side to take the lead at 7-5. The two teams then traded leads for the rest of the match. Swatik and Lewis were down by a score of 13-11, on the bad side, when they scored to make the score 12-13 as they went to the good-side. Swatik then served a spader to tie the score at 13-all. They then went up 14-13 on another Swatik spader (he had five in the match). They were now serving for the match win on the good-side, but Loiola and Rego fought back to tie the score at 14-14. The Brazilians then took the lead at 15-14. Swatik and Lewis fought back to tie the score at 15-all and then took the lead at 16-15, with a service winner by Swatik, on the bad-side. Serving for the match, Swatik hit the ball into the net. After several side-outs, Rego, on the good-side, served two quick "spaders" in a row for a 17-16 lead. Rego then served another tough serve that was passed badly, putting Swatik and Lewis in trouble. The ball came back over the net to Rego and Loiola, Rego buried it in the sand for the 18-16 victory. Loiola and Rego split $10,417.00 for their win. Swatik and Lewis split $5,937.00 for their effort. The top seeded team of Karch Kiraly and Adam Johnson were stunned by Loiola and Rego in the Semi-finals 15-7. Loiola and Rego were flawless as they went out to a 12-0 lead before Karch and Adam were able to score. Lewis and Swatik defeated Canyon Ceman and Mark Kerins 15-13 in the other Semi-final match.

3rd Place: Karch Kiraly and Adam Johnson
4th Place: Canyon Ceman and Mark Kerins
5th Place: Bill Boullianne and Ian Clark
5th Place: Eduardo Bacil and Stein Metzger

BELMAR NEW JERSEY
July 18th-19th, 1998

A "Marathon match" was the highlight of opening day at the 1998 Belmar $50,000.00 Sunkist Men's Open, in Jersey, at 5th Street and Ocean Avenue in Belmar Beach NJ. In a second-round match, Karch Kiraly and partner Adam Johnson, the top seeds, won a three-hour marathon match 9-11, 10-8, and 10-8 over the 15th-seeds Lee LeGrand and Matt Lyles to advance to the quarter-finals. This match was a throwback to some of the great matches back in the '60s, '70s and early '80s. Matches then used to be three games to 11, but at that time, players didn't jump-serve and there wasn't blocking the way it is today. Many of the fans that watched this match feel that it could be considered one of the all-time greats, it was definitely the best of this year. The match kept the large crowd at the center court transfixed until its conclusion. Johnson served an ace for the winning point in the second game, then he and Kiraly jumped to a 4-0 lead in the deciding game to six points, win by two. The 4-0 lead for Kiraly and Johnson came with just 38 seconds left on the four minutes rally clock. Although he was cramping, LeGrand delivered a tough serve and then a kill on the ensuing overpass to make it 4-1, Lyles then blocked Kiraly with 23 seconds left to make the score 4-2, LeGrand tapped a ball over close to the net after a long rally for 4-3 with 8.5 seconds to go and as the rally clock ran out, they tied the score on a block by LeGrand. At this point the clock was not a factor, since neither team could win without gaining a two-point led, no matter how long they played. And although LeGrand and Lyles were able to keep tying the game, they never gained a game-point opportunity. Both teams were feeling the heat of the single elimination format. "We always seemed to have the advantage or were tied," Kiraly said. The match finally ended at 5:34 p.m., about three hours after it started, on two successive errors by LeGrand and Lyles. First, LeGrand hit an overpass just out, then Lyles went up to hit and couldn't get the ball over the net. Lyles fell to the sand and didn't get up for a few minutes. This 32-team single elimination AVP event was won by Kent Steffes and Mike Whitmarsh. This was the 110th tournament championship for Steffes.

The championship match was played on center court with hot and humid conditions. The temperature was 87 degrees at the start of the final match. Adam Johnson and Mike Whitmarsh both received fluid replacement via IV treatment prior to the final match. Steffes and Mike Whitmarsh, the 2nd-seeds, had now won both finals they reached this year. Whitmarsh and Steffes made it 2-for-2 in finals since they teamed up five weeks ago on the AVP Tour by beating Karch Kiraly and Adam Johnson 11-4, 9-7 in the final. Steffes and Whitmarsh had also won at Chicago two weeks ago and finished ninth in their other three tournaments together. After the easy first game victory, the pair proved they are also able to win the close ones with their second-game victory over Kiraly and Johnson. Although, that game became close thanks to some tough serving by Johnson, just when it seemed Whitmarsh and Steffes were going to romp as they jumped out to an 8-3 lead. Johnson had an ace to make it 8-4 for a side change that sent him and Kiraly to the bad side with just 57 seconds left on the rally clock. But Johnson served another ace, and two more tough serves kept Whitmarsh from offensive hits, allowing defensive plays that were converted into two more points and an 8-7 score with 36 seconds left. The score remained there, until the clock ran out, which meant that the first team to get a two-point lead would win. Two serves later, Whitmarsh got the winning point after getting a partial block on a hit, allowing Steffes to set him for a kill down the middle. Whitmarsh had two blocks for points in the second game, plus several other touches and some defensive plays that he and Steffes converted. Steffes and Whitmarsh earned $10,000.00 for their first place efforts, while Kiraly and Johnson earned $5,700.00 for second. Whitmarsh and Steffes beat Canyon Ceman and Mark Kerins 11-4 and 11-9 in the quarter-finals and Dax Holdren and Todd Rogers 10-8 and 11-5 in the semifinals, after breezing through two matches in the opening rounds of this two-day event. Whitmarsh's blocking was a key element in the wins all weekend. Kiraly and Johnson, meanwhile, struggled all the way to the final. They had the three-hour, three-game match, in the second round, then they had another three-game victory, 9-11, 11-6, and 6-2, over the 7th-seeds Bill Boullianne and Ian Clark in the quarter-finals. Kiraly and Johnson went on to beat Brian Lewis and David Swatik 8-5 and 9-7 in the semifinals.

3rd Place: Brian Lewis and David Swatik
3rd Place: Dax Holdren and Todd Rogers
5th Place: Dain Blanton and Eric Fonoimoana
5th Place: Roberto Lopes and Franco Neto
5th Place: Bill Boullianne and Ian Clark
5th Place: Canyon Ceman and Mark Kerins

MINNEAPOLIS MINNESOTA
July 25th-26th, 1998

The 1998 AVP Minneapolis Miller Lite Open was played at the Target Center parking lot. The 17th stop of the 1998 AVP Tour was won by second year "Pro's" Dax Holdren and Todd Rogers. Holdren and Rogers were the third seeded team. This tournament was the anniversary of Holdren and Rogers' first finals appearance, last year's 15-4 loss to Karch Kiraly and Adam Johnson in Hermosa Beach, California. Holdren and Rogers were co-rookies of the year last season but looked like veterans during the championship match.

In the championship match, against the 4th-seeded Brazilian team, of Franco Neto and Roberto Lopes, Holdren and Rogers rallied from a 3-0 deficit. Holdren came up with two aces, and Rogers tried three consecutive jump serves. Neto and Lopes, dived in the sand to return Rogers' tough serves. Holdren took advantage, attacking on the second hit while Neto and Lopes were scrambling back into position. Holdren put away another weak return for a 5-3 lead. Neto suffered cramps on the play when attempting to block Holdren's spike and was treated for more than 10 minutes. The referee was going to call the match, but Neto returned to the game and continued to play. Rogers went down on the next play, also because of cramps, but he was also able to continue. Holdren and Rogers sealed the victory four sideouts later as Lopes' spike went into the net. Holdren and Rogers, went on to win their first championship at the Association of Volleyball Professionals' Miller Lite Open in downtown Minneapolis with a 10-8, 5-7, 6-3 victory over Brazilians, Neto and Lopes. This championship match was the second championship appearance this season for Holdren and Rogers. They lost in three games to Jose Loiola and Kent Steffes in May. Holdren and Rogers earned $10,000.00 for their first place win. Lopes and Neto earned $5,700.00 for second place. Earlier, Holdren and Rogers had extended some semi-final problems for the top-seeded team of Dain Blanton and Eric Fonoimoana with a 9-6, 4-10, 5-3 win, in the semifinals. Blanton and Fonoimoana have reached the semifinals eight times this season and advanced only twice. The men's-semi final and final were televised on the Fox Sports Network.

3rd Place: Dain Blanton and Eric Fonoimoana
3rd Place: Kevin Martin and Eduardo Garrido
5th Place: Brian Lewis and David Swatik
5th Place: Canyon Ceman and Mark Kerins
5th Place: Troy Tanner and Henry Russell
5th Place: Brent Frohoff and Rob Heidger

Note: seven players who have won the past 14 titles on the tour were playing elsewhere this weekend. Karch Kiraly and Johnson were at the Goodwill Games in New York. Kent Steffes and Mike Whitmarsh, Jose Loiola and Emanuel Rego, Ian Clark and Bill Boullianne, along with Carl Henkel and Kevin Wong were all at the FIVB event in Marseille, France.

MILWAUKEE WISCONSIN
August 1st-2nd, 1998

The 18th stop of the 1998 Miller Lite/AVP Pro Beach Volleyball Tour had a 32-team field competing over two days in a double elimination format. The first seeded team of Karch Kiraly and Adam Johnson took home their fourth victory of the season together, as they defeated the second seeded tandem of Brian Lewis and David Swatik 13-9 to win $10,416.00 as their share of the $50,000.00 tournament on Bradford Beach. Kiraly and Johnson were able to bounce back from an 13-11 loss in their semifinal match against Lewis and Swatik earlier in the day to capture this tour victory.

After a strong start in the final with a 7-4 advantage Kiraly and Johnson saw Lewis and Swatik, turn up the heat on Bradford Beach by climbing back to within two points at 11-9 before shutting them down for the remainder of the match. Lewis and Swatik were handed their first loss of the tournament in the final match after a strong showing in Milwaukee as they earned $5,937.00 for their efforts. The semifinal match, in the loser's bracket, saw Kiraly and Johnson pull-out a close victory over the Brazilian team of Franco Neto and Roberto Lopes, defeating Lopes and Neto 13-11, to advance to the finals for their match against Lewis and Swatik. Neto and Lopes lost their second match of the tournament after fighting their way back through the loser's bracket by winning six matches to take home a third place finish and $4,703.00. In the quarterfinal match, Lewis and Swatik pulled out a win by defeating the previous tournament winners in Minneapolis, fourth-seeds Dax Holdren and Todd Rogers 12-9, to advance to their semifinal match.

3rd Place: Franco Neto and Roberto Lopes
4th Place: Dax Holdren and Todd Rogers
5th Place: Aaron Boss and Albert Hannemann
5th Place: Bill Boullianne and Ian Clark

ATLANTA GEORGIA
August 7th-9th, 1998

In Atlanta, it was just another day at the beach for Karch Kiraly. Every time that Kiraly has played in Atlanta, he's left with a lot more money in his wallet. Kiraly has never lost in the five tournaments he's played in at Atlanta. On the final day of the Miller Lite Beach Challenge at MetLife Park, Hammond Dr. at Perimeter Center Parkway in Dunwoody Georgia, it was no different for Kiraly and partner Adam Johnson.

In the championship match, after an undefeated run, the top-seeded team defeated the eleventh-seeded team of Brent Frohoff and Rob Heidger 15-12 and will return to California sharing $10,416.00. After nearly two days of predictable wins by the top seeds, the quarter-final round in Atlanta was filled with surprises. To get to the championship final, Brent Frohoff and Rob Heidger knocked off the third-seeded team of Brian Lewis and

ANDRE GOMES
Brazilian Andre Gomes teamed-up with countryman Jose Loiola to win the AVP Tour event in San Antonio Texas. Gomes also had three additional top three finishes in 1998. Above photo, Gomes challenges the block of Eric Fonoimoana.
Photo Courtesy of the AVP

EMANUEL REGO
Brazilian Emanuel Rego showed great skil on the 1998 AVP Tour, by advancing to 8 championship matches, winning 4 times. Above photo, Rego reaches over the net to block the attack of Brian Lewis.
Photo Courtesy of the AVP

David Swatik by a score of 15-4, then they knocked-off the fourth-seeded team of Franco Neto and Roberto Lopez 15-9, the sixth-seeded Bill Boullianne and Ian Clark 15-4, But the duo didn't stop there, as they were winning 9-6 in their semifinal match against the tenth-seeded team of Aaron Boss and Albert Hannemann, the match was postponed until the next morning at 8:30 because of lightning. They eventually won by a score of 15-9. Boss and Hannemann pulled an upset of their own to reach Saturday's semifinals in the winner's bracket, defeating the second-seeded team of Dain Blanton and Eric Fonoimoana in the quarter-finals. The top-seeded team of Kiraly and Johnson took a more unconventional route to the finals by hammering the fourth-seeded team of Brazil's Roberto Lopes and Franco Neto 15-2 to earn a spot in the final of the winner's bracket. In front of a crowd of 1,600 at stadium court against Lopes and Neto, Kiraly and Johnson jumped out to an 8-2 lead before four straight Johnson aces ended any hope for a comeback by the Brazilians. During the final match, Kiraly's winning streak was in jeopardy, as Heidger's back-to-back blocks against Johnson gave Frohoff and Heidger a 9-5 lead. After the blocks, Johnson and Kiraly went on a 4-0 run and tied the score at 9-9 when Karch hit a shot over Heidger that found the back line. Frohoff and Heidger regained the lead at 12-9, then were left in the dust as Johnson and Kiraly ran off six straight points to capture the championship. The loss ended an upset-filled tournament run for Frohoff and Heidger. This was the best Frohoff had played in a long time. Frohoff had missed, all of last season, because of a knee injury. Fro and Heidger took home $5,937.00 for their fine effort.

3rd Place: Franco Neto and Roberto Lopez
4th Place: Aaron Boss and Albert Hannemann
5th Place: Dax Holdren and Todd Rogers
5th Place: Eduardo Garrido and Kevin Martin

HERMOSA BEACH CALIFORNIA
August 14th-16th, 1998

The 20th stop of the 1998 Miller Lite/AVP Pro-Beach Volleyball Tour was a 48-team field that competed over three days in a double elimination format. The event took place at the Hermosa Beach Pier at Pier Avenue and "The Strand". Top-seeds, Adam Johnson and Karch Kiraly earned $10,416.00 for their championship match victory over the second-seeded team of Jose Loiola and Emanuel Rego. Loiola and Rego split $5,937.00 for their efforts. The championship match was one of the most exciting finishes in the history of the AVP as the lead went back and forth on several occasions.

3rd Place: Roberto Lopes and Franco Neto
4th Place: Kent Steffes and Mike Whitmarsh
5th Place: Brian Lewis and David Swatik
5th Place: Dax Holdren and Todd Rogers

BRENT DOBLE & ERIC WURTS
Brent Doble and Eric Wurts teamed-up to supply some worthy competition on the 1998 AVP Tour, finishing within the top five on a couple of occasions. Above photo, Doble passing the ball to Wurts.

Photo Courtesy of the AVP

BILL BOULLIANNE
On the 1998 AVP Tour, Bill "Beef" Boullianne was a top five finisher 10 times. He also finished within the top 20 of the AVP point list. Above photo, "Beef" smacks the ball past the block of Adam Johnson.

Photo Courtesy of "Couvi"

SAN DIEGO CALIFORNIA
August 21st-23rd, 1998

The third seeded team of Kent Steffes and Mike Whitmarsh were the winners at the 1998 San Diego Open, played at the Del Mar Fairgrounds in Del Mar, California. After eight previous attempts to win on his home turf, Whitmarsh secured his first San Diego championship. The team of Whitmarsh and Steffes rallied late in the match to defeat Brazilians Jose Loiola and Emanuel Rego 12-10 in overtime to win this Sunkist Open. Loiola and Rego were the second seeds. Whitmarsh and Steffes split $10,416.00 with the victory. With the stadium thermometer reading 87 degrees, the championship match was played in front of a disappointing crowd of only 1,000 fans. The match was a thriller. With the score tied at 4-4, neither team led by more than two points the rest of the way. Loiola aced Whitmarsh three times to increase the Brazilians lead to 10-8. Whitmarsh and Steffes rallied to tie the match 10-10 as the clock elapsed. Steffes served an ace that gave the Americans an 11-10 lead. After eight sideouts, Whitmarsh blocked Loiola for the win.

3rd Place: Brian Lewis and David Swatik
3rd Place: Dain Blanton and Eric Fonoimoana
5th Place: Brent Doble and Adam Jewell
5th Place: Dax Holdren and Todd Rogers
5th Place: Canyon Ceman and Mark Kerins
5th Place: Roberto Lopes and Franco Neto

MUSKEGON MICHIGAN
August 28th-30th, 1998

The final event of the 1998 AVP season was the AVP Tour Championships at Pere Marquette Park Beach in Muskegon Michigan. After a cold, wet start the second day of competition more than made up for it on the beach in Muskegon. With temperatures reaching 90 degrees and not a cloud in the sky, over 5,000 spectators came to watch as the conditions were perfect for underdogs to knock off the top seeds in the winners' bracket, and were also perfect for the top seeds to knock each other around off the court. An estimated 10,000 fans showed up for the entire three-day tournament in Muskegon. Most of the players on the tour spent the previous night in a "party-hardy", "last-day-in-the-wilderness" mood. With the future of the AVP up in the air, the players just wanted to make the most of what they perceived to possibly be the last AVP event ever. If any of the teams seemed particularly sluggish the next morning, one of the taverns in downtown Grand Haven may have been to blame. A large group of players, presumably ready to cut loose after a grueling, 21-city tour, partied into the wee hours of Saturday morning. Kent Steffes and Mike Whitmarsh, the second-seeds, were eliminated from the tournament when Steffes initiated a fight in the players' area with Brian Lewis. The altercation caused a near-hour delay on the stadium court. Steffes was kicked out of the AVP Tour Championships tournament for a "serious code violation". Steffes and longtime rival Lewis exchanged words just before Lewis and his partner David Swatik were scheduled to take the court for their winners' bracket semifinal match. The words escalated into pushing and shoving, punches were thrown and at least one table was knocked over. AVP officials then restored the peace briefly, before Lewis charged Steffes about 15 minutes later. Lewis wrestled Steffes to the ground and put him into a submissive hold before he was restrained. Muskegon police were then called in and took statements from both players and witnesses in the tent. No arrests were made. Lewis came away from the fight with a gash over his left eye before a semifinal match with Ceman and Kerins. Lewis courageously played the next match, but the cut near his eye started bleeding profusely, forcing him to take a medical timeout and get more treatment at court-side. Lewis and partner David Swatik lost that match by a score of 15-13. Lewis shook off his injury when he and Swatik breezed past Frohoff and Heidger 15-10 in the losers' semifinals. They then faced Loiola and Rego in the second losers' semifinal, almost eliminating the top seeds after taking a 14-11 lead. But the Brazilians fought back for an exciting 16-14 win. The disqualification automatically advanced the eleventh-seeds Nick Hannemann and Henry Russell to the winners' bracket final. They faced Ceman and Kerins. Ceman and Kerins defeated Hannemann and Russell 15-13 to reach the championship match. Hannemann and Russell had started their day off well, handing Kiraly and Blanton their first loss of the tourney in the winners' quarter-finals, 10-6. Russell did a good job passing as he and Hannemann sided out well all-tournament long. The ninth-seeded team of Brent Frohoff and Rob Heidger, defeated Dain Blanton and Karch Kiraly by a score of 12-10 in the losers' quarterfinal. Frohoff and Heidger led 5-0 and 8-4, but Kiraly and Blanton worked their way back to a 10-9 lead before Frohoff and Heidger finished them off. The biggest upset of the day came when the eighth-seeded team of Canyon Ceman and Mark Kerins beat the top-seeds Jose Loiola and Emanuel Rego 16-14 in the winners' bracket. Loiola and Rego were up by scores of 8-2 and 14-9, but Ceman and Kerins took advantage of the situation and finished them off. Loiola and Rego went on to beat Brent Doble and Adam Jewell, ranked 15th, in the losers' bracket and then took out fellow Brazilian's, Eduardo Garrido and Franco Neto, sixth-seeds, in the losers' quarter-finals. Kiraly and Blanton still had a shot at the title after their previous loss by beating the fifth-seeds, Dax Holdren and Todd Rogers, 15-10 in the losers' bracket before losing to Frohoff and Heidger.

In the championship match, Ceman and Kerins, the only undefeated team left in the tournament, defeated Loiola and Rego in a dramatic final match, 15-12. They did it, mainly on the strength of their serving. Ceman and Kerins could have overwhelmed the Brazilians in the final after jumping out to a 6-2 lead. They built the lead to 11-5, but Loiola and Rego went on a 7-1 run to tie the match at 12-12. Ceman and Kerins got back on track as they hit shoots on the line twice to go up 14-12 for match-point. After several hard-fought sideouts, Loiola sent a spike long to end the match. After the win, Ceman took a victory lap, "High-Fiving" the crowd. It was the third career win for Ceman and the second for Kerins, winning $10,416.00. Loiola, split $5,937.00 with Rego.

3rd Place: Nick Hannemann and Henry Russell
4th Place: Brian Lewis and David Swatik
5th Place: Kent Steffes and Mike Whitmarsh
5th Place: Brent Frohoff and Rob Heidger

MEN'S TOURNAMENT RESULTS
1998-FIVB

MAR DEL PLATA ARGENTINA
January 16th-18th, 1998

The 1998 FIVB Men's Pro-Beach Volleyball Tour started at Mar del Plata Argentina with a purse worth $170,000.00. The surprise winners were the brother's Martin and Paul Laciga, from Switzerland. Their share of the purse was $20,000.00. First there was a "Qualification Tournament" that was played January 14 to January 15, 1998. The Main Draw was played January 16 to January 18, 1998. There were 40 matches played on the first day of the Main Draw and 18 matches played on the second day. The semifinals and finals (four matches) were played on January 18th, 1998. The stadium was constructed over the Playa Briston itself and had a capacity for 4,000 people distributed on four outside courts in the sand, plus a VIP roofed main court. The VIP area lodged 400 guests and journalist from several various media. There were more than fifteen "offices" that functioned in tents, two of them working as press room for accredited media and one more as an interview room. In the championship match the Swiss team of Laciga and Laciga outlasted the Brazilian team of Paulo Emilio Silva Azevedo and Paulo Roberto "Paulao" Moreira da Costa, in three games, by scores of 12-5, 11-12, and 12-10. Laciga and Laciga started the tournament with a victory over the French team of Guilherm Deulofeu and Eric Guissart by a score of 15-3. They went on to win their next six matches: 15-7 over the German team of Jorg Ahmann and Oliver Oetke, 15-4 over the Argentine team of Pedro Ramon Depiaggio

PAUL LACIGA & MARTIN LACIGA
The team of Paul Laciga and Martin Laciga, the brothers from Switzerland, played well on the 1998 FIVB Tour. They had 7 top five finishes, including a win at the Mar Del Plata Argentina event. Above photo, Martin blocks while Paul is ready on defense.
Photo Courtesy of the FIVB

EMANUEL REGO & JOSE LOIOLA
The players from Brazil dominated the 1998 FIVB Tour, winning 11 of 16 FIVB events. The top team was Emanuel Rego and Jose Loiola, winning 4 FIVB "Gold-Medals" in 1998. Above photo, Loiola hits a set from Rego into the block of Mike Whitmarsh.
Photo Courtesy of "Couvi"

and Pablo Javier Guemberena, 15-11 over the Brazilian team of Z-Marco Nobrega and Ricardo Alex Costa Santos, 15-5 over the Norwegian team of Jan Kvalheim and Bjorn Maaseide, then in the semifinals they defeated the top 1998 AVP team in the U.S.A., Brazilian's Emanuel Rego and Jose Loiola, by a score of 16-14. They then won their seventh straight match in the finals, splitting $32,000.00 for their Gold Medal effort. Paulo Emilio and Paulo won their semifinal match 15-13 Over compatriots Para Ferreira Souza and Guilherme Marques. Paulo Emilio and Paulo split $23,000.00 for their Silver Medal effort.

3rd Place: Emanuel Rego and Jose Loiola-Bra
4th Place: Para Ferreira Souza and Guilherme Marques-Bra
5th Place: Esteban Martinez and Martine Conde-Arg
5th Place: Jan Kvalheim and Bjorn Maaseide-Nor

The best finish by a U.S.A. team was seventh place by Bill Boullianne and Eric Fonoimoana, with a 3 win 2 loss record. Their victories were: 15-4 over the Austrian team of Gernot Leitner and Stamm, 15-8 over the U.S.A. team of Sinjin Smith Ricci Luyties, 15-12 over the Argentine team of Jose Luis Salema Abrantes and Mariano Baracetti. Boullianne and Fonoimoana opened the tournament with a 12-15 loss to the French team of Christian Penigaud and Jean-Philippe Jodard. They finished the tournament with another 12-15 loss to the Brazilian team of Para and Guilherme. The next best finish by a U.S.A. team was 13th by Carl Henkel and Stein Metzger. They finished with a 2 win and 2 loss record. Their wins were 17-15 over the team of Luis Miguel Barbosa Maia and Jose Carlos Pereira Brenha Alves, from Portugal then a 15-9 win over the Cuban team of Juan Miguel Rosell Milanes and Chambers. Their losses were: 12-15 against Depiaggio and Guemberena from Argentina; 6-15 loss courtesy of fellow U.S.A. countrymen Boullianne and Fonoimoana. There were two U.S.A. teams in the 17th spot: Sinjin Smith and Ricci Luyties along with Kent Steffes and Dain Blanton.

VINA DEL MAR CHILI
February 6th-8th, 1998

The 1998 FIVB Men's Pro-Beach "Challenger" was won by the Brazilian team of Luiz Antonio "Lula" Barbosa da Silva and Francismar Adriano Dias Garrido. In the one hour and six minute championship match, they defeated the American team of Sinjin Smith and Ricci Luyties by a score of 15-12. They earned $4,000.00 and the Gold Medal for their efforts. The fifty minute third place match, was won by the Canadian team of John Child and Mark Heese, 15-7 over the Argentine team of Esteban Martinez and Martine Conde. Lula and Adriano made it to the finals by defeating Martinez and Conde 15-12 in their 52 minute semifinal match. Smith and Luyties made it to the finals by defeating Child and Heese 15-8 in their 40 minute semifinal match. Smith and Luyties made it to the finals undefeated. First they beat-up on Ohlsson and Ortiz, from Chili 15-5. Then they outlasted the Austrian team of P. Schroffenegger and T. Schroffenegger 15-12. In their next match they handled the Italian team of Raffaelli and Pimponi 15-9. Martinez and Conde from Argentina were Smith and Luyties next victims with a score of 15-6. Next they earned their way into the semi's by defeating the German team of Dieckmann and Dieckmann 15-10.

3rd Place: John Child and Mark Heese-Canada
4th Place: Esteban Martinez and Martine Conde-Arg
5th Place: Charles Dieckmann and Markus Dieckmann-Ger
5th Place: Andrea Raffaelli and Maurizio Pimponi-Italy

Pete Gray and Ian Clark, from the USA, also participated. In their first match they easily defeated Iglesias and Cabero from Chile 15-3. They lost their second match 6-15 to Jarry and Yoyo Grimalt, also from Chile. After the loss, they won their third and fourth matches, 15-13 over the Brazilian team of Marcio Araujo and Reis Castro and 17-16 over the Russian team of Dmitri Karasev and Oleg Kiselev. In their fourth and final match, they were eliminated from the tournament, finishing in ninth place, after losing to Raffaelli and Pimponi from Italy.

RIO DE JANERIO BRAZIL
February 12th-15th, 1998

The third tournament of the 1998 FIVB Men's Pro-Beach Volleyball World Tour was in Copacabana, Rio de Janeiro, Brazil. It started with 46 matches in the qualifying round. There were eight teams that qualified to join 24 other teams in the main draw of the 32 team competition. The potent heat of Rio De Janeiro's summer made it impossible for the teams to play at noon. It was the first time on the FIVB World Circuit, the competition had an interruption to allow the players to avoid the hottest time of the day. After the heat of the qualifying tournament, the temperatures in Rio were reduced as rain fell all day during the first day of the main draw. The 32 teams qualified in the main draw played 40 matches the first day. In the first semi-final match, Z-Marco and Ricardo defeated Kvalheim and Maaseide 15-12, in a fort-four minute match. In the second semi-final match, Emanuel and Loiola defeated Roberto Lopes and Franco 15-7 in forty-three minutes. After two days of rain and cloudy weather, the sun came back to Rio and a crowd of 7,000 people came to the arena in Copacabana to watch the final match between the two Brazilian teams.

In the finals of the main draw, with his new partner, Ricardo, Ze Marco beat Emanuel, his former partner now playing with Jose Loiola, to win the championship. In the first set the two teams started well, with Ze Marco and Ricardo taking an early lead of 5-2, but good spikes from Loiola made the difference. Loiola and Emanuel tied the set at 7-7 and then took the lead to win the first set by 12-9, in 40 minutes. In the second set Ze Marco and Ricardo put their game together, as the 23 year old Ricardo, playing for the first time in a final of an FIVB World Circuit event, seemed to be less nervous. Emanuel and Loiola led the score in the beginning at 5-1, but Ze Marco and Ricardo tied it at 5-5, 6-6 and 9-9. Then, the good blocks of Ricardo helped his team to win the game 12-9, in 37 minutes. In the third game tie-breaker, again the concentration of Ze Marco and Ricardo paid off. The set was 6-6 when they took the lead at 7-6, 8-6 and 9-7. They went on to win the game and match with a 12-10 score in 11 minutes as Loiola made a service error at match-point. Up to this point, Jose Loiola, the 1997 "king of the beach" on the AVP Tour, had never won in Rio. Three Brazilian teams took Gold, Silver and Bronze in the competition here at Copacabana Beach. In the one hour and twenty-eight minute championship match, Ze Marco and Ricardo won the gold medal and the first place prize money of $32,000.00. The total prize money for this event was set at $170,000.00. Copacabana, Rio de Janeiro, Brazil has hosted this competition since 1987 with the American team of Sinjin Smith and Randy Stoklos holding the record for victories, with five titles.

There were teams from 17 countries playing in this tournament: Brazil, USA, Switzerland, Argentina, Norway, Italy, Canada, Germany, France, Portugal, Austria, Australia, Russia, Puerto Rico, Japan, Czech Republic and Spain. The tournament was observed by Jackie Murdoch and John Quinlan, members of the

Sydney Olympic Games Organizing Committee. They intend to use the arena in Rio as a model for the 2000 Olympic Games.

3rd Place: Roberto Lopes and Franco Neto-Bra
4th Place: Jan Kvalheim and Bjorn Maaseide-Nor
5th Place: Jose "Duda" Macedo de Abreu and "Fred" Doria de Souza-Bra
5th Place: Paulo Emilio Silva Azevedo and Carlos Eduardo Dias Garrido-Bra
The best finish for a U.S.A. team was a ninth place finish by Steffes and Boullianne. Other U.S.A. finishers: Blanton and Fonoimoana along with Sinjin Smith and Luyties were in 13th place, while Canyon Ceman and Ian Clark along with Carl Henkel and Stein Metzger were in 17th place.

TORONTO CANADA
June 19th-21st, 1998

There were 35 countries, a total of 138 teams, that took part in the Labatt Blue Toronto Open (the most "ethnically diverse" city in the world). This was the third edition of the FIVB's World Tour and the first ever FIVB World Tour event to come to Canada. There was an unprecedented $340,000.00 in prize money, equally divided between Men and Women. There were 53 men's teams seeded for the Qualification Tournament, all vying for the precious 8 spots available in the 32 team main draw. With the sun shining, along with hot humid 80 degree weather, the tournament was staged at the "International Beach Village" on the beach of Ashbridge's Bay. The Canadians showed strong support by filling the 5,000 seat stadium court and crowded the secondary stadium courts (six additional competition courts). The fans supported the excitement, spectacular play, along with the variety of other attractions. There were 40 men's matches played on the first day of the main draw when the 32 teams were reduce to 16. Four different countries were represented in the Men's final four. The Brazilian team of Emanuel and Loiola vs Bosma and Diez, from Spain, along with the Argentine team of Martinez and Conde vs Kvalheim and Maaseide from Norway. Bosma and Diez earned $15,000.00 and took the bronze medal away from the Norwegians in a close 15-13 match for third place. The Norwegians took home $12,000.00 for their fourth place finish. The gold medal match was a South-American match-up with the top seeded Brazilian team of Emanuel and Loiola taking on their neighbors to the South, Argentines, Martinez and Conde. The Argentinians earned $32,000.00, as they came out on top 15-10, in a match that was highlighted by great digs and awe-inspiring net play. The Brazilians earned $23,000.00 for their second place effort. All of the matches, including the final match, were played in "FORMAT-A" (1 game to 15 points with a 2 point lead. If there was a 16-16 tie, the team that scored the 17th point won the game and the match with only a one-point lead).

3rd Place: Javier Bosma Minguez and Fabio Diez-Spain
4th Place: Jan Kvalheim and Bjorn Maaseide-Nor
5th Place: Lee Zahner and Julien Prosser-Aus
5th Place: Paul Laciga and Martin Laciga-Swiss

Top U.S.A. finishers were Blanton and Fonoimoana in 7th place. They were followed by Smith and Luyties in ninth place while Carl Henkel and Kevin Wong were in 13th place.

BERLIN GERMANY
July 3rd-5th, 1998

The 1998 $170,000.00 German Men's Open in Berlin was the fourth stage of the 1998 Men's FIVB World Tour. The tournament was staged on Berlin's "Schloplatz" for the second time in three years. The event started, in rainy conditions, with 60 matches on the first day of qualification rounds. The matches were staged on the "Center Court" and three side courts. There were more than 2,000 spectators watching the exciting international qualifying matches. On the second day of qualifying, there were over 2,500 spectators watching as the final eight teams earned their way into the main draw. On a cold and cloudy day, the first day of the main draw, saw the winner's of Toronto's men's FIVB event, the 7th-seeded team from Argentina, Esteban Martinez and Martin Conde, eliminated. During the 40 matches of play, more than 4,000 spectators enjoyed net-action and a lot of great defense on all of the tournament courts. The third day of main draw action was played in constant rain, strong winds, and temperatures at less than 60 degrees. As the sun peeked through the clouds, the rain stopped for the championship match. The tournament finished with a big surprise. In the championship match, the victory of the Norwegians Kjemperud and Hoidalen, over the Brazilians Guilherme and Paro, surprised everybody. Until now, this Scandinavian team had never reached the semi-finals of a World Tour Event. As the 25th-seeds in the main draw, they defeated the 2nd-

JORRE ANDRE KJEMPERUD
On the 1998 FIVB Tour, Norwegian Jorre Andre Kjemperud was a force to contend with. Kjemperud teamed-up with compatriot Vegard Hoidalen to win the Berlin Germany event. Above photo, Kjemperud cuts the ball past the block og USA's Chip McCaw.
Photo Courtesy of the FIVB

seeded team two straight games in the one and one-half hour final. The scores were 12-4 and 12-8. The two Norwegians served more than ten spaders in the final and they played very solid side-out volleyball. Not surprisingly, Hoidalen finished the tournament with another spader. There were over 4,500 spectators that enjoyed the finals. The total attendance for all five days was estimated at 18,000. Kjemperud and Hoidalen earned their way into the championship match by defeating another Brazilian duo in the semi-finals. In their 36-minute Semi-final match, they defeated 3rd-seeded Z-Marco and Ricardo by a score of 15-5. Kjemperud and Hoidalen earned $32,000.00 for their gold medal performance. In their 45-minute Semi-final match, Guilherme and Para de Souza defeated Palinek and Kubala, from the Czech Republic, by a score of 15-7. Z-Marco and Ricardo defeated Palinek and Kubala by a score of 15-7 in a 41-minute match to determine third place.

3rd Place: Z-Marco Nobrega and Ricardo Alex Costa Santos-Bra
4th Place: Michal Palinek and Premysl Kubala-Czech
5th Place: Paul Laciga and Martin Laciga-Swiss
5th Place: Carl Henkel and Kevin Wong-USA

The U.S.A. team of Sinjin Smith and Ricci Luyties finished in 13th place.

JONA SWITZERLAND
July 4th-5th, 1998

There was a "Sattellite" tournament staged in Jona Switzerland. The winner's of the tournament were Igor Stejskal and Petr Chromy, from the Czech Republic. The first place check was in the amount of $2,000.00. In the Championship match, Stejskai and Chromy outlasted the American team of Morgan Chapman and Greg Ryan. The final scores were 12-9 and 12-8.

3rd Place: Amaury Velasco and Willie De Jesus-PR
4th Place: Robert Nowotny and Stefan Potyka-Austria
5th Place: Victor Anfilloff and Shaun Blackman-Aus
5th Place: Patrick Egger and Bernhard Vesti-Swiss

LIGNANO ITALY
July 17th-19th, 1998

The 1998 FIVB $170,000.00 Men's Pro-Beach Volleyball Event at Lignano Sabbiadora Italy began with a qualifying tournament. The "Maxicono Cup" qualifier showcased 74 teams from 30 different countries. During the first day of qualification, in front of 5,000 spectators, there were 65 matches played. On the second day of qualification there were 12 matches played by 16 teams that decided the eight teams that went into the main draw. Under a hot sun, in front of over 6,000 spectators, the first day of the main draw featured 40 matches. There were 18 matches played on the second day of the main draw. During the 18 matches more than 7,000 spectators enjoyed spectacular net-action and a lot of great defense during all of the action. On the final day of main draw action, more than 7,000 people crowded the beach arena for the fifth FIVB men's tournament of the season. The morning semifinal matches featured the four remaining teams. In the first semifinal, the winner's of the loser's bracket, Paul Laciga and Martin Laciga from Switzerland defeated the Brazilian team of Jose Loiola and Emanuel Rego in one hour and ten minutes by a score of 15-7. In the other semifinal, the Brazilian team of Guilherme Marques and Para Ferreira Souza defeated the Spanish team of Javier Bosma and Fabio Diez in one hour and 24 minutes by a score of 16-14. In the thirty-seven minute match for third place, Emanuel and Loiola defeated Bosma and Diez by a score of 15-7. In the championship match, the current leaders of the "World Rankings", Guilherme and Para of Brazil won the "Gold-Medal" and $32,000.00 by defeating the Swiss brothers Laciga and Laciga in two straight games, 12-6 and 12-8. The final match lasted one hour and twenty-six minutes. Laciga and Laciga earned $23,000.00 for their silver medal performance.

3rd Place: Jose Loiola and Emanuel Rego-Bra
4th Place: Javier Bosma and Fabio Diez-Spain
5th Place: Ricardo Lione and Andrea Ghiurghi-Italy
5th Place: Luis Maia and Joao Brenha-Port

There were two U.S. teams that competed in the main draw. Sinjin Smith and Ricci Luyties finished in 7th place with a 3 win 2 loss record. Carl Henkel and Kevin Wong finished in 13th place with a 2 win 2 loss record. Smith and Luyties record included a first round 15-7 win over the Norwegian team of Andre' Kjemperud and Vegard Hoidalen, followed by a 15-9 win over the Polish team of Bachorski and Bulkowski. They then lost to the tournament champions Para and Guilherme by a score of 15-3. They followed with a 15-13 win over the Canadian team of Holden and Leinemann and they were eliminated from the tournament 15-12 by the Italian team of Lione and Ghiurghi. Henkel and Wong opened with a 15-3 win over the Russian team of Kouchnerev and Karasev, followed by a 15-12 loss to Lione and Ghiurghi. They came back with a 15-8 win over Brazil's Giovane and Tande, but were eliminated with a 15-12 loss at the hands of the German team of Charles Dieckmann and Markus Dieckmann.

MARSEILLE FRANCE
July 24th-26th, 1998

The next $170,000.00 FIVB Men's Beach Volleyball World Tour event was staged in Marseille France. The Brazilian team of Ze-Marco and Ricardo took home the gold medal along with the first place check of $40,000.00. In the championship match, Ze-Marco and Ricardo outlasted the German team of Jorg Ahmann and Axel Hager, by scores of 12-11 and 12-10. The Brazilians made it into the final with a three set semifinal victory over Americans Ian Clark and Bill Boullianne. The scores were 10-12, 12-0, and 13-11. The Germans also made it into the final with a three set semifinal victory over Brazilians Paulo Emilo and Paulao. Their scores were 12-8, 9-12, and 12-10.

3rd Place: Ian Clark and Bill Boullianne-USA
4th Place: Paulo Emilo and Paulo Moreira-Bra
5th Place: Car Henkel and Kevin Wong-USA
5th Place: Giovane Gavio and Alexandre Tande-Bra
5th Place: Miguel Luis Maia and Joao Carlos Brenha-Port
5th Place: Bernhard Vesti and Markus Egger-Swiss

Americans Kent Steffes and Mike Whitmarsh finished in ninth place.

KLAGENFURT AUSTRIA
July 31st-August 2nd, 1998

The FIVB Beach Volleyball Men's World Tour staged it's 7th event of the season on the Klagenfurt Beach Volleyball Area at Wurther Lake in Klagenfurt Austria. Over the course of the tournament, more than 30,000 spectators attended. Brazilian defending champion, Emanuel Rego, and his new partner Jose Loiola came out on top at the 2nd Austria Open, to win their first tournament together. In the 81 minute final of this $170,000.00 event, they defeated Eric Fonoimoana and Dain Blanton, from the U.S.A., by scores of 12-8 and 12-3. The two Brazilians were so thrilled that threw their hats into the crowd after they converted their fourth match-point for the win. Loiola and Rego split $32,000.00 prize money, while Blanton and Fonoimoana split $23,000.00 for their efforts. In the match for third place, despite the tropical heat, the Norwegian team of Kvalheim and Maaseide kept their cool during the match, played in front of 4,500 spectators inside the attractive Werthersee Stadium. The North Europeans took advantage of Paulao's ankle injury (a cancellation of the game was even discussed), came back from four points behind at 7-11 and finally made use of their seventh match-point to win the game 16-14 after 73 minutes. The two Scandinavians were thrilled with their best result on this year's FIVB World Tour, after two fourth places in Toronto and Rio. Runners-up Fonoimoana and Blanton cruised their way into the tournament by easily beating their semi-final opponents Paulo Emilio and Paulao by a score of 15-3 in 51 minutes. The game was very close at first, but then the Brazilians play deteriorated. The second semi-final was also won pretty clearly. Last year's winner Rego and his new partner Loiola beat the Norwegian pair 15-8 in 55 minutes. This victory moved Rego and Loiola two places higher in the FIVB World Ranking to 4th place.

3rd Place: Jan Kvalheim and Bjorn Maaseide-Nor
4th Place: Paulo Emilo and Paulo Moreira-Bra
5th Place: Jorg Ahmann and Axel Hager-Ger
5th Place: Z-Marco Nobrega and Ricardo Alex Costa Santos-Bra

U.S.A. team results from the first day of main draw competition at the 1998 Beach Volleyball World Tour Klagenfurt Austria Men's Open: Eric Fonoimoana and Dain Blanton 15-12 over Charles Dieckmann and Markus Dieckmann, from Germany. Fonoimoana and Blanton 15-9 over Kent Steffes and Mike Whitmarsh. Steffes and Whitmarsh 15-5 over Russians Kouchnerev and Karasev. Steffes and Whitmarsh 15-5 over Kjemperud and Hoidalen from Norway. Carl Henkel and Kevin Wong 15-10 over Canadians Holden and Leinemann. Henkel and Wong 15-5 over Brazilians Para and Guilherme. The AVP team of Rego and Loiola (both USA residents)15-12 over Velasco-De Jesus from Puerto Rico and 15-8 over Child and Heese from Canada. U.S.A. team results from the second day of main draw competition at the 1998 Beach Volleyball World Tour Klagenfurt Austria Men's Open: Steffes and Whitmarsh 15-6 over Brazilians Para and Guilherme. Steffes and Whitmarsh 10-15 losers to the Brazilian team of Z-Marco and Ricardo. Henkel and Wong 12-15 losers to the German team of Ahmann and Hager. Fonoimoana and Blanton 15-10 over Henkel and Wong. Fonoimoana and Blanton 15-11 over Rego and Loiola. Rego and Loiola 15-9 over Z-Marco and Ricardo. Final U.S.A. finishers: Fonoimoana and Blanton finished in 2nd place. Henkel and Wong along with Steffes and Whitmarsh finished in 9th place.

ESPINHO PORTUGAL
August 7th-9th, 1998

The Men's $200,000.00 FIVB World Tour event in Praia da Ba, Espinho Portugal enjoyed excellent weather conditions along with great fan support. Over the duration of the tournament, there was a total of 60,000 fans in the Beach Volleyball stadium. There was a two-day Qualification Tournament, followed by three days of main draw action. There were over 70 matches in the main draw. The event started off with a high level of play in the Qualification Tournament. It was raised even higher on the first day of the main draw with four matches lasting over one hour play. The match between the first placed team in the World rankings, Brazilians Rogrio "Para" Ferreira de Souza and Guilherme Luiz Marquez vs the ninth best, Jose Luis Salema Abrantes and Mariano Baracetti, from Argentina, was one of the longest with a duration of one hour and fifteen minutes. The match involving the American team of Sinjin Smith and Ricci Luyties against the Norwegian team of Jorre Andre' Kjemperud and Vegard Hoidalen was played even longer at one hour and twenty-three minutes! The team from Norway won by a score of 17-16, knocking Smith and Luyties out of the tournament with a seventeenth place finish. Smith and Luyties had lost in the first round to the team of Premsyl Kubala and Mical "Palda", from the Czech Republic, in another long (one hour and ten minutes) close match, by a score of 16-14. They then won their second match against the Russian team of Michel Kouchnerev and Dmitri Karasev, in a thirty-five minute match, by a score of 15-2. On the first day of the main draw, there were no big surprises as the top teams won their matches. In the two semi-final matches: Steffes and Whitmarsh defeated Brazilians Para and Guilherme 15-9, in a seventy-five minute match, while Brazilians Rego and Loiola defeated the Swiss team of Laciga and Laciga 15-10, in a fifty-five minute match. On the final day of competition, the Brazilian team of Emanuel Rego and Jose Loiola won the Men's Portugal Open. In the, one hour and ten minute, championship match, they defeated the American team of Kent Steffes and Mike Whitmarsh by scores of 12-8 and 12-9. The victory gave Rego and Loiola the $40,000.00 first place prize-money, the largest of the 1998 FIVB World Tour. In the first game, Steffes and Whitmarsh went out to a 5-1 lead, but Rego and Loiola came back and tied it at 8-all. The Brazilians then scored the next four points to win the first game 12-8. In the second game the American team took the advantage at 7-4, but the constant support given to the Brazilians by the local fans helped inspire Loiola and Rego to victory.

3rd Place: Rogrio "Para" de Souza and Guilherme Luiz Marquez-Bra
4th Place: Paul Laciga and Martin Laciga-Swiss
5th Place: Eduardo Martinez and Martin Conde-Arg
5th Place: Luis Maia and Joao Brenha-Port

The American team of Kevin Wong and Carl Henkel settled for a 9th place.

OSTEND BELGIUM
August 14th-16th, 1998

The sun and great weather welcomed the first day of the main draw competition at the Ostend $170,00.00 FIVB Men's Beach Volleyball World Tour. This ninth stage of the 1998 FIVB Tour began beautifully at Ostend, the Queen of Belgian beaches. The Belgian National champions, Pascal Delfosse and Jacky Kempenaers, were staged on the main court. They played well, easily defeating the Australian team of Victor Anfiloff and Andrew Schacht, by a score of 15-5. The Belgian crowd was thrilled to see a home team play so well. For the first time in four years, the Main Draw of FIVB World Tour Beach Volleyball in Ostend was played under cloudy skies. This didn't prevent the players from playing sensational beach volleyball. During the second day of main draw competition, eight undefeated teams battled to see who was to make it to the championship match. The American team of Bill Boullianne and Ian Clark, played superb beach volleyball, by asserting a 15-6 win over the Australian pair of Zahner and Prosser. In the first semi-finals match, Brazilians Z-Marco and Ricardo outlasted Americans Boullianne and Clark, by a score of 15-11, in one hour and eleven minutes. The second semi-final match, saw Maia and Brenha handle Child and Heese in forty minutes by a score of 15-9. On a sunny day, the final day of the Belgian FIVB event began with four of the best teams in the world poised to compete in front of a turn-away crowd and a live broadcast on the main national TV channels. The championship match was contested by two teams of Portuguese expression, Z-Marco and Ricardo from Brazil against Maia and Brenha from Portugal. Maia and Brenha surprised the Brazilian champions by taking charge in the first game, winning 12-9. The second game saw Maia and Brenha take a 3-1 lead, before Z-Marco and Ricardo made some great blocks and digs, on their way to a 12-6 win. In the third game tie-breaker, the Portuguese team held on for a 13-11 win. Along with their first place prize of $32,000.00, they earned their first international tournament championship.

3rd Place: John Child and Mark Heese-Canada
4th Place: Bill Boullianne and Ian Clark-USA
5th Place: Jorg Ahmann and Axel Hager-Ger
5th Place: Lee Zahner and Julien Prosser-Aus

Americans Carl Henkel and Kevin Wong along with Sinjin Smith and Ricci Luyties were in the seventeenth spot.

LAUSANNE-VIDY SWITZERLAND
August 14th-16th, 1998

The $30,000.00 "Challenger" event, in Lausanne-Vidy Switzerland, was won by the Brazilian team of Jan Ferreira De Souza and Federico "Fred" Doria de Souza. In the championship match, they outlasted compatriots Dennys Pardes Gomes and Luiz "Luizao" Correa De Jesus, by a score of 17-15, winning $4,000.00 for their efforts.

3rd Place: Morgan Chapman and Greg Ryan-USA
4th Place: Alessandro Rigo and Massimo Marino-Italy
5th Place: Patrick Heuscher and Stephan Kobel-Swiss
5th Place: Martin Fluckiger and Stephan Zimmerman-Swiss

MOSCOW RUSSIA
August 21st-23rd, 1998

The Men's $170,000.00 Men's FIVB World Tour event in Moscow Russia was won by Brazilians Para and Guilherme. Along with the gold medal, they split the $40,000.00 first place check. In the three set championship match, Para and Guilherme defeated the Argentine team of Martinez and Conde. The scores were 12-3, 5-12, and 12-9. The Brazilians earned their way into the final match by defeating the Swiss team of Laciga and Laciga in the semifinals. Martinez and Conde moved into the final by defeating the German team of Ahmann and Hager, 15-6, in their semifinal match.

3rd Place: Jorg Ahmann and Axel Hager-Ger
4th Place: Paul Laciga and Martin Laciga-Swiss
5th Place: Jan Kvalheim and Bjorn Maaseide-Nor
5th Place: Paulo Emilo and Paulo Moreira-Bra

Three American teams finished in thirteenth place. The teams were Carl Henkel and Kevin Wong, Sinjin Smith and Ricci Luyties along with Bill Boullianne and Ian Clark.

ALBENA BULGARIA
August 21st-23rd, 1998

The Albena Bulgaria $30,000.00 "Challenger" event took place. The Italian team of Alissandro Rigo and Massimo Marino won by injury default over the German team of Pierre-Andre' Froehlich and Andreas "Andy" Scheuerpflug. The winner's took home $4,000.00 for their efforts.

3rd Place: Tom Englen and Niclas Tornberg-Sweden
4th Place: Takuya Noguchi and Taichi Morikawa-Japan
5th Place: Fabio Galli and Matteo De Cecco-Italy
5th Place: Bjorn Berg and Simon Dahl-Sweden

The only American team participating, Greg Ryan and Morgan Chapman, finished in ninth place.

CANARY ISLANDS TENERIFE SPAIN
September 3rd-6th, 1998

The first day of main draw competition at the 1998 Beach Volleyball World Tour Spain Men's Open, saw the Australian team of Lee Zahner and Julien Prosser put two strong American AVP teams into the looser's bracket. First they defeated the team of Karch Kiraly and Mike Whitmarsh in a 53 minute match by a score of 16-14. The Australian's then went on to defeat the U.S.A. duo of Dain Blanton and Eric Fonoimoana, also top players from the AVP. The Australians won by a score of 17-15 in another match that lasted 53 minutes. Before losing to the Australians, Kiraly and Whitmarsh beat-up on the Puerto Rican team of Amaury Velasco and Willie "Toro" De Jesus Torres, by a score of 15-3. After losing to the Australians, Blanton and Fonoimoana defeated Velasco and De Jesus, by a score of 15-9. Another American team lost in the first day of competition, but this time it was to another America team. The team of Sinjin Smith and Ricci Luyties lost to Carl Henkel and Kevin Wong by a score of 15-17 in a 68 minute match. After their loss to Henkel and Wong, Smith and Luyties defeated the Japanese team of Takuya Noguchi and Taichi Morikawa by a score of 15-6. Henkel and Wong then lost to the Brazilian team of Emanuel Rego and Jose Loiola, 13-15. Ian Clark and Bill Boullianne were the only team from the U.S.A. to go through the first day of main draw competition without a loss as they posted a 15-6 win over Germany's Charles Dieckmann and Markus Dieckmann. Clark and Boullianne, then defeated Brazil's Para and Guilherme, by a score of 15-8. On the second day, of the main draw competition, teams from the U.S.A. had the following results: Henkel and Wong 15-8 over Brazilians Jan and Paulaol. Henkel and Wong 15-9 over Italians Lione and Ghiurghi. Kiraly and Whitmarsh 15-5 over Germans Dieckmann and Dieckmann Germany. Kiraly and Whitmarsh 15-8 over Canadians Holden and Chaloupka. Blanton and Fonoimoana 15-5 over Brazilians Para and Guilherme. Blanton and Fonoimoana 15-7 over Kjemperud and Hoidalen, from Norway. Clark and Boullianne 15-12 over Kvalheim and Maaseide, from Norway. Smith and Luyties 15-13 over Salema and Baracetti, from Argentina. Smith and Luyties lost 15-17 to Spaniards Bosma and Diez. The AVP team of Rego and Loiola, from Brazil, defeated Martinez and Conde, from Argentina by a score of 15-11. On the third day of the main draw competition, teams from the U.S.A. had the following results: Henkel and Wong 15-10 over Norwegians Kvalheim and Maaseide. Henkel and Wong then lost to Kiraly and Whitmarsh by a score of 15-3. Kiraly and Whitmarsh 15-8 over Canadians Child and Heese. Kiraly and Whitmarsh 17-15 over the Swiss team of Laciga and Laciga. Clark-Boullianne 15-5 over Brazilians Z-Marco and Ricardo. Blanton and Fonoimoana lost to the Brazilian team of Rego and Loiola by a score of 15-5. Rego and Loiola then defeated Bosma and Diez from Spain, then compatriots Marco and Ricardo, by scores of 15-9 and 16-14 respectively. Two North American teams, one Argentine and one Brazilian, passed to semi-finals. Americans Clark and Boullianne and the Argentines Martinez and Conde were the first two teams to qualify for the semi-finals of the

"Beach Volleyball World Tour Spain Open." They reached the semi-finals without losing a match. Through the losers bracket, Kiraly and Whitmarsh along with Brazilians Rego and Loiola were the other semi-finalists, with each looser's bracket finalist, pitted against the winner's bracket finalist. Clark and Boullianne defeated Brazilians Ze Marco and Ricardo 15-5 in 35 minutes while Martinez and Conde defeated the Laciga brothers 15-13 in 43 minutes, but not easily. The Swiss team protested to no avail. They then played tentatively and lost their sharpness as Martinez and Conde forced the Swiss team to make several mistakes and capture the victory. The Swiss team then went on to loose a grueling match against the Americans Kiraly and Whitmarsh, by a score of 15-17. There was a match that took place, with four "1996 Beach Volleyball Olympic-medalist," Karch Kiraly and Mike Whitmarsh (gold & silver) defeating the Canadians John Child and Mark Heese (bronze) 15-8. In another match, the American Fonoimoana against Brazilian Loiola, both "King of the Beach" winners. Last years "K of B" Loiola and partner Rego, defeating Blanton and current "KOB" Fonoimoana 15-5 in 30 minutes. In Las Teresitas, on the final day of the main draw competition, there was another capacity crowd including FIVB President Rubin Acosta in attendance, providing a huge party atmosphere. In the semi-finals, Kiraly and Whitmarsh outlasted Clark and Boullianne by a score of 15-13 in a 45 minute match. It was a strategic match that Clark and Boullianne started strong with a 6-2 lead. Then Kiraly and Whitmarsh changed their tactics and started to attack with finesse instead of power. The score was tied the same as the game, but the result was still undecided, even when Kiraly and Whitmarsh were ahead 13-12. Two awesome blocks by Whitmarsh decided the match at 15-13. In the other semifinal match, Rego and Loiola beat up the Argentine team of Martinez and Conde by a score of 15-3. In the all AVP-Championship match, that lasted 70 minutes, Rego and Loiola prevailed over Kiraly and Whitmarsh by scores of 12-4 and 12-10. The first game, as the score showed, was a game in which the Brazilian power was the key, rattling the Atlanta Olympic medalists. In the second game the team from the U.S.A. played better, but Rego and Loiola continued to display their power as they played at an even higher level to capture the victory.

3rd Place: Ian Clark and Bill Boullianne-USA
4th Place: Eduardo Martinez and Martin Conde-Arg
5th Place: Z-Marco Nobrega and Ricardo Alex Costa Santos-Bra
5th Place: Paul Laciga and Martin Laciga-Swiss

Final U.S.A. finishers: Kiraly and Whitmarsh second place. Clark and Boullianne third place. Henkel and Wong seventh place. Blanton and Fonoimoana ninth place. Smith and Luyties thirteenth place.

ALANYA TURKEY
September 11th-13th, 1998

The FIVB Beach Volleyball Men's World Tour staged its next $170,000.00 event in Alanya Turkey. The Brazilian team of Jose Loiola and Emanuel Rego took the gold medal and $40,000.00 first place prize money. In the championship match, Loiola and Rego handled the Canadian team of Mark Heese and John Child, by scores of 12-7 and 12-8. In the semifinals, Rego and Loiola made it into the final by defeating compatriots ZeMarco and Ricardo, 15-13. Heese and Child made it into the finals with a 15-11 victory over Brazilians Rogerio "Para" de Souza Ferreira and Marques Guilherme Luiz.

3rd Place: Z-Marco Nobrega and Ricardo Alex Costa Santos-Bra
4th Place: Rogerio "Para" de Souza Ferreira and Guilherme Luiz-Bra
5th Place: Lee Zahner and Julien Prosser-Aus
5th Place: Luis Maia and Joao Brenha-Port

The top finish by an American team was seventh by Dain Blanton and Eric Fonoimoana. Additional USA finishes, included: Ian Clark and Bill Boullianne in ninth place, Sinjin Smith and Ricci Luyties in seventeenth place, Carl Henkel and Kevin Wong in twenty-fifth place.

VITORIA BRAZIL
December 3rd-6th, 1998

The final Men's FIVB World Series event took place at Vitoria Brazil. The Brazilian team of Rogerio "Para" de Souza Ferreira and Marques Guilherme Luiz were the winners of the gold medal and first place check worth $40,000.00. In the three set championship match, Para and Guilherme outlasted compatriots Franco Neto and Roberto Lopes. The final scores were 10-12, 12-11, and 21-19. Para and Guilherme moved to the final match by outlasting the Swiss team of Laciga and Laciga, in the semifinals, by a score of 15-13. Franco and Lopes got there with a 15-7 semifinal victory over Salema and Baracetti, from Argentina.

3rd Place: Jose Luis Salema Abrantes and Mariano Baracetti-Arg
4th Place: Paul Laciga and Martin Laciga-Swiss
5th Place: Jose Loiola and Emanuel Rego-Bra
5th Place: Eduardo Esteban "Mono" Martinez and Martin Alejo Conde-Arg

The best American finish was by Carl Henkel and Kevin Wong along with Ian Clark and Bill Boullianne, in ninth place. Additional American finishes, included: Dain Blanton and Eric Fonoimoana along with Canyon Ceman and Adam Jewell in thirteenth place. Sinjin Smith and Rob Heidger finished in the twenty-fifth spot.

ANDRE KJEMPERUD & VEGARD HOIDALEN
Norwegians Andre Kjemperod and Vegard Hoidalen were the surprise team on the 1998 FIVB Tour when they won the "Gold-Medal" at the 1998 FIVB Tour event in Berlin Germany. Above photo, Kjemperod (left) and Hoidalen (right) celebrate a win.
Photo Courtesy of the FIVB

MEN'S TOURNAMENT RESULTS
1998-GOODWILL GAMES

NEW YORK U.S.A
July 22nd-26th, 1998

Since it's inception in 1986, the **Goodwill Games** have alternated between the U.S.A. and Russia. The first took place in Moscow Russia. Other past sites include the U.S.A.'s Seattle Washington in 1990 and Russia's Saint Petersburg Russia in 1994. The 1998 Goodwill Games featured two-man beach volleyball as an event. The Goodwill Games men's beach volleyball competition is a sanctioned event on the FIVB Beach Volleyball World Tour and featured $100,000.00 in prize money. The men's event took place at Wollman Rink Stadium, located in South Central Park in the heart of Manhattan. The stadium was filled with almost 500 tons of sand as it was transformed into a 3,000 seat beach court with skyscrapers in the background. The top seven ranked men's teams in the FIVB Beach Volleyball World Ranking plus a wild card team from the U.S.A. competed for the $100,000.00 prize money. The Participating teams were:

GROUP A
U.S.A.: Karch Kiraly and Adam Johnson (wildcard)
U.S.A.: Sinjin Smith and Ricci Luyties
Brazil: Para Ferreira Souza and Guilherme Marques
Canada: John Child and Mark Heese

GROUP B
Norway: Jan Kvalheim and Bjorn Maaseide
Argentina: Esteban Martinez and Martin Conde
Switzerland: Martin Laciga and Paul Laciga
Australia: Julien Prosser and Lee Zahner

Each group of four teams played a round-robin competition of three matches within its own group. The first and second place finishers from each group advanced to the medal round that determined places one through four.

Norwegians Jan Kvalheim and Bjorn Maaseide, opened with a win 15-13 win over Australians Julien Prosser and Leo Zahner. Kvalheim and Maaseide, the third-ranked team on the 1998 FIVB Tour, rallied from a 10-8 deficit

KARCH KIRALY
Karch Kiraly teamed-up with Adam Johnson at the 1998 Goodwill Games, staged in New York City. Kiraly and Johnson lost in the championship match to the Brazilian team of Guilherme Marques and Rogerio Para. Above photo. Kiraly attacking the ball.
Photo Courtesy of the FIVB

GUILHERME MARQUES
Brazilian Guilherme Marques paired-up with countryman Rogerio Para Ferreira to win the "Gold-Medal" at the 1998 Goodwill Games, staged in New York's Central Park. Above photo, Marques challenges the block of Karch Kiraly.
Photo Courtesy of the FIVB

to tie the match at 10-all. The two teams were still tied at 13-all as the 1994 Goodwill winners scored the last two points of the match.

Also during the men's opening round, which was played in hazy, hot and humid 94 degree weather, beach volleyball teams of Martin Conde and Esteban Martinez from Argentina along with the U.S.A.'s Adam Johnson and Karch Kiraly scored round-robin pool play wins. In their opening "Group B" match, Conde and Martinez, ran off 7 straight points against Martin and Paul Laciga of Switzerland to take a commanding 13-5 lead. The Argentina tandem posted a 15-6 win. Kiraly and Johnson scored a 15-8 win over John Child and Mark Heese of Canada in a Group "A" match.

The Brazilian team of Guilherme and Para showed how strong they were when they opened with a 15-2 win over the American team of Sinjin Smith and Ricci Luyties.

On the second day of competition, the Brazilians downed Johnson and Kiraly 15-3 in Group A play. Guilherme and Para were they only unbeaten team, in the 1998 Goodwill Games, posting a 3-0 record in round-robin play along with Saturday's victory over their South American rivals Johnson and Kiraly were 3-1 this week, including a 2-1 pool play mark. Martin Conde and Esteban Martinez of Argentina won their second men's beach volleyball match of the 1998 Goodwill Games on this second day, while Canadian's John Child and Mark Heese posted their first win. The second day's afternoon session was delayed for 90 minutes due to rain after Conde and Martinez upset Norway's Jan Kvalheim and Bjorn Maaseide 16-14 in a 79-minute, 105-sideout match. The Argentina tandem took an 11-9 lead 56 minutes into the match before Kvalheim and Maaseide rallied to take a 14-13 edge with 63 minutes gone in the match. Conde and Martinez scored the final three points of the match with a pair of Conde kills. After the rain-delay, Child and Heese led from the start to down Ricci Luyties and Sinjin Smith of the U.S.A. 15-5.

The third day of competition brought an all-American a 63-minute match that featured four ties and 84-sideouts, Johnson and Kiraly rallied from a 3-0 deficit at the start to take an 11-7 lead over Ricci Luyties and Sinjin Smith. The match was tied at 12-12 and 14-14 before Johnson's service ace and Kiraly's kill netted the win. Martin and Paul Laciga of Switzerland eliminated Jan Kvalheim and Bjorn Maaseide of Norway from medal contention, lifting Conde and Martinez into the medal round. The Laciga's rallied from a 14-11 deficit to score a 16-14 decision over Kvalheim and Maaseide to oust the Goodwill Games defending champions from medal contention. The Norwegians had to win the match by four points or better against the Swiss to advance. It was not to be as the Laciga's mounted a "tremendous" comeback to tie Kvalheim and Maaseide in the Group B standings with 1-2 marks. The Norwegians had a better point differential (minus-2 to minus-9) to earn a spot in the fifth-sixth playoff, while the Laciga's played for seventh in the overall Goodwill Games standings.

With the Swiss win, Conde and Martinez advanced as the second-place Group B team while Prosser and Zahner of Australia won the pool. Both teams tied with 2-1 marks with the Aussies having a point differential edge (plus-8 to plus-3). Prosser and Zahner downed Conde and Martinez 15-7 in the third days first match before the Brazilians rallied to defeat John Child and Mark Heese of Canada 15-11. Guilherme and Para, the top-rated team on the 1998 FIVB Beach Volleyball World Tour, were down 6-0 to the Canadians before rallying to take a 10-9 lead. The two teams were tied at 11-11 before Brazil scored the last four points.

On the fourth day of competition, Kiraly and Johnson advanced to the finals with a 12-2 and 12-10 semi-final win over Australian's Julien Prosser and Leo Zahner in a 77-minute semi-final match. They led from the start to win the first set easily. Prosser and Zahner made a match of it in the second set by tying Johnson and Kiraly at 9 all and 10 all, before succumbing to the pressure of the match. In the other semi-final match, Guilherme and Para, the top-ranked team on the 1998 FIVB Beach Volleyball World Tour, downed Conde and Martinez of Argentina 12-5 and 12-10 in a 79-minute contest. The Brazilians led from the start in each game as Conde and Martinez made it interesting, in the second game, after trailing 11-4.

On the fifth day of competition, in the championship match, Brazilians Guilherme Marques and Para Ferreira captured the Gold medal at the 1998 Goodwill Games in Central Park at Wollman Rink. The Brazilians scored a 12-11 and 12-4 win over Americans Adam Johnson and Karch Kiraly to share the $30,000.00 first-

FAN SUPPORT
In New York Cities Central Park, There was no shortage of patriotism at the 1998 Goodwill Games. Above photo, the USA teams of Karch Kiraly with Adam Johnson and Sinjin Smith with Ricci Luyties enjoyed the support from these USA fans.
Photo Courtesy of the FIVB

place prize. Kiraly and Johnson settled for the $20,000.00 second-place prize in this $100,000.00 FIVB Beach Volleyball World Tour event. The Brazilian's won the 55-minute first set 12-11 on Para's block of Johnson. Guilherme and Para had led 11-9 before the United States tied the count at 11 all. They led from the start in the 52-minute second set to capture the Gold Medal. Guilherme and Para, were the only unbeaten team in the 1998 Goodwill Games with a 5-0 record.

Earlier, In the Goodwill Games' Bronze medal match, Argentina's Martin Conde and Esteban Martinez downed Julien Prosser and Leo Zahner of Australia 12-11 and 12-9 to share the $15,000.00 third-place prize money. The Aussies shared $11,000.00 for fourth place.

Norway's Jan Kvalheim and Bjorn Maaseide scored a 15-13 win over John Child and Mark Heese of Canada to capture fifth-place. The Norwegians, who won the 1994 Goodwill Games Gold medal in St. Petersburg, Russia, shared the $8,000.00 purse for fifth-place while Child and Heese, the Bronze medalists at the 1996 Atlanta Olympic Games, split $7,000.00 for sixth. Martin and Paul Laciga of Switzerland scored a 15-7 win over Ricci Luyties and Sinjin Smith of the United States to earn seventh-place in the competition. The Swiss split $5,000.00 while Luyties and Smith shared $4,000.00.

Both medal matches featured the FIVB's Format B with two out of three sets to 12 points. The first two sets must be won with a minimum lead of two points with a point limit at the 12-point cap. The deciding set featured the rally scoring system to 12 points with a minimum lead of two points. There was no point cap for the deciding set.

SINJIN SMITH
Sinjin Smith still had some levitation left in him, at the 1998 Goodwill Games, where he finished in 8th place with Ricci Luyties. Above photo, Smith makes an all-out effort to levitate for the diving-dig.
Photo Courtesy of the FIVB

1998 GOODWILL GAMES
MEN'S BEACH VOLLEYBALL RESULTS:

DAY #1
July 22nd, 1998
MEN'S GROUP "A" MATCHES:
GAME #1: The American team of Kiraly and Johnson defeated the team from Canada, Child and Heese, by a score of 15-8.
GAME #2: The Brazilian team of Para and Guiherme defeated the American team of Sinjin Smith and Luyties by a score of 15-2.

MEN'S GROUP "B" MATCHES:
GAME #1: The Norweigian team of Kvalheim and Maaseide defeated the Australian team of Prosser and Zahner by a score of 15-13.
GAME #2: The Argentine team of Martinez and Conde defeated the Swiss team of M. Laciga and P. Laciga by a score of 15-6.

DAY #2
July 23rd, 1998
MEN'S GROUP "A" MATCHES:
GAME #1: The Canadian team of Child and Heese defeated the American team of Sinjin Smith and Luyties by a score of 15-5.
GAME #2: The Brazilian team of Para and Guilherme defeated the American team of Kiraly and Johnson by a score of 15-3.

MEN'S GROUP "B" MATCHES:
GAME #1: The Argentine team of Martinez and Conde defeated the team from the Norway, Kvalheim and Maaseide, by a score of 16-14.
GAME #2: The Australian team of Prosser and Zahner defeated the Swiss team of M. Laciga and P. Laciga by a score of 15-13.

DAY #3
July 24th, 1998
MEN'S GROUP "A" MATCHES:
GAME #1: The Brazilian team of Para and Guilherme defeated the team from the Canada, Child and Heese, by a score of 15-11.
GAME #2: In an all-American match-up, the team of Kiraly and Johnson defeated the team of Sinjin Smith and Luyties by a score of 16-14.

MEN'S GROUP "B" MATCHES:
GAME #1: The Australian team of Prosser and Zahner defeated the team from Argentina, Martinez and Conde, by a score of 15-7.
GAME #2: The Swiss team of M. Laciga and P. Laciga defeated the Norwegian team of Kvalheim and Maaseide by a score of 16-14.

DAY #4
July 25th, 1998
GAME FOR 7TH AND 8TH PLACE
The Swiss team of M. Laciga and P.Laciga defeated the American team of Sinjin Smith and Luyties by a score of 15-7.

GAME FOR 5TH AND 6TH PLACE
Kvalheim-Maaseide, from Norway, defeated Child and Heese, from the Canada, by a score of 15-13.

SEMI-FINAL MATCHES:
GAME #1: The American team of Kiraly and Johnson outlasted the Australian team of Zahner and Prosser by scores of 12-2, 12-10.
GAME #2: The Brazilian team of Para and Guilherme defeated the Argentine team of Martinez and Conde by scores of 12-5 and 12-10.

DAY #5
July 26th, 1998
BRONZE MEDAL GAME
The team of Martinez and Conde, from Argentina, won the 1998 Goodwill Games Bronze Medal, for beach volleyball, by defeating the Australian team of Zahner and Prosser by scores of 12-11 and 12-9, in the match for third place.

GOLD MEDAL GAME
The Brazilian team of Para and Guilherme won the 1998 Goodwill Games Gold Medal, for beach volleyball, with their victory over the American team of Kiraly and Johnson by scores of 12-11 and 12-4, in the match for the championship.

MEN'S TOURNAMENT RESULTS
1998-CBVA

PLAYA DEL REY CALIFORNIA
March 21st, 1998
PLAYA DEL REY MEN'S AAA
1st Place: Mark Paaluhi and Nick Hannemann
2nd Place: Carl Henkel and Bruk Vandeweghe
3rd Place: John Anselmo and Shawn Davis
3rd Place: Greg Ryan and Doug Smith

CAPISTRANO CALIFORNIA
April 18th, 1998
CAPISTRANO BEACH MEN'S AAA
1st Place: Justin Pearlstrom and Mike Garcia
2nd Place: Dane Pearson and Scott Davenport
3rd Place: Duane Cameron and Sean Fallowfield

PLAYA DEL REY CALIFORNIA
April 25th, 1998
PLAYA DEL VOLLEYBALL FESTIVAL MEN'S AAA
1st Place: Jose Pepe Delahoz and Juan Rodriguez
2nd Place: Justin Perlstrom and Mike Garcia
3rd Place: Scott Davenport and dane Pearson
3rd Place: Doug Grove and Dave Becker

SANTA MONICA CALIFORNIA
May 2nd, 1998
SANTA MONICA PIER MEN'S AAA
1st Place: Julien Prosser and Lee Zahner
2nd Place: John Hirbar and Dan Ortega
3rd Place: Brian Meckna and John Braunstein
3rd Place: Jon Beerman and Erik Pichel

SAN DIEGO CALIFORNIA
May 16th-17th, 1998
The 1998 Ocean Beach "Bud Light Volleyball Festival" Men's "AAA" was won by Juan Rodriguez and Jose "Pepe" DeLahoz. In the championship final, they defeated the German team of Axel Hager and Jorge Ahman. George Stepanof was the tournament director of this tournament that had 18 teams participate.
3rd Place: Kenny Lentin and Mike Rosen
3rd Place: Lavelle Carter and Said Souikane

PLAYA DEL REY CALIFORNIA
May 9th, 1998
PLAYA DEL REY MEN'S AAA
1st Place: Pepe Delahoz and Jeff Rodriguez
2nd Place: Jason Hughes and Christian Kiernan
3rd Place: Randall Koerv and Jack Quinn

SANTA CRUZ CALIFORNIA
May 23rd-24th, 1998
The "Cal-King" Pro Beach Volleyball Tour kicked off their 1998 summer beach volleyball season in Santa Cruz, California on the weekend of May 23th-24th. This inaugural event saw a final that took on an "International" flair rather than the expected Nor-Cal versus So-Cal battle. In the championship match, the Canadian twosome of Evi Matthews and Mark Reilly soundly defeated their Brazilian counterparts, Wesley Defreitas and Pedro Brazao. The Brazilians, in California for the

MARK PAALUHI
Mark Paaluhi paired-up with Nick Hannemann to win the championship match, against Carl Henkel and Bruk vandeweghe, at the 1998 Playa Del Rey Men's "AAA" tournament. Above photo, Paaluhi challenges the block of Kevin Wong at an AVP event.
Photo Courtesy of "Couvi"

JOHN ANSELMO
John Anselmo teamed-up with Shawn Davis for a third place finishe at the 1998 Playa Del Rey Men's "AAA" tournament. They were tied with Greg Ryan and Doug Smith. Above photo, Anselmo, an excellent passer, gets ready to pass the ball.
Photo Courtesy of the AVP

summer from Brazil, had marched through the rest of the field with their power game and ripping jump serves. The Canadians, however, had the Brazilians' number supported by steady side-out play and plenty of tough serving of their own while jumping out to a 11-0 lead in the final before waltzing the rest of the way for the $1,000.00 first place prize money and the prestige of being the best on the beach. An estimated 20,000 Memorial Day weekend vacationers were exposed to the first ever CAL-KING event in Santa Cruz. The tournament saw eight teams advance from pool play on the first day of competition to make it to the double elimination format on the final day. The competition was intense on both days.

3rd Place: Sean Scott and Mike "Rock" Matterocci
4th Place: Sean DeLapp and Kjell Nillsen

SANTA MONICA CALIFORNIA
June 6th, 1998
WILL ROGERS MEN'S AAA

1st Place: Jasiu Bulkowski and Bart Bachorski
2nd Place: Koh Ozaki and Tomohisa
3rd Place: Christian Kiernan and Shane Davis

SAN DIEGO CALIFORNIA
May 30th, 1999

The 1999 Ocean Beach "Redsand" Men's "AAA" was won by John Braunstein and Chris Oitzak. In the championship match, they defeated Ken Lentin and Mike Rosen. George Stepanof was the tournament director of this tournament that had 25 teams participate. 3rd Place: Chris Walmer and Curtis Jacson

SANTA CRUZ CALIFORNIA
June 13th, 1998
SANTA CRUZ BUD LIGHT VOLLEYBALL FESTIVAL
Men's AAA

1st Place: Chris Larson and Andrew Cavanaugh
2nd Place: Ernie Sandidige and Nathan Brown
3rd Place: John Hancock and Jeff Alzina
3rd Place: Tate Walthall and Zachary Small

DOHENY BEACH
June 13th, 1998
Men's AAA

1st Place: Brent Doble and Dan Castillo
2nd Place: Scott Friederichsen and Troy Tanner
3rd Place: Sean Fallowfield and Scott Lane

HERMOSA BEACH CALIFORNIA
June 13th-14th, 1998

The Cal-King Pro Beach Volleyball Tour's second event was staged in the lively and picturesque beach town of Hermosa Beach. Hermosa does not take its beach volleyball lightly, they flat out worship the sport as well as the players that the town harbors who just happen to be the cream of the crop in beach volleyball. Cal-King matches are played old school style with games to 15, win by two, and no point cap. Cal-King events also include a double final. In the championship match, the highly ranked and favored AVP squad of Henry Russell and Mark Kerins, winners of the Cape Cod Massachusetts AVP event held less than a year ago, was not able to claim the King of the Beach honors as the hot team of Juan "El Guapo" Rodriguez and Mike Garcia, fresh off their ninth place AVP finish in Sacramento the week before, took home the Hermosa Cal-King crown. There was a nice crowd that turned out to witness this top quality event. The crowd was not disappointed. On center court they saw three overtime matches in a row starting with the 18-16 winners bracket final match. Rodriguez and Garcia were able to prevail over the team of Russell/Kerins despite being down 15-14 as they fought off a number of match point tries by Russell and Kerins and were able to salvage victory. Then in the loser's bracket final, Russell and Kerins were able to turn the tables on the talented AVP team of Mark Paaluhi and Leland Quinn, by rallying from a 14-11 deficit to take the match by another 18-16 score, this time in their favor. The long matches might have taken it out of Russell and Kerins who put up a valiant effort in the final before eventually falling to the winning team of Rodriguez and Garcia. The winners collected $1,000.00 for their effort.

LAGUNA BEACH CALIFORNIA
June 20th, 1998
LAGUNA BEACH MEN'S AAA

1st Place: Brian Meckna and Dave Becker
2nd Place: Anthony Medel and Jason Lee
3rd Place: Scott Sjoquist and Matthew Taylor

CORONA DEL MAR CALIFORNIA
July 11th, 1998

The 1998 Corona del Mar Men's "AAA" was won by Mark Williams and Larry Witt. In the championship match, they defeated Jack Quinn and Randall Koerv.
3rd Place: Brian Meckna and Dave Becker

CAPISTRANO BEACH CALIFORNIA
July 18th, 1998

The 1998 Capistrano Beach Men's "AAA" was won by Jessie Brown and Aaron Hansen. In the championship match, they defeated Brian Meckna and Dave Becker.
3rd Place: William Harris and Bob Baker

VENTURA CALIFORNIA
July 11th, 1998
Ventura Cal Cup Men's Open

1st Place: Mike Rosen and Dave Counts
2nd Place: Steve Vanderveen and Shawn Essert
3rd Place: Laurence Ceccerelli and Jason Lee
3rd Place: Anthony Medel and Raymond Morain

CORONA DEL MAR CALIFORNIA
July 11th, 1998
Men's AAA Corona del Mar

1st Place: Larry Witt and Mark Williams
2nd Place: Jack Quinn and Randall Koerv
3rd Place: Dave Becker and Brian Meckna

CAPISTRANO BEACH CALIFORNIA
July 18th, 1998
Men's AAA Capistrano Beach

1st Place: Jesse Brown and Aaron Hanson
2nd Place: Brian Meckna and Dave Becker
3rd Place: William Harris and Bob Baker

SANTA CRUZ CALIFORNIA
July 25, 1998
Men's AAA Santa Cruz

1st Place: Sean Delapp and Jason Faughn
2nd Place: Mark Tanner and Phil Melese
3rd Place: Sean Wilson and Dave Werdmuller

MANHATTAN BEACH CALIFORNIA
July 25th, 1998
Manhattan Open - Men's AAA

1st Place: Sean Scott and Pepe Delahoz
2nd Place: Tim Hovland and Brandon Taliaferro
3rd Place: Chris Makos and Andrew Vazquez

TOP PHOTOS: Left: Eric Fonoimoana attacking the ball. **Center:** Dain Blanton serving one of the hardest jump-serves on the AVP Tour. **Right:** Troy Tanner attacking the block of Eric Fonoimoana.

MIDDLE PHOTOS: Left: Bill "Beef" Boullianne spiking the ball. **Center:** Emanuel Rego gets above the net to reject the hit by Adam Johnson. **Right:** Mark Paaluhi hits the ball past the block of Lee LeGrande.

1998 MEN'S BEACH VOLLEYBALL ACTION

BOTTOM PHOTOS: Left: Jim Nichols reaches above the net to spike the ball. **Center:** Dax Holdren attacking the block of Kent Steffes. **Right:** Brian "Lewey" Lewis, one of the all-time best AVP Tour setters, dishing-up some nectar.
Top photos courtesy of "Couvi" Middle and Bottom Photo's Courtesy of the AVP

WOMEN'S BEACH VOLLEYBALL
1998

WPVA

In 1998, the Women's Professional Volleyball Association (WPVA) announced that San Diego investor Charles Jackson was withdrawing his financial support to do seven women's beach volleyball events in 1998. Jackson's plan was to combine the women's two person and four person players in a series of seven events throughout the country. Although citing that difficulty of securing television coverage and sponsorship so late in the year as the reasons for his withdraw, sources claim lack of cooperation from the WPVA was the primary reason for his pull-out. With a tour already delayed till after June, and prospects of a prize purse that will barely cover the player's costs, this is the latest in a series of problems that plagued the failing league. The Womens Professional Volleyball Association (WPVA) was formed in 1986 in order to administer, govern, and protect the integrity of Women's Professional Beach Volleyball. The WPVA was dissolved on April 6, 1998 after 11 seasons.

1998 WPVA SCHEDULE

WHEN:	WHERE:
April 4-5	Deerfield Beach, Fla.
April 18-19	Clearwater, Fla.
May 2-3	South Padre, Texas
May 16-17	Austin, Texas
May 30-31	Hermosa Beach, CA
June 13-14	San Jose, CA
June 27-28	San Diego, CA
July 4-5	Chicago, Ill.
July 11-12	Muskegon, Mich.
July 25-26	Huntington Beach CA
August 15-16	Vancouver, B.C.
August 22-23	UCLA event
Sept. 5-6	site TBD
Sept. 12-13	Las Vegas or New York
Sept. 26-27	Kauai or Maui, HI

THE ABOVE SCHEDULE WAS CANCELED!!!

LISA ARCE
In 1998, Without a Domestic Tour to show her tallents, last year's top WPVA team, Lisa Arce with Holly McPeak, took advantage of the opportunity to play at the 1998 "Best-Of-The-Beach" event in Huntington Beach CA. McPeak finishe 3rd, while Arce was the big winner, collecting $30,000.00 for her efforts. Above photo, Arce puts-up a huge block against McPeak's hit.
Photo Courtesy of Frank Goroszko

BARBRA FONTANA & HOLLY McPEAK
In 1998, Without a Domestic Tour to compete on, Barbra Fontana, along with Holly McPeak, Lisa Arce as well as others, took advantage of the opportunity to play at the 1998 "Best-Of-The-Beach" event in Huntington Beach CA. Fontana finished 2nd while McPeak finishe 3rd. Above photo, McPeak attempts to poke the ball over the block of Fontana.
Photo Courtesy of Frank Goroszko

AMERICAN VOLLEYBALL LEAGUE

After the demise of the female player's WPVA domestic tour, the United States' women's pro beach volleyball players were almost "saved" by Trident Media Group, Inc. of Carlsbad, California with the formation of the Trident's American Volleyball League. The AVL was licensed by Trident to host the women's professional beach volleyball tour in the United States. The AVL's mission was to provide a stable environment for the women pro-beach volleyball players to perform, including world class venues, and substantial prize packages. The American Volleyball League was scheduled to kick off its first event, the $100,000 Del Mar Open, at the Del Mar Open Air Arena, in Del Mar, California, on August 28-30th, 1998 The event was supposed to be a thirty-two (32) team open competition, but the tournament was canceled along with the proposed 1999 AVL schedule.

AVL-1999
(American Volleyball League)
1999 Proposed AVL Schedule

WHEN	WHERE
March 26-28	Daytona Beach, Florida
April 2-4	Deerfield Beach, Florida
April 9-11	Clearwater, Florida
April 27- May 1	Louisville, Kentucky
May 7-9	Indianapolis, Indianapolis
May 21-23	Texas site to be announced
June 7-9	Milwaukee, Wisconsin or Muskegon, Michigan
July 9-11	Seattle, Washington
August 13-15	Atlantic City, New Jersey
August 27-29	Del Mar, California
September 10-12	Las Vegas, Nevada

THE ABOVE SCHEDULE WAS CANCELED!!

1998 BEST OF THE BEACH
HUNTINGTON BEACH CALIFORNIA
July 17th-19th, 1998

The only chance, for the top American women beach players to win some prize money, domestically, came at the 1998 "OP Beast of the Beach Invitational." The event featured the following players: #1 seed Lisa Arce, #2 seed Holly McPeak, #3 seed Nancy Reno, #4 seed Barbra Fontana, #5 seed Linda Hanley, #6 seed Angela Rock, #7 seed Karrie Poppinga, #8 seed Christine Schaefer, #9 seed Krista Blomquist, #10 seed Deb Richardson, #11 seed Gayle Stammer, #12 seed Gail Castro, #13 seed Elaine Youngs, #14 seed Patti Dodd.

Top-seeded Lisa Arce won the 1998 OP Best of the Beach Invitational after winning all three of her matches in Sunday's final round. Despite being seeded first via a coin flip with Holly McPeak, Arce entered the final round in third place based on tiebreakers from Saturday's play. Arce's fate wasn't in doubt for long as she captured her 12th career title by winning all three matches handily, as no team scored more than 10 points against her. With this victory, Lisa had earned 11 titles in the last 17 domestic beach volleyball events. The competition kicked off the Op Beach Festival in Huntington Beach, California. "P.S. Star-Games" a Marina del Rey sports marketing and management company staged the three-day competition that featured 14 of the top ranked players in women's pro-beach volleyball.

Arce won a total of $30,000.00, by far the largest single payday in domestic women's pro beach volleyball. The previous high was $15,750.00 by McPeak and Nancy Reno in New York in 1996. Sixth-seeded Angela Rock finished second, earning $15,000.00. Holly McPeak, who was the second seed, tied for third along with Barbra Fontana. They took home $13,000.00 each. Arce, McPeak and Fontana all reside in Manhattan Beach, and all three are graduates of Mira Costa High School. When the three players finished with a 1-2 record, tying for second place, as point differential from their first six matches was used to determine placement. Rock ended with a +5 mark, while McPeak and Fontana both had +3 tallies. The final day's opening match saw Arce reunited with her usual partner, McPeak. Arce and McPeak used their chemistry to claim a 15-10 victory. There were four ties early, but Arce and McPeak outlasted Fontana and Rock down the stretch. Arce had three blocks in the match while McPeak added three points directly from serves. In the second match, between McPeak and Fontana vs Arce and Rock, the score was tied at 1-1 and 2-2 when Arce and Rock reeled off seven straight points in route to a 15-4 win. Rock helped the cause by recording 13 kills.

In the last match of the day, Arce and Fontana went on a 5-0 run to take a 10-5 lead over McPeak and Rock. The match had 76 sideouts when the nine-minute playing clock expired with Arce and Fontana holding a 12-9 lead. Fontana led the way with a "tournament-best" 24 kills and added 12 digs. The $100,000.00 OP Best of the Beach Invitational was televised Nationally, on a delayed basis, on ESPN and ESPN 2. Chris Marlowe and veteran player Chris Schaefer provided the commentary.

TOURNAMENT SUMMARY
1st Day -Friday
Patti Dodd and Deb Richardson defeated Kerri Poppinga and Gail Stammer 15-3.
Gail Castro and Chris Schaefer defeated Krista Blomquist and Elaine Youngs 15-10.
Richardson and Stammer defeated Dodd and Poppinga 15-8.
Schaefer and Youngs defeated Blomquist and Castro 15-4.
Poppinga and Richardson defeated Dodd and Stammer 15-12.
Castro and Youngs defeated Blomquist and Schaefer 15-9.
Richardson and Schaefer advanced.

2nd Day Saturday
Nancy Reno and Angela Rock defeated Holly McPeak and Deb Richardson 14-12 as time expired.
Lisa Arce and Elaine Youngs defeated Barbra Fontana and Linda Hanley 14-12 as time expired.
McPeak and Rock defeated Reno and Richardson 15-8.
Fontana and Youngs defeated Arce and Hanley 15-9.
McPeak and Reno defeated Rock and Richardson 15-8.
Arce and Fontana defeated Hanley and Youngs 15-3.
Fontana, McPeak, Arce, and Rock advanced to the final day of competition.

3rd Day Sunday
Lisa Arce and Holly McPeak defeated Fontana and Rock 15-10. Arce and Rock defeated Fontana and McPeak 15-4. Arce and Fontana defeated McPeak and Rock 12-9 as the time clock expired.

FIVB

The 1998 FIVB Pro-Beach Volleyball Season included six new events on the World Tour Calendar. Players from more than 50 countries competed for more than $4 million in prize money. There were 9 women's events carrying a total jackpot of $1,550,000.00. The women gained parity with the men with eight of the nine events being worth $170,000.00, an increase of $50,000.00 on the 1997 figure. The newly-introduced Canadian Open carried the biggest prize money of $190,000.00. The Canadian Open, which was staged in Toronto June 19th-21st, 1998 also appeared on the men's calendar for the first time. The other new women's event was the China Open which was introduced on the women's circuit. A women's beach volleyball tournament was included in the Goodwill Games, played on the courts set-up in New York's Central Park. There was $100,000.00 in prize money. Each to the eight best nations in the World Ranking from July 29th-August 2nd, 1998 participated.

1998 FIVB WOMEN PLAYERS
TOP 50 FIVB WOMEN PLAYERS
(Start OF 1998)

Adriana Behar-Brazil	Shelda-Brazil
Adriana Samuel-Brazil	Monica-Brazil
Lisa Arce -USA	Holly McPeak-USA
Jackie Silva-Brazil	Sandra Pires-Brazil
Cook-AUS	Pottharst-AUS
Friedrichsen-GER	Musch-GER
Barbra Fontana-USA	Bruschini-ITA
Solazzi-ITA	Nancy Reno-USA
Celbova -CZE	Dosoudilova-CZE
Linda Hanley-USA	Liz Masakayan-USA
Elaine Youngs-USA	Kerrie Poppinga-USA
Angela Rock-USA	Fenwick-AUS
Drakich-CAN	Adriana Bento-Brazil
Takahashi-JPN	Manser-AUS
Magda-Brazil	Siomara-Brazil
Dumont-CAN	Bragado-USA
Clarke-AUS	Karolyn Kirby-USA
Schaefer-USA	Traton-AUS
Ishizaka-JPN	Ana Richa-Brazil
Gattelli-ITA	Perrotta-ITA
Nascimento-ITA	Kadijk R.-NED
Schoon Kadijk-NED	Huygens Tholen-AUS
Wilson-AUS	Hudcova-CZE
Tobiasova-CZE	Blomquist-USA
De Marinis-ITA	Teru Saiki-JPN

1998 FIVB BEACH VOLLEYBALL SCHEDULE
WOMEN

When	Where	Prize Money
Feb 26- Mar1	Rio de Janerio Brazil	$ 80,000.00
June 19-21	Toronto Canada	$100,000.00
Jul 3-5	Vasto Italy	$ 80,000.00
Jul 23-26	Marseille France	$ 80,000.00
July 29-Aug 2	New York U.S.A. Goodwill Games	$100,000.00
July 31-Aug 2	Espinho Portugal	$ 80,000.00
Aug 7-9	Osaka Japan	$ 80,000.00
Aug 14-16	Pusan Korea	$ 80,000.00
TBA	China	$ 80,000.00
Oct 22-25	Salvador Brazil	$ 80,000.00
Nov 13-15	Kuah Mas (Langkawi)	$ 80,000.00

INDIVIDUAL FIVB TOURNAMENT FINISHES
1998

Player	1st	2nd	3rd	4th	5th
Lisa Arce	0	1	2	0	1
SheldaKellyBruno Bede	5	2	0	0	0
AdrianaBrandao Behar	5	2	0	0	0
Laura Bruschini	0	0	0	2	0
Angela Clarke	0	0	0	0	2
Natalie Cook	0	0	0	0	3
Liane Fenwick	0	0	0	0	1
Maike Friedrichsen	0	0	0	1	2
Linda Robertson Hanley	1	1	0	3	1
Barbra Fontana	1	1	0	3	1
Tania Gooley	0	0	0	0	2
DeboraSchoon Kadijk	0	0	0	0	1
R. Kadijk	0	0	0	0	1
Karolyn Kirby	0	0	0	0	1
Pauline Manser	0	1	1	1	0
Liz Masakayan	0	0	0	0	3
Holly McPeak	0	1	2	0	1
Danja Musch	0	0	0	1	2
SandraTavares Pires	2	2	3	0	0
KerriAnn Pottharst	0	1	1	1	0
Nancy Reno	0	0	1	0	0
Monica Rodrigues	0	1	1	1	2
Mika Teru Saiki	0	0	0	0	1
AdrianaRamos Samuel	2	2	2	0	1
Nicole Sanderson	0	0	0	0	2
Ulrike Schmidt	0	0	0	0	1
JacquelineLouise"Jackie"Cruz Silva	0	1	2	1	1
Annamaria Solazzi	0	0	0	2	0
Gudula Staub	0	0	0	0	1
Yukiko Takahashi	0	0	0	0	1
Ali Wood	0	0	0	0	1
Elaine Youngs	0	0	1	0	2

CBVA

Because of the demise of domestic women's professional beach volleyball tours, some of the top women beach player's participated on the CBVA Tour. The list below consist of some of the most successful players on the 1998 CBVA Tour.

Krysta Attwood	Mary Baily
Sarah Beyer	Andrea Beylen
Lynda Black	Vicki Bonin
Joy Burkholder	JB Burrell
Linda Burton	Carrie Busch
Jackie Campbell	Gail Castro
Alicia Chung	Ilga Clemins
Evelyn Conley	Erin Deiters
Guylaine Dumont	Rachel Errthum
Karen Helyer	Laura Higgins
Valinda Hilleary	Judy Hissong
Jennifer Holdren	Sue Holmes
Cassie Hyatt	Julie James
Jenny Johnson	Deia Kadlubek
Angie Kammer	Rhonda Kottke
Tracy Lindquist	Christine Lusser
Nancy Mason	Sandy Matthews
Jackie McCabe	Marsha Miller
Michelle Morse	Stephanie Nelson
Chastity Nobriga	Barb Nyland
Barb Ovellette	Liz Pagano.
Jenny Pavley	Helen Reale
Charlotte Roach	Amy Robertson
Kristin Schritter	Beth Schuler
Leanne Schuster	Julie Sprague
Monica Stewart	Kathy Tough
Lisa Westlake	Wendy Whiting
Bonnie Williams	Terri Willis
Ali Wood	Lina Yanchulova
Petia Yanchulova	Chrissie Zartman

WOMEN'S TOURNAMENT RESULTS
1998-FIVB

RIO DE JANERIO BRAZIL
February 26th- March 1st, 1998

The Brazilian team of Adriana Behar and Shelda Bede won the $170,000.00 FIVB Women's Beach Women's Open, in Copacabana, Brazil. This was the first tournament of the 1998 FIVB Beach Volleyball World Tour. On a hot Rio summer day, Behar and Bede beat the Australian team of Pauline Manser and Kerri Pottharst, 12-3 and 12-8, earning their first Rio Championship. Adriana and Shelda, champions of last years FIVB World Tour, took home $32,000.00 and 340 points in the World ranking for their first place effort. In the first game of the championship match, Behar and Bede easily won in 24 minutes by a score of 12-3. They utilized a very good serve and took advantage of some mistakes by the Australian team. In the 64 minute second game, Manser and Pottharst played much better. Adriana and Shelda won by a score of 12-8. The Brazilian team utilized a good serve and patience to win in two games. They celebrated the championship along with a crowd of almost 7,000 beach volleyball fans. Another Brazilian team was in third place. In the first match of the final day, Jackie Silva and Sandra Tavares Pires defeated the German team of Maike Friedrichsen and Danja Musch in a 37 minute match for the "Bronze-Medal" by a score of 15-6. Thirty-two teams from 13 countries took part in the main draw: Brazil, Australia, Germany, France, Portugal, Japan, The Netherlands, Czech Republic, United States, Mexico, Italy, Canada and Denmark.

3rd Place: Sandra Pires and Jackie Silva-Bra
4th Place: Maike Friedrichsen and Danja Musch-Ger
5th Place: Natalie Cook and Angela Clarke-Aus
5th Place: Adriana Samuel and Monica Rodrigues-Bra

Top American finishes: two teams from the U.S.A., Fontana and Hanley along with Masakayan and Kirby finished in seventh place. Ninth place went to McPeak and Arce, thirteenth place for Kerrie Poppinga and Angela Rock, while Nancy Reno and Elaine Youngs finished in seventeenth place. Match results of U.S.A. teams: McPeak and Arce defeated Norma Teresa "Teresita" Villareal Saenz and Blanca Nelia Trevino Flores from Mexico 15-1, Natalie Cook and Angela Clarke from Austrailia 15-9. They then lost to the German team of Friedrichsen and Musch 14-16, then to the Australian team of Manser and Pottharst 11-15. Fontana-Hanley defeated the Canadian team of Storch and Gougeon 15-4, the Brazilian team of Gerusa and Rejane 15-5. Then lost to the Brazilian team of Silva and Sandra Pires 2-15. They then won again against Schoon Kadijk and R. Kadijk, from the Netherlands, 15-7. They were put out of the tournament with a loss to the Australian team of Manser and Pottharst by a score of 7-15. Reno and Youngs started out the tournament with a win over Jorgensen and Sommer, from Denmark, 15-3. They lost their next two matches 15-10 to the Brazilian team of Adriana Bento and Ana Richa, then 15-7 to the Canadian team of Dumont and Tough. Masakayan and Kirby started off with a 15-2 win over the Italian team of De Marinis and Nascimento and a 15-5 win over Ishizaka and Rii Seike from Japan. They followed with an 11-15 loss to the Brazilian team of Adriana Behar and Shelda. They then defeated Gerusa and Rejane, also from Brazil, 15-13. Masakayan and Kirby were then eliminated from the tournament with a 6-15 loss to the Australian team of Cook and Clarke. Poppinga and Rock started the tournament off with a 15-7 win over the Japanese team of Ishizaka and Rii Seike and then a 15-13 win over De Marinis and Nascimento from Italy. They followed their two wins with two losses. Poppinga and Rock first lost to Dosoudilova and Celbova 15-6, from the Czech Republic, followed by a 9-15 loss to the Australian team of Cook and Clarke.

SHELDA BEDE & ADRIANA BEHAR
The Brazilian team of Shelda Kelly Bruno Bede and Adriana Brandao Behar were the top women's team on the 1998 FIVB Tour. As a team they advanced to 7 "Gold-Medal" matches, winning 5 times. Above photo, Bede (left) and Behar (right) celebrate another championship.
Photo Courtesy of the FIVB

TORONTO CANADA
June 19th-21st, 1998

The first ever Women's FIVB World Tour event staged in Canada, offered a total purse of $170,000.00. There were 37 women's teams seeded for the Qualification Tournament, all vying for the precious 8 spots available in the 32 team main draw. The "Labatt Blue" Toronto Women's Open FIVB tournament was staged at the "International Beach Village" on the beach of Ashbridge's Bay. The weather was hot and humid with temperatures at almost 80 degrees along with plenty of sunshine. The Canadian crowd showed strong support as there were more than 5,000 fans supporting the excitement and spectacular play. There were 8 Canadian Teams that took part in the Qualifier. There were 40 women's matches played on the first day of the main draw when the 32 teams were reduce to 16. The top-ranked WPVA team of Liz Masakayan and Karolyn Kirby were seeded first in the qualifying round. The big question in the Women's Qualifier was which one of the three entered from the U.S.A. would advance to the Main Draw to join their four already qualified counterparts. The U.S.A. was well represented with five teams making it to the Main Draw. Along with Masakayan and Kirby, the U.S.A. was led by Lisa Arce and Holly McPeak, Linda Hanley and Barbra Fontana, Kerrie Poppinga and Angela Rock, Nancy Reno and Elaine Youngs. The only Canadian team to advance in the Main Draw was the duo of Guylaine Dumont and Kathy Tough. The teams from the U.S.A. and Brazil continued to show their dominance on the world circuit by qualifying two teams each for the semi-finals. The American team of Barbra Fontana and Linda Hanley thrilled the capacity crowd, which included I.O.C. Member Carol Anne Letheren in attendance, with their win over Australia's surprising duo, the unseeded fifth place finishers, Tania Gooley and Nicole Sanderson.

In the championship match, Brazil stole the show, as the two top seeds Adriana Behar and Shelda Bede battled Sandra Pires and Adriana Samuel. The match lasted over an hour with Pires and Samuel squeaking by their countrywomen by a score of 17-16. Pires and Samuel took home $32,000.00 and the Gold Medal for their efforts, while Behar and Shelda earned $23,000.00 along with their Silver Medal. The bronze medal match was an all U.S.A. affair as Arce and McPeak faced off on center-court against Fontana and Hanley, with Arce and McPeak winning 15-4. Arce and McPeak took home $15,000.00 along with the Bronze Medal. Fontana and Hanley earned $12,000.00 for their fourth place effort. All of the matches, including the final match, were played in "FORMAT-A" (1 game to 15 points with a 2 point lead. If there was a 16-16 tie, the team that scored the 17th point won the game and the match with only a one-point lead). In all there were teams from 35 countries entered in this tournament.

3rd Place: Holly McPeak and Lisa Arce-USA
4th Place: Barbra Fontana and Linda Hanley-USA
5th Place: Monica Rodrigues and Jackie Silva-Bra
5th Place: Tania Gooley and Nicole Sanderson-Aus The U.S.A. teams of Reno and Youngs along with Poppinga and Rock finished seventh and thirteenth respectively.

VASTO ITALY
July 3rd-5th, 1998

The $170,000.00 FIVB Beach Volleyball event in Vasto Italy, the "Omnitel Cup" FIVB Women's World Tour, which was the Italian leg of the 1998 FIVB Women's World Tour. Was won by the Brazilian team of Adriana Behar and Shelda Bede.

Krista Blomquist and Ali Wood of the United States advanced to the main draw. Blomquist and Wood won four matches in the qualifying rounds of the third FIVB women's beach event of 1998. Due to the extreme heat the players consumed over 1,200 bottles of water. The matches continued until 8pm due to the large number of teams competing. There were a total of 42 teams in the two day qualifying rounds, of which a total of eight teams made it into the main draw. The crowds, exceeded 1500 people throughout the qualifying, created an exciting frame for the sixty matches played during the qualifying tournament. In the main draw, hampered by strong winds. The Semi-final matches were played infront of a boisterous crowd of 2,000.

In the almost one and one half hour championship match, the first seeded team of Behar and Shelda easily defeated Jackie Silva and Monica Rodrigues in two straight matches 12-4 and 12-5. In the 52 minute match for third place, the Brazilian team of Adriana Samuel and Sandra Pires made it a one-two-three sweep for Brazil with a 15-11 win over Fontana and Hanley. The final matches were played under clear and sunny skies with the temperature at a comfortable 80 degrees. During the awards ceremony, the Podium was colored entirely in gold and green (Brazil's National colors) as Behar and Shelda took home $32,000.00 and the Gold Medal for their winning efforts. Silva and Monica earned $23,000.00 along with their Silver Medal. Coverage of the event was from both National and regional newspapers like Gazzetta dello Sport, Il Messaggero, Il Tempo, il Centro and Radio RAI2 along with the National Network RAI. There were broadcast of some images of Vasto at 6.30 pm during the television news on Channel 2 and further comments were broadcast on RAI3 at 7.45 pm and 10.45 pm.

3rd Place: Adriana Samuel and Sandra Pires-Bra
4th Place: Barbra Fontana and Linda Hanley-USA
5th Place: Ali Wood and Krista Blomquist-USA
5th Place: Liz Masakayan and Karolyn Kirby-USA
The top rated U.S.A. team of Holly McPeak and Lisa Arce finished in ninth place after McPeak injured her ankle in a 12-15 losing effort against fellow Americans Blomquist and Wood. The U.S.A. team of Nancy Reno and Elaine Youngs finished in 13th place.

MARSEILLE FRANCE
July 23rd-26th, 1998

The Brazilian "Carioca" girls had another clean sweep on the podium! This time it was the $170,000.00 French Open, in Marseilles France. The same six Brazilian athletes as at the previous Open, in Italy, were on the winner's stage, but in a different order. In the semi-finals, the Brazilian team of Adriana Behar and Shelda Bede played for eighty-eight minutes before defeating the U.S.A. team of Linda Hanley and Barbra Fontana by scores of 12-6 and 12-11. In another semi-final match, two Brazilian teams fought for the right to go into the championship final. In the one hour and fourteen minute match, Sandra Pires and Adriana Samuel defeated Monica Rodriguez and Jackie Silva, by scores of 12-6 and 12-10.

During the one hour and fifteen minute championship match, the "Mistral," the indicative wind of Marseilles, escalated. Samuel and Pires were able to handle it the best, as they defeated compatriots Adriana Behar and Shelda Bede in two straight sets. The scores were 12-9 and 12-7. The winner's split thje $32,000.00 first place prize. In the bronze medal match, versus the USA team Linda Hanley and Barbra Fontana, it took Rodrigues and Silva eighty minutes to complete the Brazilian clean sweep. Although the Americans had a 11-10 lead in the second set, they failed to keep the momentum and had to settle for fourth place. This was the third consecutive time that Hanley and Fontana finished an FIVB tournament in fourth place.

3rd Place: Monica Rodrigues and Jackie Silva-Bra
4th Place: Barbra Fontana and Linda Hanley-USA
5th Place: Lisa Arce and Holly McPeak-USA
5th Place: Maike Friedrichsen and Danja Musch-Ger
5th Place: Yukiko Takahashi and Mika Teru Saiki-Japan
5th Place: Tania Gooley and Nicole Sanderson-Aus

ESPINHO PORTUGAL
July 31st - August 2nd, 1998

Barbra Fontana and Linda Hanley of the United States won their second FIVB Beach Volleyball World Tour together Sunday (August 2) by defeating Brazilians Sandra Pires and Adriana Samuel 11-12, 12-5 and 13-11, in an 89-minute championship match. Fontana and Hanley had not won an FIVB event in 12 events since winning in their first international event together November 19, 1995 in Santos, Brazil. The Americans took home $32,000.00 for their winning effort. The Americans win also snapped a run of six-straight FIVB events captured by women's teams from Brazil. The USA also captured third-place as Nancy Reno and Elaine Youngs defeated Monica Rodrigues and Jackie Silva of Brazil 17-15 in 48 minutes. Reno and Youngs had lost their semi-final match to Fontana and Hanley 15-2 in 20 minutes while Pires and Samuel were downing Rodrigues and Silva 16-14 in 53 minutes. This FIVB event was staged at the same time as the 1998 Goodwill Games in New York where Bede and Behar of Brazil played Pauline Manser and Kerri Pottharst of Australia in the Gold medal match. Arce and McPeak claimed the Goodwill Games Bronze medal by defeating Laura Bruschini and Annamaria Solazzi of Italy 12-11 and 12-3.

3rd Place: Nancy Reno and Elaine Youngs-USA
4th Place: Monica Rodrigues and Jackie Silva-Bra
5th Place: Ulrike Schmidt and Gudi Staub-Ger
5th Place: Natalie Cook and Liane Fenwick-Aus

OSAKA JAPAN
August 7th-9th, 1998

During the final day of competition, rain in the morning threatened the $170,000.00 Women's FIVB World Tour event, in Osaka Japan. Half of an hour before play was due to start, the skies cleared to a warm humid still day. In an all Brazil championship final, a large noisy crowd of 2000 turned out in the hot sun, to cheer both sides on. Behar and Bede versus Pires and Samuel exchanged points early in the first game. At 5-5, after 27 minutes, a break was made and Behar and Bede edge to an 8-5 lead. They managed to hold this lead with some powerful accurate serving by Bede, to win the game 12-8 in 48 minutes. The second game was a different story as Behar and Bede both served extremely tough, putting pressure on Pires and Samuel. Then at 12-11, they regained their confidence, to finish the match 15-12 in 63 minutes. The winner's split the first-place check of $32,000.00. In the match for third place, McPeak and Arce had a tough match with Italians Laura Bruschini and Annamaria Solazzi. The Italians started quickly and led 4-1, but McPeak and Arce fought back to win the next 10 points. On defense, Arce formed a wall at the net, while McPeak was dominating the back court like a cat. The Americans convincingly won the game 15-6 in 60 minutes.

3rd Place: Holly McPeak and Lisa Arce-USA
4th Place: Laura Bruschini and Annamaria Solazzi-Italy
5th Place: Debora Schoon Kadijk And R. Kadjk-Net
5th Place: Linda Hanley and Barbra Fontana-USA
Additional USA finishes: Nancy Reno and Elaine Youngs in seventh place. Liz Masakayan and Karolyn Kirby in ninth place. Krista Blomquist and Ali Wood in thirteenth place.

ELAINE YOUNGS
Elaine "EY" Youngs provided some worthy competition on the 1998 FIVB Women's Tour. Her best finish was a third at the Espinho Portugal event. Above photo, "EY" challenges the block of Brazilian Shelda Bede.
Photo Courtesy of the FIVB

DALIAN CHINA
August 12th-16th, 1998

The FIVB Women's Pro-Beach Volleyball Tour went to Dalian China for the next $170,000.00 tournament. The event was staged at the China Dalian Golden Pebble Beach volleyball Sport Center located in China Dalian Golden Pebble Beach National Resort. The beach volleyball Sport Center is located on a natural beach, where the courts were set up for play. The event started off with the qualifying rounds, filling the six remaining spots in the Main Draw. Two Chinese teams advanced to the Main Draw, along with American's Krist Blomquist and Ali Wood. The powerful Brazilian pair of Adriana Behar and Shelda Bede won comfortably in their semifinal match, 15-2, over the Italian team of Laura Bruschini and Annamaria Solazzi.

In the championship match, they outclassed the American duo of Lisa Arce and Holly McPeak, 12-5 and 12-6, proving their unshakable position as the worlds number one ranked players. Arce and McPeak made it into the final by winning their semi-final match 15-10 over the Australian team Pauline Manser and Kerri-Ann Pottharst. The match for third place reflected the closeness of the tours playing level. The Australian team Manser and Pottharst stopped further attempts by the Italian team of Bruschini and Solazzi, winning 15-10 in 50 minutes. There was an awards ceremony held immediately after the final match. Behar was awarded "the Best Player" of the tournament, and Zhang Jingkun was awarded "the Best Chinese Player." Behar also shared the first place prize of $32,000.00 with her partner Bede.

3rd Place: Pauline Manser and Kerri-Ann Pottharst-Aus
4th Place: Laura Bruschini and Annamaria Solazzi-Italy
5th Place: Maike Friedrichsen and Danja Musch-Ger
5th Place: Liz Masakayan and Elaine Youngs-USA
Americans Barbra Fontana and Annett Davis finished in seventh place, while Krista Blomquist and Ali Wood were in ninth place.

JONA SWITZERLAND
August 14th-16th, 1998

There was a Women's "Satellite" tournament staged in Jona Switzerland. The winner's of the tournament were Americans Gracie Santana and Donalee Bragado. In the championship match, Santana and Bragado outlasted Schlaefli and Benoit, from Switzerland, by the score of 12-8 in both games. For winning, the Americans each took home a check for $2,000.00. In the semifinals, Santana and Bragado won 15-11 over the Swiss team of Denisa Koeliker and Annalea Hartman. Schlaefli and Benoit won their semifinal match over compatriots Gerson and Schneiter, 15-10. In the all Swiss match for third place, Gerson and Schneiter were outplayed by Koelliker and Hartman by a score of 15-8.

3rd Place: Denisa Koelliker and Annalea Hartman-Swiss
4th Place: Cornelia Gerson and Evelyne Schneiter-Swiss
5th Place: Radana Foltnova and Lucie Svarcova Czech
5th Place: Patricia Dormann and Simone Gasser-Swiss

SALVADOR BRAZIL
October 29th - Novemberr 1st, 1998

The FIVB Women's Pro-Beach Volleyball Tour went to Salvador Brazil for the next $170,000.00 tournament. Brazilians Adriana Behar and Shelda Bede won another "Gold-Medal" and the $32,000.00 first place money. In the one and a half hour championship match, Bede and Behar outlasted the American team of Linda Hanley and Barbra Fontana, by scores of 12-7 and 12-9. In the semifinals, Bede and Behar defeated compatriots Sandra Pires and Adriana Samuel, 15-8, while Hanley and Fontana earned their way into the final with a 15-11 win over Australians Kerri-Ann Pottharst and Pauline Manser. In the match for third place, Pottharst and Manser were outplayed by Pires and Samuel, 15-4. Fifth place went to Americans Liz Masakayan and Elaine Youngs along with Australians Natalie Cook and Angela Clarke.

3rd Place: Sandra Pires and Adriana Samuel-Bra
4th Place: Kerri-Ann Pottharst and Pauline Manser-Aus
5th Place: Natalie Cook and Angela Clarke-Aus
5th Place: Liz Masakayan and Elaine Youngs-USA
Additional USA finishes: Jenny Jordan and Annett Davis were in ninth place while Wendy Stammer and Gabrielle "Gabby" Reece along with Ali Wood and Krista Blomquist were in 25th place.

NATALIE COOK
Australian Natalie Cook played some competive beach Volleyball on the 1998 FIVB Women's Tour, finishing within the top five 3 times. Above photo, Cook gets down in the sand to make a dig.
Photo Courtesy of "Couvi"

TANIA GOOLEY
Australian Tania Gooley gave some nice performances on the 1998 FIVB Women's Tour, including a couple of top five finishes. Above photo, Gooley stretches-out to dig the ball.
Photo Courtesy of the FIVB

WOMEN'S TOURNAMENT RESULTS
1998-GOODWILL GAMES

NEW YORK U.S.A.
July 29th-August 2nd, 1998

Since their inception in 1986, the Goodwill Games have alternated between the U.S.A. and Russia. The first took place in Moscow Russia. Other past sites include the U.S.A.'s Seattle Washington in 1990 and Russia's Saint Petersburg Russia in 1994. The 1998 Goodwill Games featured two-woman beach volleyball as an event. The Goodwill Games women's beach volleyball competition is a sanctioned event on the FIVB Beach Volleyball World Tour and featured $100,000.00 in prize money. The women's event took place at Wollman Rink Stadium, located in South Central Park in the heart of Manhattan. The stadium was filled with almost 500 tons of sand as it was transformed into a 3,000 seat beach court with skyscrapers in the background. The top seven ranked women's teams in the FIVB Beach Volleyball World Ranking plus a wild card team from the U.S.A. competed for the $100,000.00 prize money. The Participating teams were:

GROUP A
U.S.A.: Karolyn Kirby and Liz Masayakyan*
Brazil: Adriana Behar and Shelda Bede
Australia: Pauline Manser and Kerri-Ann Pottharst
Canada: Guylaine Dumont and Kristine Drakich
* = wild card

GROUP B
U.S.A.: Lisa Arce and Holly McPeak
Italy: Annamaria Solazzi and Laura Bruschini
Czech Republic: Sona Dosoudilova and Eva Celbova
Germany: Maike Friedrichsen and Danja Musch

Each group of four teams played a round-robin competition of three matches within its own group. The first and second place finishers from each group advanced to the medal round that determined places one through four.

Eight women's beach tandems began competing July 29th, 1998 with the Gold and Bronze medal matches played on August 2nd, 1998. The women had competed in an FIVB Beach Volleyball World Tour event the prior week in Marseille, France before invading Wollman Rink.

The Australian team of Pauline Manser and Kerri-Ann Pottharst advanced to the finals with a 12-11, 11-12 and 12-6 win over Lisa Arce and Holly McPeak in the first semi-final match that lasted 97 minutes. The Brazilian team of Bede and Behar, the top-ranked team on the FIVB tour, downed the Italian team of Laura Bruschini and Annamarie Solazzi 12-5 and 12-7 in 67 minutes in the second semi-final match. The Brazilians had total control in both sets with Bruschini and Solazzi, who were competing in their first ever FIVB semi-final together.

Shelda Bede and Adriana Behar captured the 1998 Goodwill Games Beach Volleyball Gold medal, in the women's competition, by defeating the Australians Pauline Manser and Kerri Pottharst 12-9 and 12-5. Bede and Behar, the top-ranked team on the FIVB Beach

ADRIANA BEHAR
Brazilian Adriana Behar paired-up with compatriot Shelda Bede to win the "Gold-Medal" match at the 1998 Goodwill Games, staged in New York's Central Park. In the championship match, Behar and Bede defeated the Australian team of Pauline Manser and Keri-Ann-Potharst by scores of 12-9 and 12-5. Above photo Behar shows the kind of effort necessary to win a "Gold-Medal"
Photo Courtesy of the FIVB

Volleyball World Tour, shared the $30,000.00 first-place prize by winning the 76-minute match while the fourth-seeded Manser and Pottharst split $20,000.00 for second-place.

Lisa Arce and Holly McPeak of the U.S.A. went on to claim the Bronze medal in the 1998 Goodwill Games women's beach volleyball competition. The second-seeded Arce and McPeak downed Bruschini and Solazzi of Italy 12-11 and 12-3 in 72 minutes to share $15,000.00 for finishing third in the FIVB-sanctioned event. The Italians, who posted their best ever finish in a FIVB Beach Volleyball World Tour event, split $11,000.00 for fourth-place.

In the playoff matches at Wollman Rink, Germany's Maike Friedrichsen and Danja Musch netted fifth place as they rallied for a 16-14 win over the fifth-seeded American team of Karolyn Kirby and Liz Masakayan. The USA pair had won the inaugural women's Goodwill Games beach volleyball title in 1994 at St. Petersburg, Russia. The third-seeded Friedrichsen and Musch split $8,000.00 for fifth while Kirby and Masakayan split $7,000.00. Eva Celbova and Sona Dosoudilova of the Czech Republic netted seventh-place in the 1998 Goodwill Games by rallying to defeat Canadians Kristine Drakich and Guylaine Dumont 16-14. Celbova and Dosoudilova shared $5,000.00 for finishing seventh while the Canadians split $4,000.00.

All medal matches featured the FIVB's Format B with two out of three sets to 12 points. The first two sets had to be won with a minimum lead of two points with a point limit of 12-points as a cap. The deciding set featured the rally scoring system to 12 points with a minimum lead of two points. There was no point cap for the deciding set.

EVA CELBOVA & SONA DOSOUDILVOA
Eva Celbova (left) and Sona Dosoudilvoa (right), from the Czech Republic had a good time participating in the 1998 Goodwill Games, winning the game for 7th place.
Photo Courtesy of the FIVB

WOMEN'S TOURNAMENT RESULTS
1998 - GOODWILL GAMES

DAY #1
July 29th, 1998
WOMEN'S GROUP "A" MATCHES:
GAME #1: The Australian team of Manser and Pottharst defeated Kirby and Masakayan, from the U.S.A. by a score of 15-10.
GAME #2: The American team of Arce and McPeak defeated the Italian team of Bruschini and Solazzi by a score of 15-4.

WOMEN'S GROUP "B" MATCHES:
GAME #1: The German team of Friedrichsen and Musch defeated the team from the Czech Republic, Dosoudilova and Celbova by a score of 15-4.
GAME #2: The Brazilian team of Adriana Behar and Shelda defeated the Canadian team of Drakich and Dumont by a score of 15-1.

DAY #2
July 30th, 1998
WOMEN'S GROUP "A" MATCHES:
GAME #1: The American team of Arce and McPeak defeated the team from the Czech Republic, Dosoudilova and Celbova, by a score of 15-9.
GAME #2: The American team of Kirby and Masakayan defeated the Canadian team of Drakich and Dumont by a score of 15-5.

WOMEN'S GROUP "B" MATCHES:
GAME #1: The Brazilian team of Adriana Behar and Shelda defeated the Australian team of Manser and Pottharst by a score of 15-9.
GAME #2: The Italian team of Bruschin and Solazzi defeated the German team of Friedrichsen and Musch by a score of 15-10.

DAY #3
July 31st, 1998
WOMEN'S GROUP "A" MATCHES:
GAME #1: The Brazilian team of Adriana Behar and Shelda defeated the American team of Kirby and Masakayan by a score of 15-9.
GAME #2: The American team of Arce and McPeak defeated the German team of Friedrichsen and Musch by a score of 15-11.

WOMEN'S GROUP "B" MATCHES:
GAME #1: The Italian team of Bruschini and Solazzi defeated the team from the Czech Republic, Dosoudilova and Celbova, by a score of 15-7.
GAME #2: The Australian team of Manser and Pottharst defeated the Canadian team of Drakich and Dumont by a score of 15-8.

DAY #4
August 1st, 1998
GAME FOR 7TH AND 8TH PLACE
Dosoudilova-Celbova, from the Czech Republic, defeated the team of Dumont and Drakich, from Canada, by a score of 16-14.

GAME FOR 5TH AND 6TH PLACE
Friedrichsen and Musch, from Germany, defeated Kirby and Masakayan, from the U.S.A. by a score of 16-14.

SEMI-FINAL MATCHES:
GAME #1: The Australian team Manser and Pottharst outlasted the U.S.A. team of McPeak and Arce by scores of 11-12, 12-11, and 12-6.
GAME #2: The Brazilian team of Adriana Behar and Shelda defeated the Italian team of Bruschini and Solazzi by scores of 12-5 and 12-7.

DAY #5
August 2nd, 1998

BRONZE MEDAL GAME
The American team of McPeak and Arce won the 1998 Goodwill Games Bronze Medal, for beach volleyball, by defeating the Italian team of Bruschini and Solazzi by scores of 12-11 and 12-3, in the match for third place.

GOLD MEDAL GAME
The Brazilian team of Adriana Behar and Shelda won the 1998 Goodwill Games Gold Medal, for beach volleyball, with their victory over the Australian team of Manser and Pottharst by scores of 12-9 and 12-5, in the match for the championship.

WOMEN'S TOURNAMENT RESULTS
1998-CBVA

SANTA MONICA CALIFORNIA
March 14th, 1999
The Women's State Beach XOTX "AAA" was won by the team of Jenny Pavley and JB Burrell. In the championship match, they defeated Mary Baily and Helen Reale.

PLAYA DEL REY CALIFORNIA
March 21st, 1999
The Playa Del Rey Balksters Challenge Women's "AAA" was won by Nancy Mason and Carrie Busch. In the championship match, they out-pointed Marsha Miller and Jennifer Holdren.

CAPISTRANO CALIFORNIA
April 18th, 1999
The 1999 Capistrano Maui Life Women's "AAA" was won by Valinda Hilleary and Alicia Chung. In the championship match, they defeated Stephene Nelson and Liz Pagano.

PLAYA DEL REY CALIFORNIA
April 25th, 1999
The Playa Del Rey Bud Light CBVA Volleyball Festival Women's "AAA" was won by Leanne Schuster and Nancy Mason. In the championship match, they out-scored Carrie Busch and Kristin Schritter.

SANTA MONICA CALIFORNIA
May 3rd, 1999
The Santa Monica Pier Women's "AAA" was won by the team of Kristin Schritter and Julie Sprague. In the championship match, they defeated Laura Higgins and Barb Nyland.

PLAYA DEL REY CALIFORNIA
May 9th, 1999
The Playa Del Rey Summit Ski & Cycle Challenge Women's "AAA" was won by Helen Reale and Mary Baily. In the championship match, they outlasted Marsha Miller and Rhonda Kottke.

SAN DIEGO CALIFORNIA
May 16th, 1998
The 1998 Ocean Beach Bud Light CBVA Volleyball Festival Women's "AAA" was won by Gail Castro and Lynda Black. In the championship match they defeated Kristin Schritter and Ali Wood. Third place went to Julie James and Liz Pagano along with Jenny Pavley and Jenny Johnson. This tournament was directed by George Stepanof.

SAN DIEGO CALIFORNIA
May 30th, 1998
The 1998 Ocean Beach "Redsand" Women's "AAA" was won by Kathy Tough and Guylaine Dumont. In the championship match they defeated Lynda Black and Angie Kammer. Third place went to Lina Yanchulova and Petia Yanchulova along with Christine Lusser and Barb Ovellette. George Stepanof was the tournament director. There were 13 teams entered in this tournament.

SANTA CRUZ CALIFORNIA
June 13th, 1999
The Santa Cruz Bud Light CBVA Volleyball Festival Women's "AAA" was won by the team of Ilga Clemins and Jackie McCabe. In the championship match, they out-pointed Charlotte Roach and Jackie Campbell.

CORONA DEL MAR CALIFORNIA
June 13th, 1999
The Corona Del Mar Women's "AAA" was won by Monica Stewart and Wendy Whiting. In the championship match, they defeated Linda Burton and Amy Robertson.

SANTA MONICA CALIFORNIA
July 11th, 1999
The Will Rogers Smack Sportswear Women's "AAA" was won by Karen Helyer and Vicki Bonin. In the championship match, they out-scored JB Burrell and Bonnie Williams.

NANCY MASON
Nancy Mason paired-up with Leanne McSorley to win the CBVA Women's "AAA" event in Playa Del Rey. Mason also won the Playa Del Rey "Balksters" "AAA" Women's Challenge with Carrie Busch. Above photo, Mason goes to the line, to make the pass.
Photo Courtesy of "Couvi"

VENTURA CALIFORNIA
July 11th, 1998

The 1998 "Ventura Cal Cup Women's Open "AAA" was won by the team of Laura Higgins and Judy Hissong. In the championship match, they defeated Deia Kadlubek, and Terri Willis. The third place tie went to the teams of Rachel Errthum and Lisa Westlake along with Joy Burkholder and Casie Hyatt.

LAGUNA BEACH CALIFORNIA
July 18th, 1998

The 1998 Laguna Laguna Beach Women's Open "AAA" was won by Liz Pagano and Evelyn Conley. In the championship match, they defeated Erin Deiters and Michelle Morese. The third place tie went to the teams of Chastity Nobriga and Stephanie Nelson along with Krysta Attwood and Beth Schuler.

SANTA CRUZ CALIFORNIA
July 25th, 1998

The Santa Cruz Chiro & Sports Therapy Women's "AAA" was won by the team of Sarah Beyer and Ilga Clemins. In the championship match, they defeated Sue Holmes and Andrea Beylen.

MANHATTAN BEACH CALIFORNIA
August 8th, 1998

The Bud Light Manhattan Beach CBVA Volleyball Festival Women's "AAA" event was won by the team of Liz Pagano and Marsha Miller. In the championship match, they outlasted Helen Reale and Mary Baily.

MANHATTAN BEACH CALIFORNIA
September 5th, 1998

The Bud Light Manhattan Beach Cal Cup and US Nationals Women's "AAA" event was won by Helen Reale and Mary Baily. In the championship match, they defeated Jenny Pavley and JB Burrell.

HERMOSA BEACH CALIFORNIA
September 12th, 1998

The Hermosa Beach Sunsets Separates/Good Stuff Women's "AAA" was won by Chastity Nobriga and Michelle Morse. In the championship match, they outpointed Tracy Lindquist and Chrissie Zartman.

PLAYA DEL REY CALIFORNIA
September 19th, 1998

The Playa Del Rey Gordon's Market Fall Festival Women's "AAA" was won by the team of Chastity Noberiga and Sandy Matthews. In the championship match, they defeated Erin Deiters and Michelle Morse.

MIXED-DOUBLE'S TOURNAMENT RESULTS
1999 - CBVA
SANTA MONICA CALIFORNIA
March 15th, 1998

The March 15th, 1999 State Beach Reverse Coed "AAA" was won by beach volleyball legend Bob Vogelsang and Nicole Midwin. In the championship match, they outlasted Tim Nestlerode and Michelle Nestlerode.

HERMOSA BEACH CALIFORNIA
April 18th, 1998

The April 8th, 1999 Speedo Hermosa Beach Coed Open was won by the team of Cody Cowell and Christina Gage. In the championship match, they outscored Brian Meckna and Therese Butler.

PLAYA DEL REY CALIFORNIA
April 26th, 1998

The Playa Del Rey Bud Light Volleyball Festival Coed "AAA" was won by the team of Brian Meckna and Therese Butler. In the championship match, they defeated Doug Foust and Lisa DelGiudice.

SAN DIEGO CALIFORNIA
May 17th, 1998

The 1998 Ocean Beach "Bud Light CBVA Volleyball Festival" Mixed-Doubles "AAA" was won by Jack Quinn and Susie Turner. In the championship final, they defeated Jeremie Simkins and Cherry Simkins. Third place went to Sean Burke and Caron Janc. George Stepanof was the tournament director of this tournament that had only six teams participate.

SAN DIEGO CALIFORNIA
June 14th, 1998

The team of Ericholman and Gina Peterman won the 1998 Mission Beach Redsand AAA Mixed-Doubles Tournament. In the championship final, they defeated Jeremie Simkins and Cherry Simkins. Third place went to Jeff Smith and Andrea Vanschmus. Tournament director George Stepanof recorded that the conditions were sunny and "Perfect" during this tournament that only had five teams entered.

PLAYA DEL REY CALIFORNIA
June 20th, 1998

The June 20th, 1999 Playa Del Rey Coed "AAA" was won by Bob Vogelsang and Marjoree Hebrard. In the championship match, they outlasted Ron Spohn and Niki Jablowski.

MANHATTAN BEACH CALIFORNIA
July 4th, 1998

The Marine Avenue Smack Sportswear Coed "AAA" was won by the team of Imran Nadir and Marsha Miller. In the championship match, they defeated Tagore Evans and Dianna Evans. Third place went to the team of Travis Ferguson and Heidi Ferguson.

MANHATTAN BEACH CALIFORNIA
July 19th, 1998

The 1998 Dion Gallery Rosecrans Coed AAA was won by the team of Shawn Davis and Ann Vallas. In the championship match, they defeated Ron Spohn and Niki Jablowski.

VENTURA CALIFORNIA
September 19th-20th, 1998

The California Beach Party Ventura Coed "AAA" was won by Todd Rogers and Deia Kadlubek Kidd. In the championship match, they outlasted Cody Cowell and Christina Gage Cowell.

PLAYA DEL REY CALIFORNIA
September 20th, 1999

The Playa Del Rey Coed "AAA" was won by the team of Tom Slauterbreck and JB Burrell. In the championship match, they defeated Rifat Agi and Ashley Kuehn. John and Sherry Anselmo were in the third spot.

TOP PHOTOS: Left: Linda Hanley attacking the block of Nancy Reno. **Center:** Christine Schaefer hits a set from partner Kerri Poppinga. **Right:** Nancy Reno avoids the block of Barbra Fontana.

MIDDLE PHOTOS: Left: Karolyn Kirby hitting the ball towards the defense of Linda Hanley. **Center:** Lisa Arce passing the ball. **Right:** Nancy Reno gets above the net for the attack.

1998 WOMEN'S BEACH VOLLEYBALL ACTION

BOTTOM PHOTOS: Left: Liz Masakayan tries to poke the ball over the block of Nancy Mason. **Center:** Angela Rock winds-up for the spike. **Right:** Patty Dodd tries to slice the ball past the block of Nancy Reno.

Photo's Courtesy of the AVP

ADDITIONAL VOLLEYBALL INFORMATION
1998

MOTHERLOAD TOURNAMENT
ASPEN COLORADO
September 7th, 1998

Curtis Griffin and Eric Moore captured their fourth-straight Men's Open at the 26th Motherload Volleyball Classic. They won seven-straight matches to earn the title. Griffin (Boulder, Colorado) and Moore (Salt Lake City, Utah), had now won 11-straight Motherload Men's Open matches. In the championship match, they downed fourth-seeded Mark Presho and Matt Unger 15-5. Griffin and Moore led from the start by jumping to 6-0 and 10-1 leads. Presho (Huntington Beach, California) and Unger (Pacific Palisades California) advanced to the finals with an 11-6 win over third-seeded Ryan Post (Denver, Colorado) and Dane Hansen (Lakewood, Colorado). Post and Hansen finished in the third spot.

In the Men's Seniors (45 and older) championship match, David King (San Cruz, California and Dan Sayler (San Luis Obispo, California) defeated Jack Flora (Denver, Colorado) and Mike Wirsing (Winter Park, Colorado). Jon Lee (Santa Barbara, California) and Jeff Rydberg (Santa Barbara, California) finished in third place.

In the Men's Masters (37 and older) championship match, Anthony Jenkins (Wichita, Kansas) and Doug White (Los Angeles, California) defeated Eric Anderson (Los Gatos, California) and Kent Kitchel (Santa Cruz, California). Jack Hinton (Long Beach, California) and Bill Stetson (Manhattan Beach, California) finished in third place.

In the Men's Seniors (50 and older) championship match, Danny Patterson (Aspen, Colorado) and Byron Shewman (San Diego, California) defeated Steve Anderson (Denver, Colorado) and Denice Dempsey (Lakewood, Colorado). The third spot was filled by David Fuchs (Chicago, Illinois) and Ahmed Vassoughi (Chicago, Illinois).

In the Women's Open division, second-seeded Nancy Mason (Belleville, Illinois) and Leanne Schuster (Tempe, Arizona) scored two upset wins over defending champions Valinda Hilleary (Littleton, Colorado) and Pat Keller (Sarasota, Florida) to capture the Women's Open title. In the championship match, Mason and Schuster scored a 15-5 win over Hilleary and Keller. Mason and Schuster jumped to a 6-2 lead and scored eight-straight points to increase their advantage to 14-3 in the championship match over Hilleary and Keller, who netted Motherload Women's Open titles in 1993 and 1997. Hilleary and Keller, who had dropped a 15-13 decision to Mason and Schuster earlier Monday in the finals of the championship bracket, advanced to the finals with an 11-4 win over Erin Deiters (Green Bay, Wisconsin) and Deanna Johnson (San Diego, California). Deiters and Johnson finished in the third spot. A total of 591 pro-am teams competed in the five-day event, including 394 men's and 197 women's tandems.

CUERVO TOUR CHAMPIONSHIPS
FORT LAUDERDALE FLORIDA

James Fellows and James Van Zweitan won men's division at the 1998 "Cuervo" Tour Championship. In an exciting championship match, they outlasted this years Manhattan Beach Open winners, Sean Scott and Pepe De La Hoz, by a score of 18-16.

Jennifer Johnson and Annette-Buckner-Davis won the women's division at the 1998 "Cuervo" Tour Championship. In the championship match, they easily defeated Stephanie Nelson and Liz Pagona by a score of 15-3.

ADDITIONAL
BEACH VOLLEYBALL INFORMATION

There were various beach volleyball National Circuits in Europe that were taking place in 1998, including:

The Russian National Beach Volleyball Circuit for Men and Women took place in five different cities including: Krasnodar, Taganrog, Moscow, Riazan, and Sosnovi Bor.

The Austrian National Beach Volleyball Circuit for Masters and Championships, Men and Women took place at five different events including: Generali Masters Wien, Raiffeisen Masters Wolfurt, Ischgl Masters Ischgl, Casinos Masters Velden, and Austrian Championship at Neusiedler See.

The Circuito Nacional De Duplas for Men took place in ten different Italian Cities while for the Women there were four events in three Italian Cities. The Men's events took place in Lamego, Foz do Arelho (Caldas da Rainha), Praia das Macas (Sintra), Porto Santo (Madeira), Fos do Douro (Porto), Penacova, Figueira da Foz, Ponte de Lima, Praia da Rocha (Portimao), and Nazare. Women: Matosinhos, Penacova, and Figueira da Foz.

The Tuborg Swiss Beach Volleyball Tour for Men and Women took place in five different cities: Basel (Barfusserplatz), Locarno (Piazza Grande), Lausanne (Vidy), Luzern (Tivoli), and Bern (Bundesplatz).

LAGUNA BEACH CALIFORNIA
1998

The 1998 Laguna Beach Men's Open was an amateur "AAA" tournament. David Becker and Brian Meckna were the winners. In the championship match, they defeated they defeated Anthony Medel and Jason Lee.

3rd Place: Matt Taylor and Scott Sjoquist
4th Place: Evan Hook and Scott Lane

MEN'S BEACH VOLLEYBALL
1999

1999 MEN'S AVP TOUR SCHEDULE

DATE	CITY/STATE	EVENT SITE	PRIZE MONEY
May 1st-2nd, 1999	Clearwater, Forida*	Hilton Clearwater	$ 75,000.00
May 22nd-23rd, 1999	New Orleans, Louisiana	Coconut Beach	$ 75,000.00
June 5th-6th, 1999	Dallas, Texas	West End	$ 75,000.00
June 11th-13th, 1999	Hermosa Beach, California*	Hermosa Pier	$ 75,000.00
June 26th-27th, 1999	Belmar, New Jersey	Belmar Beach	$ 75,000.00
July 3rd-4th, 1999	Chicago, Illinois*	North Avenue	$ 75,000.00
July 10th-11th, 1999	Muskegon, Michigan*	Muskegon Beach	$ 75,000.00
July 31st-August 1st, 1999	Santa Barbara, California	East Beach	$ 75,000.00
August 13th-14th, 1999	Louisville. Kentucky	The Brewery	$ 75,000.00
August 21st-22nd, 1999	Cleveland, Ohio	Nautica Center	$ 75,000.00
August 28th-29th, 1999	Manhattan Beach, California*	Manhattan Pier	$100,000.00
September 17th-19th, 1999	Las Vegas, Nevada**	Hard Rock Hotel	$150,000.00

* = Both Men and Women's tournaments
** = King and Queen of the Beach tournaments

1999 AVP ACTION

In 1999, the AVP Tour provided action on and off the beach volleyball court. Off the court there was an effort to initate a new "Strategic Plan" for the AVP, including new management with Bill Berger running the show along with Dan Vrebalovich. On the court there was plenty of action at all 12 of the venue sites. Above photo, Stein Metzgar passing the ball to partner Carlos Loss during the 1999 Santa Barbara event.
Photo Courtesy of "Couvi"

AVP

At the end of 1998 there was a tremendous amount of speculation as to the fate of the AVP and beach volleyball in America. The media professed that the AVP had a laundry list of problems without any real solutions. The AVP's 1999 "Strategic Plan" regarding its future started with a complete management and financial transition. The AVP Board of Directors initiated a go forward plan with a new management team, spearheaded by Bill Berger who had been involved in the business of volleyball for the past 10 years. Berger, along with volleyball veteran Dan Vrebalovich introduced the AVP Board of Directors to an investment team that assisted the management team in rebuilding the once great AVP. Berger and Vrebalovich assembled an impressive management team experienced in sports marketing.

In the past, the AVP had been a dynamic property which provided hundreds of hours of entertaining television, wild and fun events, sponsor value, and an opportunity for cities all over the country to take pride in the local nature of the events. The AVP became endeared by the media as the sport with enough credibility yet a "California Lifestyle" theme with a grass roots "vibe" that made it the sweetheart for several years. On the victory stand of the 1996 Olympic Games, Karch Kiraly and Kent Steffes represented the U.S.A. and indirectly the AVP, showing the world that the sport had grown up.

Unfortunately, as the sport matured, it began to lose its charm, and more specifically, what made it so appealing. The AVP decided that it would brave it alone in the sports world, alienating or ignoring the various volleyball constituencies (USAV, NCAA, FIVB, High Schools, AVA, etc.). Thus limiting the overall development programs that so many other sports revel in.

The 1999 AVP main sponsors were Speedo, Sunkist, and Wilson. The sponsors, along with the AVP and their "Strategic Plan," the 1999 season was successful in bringing the beach volleyball fans a professional tour.

The AVP's New Strategic Plan covered the current situation of the game since its inception in 1983 to its peak, in the late 1980's and early 1990's and finally to the AVP as it stood in 1999.

The AVP's plan included the creation of a consumer-friendly viewing environment for volleyball fans while

DAN VREBALOVICH
The 1999 AVP Tour, along with Bill Berger and Dan Vrebalovich assembled an impressive management team to run the AVP. Above photo, Vrebalovich shows his winning style as he challenges the block of Tim Hovland.
Photo Courtesy of Dennis G. Steers

DAVID SWATIK
David Swatik was voted the 1999 AVP Tour's "Most Improved Player" in fact he improved so much he was the 1999 "King of the Beach" winner. Above photo, During the 1999 Hermosa Beach event, Swatik attacks the block of Adam Jewell.
Photo Courtesy of "Couvi"

maximizing sponsorship exposure. At some events they reduced, and in some cases eliminated bleacher seating charges to ensure access for all volleyball fans. Court-side "in-the-sand" seating was re-established to recapture the social interaction, feeling of a "fun-in-the-sun" beach.

The 1999 AVP Tour took the first step to establish annual consistency in events, where the date and location will ensure appropriate lead-times and delivery of event value to constituents so as to develop strong relationships with AVP event communities and gain cooperative involvement.

Local media relationships were developed to all aspects of promoting the league and its many event stops. The players were drafted to aggressively promote in all aspects of the league and its many event stops so as to develop and promote the wide range of personalities that make up AVP tour players and work to establish the players as "household names."

In 1999, the AVP made an effort to deliver the highest level of consistent sponsorship value, measured throughout the AVP season; while they tried to remain flexible to the changing goals and expectations of the sponsors differing levels based on sponsor commitments.

The AVP began its plan to integrate with all levels of amateur volleyball to deliver more value for sponsors and to provide feeder-system for future AVP players and US Olympians. This brought about the landmark merger between AVP and the AVA which vertically blended outdoor volleyball into one powerful entity by using the marketing power of the AVP to expand the AVA's 2,500 tournaments and 75,000 participants far beyond 1998 levels. In 1999, the AVP recognized that a cooperative relationship with the USAV was instrumental in developing future Olympic beach volleyball players. The AVP began looking forward to developing a mutually beneficial flow chart with USAV. The AVP, in conjunction with the Amateur Volleyball Association (AVA) and the Amateur Athletic Union (AAU), created an 8 stop youth beach volleyball tour to coincide with AVP venues.

The AVP handed out three awards to players in 1999. The "Most Valuable Player" was Karch Kiraly. The "Most Improved Player" award went to David Swatik and the "Rookie of the Year" award went to Sean Scott. Swatik improved so much, he won the 1999 King of the Beach title in Las Vegas Nevada.

SEAN SCOTT
Sean Scott was awarded the AVP Tour's "Rookie of the Year" in 1999. Scott's aggresive play at the net helped him get this honor. Above photo, Scott gets above the net for another successful block.
Photo Courtesy of "Couvi"

KARCH KIRALY
In 1999, Karch Kiraly was voted the "Most Valuable Player" on the AVP Tour. Karch advanced to 5 championship matches, winning 4 times, all with Adam Johnson. Above photo, during the 1999 S.B. event, Karch passing the ball from the 805 area code.
Photo Courtesy of Frank Goroszko

INDIVIDUAL AVP TOURNAMENT FINISHES
1990-1999

Player	1st	2nd	3rd	4th	5th
Pete Aroncheck	1	0	0	0	0
Scott Ayakatubby	12	19	20	12	27
Eduardo Bacil	1	10	11	12	27
Dain Blanton	2	8	13	5	13
Mike Boehle	1	0	0	0	0
Aaron Boss	0	0	0	1	4
Bill Boullianne	1	3	14	10	31
Paul Boyd	0	0	0	0	1
Eric Boyles	0	0	1	1	1
John Brajevic	0	0	0	0	2
Daniel Cardenas	0	0	0	0	1
George Carey	0	0	0	0	1*
Dan Castillo	0	0	0	2	3
Canyon Ceman	3	4	11	7	13
Robert Chavez	0	0	0	1	2
Ian Clark	0	0	2	3	18
Roger Clark	0	0	1	2	10
Robert Curci	0	0	0	0	1*
Shawn Davis	0	1	1	0	1
Pepe DeLaholz	0	0	0	0	1
Brent Doble	0	0	1	0	6
Mike Dodd	19	33	41	25	31
Rudy Dvorak	0	1	0	0	8
John Eddo	1*	3*	1	1	5*
Mark Eller	0	1*	1	0	0
Sean Fallowfield	0	2*	1	1	0
Andy Fishburn	0	0	1	0	0
Eric Fonoimoana	3	6	16	14	29
Doug Foust	0	0	0	1	4
Scott Friederichsen	0	0	1	5*	17
Brent Frohoff	9	23	25	11	34
Mike Garcia	0	0	0	0	1
Eduardo Garrido	0	0	2	0	6
Brian Gatzke	0	0	1	0	10
Andre Gomes	1	0	3	0	1
Wally Goodrick	0	0	2	4	2*
Marques Guilherme	0	0	0	1	1
John Hanley	1	4	5	7	11
Albert Hannemann	0	1	0	1	2
Nick Hannemann	0	0	1	0	3
Leif Hanson	2*	2*	1	2	14*
Rob Heidger	0	3	11	2	15
Dax Holdren	2	2	3	5	16
Tim Hovland	9*	16*	5	8	22
Brian Ivie	0	0	1	1	4
Al Janc	1*	1*	0	4*	8
Adam Jewell	0	0	0	0	2
Adam Johnson	38*	35	28	26	29
Mark Kerins	2	1	3	4	8
Karch Kiraly	**104**	**31**	**22**	**8**	**11**
Lee LeGrand	0	0	1	0	7
Brian Lewis	6	23	28	16	39
Jose Loiola	32	23*	17	14	20
Roberto Lopes	0	3	5	1	2
Carlos Loss	0	1	0	0	4
Ricci Luyties	7	9	13	23	36
Matt Lyles	0	0	1	0	2
Kevin Martin	0	0	2	1	12
Owen McKibben	0	0	1	1	1
Owen McKibben	0	0	0	0	1
Larry Mear	0	3	0	3	10
Stein Metzger	0	2	0	0	4
Craig Moothart	0	0	2	2*	14
Franco Neto	1	3	5	1	3
Jim Nichols	0	0	0	2	0
Raul Papaleo	0	0	0	0	4
Rogerio Para de Souza	0	0	0	1	1
Justin Perlstrom	0	0	0	0	1
Pat Powers	3	5	9	11	18
Emanuel Rego	5	5	4	0	1
Jeff Rogers	0	1	1	0	7
Todd Rogers	2	2	4	5	16
Henry Russell	1	1	3	1	4
Todd Schaffer	0	1*	0	0	0
Mike Schlegel	0	0	0	0	1
Wayne Seliqson	0	0	1	0	2
Dane Selznick	0	0	1	0	0
Sinjin Smith	33*	22	14*	8	6
Andrew Smith	0	1	1	9	8
Matt Sonnichsen	0	0	0	1	1
Kent Steffes	**104***	**29***	**16**	**12**	**15**
Jon Stevenson	0	0	3	3*	7
Randy Stoklos	39*	42	26*	17	19
Bill Suwara	0	0	0	0	1
David Swatik	4	3	5	5	14
Troy Tanner	0	9	13*	5	21
Steve Timmons	0	1	2	1	6
Matt Unger	0	0	0	0	5
Bruk Vandeweghe	1	3	5	11	9
Dan Vrebalovich	2	1	6*	6	22
Tim Walmer	1*	2*	1	5*	10
Wes Welch	0	2	6	2	8
Mike Whitmarsh	21	30	29	23	42
Kevin Wong	0	1	0	0	5
Eric Wurts	1*	4	4	3	11
Chris Young	0	0	0	0	1

(list does **NOT** include Goodwill Games or FIVB events)

1999 INDIVIDUAL AVP TOURNAMENT FINISHES

Player	1st	2nd	3rd	4th	5th
Eduardo Bacil	0	0	0	0	5
Dain Blanton	1	4	1	1	2
Aaron Boss	0	0	0	0	1
Bill Boullianne	0	0	0	1	1
Paul Boyd	0	0	0	0	1
Dan Castillo	0	0	0	0	1
Canyon Ceman	0	1	3	0	0
Ian Clark	0	0	0	1	1
Pepe DeLaholz	0	0	0	0	1
Brent Doble	0	0	1	0	4
Eric Fonoimoana	1	3	2	1	2
Brent Frohoff	0	0	0	0	3
Eduardo Garrido	0	0	0	0	3
Nick Hannemann	0	0	0	0	1
Dax Holdren	1	0	2	2	2
Brian Ivie	0	0	0	0	1
Adam Jewell	0	0	0	0	1
Adam Johnson	4	1	2	1	0
Mark Kerins	0	0	2	0	3
Karch Kiraly	4	1	2	1	0
Lee LeGrand	0	0	1	0	4
Brian Lewis	1	1	2	1	2
Jose Loiola	0	2	3	0	0
Roberto Lopes	0	1	0	0	0
Carlos Loss	0	1	0	0	4
Ricci Luyties	0	0	0	0	2
Matt Lyles	0	0	1	0	1
Kevin Martin	0	0	1	0	3
Stein Metzger	0	1	0	0	0
Franco Neto	1	1	0	0	1
Emanuel Rego	0	2	3	0	0
Todd Rogers	1	0	3	2	2
Henry Russell	0	0	0	0	1
Wayne Seliqson	0	0	1	0	2
David Swatik	4	1	0	0	2
Mike Whitmarsh	3	1	1	1	2

(list does **NOT** include Goodwill Games or FIVB events)

FIVB
1999 MEN'S FIVB TOUR SCHEDULE

DATE	CITY/COUNTRY/EVENT SITE	PRIZE MONEY
January 13th-17th, 1999	Mar Del Plata Arg. Playa Bristol	$170,000.00
April 7th-11th, 1999	Acapulco Mex. Tamarindo Playa	$170,000.00
May 15th-16th, 1999**	Huntington Beach Ca. USA-Pier	$100,000.00
June 16th-20th, 1999	Toronto Canada Woodbine Beach	$170,000.00
June 23rd-27th, 1999	Moscow Russia Troparevo Park	$170,000.00
June 30th-July 4th, 1999	Berlin Germany Jannowitzbruske	$170,000.00
July 7th-11th, 1999	Stavanger Norway Vaagen Ctr.	$170,000.00
July 14th-18th, 1999	Ligano Italy Sabbiadoroos Beach	$170,000.00
July 20th-25th, 1999*	Marseille France Plage du Prado	$300,000.00
July 28th-August 1st, 1999	Klagenfurt Austria Strandbad Sds	$170,000.00
August 4th-8th, 1999	Esphinho Portugal Praia de Baia	$170,000.00
August 11th-15th, 1999	Ostend Belgium Grote Shand Bch	$170,000.00
August 18th-22nd, 1999	Tenerife, Canary Islands, Spain Las Teresitas Beach	$170,000.00
Sept. 11th-12th, 1999**	San Diego, California, USA Crown Point	$100,000.00
Nov. 30th-Dec. 5th, 1999	Vitoria Brazil Camburi Beach	$170,000.00

* = World Championships
** = FIVB Registered "Olympic Challenge" Tournaments

One of the many interests of the 1999 FIVB Beach Volleyball World Tour was the struggle for the Olympic tickets, and especially the "fratricidal" rivalry between the plethora of good teams of the power countries Brazil and USA. Actually, because of the country quota rule, each nation was only able to qualify 2 teams for Sydney (except host Australia that could have had up to 3 representatives). The Men's FIVB World Tour events from Jan. 1, 1999 to Aug. 15, 2000 determined the 24 men's and 24 women's teams that competed at the 2000 Sydney Olympic Games (Sept. 16-26). A total of 12 men's and 10 women's events entering into this qualification process were played before the August 15th deadline

Including the 1999 Olympiad, there were a total of 15 Men's FIVB Tour events in 1999. The total prize money on the 1999 Men's FIVB Tour was at $2,130,000.00. The Prize Money for each World Tour event was $170,000.00. With the exception of the U.S.A. events, staged in Huntington Beach and San Diego. Each of these California events had a purse of $100,000.00. The World Championships in Marseille France had a purse of $300,000.00.

The Brazilian team of Jose Loiola and Emanuel Schaefer Rego established the all-time FIVB Men's Beach Volleyball Tour tournament win streak. In 1999 they won six tournament championships in a row. The streak included twenty-one consecutive match victories. Loiola and Rego outclassed the rest of the field by advancing to the finals of 9 events, winning a total of 7 events.

IAN CLARK & BILL BOULLIANNE
Ian Clark and Bill Boullianne were the only American team able to win an FIVB "World Tour" event in 1999. They won the Mexican Open, in Acapulco Mecixo. Above photo, Clark hits a set from Boullianne.
Photo Courtesy of "Couvi"

EMANUEL REGO & JOSE LOIOLA
In 1999, Emanuel Rego and Jose Loiola paired-up on both the AVP and FIVB Tour's. They had the most success on the FIVB Tour, advancing to 9 finals, winning 7 times. Above photo, Rego hits a set from Loiola into the block of Nick Hanneman.
Photo Courtesy of "Couvi"

Jose Z-Marco Melo Ferreira Nobrega and Ricardo Alex Costa Santos, also from Brazil was the team with the second best total of FIVB championships, winning 3 events. The Portugese team of Joao Carlos Pereira Brenha Alves and Luis Miguel Barbosa Maia were also able to win a World Tour championship in 1999. They won the, as the 20th seeded team at the Russian Open at Troparevo Recreational Park, in Moscow Russia. Bill Boullianne and Ian Clark were the only American team able to win a FIVB World Tour event in 1999. They won the $170,000.00 Men's Mexican Open, in Acapulco Mexico, on the beach at Playa Tamarindos. The teams of Karch Kiraly and Adam Johnson along with Kevin Wong and Rob Heidger were each able to gain wins at the FIVB sanctioned U.S.A. Alero Beach Volleyball Series. Kiraly and Johnson won in Huntington Beach while Wong and Heidger won in San Diego.

With Ze'Marco and Ricardo's "Gold-Medal" performance, Brazil won 11 of the 13 FIVB Beach Volleyball World Tour "open" men's events in 1999. Only the Gold Medals by Bill Boullianne and Ian Clark of the United States in Mexico and Maia and Brenha in Russia prevented a "clean" sweep for the Brazilians. The season ending Brazilian Open was the 100th Men's FIVB Beach Volleyball World Tour event. A total of 46 men from nine countries had earned "Gold-Medals" on the beach. Brazil, which had now won 61 FIVB Beach Volleyball World Tour events in the 12-year history of the circuit, had been represented in 29-straight international championship matches. The last time a Brazilian team had not reached the finals was September 7, 1997 in Tenerife, Canary Islands. Brazil also has had a team in a FIVB "final four" in each of the last 44 international events since being denied a semi-final berth in the 1996 Portugal event.

INDIVIDUAL FIVB TOURNAMENT FINISHES
1999

Player	1st	2nd	3rd	4th	5th
Dain Blanton	0	0	0	2	1
Joao Carlos Pereira Brenha Alves	1	0	0	1	0
Bill Boullianne	1	0	0	0	0
John Child	0	0	1	0	1
Ian Clark	1	0	0	0	0
Martin Alejo Conde	0	1	1	3	0
Roberto Lopes da Costa	0	0	1	0	0
Fabio Diez	0	1	1	0	2
Eric Fonoimoana	0	0	0	2	1
Giovane Gavio	0	0	1	0	1
Mark Heese	0	0	1	0	1
Rob Heidger	1	0	1	1	2
Carl Henkel	0	0	0	0	2
Adam Johnson	0	0	0	1	3
Karch Kiraly	0	0	0	1	3
Jan Kvalheim	0	0	0	0	1
Martin Laciga	0	1	0	3	4
Paul Laciga	0	1	0	3	4
Jose Loiola	**7**	**2**	**1**	**0**	**0**
Bjorn Maaseide	0	0	0	0	1
Luis Miguel Barbosa Maia	1	0	0	1	0
Luiz Guilherme Marquez	0	5	2	1	2
Eduardo Esteban "Mono" Martinez	0	1	1	3	0
Javier Bosma Minguez	0	1	1	0	2
Jose Franco Vieira Neto	0	0	1	0	0
Jose Z-Marco Melo Ferreira Nobrega	3	3	3	1	0
Julien Prosser	0	0	1	0	4
Ricardo Alex Costa Santos	3	3	3	1	1
Emanuel Rego Scheffer	**7**	**2**	**1**	**0**	**0**
Sinjin Smith	0	0	0	0	2
Rogrio "Para" Ferrirs de Souza	0	5	2	1	2
Alexandre Tande Ramos	0	0	1	0	1
Kevin Wong	1	0	1	1	2
Lee Zahner	0	0	1	0	4

ADAM JOHNSON & KARCH KIRALY
Adam Johnson and Karch Kiraly won the FIVB sanctioned U.S.A. Alero Beach Volleyball Series event in Huntington Beach California, Above photo, Karch hits a set from Johnson, towards the defense of Canyon Ceman (left) and Brian Lewis (right).
Photo Courtesy of "Couvi"

ROB HEIDGER & KEVIN WONG
Rob Heidger and Kevin Wong won the FIVB sanctioned U.S.A. Alero Beach Volleyball Series event in San Diego California. Above photo, Heidger (left) and Wong fight for the ball during an event when the were on opposite sides of the net.
Photo Courtesy of "Couvi"

MEN'S TOURNAMENT RESULTS
1999-AVP

CLEARWATER, FLORIDA
May 1st-2nd, 1999

The first stop of the 1999 AVP Tour was staged at the "Hilton" in Clearwater Florida. Thirty-two teams competed in a single elimination format. This $75,000.00 event was won by the team of Dain Blanton and Eric Fonoimoana. Their share of the purse was $20,000.00. In the championship match, Blanton and Fonoimoana handed Karch Kiraly and Adam Johnson a 15-8 defeat. Kiraly and Johnson split $10,000.00 for their second place finish. The finals were televised on FOX Sports Net.

3rd Place: Emanuel Rego and Jose Loiola
3rd Place: Dax Holdren and Todd Rogers
5th Place: Kevin Martin and Mark Kerins
5th Place: Brent Frohoff and Ricci Luyties
5th Place: Aaron Boss and Dan Castillo
5th Place: Ian Clark and Bill Boullianne

NEW ORLEANS, LOUISIANA
May 22nd-23rd, 1999

The second stop of the 1999 AVP Tour was staged on Coconut Beach in New Orleans Louisiana. Thirty-two teams competed over two days, in a double elimination format. This $75,000.00 event was won by the team of Karch Kiraly and Adam Johnson. Their share of the purse was $18,000.00. In the championship match, Kiraly and Johnson handed Dain Blanton and Eric Fonoimoana a 15-8 defeat. Blanton and Fonoimoana split $11,000.00 for their second place finish. The finals were televised on FOX Sports Net.

3rd Place: Emanuel Rego and Jose Loiola
4th Place: Bill Boullianne and Ian Clark
5th Place: David Swatik and Mike Whitmarsh
5th Place: Todd Rogers and Dax Holdren

DALLAS, TEXAS
June 5th-6th, 1999

The third stop of the AVP Pro Beach Volleyball Tour was supposed to be a 32-team double elimination tournament, competed over two days, but the 1999 Dallas Open marked a new era of prudent and creative financial management for the AVP. The AVP made life a little bit better for the players and the fans in the process. With a mid-week qualifier, played on Sorrento Beach in Santa Monica California, players were able to compete for the right to join the "Elite Eight" in Dallas for the weekend. Four teams advanced to play in Dallas joining the top four seeds who were directly in the event.

ERIC FONOIMOANA & DAIN BLANTON
Eric Fonoimoana and Dain Blanton started the 1999 ABP Tour off on the right foot, winning the Clearwater Beach Florida event. Above photo, Fonoimoana hits a set from Blanton, past the block of Carl Henkel towards the defense of Sinjin Smith.
Photo Courtesy of "Couvi"

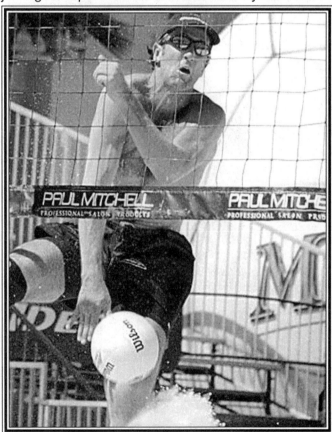

CANYON CEMAN
Canyon Ceman played well enough to finish within the top three places at four 1999 AVP Tour tournaments. Ceman's best 1999 finish was a second place, at the Belmar NJ event, with Brian Lewis. Above photo, Ceman attacking the ball.
Photo Courtesy of "Couvi"

The players who didn't make it, received equal prize money to their finish as if the whole event had been played in Dallas. The only difference was, no travel expenses and the weekend off. The fans in Dallas enjoyed the intimacy and quality of play that a one court venue provides, and the competition was focused. The Dallas Open was a very successful experiment. The AVP considered utilizing this system and improve the mid-week qualifiers making them special events unto themselves, market the qualifiers, and keep the positive vibrations flowing. The only Achilles heel to this system was that it seemed virtually impossible to surpass the top four teams in points as they were guaranteed a high finish every week-end. The four teams that qualified for Dallas were Carlos Loss and Eduardo Bacil, Henry Russell and Nick Hannemann, Brent Frohoff and Ricci Luyties, along with Brent Doble and Lee LeGrande.

The AVP $75,000.00 Dallas Open was played on one court that was set up at "West End." The winners of the tournament and the $18,000.00 first place prize were Karch Kiraly and Adam Johnson. In the championship match, Kiraly and Johnson defeated Dain Blanton and Eric Fonoimoana. Last year's winners were Jose Loiola and Kent Steffes. This years final was televised on FOX Sports Net

3rd Place: Jose Loiola and Emanuel Rego
3rd Place: Mike Whitmarsh and Brian Lewis
5th Place: Carlos Loss and Eduardo Bacil
5th Place: Henry Russell and Nick Hannemann
5th Place: Brent Frohoff and Ricci Luyties
5th Place: Brent Doble and Lee LeGrand

HERMOSA BEACH, CALIFORNIA
June 9th-13th, 1999

On the north side of the Hermosa Beach Pier, the $75,000.00 Hermosa Beach Men's Open was staged. This was the fourth stop of the 1999 AVP Tour. The event was staged in conjunction with the 1999 "Hermosa Beach Bash." It was a circus atmosphere, with an "Inline Skate-BMX-Skateboard Bowl" set up next to the volleyball stadium. The courts were lined with bright blue beach chairs, in addition to blaring music and lots of people on the surrounding courts of sand. There were approximately 20,000 attendees at this AVP Sideout Hermosa Beach tournament. The crowd was nothing short of huge, with people milling around everywhere, all over the tournament venue as well as all up and down the famed Hermosa Beach Strand. The temperatures stayed relatively cool, which was a welcome relief from last weekend at the Dallas tournament

In the winner's bracket final Jose Loiola and Emanuel Rego defeated Mike Whitmarsh and David Swatik by a score of 15-8. In the loser's bracket final Whitmarsh and Swatik earned their way into the championship match by defeating Lee LeGrande and Brent Doble 12-8. In the championship match, after falling into the loser's bracket earlier in the day, Whitmarsh and Swatik rallied to score an exciting 14-12 win over Loiola and Rego to capture the win and split the $20,000.00 first place check.

3rd Place: Lee LeGrande and Brent Doble
4th Place: Karch Kiraly and Adam Johnson
5th Place: Dax Holdren and Todd Rogers
5th Place: Dain Blanton and Eric Fonoimoana

HENRY RUSSELL
On the 1999 AVP beach volleyball tour, Henry Russell presented a huge stumbling block for the opposition. Above photo, Russell gets above the net to reject the ball.
Photo Courtesy of "Couvi"

KEVIN MARTIN & BILL BOULLIANNE
With different partners, Bill Boulianne and Kevin Martin both provided some worthy competition on the 1999 AVP Tour, finishing within the top five 2 and 4 times respectively. Above photo, Martin cuts the ball past the block of Boullianne.
Photo Courtesy of "Couvi"

BELMAR, NEW JERSEY
June 26th-27th, 1999

The 1999 Belmar Beach $75,000.00 AVP Men's Open was won by Mike Whitmarsh and David Swatik this was their second tournament championship in a row. This was also the third year in a row that Whitmarsh has won the Belmar Open, all with different partners. He won in 1997 with Canyon Ceman and in 1998 with Kent Steffes. In the championship match, the "Whit" and "Swatty" easily defeated Ceman and Lewis by a score of 15-6. The winners split $18,000.00 for their efforts.

3rd Place: Karch Kiraly and Adam Johnson
3rd Place: Dax Holdren and Todd Rogers
5th Place: Kevin Martin and Mark Kerins
5th Place: Dain Blanton and Eric Fonoimoana
5th Place: Eduardo Bacil and Eduardo Garrido
5th Place: Brian Ivie and Brent Frohoff

CHICAGO, ILLINOIS
July 3rd-4th, 1999

Chicago's North Beach, at North Avenue, was the site for the $75,000.00 AVP Chicago Open. During the championship match, there was a chant of "USA, USA" that was fitting for the occasion. Not only was it the 4th of July, but at center court, inside the temporary stadium, hundreds of fans witnessed the, record-breaking performance, of the greatest player to ever set foot on the sand. The man in the pink "Speedo" hat, Karch Kiraly and partner Adam Johnson, defeated the all-Brazilian team of Roberto Lopes and Franco Neto 15-7 to win the AVP-Paul Mitchell Grand Slam event. Fittingly Kiraly served for the winning point but was perplexed when Lopes and Neto did not play the ball. The point was awarded to Kiraly and Johnson for the championship. This gave Kiraly his 140th tournament championship. He also split the $18,000.00 first place check with his partner.

3rd Place: Dain Blanton and Eric Fonoimoana
4th Place: Dax Holdren and Todd Rogers
5th Place: Eduardo Bacil and Eduardo Garrido
5th Place: Stein Metzgar and Carlos Loss

MUSKEGON MICHIGAN
July 10th-11th, 1999

The world's Michigan's "Muskegon Beach" was the site of the next $75,000.00 Men's AVP event. The $18,000.00 first place prize went to the team of Brian Lewis and Franco Neto. In the championship match, the ydefeated Dax Holdren and Todd Rogers, in an excitingchampionship final. Holdren and Rogers received a check in the amount of $11,000.00 for their second place finish.

3rd Place: Lee LeGrande and Brent Doble
4th Place: Karch Kiraly and Adam Johnson
5th Place: Eric Fonoimoana and Dain Blanton
5th Place: Stein Metzger and Carlos Loss

SANTA BARBARA, CALIFORNIA
July 31st-August 1st, 1999

The world's best players from the Association of Volleyball Professional (AVP) participated in the eighth stop of the 1999 AVP Pro Beach Volleyball Tour. The $75,000.00 "Karch Kiraly Classic" had 32 men's teams that competed over two days in a double elimination format. In the championship match, Karch Kiraly and Adam Johnson defeated Carlos Loss and Stein Metzgar, by a score of 15-7. This was Kiraly's 141 tour championship win. Kiraly and Johnson split $20,000.00, Loss and Metzgar split $11,000.00. The finals were televised on FOX Sports Net.

3rd Place: Canyon Ceman and Brian Lewis
4th Place: Dax Holdren and Todd Rogers
5th Place: Brent Doble and Lee LeGrande
5th Place: Mark Kerins and Kevin Martin

LOUISVILLE, KENTUCKY
August 13th-14th, 1999

The ninth stop of the 1999 AVP Tour was at The Brewery, in Louisville Kentucky for the $75,000.00 Men's Louisville Open.

Prior to this event, on Tuesday, August 10th, 1999, there were twenty-eight men's teams competing on Sorrento Beach, California in a single elimination format to earn four positions in the Louisville tournament. The top four ranked teams on the AVP Tour got an automatic bye to Louisville, to meet the four teams that qualified at Sorrento Beach. The four teams to qualify were: Matt Lyles and Wayne Seligson, Eduardo Bacil and Eduardo Garrido, Paul Boyd and Pepe Delahoz, along with

BRENT DOBLE & MIKE WHITMARSH
Brent Doble paired-up with Lee Legrande for 5 top five finishes. Mike Whitmarsh teamed-up with David Swatik to advance to 4 finals, winning 3 times. Above photo, Whitmarsh challenges the block of Doble, during the 1999 Hermosa Beach CA event.
Photo Courtesy of Frank Goroszko

Carlos Loss and Stein Metzger. A total of eight teams then competed in Louisville in a single elimination format over two days.

In the championship match, the first seeded team of Todd Rogers and Dax Holdren outlasted the third seeded team of Mike Whitmarsh and David Swatik 12-10. The winner's earned $18,000.00 for their effort. The finals were televised on FOX Sports Net.
3rd Place: Mark Kerins and Canyon Ceman
3rd Place: Matt Lyles and Wayne Seligson
5th Place: Franco Neto and Brian Lewis
5th Place: Stein Metzgar and Carlos Loss
5th Place: Eduardo Bacil and Eduardo Garrido
5th Place: Paul Boyd and Pepe Delahoz

CLEVELAND, OHIO
August 21st-22nd, 1999

At Cleveland's Nautica Center, the $75,000.00 AVP "Tournament of Champions" beach volleyball tournament was staged. The world's best players from the Association of Volleyball Professionals participated in the tenth stop of the 1999 AVP Pro Beach Volleyball Tour.

Prior to this event, on Tuesday, August 17th, 1999 twenty-eight men's teams competed in Sorrento Beach, California in a single elimination format to earn four positions in the Cleveland tournament. The top four ranked teams on the AVP Tour received an automatic bye to Cleveland, to be met by the four teams competing in Sorrento Beach. The four teams to qualify were: Matt Lyles and Wayne Seligson, Brent Doble and Lee LeGrande, Mark Kerins and Kevin Martin, along with Carlos Loss and Stein Metzger. A total of eight teams then competed in Cleveland in a single elimination format over two days.

In the championship match, the fourth seeded team of Brian Lewis and Franco Neto defeated the second seeded team of Eric Fonoimoana and Dain Blanton, by a score of 15-8. The winners earned $18,000.00 for their effort. The finals were televised on FOX Sports Net. Last years winners, Jose Loiola and Emanuel Rego were playing an FIVB event Tenerife, Canary Islands, Spain.
3rd Place: Todd Rogers and Canyon Ceman
3rd Place: Mark Kerins and Kevin Martin
5th Place: Mike Whitmarsh and David Swatik
5th Place: Stein Metzgar and Carlos Loss
5th Place: Matt Lyles and Wayne Seligson
5th Place: Brent Doble and Lee LeGrande

MANHATTAN BEACH, CALIFORNIA
August 28th-29th, 1999

Prior to the 1999 $100,000.00 AVP Manhattan Beach Open, David Swatik and Mike Whitmarsh were so frustrated with their play on the AVP Tour that they considered changing partners, heading into the tournament. The duo decided to stick it out together, and when it was all over Sunday, Swatik and Whitmarsh stood united, waving to an appreciative crowd while holding a $22,000.00 check for winning the tournament championship at the Manhattan Beach Pier.

In the championship match, Loiola and Rego took an early lead, but Swatik and Whitmarsh went ahead, 7-6, on Swatik's third ace and would never trail again. Rego managed to tie the match at 13 with a cross-court kill, but he then hit wide and into the net on the next two points to give Swatik and Whitmarsh the title. The 15-13 victory over Brazilians Jose Loiola and Emanuel Rego in what turned out to be a rematch of the Hermosa Beach Open final was especially sweet for Swatik, a Manhattan Beach local, whose seven jump-serve aces made the difference. Swatik, after each of his jump-serve aces, pumped his arms as if he were Hulk Hogan, drawing roars of approval from the crowd. Both players felt honored to be up on the pier (where tournament winners are listed by bronze plaques) with all of the legends of beach volleyball.
3rd Place: Karch Kiraly and Adam Johnson
4th Place: Dain Blanton and Eric Fonoimoana
5th Place: Adam Jewell and Eduardo Bacil
5th Place: Brent Doble and Lee LeGrande

LAS VEGAS, NEVADA
September 17th-19th, 1999

The 1999 "King-of-the-Beach" $150,000.00 invitational tournament was played on the "Sands" of the Hard Rock Hotel's parking lot in Las Vegas Nevada. David Swatik completed his best AVP season ever by winning the 1999 "King-of-the-Beach" crown. Swatik did it in style, winning all six games that he played in over two days of play. He demonstrated his versatility by winning his games playing with five different partners.

By the second game of the final day of competition, Swatik was far enough ahead of the other competitors that he actually claimed "King" status while the other players were competing to determine second through fourth place. In the first match of the final day, Swatik was teamed with Eric Fonoimoana against Dain Blanton and Mike Whitmarsh. "Swattty" and "Foni" were leading 11-7 with only 17 seconds on the clock. After an excellent dig by Blanton, and a couple of quick mistakes by "Swatty" and "Foni" the game went into overtime, with "Swattty" and "Foni" pulling off the 12-10 win. After this first game, Fonoimoana was the only player with enough points to contest Swatik for the title. In the deciding match, Swatik and Blanton defeated Fonoimoana and Whitmarsh by a score of 14-10. Swatik earned $47,000.00 for his "Royal" performance. Blanton edged past Fonoimoana for second place and a check for $25,000.00, while Fonoimoana settled for third place and $20,000.00. Fourth place went to Whitmarsh along with $15,500.00. Brian Lewis was in the fifth spot, earning $14,000.00.
1st Place: David Swatik
2nd Place: Dain Blanton
3rd Place: Eric Fonoimoana
4th Place: Mike Whitmarsh
5th Place: Brian Lewis

MEN'S TOURNAMENT RESULTS
1999-FIVB

MAR DEL PLATA ARGENTINA
January 13th-17th, 1999

The first stop of the 1999 FIVB Beach Volleyball World Tour was the Men's Argentina Open, at Mar del Plata. The event was won by the Brazilian team of Emanuel Scheffer Rego and Jose Loiola. In the championship match, Rego and Loiola, sent the Argentinean fans home disappointed, when the top-seeded team scored a 12-7 and 12-6 win over Esteban Martinez and Martin Conde, from Argentina, to capture the Gold Medal in this $170,000.00 FIVB Beach Volleyball World Tour event. The 76-minute-match on Bristol Beach earned Emanuel and Loiola the $30,000.00 first-place prize in the first of 13 scheduled FIVB Beach Volleyball World Tour events on the 1999 calendar. The third-seeded Martinez and Conde, who had won seven-straight matches on their home sand after dropping their opening game Friday, shared $20,000.00 for second. This opening event was the first opportunity to play with the new rules that were introduced to the World Tour, particularly the limitation of time between 2 rallies to 12 seconds and the reduction to 2 time-outs per match or set (instead of 4). These changes proved to be appropriate as they added tempo to the games which pleased the over 40,000 spectators witnessing the event in the volleyball stadium. There was live coverage of the final by the TV Channel ESPN SUR.

3rd Place: Rogerio Para and Guilherme Marques-Bra
4th Place: ZeMarco de Melo and Ricardo Santos-Bra
5th Place: John Child and Mark Heese-Canada
5th Place: Carl Henkel and Kevin Wong-USA

Additional American team finishes included a seventh place finish by the team of Sinjin Smith and Rob Heidger. Dain Blanton and Kent Steffes were in ninth place, while Mike Whitmarsh and Eric Fonoimoana were in seventeenth place.

This event began the qualification process to determine entries for the 2000 Sydney Olympic Games with final selections to be determined August 15th, 2000. The top ten rankings, with results from this tournament were:

FIVB TOP 10 MENS' TEAM WORLD RANKING 1999
(dated January 18th, 1999)

Teams	Country	Points
1. Para-Guilherme	BRA	2348.00
2. Emanuel-Loiola	BRA	2306.50
3. Martinez-Conde	ARG	1996.50
4. M.Laciga-P.Laciga	SUI	1901.50
5. ZeMarco-Ricardo	BRA	1841.50
6. Kvalheim-Maaseide	NOR	1590.50
7. Child-Heese	CAN	1546.50
8. Maia-Brenha	POR	1392.00
9. Bosma-Diez	ESP	1336.00
10. Henkel-Wong	USA	1281.00

RICARDO ALEX COSTA SANTOS
Brazilian Ricardo Santos began to provide some enormous competition on the 1999 FIVB Tour. Ricardo advanced to 6 "Gold-Medal" matches winning 3 times. Above photo, Ricardo challenges the block of 6'8" Sascha Heyer, from Switzerland.
Photo Courtesy of "Couvi"

EMANUEL REGO
On the 1999 FIVB Tour, Brazilian Emanuel Rego paired-up with compatriot Jose Loiola to win six "Gold-Medal" matches in a row. Their win streak included twenty-one consecutive match victories. Above photo, Rego gets down low to make a pass.
Photo Courtesy of Frank Goroszko

ACAPULCO, MEXICO
April 7th-11th, 1999

The second stop of the 1999 FIVB Beach Volleyball World Tour was the $170,000.00 Men's Mexican Open, in Acapulco Mexico. The event was won by the American team of Ian Clark and Bill Boullianne. They were the fourteenth seeds in the 32-team Main Draw competition on the beach at Playa Tamarindos. The Americans posted a pair of upset wins over a pair of Brazilian rivals to capture the U.S.A's first men's FIVB Beach Volleyball World Tour Gold medal in 29 international events. Twice they posted wins of 15-10 over two Brazilian teams, including a 51-minute victory over fifth-seeded Para Ferreira and Guilherme Marques in the Gold medal match. The Americans utilized tough serving all through the match. With the win, Clark and Boullianne shared the $30,000.00 first-place prize while Para and Guilherme split $20,000.00 for their Silver medal effort. The win by Clark and Boullianne put an end to five-straight FIVB men's beach titles for Brazil. This was the first international championship match for Clark and Boullianne. They posted a 6-0 match mark and were now 2-0 against Para and Guilherme, the No.1-ranked team on the FIVB Tour. This was the 17th FIVB Gold medal match for Para and Guilherme. The duo had won seven international titles together, including four last season. The Brazilians were the reigning FIVB Beach Volleyball World Champions after winning the crown in 1997 in Los Angeles. The five-day beach volleyball event started with 53 men's teams attempting to qualify for the Main Draw. This event was the first of three combined tournaments with women on the FIVB Beach Volleyball World Tour this season. There were over 50,000 spectators that attended this event.

3rd Place: ZeMarco de Melo and Ricardo Santos-Bra
4th Place: Paul Laciga and Martin Laciga-Swiss
5th Place: Karch Kiraly and Adam Johnson-USA
5th Place: Sinjin Smith and Rob Heidger-USA

Additional American finishes: Dain Blanton and Kent Steffes finished in 9th place. Carl Henkel and Kevin Wong finished in 17th place. Eric Fonoimoana and Mike Whitmarsh finished in a distant 25th place.

HUNTINGTON BEACH CALIFORNIA USA
May 15th-16th, 1999

The 1999 Men's Oldsmobile Alero Beach Volleyball Series at Huntington Beach was won by Karch Kiraly and Adam Johnson. Kiraly and Johnson won their 11th pro title together at this four-day, $100,000.00 event. In the championship match of this U.S. Olympic challenge event, Kiraly and Johnson overcame a challenge from the team of Carl Henkel and Kevin Wong. Seeded second in the men''s competition, Kiraly and Johnson won their first event in their last five tournaments together at The Pier by downing third-seeded Carl Henkel and Kevin Wong 15-9 in a 35-minute, 32-sideout title match. Kiraly and Johnson led from the start to split the $20,000.00 first-place prize while Henkel and Wong shared $14,000.00 for their best finish together. Kiraly earned his 137th pro beach title as he continues to chases beach legend Sinjin Smith for the all-time domestic mark. Smith, a 23 year veteran of tournament play, just turned 42 years old. He had 139 pro titles with his last win in 1993 with Randy Stoklos in Fort Myers, Florida.

This Oldsmobile Alero Beach Volleyball Series opener was the fourth 1999 event for the United States men. Sponsored by Oldsmobile Alero, the nine-event Oldsmobile Alero Beach Volleyball Series was developed in partnership with USA Volleyball (USAV) and the United States Olympic Committee (USOC), to determine the athletes who will represent the United States on the FIVB Beach Volleyball World Tour and ultimately identify those to compete in the 2000 Sydney Australia Olympic Games.

3rd Place: Sinjin Smith and Rob Heidger-USA
4th Place: Brent Doble and Lee LeGrande-USA
5th Place: Ricci Luyties and Brent Frohoff-USA
5th Place: Dax Holdren and Todd Rogers-USA

In seventh place was the U.S.A. team of Scott Friederichsen and Kevin Martin.

TORONTO CANADA
June 16th-20th, 1999

On Toronto's Woodbine Beach, on Ashbridges Bay, the FIVB Men's $170,000.00 Labatt Blue Toronto was won by the Brazilian team of ZeMarco deMelo and Ricardo Santos. This was their first FIVB Beach Volleyball World Tour title of the 1999 season. This event was the second of three combined men and women's events on the 1999 FIVB Beach Volleyball World Tour. In the championship match, they defeated fellow countrymen Emanuel Scheffer Rego and Jose Loiola by a score of 15-10. The 54-minute title match featured 80 sideouts, five ties and two lead changes with ZeMarco and Ricardo taking the lead for good at 9-8 on an Emanuel hitting error that started a six point run to increase their lead to 14-8. ZeMarco scored the winning point with a hard spike that hit on the back line. The winner's split $30,000.00, while the runner-ups split $20,000.00 for their efforts.

3rd Place: Rob Heidger and Kevin Wong-USA
4th Place: Karch Kiraly and Adam Johnson-USA
5th Place: Jan Kvalheim and Bjorn Maaseide-Nor
5th Place: Paul Laciga and Martin Laciga-Swiss

Additional American finishes: Ian Clark and Bill Boullianne were in ninth place. Dain Blanton and Eric Fonoimoana along with Sinjin Smith and Car Henkel were in seventeenth place.

MOSCOW RUSSIA
June 23rd-27th, 1999

The $170,000.00 Men's FIVB Russian Open at Troparevo Recreational Park, in Moscow Russia, was won by the 20th-seeded team of Luis Maia and Joao Brenha of Portugal. The Portugese duo won six-straight matches in the second annual Russian Open with each upset victory being over a higher seeded team in the Main Draw competition. This was their second international title. In the championship match, Maia and Brenha completed their upset escapade by defeating the third-seeded Brazilian team of ZeMarco de Melo and Ricardo Santos, in the the 52-minute match by a score of 15-9, to capture the "Gold-Medal" and $30,000.00 first place prize. ZeMarco and Ricardo, shared the $20,000.00 second place check along with the Silver Medal.

3rd Place: Emanuel Rego and Jose Loiola-Bra
4th Place: Eduardo Martinez and Martin Conde-Arg
5th Place: Paul Laciga and Martin Laciga-Swiss
5th Place: Rogerio Para and Guilherme Marques-Bra

Additional American finishes: Sinjin Smith and Carl Henkel were in seventh place. Bill Boullianne and Ian Clark along with Rob Heidger and Kevin Wong, were in twenty-fifth place.

BERLIN GERMANY
June 30th-July 4th, 1999

The fifth of 13 stops on the 1999 men's FIVB Beach Volleyball World Tour, was played under mostly sunny skies, on the Platz an der Jannowitzbrucke. The $170,000.00 FIVB Men's 1999 Berlin Open, was won by Brazilians, ZeMarco de Melo and Ricardo Santos, as they became the first two-time winners on the 1999 FIVB Beach Volleyball World Tour. In the championship match, first seeds ZeMarco and Ricardo defeated fourth-seeded Martin and Paul Laciga of Switzerland 15-11 in the 53-minute final. The win netted ZeMarco and Ricardo the $30,000.00 first-place prize. More than 15,000 spectators viewed the final. The Lacigas shared $20,000.0 with their second place finish.

3rd Place: Javier Bosma and Fabio Diez-Spain
4th Place: John Child and Mark Heese-Canada
5th Place: Kevin Wong and Rob Heidger-USA
5th Place: Gavio Giovane and Alxandre Tande-Bra
Additional American finishes: Sinjin Smith and Carl Henkel were in 17th place while Bill Boullianne and Ian Clark were in 25th place.

STAVANGER NORWAY
July 7th-11th, 1999

The inaugural Phillips Men's Open, was staged at the Vaagen City Center, in Stavanger Norway. This $170,000.00 FIVB Beach Volleyball World Tour event was won by Brazilians Emanuel Rego Scheffer and Jose Loiola. The finals were played under sunny skies and witnessed by a "sold out" crowd of 3,000-plus fans, who had purchased $25 tickets for final four matches. In the championship match, Emanuel and Loiola rallied from 11-8 and 13-11 deficits to snare the Gold Medal and the $30,000.00 first-place prize. They defeated compatriots, number four seeds, Para Ferreira and Guilherme Marques 15-13. Para and Guilherme, who gave up four-straight points after gaining a 13-11 lead, split $20,000.00 for second-place. More than 70,000 fans watched the five days of competition, as Norway hosted, its biggest volleyball event in its history.

3rd Place: ZeMarco de Melo and Ricardo Santos-Bra
4th Place: Paul Laciga and Martin Laciga-Swiss
5th Place: Julien Prosser and Lee Zahner-Aus
5th Place: Gavio Giovane and Alxandre Tande-Bra
Sinjin Smith and Carl Henkel, Bill Boullianne and Ian Clark, along with Rob Heidger and Kevin Wong, all three American teams, were in 17th place.

LIGANO ITALY
July 14th-18th, 1999

On Sabbiadoroos Beach in Lignano Sabbiadoro Italy, Brazilians Emanuel Scheffer and Jose Loiola rebounded from a second-round loss to win seven-straight matches enroute to capturing their second-straight FIVB Beach Volleyball World Tour "Gold-Medal." In the championship match, Emanuel and Loiola outlasted compatriots Para Ferreira and Guilherme Marques 15-13 at the $170,000.00 Italian Men's Open final. The match was played before a standing room-only crowd of 4,500 in near-perfect weather conditions, for the All-Brazilian final. Para and Guilherme were playing in their 19th FIVB Beach Volleyball World Tour championship match in 54 career events together. The Brazilians had now posted a 29-11 match record for the 1999 season with $92,000.00 in combined earnings.

3rd Place: Eduardo Martinez and Martin Conde-Arg
4th Place: Rob Heidger and Kevin Wong-USA
5th Place: ZeMarco de Melo and Ricardo Santos-Bra
5th Place: Javier Bosma and Fabio Diez-Spain
Additional American finishes: Dain Blanton and Eric Fonoimoana along with Sinjin Smith and Car Henkel finished in 9th place. Ian Clark and Bill Boullianne along with Karch Kiraly and Adam Johnson were in 17th place.

MARSEILLE FRANCE
July 20th-25th, 1999

On Plage du Prado in Marseille France, the Men's FIVB $300,000.00 World Championship of Beach Volleyball was won by the Brazilian team of Emanuel Rego Scheffer and Jose Loiola. The FIVB Beach Volleyball World Championships were played before an estimated 70,000 spectators over a seven-day period. In the championship match, played before a packed Plage du Prado Centre Court of 5,000 spectators and near-perfect weather, the Brazilians broke open a tight match by scoring the last six points in route to a 15-8 win over Martin and Paul Laciga of Switzerland. Loiola and Emanuel were really focused and were able to handle the Swiss team's big service game. The Swiss are a big and strong team and they kept the pressure on throughout the match, but the Brazilians conditioning paid off in the end. The 50-minute win netted the second-seeded Emanuel and Loiola their biggest paycheck ever as they split $60,000.00 for their third-straight win on the FIVB Beach Volleyball World Tour. The Laciga's also earned their biggest paycheck with $39,000.00 for second place. Loiola and Emanuel credited their American coach, Jim Menges, for helping them develop consistent play. Menges is a beach volleyball legend that knows the game. He uses his knowledge and experience to prepare Loiola and Emanuel both physically and mentally.

3rd Place: Javier Bosma and Fabio Diez-Spain
4th Place: Rogerio Para and Guilherme Marques-Bra
5th Place: Karch Kiraly and Adam Johnson-USA
5th Place: Julien Prosser and Lee Zahner-Aus
Additional American finishes: Rob Heidger and Kevin Wong were in 7th place along with Sinjin Smith and Carl Henkel. Dain Blanton and Eric Fonoimoana were in 9th place while Ian Clark and Bill Boullianne were in 17th place.

KLAGENFURT AUSTRIA
July 28th-August 1st, 1999

On the Strandbad Sands in Klagenfurt Austria, Brazilian Emanuel Scheffer Rego captured his third-straight "Austrian Wash & Go Men's Open" championship with partner Jose Loiola. In the one hour championship match, Emanuel and Loiola defeated compatriots ZeMarco de Melo and Ricardo Santos 15-11. At this $170,000.00 FIVB event, the stadium was jam-packed with 8,000 spectators, as the top-seeded Emanuel and Loiola won their fourth-straight title this season. Loiola and Emanuel, the only team to win four-straight international men's events, split the $30,000.00 first-place purse. ZeMarco and Ricardo shared the $20,000.00 second-place prize.

3rd Place: Rogerio Para and Guilherme Marques-Bra
4th Place: Dain Blanton and Eric Fonoimoana-USA
5th Place: Kevin Wong and Rob Heidger-USA
5th Place: Julien Prosser and Lee Zahner-Aus
Additional American finishes: Sinjin Smith and Carl Henkel were in 17th place while Ian Clark and Bill Boullianne were a distant 25th.

ESPHINHO PORTUGAL
August 4th-8th, 1999

On Praia de Baia in Espinho, Portugal the top-seeded team of Emanuel Scheffer Rego and Jose Loiola, from Brazil, captured their fifth-straight FIVB Beach Volleyball World Tour title. In the championship match, Emanuel and Loiola defeated second seeds Para Ferreira and Guilherme Marques, 15-8 in the 30-minute all-Brazilian final. Emanuel and Loiola, split the $30,000.00 first place check. Emanuel, who has won a record 25 FIVB Beach Volleyball World Tour titles, and Loiola defeated Para and Guilherme in a Gold Medal match for the third-time in the last six weeks. With two teams in the finals, Brazil had a tandem in FIVB Beach Volleyball World Tour Gold Medal match for the 26-straight event. Loiola, winning his 10th FIVB Beach Volleyball World Tour title moved into a fifth-place tie on the all-time list with Americans Sinjin Smith and Randy Stoklos. Brazil won all three medals at this $170,000.00 Portugal Open for the second-straight week on the FIVB Tour this season and the eighth-time in the 12-year history of the international circuit.

3rd Place: ZeMarco de Melo and Ricardo Santos-Bra
4th Place: Eduardo Martinez and Martin Conde-Arg
5th Place: Dain Blanton and Eric Fonoimoana-USA
5th Place: Paul Laciga and Martin Laciga-Swiss
Additional American finishes: Adam Johnson and Karch Kiraly along with Sinjin Smith and Carl Henkel were in ninth place. Rob Heidger and Kevin Wong were in seventeenth place.

OSTEND BELGIUM
August 11th-15th, 1999

On Grote Shand Beach, in Ostende Belgium, top-seeded Emanuel Scheffer Rego and Jose Loiola captured their sixth-straight 1999 FIVB Beach Volleyball World Tour event. The Spa Beach Volleyball 1999 of Belgium was the 11th of 13 men's events on the FIVB Beach Volleyball World Tour. In the championship match, they defeated compatriots ZeMarco de Melo and Ricardo Santos in the $170,000.00 Belgium Spa Beach Volleyball event. With improved conditions from prior wet and windy weather, Emanuel and Loiola used the wind to their advantage, as they made very few mistakes as they scored a 12-9 and 12-5 decision in 53 minutes over ZeMarco and Ricardo. They had now won their last 22 matches on the FIVB Beach Volleyball World Tour. Emanuel and Loiola split the $30,000.00 first-place prize while ZeMarco and Ricardo shared $20,000.00 for second placel.

3rd Place: Julien Prosser and Lee Zahner-Aus
4th Place: Dain Blanton and Eric Fonoimoana-USA
5th Place: Para Ferreira and Guilherme Marques-Bra
5th Place: Additional American finishes: Rob Heidger and Kevin Wong were in seventh place. Karch Kiraly and Adam Johnson were in ninth place. Sinjin Smith and Carl Henkel were in seventeenth place.

LUIS MIGUEL BARBOSA MAIA
Luis Maia, from Portugal, showed that he was capable of siding-out against all of the competition on the 1999 FIVB Tour. Maia teamed-up with compatriot Carlos Brenha to win the Fivb event in Moscow Russia. Above photo, Maia slices another side-out.
Photo Courtesy of the FIVB

LEE ZAHNER
Australian Lee Zahner teamed-up with fellow countryman Julien Prosser to provide some worthy competition on the 1999 FIVB Tour. Zahner and Prosser finmished within the top five 5 times, including a 3rd at the Belgium event. Above photo, Zahner digging
Photo Courtesy of the FIVB

TENERIFE, CANARY ISLANDS, SPAIN
August 18th-22nd, 1999

On Las Teresitas Beach, in Tenerife, Canary Islands Spain, the Brazilian's continued their FIVB Beach Volleyball World Tour superiority as the South Americans posted another medal sweep at the $170,000.00 Spanish Open. This was the 12th of 13 events and tenth-straight week of arduous competition on the 1999 FIVB Beach Volleyball World Tour. In the championship match, of the fifth annual Spanish Open, ZeMarco de Melo and Ricardo Santos scored a 15-8, 47-minute win over second-seeded compatriots Para Ferreira and Guilherme Marques to share the $30,000.00 first-place prize. Para and Guilherme shared $20,000.00 for netting the "Silver-Medal."

3rd Place: Giovane Gavio and Tande Ramos-Bra
4th Place: Paul Laciga and Martin Laciga-Swiss
5th Place: Karch Kiraly and Adam Johnson-USA
5th Place: Julien Prosser and Lee Zahner-Aus
Additional American finishes: Sinjin Smith and Carl Henkel were in seventh place, while Rob Heidger and Kevin Wong settled for a ninth place

MARTIN ALEJO CONDE
Martin Conde teamed-up, with fellow Argentine "Mono" Esteban Martinez, to compete on the 1999 FIVB Tour. They finished within the top five on five occasions. Their best finish was a 2nd at Mar Del Plata Argentina. Above photo, Conde passing the ball.
Photo Courtesy of the FIVB

SAN DIEGO, CALIFORNIA, USA
September 11th-12th, 1999

Americans, Rob Heidger and Kevin Wong captured the Oldsmobile Alero Beach Volleyball Series Gold Medals, winning the $150,000.00 Bank of America "U. S. Olympic Cup" at Crown Point Shores, on Mission Bay, in San Diego California. In the championship match, Heidger and Wong, the sixth-ranked team on the FIVB Beach Volleyball World Tour, scored a 15-10 win in 43 minutes over Spain's Javier Bosma and Fabio Diez to share the $20,000.00 first-place prize. Heidger and Wong, who teamed up together in June of this year, scored their first professional win on Wong's 27th birthday. Bosma and Diez, who entered this event as the fifth-ranked international tandem, split $14,000.00 along with the "Silver-Medal." The "Gold-Medal" match was tied seven times before the Americans scored four-straight points to take a 13-9 lead. Bosma and Diez turned the tide as they cut the lead to 13-10, but Heidger and Wong scored two-straight points to end the match.

3rd Place: John Child and Mark Heese-Canada
4th Place: Martin Conde and Esteban Martinez-Arg
5th Place: Sinjin Smith and Carl Henkel-USA
5th Place: Paul Laciga and Martin Laciga-Swiss
The American teams of Morgan Chapman and Greg Ryan along with Mike Mattarocci and Devin Poolman were in seventh place. Note: the top AVP teams were not allowed to participate in the tournament due to contract restraints with the AVP. The AVP players were banned form playing on the Alero Tour because the AVP viewed it as a competing tour. If the AVP players participated in the event, it was possible that they would have been fined as well as suspended.

VITORIA BRAZIL
November 30th-December 5th, 1999

Third-seeded Ze'Marco de Melo and Ricardo Santos captured their second-straight FIVB Beach Volleyball World Tour Gold Medal by upsetting top-seeded Emanuel Rego Scheffer and Jose Loiola in the finals of the $170,000.00 Brazilian Open. The title was the sixth FIVB Beach Volleyball World Tour Gold Medal for Ze'Marco de Melo and Ricardo Santos as the pair netted the $30,000.00 first-place prize by defeating Emanuel and Loiola 12-9 and 12-6 in the 81-minute match on Camburi Beach before a standing room-only crowd of 5,000. Emanuel and Loiola shared $20,000.00 for the Silver Medal finish. Brazil scored a clean sweep of the medals for the fifth-time this season as eighth-seeded Franco Neto and Roberto Lopes captured the $15,000.00 third-place prize by defeating 14th-seeded Luis Maia and Joao Brenha of Portugal 15-11 in the 48-minute Bronze Medal match. Maia and Brenha shared $11,000.00 for fourth-place. "The Gold Medal match was played under cloudy skies (79 degrees F). "Ze'Marco and Ricardo played extremely well. The serving was the key to the match as they kept Rego and Loiola off-balance with their short serves. The title was the fourth this season for Ze'Marco and Ricardo as their win prevented Emanuel and Loiola from tying the FIVB Beach Volleyball World Tour record for most wins in a season. Franco and Roberto Lopes, who had won 13 FIVB events, set the mark with eight titles during the 1995-1996 season. Emanuel and Loiola had won 11 international "Gold-Medals" together.

3rd Place: Franco Neto and Roberto Lopes-Bra
4th Place: Luis Maia and Joao Brenha-Por
5th Place: Oliver Stamm and Nikolas Berger-Austria
5th Place: Paul Laciga and Martin Laciga-Swiss

TOP PHOTOS: Left: Adam Jewell challenging the block of Aaron Boss. **Center:** Dan Castillo jump serving. **Right:** Two beach volleyball "Celebrities" Karch Kiraly (left) and Gabriel Reece, take a break from the fanfare.

MIDDLE PHOTOS: Left: Mike Dodd challenging the block of Eric Fonoimoana. **Center:** Brazilian Andre Gomes hits the ball past the block of Nick Hannemann. **Right:** Mark Paaluhi spiking the ball towards the block of Jason Pursley.

1999 MEN'S BEACH VOLLEYBALL ACTION

BOTTOM PHOTOS: Left: Tim Hovland shows that he can still play the game of beach volleyball in 1999, as he hits the ball past the block. **Center:** Wayne Seligson (left) jousting with Paul Baxter (right). **Right:** Eduardo Bacil attacking the ball.

Top Photos Courtesy of Tim Andexler. Middle and Bottom Photos Courtesy of "Couvi"

WOMEN'S BEACH VOLLEYBALL
1999

AVP

When the American Volleyball League failed to get off the ground, the AVP announced, in conjunction with the Men's AVP Tour, six Women's AVP events. The 1999 Women's AVP Tour schedule included stops in Clearwater Florida, Hermosa Beach California, Chicago Illinois, Muskegon Michigan, Manhattan Beach California, and the "Queen of the Beach" event in Las Vegas Nevada.

Liz Masakayan and Elaine Youngs took charge of the Women's 1999 AVP Tour, winning the first three tournaments. They won events in Clearwater Florida, Hermosa Beach California and Chicago Illinois.

The only other team to win on the tour was Jennifer Johnson Jordan and Annett Buckner-Davis, winning Michigan's "Muskegon Beach" event. The remaining events included the Queen of the Beach qualifier at Manhattan Beach, where the four qualifiers for the Queen of the Beach event were, Lisa Arce, Holly McPeak, Barbara Fontana and Jen Meredith. The final AVP Women's event was the Queen of the Beach tournament. The winner there was Holly McPeak.

1999 WOMEN'S AVP TOUR SCHEDULE

DATE	CITY/STATE/EVENT SITE	PRIZE MONEY
May 1st-2nd, 1999*	Clearwater, Florida/Hilton	$ 75,000.00
June 11th-13th, 1999*	Hermosa Beach, CA/Pier	$ 75,000.00
July 3rd-4th, 1999*	Chicago, IL/North Avenue Beach	$ 75,000.00
July 10th-11th, 1999*	Muskegon, MI/Muskegon Beach	$ 75,000.00
August 28th-29th, 1999*	Manhattan Beach, CA/Pier	$100,000.00
Sept. 17th-19th, 1999**	Las Vegas, NV/Hard Rock Hotel	$150,000.00

* = Both Men and Women's tournaments
** = King and Queen of the Beach tournaments

INDIVIDUAL AVP TOURNAMENT FINISHES
WOMEN-1999

Player	1st	2nd	3rd	4th	5th
Lisa Arce	0	1	2	1	0
Krista Blomquist	0	0	0	0	1
Annett Buckner-Davis	1	2	1	0	0
Patty Dodd	0	0	0	1	2
Barbra Fontana	0	1	3	0	0
Linda Hanley	0	1	0	0	2
Janice Harrer	0	0	0	0	2
Valinda Hillary	0	0	0	0	1
Jennifer Johnson Jordan	1	2	1	0	0
Liz Masakayan	3	0	0	1	0
Nancy Mason	0	0	0	0	1
Holly McPeak	1	0	2	0	2
Jen Meredith	0	1	0	0	1
Kerri Pottharst	0	0	0	1	0
Gabrielle Reece	0	0	1	0	2
Nancy Reno	0	1	1	0	2
Angela Rock	0	0	0	1	2
Leanne Schuster	0	0	0	0	1
Ali Wood	0	0	0	1	0
Lia Young	0	0	0	0	1
Elaine Youngs	3	0	0	1	0

GABRIELLE REECE
Gabreielle Reece teamed-up with Linda Hanley on the 1999 AVP Women's Tour, for some "2-Person" beach volleyball. Their best finish was a third at the Chicago event. Above photo, Reece hits a set from Hanley into the block of Marsha Miller.
Photo Courtesy of "Couvi"

ELAINE YOUNGS & LIZ MASAKAYAN
In 1999, Elaine Youngs and Liz Masakayan were the top team on the abbreviated AVP Women's Tour. They advanced to 3 finals, winning each time. Above photo, Masakayan (right) digs the ball as Youngs gets into position at the 1999 Hermosa Beach event.
Photo Courtesy of "Couvi"

AVL
(American Volleyball League)

The 1999 Women's Beach Volleyball Tour was struggling. The newly formed American Volleyball League proposed a very tentative ten event schedule, for women's pro-beach volleyball, from March 26th - September 12, 1999. The tour was offering a total of $600,000.00 in prize money. Unfortunately the league never got off its feet when the players could not agree on how to distribute the prize money.

1999 Proposed AVL Schedule
(cancelled)

DATE	WHERE
March 26-28	Daytona Beach, Florida
April 2-4	Deerfield Beach, Florida
April 9-11	Clearwater, Florida
April 27- May 1	Louisville, Kentucky
May 7-9	Indianapolis, Indianapolis
May 21-23	Texas site to be announced
June 7-9	Milwaukee, Wisconsin or Muskegon, Michigan
July 9-11	Seattle, Washington
August 13-15	Atlantic City, New Jersey
August 27-29	Del Mar, California
September 10-12	Las Vegas, Nevada

FIVB
1999 WOMEN'S FIVB TOUR SCHEDULE

DATE	CITY/COUNTRY/EVENT SITE	PRIZE MONEY
April 7th-11th, 1999	Acapulco Mex./Tamarindo Playa	$170,000.00
May 15th-16th, 1999	Huntington Beach, CA. USA/Pier Olympic Challenge event	$100,000.00
June 16th-20th, 1999	Toronto Canada/Woodbine Beach	$170,000.00
June 24th-27th, 1999	Virginia Beach, VA, USA/Beach Olympic Challenge event	$100,000.00
July 20th-25th, 1999*	Marseille France/Plage du Prado	$300,000.00
July 30th-Aug 1st, 1999	Esphinho Portugal Praia de Baia	$170,000.00
August 4th-8th, 1999	Osaka Japan/Tannowa Beach	$170,000.00
Sept. 11th-12th, 1999	San Diego, CA, USA/Crown Point Olympic Challenge event	$100,000.00
August 11th-15th, 1999	Dalian, China/Golden Pebble Bch	$170,000.00
November 2nd-4th, 1999	Salvador de Bahia Brazil/ Armacao Beach	$170,000.00

* = World Championships

The 1999 Women's FIVB World Tour included 7 events in 7 countries. Total prize money for the women was nearly $1,500,000.00. The World Championships at Plage du Prado in Marseille France was worth $300,000.00.

The World Championships and Open events included in the World Tour Calendar between January 1, 1999 and August 15, 2000 were all valid for the Olympic

LISA ARCE & BARBRA FONTANA
Lisa Arce and Barbra Fontana paired-up for the 1999 beach tour, playing in both the AVP and FIVB sanctioned events. Their only championship came at the Alero Series Huntington Beach event. Above photo, Arce spikes the set from Fontana.
Photo Courtesy of Frank Goroszko

ANNA PAULA CONNOLLY
Brazilian Anna Paula Connolly teamed-up with compatriot Jackie Silva for a third place finish at the FIVB Women's Tour event staged Osaka Japan. Above photo, Connolly leaps at the net to attack the ball.
Photo Courtesy of "Couvi"

Qualification of Beach Volleyball athletes for the Olympic Games 2000 in Sydney. The FIVB Beach Volleyball World Tour determined the 24 women's and 24 men's beach volleyball teams.

The team of Shelda Kelly Bruno Bede and Adriana Brandao Behar outclassed the rest of the field, by advancing to the finals at 6 international events, winning 5 times. Only two other teams were able to win "Gold-Medal" matches on the 1999 Women's FIVB World Tour. Americans Annette Buckner Davis and Jenny Johnson Jordan teamed-up together to win on Praia de Baia, in Espinho Portugal, while compatriots Holly McPeak and Nancy Reno won at Woodbine Beach Park on Ashbridges Bay in Toronto Canada.

Behar and Bede, who captured the FIVB Beach Volleyball World Tour's point title for the third-straight season, also played in their 16th-straight international Gold Medal match. At seasons-end, Behar and Bede had won their last 31 matches on the FIVB Beach Volleyball World Tour and had compiled a 201-36 career match mark (84.8 winning percentage), winning 100 of their last 105 international matches. Behar and Bede finished 1999 with a 45-2 match mark and $200,000.00 in earnings. Arce and Fontana completed their first season together with a 1999 international match mark of 25-13 with $54,500 in combined earnings.

INDIVIDUAL FIVB TOURNAMENT FINISHES
1999

Player	1st	2nd	3rd	4th	5th
Lisa Arce	1	0	0	2	5
SheldaKellyBruno Bede	5	1	0	0	0
AdrianaBrandao Behar	5	1	0	0	0
Eva Celbova	0	0	0	0	1
Angela Clarke	0	0	1	0	0
Ana Paula Connolly	0	0	1	0	0
Natalie Cook	0	2	1	1	0
Annette Buckner Davis	1	3	1	0	1
Carrie Busch	0	0	0	1	0
Sonja Dosoudilova	0	0	0	0	1
Maike Friedrichsen	0	0	0	0	1
Linda Robertson Hanley	0	1	1	0	2
BarbraFontana Harris	1	0	0	2	5
Jenny Johnson Jordan	1	3	1	0	1
Pauline Manser	0	1	0	0	0
Liz Masakayan	1	1	3	0	2
Holly McPeak	1	0	1	1	0
Danja Musch	0	0	0	0	1
SandraTavares Pires	0	0	1	5	1
KerriAnn Pottharst	0	3	0	1	0
Gabrielle Reece	0	0	1	0	0
Nancy Reno	1	1	1	1	2
Mika Teru Saiki	0	0	0	0	2
AdrianaRamos Samuel	0	0	1	5	1
Ulrike Schmidt	0	0	0	0	1
Leanne Schuster	0	0	0	1	0
JacquelineLouise"Jackie"Cruz Silva	0	0	1	0	0
Gudula Staub	0	0	0	0	1
Yukiko Takahashi	0	0	0	0	2
Elaine Youngs	1	1	3	0	2

(includes Olympic challenge events)

ELAINE YOUNGS & HOLLY McPEAK
Elaine Youngs and Holly McPeak encountered each other on both the AVP and FIVB Women's Tour's, with McPeak winning 2 events and Youngs winning 4 events. Above photo, McPeak encounters the block of Youngs.
Photo Courtesy of the AVP

SANDRA PIRES & BARBRA FONTANA
On the 1999 FIVB Women's Tour, Brazilian Sandra Pires battled for victories against the USA's Barbra Fontana. Pires had 7 top five FIVB finishes, while Fontana had 8 top five FIVB sanctioned finishes. Above photo, Pires challenges the block of Fontana.
Photo Courtesy of the FIVB

WOMEN'S TOURNAMENT RESULTS
1999-AVP

CLEARWATER, FLORIDA
May 1st-2nd, 1999

The Women's 1999 AVP Hilton Clearwater Beach $75,000.00 event was won by the team of Liz Masakayan and Elaine Youngs. They earned $20,000.00 for their championship effort. In the championship match, they outlasted Annett Buckner Davis and Jennifer Johnson Jordan. The second place team of Davis and Jordon earned $10,000.00 for their efforts.

3rd Place: Lisa Arce and Barbra Fontana
3rd Place: Nancy Reno and Holly McPeak
5th Place: Jenn Meredith and Leanne Schuster
5th Place: Janice Harrer with Lia Young
5th Place: Angela Rock with Patty Dodd
5th Place: Linda Hanley and Gabrielle Reece

HERMOSA BEACH, CALIFORNIA
June 11th-13th, 1999

The Women's 1999 AVP Hermosa Beach $75,000.00 event was won by the team of Liz Masakayan and Elaine Youngs. They earned $20,000.00 for their championship effort. In the championship match, they outlasted Lisa Arce and Barbara Fontana. The second place team of Arce and Fontana earned $12,000.00 for their efforts.

3rd Place: Anette Davis and Jenny Jordan
4th Place: Ali Wood and Kerri Pottharst
5th Place: Angela Rock with Patty Dodd
5th Place: Holly McPeak and Nancy Reno

CHICAGO, ILLINOIS
July 3rd-4th, 1999

North Avenue Beach, in Chicago Illinois, was the site of the next Women's $75,000.00 AVP event. For the third event in a row, Liz Masakayan and Elaine Youngs, took the top prize. This time in the amount of $18,000.00. In the championship match, Masakayan and Youngs outpointed Jennifer Johnson Jordan and Annette Buckner Davis. Jordan and Davis earned $11,000.00 for their second place finish.

3rd Place: Holly McPeak and Gabrielle Reece
4th Place: Patty Dodd and Angela Rock
5th Place: Linda Hanley and Nancy Reno
5th Place: Nancy Mason and Krista Blomquist

MUSKEGON, MICHIGAN
July 10th-11th, 1999

Michigan's "Muskegon Beach" was the site of the next $75,000.00 Women's AVP event.

The seeding's were as follows:
1. Liz Masakayan and Elaine Youngs
2. Jennifer Johnson Jordan and Annett Buckner-Davis
3. Lisa Arce and Barbara Fontana
4. Holly McPeak and Gabrielle Reece
5. Linda Hanley and Nancy Reno
6. Kerri Pottharst and Patty Dodd

ELAINE YOUNGS
Elaine "EY" Youngs paired-up with Liz Masakayan as the top team on the women's abridged 1999 AVP Tour. "EY" managed to capture three of the four tournament championships that were available. Above photo, "EY" attacks with her jump serve.
Photo Courtesy of "Couvi"

LINDA HANLEY
On the 1999 Women's AVP Tour, Linda Hanley played well enough to advance to the championship match of the Muskegon Michigan event, where she finished in second place. Above photo, Hanley dives into the sand to make a dig.
Photo Courtesy of Frank Goroszko

The $18,000.00 first place prize went to the team of Jennifer Johnson-Jordan and Annett Buckner-Davis. In the championship match, the defeated Linda Hanley and Nancy Reno, in a back-and-forth championship final. Reno and Hanley received a check in the amount of $11,000.00 for their second place finish.

3rd Place: Barbra Fontana and Lisa Arce
4th Place: Liz Masakayan and Elaine Youngs
5th Place: Valinda Hillary and Janice Harrer
5th Place: Holly McPeak and Gabrielle Reece

MANHATTAN BEACH, CALIFORNIA
August 28th-29th, 1999

On the same weekend as the Men's AVP Manhattan Open, 12 women competed in a round robin format to qualify for the "Queen of the Beach" tournament in Las Vegas NV. The best players from each of the three pools on Saturday advanced to the Las Vegas event. The second best player from each of the three pools on Saturday, plus the highest placing third place player advanced to a final pool of four players on Sunday. One player from Sunday's pool advanced to the Queen of the Beach. The four qualifiers for the Queen of the Beach event were, Lisa Arce, Holly McPeak, Barbara Fontana and Jen Meredith.

LAS VEGAS, NEVADA
September 17th-19th, 1999

The Hard Rock Hotel and Casino, in Las Vegas NV, was the site, for the $150,000.00 AVP's 1999 "King and Queen of the Beach" event. On the women''s side, Holly McPeak took care of business early, winning the first game of the second day, 13-10, with Jen Meredith over Lisa Arce and Barbara Fontana. This win, coupled with Saturdays 15-11 win for McPeak and Arce over Fontana and Meredith, placed McPeak in the lead, with Arce having to win the final game by more than 2 points to reach McPeak. The game started out as though McPeak and Fontana would run away with an easy win. But after the 7-3 side switch, Meredith and Arce stormed back to challenge at 8-8. But the ball control, defense, and shot making of McPeak and Fontana prevailed and McPeak was guaranteed the tournament victory after taking a 13-10 lead on a fantastic dig by McPeak and set by Fontana. It was a satisfying point on which to earn the title, and the crowd responded with an uproarious ovation.

1st Place: Holly McPeak
2nd Place: Barbra Fontana
3rd Place: Jennifer Meredith
4th Place: Lisa Arce
5th Place: Linda Hanley

ELAINE YOUNGS & BARBRA FONTANA
During the 1999 Women's AVP Tour, Elaine "EY" Youngs and Barbra Fontana confronted each other on several occasion. Youngs finished with 3 championship, while Fontana was unable to secure one. Above photo, "EY" and Fontana joust for the ball.
Photo Courtesy of Frank Goroszko

NANCY RENO & ANNETTE DAVIS
Nancy Reno and Annette Davis were participants on the 1999 Women's AVP Tour. They challenged each other everytime that they met. Above photo, Reno challenges the block of Davis, during the 1999 Hermosa Beach event.
Photo Courtesy of "Couvi"

WOMEN'S TOURNAMENT RESULTS 1999-FIVB

ACAPULCO MEXICO
April 7th-11th, 1999

On "Playa Tamarindo" in Acapulco Mexico, Top-seeded Adriana Behar and Shelda Bede of Brazil won the inaugural $170,000.00 FIVB Women's Mexican Open. The five-day two-person beach volleyball event started with 35 women's teams attempting to qualify for the eight available spots in the 32-team Main Draw. There were, a total of 59 women's tandems from 21 countries that competed in the tournament. This event was the first of three combined tournaments with the men on the FIVB Beach Volleyball World Tour this season. There were over 50,000 spectators that attended this event.

In the championship match, The number one ranked team on the FIVB Women's Beach Volleyball World Tour, Adriana Behar and Shelda Bede, fell behind 5-3 and 8-6 before they rallied and scored nine of the last 12 points to secure a 15-11 win over fourth-seeded Pauline Manser and Kerri Pottharst of Australia. The winners netted the $30,000.00 first-place prize while Manser and Pottharst split $20,000.00 for second-place. Behar and Bede have now won 34-straight matches on the FIVB Tour.

3rd Place: Natalie Cook and Angela Clarke-Aus
4th Place: Sandra Pires and Adriana Samuel-Bra
5th Place: Lisa Arce and Barbra Fontana-USA
5th Place: Liz Masakayan and Elaine Youngs-USA
Additional U.S. finishes: Holly McPeak and Nancy Reno were in 9th place, while Linda Hanley and Gabrielle "Gabby" Reece were in 17th place.

HUNTINGTON BEACH CALIFORNIA USA
May 15th-16th, 1999

The 1999 Women's Oldsmobile Alero Beach Volleyball Series, four-day event at Huntington Beach, was won by Lisa Arce and Barbra Fontana. In the championship match of this U.S. Olympic challenge event (sanctioned by the FIVB), Arce and Fontana scored the last five points of the 50-minute, 76-sideout match, to defeat fifth-seeded Annett Buckner-Davis and Jenny Johnson-Jordan 15-12. (Buckner-Davis is the daughter of Cleveland Buckner, who played for the New York Knicks of the National Basketball Association. Johnson-Jordan is the daughter of former UCLA athlete and Olympic Decathlon champion Rafer Johnson. Rafer won a decathlon Silver Medal at the 1956 Melbourne Games, and a Gold Medal at the 1960 Rome Games). The match featured eight ties and seven lead changes as Arce and Fontana rallied from a 12-10 deficit.

3rd Place: Liz Masakayan and Elaine Youngs-USA
4th Place: Holly McPeak and Nancy Reno-USA
5th Place: Linda Hanley and Gabriel Reece-USA
5th Place: Krista Blomquist and Ali Wood-USA

TORONTO CANADA
June 16th-20th, 1999

At Woodbine Beach Park on Ashbridges Bay in Toronto Canada, Americans Holly McPeak and Nancy Reno won the $170,000.00 FIVB Women's "Labatt Blue" Toronto Open. In the championship match, McPeak and Reno registered an upset by defeating Shelda Bede and

1999 ALERO BEACH VOLLEYBALL SERIES-HUNTINGTON BEACH CALIFORNIA
Huntington Beach California was the host for an Alero Beach Volleyball Series event. The winners of the "Gold-Medal" match were Lisa Arce and Babra Fontana, when they rallied from a 12-10 deficit to defeat the team of Jenny Johnson Jordan and Annett Buckner Davis, by a score of 15-12. Above photo, Fontana is ready at the net as Arce jump serves towards the team of Davis (left) and Jordan (right), during the championdhip match of the 1999 Huntington Beach event.

Photo Courtesy of Frank Goroszko

Adriana Behar of Brazil 15-8 to win the "Gold-Medal" and $30,000.00 first place check. They started out slow, trailing 3-2 early, but took the lead at 7-6 and never relinquished it again in the 55-minute match. The title marked the seventh international title for McPeak and Reno. Bede and Behar split $20,000.00 for second-place.
3rd Place: Annett Buckner-Davis and Jenny Johnson-Jordan-USA
4th Place: Sandra Pires and Adriana Samuel-Bra
5th Place: Lisa Arce and Barbra Fontana-USA
5th Place: Maike Friedrichsen and Danja Musch-Ger
Additional American finishes: Linda Hanley and Gabrielle "Gabby" Reece were in 17th place, while Liz Masakayan and Elaine Youngs were a distant 25th.

VIRGINIA BEACH, VIRGINIA USA
June 24th-27th, 1999

The 1999 Oldsmobile Women's Alero Beach $100,000.00 Volleyball Series at Virginia Beach was won by Liz Masakayan and Elaine Youngs. In the championship match of this U.S. Olympic challenge event. After jumping to a 2-0 lead, Masakayan and Youngs fell behind 10-6 in the 39-minute, 46-sideout final against the new team of Linda Hanley and Nancy Reno. Then after seven-straight sideouts, the winners scored five-straight points on Masakayan's serve. Masakayan and Youngs continued on a nine-point run when Reno hit two spikes wide, while a Masakayan dig and a Youngs cut shot "nailed" the 15-10 victory. The winners split $20,000.00 for their efforts. The title was the third domestic title this season for the Masakayan and Youngs partnership and the 40th career title for Masakayan.
3rd Place: Holly McPeak and Gabrielle Reece-USA
4th Place: Carrie Busch and Leanne Schuster-USA
5th Place: Lisa Arce and Barbra Fontana-USA
5th Place: Annett Buckner-Davis and Jenny Johnson-Jordan-USA

MARSEILLE FRANCE
July 20th-25th, 1999

In Marseille France, Adriana Behar and Shelda Bede, from Brazil, captured the Gold Medal at the $300,000.00 FIVB Women's Beach Volleyball World Championships, before a jammed-pack Plage du Prado Center Court crowd of 5,000 fans. In the championship match Behar and Bede outlasted the American team of Annett Buckner Davis and Jenny Johnson Jordan, with a 15-11 win in 30 minutes over the eighth-seeded team. Behar and Bede shared the $60,000.00 first-place prize for their biggest check in their careers. The championship win was the Brazilians' 12th FIVB Beach Volleyball World Tour title to tie the mark for most career team wins. Sandra Pires and Jackie Silva of Brazil established the mark in 1997. The Silver Medal was Buckner-Davis and Johnson-Jordan best international finish and earned them their largest beach volleyball paycheck at $39,000.00.
3rd Place: Liz Masakayan and Elaine Youngs-USA
4th Place: Sandra Pires and Adriana Samuel-Bra
5th Place: Ulrike Schmidt and Gudula Staub-Ger
5th Place: Yukiko Takahashi and Teru Saiki-Japan
Additional American finishes: Linda Hanley and Nancy Reno finished in 13th place. Lisa Arce and Barbra Fontana, along with Gabrielle "Gabby" Reece and Holly McPeak, finished in 17th place. Karolyn Kirby and Patty Dodd were in a distant 25th place.

ADRIANA BRANDO BEHAR
In 1999, Brazil's Adriana Behar was paired-up with compatriot, Shela Bede, on the Women's FIVB Tour. They advanced to 6 "Gold-Medal" matches, winning 5 times. Above photo, Behar spiking the ball.
Photo Courtesy of the FIVB

JENNIFER JOHNSON JORDAN
In addition to winning on the Women's AVP Tour, Jenny Jordan paired-up with Annette Davis to also win an FIVB Women's event. They won the Esphinho Portugal event. Above photo, Jordan attempts to poke the ball over the block of Elaine Youngs.
Photo Courtesy of Frank Goroszko

ESPHINHO PORTUGAL
July 30th-August 1st, 1999

On Praia de Baia, in Espinho Portugal, third-seeded Annette Buckner Davis and Jenny Johnson Jordan of the United States captured their first international beach volleyball crown. Their first win came at the $170,000.00 FIVB Women's Portugal Open before a jam-packed Praia da Baia Center Court with 6,000 spectators. In the 45 minute championship match, Buckner-Davis and Johnson-Jordan downed second-seeded Natalie Cook and Kerri Pottharst of Australia 15-12. They started slow, but played well at the end to earn their biggest win ever. The Aussies are a big and strong hitting team and Cook was playing great defensively. The Americans had a 14-8 lead in the finals, but the Australians didn't quit until the match was over.

3rd Place: Liz Masakayan and Elaine Youngs-USA
4th Place: Lisa Arce and Barbra Fontana-USA
5th Place: Sandra Pires and Adriana Samuel-Bra
5th Place: Linda Hanley and Nancy Reno-USA
The American team of Marla O'Hara and Ali Wood, finished in 25th place.

OSAKA JAPAN
August 4th-8th, 1999

On Tannowa Beach, in Osaka Japan, top-seeded Adriana Behar and Shelda Bede of Brazil successfully defended their Japanese Open title at the $170,000.00 FIVB Women's Japan Open. This event was the fifth of seven events on the 1999 FIVB Beach Volleyball World Tour. In the championship match, Behar and Bede defeated the Australian team of fourth-seeded Natalie Cook and Kerri Pottharst, by scores of 12-10 and 12-1. The Brazilians had now won eight of 10 games from the Aussies. This time it was not easy. They made a lot of errors and had to rally from a 10-7 deficit in the first game, scoring the final five points against Cook and Pottharst to secure the win. The second game, in the best-of-three title match, was never close as the Brazilian's serving was outstanding and Bede elevated her defense, winning their 19th-straight match on the 1999 FIVB Beach Volleyball World Tour. Behar and Bede, had now won a record 14 international titles in 32 career starts together. The winner's split the $30,000.00 first-place prize while the Aussies claimed their second-straight "Silver-Medal" to share the $20,000.00 second-place purse.

3rd Place: Jackie Silva and Ana Paula Connolly-Bra
4th Place: Sandra Pires and Adriana Samuel-Bra
5th Place: Lisa Arce and Barbra Fontana-USA
5th Place: Liz Masakayan and Elaine Youngs-USA
The U.S.A. teams of Linda Hanley and Nancy Reno along with Annett Buckner-Davis and Jenny Johnson-Jordan were tied in seventh place.

SAN DIEGO, CALIFORNIA USA
September 11th-12th, 1999

Brazilians, Adriana Behar and Shelda Bede, captured the Oldsmobile Alero Beach Volleyball Series "Gold-Medals" at Crown Point Shores, on Mission Beach in San Diego California. This event was the $150,000.00 Bank of America "U. S. Olympic Cup." In the Gold Medal match, the top two women's teams on the FIVB Beach Volleyball World Tour battled for the $20,000 first-place prize. Behar and Bede withstood a strong challenge from Americans Annette Buckner Davis and Jenny Johnson Jordan, winning, 15-12 in 44 minutes.

3rd Place: Linda Hanley and Nancy Reno-USA
4th Place: Natalie Cook and Kerri Pottharst-Aus
5th Place: Yukiko Takahashi and Teru Saiki-Japan
5th Place: Lisa Arce and Barbra Fontana-USA

SALVADOR DE BAHIA BRAZIL
November 2nd-7th, 1999

It was host Brazil's day on the sands of Armacao Beach as the South American tandems of Adriana Behar and Shelda Bede along with Sandra Pires and Adriana Samuel captured the two medal matches in the $170,000.00 Brazilian Open. The seventh of 7 women's events on the 1999 FIVB Beach Volleyball World Tour concluded with the top-seeded Behar and Bede outlasting sixth-seeded Liz Masakayan and Elaine Youngs 12-9 and 12-9 in 95 minutes to capture the Gold Medal and the $30,000 first-place prize. Youngs, who had posted two thirds and two fourths with Masakayan in 12 previous FIVB Beach Volleyball World Tour events together, was playing in her first international final as the pair split $20,000.00 for earning the Silver Medal. Masakayan had played in six previous FIVB Gold Medal matches, winning three times with Karolyn Kirby.

3rd Place: Sandra Pires and Adriana Samuel-Bra
4th Place: Lisa Arce and Barbra Fontana-USA
5th Place: Linda Hanley and Nancy Reno-USA
5th Place: Eva Celbova and Sonja Dosoudilova-Czech

HOLLY McPEAK
In 1999, Holly McPeak won championships on both the Women's AVP and FIVB Tour's. On the AVP Tour, Holly won the "Queen of the Beach" and on the FIVB Tour, she won the "Gold-Medal" in Toronto Canada. Above photo, McPeak attacking the ball.
Photo Courtesy of "Couvi"

TOP PHOTOS: Left: Nancy Mason (left) and Liz Masakayan (right) "Joust" for the ball. **Center:** Annette Davis spikes the ball past the block of Nancy Reno. **Right:** Holly McPeak challenging the block of Linda Hanley.

MIDDLE PHOTOS: Left: Nancy Reno takes a break from the action. **Center:** Brazilian Sandra Pires reaches for the attack. **Right:** Brazilian Shelda Bede steadys herself for the dig.

1999 WOMEN'S BEACH VOLLEYBALL ACTION

BOTTOM PHOTOS: Left: Marla O'Hara is at the net and ready for action. **Center:** Leanne Schuster McSorley getting ready for action. **Right:** Gabby Reece covering the net.

Top Photos Courtesy of the AVP. Middle Photos Courtesy of the FIVB. Bottom Photos courtesy of "Couvi"

ADDITIONAL VOLLEYBALL INFORMATION
1999

MEN'S TOURNAMENT RESULTS
1999 - CBVA

SANTA MONICA CALIFORNIA
March 27th, 1999

Dan Ortega and Adam Jewell were the winner's of the Men's AAA, staged at the Santa Monica Pier. In the championship match, they defeated Jack Quinn and Randall Koerv.
3rd Place: Brian Meckna and Dave Becker

PLAYA DEL REY CALIFORNIA
April 10th, 1999

The Men's AAA at Playa del Rey ended in a tie. The teams of Chris Makos and Jerry Graham along with Paul Boyd and Scott Davenport were the dual winner's.
3rd Place: Rifat Agi. and John Anselmo

DOHENY CALIFORNIA
April 17th, 1999

The Men's AAA, staged at Doheny State Beach, was won by the German team of Jorg Ahman and Axel Hager. In the championship match, they defeated Everett Matthews and Dave Counts.
3rd Place: Craig Geibel and Scott Murdoch

PLAYA DEL REY CALIFORNIA
April 24th, 1999

The Festival-Men's Playa del Rey AAA was won by Jorg Ahman and Axel Hagar. In the championship match, they outlasted Nate Heidger and Paul Baxter.
3rd Place: Anthony Medel and Chris Larson

PLAYA DEL REY CALIFORNIA
May 8th, 1999

This Men's Playa del Rey AAA was won by the Canadian team of Brian Gatzke and Dan Lewis. In the championship match, they outplayed Andrew Vasquez and Jeff Carlucci.
3rd Place: Christian "K-9" Kiernan and Tony Zapata.

SAN DIEGO CALIFORNIA
May 15th-16th, 1999

The 1999 Ocean Beach "Bud Light Volleyball Festival" Men's "AAA" was won by The Canadian team of Brian Gatzke and Dan Lewis. In the championship final, they defeated Mark Paaluhi and Nick Hannemann. George Stepanof was the tournament director of this tournament that had 17 teams participate.
3rd Place: Christian "K-9" Kiernan and Tony Zapata.
3rd Place: Lavelle Carter and Said Souikane

JOHN ANSELMO
In 1999, John Anselmo participated in some AVP events. He also provided some worthy competition in some CBVA Tournaments, including a third at the Playa Del Rey CA "AAA" event, with Rifat Agi. Above photo, Anselmo attacking the ball.
Photo Courtesy of "Couvi"

JASON PURSLEY
In 1999, Jason Pursley took part in some AVP events. He also provided some noteworthy competition in some CBVA Tournaments, including a third at the Santa Monica State Beach "Cal-King" event. Above photo, Pursley passing the ball.
Photo Courtesy of "Couvi"

HERMOSA BEACH CALIFORNIA
May 22nd, 1999

The CBVA Men's AAA, played north of the Hermosa Beach Pier, was won by the team of Steve Simpson and Chris Magill. In the championship match, they outplayed the veteran team of Chris Larson and Andrew Cavanaugh.

3rd Place: Chad Convis and Eddie Convis

SAN DIEGO CALIFORNIA
May 29th, 1999

The 1999 Ocean Beach "Redsand" Men's "AAA" was won by Dave Wisinski and Everette Mathews. In the championship match, they defeated Matt Olson and Rich Smith. George Stepanof was the tournament director.

3rd Place: Brandon Smeltzer and Sean Rosenthal
3rd Place: Dismas Abelman and Ken Lentin

SANTA CRUZ CALIFORNIA
May 29th-30th, 1999

The Santa Cruz Cal-King Pro Beach Volleyball Tour saw the real boys of summer come out in full force. After a cold day of hard-fought volleyball on Saturday the survivors were rewarded with a gorgeous day for beach volleyball on Sunday. "Pepe" Delahoz and his partner Leland Quinn ultimately prevailed over the team of Scott Davenport and Collin Smith. The two teams battled it out in three matches to determine who would be crowned the "CAL-KING" In the finals of the winner's bracket, Davenport and Smith won 15-11. The loss sent Delahoz and Quinn into the contenders bracket to face Devon Poolman and his young partner Brad Griffith. Pollman and Griffith had just won a hotly contested match against Santa Cruz local favorites and fourth place finishers Kjell Nilssen and Sean DeLapp. These two battled hard all weekend, but didn't have enough left against the eventual champs to be and wound up in third for the tournament.

The Santa Cruz crowd that gathered for the championship was not disappointed as both teams rose to the occasion and put on quite a display of top notch beach volleyball. Pepe and Leland took command early only to see their 8-2 lead slip away into a 14-14 tie with the inspired comeback play of Smith and Davenport. LaVelle Carter was on the microphone and did his best to pump up the laid back Santa Cruz crowd. The crowd seemed to favor Smith and Davenport, but a couple of tough serves by the big lefty Leland ended things at 16-14 and forced a double final. Delahoz and Quinn scored right away on the first play and never looked back in the final game to seven. Davenport and Smith sided out well, but Delahoz and Quinn slowly pulled away until Quinn terminated the contest. Leading 6-2 on game-point, the big guy threw up a monster block against Smith which Davenport was able to cover. However, the ball floated back up to the net and with a small hop step Leland put it "STRAIGHT DOWN" for the win. A plea for a net call by Smith was to no avail and Delahoz and Quinn were the Kings of California in Santa Cruz.

3rd Place: Devon Poolman and Brad Griffith
4th Place: Kjell Nilssen and Sean DeLapp
5th Place: Desjardens and Desjardens
5th Place: Harris and Alzina

SANTA MONICA CALIFORNIA
June 5th, 1999

The 1999 State Beach "AAA" was won by the team of Andrew Vazquez and Jeff Carlucci. In the championship match, they defeated Craig Geibel and Scott Murdock.

SANTA CRUZ CALIFORNIA
June 12th, 1999

The 1999 Santa Cruz "AAA" was won by the team of Christian Larson and Andrew Cavanaugh. In the championship match, they defeated Chad Convis and Anthony Medel.

DOHENY CALIFORNIA
June 12th, 1999

The 1999 Men's Doheny "AAA" was won by Dan Styles and Lavelle Carter. In the championship match, they defeated Branden Meltzer and Sean Rosenthal.

LAGUNA BEACH CALIFORNIA
June 19th, 1999

The 1999 Laguna Beach Men's "AAA" was won by Matt Lyles and Erik Moore. In the championship match, they outlasted Justin Pearlstrom and Mike Miner.

HUNTINGTON BEACH CALIFORNIA
June 19TH-20th, 1999

The 1999 Huntington Beach Cal-King Pro Beach Volleyball Tour event was won by the team of Lewis and Diehl. In the championship match, they defeated Mark Paaluhi and Steve Simpson by a score of 15-3. The third spot went to the team of Scott Davenport and Paul Boyd.

3rd Place: Scott Davenport and Paul Boyd
4th Place: Koerv and Rafat Agi
5th Place: Jason Pursley and John Anselmo
5th Place: Desjardins and Ely Fairfield

SANTA CRUZ CALIFORNIA
July 10th, 1999

The July 10th, 1999 Santa Cruz "AAA" was won by Phil Melese and Russell Tanner. In the championship match, they defeated Ben Saltzman and Tom Jackson.

CORONA DEL MAR CALIFORNIA
July 10th, 1999

The 1999 Corona "AAA" was won by the team of Ken Lentin and Levi Gundert. In the championship match, they out-pointed Sean Rosenthal and Branden Meltzer.

CAPISTRANO CALIFORNIA
July 17th, 1999

The 1999 Capistrano "AAA" was won by Michael Scales and Corin Bemus. In the championship match, they defeated Scott Kiedaisch and Dan Skilins.

SANTA MONICA CALIFORNIA
July 17th-18th, 1999

The 1999 Santa Monica State Beach Cal-King Pro Beach Volleyball Tour event was won by the team of Paul Boyd and Adam Jewell. In the championship match, they out-pointed Jason Stimpfig and Ken Lynch 15-10 and 7-1.

3rd Place: Jason Pursley and Steve "Texas" Simpson
4th Place: Chad Convis and Jeff Carlucci
5th Place: Scott Davenport and Ely Fairfield
5th Place: Adam Renfree and Larry Witt

MANHATTAN BEACH CALIFORNIA
July 24th, 1999

The 1999 CBVA Festival Men's "AAA" Manhattan Beach event was won by Scott Davenport and Paul Boyd. In the championship match, they defeated Chad Convis and Pete Goers.

SANTA BARBARA CALIFORNIA
August 13th-14th, 1999

Andrew Cavanaugh and Chris Larson captured their second beach volleyball tournament title of the 1999 season when they won the USA Masters Championship (35-44 age group) at East Beach. In the championship match, they defeated Gary Heinemman and Alan Jones, 15-3, to take the $1,000.00 first prize.
3rd Place: Eric Anderson and Greg Soulagers

In the 45-54 age group, Jeff Rydberg and Bill Wallace held off Dan Salyer and Mark Tanner by a score of 15-13 earning their first place check of $1,000.00.
3rd Place: Gary Hooper and Jon Roberts

Orey Higgins and Jim Ginter defeated Archie Allen and Ken Venturi, 15-10, in the 55 and over age group. Allen and Venturi upset beach legends Butch May and Bob Vogelsang in the semifinals by a score of 15-10.

WOMEN'S TOURNAMENT RESULTS
1999 - CBVA

SANTA MONICA CALIFORNIA
March 13th, 1999

The CBVA Women's AAA event, staged at Will Rogers State Beach, was won by the team of Karen Helyer and Laura Higgins. In the championship match, they out-pointed Monique Oliver and Melissa Coutts.
3rd Place: Terri Willis and Sara Schroeder
3rd Place: Vasdiki Karadesiov and Efrosyne Sfyri

SANTA MONICA CALIFORNIA
March 27th, 1999

The March 27th, 1999 Santa Monica Women's "AAA" was won by the team of Marsha Miller and Jenny Pavley. In the championship match, they out-scored Kathy Tough and Janette Solecki.

PLAYA DEL REY CALIFORNIA
April 10th, 1999

The April 10th, 1999 Women's "AAA" in Playa del Rey was won by Stephanie Cox and Angie Kammer. In the championship match, they defeated Bonnie Bright and Sarah Schroeder.

DOHENY CALIFORNIA
April 18th, 1999

The April 18th, 1999 Women's "AAA" at Doheny State Beach was won by Sara Schroeder and Bonnie Bright. In the championship match, they out-played Sandi Enriquez and Kim Zuffelato.

STEVE SIMPSON
Steve "Texas-Steve" Simpson utilized his excellent blocking technique to provide plenty of competitive beach volleyball on the 1999 CBVA Tour, including a championship. Above photo, "Texas-Steve" reaches over the net to block the hit by Kyle Denitz.
Photo Courtesy of "Couvi"

ANDREW CAVANAUGH & CHRIS LARSON
Andrew Cavanaugh and Chris Larson won the 1999 USA Masters Championship (35-44 years) on East Beach in Santa Barbara California. Above photo, Larson hits a set from Cavanaugh towards the block of Brian Ivie.
Photo Courtesy of "Couvi"

SAN DIEGO CALIFORNIA
April, 1999
The 1999 Ocean Beach Women's Open was won by Deanna Johnson and Shannon Terry-Nembach. In the championship match, they defeated the Australian team of Kerry Pottharst and Natalie Cook. There were 30 teams entered in this tournament that was directed by George Stepanof. There were over 2,000 spectators watching this event, with an additional 15,000 "walk-bys."
3rd Place: Lynda Johnson and Dianna Evans
3rd Place: Kamila Pavlaskova and Christine Lussier

PLAYA DEL REY CALIFORNIA
April 24th, 1999
The 1999 "Festival" Women's "AAA" in Playa del Rey was won by the team of Sarah Schroeder, Sarah and Bonnie Bright. In the championship match, they out-scored Chastity Nobriga, and Robyn Ahmow.

PLAYA DEL REY CALIFORNIA
May 8th, 1999
The 1999 Women's "AAA" in Playa del Rey was won by Christine Lussier and Leila Brown. In the championship match, they defeated Sandy Matthews and Gina Pillitiere.

SAN DIEGO CALIFORNIA
May 15th-16th, 1999
The 1999 Ocean Beach "Bud Light Volleyball Festival"

MONIQUE OLIVER
Monique Oliver was one of the WPVA palyers that found refuge on the Women's CBVA Tour. Oliver played competitive beach volleyball whil;e competing in CBVA tournaments. Above photo, Oliver attacks with her jump serve.
Photo Courtesy of Frank Goroszko

Women's "AAA" was won by Karen Hlyer and Laura Higgins. In the championship match they defeated Deanna Johnson and Erin Deiteas. Tournament director, George Stepanof recorded that there were 19 teams that participated in this tournament.
3rd Place: Caron Janc and Barbara Nyland
3rd Place: Jackie Signor and Sara Beyer

CORONA DEL MAR CALIFORNIA
May 22nd, 1999
The 1999 Women's "AAA" in Corona Del Mar was won by the team of Barb Broem-Ovellette and Christine Lussier. In the championship match, they out-played Linda Burton and Monica Stewart.

SAN DIEGO CALIFORNIA
May 29th, 1999
The 1999 Ocean Beach "Redsand" Women's "AAA" was won by Katie Lindquist and Tracy Lindquist. In the championship match they defeated Karen Reitz and Barbara Nyland. George Stepanof was the tournament director.
3rd Place: Susie Turner and Karen Helyer
3rd Place: Lynn Jomphe and Celine Landry

SANTA CRUZ CALIFORNIA
June 12th, 1999
The 1999 Women's "AAA" at Santa Cruz was won by Allison Block and Susie Turner. In the championship match, they defeated Sue Holmes and Andrea Beylen.

SANTA BARBARA CALIFORNIA
June 26th, 1999
The 1999 Women's "AAA" in Santa Barbara was won by the team of Lina Yanchulova and Petia Yanchulova. In the championship match, they out-lasted Bonnie Bright and Sarah Schroeder.

SANTA CRUZ CALIFORNIA
July 10th, 1999
The 1999 Women's "AAA" in Santa Cruz was won by Andrea Beylen and Sue Holmes. In the championship match, they defeated Jackie Signor and Kathy King.

SANTA MONICA CALIFORNIA
July 10th, 1999
The 1999 Women's "AAA" at Will Rogers State Beach was won by the team of Jenny Pavely and Marsha Miller. In the championship match, they out-played Lina and Petia Yanchulova.

LAGUNA BEACH CALIFORNIA
July 17th, 1999
The 1999 Women's "AAA" in Laguna Beach was won by Monica Stewart and Linda Burton. In the championship match, they defeated Jennifer Marzahl-Francisco and Lael Fresenius.

MANHATTAN BEACH CALIFORNIA
July 24th, 1999
The 1999 CBVA Festival Women's "AAA" at the Manhattan Beach Pier was won by Mary Baily and Helen Reale. In the championship match, they out-played Leila Brown and Sandy Matthews.

MIXED-DOUBLE'S TOURNAMENT RESULTS
1999 - CBVA
HERMOSA BEACH CALIFORNIA
May 23rd, 1999

The May 23rd, 1999 Coed OPEN, at the Hermosa Beach Pier, was won by John Stagler and Gay Nicholson. In the championship match, they defeated Greg Runcie and Elaine Cooke.

SANTA MONICA CALIFORNIA
June 6th, 1999

The June 6th, 1999 Coed "AAA" at Will Rogers State Beach, was won by Jason Stimpfig and Laurie Rusher Stimpfig. In the championship match, they out-scored Geremie Simkins and Cherry Simkins.

SANTA CRUZ CALIFORNIA
June 13th, 1999

The June 13th, 1999 99Coed "AAA" in Santa Cruz was won by Ben Saltzman and Tawnya Sargent. In the championship match, they defeated Chris Wehman and Bonnie Dahm.

MANHATTAN BEACH CALIFORNIA
July 3rd, 1999

The July 3rd, 1999 Coed "AAA" at Marine Avenue was won by Brett Coordt and Denise Black. In the championship match, they out-pointed Shane Davis and Michelle Morse.

HERMOSA BEACH CALIFORNIA
July 11th, 1999

The July 11th, 1999 Coed "AAA" at the Hermosa Beach Pier was won by the team of Jason Stimpfig and Laurie Rusher Stimpfig. In the championship final, they out-pointed John Stadler and Suzanne Radcliff.

MANHATTAN BEACH CALIFORNIA
July 24th, 1999

The July 24th, 1999 CBVA Festival Coed "AAA" in Manhattan Beach was won by Randall Koerv and Michelle Morse. In the championship match, they defeated Aaron Watchfogel and Jennifer Holdren.

JASON STIMPFIG
In 1999, Jason Stimpfig utilized his all-around skill to qualify for several AVP events. He also won the Santa Monica and Hermosa Beach "AAA" Mixed-Doubles events in 1999 with partner Laurie Rusher Stimpfig. Above photo, Jason attacking the ball.
Photo Courtesy of "Couvi"

KENNY LYNCH & JASON STIMPFIG
Kenny Lynch and Jason Stimpfig teamed-up to advance to the finals of the 1999 "Cal-King" event on Santa Monica's State Beach, finishing in second place. Above photo, Stimpfig goes all-out to dig the ball for partner Kenny Lynch.
Photo Courtesy of "Couvi"

BEACH VOLLEYBALL AVP-FIVB
2000 and BEYOND

AVP

In the 21st Century, The Association of Volleyball Professionals continued to struggle. By the end of the 2000 beach volleyball season, the AVP Tour was in big trouble and filled for bankruptcy. Then in May of 2001, Leonard Armato announced his latest involvement with the financially struggling sport of pro beach volleyball. Armato announced that he had acquired the Association of Volleyball Professionals. Armato then unified the competing beach volleyball circuits into one domestic AVP Tour, featuring both men's and women's competition. Armato originally founded the AVP in 1983 and led it to surprising heights, with $100,000.00 first-place-prize purses, live network TV, recognizable stars such as Sinjin Smith and Karch Kiraly. Armato left the AVP in 1989, as a "Sports-Agent" for many of the top sports figures, including the LA Lakers Shaquille Oneil.

When beach volleyball gained Olympic status it seemed to give the sport a stamp of approval, and it was a big hit in Atlanta in 1996. But sponsorship and TV money went by the way-side in the late 1990's, and by the end of 1998, the AVP had to declare bankruptcy, after barely surviving the last two years with drastic cuts in events and prize money.

Armato's plan has unified, and restored communications with sponsors as well as reestablishing the necessary political ties, while going forward with a huge marketing plan. The Association of Volleyball Professionals (AVP) was able to convince all of the U.S. players to sign-on to the new road ahead, including the number one team on the women's International FIVB Pro Beach Volleyball Tour, Misty May and Kerri Walsh, when they signed an exclusive contract with the AVP Tour effective for the 2003 season. Armato had tough negotiations with veteran AVP players such as Karch Kiraly and Mike Whitmarsh over adopting FIVB rules, with the smaller court, different ball, rally scoring. In the end, though, the players had no alternative and the new rules were adopted. The AVP now stands alone as the only professional beach volleyball tour in the country. It now follows the regulations set forth by USA Volleyball and the Federation International de Volleyball (FIVB) and allows its players to compete in official tournaments en route to the 2004 Olympics.

The AVP Pro Beach Volleyball Tour and USA Volleyball's new working arrangement has further increased the popularity of the outdoor game. The two organizations

LEONARD ARMATO
New AVP CEO Leonard Armato had a lot to talk about when he took-over the AVP in 2000. Armato announced a new and revamped AVP, with a new schedule made possible by new sponsors and and TV Support.
Photo Courtesy of "Couvi"

KERRI WALSH & MISTY MAY
Kerri Walsh and Misty May finally "signed-on" to play on the AVP Tour, with an exclusive contrat for the 2003 season. Above photo, Annette Davis challenges the block of Walsh while May gets ready to make the play on defense.
Photo Courtesy of "Couvi"

formed a working committee comprised of four members from the AVP and four members from USA Volleyball. They meet on a regular basis. The AVP component is represented by Bruce Binkow (Chief Marketing Officer), Andy Reif (Chief Operating Officer), Jeffrey R. David (Director of Grassroots Marketing) and Al Lau (Director of Player Relations). USA Volleyball representatives to the committee include Rebecca Howard (Chief Executive Officer), Kerry Klostermann (Secretary General), John Kessel (Director, Coaching Education, Disabled, Grassroots and Beach Programs) and Margie Mara (Associate Executive Director).

The first tournament under the reorganized AVP was June 8-10, 2001 in Hermosa Beach, California, where both men and women players participated. In all, the 2001 schedule included eight events (five with men and women, three with men only). Total prize money was nearly $1 million. All events were shown tape-delayed on Fox Sports Net. The AVP entered its 20th season, in 2003, the AVP and was comprised of over 150 of the best men's and women's pro beach volleyball players in the U.S., and arguably, the world. By 2004 the players had agreed to and signed a new contract that provided for the continued growth of the AVP.

FIVB

The Federation International de Volleyball (FIVB), guided by President Dr. Rubéén Acosta, is the recognized international organization for beach volleyball. The FIVB has come a long way from the dusty-old YMCA gymnasium of Holyoke, Massachusetts, USA, where visionary, William G. Morgan, invented the sport back in 1895 and on through the "Golden-Years" of beach volleyball, when the first "King of the Beach" Gene Selznick took the game to new heights. It has seen the start of two centuries and the dawn of a new millennium. Volleyball is now one of the big three international sports, and the FIVB, with its 218 affiliated national federations, is the largest international sporting federation in the world. In the 21st Century, The FIVB and the Beach Volleyball phenomenon, although hugely visible, is still just in its infancy. From the first FIVB World Tour event just over ten years ago, to the overwhelming spectator and television success of beach volleyball at the Atlanta 1996 and Sydney 2000 Olympic Games, Beach Volleyball has opened up Volleyball to a completely new market and opportunities. Over the last decade particularly, Volleyball has witnessed unprecedented growth. The success of the Olympic Games and the level of participation at all levels internationally continues to grow exponentially. Teams representing more than 50 countries took part in the Olympic Games qualification process for the 2000 Olympic Games in

JOHN KESSEL
John Kessel is a strong proponent for beach volleyball. From 1990 "Kess" has been working for the National Governing Body of the sport, USA Volleyball. He is currently the Director of Beach Volleyball, Education and Grassroots Programs. Volleyball magazine named him as one of the 50 most important people in the sport of volleyball in the first 100 years.
Photo Courtesy of John Kessel

OLYMPIC BEACH VOLLEYBALL
Beach volleyball, through the FIVB reached new heights when it was included as an event in the Olympics. Above photo, beach volleyball legend and first "King of the Beach" Gene Selznick (right), along with his son Dane, enjoy the 2000 Olympics in Australia, in front of a nice crowd, in the stadium on Bondi Beach. Gene and Dane are both active beach volleyball coaches.
Photo Courtesy of Dane Selznick

Sydney where the top 24 men's and 24 women's teams in the world competed on Australia's Bondi Beach in the most important competition in the world. It was a fantastic venue with a stadium of 10,000 spectators and modern facilities set up offering the top-class event. Following the phenomenal success of the Beach Volleyball performance during the Sydney Olympics, the IOC Executive Committee declared Beach Volleyball an official part of the Olympic program. The Athens Olympic Games Organizing Committee confirmed that Beach Volleyball was to be included in the Olympic Games program in 2004.

The 2000 FIVB Beach Volleyball World Tour featured 26 events totaling four million dollars in prize money. The Women's Tour had a tremendous increase in the number of tournaments from seven in 1999, up to twelve in 2000. Men and women athletes were given the same opportunities. The FIVB reached an agreement with Turner Inc. to include beach volleyball into the 2001 Goodwill Games in Brisbane, Australia.

For the first time, on the Men's and Women' FIVB Tour's, the players were treated with complete equality when both tours scheduled the same number of events, as well as equal prize money from the $4,550,000.00 that was distributed ($2,275,00.00 each, for men and women). The twenty-four FIVB Tour events of the 2001 were covered with a particularly large television exposure creating more and more interest for a spectacular sport, proved at the Sydney Games 2000.

The Men's FIVB 2001 World Tour of Beach Volleyball staged twelve events, including the Goodwill Games in Brisbane Australia. There were events in eleven countries with a total purse of over one million dollars. After two successful years in Volleyball, the Rally Point System (RPS) was started in Beach Volleyball. The matches were/are played in two sets of 21 points and an eventual third decisive set with 15 points. In order to prolong spectacular rallies. The Playing court's new dimensions of 16x8m (instead of 18x9m) reducing it to 8x8 meters per side, was instituted to be tested for one year, and by 2004 it was still in use. The preceding rule changes were researched and recommended by volleyball legend Sinjin Smith, the President of the FIVB's Beach Volleyball Council.

The Men's FIVB 2002 World Tour of Beach Volleyball staged ten events. There were events in nine countries with a total purse of $3.3 million (split with the Women's 11 event FIVB World Tour). This was the first year that the women's tour featured more events (11) and more prize money, than the men's tour (10).

The Men's FIVB 2003 World Tour of Beach Volleyball staged eleven events, including the XIV Pan American Games in Santo Domingo and four "Grand Slam" events as well as the World Championships, which offered $800,000.00 in prize money. The event was played on Copa Cabana in Rio de Janeiro Brazil. There were events in eleven countries with a total purse of $2,500,000.00. FIVB events from January 2003 until July 2004 are part of the Olympic qualification process. Also groundbreaking agreement with the USA's Association of Volleyball Professionals (AVP), opened the way for a Grand Slam event in Los Angeles that was a season highlight. The FIVB calendar also include Challenger and Satellite events. The demand for Challenger and Satellite events was a sign of the growing popularity of beach volleyball in many countries. Challenger and Satellite tournaments are a perfect launch pad for up-and-coming players to gain international experience. The Women's FIVB 2003 World Tour of Beach Volleyball staged thirteen events, including the XIV Pan American Games in Santo Domingo and four Grand Slam events. There were events in thirteen countries with a total purse of $2,500,000.00.

SINJIN SMITH
Beach volleyball legend and FIVB Beach Volleyball Council President, Sinjin Smith, in an effort to make the game more exciting to the public researched and recommended rule changes for the FIVB. Above photo, the ever-ready Sinjin Smith.
Photo Courtesy of Dennis G. Steers

In Lausanne, Switzerland, the International Volleyball Federation (FIVB) increased the schedule for the 2004 Swatch-FIVB World Tour, with five more events than the 2003 schedule. The 2004 season was a landmark for Beach Volleyball, with an impressive 27 tournaments (15 men and 12 women), worth $5,480,000.00 in Prize Money and Bonus Pool.

TOP PHOTOS: Left: Larry "Dizzel" Witt attacking the ball. **Center:** Adam Jewell hitting the ball over the defense of Jeff Nygard. **Right:** Brian "Lewy" Lewis attacking the ball.

MIDDLE PHOTOS: Left: Dain Blanton attacking the block of Kevin Wong. **Center:** Scott "Ack" Ayakatubby attacking with a jump-serve. **Right:** During the block attempt, Sean "Rosey" Rosenthal takes a look above the net.

BEACH VOLLEYBALL 2000 AND BEYOND

BOTTOM PHOTOS: Left: Carl "Carlton" Henkel gets above the net to pound the ball. **Center:** George Roumain follows-through after attacking the ball. **Right:** Canyon Ceman spiking the ball past the block of Brent Doble.

Photo's Courtesy of "Couvi"

MEN'S BEACH VOLLEYBALL 2000

AVP

In 2000, the AVP Pro-Beach Volleyball tournament schedule included eleven AVP Tour events, with total prize money at $825,000.00. In 2000, California was back on top with most AVP Tour events staged with six. The five additional events were staged in five different states. Florida, Illinois, Michigan, and New Jersey all staged one AVP Tour event. The fifth out-of-State" event was the King and Queen of the Beach event, staged in Las Vegas Nevada.

In 2000, Jose Loiola and Emanuel Rego were the top team with three tournament championships. After advancing to four finals they won their three events. Their wins came at the Hermosa Beach, Manhattan Beach and the U.S. Open in Seal Beach. Dax Holdren and Todd Rogers also advanced to four finals, winning twice. Their wins came at the Chicago Illinois and Muskegon Michigan AVP Tour events. There were six different teams that won one AVP Tour event in 2000. Brent Doble and Lee LeGrande won the Tournament of Champions in Del Rey Beach Florida. Dain Blanton and Eric Fonoimoana won the Santa Cruz Open. Canyon Ceman and Brian Lewis won the Huntington Beach Open. Lee LeGrande and Franco Neto won the Karch Kiraly Classic in Santa Barbara California. Canyon Ceman and Mike Whitmarsh won the Belmar Beach Open. Karch Kiraly and Adam Johnson won the Virginia Beach Open. Mike Whitmarsh was "Crowned" the 2000 AVP King of the Beach. Barbra Fontana was "Crowned" the 2000 AVP Queen of the Beach.

2000 INDIVIDUAL AVP TOURNAMENT FINISHES

Player	1st	2nd	3rd	4th	5th
Paulo Emilo Silva Azvedo	0	0	0	0	1
Eduardo Bacil	0	0	2	2	0
Dain Blanton	1	1	0	0	1
Canyon Ceman	2	2	3	5	0
Ian Clark	0	0	0	0	1
Brent Doble	1	0	3	0	2
Eric Fonoimoana	1	1	0	0	1
Brent Frohoff	0	1	0	0	0
Eduardo Garrido	0	0	0	0	1
Nick Hannemann	0	1	0	0	1
Dax Holdren	2	2	0	1	3
Adam Jewell	0	1	0	0	1
Adam Johnson	1	1	1	1	3
Mark Kerins	0	0	0	1	0
Karch Kiraly	1	1	1	1	1
Lee LeGrand	2	1	1	1	2
Brian Lewis	1	2	2	2	2
Jose Loiola	**3**	**2**	**1**	**0**	**0**
Kevin Martin	0	0	0	1	0
Stein Metzger	0	0	3	0	2
Franco Neto	1	1	1	1	1
Emanuel Rego	**3**	**2**	**1**	**0**	**1**
Todd Rogers	2	1	0	1	3
Fred Souza	0	0	2	2	0
David Swatik	0	0	0	0	1
Matt Unger	0	0	0	1	0
Mike Whitmarsh	2	1	1	3	1
Larry Witt	0	1	0	0	0

2000 BEACH VOLLEYBALL ACTION

The 2000 AVP Tour included eleven beach volleyball events worth over $800,000.00. The crowds were large at all of the events, including the 2000 Manhattan Beach Open, which went back in time, staging an "Old-School" type of tournament, without large stands. In the above photo, during the championship match, Mike Whitmarsh hits a set from Canyon Ceman, towards the defense of Jose Loiola (left) and Emanuel Rego (right).

Photo Courtesy of Frank Goroszko

FIVB

The Men's FIVB 2000 World Tour of Beach Volleyball staged sixteen events, including one USAV event (sanctioned by the FIVB) and the Olympics, on Bondi Beach, outside of Sydney Australia. There were events in fourteen countries with a total purse of over two and one quarter million dollars. The FIVB events were staged in Mar Del Plata Argentina, Guaruja Brazil, Macau, Rosarito Mexico, Deerfield Michigan U.S.A., Toronto Canada, Tenerife Spain, Chicago Illinois U.S.A., Stavanger Norway, Lignano Italy, Marseille France, Espinho Portugal, Klagenfurt Austria, Ostende Belgium, Sydney Australia and Vitoria Brazil. The 2000 FIVB Beach Volleyball World Men and Women's Tour featured 31 events (including one USAV event sanctioned by the FIVB and the Olympics) totaling four million dollars in prize money. The Women's Tour had a tremendous increase in the number of tournaments from seven in 1999, up to fifteen in 2000 (including two USAV events sanctioned by the FIVB and the Olympics).

The top team, on the 2000 FIVB Men's World Tour, was Brazil's ZeMarco de Melo and Ricardo Santos. They advanced to nine "Gold-Medal" matches, winning five times, while earning over one quarter of a million dollars. Brazil's Jose Loiola and Emanuel Rego were the number two team on the 2000 FIVB Men's Tour. Rego and Loiola advanced to five "Gold-Medal" Matches, winning four times, while earning over $180,000.00. Another Brazilian team was in the top three as Marcio Araujo and Benjamin Insfran advanced to five "Gold-Medal" matches, winning twice, while earning over $150,000.00. The Swiss team of Stefan Kobel and Patrick Heuscher were in the fourth spot as they advanced to three "Gold-Medal" matches, winning twice. There were five additional teams that each won one "Gold-Medal" on the 2000 FIVB Men's World Tour. There were two more teams from Switzerland, Martin Laciga with Paul Laciga and Markus Egger with Sascha Heyer. There were also two American teams that won, Dain Blanton with Eric Fonimoana, winning the Olympic "Gold-Medal" and Dax Holdren with Todd Rogers. Jose Salema and Mariano Baracetti, from Argentina, also won a "Gold-Medal" on the 2000 FIVB Tour.

NEW FIVB RULES

FIVB President, Dr. Ruben Acosta made the rules one of the top stories of 2000. In 1999, it was the uniforms and the let serve. This year it was the new rules for beach volleyball, including rally scoring and a smaller court size. These rules had volleyball fans talking all summer long. It is said that the rules "came down from the mountain" (the Swiss Alps in this case) and were instituted in 2001. The FIVB had decided on the following: Rally Point System to be used immediately and throughout the 2001 season with 2 sets to 21 points each and an eventual 15 points tie break. The playing Court was reduced to 8x8 meters per side aiming to prolong rallies. The effects of the new rules were presented to the FIVB Congress in 2002 and the decision was made to continue utilizing them.

LAUSANNE SWITZERLAND
September 13th, 2000

Dr. Ruben Acosta Hernandez, FIVB President for the past 16 years, was elected to the elite ranks of the International Olympic Committee at the 111th IOC Session in Sydney Australia. Dr. Acosta's election had been proposed by the IOC Executive Board and received the full approval of the IOC Session. IOC President H.E. Juan Antonio Samaranch was a strong supporter of Dr. Acosta telling delegates at the last FIVB Congress in Seville: "We are ready to welcome your President as an IOC member. The FIVB is a great Federation in the Olympic movement." Dr. Acosta has had a long association with the Olympic Games as an Executive member of the Mexican Olympic Committee since 1966, and then as General Vice Director of Sports in the Organizing Committee of the 1968 Mexico Olympics in charge of sports technical organization for the Games. A recipient of the Olympic Order granted at the 93rd IOC Session in Calgary, he attended every Olympic Games since 1968 in addition to being the FIVB Control Committee member or president at the Munich 1972, Montreal 1976, Moscow 1980, Los Angeles 1984, Seoul 1988, Barcelona 1992, Atlanta 1996 Olympics - a role he will again perform in Sydney 2000. A 66-year-old lawyer, Acosta was born in Jerez, Zacatecas in the

Z-MARCO DE MELO
Brazil's Z-Marco de Melo paired-up with compatriot Ricardo Santos as the top team on the 2000 FIVB World Tour. As a team, Z-Marco and Santos advanced to 9 "Gold-Medal" matches, winning 5 times. Above photo, Z-Marco passing the ball.
Photo Courtesy of the FIVB

Northern part of Mexico, the sixth son of a prominent Mexican educator. He initiated his education in a military school in San Luis Potosi where he studied languages. He is fluent in Spanish, English, French and Italian - and graduated in Pedagogy and the Sciences of Education. At the Universidad A.P. he obtained a Bachelor's Degree in Social Sciences. Later he completed law studies at the National University of Mexico, graduating with a thesis on Criminal Law. From 1957 to 1967, Dr. Acosta was engaged in his career as an educator, lecturer and lawyer. During the same period he completed his MBA studies in the USA while working as a company lawyer for General Electric Co. from 1963 to 1973 before branching out as a legal counselor in administration, civil and trade laws. He has been associated with sports since 1948, first as a Volleyball, Baseball and Basketball player and then university coach and national referee in local and national competitions. In this period he was elected Executive Member of the National Sports Confederation and the Mexican Olympic Committee. He became a member of the FIVB Board of Administration in 1966 and was elected in 1984 President of the International Volleyball Federation for the first time, being re-elected successively in Seoul 1988, Barcelona 1992, Athens, 1994 and lately Tokyo, 1998.

LAUSANNE SWITZERLAND
January 18th, 2001

The International Olympic Committee confirmed the status of Beach Volleyball as a full Olympic discipline as from the Olympic Games of Athens in 2004. In a letter sent this week, Juan Antonio Samaranch, President of the IOC has officially informed Dr. Rubéén Acosta, President of the International Volleyball Federation (FIVB) of the decision taken last month by the Executive Board of the IOC in favour of Beach Volleyball.

THE OLYMPICS
September, 2000

The Gold Medal Matches, of beach volleyball, at the Sydney Olympics was the highlight of the 2000 beach volleyball calendar. The event at the Sydney Olympics was staged on one of Australia's most spectacular beaches, Bondi Beach. The tournament was a complete success. Sell out crowds every day. Exciting play in almost every match. Beach volleyall could not have had a better showcase. Both "Gold-Medal" matches (men and women) went the distance. Both had drama and come-from-behind-upsets. In the men's event, the USA's Dain Blanton and Eric Fonoimoana finally showed that the potential everyone knew they possessed was for real, as they defeated the favored Brazilian team of Ricardo Santos and Ze'Marco de Melo for the gold.

Beach volleyball's team of the year had to be Dain Blanton and Eric Fonoimoana. Blanton and Fonoimoana surprised a lot of people in 2000 by "apparently" coming out of nowhere, to take home the "Gold-Medal" at the 2000 Olympics in an exciting upset win over Brazil's Ricardo Santos and Ze'Marco de Melo. They were a solid team, having won events on the domestic tour together. But on the international tour, while they had some good results, they had never played consistent. That all changed at the final FIVB qualification tournament in Belgium, where they needed a strong finish to qualify and they got it, taking third in the event. That finish gave them the confidence they needed for the Olympics. Once they got to the Games, they played solid throughout the tournament. They stayed focused and never lost site of their goal. Their gold medal winning match was one of the highlights of the Games and had fans on the edge of their seats throughout the entire match. Their year ended on another high note as well, when they were named the Team of the Month by the United States Olympic Committee in October, and when they got to visit the White House to meet the President with other top USA Olympians. Blanton and Fonoimoana had made a statement to the rest of the USA beach volleyball world that they were ready to take the next step and try to become the No. 1 team in the USA in 2001.

ERIC FONOIMOANA
Eric Fonoimoana was "all-business" when he teamed-up with Dain Blanton to win the "Gold-Medal" at the 2000 Olympics on Bondi Beach in Australia. Above photo, during a break in the action, Fonoimoana is focused for the win.
Photo Courtesy of "Couvi"

As mentioned previously, 2000 was the year of the Olympic Games in Sydney where the top 24 men's and 24 women's teams in the world competed on Bondi Beach in the most important competition in the world. The qualifying for the 2000 Sydney Australia Olympiad showcased teams that represented more than 50 countries that took part in the Olympic Games qualification process. The World Council clarified that the 8 best results would count for the Olympic Games qualification process were 8 team results. European players could include one of the CEV (European Volleyball Confederation) Tour's Finals, either 1999 or 2000 edition, in their 8 best performances to count towards the Olympic qualification. The CEV Final 2000 was scheduled in Palma de Mallorca July 15-16 for women and July 17-18 for men. The Olympic Beach Volleyball tournaments were scheduled September 16-26 on Bondi Beach, in Sydney, Australia.

The Olympic venue included a stadium where 10,000 spectators witnessed a electrifying event, when in the "Gold-Medal" match, Americans Eric Fonoimoana and Dain Blanton made a spectacular come-back to snatch the "Gold-Medal" when they defeated Brazil's ZeMarco de Melo and Ricardo Santos by the scores of 12-11 and 12-9. In the "Bronze-Medal" match, Germany's Vince Ahmann and Axel Hager defeated Portugal's Joao Brenha Miguel Maia by scores of 12-9 and 12-6. In the Women's Division, The "Bronze-Medal" match was won by Brazil's Sandra Pires and Adriana Samuel when they outclassed Japan's Mika Saiki and Yukiko Takahashi, by scores of 12-4 and 12-6. In the "Gold-Medal" match Australia's Nathalie Cook and Kerri Pottharst, outlasted Brazil's Adriana Behar Shelda Bede, by scores of 12-11 and 12-10.

2000 INDIVIDUAL FIVB TOURNAMENT FINISHES

Player	1st	2nd	3rd	4th	5th
Vince Ahman	0	0	1	0	0
Marcio Araujo	2	3	1	1	2
Mariano Baracetti	1	0	0	1	0
Dain Blanton	1	0	2	0	1
Joao Carlos Pereira Brenha Alves	0	0	0	1	2
Jefferson Bellaguarda	0	0	1	1	1
Bjorn Berg	0	1	0	0	0
Nikilas Berger	0	0	0	0	1
Aaron Boss	0	0	0	0	1
Bill Boullianne	0	1	0	0	0
John Child	0	1	1	1	2
Ian Clark	0	1	0	0	0
Martin Alejo Conde	0	0	0	1	1
Roberto Lopes da Costa	0	0	1	0	0
Fabio Diez	0	0	0	0	1
Eric Fonoimoana	1	0	2	0	1
Simon Dahl	0	0	0	0	1
Giovane Gavio	0	0	0	0	1
Axel Hager	0	0	1	0	0
Mark Heese	0	1	1	1	2
Rob Heidger	0	1	0	1	2
Carl Henkel	0	1	0	0	1
Vegard Hoidalen	0	1	0	3	1
Dax Holdren	2	0	0	0	0
Benjamin Insfran	2	3	1	1	2
Adam Johnson	0	0	0	0	1
Karch Kiraly	0	0	0	0	1
Jorre Kjemperud	0	1	0	3	1
Mikhail Kouchnerev	0	0	1	0	2
Jan Kvalheim	0	0	0	0	1
Martin Laciga	1	2	3	1	5
Paul Laciga	1	2	3	1	5
Martin Lebl	0	0	0	1	0
Jose Loiola	4	1	3	0	1
Roberto Lopes	0	0	0	1	0
Bjorn Maaseide	0	0	0	0	1
Luis Miguel Barbosa Maia	0	0	0	1	2
Eduardo Esteban Martinez	0	0	0	1	1
Stein Metzger	0	0	0	0	1
Javier Bosma Minguez	0	0	0	0	1
Paulao Morrira	0	0	1	1	1
Jose Franco Vieira Neto	0	0	1	1	0
Jose Z-Marco Melo Nobrega	6	4	0	2	3
Oliver Oetke	0	0	0	1	1
Michal Palinek	0	0	0	1	0
Maurizio Pimponi	0	0	0	0	1
Julien Prosser	0	0	2	0	0
Jose Salema	1	0	0	1	0
Ricardo Alex Costa Santos	6	4	0	2	3
Emanuel Rego Scheffer	4	2	3	0	1
Andreas Scheuerpflug	0	0	0	1	1
Sinjin Smith	0	1	0	0	1
Oliver Stamm	0	0	0	0	1
Andrea Raffaelli	0	0	0	0	1
Alexandre Tande Ramos	0	1	0	0	1
Todd Rogers	2	0	0	0	0
David Swatik	0	0	0	0	1
Mike Whitmarsh	0	0	0	0	1
Kevin Wong	0	1	0	1	2
Lee Zahner	0	0	2	0	0

(Above list includes Olympic Challenge series as well as the Olympics)

DR. RUBEN ACOSTA
In 2000, FIVB President Dr. Ruben Acosta presented several new beach volleyball rule changes. Dr. Acosta was also proud to present beach volleyball at the 2000 Olympiad. Above photo, Dr. Acosta (left) attending an FIVB event with FIVB Beach Volleyball Coordinator Angelo Squeo (right).
Photo Courtesy of the FIVB

MEN'S TOURNAMENT RESULTS
2000-AVP

DEL REY BEACH FLORIDA
April 28th-30th, 2000

The $75,000.00 Sunkist AVP Tournament of Champions, staged at the Del Rey Tennis Center, was won by the team of Brent Doble and Lee Legrande. The tournament format was double elimination, one game to 15, win by two, no clock and no point cap. In the championship match they defeated Canyon Ceman and Brian Lewis 11-7, 4-11 and 8-6. The winner's earned $16,000.00. Television coverage was carried by the FOX Sports Network, via tape delay.

3rd Place: Jose Loiola and Emanuel Rego
4th Place: Mark Kerins and Kevin Martin
5th Place: Mike Whitmarsh and David Swatik
5th Place: Dax Holdren and Todd Rogers

SANTA CRUZ CALIFORNIA
May 26th-28th, 2000

The $75,000.00 AVP Yahoo Sports Santa Cruz Open, staged on Main Beach, was won by the team of Eric Fonoimoana and Dain Blanton. The tournament format was double elimination, one game to 15, win by two, no clock and no point cap. In the championship match they defeated Jose Loiola and Emanuel Rego. The winner's earned $16,000.00. Fox Sports Net televised the finals, via tape delay.

3rd Place: Canyon Ceman and Brian Lewis
4th Place: Karch Kiraly and Adam Johnson
5th Place: Brent Doble and Lee Legrande
5th Place: Ian Clark and Stein Metzgar

HERMOSA BEACH CALIFORNIA
June 8th-11th, 2000

The Mervyns Beach Bash $75,000.00 AVP Sideout Hermosa Beach Open, was staged on the north side of the Pier. The tournament format was double elimination, one game to 15, win by two, no clock and no point cap. The event was won by the team of Jose Loiola and Emanuel "Bones" Rego. In the championship match they defeated Dax Holdren and Todd Rogers by a score of 15-6. The game was close in the beginning with Loiola's big dig and Roger's off speed shot. Loiola and Rego went ahead 5-2 with the help of Regos' powerful serve. Dax also made an ace to make the score 5-3. Holdren and Rogers tried to draw from the cheering group of friends and family that were chanting "USA-USA-USA-USA" but Brazil's Rego quickly answered the chant with a nice block. From there on, Loiola and Rego seemed unstoppable making the score 12-5. Holdren and Rogers regained some strength and Dax's block and spike kept the Brazilians from scoring the next point for a while. Dax's ace got them the 6th point, but that's all they could do against the powerful Brazilian team. Rego and Loiola won the final at 15-6 with a well timed block by Rego. The winner's earned $16,000.00. Fox Sports Net televised the finals, via tape delay.

3rd Place: Canyon Ceman and Brian Lewis
4th Place: Eduardo Bacil and Fred Souza
5th Place: Karch Kiraly and Adam Johnson
5th Place: Dain Blanton and Eric Fonoimoana

EMANUEL REGO & JOSE LOIOLA

Emanuel Rego and Jose Loiola were the top team on the 2000 AVP Tour. Rego and Loiola advanced to four championship matches, winning 3 times. Above photo, During the AVP Tour stop in Hermosa Beach California, Rego hits a set from Loiola towards the block of Henry Russell. Nick Hannemann is ready on defense. Rego and Loiola won the event when they defeated Dax Holdren and Todd Rogers by the score of 15-6 in the championship match.

Photo Courtesy of "Couvi"

HUNTINGTON BEACH CALIFORNIA
June 16th-18th, 2000

The $75,000.00 AVP Huntington Beach Open, was staged on the south side of the Pier. The tournament format was double elimination, one game to 15, win by two, no clock and no point cap. The event was won by the team of Canyon Ceman and Brian Lewis. In the championship match they defeated Karch Kiraly and Adam Johnson by a score of 15-6. The winner's earned $16,000.00. Fox Sports Net tape delayed the finals.

3rd Place: Eduardo Bacil and Fred Souza
4th Place: Matt Unger and Mike Whitmarsh
5th Place: Lee LeGrande and Franco Neto
5th Place: Brent Doble and Stein Metzger

CHICAGO ILLINOIS
June 23rd-25th, 2000

The $75,000.00 AVP Chicago Open, was staged on North Beach. The tournament format was double elimination, one game to 15, win by two, no clock and no point cap. The event was won by the team of Dax Holdren and Todd Rogers. In the championship match, in front of a jam-packed beach crowd, they defeated Jose Loiola and Emanuel "Bones" Rego by a score of 16-14. The winner's earned $16,000.00. Fox Sports Net televised the finals, via tape delay.

3rd Place: Karch Kiraly and Adam Johnson
4th Place: Canyon Ceman and Brian Lewis
5th Place: Brent Frohoff and Larry Witt
5th Place: Mike Whitmarsh and Matt Unger

SANTA BARBARA CALIFORNIA
July 7th-9th, 2000

The $75,000.00 AVP Karch Kiraly Classic, was staged on East Beach in Santa Barbara California. The tournament format was double elimination, one game to 15, win by two, no clock and no point cap. The event was won by the team of Lee LeGrande and Franco Neto. In the championship match they overwhelmed Dax Holdren and Todd Rogers by the score of 15-3. The winner's earned $16,000.00. TV via Fox Sports Net.

3rd Place: Brent Doble and Stein Metzger
4th Place: Canyon Ceman and Brian Lewis
5th Place: Karch Kiraly and Adam Johnson
5th Place: Brent Frohoff and Larry Witt

MUSKEGON MICHIGAN
July 14th-16th, 2000

The $75,000.00 Sunkist AVP Muskegon Open, was staged at Marquette Park, next to the Pier, in Muskegon Michigan. The tournament format was double elimination, one game to 15, win by two, no clock and no point cap. The event was won by the team of Dax Holdren and Todd Rogers. In the championship match they out-lasted Lee LeGrande and Franco Neto by the score of 15-9. The winner's earned $16,000.00. Fox Sports Net televised the finals, via tape delay.

3rd Place: Brent Doble and Stein Metzger
4th Place: Canyon Ceman and Mike Whitmarsh
5th Place: Brent Frohoff and Larry Witt
5th Place: Eduardo Bacil and Fred Souza

TODD ROGERS & DAX HOLDREN
Todd Rogers and Dax Holdren stepped-up for a couple of tournament championships on the 2000 AVP Tour. They won the Chicago IL and Muskegon MI events. Above photo, Adam Johnson hits into the block of Rogers. Dax is ready on defense.
Photo Courtesy of Tim Andexler

JOSE LOIOLA & HENRY RUSSELL
On the 2000 AVP Tour, Jose Loiola made a habit of rejecting the ball at the net, while winning three AVP Tour events with Emanuel Rego. In the above photo, Loiola gets above the net as Henry Russell challenges the block.
Photo Courtesy of Tim Andexler

BELMAR BEACH NEW JERSEY
July 21st-23rd, 2000

The $75,000.00 Sunkist AVP Belmar Open, was on Belmar Beach in Belmar New Jersey. The tournament format was double elimination, one game to 15, win by two, no clock and no point cap. The event was won by the team of Canyon Ceman and Mike Whitmarsh. In the championship match they out-scored Adam Jewell and Nick Hannemann 15-9. The winner's earned $16,000.00. Fox Sports Net televised the finals, via tape delay.

3rd Place: Brent Doble and Stein Metzger
4th Place: Eduardo Bacil and Fred Souza
5th Place: Lee Legrand and Franco Neto
5th Place: Adam Johnson and Brian Lewis

VIRGINIA BEACH VIRGINIA
July 28th-30th, 2000

The $75,000.00 AVP Virginia Beach Open, was staged on Fourth Street Beach in Virginia Beach Virginia. The tournament format was double elimination, one game to 15, win by two, no clock and no point cap. The event was won by the team of Karch Kiraly and Adam Johnson. In the double final championship match they controlled Larry Witt and Brent Frohoff by the scores of 11-2 and 7-2. The winner's earned $16,000.00. Fox Sports Net televised the finals, via tape delay.

3rd Place: Canyon Ceman and Mike Whitmarsh
4th Place: Lee Legrand and Franco Neto
5th Place: Dax Holdren and Todd Rogers
5th Place: Brent Doble and Stein Metzger

CANYON CEMAN
On the 2000 AVP Tour, Canyon Ceman won two events with two different partners. With Brian Lewis he won the Huntington Beach evewnt and With Mike Whitmarsh he won the Belmar NJ event. Above photo, Ceman braces himself for the pass.
Photo Courtesy of Frank Goroszko

SEAL BEACH CALIFORNIA
August 18th-20th, 2000

The $75,000.00 Sunkist AVP Seal Beach Open, was staged in Seal Beach California, next to the Pier. The tournament format was double elimination, one game to 15, win by two, no clock and no point cap. The event was won by the team of Jose Loiola and Emanuel Rego. In the extended championship match they out-lasted Dain Blanton and Eric Fonoimoana by the score of 19-17. The winner's earned $16,000.00. Fox Sports Net televised the finals, via tape delay.

3rd Place: Lee Legrande and Franco Neto
4th Place: Canyon Ceman and Mike Whitmarsh
5th Place: Dax Holdren and Todd Rogers
5th Place: Nick Hannemann and Adam Jewell

MANHATTAN BEACH CALIFORNIA
August 25th-27th, 2000

The $75,000.00 Sunkist AVP Manhattan Beach Open, was staged on the south side of the Pier in Manhattan Beach California. The tournament format was double elimination, one game to 15, win by two, no clock and no point cap. The event was won by the team of Jose Loiola and Emanuel Rego. In the arousing championship match they out-pointed Canyon Ceman and Mike Whitmarsh by the score of 15-13. The winner's earned $16,000.00. Fox Sports Net televised the finals, via tape delay.

3rd Place: Eduardo Bacil and Fred Souza
4th Place: Dax Holdren and Todd Rogers
5th Place: Brian Lewis and Adam Johnson
5th Place: Paulo Emilio Silva Azvedo and Eduardo Garrido

LAS VEGAS NEVADA
October 5th-8th, 2000

The $175,000.00 AVP King of the Beach, was staged on the "industrial" sand, in the parking lot of the Hard Rock Hotel and Casino, in Las Vegas Nevada. The "Crown" was won by Mike Whitmarsh, who collected $40,000.00 in prize money. In a tie for second place, the runner-ups were Brian Lewis and Dax Holdren. Lewis collected $31,000.00 and Holdren $26,500.00. Canyon Ceman was in the fourth spot. Fox Sports Net televised the finals, via tape delay.

1st Place: Mike Whitmarsh
2nd Place: Brian Lewis
2nd Place: Dax Holdren
4th Place: Canyon Ceman
5th Place: Emanuel Rego
6th Place: Lee LeGrande
7rd Place: Franco Neto
8th Place: Todd Rogers
9th Place: Stein Metzger

MEN'S TOURNAMENT RESULTS 2000-FIVB

MAR DEL PLATA ARGENTINA
January 12th-16th, 2000

Arousing action was in evidence during the finish of the $150,000.00 FIVB 2000 Argentina Beach Volleyball Men's Open in Mar del Plata, Argentina. The 10th-seeded local team of Mariano Baracetti and Jose Salema claimed the "Gold-Medal" by defeating the top-seeded team of Ze Marco de Melo and Ricardo Santos, from Brazil, by the score of 15-13. The 4th-seeded Australian pair of Julien Prosser and Lee Zahner clinched the "Bronze-Medal" by beating the 8th-seeded Brazilians Franco Neto and Roberto Lopes, who had to go through the never-easy qualification tournament to reach the final-four level.

3rd Place: Julien Prosser and Lee Zahner-Australia
4th Place: Roberto Lopes and Franco Neto-Brazil
5th Place: Martin Laciga and Paul Laciga-Switzerland
5th Place: Maurizio Pimponi and Andrea Raffaelli-Italy

GUARUJA BRAZIL
January 18th-23rd, 2000

History was made at the $150,000.00 FIVB 2000 Brazil Beach Volleyball Men's Open. For only the second time in FIVB World Tour history, a team that had advanced to the Main Draw through the qualification tournament captured the "Gold-Medal" (the first time was in 1998 when Brazil's Ze Marco de Melo and Ricardo Santos won in Rio de Janeiro, Brazil). In the almost 1 ½ hour "Gold-Medal" match, the 56th FIVB ranked team of Marcio Araujo and Benjamin Insfran, from Brazil, beat the Swiss team of Paul Laciga and Martin Laciga, by the scores of 12-6 and 12-5. The Swiss brothers Laciga and Laciga finished as the runner-ups while Brazilians Emanuel Rego and Jose Loiola clinched the "Bronze-Medal."

3rd Place: Jose Loiola and Emanuel Rego-Brazil
4th Place: Oliver Oetke and Andreas Scheuerpflug-Germany
5th Place: Ze Marco de Melo and Ricardo Santos-Brazil
5th Place: Giovane Gavio and Tande Ramos-Brazil

PAULAO MORRIRA
Brazilian Paulao Morrira paried-up with compatriot Jefferson Bellaguarda, on the 2000 FIVB Tour. They had a best finish of third at the Klagenfurt Austria event. Above photo, Paulao challenges the block of Eduardo Esteban Martinez from Argentina.
Photo Courtesy of the FIVB

MARIANO BARACETTI
Argentine Mariano Baracetti teamed-up with compatriot Jose Salema to win the "Gold-Medal" match at the 2000 FIVB event in Mar del Plata Argentina. Above photo, Baracetti follows-thru after attacking the ball.
Photo Courtesy of the FIVB

DEERFIELD BEACH FLORIDA
April 13th-16th, 2000

The Men's USAV $100,000.00 Oldsmobile Olympic Challenge Series, sanctioned by the FIVB, was won by Dax Holdren and Todd Rogers. The event was staged on Deerfield Beach Florida U.S.A. In the championship match, Holdren and Rogers out-lasted Bill Boullianne and Ian Clark. In the match for third place, Dain Blanton and Eric Fonoimoana defeated Rob Heidger and Kevin Wong. The winner's split $20,000.00 for their "Gold-Medal" performance.

3rd Place: Dain Blanton and Eric Fonoimoana-USA
4th Place: Rob Heidger and Kevin Wong-USA
5th Place: David Swatik and Mike Whitmarsh-USA
5th Place: Aaron Boss and Stein Metzger-USA

MACAU CHINA
May 24th-28th, 2000

The Men's $150,000.00 FIVB 2000 Macau Beach Volleyball Men's Open, in Macau China, was won by Brazil's Ze Marco de Melo and Ricardo Santos. In the all-Brazilian championship match, Z-Marco and Santos out-pointed Marcio Araujo and Benjamin Insfran. In the "Bronze-Medal" match, another Brazilian team, Roberto Lopes and Franco Neto defeated Vegard Hoidalen and Jorre Kjemperud, from Norway. The winner's split $20,000.00 for their "Gold-Medal" performance.

3rd Place: Roberto Lopes and Franco Neto-Brazil
4th Place: Vegard Hoidalen and Jorre Kjemperud-Norway
5th Place: Martin Laciga and Paul Laciga-Switzerland
5th Place: Martin Conde and Eduardo Martinez-Argentina

ROSARITO MEXICO
May 31st-June 4th, 2000

At the 2000 FIVB $150,000.00 Mexico Open, on Rosarito Beach, Mexico, for the third-time since 1996, a qualifying team for a men's FIVB Beach Volleyball World Tour Main Draw claimed a "Gold-Medal" when American's Dax Holdren and Todd Rogers completed a "perfect" weekend by capturing the Mexican Open on Rosarito Beach. In the championship match, Holden and Rogers defeated compatriots Rob Heidger and Kevin Wong. The winner's claimed the first place prize of $26,000.00. In the "Bronze-Medal" match, the Brazilian team of Marcio Araujo and Benjamin Insfran defeated the Swiss team of Martin Laciga and Paul Laciga.

3rd Place: Marcio Araujo and Benjamin Insfran-Brazil
4th Place: Martin Laciga and Paul Laciga-Switzerland
5th Place: Ze Marco de Melo and Ricardo Santos-Brazil
5th Place: Sergey Ermishin and Mikhail Kouchnerev-Russia

JAVIER BOSMA MINGUEZ
Spain's Javier Bosma Minguez teamed-up with compatriot Fabio Diez to provide some stiff competition on the 2000 FIVB World Tour. Above photo, Bosma challenges the block of American Eric Fonoimoana.
Photo Courtesy of the FIVB

SERGEY ERMISHIN
Russian Sergey Ermishin teamed-up with compatriot Mikhail Kouchnerev for some success on the 2000 FIVB World Tour. They had a best finish of third at the FIVB event in Tenerife Spain. Above photo, Ermishin attacking the ball.
Photo Courtesy of the FIVB

TORONTO CANADA
June 14th-18th, 2000

The 2000 FIVB $150,000.00 Nokia Open was the stage for fifth seeded Emanuel Rego Scheffer and Jose Loiola of Brazil. They staged one of the most amazing comebacks in the history of the FIVB Beach Volleyball World Tour here when they captured the men's "Gold-Medal" at Woodbine Beach Park on Ashbridges Bay, in Toronto Canada. After finishing second in the previous two Nokia Opens, Emanuel and Loiola rallied, in the championship match, from 9-0, 10-5 and 14-8 deficits to score a 16-14 win in 63-minutes over the 9th-seeded Canadian team of John Child and Mark Heese. This "Gold-Medal" finish snapped a streak of five FIVB Beach Volleyball World Tour events where Rego and Loiola had not finished first, including a career-worst placement of 13th in the last men's international event in Mexico. The win was worth $26,000.00 for Emanuel and Loiola while Child and Heese split $18,000.00. Australia captured the "Bronze-Medal" when Julien Prosser and Lee Zahner rallied from 5-0, 8-2, 11-4, 13-7 and 14-11 deficits to defeat Ze'Marco de Melo and Ricardo Santos 17-16 in 52 minutes.

3rd Place: Julien Prosser and Lee Zahner-Australia
4th Place: Ze Marco de Melo and Ricardo Santos-Brazil
5th Place: Marcio Araujo and Benjamin Insfran-Brazil
5th Place: Oliver Oetke and Andreas Scheuerpflug-Germany

TENERIFE SPAIN
June 21st-25th, 2000

It was a Swiss weekend in Tenerife Spain at the Men's 2000 FIVB $150,000.00 Spain Open. "Team-Brothers" Paul and Martin Laciga held-on to win the "Gold-Medal" as well as $26,000.00 in prize money. In the championship match they out-lasted Brazil's Marcio Araujo and Benjamin Insfran. In the "Bronze-Medal" match, the Russian team of Sergey Ermishin and Mikhail Kouchnerev defeated Ze Marco de Melo and Ricardo Santos, from Brazil.

3rd Place: Sergey Ermishin and Mikhail Kouchnerev-Russia
4th Place: Ze Marco de Melo and Ricardo Santos-Brazil
5th Place: Nikolas Berger and Oliver Stamm-Austria
5th Place: Joao Brenha and Luis Maia-Portugal

CHICAGO ILLINOIS
June 28th-July 2nd, 2000

It was another Brazilian weekend on the 2000 Men's FIVB World Tour, in Chicago Illinois, at the $200,000.00 Oldsmobile Grand Slam. In an all-Brazilian final, Jose Loiola and Emanuel Rego won the "Gold-Medal" over compatriots Ze Marco de Melo and Ricardo Santos. The winners collected $32,000.00 while the runner-ups settled for $22,000.00.

3rd Place: Martin Laciga and Paul Laciga-Switzerland
4th Place: Mariano Baracetti and Jose Salema-Argentina
5th Place: Marcio Araujo and Benjamin Insfran-Brazil
5th Place: Vegard Hoidalen and Jorre Kjemperud-Norway

STAVANGER NORWAY
July 5th-9th, 2000

The top seed in the world, Ze Marco de Melo and Ricardo Santos, from Brazil, played trough the 2000 Phillips $150,000.00 Stavanger Open, without a loss, earning the "Gold-Medal" and $26,000.00 in prize money. The event was staged in Stavanger Norway. In the championship match Ze Marco and Santos utilized aggressive serves and tremendous blocking to defeat compatriots Marcio Araujo and Benjamin Insfran. This was Ze Marco and Ricardo's eighth victory together, their second this year, and they strengthened their position on the top of the world ranking. The 62nd and last match in Stavanger 2000 ended in 46 minutes, and 3500 spectators were given beach volleyball on the highest level, with serve aces, blocks, as well as line-shots.

3rd Place: Jose Loiola and Emanuel Rego-Brazil
4th Place: Martin Conde and Eduardo Martinez-Argentina
5th Place: Joao Brenha and Luis Maia-Portugal
5th Place: Carl Henkel and Sinjin Smith-USA

LIGNANO ITALY
July 12th-16th, 2000

The 2000 FIVB $150,000.00 Italian Open, staged in Lignano Sabbiadoro Italy, was another "Gold-Medal" performance for the Brazilian team of Ze'Marco de Melo and Ricardo Santos, who defeated the Swiss team of Martin Laciga and Paul Laciga. This was their third "Gold-Medal" on the 2000 World Tour, after Macau China and Stavanger Norway. This win helped them confirm their first place position in the international ranking. The prize money for the first place was $26,000.00 and 170 points for the personal ranking. In the championship match, the second place Laciga brothers fell to the awesome force and the consistent play of the winners. Santos was especially strong at the net, with his huge block. The final score was 15-3.

3rd Place: John Child and Mark Heese-Canada
4th Place: Marcio Araujo and Benjamin Insfran-Brazil
5th Place: Jose Loiola and Emanuel Rego-Brazil
5th Place: Rob Heidger and Kevin Wong-USA

MARSEILLE FRANCE
July 19th-23rd, 2000

The 2000 FIVB $150,000.00 French Open, staged in Marseille France, was another "Gold-Medal" performance for the Brazilian team of Ze'Marco de Melo and Ricardo Santos. This time they defeated Vegard Hoidalen and Jorre Kjemperud, from Norway. This was their fourth "Gold-Medal" on the 2000 World Tour. They collected another $26,000.00 for their "Gold-Medal" performance. In the championship match, they utilized the blocking ability of Santos and the defensive expertise of Ze Marco to out-play the team from Norway.

3rd Place: Jose Loiola and Emanuel Rego-Brazil
4th Place: Martin Lebl and Michal Palinek-Czech Republic
5th Place: Sergey Ermishin and Mikhail Kouchnerev-Russia
5th Place: Jan Kvalheim and Bjorn Maaseide-Norway

ESPINHO PORTUGAL
July 26th-30th, 2000

The last day of the competition at the Men's FIVB $150,000.00 Portugal Open was a spectacular demonstration of beach volleyball combined with fan support and excitement. On this beautiful and warm day, the stadium was packed with an exuberant crowd for the "Gold-Medal" match. In the all-Brazilian championship match, the fans watched as Ze Marco de Melo and Ricardo Santos played magnificently, while overpowering compatriots Emanuel Rego and Jose Loiola by the score of 15-6. The winner's shared $26,000.00 for their efforts. Earlier, in the semi-finals, the both Brazilian teams easily handled their opponents. Emanuel and Loiola won 15-9 over Canadians John Child and Mark Heese, while Ze Marco and Ricardo knocked out Paul Laciga and Martin Laciga by a score of 15-10. In the "Bronze-Medal" match, the Laciga brothers played a high-level match to out-play the Canadians by a score of 15-4.

3rd Place: Martin Laciga and Paul Laciga-Switzerland
4th Place: John Child and Mark Heese-Canada
5th Place: Jefferson Bellaguarda and Paulao Moreira-Brazil
5th Place: Dain Blanton and Eric Fonoimoana-USA

KLAGENFURT AUSTRIA
August 2nd-6th, 2000

On a sunny day, at the 2000 Men's FIVB $150,000.00 Austrian Open, in-front of 13.000 spectators creating the energetic atmosphere in the stadium of Klagenfurt, two powerful Brazilian teams provided another sensational "Gold-Medal" match. World Champions Emanuel Rego and Jose Loiola held-on to out-score top seeded Zé-Marco de Melo and Ricardo Santos. In the championship match, on one side of the net Ricardo did a good job of blocking as his team rallied from a 12-5 deficit to take a 13-12 lead over Emanuel and Loyola. On the other side of the net Emanuel was consistent to the finish as he executed two deadly shots against Zé-Marco to gain the last two points in the 15-13 victory.

3rd Place: Jefferson Bellaguarda and Paulao Moreira-Brazil
4th Place: Vegard Hoidalen and Jorre Kjemperud-Norway
5th Place: Martin Laciga and Paul Laciga-Switzerland
5th Place: Adam Johnson and Karch Kiraly-USA

OSTENDE BELGIUM
August 9th-13th, 2000

Brazilians Emanuel Rego and Jose Loiola were "on fire" during the "Gold-Medal" match, on the center court of Ostende Beach, at the 2000 Men's FIVB $150,000.00 Belgium Open. In the championship match, to the beat of the Brazilian Samba, Emanuel and Loiola dominated the final match of this tournament against Americans Carl Henkel and Sinjin Smith. Henkel and Smith started-out slow and were down 5-0 and never managed to turn the score to their advantage. Henkel struggled as he was unable to block the attacks from the Brazilians. Without their preferred weapon and serving badly, the American duo had to give up the game to the opponents 15-8. The winners received $26,000.00 along with the championship. This Belgian Men's Open in Ostend, was the last official FIVB World Tour tournament taken into account for the 2000 Olympic Games in Sydney Australia.

3rd Place: Dain Blanton and Eric Fonoimoana-USA
4th Place: Vegard Hoidalen and Jorre Kjemperud-Norway
5th Place: Martin Laciga and Paul Laciga-Switzerland
5th Place: John Child and Mark Heese-Canada

SYDNEY AUSTRALIA
September 16th-26th, 2000

The ninth ranked team of Eric "Fonoi" Fonoimoana and Dain Blanton, from the U.S.A. are now Olympic "Gold-Medallists" by virtue of an upset victory over the Brazilian team of Ze Marco De Melos and Ricardo Santos in the final of the 2000 Olympiad's presentation of beach volleyball on Bondi Beach in Sydney Australia. In the "Gold-Medal" match Blanton and Fonoimoana raised their level of play and consistency to surprise the Brazillian team of Ze Marco De Melos and Ricardo Santos in the final. The winner's utilized a consistent side-out play throughout the match. In the first game, the US held of Brazil to win by a close 12-11 score. Blanton and Fonoimoana continued their consistent play in the second game as Blanton's sideout attack was unstoppable. The 66-minute second game featured 97 side outs as Blanton and Fonoimoana jumped to a 4-1 lead with the Brazilians tying the score at 4-4. Blanton and Fonoimoana regained the lead for good with a three-point run. Ze'Marco, who has won the second-most international titles (26 to Brazil's Emanuel Rego's 30), and Ricardo cut the American's lead to 8-7 and 10-9. Fonoimoana ended the 101-minute Gold Medal match with an aggressive attack that reached the opponents sand for the 11th point. Foni then made a block for the championship point. In the "Bronze-Medal" match, the German team of Vince Ahmann and Axel Hager defeated Portugals Luis Maia and Joao Brenha by scores of 12-9, 12-6 . Earlier, during the semi-finals, Blanton and Fonoimoana defeated Luis Maia and Joao Brenha, from Portugal 15-12, while Ze Marco and Ricardo out-scored Ahmann-Hager, 15-5.

3rd Place: Vince Ahmann and Axel Hager-Germany
4th Place: Luis Maia and Joao Brenha-Portugal
5th Place: Martin Laciga and Paul Laciga-Switzerland
5th Place: John Child and Mark Heese-Canada
5th Place: Javier Bosma-Fabio Diez-Spain
5th Place: Kevin Wong-and Rob Heidger-USA

VITORIA BRAZIL
November 28th-December 3rd, 2000

The 4000 spectators at the 2000 Men's FIVB $150,000.00 Brazil Open were delighted with the all-Brazilian "Gold-Medal" match, on Camburi Beach in Vitoria Brazil. In the last championship match of the 2000 FIVB World Tour, Brazilians Marcio Araujo and Benjamin Insfran defeated compatriots Tande Ramos and Emanuel Rego in the hard-fought games to capture the "Gold-Medal" along with the $26,000.00 first place check.

3rd Place: Martin Laciga and Paul Laciga-Switzerland
4th Place: Jefferson Bellaguarda and Paulao Moreira-Brazil
5th Place: Ze Marco de Melo and Ricardo Santos-Brazil
5th Place: Bjorn Berg and Simon Dahl-Sweden

TOP PHOTOS: Left: Lee "LL" LeGrande passing the ball. **Center:** Larry "Dizzel" Witt passing the ball. **Right:** Sean Scott passing the ball.

MIDDLE PHOTOS: Left: Brazilian Fred Souza rejecting the ball. **Center:** Dax Holdren challenging the block of Dain Blanton. **Right:** Dual citizen (Brazilian and American) Jose Loiola passing the ball.

2000 MEN'S BEACH VOLLEYBALL ACTION

BOTTOM PHOTOS: Left: Norway's Vegard Hoidalen reaches high to pass the ball. **Center:** Martin Conde, from Argentina, passing the ball. **Right:** Germany's Axel Hager concentrates as he passes the ball.

Top and Middle Photos Courtesy of Frank Goroszko. Bottom Photos Courtesy of the FIVB

WOMEN'S BEACH VOLLEYBALL 2000

The Womens Professional Volleyball Association (WPVA) was formed in 1986 and began in 1987 in order to administer, govern, and protect the integrity of Women's Professional Beach Volleyball. A group of women that included former Olympic and collegiate All-American volleyball players joined together at the end of 1986 to form the WPVA. Led by Pepperdine volleyball coach Nina Matthies, the formation of the WPVA was the first step in organizing the women's pro beach volleyball events which had previously been played as armature games or as the accompaniment to the men's professional game. With a membership of more than 225 active female athletes, in 1996, the WPVA was the third largest professional league for women and served as the sanctioning body for the participation of the United States top female beach volleyball players in world-wide competition.

In 1997 the WPVA organization included: Board of Directors, Bussiness Affairs Department, Event Management Department, Public Relations Department, and an Operations Department. The 1997 WPVA Board of Directors consisted of: Krista Blomquist, Linda Hanley, Helen Reale, Angela Rock, Jay Brooks, Bobby Clark, Chris Lancey, Nancy Lengel, Paul Leroue, and Teresa Saputo. The 1997 WPVA Business Affairs Department consisted of: Executive Director Nancy Lengel, Marketing Director Kelly Watson, and Administrative/Marketing Manager Angela Guerra. The 1997 WPVA Public Relations department consist of: Information Director Tim Simmons and Operations/Information Manager Sue Carpenter.

In 1998 the Women's Pro Beach Volleyball tour, the WPVA entered into "voluntary dissolution." By 1999, in the USA, there was no domestic women's professional tour for American players to participatein The only professional tour was the international FIVB Tour. Then in the year 2000, Beach Volleyball America (BVA) was formed.

NINA GROUWINKEL MATTHIES
In 1986, Nina Grouwinkel Matthies was instrumental in getting the WPVA started. Her efforts were the foundation of women's professional beach volleyball. Above, Nina is "ever-steady" as she passes the ball.
Photo Courtesy of Bruce Hazelton

LINDA ROBERTSON HANLEY
Linda Robertson Hanley was involved in beach volleyball well before the WPVA. She was also on the Board of Directors when it was thriving and she was still involved after its dissolution. Above photo, Hanley hits a set from Nina Grouwinkel Matthies.
Photo Courtesy of Bruce Hazelton

Women's professional beach volleyball was made available through the BVA, which staged seven events, with a total purse of $525,000.00. The BVA events were all staged in California at Oceanside, Santa Monica, Hermosa Beach, Seal Beach, Pismo Beach, Long Beach and San Diego. In addition to the BVA events the AVP staged the "Queen of the Beach" event in Las Vegas Nevada. The top team on the 2000 BVA Tour was Annette Davis and Jenny Jordan. They entered five BVA events, advancing to the championship match three times, winning two events, along with two third place finishes. They earned $55,500.00 in prize money. The team of Lisa Arce and Barbra Fontana was in second place, entering six BVA events, advancing to three finals, winning twice along with one third place finish. Arce and Fontana earned $54,000.00 in prize money. There were three additional teams, that won one event each, on the 2000 BVA Tour. They were the teams of Holly McPeak with Misty May, Nancy Reno with Elaine Youngs and Carrie Busch with Leanne Schuster McSorley. Barbra Fontana won the "Queen of the Beach" event.

In 2000, the Federation Internationale de Volleyball (FIVB), the international governing body of the sport of volleyball worldwide endorsed Beach Volleyball America (BVA) and the BVA Pro Beach Volleyball Tour as its official men's and women's US National Tour for the sport of beach volleyball. The FIVB has over 218 member countries and oversees the administration and promotion of the FIVB World Tour, which offers close to $5 million in prize money distributed equally between male and female competitors. The FIVB World Tour serves as the official Olympic qualification tour for the sport of beach volleyball.

The new women's pro beach volleyball league named the BVA Tour was formed by Charlie Jackson, a software entrepreneur and member of USAV board of directors funded and initiated this tour. Jackson was the chairperson the USAV International Beach Volleyball Commission. The purpose of the BVA was to create a growth in Women's beach volleyball in the US. The BVA was to be closely knit with the FIVB and the Olympic Challenge Series (OCS) to maximize opportunities for the women and avoid schedule conflicts. The format was to have 24 teams at each event, competing for over $500,000 in prize money. The top 16 teams in the country were automatically seeded into two-day double elimination tournaments, with the last 8 from a qualifier. In 2000, the team of Misty May and Holly McPeak, which, had teamed up late in 1999, gave all of the other top USA women's teams a one year head start towards qualification for the Olympics. Not giving them much chance of catching the top two USA teams with only 10 qualifying events to go. With the help of beach volleyball legend Gene Selznick's coaching and veteran McPeak tutoring May, the duo caught-up fast. In only their third tournament, the Oldsmobile Beach Volleyball Olympic Challenge Series (OCS) event in Deerfield Beach, Florida, they played through a strong field and then defeated Lisa Arce and Barbra Fontana to win their first title. By the time the Olympics rolled around, not only did they make the USA Olympic team, they were arguably the best team in the world. In the period between their first win and the Olympics, they had four second place finishes (FIVB Mexico, Canada, Switzerland, and China) and two more wins (FIVB Chicago and Germany). Unfortunately, May also pulled a stomach muscle in the FIVB Germany tournament and while she seemingly was recovered by the time the Olympic got

ANNETTE DAVIS & JENNY JORDAN
Annette Buckner Davis and Jenny Johnson Jordan advanced to 3 championship matches on the 2000 BVA Tour. They won twice. Above photo, Davis hits a set from Jordan, past the block of Elaine Youngs.
Photo Courtesy of "Couvi"

BARBRA FONTANA & LISA ARCE
Barbra Fontana and Lisa Arce fought their way into 3 championship matches on the 2000 BVA Tour. They won twice. In the above photo, Arce chases down the ball to make a dig for Fontana.
Photo Courtesy of "Couvi"

underway, anyone watching them play realized that she was not 100 %. In the end, they finished fifth. This past November, completely healed and back on top of their game, May and McPeak stormed through the field at the season ending FIVB Brazil tournament to win their fourth title of the year and set the stage for next year when they will try to dethrone Adriana Behar and Shelda Bede of Brazil, the No. 1 team in the world for the last four years. May and McPeak definitely had the potential to become one of the great teams in the history of the women's game, but in 2001 May elected to team-up with best friend Kerri Walsh, for what now looks like might be the best women's beach volleyball team of all-time.

2000 INDIVIDUAL BVA TOURNAMENT FINISHES

Player	1st	2nd	3rd	4th	5th
Lisa Arce	2	1	1	0	0
Annett Buckner-Davis	2	1	2	0	0
Carrie Busch	1	0	1	0	1
Stephanie Cox	0	0	1	0	4
Kathy Eldridge	0	0	1	0	4
Barbra Fontana	3	1	1	0	0
Linda Hanley	0	1	0	2	4
Jennifer Johnson Jordan	2	1	2	0	0
Karolyn Kirby	0	0	0	0	2
Liz Masakayan	0	0	0	1	2
Nancy Mason	0	1	0	2	0
Misty May	1	1	1	0	0
Holly McPeak	1	1	2	1	1
Leanne Schuster McSorley	1	1	0	2	0
Jen Meredith	0	0	2	0	0
Mazrsha Miller	0	0	0	0	1
Marla O'Hara	0	0	0	0	1
Jenny Pavley	0	0	1	0	0
Kerri Poppinga	0	0	0	1	4
Nancy Reno	1	3	0	2	0
Kristen Schritter	0	0	0	0	1
Rachel Wacholder	0	1	0	1	0
Ali Wood	0	0	0	1	1
Lia Young	0	0	0	0	1
Elaine Youngs	1	2	0	1	1

LEANNE McSORLEY & CARRIE BUSCH
Leanne Schuster McSorley and Carrie Busch broke-through for a tournament championship at the 2000 Hermosa Beach BVA event. Above photo, Misty May challenges the block of McSorley, while Busch is ready for action on defense .
Photo Courtesy of "Couvi"

HOLLY McPEAK & MISTY MAY
Holly McPeak and Misty May teamed-up for some success on the 2000 BVA Tour. They also played well internationally, qualifying for the 2000 Olympiad. Above photo, McPeak (left) and May (right) take a break from play.
Photo Courtesy of Tim Andexler

FIVB

The Women's FIVB 2000 World Tour of Beach Volleyball staged fifteen events, including two USAV events (sanctioned by the FIVB) and the Olympics. There were events in twelve countries with a total purse of $2,050,000.00. The FIVB events were staged in Vitoria Brazil, Rosarito Mexico, Calgiari Italy, Toronto Canada, Gstaad Switzerland, Chicago Illinois U.S.A., Berlin Germany, Marseille France, Espinho Portugal, Osaka Japan, Dalan China and Fortaleza Brazil. The two USAV events were staged in the U.S. Cities of Deerfield Beach Michigan and Virginia Beach Virginia. The 2000 Olympics were staged in Sydney Australia on Bondi Beach.

The top team, on the 2000 FIVB Women's World Tour was Brazil's Shelda Bede and Adriana Behar. They advanced to seven "Gold-Medal" matches, winning four times, while earning nearly $190,000.00. American's Misty May and Holly McPeak were the number two team on the 2000 FIVB Women's Tour. May and McPeak advanced to seven "Gold-Medal" Matches, winning three times, while earning $180,000.00. Another American team was in the top three as Liz Masakayan and Elaine Youngs advanced to three "Gold-Medal" matches, winning each time, while earning nearly $120,000.00. A third American team was within the top four, as Annette Davis and Jenny Jordan advanced to two "Gold-Medal" matches, winning once. There were three additional teams that each won one "Gold-Medal" on the 2000 FIVB Women's World Tour. They were Australian's Kerri-Ann Pottharst with Natalie Cook, Brazil's Ana Paula Connelly with Monica Rodrigues and Petia Yanchulova with Lina Yanchulova, from Bulgaria.

THE 2000 OLYMPICS

The 2000 Olympics were staged in Sydney Australia. The beach volleyball took place on Sydney's most famous beach, Bondi Beach. The beach volleyball matches were staged within a secured area next to Bondi Pavilion, the surrounding park and of course the beach. There were also eight training and warm-up courts. The stadium was designed to hold 10,000 spectators. The beach volleyball competition included 84 beach volleyball players of which 48 were male, while 36 were female. There were 116 scheduled matches that took place September 16th-27th, 2000. As in the 1996 Olympics at Atlanta Beach, there were two sessions daily. The scheduled times for each session were in the morning from 8:30am-12:30pm and then in the afternoon from 2:00pm-7:30pm.

The women's event was highlighted by a spectacular upset featuring the Australian team of Natalie Cook and Kerri Pottharst winning over the best team in the world, Adriana Behar and Shelda Bede of Brazil to win the "Gold-Medal" in front of the very appreciative Australian fans. A spectacular final for the deserving gold medalists, at one of the best beach volleyball tournaments in the history of the game.

2000 INDIVIDUAL FIVB TOURNAMENT FINISHES

Player	1st	2nd	3rd	4th	5th
Lisa Arce	1	1	0	0	4
Shelda Kelly Bruno Bede	4	3	1	2	1
Adriana Brandao Behar	4	3	1	2	1
Danalee Bragado	0	0	0	0	1
Laura Bruschini	0	0	0	0	3
Adriana Benito Buczmiejuk	0	0	0	0	1
Rong Chi	0	0	1	0	0
Carrie Busch	0	0	0	0	1
Ana Paula Connolly	1	0	2	0	3
Natalie Cook	1	0	3	1	3
Annette Buckner Davis	2	1	2	3	3
Barbra Fontana	0	2	0	0	4
Tania Gooley	0	1	0	0	3
Dalixia Fernandez Grassel	0	0	0	0	1
Linda Robertson Hanley	0	0	1	1	1
Jenny Johnson Jordan	2	1	2	3	3
Rebekka Kadijk	0	0	0	0	1
Schoon Kadijk	0	0	0	0	1
Vasso Karadassiou	0	0	0	0	1
Magda Lima	0	0	0	0	1
Pauline Manser	0	1	0	0	3
Liz Masakayan	3	0	0	1	1
Misty May	4	6	0	1	2
Holly McPeak	4	6	0	1	2
Leanne Schuster McSorley	0	0	1	0	1
Nancy Mason	0	0	1	0	0
Tamara Larrea Perazza	0	0	0	0	1
Cristina Pereria	0	0	0	1	0
Sandra Tavares Pires	0	2	2	2	0
Kerri Poppinga	0	0	0	1	0
Kerri Ann Pottharst	1	0	3	1	3
Christine Pereria	0	0	0	1	0
Nancy Reno	0	0	1	1	1
Angela Rock	0	0	0	1	0
Monica Rodrigues	1	0	2	0	3
Maria Clara Rufino	0	0	0	0	1
Mika Teru Saiki	0	1	2	1	0
Adriana Ramos Samuel	0	2	2	2	0
Ulrike Schmidt	0	0	0	1	0
Maria Jose Schuller	0	0	0	1	0
Efi Sfyri	0	0	0	0	1
JacquelineLouise"Jackie"Cruz Silva	0	0	0	0	1
Anna Maria Solazzi	0	0	0	0	3
Gudula Staub	0	0	0	1	0
Yukiko Takahashi	0	1	2	1	0
Zi Xiong	0	0	1	0	0
Ali Wood	0	0	0	0	1
Elaine Youngs	3	0	0	1	1

(Above list includes Olympic Challenge series as well as the Olympics)

TANIA GOOLEY
Australian Tania Gooley played some good beach volleyball on the 2000 FIVB Tour. Her best finish was a second at the German Open with compatriot Pauline Manser. Above photo, Gooley gets sandy in-order to make a dig.
Photo Courtesy of the FIVB

WOMEN'S TOURNAMENT RESULTS
2000-BVA

OCEANSIDE CALIFORNIA
May 12th-14th, 2000

The Women's $75,000.00 BVA Volleyhut.com 2000 Oceanside Invitational, staged south of the Pier Plaza, was won by the team of Lisa Arce and Barbra Fontana. In the almost one hour championship match, they outlasted Misty May and Holly McPeak by the score of 15-13. Arce and Fontana collected the first place prize of $15,000.00, while the runner-ups collected $10,500.00. National television telecast was on Fox Sports Net.

3rd Place: Annette Davis and Jenny Jordan
4th Place: Linda Hanley and Nancy Reno
5th Place: Liz Masakayan and Elaine Youngs
5th Place: Stephene Cox and Katy Eldridge

SANTA MONICA CALIFORNIA
June 16th-18th, 2000T

The Women's $75,000.00 BVA 2000 Santa Monica Open was staged south of the Santa Monica Pier between Pico and Bicknell. The winner's were Annette Davis and Jenny Jordan. In the over one hour championship match, they held-on to defeat Nancy Reno and Linda Hanley, by the score of 15-13. Davis and Jordan collected the first place prize of $15,000.00, while the runner-ups collected $10,500.00. FOX Sports tape delayed the television telecast.

3rd Place: Misty May and Holly McPeak
4th Place: Liz Masakayan and Elaine Youngs
5th Place: Stephene Cox and Katy Eldridge
5th Place: Marla O'Hara and Kristen Schritter

HOLLY McPEAK
Holly McPeak was a consistant player on the 2000 BVA Tour. She advanced to 2 championship matches, winning the Seal Beach event with Misty May. Above photo, McPeak spikes the ball towards the defense of Leanne Schuster McSorley.
Photo Courtesy of "Couvi"

LISA ARCE
During the 2000 BVA tour, Lisa Arce was a menacing force at the net, both blocking and attacking. Arce won two titles with Barbra Fontana in 2000. Above photo, Arce follows-through after attacking the ball.
Photo Courtesy of "Couvi"

HERMOSA BEACH CALIFORNIA
June 9th-11th, 2000

The Women's $75,000.00 BVA Union Bay Hermosa Beach Open was part of the 2000 Mervyn's California Beach Bash. The beach volleyball tournament was won by the team of Carrie Busch and Leanne Schuster McSorley. In the almost one hour championship match, they out-lasted Nancy Mason and Rachel Wacholder by the score of 15-13. This was the third tournament in a row that the championship match was determined by the score of 15-13. Busch and Schuster collected the first place prize of $15,000.00, while the runner-ups collected $10,500.00. National television telecast was on Fox Sports Net.

3rd Place: Jennifer Meredith and Jenny Pavley
4th Place: Danalee Bragado and Ali Wood
5th Place: Karolyn Kirby and Karrie Poppinga
5th Place: Marsha Miller and Lia Young

SEAL BEACH CALIFORNIA
July 7th-9th, 2000

The Women's $75,000.00 BVA 2000 Seal Beach Open was staged at the Seal Beach Pier. The winner's were Misty May and Holly McPeak. In the nearly one hour championship match, they easily defeated Lisa Arce and Barbra Fontana, by the score of 15-4. May and McPeak collected the first place prize of $15,000.00, while the runner-ups collected $10,500.00. FOX Sports tape delayed the television telecast.

3rd Place: Annette Davis and Jenny Jordan
4th Place: Leanne Schuster McSorley and Nancy Reno
5th Place: Linda Hanley and Karrie Poppinga
5th Place: Stephanie Cox and Katy Eldridge

PISMO BEACH CALIFORNIA
August 12th-13th, 2000

The Women's $75,000.00 BVA 2000 Pismo Beach Open was staged just South of the Pier in Pismo Beach behind the Sea Venture Hotel. The winner's were Lisa Arce and Barbra Fontana. In the forty-two minute championship match, they narrowly defeated Leanne Schuster McSorley and Nancy Reno, by the score of 15-13. Arce and Fontana collected the first place prize of $15,000.00, while the runner-ups collected $10,500.00. FOX Sports tape delayed the television telecast.

3rd Place: Carrie Busch and Jennifer Meredith
4th Place: Nancy Mason and Rachel Wacholder
5th Place: Linda Hanley and Karrie Poppinga
5th Place: Stephanie Cox and Katy Eldridge

LONG BEACH CALIFORNIA
August 19th-20th, 2000

The Women's $75,000.00 BVA 2000 Long Beach Open was staged just South of the Belmont Pier and Belmont Olympic Plaza in Long Beach. The winner's were Nancy Reno and Elaine Youngs. In the sixty-two minute, overtime championship match, they narrowly defeated Annette Davis and Jenny Jordan, by the score of 16-14. Reno and Youngs collected the first place prize of $15,000.00, while the runner-ups collected $10,500.00. FOX Sports tape delayed the television telecast

3rd Place: Lisa Arce and Barbra Fontana
4th Place: Linda Hanley and Karrie Poppinga
5th Place: Carrie Busch and Holly McPeak
5th Place: Danalee Bragado and Ali Wood

SAN DIEGO CALIFORNIA
August 26th-27th, 2000

The Women's $75,000.00 BVA 2000 Kyocera U.S. Championships was staged on Mariner's Point in Mission Bay, San Diego California. The winner's were Annette Davis and Jenny Jordan. In the forty-four minute championship match, they were in total control when they out-played Nancy Reno and Elaine Youngs, by the score of 15-7. Davis and Jordan collected the first place prize of $15,000.00, while the runner-ups collected $10,500.00. FOX Sports tape delayed the television telecast.

3rd Place: Stephanie Cox and Katy Eldridge
4th Place: Holly McPeak and Leanne McSorley
5th Place: Linda Hanley and Karrie Poppinga
5th Place: Karolyn Kirby and Liz Masakayan

LAS VEGAS NEVADA
October 5th-8th, 2000

Barbra Fontana was "Crowned" the 2000 "Queen of the Beach" at the Women's AVP $75,000.00 Paul Mitchell Queen of the Beach event. The tournaments was staged on the man made beach at the parking lot of the Hard Rock Hotel and Casino. Fontana collected $25,100.00 along with her Queen of the Beach Crown. The top five finishes along with their prize money:

Finish	Winnings
1. Barbra Fontana	$25,100.00
2. Elaine Youngs	$13,200.00
3. Holly McPeak	$11,900.00
4. Nancy Mason	$11,400.00
5. Linda Hanley	$ 2,400.00

NANCY RENO
Nancy Reno played well on the 2000 BVA Tour. She advanced to the championship match 4 times, winning once, at the Pismo Beach event, with Leanne Schuster McSorley. Above photo, Reno challenges the block of Annette Davis.
Photo Courtesy of Frank Goroszko

WOMEN'S TOURNAMENT RESULTS 2000-FIVB

VITORIA BRAZIL
February 1st-6th, 2000

The large crowd at the 2000 Women's FIVB $150,000.00 Brazil Open were subdued during the "Gold-Medal" match, on Camburi Beach in Vitoria Brazil, when the American team of Liz Masakayan and Elaine Youngs controlled the tempo of the match against the Brazilian team of Sandra Pires and Adriana Samuel. In the sixty-five minute championship match, Masakayan and Youngs out-distanced Pires and Samuel in two sets, 12-11 and 12-1 to capture the "Gold-Medal" along with the $26,000.00 first place check. The runner-ups shared $18,000.00. In the "Bronze-Medal" match, the Japanese team of Yukiko Takahashi and Mika Teru Saiki dealt the Brazilian team of Adriana Behar and Shelda Bede a 15-12 loss, earning $14,000.00 in the process.

3rd Place: Yukiko Takahashi and Mika Teru Saiki-Japan
4th Place: Shelda Bede and Adriana Behar-Brazil
5th Place: Vasso Karadassiou and Efi Sfyri-Greece
5th Place: Misty May and Holly McPeak-USA

DEERFIELD BEACH FLORIDA U.S.A.
April 13th-16th, 2000

The Women's USAV $100,000.00 Oldsmobile Olympic Challenge Series, sanctioned by the FIVB, was won by Misty May and Holly McPeak. The event was staged on Deerfield Beach Florida U.S.A. In the championship match, McPeak and May out-scored Lisa Arce and Barbra Fontana for the victory. In the match for third place, Annette Davis and Jenny Jordan defeated Kerri Poppinga and Angela Rock to take the "Bronze-Medal" match. The winner's split $20,000.00 for their "Gold-Medal" performance.

3rd Place: Annett Davis and Jenny Johnson Jordan
4th Place: Karrie Poppinga and Angela Rock
5th Place: Linda Hanley and Nancy Reno
5th Place: Danalee Bragado and Ali Wood

KERRI POPPINGA
Kerri Poppinga paired-up with Angela Rock for a fourth place at the 2000 Deerfield Beach Florida FIVB sanctioned Olympic Challenge event. Above photo, Poppinga aggressively attacking the ball.

Photo Courtesy of the AVP

ELAINE YOUNGS
Elaine "EY" Youngs paired-up with Liz Masakayan for some success on the 2000 FIVB World Tour. They advanced to 3 "Gold-Medal" matches, winning all three times. Above photo, "EY" attacking the ball.

Photo Courtesy of "Couvi"

VIRGINIA BEACH VIRGINIA U.S.A.
May 26th-28, 2000

The Women's USAV $100,000.00 Oldsmobile Olympic Challenge Series, sanctioned by the FIVB, was won by Annett Davis and Jenny Johnson Jordan. The event was staged on Virginia Beach Virginia U.S.A. In the championship match, Davis and Jordan out-distanced Misty May and Holly McPeak, by the score of 15-5, for the victory. In the match for third place, Linda Hanley and Nancy Reno defeated Liz Masakayan and Elaine Youngs, 15-10, to take the "Bronze-Medal" match. The winner's split $20,000.00 for their "Gold-Medal" performance.

3rd Place: Linda Hanley and Nancy Reno
4th Place: Liz Masakayan and Elaine Youngs
5th Place: Lisa Arce and Barbra Fontana
5th Place: Carrie Busch and Leanne McSorley

ROSARITO MEXICO
May 31st-June 4th, 2000

There was a nice crowd at the 2000 Women's FIVB $150,000.00 Mexico Open, for the "Gold-Medal" match, on Rosarito Beach in Rosarito Mexico. The Brazilian team of Shelda Bede and Adriana Behar captured the "Gold-Medal" and the $26,000.00 first place check. In the championship match, Bede and Behar out-played the American team of Misty May and Holly McPeak, for the win. The runner-ups shared $18,000.00. In the "Bronze-Medal" match, the American team of Annette Davis and Jenny Johnson Jordan out-lasted the Brazilian team of Adriana Samuel and Sandra Pires, earning $14,000.00 for their efforts.

3rd Place: Annette Davis and Jenny Johnson Jordan-USA
4th Place: Adriana Samuel and Sandra Pires-Brazil
5th Place: Lisa Arce and Barbra Fontana-USA
5th Place: Natalie Cook and Kerri-Ann Pottharst-Australia

CAGLIARI ITALY
June 7th-11th, 2000

The stadium was full at the 2000 Women's FIVB $150,000.00 Italy Open, for the "Gold-Medal" match, in Cagliari Italy. The Brazilian team of Ana Paula Connelly and Monica Rodrigues captured the "Gold-Medal" and the $26,000.00 first place check. In the championship match, Connelly and Rodrigues out-played the American team of Annette Davis and Jenny Johnson Jordan, for the victory. The runner-ups shared $18,000.00. The "Bronze-Medal" match was an all-Brazilian affair as the team of Shelda Bede and Adriana Behar out-played their compatriots, Adriana Samuel and Sandra Pires, earning $14,000.00 with the victory.

3rd Place: Shelda Bede and Adriana Behar-Brazil
4th Place: Sandra Pires and Adriana Samuel-Brazil
5th Place: Laura Bruschini and Annamaria Solazzi-Italy
5th Place: Misty May and Holly McPeak-USA

TORONTO CANADA
June 13th-18th, 2000

After finishing second the past two seasons, on the Woodbine Beach Park Center Court, Brazilians Adriana Behar and Shelda Bede finally found the "keys" to success here by capturing the $150,000.00 Nokia Canadian Open's 2000 "Gold-Medal" match. Seeded first in the 32-team Main Draw, Behar and Bede scored a 15-12 win in 63 minutes over seventh-seeded Misty May and Holly McPeak of the United States to capture the $26,000.00 first-place prize. The runner-ups shared $18,000.00. In the "Bronze-Medal" match, Australians Kerri-Ann Pottharst and Natalie Cook out-played the American team of, Annett Davis and Jenny Johnson Jordan, earning $14,000.00 with the victory.

3rd Place: Natalie Cook and Kerri-Ann Pottharst-Australia
4th Place: Annett Davis and Jenny Johnson Jordan-USA
5th Place: Ana Paula Connelly and Monica Rodrigues-Brazil
5th Place: Tania Gooley and Pauline Manser-Australia

GSTAAD SWITZERLAND
June 21st-25th, 2000

The 2000 Women's FIVB $150,000.00 Swiss Open, staged in Gstaad Switzerland was won by the Brazilian team of Adriana Behar and Shelda Bede. In the the "Gold-Medal" match, they out-played the American team of Holly McPeak and Misty May by out-scoring them 15-11 to capture the "Gold-Medal" along with the $26,000.00 first place check. The runner-ups shared $18,000.00. In the "Bronze-Medal" match, another Brazilian team, Ana Paula Connelly and Monica Rodrigues, out-scored another American team, Annette Davis and Jenny Jordan 15-9, earning the "Bronze-Medal" as well as $14,000.00 in prize money.

3rd Place: Ana Paula Connelly and Monica Rodrigues-Brazil
4th Place: Annett Davis and Jenny Johnson Jordan-USA
5th Place: Liz Masakayan and Elaine Youngs-USA
5th Place: Rebekka Kadijk and Debora Schoon Kadijk-Netherlands

ANA PAULA CONNOLLY
Ana Paula Connolly played inspired beach volleyball on the 2000 FIVB Tour. She won the "Gold-Medal" at the Cagliari Italy event with Monica Rodrigues. Above photo, Connolly moves to the side for the dig.

Photo Courtesy of "Couvi"

CHICAGO ILLINOIS U.S.A.
June 30th-July 4th, 2000

The Women's FIVB $200,000.00 Oldsmobile U.S. Grand Slam, staged on North Avenue Beach in Chicago Illinois U.S.A. was won by the American team of Holly McPeak and Misty May. In the championship match, May and McPeak, out-played the Brazilian team of Shelda Bede and Adriana Behar. The winner's split $32,000.00 for their "Gold-Medal" performance. The runner-ups split $22,000.00. In the match for third place, Brazilians Sandra Pires and Adriana Samuel defeated Linda Hanley and Nancy Reno, from the United States, to take the "Bronze-Medal" match and collect $17,000.00.

3rd Place: Sandra Pires and Adriana Samuel-Brazil
4th Place: Linda Hanley and Nancy Reno-USA
5th Place: Natalie Cook and Kerri-Ann Pottharst-Australia
5th Place: Ana Paula Connelly and Monica Rodrigues-Brazil

BERLIN GERMANY
July 12th-16th, 2000

In front of a jam-packed stadium, at the 2000 Women's FIVB $150,000.00 German Open, for the "Gold-Medal" match, in Berlin Germany, The American team of Misty May and Holly McPeak captured the "Gold-Medal" and the $26,000.00 first place check. In the championship match, McPeak and May defeated the Australian team of Tania Gooley and Pauline Manser, for the win. The runner-ups shared $18,000.00. In the "Bronze-Medal" match, The Japanese team of Yukiko Takahashi and Mika Teru Saiki, out-played the German team of Ulrike Schmidt and Gudi Staub, earning $14,000.00 with the victory.

3rd Place: Yukiko Takahashi and Mika Teru Saiki-Japan
4th Place: Ulrike Schmidt and Gudi Staub-Germany
5th Place: Natalie Cook and Kerri-Ann Pottharst-Australia
5th Place: Annett Davis and Jenny Johnson Jordan-USA

MARSEILLE FRANCE
July 18th-22nd, 2000

Americans Annette Davis and Jenny Jordan, won the "Gold-Medal" at the 2000 Women's FIVB $150,000.00 French Open, in Marseille France, The Americans secured the "Gold-Medal" and the $26,000.00 first place check, in the championship match, when they defeated the Brazilian team of Shelda Bede and Adriana Behar. The runner-ups shared $18,000.00. In the "Bronze-Medal" match, The Brazilian team of Ana Paula Connelly and Monica Rodrigues, out-played the Australian team of Natalie Cook and Kerri-Ann Pottharst, earning $14,000.00 with the victory.

3rd Place: Ana Paula Connelly and Monica Rodrigues-Brazil
4th Place: Natalie Cook and Kerri-Ann Pottharst-Australia
5th Place: Tania Gooley and Pauline Manser-Australia
5th Place: Lisa Arce and Barbra Fontana-USA

REBKKA KADIJK
Rebbka Kadijk, from the Netherlands, was a competitive opponent on the 2000 Women's FIVB World Tour. Kadijk was able to make an appearance within the top five on one occasion. Above photo, Kadijk follows-through after attacking the ball.
Photo Courtesy of the FIVB

GUDULA STAUB
Germany's Gudula Staub provided some worthy competition on the 2000 Women's FIVB World Tour. Staub had a best finish of fourth at the Berlin Germany event. Above photo, Staub reaches over the net to make a block.
Photo Courtesy of the FIVB

ESPINHO PORTUGAL
July 25th-29th, 2000

Americans Liz Masakayan and Elaine Youngs, won the "Gold-Medal" in an All-American final, at the 2000 Women's FIVB $150,000.00 Portugal Open, in Espinho Portugal, Youngs and Masakayan won the "Gold-Medal" and the $26,000.00 first place check, in the championship match, when they defeated compatriots Lisa Arce and Barbra Fontana. The runner-ups shared $18,000.00. In the "Bronze-Medal" match, The Australian team of Natalie Cook and Kerri-Ann Pottharst, won the "Bronze-Medal" and $14,000.00, when they defeated Annette Davis and Jenny Jordan, from the United States.

3rd Place: Natalie Cook and Kerri-Ann Pottharst-Australia
4th Place: Annett Davis and Jenny Johnson Jordan-USA
5th Place: Shelda Bede and Adriana Behar-Brazil
5th Place: Ana Paula Connelly and Monica Rodrigues-Brazil

OSAKA JAPAN
August 2nd-6th, 2000

The Brazilian team of Shelda Bede and Adriana Behar, won the "Gold-Medal" at the 2000 Women's FIVB $150,000.00 Japan Open, in Osaka Japan, Bede and Behar won the "Gold-Medal" and the $26,000.00 first place check, in the championship match, when they defeated the Japanese team of Yukiko Takahashi and Mika Teru Saiki. The runner-ups shared $18,000.00. In the "Bronze-Medal" match, The Australian team of Natalie Cook and Kerri-Ann Pottharst, won the "Bronze-Medal" and $14,000.00, when they defeated Misty May and Holly McPeak, from the United States.

3rd Place: Natalie Cook and Kerri-Ann Pottharst-Australia
4th Place: Misty May and Holly McPeak-USA
5th Place: Lisa Arce and Barbra Fontana-USA
5th Place: Annett Davis and Jenny Johnson Jordan-USA

DALIAN CHINA
August 9th-13th, 2000

Holly McPeak and Misty May from the USA did not win the the "Gold-Medal" at the 2000 Women's FIVB $150,000.00 China Open, in Dalian China. But they did qualify for the Sydney 2000 Olympic Games, when they defeated the Chinese team of Rong Chi and Zi Xiong in an exciting semi-final match, by the score of 17-16, earning them a spot for participation in the Sydney Olympic Games. The victory for McPeak and May was exceptionally dramatic as they rebounded from a 14-8 deficit in front of 3500 Chinese spectators. In the "Gold-Medal" match Liz Masakayan and Elaine Youngs, also from the USA, defeated McPeak and May 15-7, to capture the "Gold-Medal" in the all-American final. In the "Bronze-Medal" match Xiong and Chi prevailed over the Portuguese team of Maria Jose and Cristina Pereira by the score of 15-8. This "Bronze-Medal" for Xiong and Chi was their first-ever FIVB World Tour medal.

3rd Place: Rong Chi and Zi Xiong-China
4th Place: Cristina Pereira and Maria Jose Schuller-Portugal
5th Place: Laura Bruschini and Annamaria Solazzi-Italy
5th Place: Dalixia Fernandez Grasset and Tamara Larrea Peraza-Cuba

SYDENY AUSTRALIA
September 16th-25th, 2000

The Women's FIVB XXVII Olympic Games, on Bondi Beach in Sydney Australia showcased the Olympic Women's Beach Volleyball Gold Medal Match, when Australians Natalie Cook and Kerri Pottharst ended their four-year mission to win beach volleyball's most coveted prize by winning the Sydney 2000 Olympic Games Gold Medal before the "home-crowd" by defeating Adriana Behar and Shelda Bede of Brazil. The Bronze Medallists in beach volleyball at the 1996 Atlanta Olympic Games, Cook and Pottharst scored 12-11 and 12-10 wins in 75 minutes over Behar and Bede before 10,000 enthusiastic fans on the Bondi Beach Center Court. Brazil served Kerri Pottharst through out the first set and gleaned uncharacteristic passing errors from the big Australian but Natalie Cook managed to keep her composure in front of the ten thousand strong crowd and feed Pottharst sets from which she hit winners. This accompanied by Pottharst's big serving kept the Australians within striking distance of the Brazilians. While the Australians were half a step slower then Bede and Adriana in defiance they clearly ruled the net and the made the Brazilians pay for their decision not to block much of the Australian attack in the first game. In the second game the Australians looked flustered while the Brazilian team kept their calm but again Pottharst and Cook pulled themselves out of the deficit and through to a win with a mixture of big serving and patience. A successful Pottharst attack followed by her serving ace earned the Australians a 10-10 tie. Pottharst closed out the scoring with another ace and another successful attack to end the 36-minute second set, earning the Aussies the "golden" spot on the Bondi Beach podium. In the "Bronze-Medal" match, the Brazilian team of Sandra Pires and Adriana Samuel out-scored the Japanese team of Yukiko Takahashi and Mika Teru Saiki 12-4 and 12-6.

3rd Place: Sandra Pires and Adriana Samuel-Brazil
4th Place: Yukiko Takahashi and Mika Teru Saiki-Japan
5th Place: Annette Davis and Jenny Johnson Jordan-USA
5th Place: Misty May and Holly McPeak-USA
5th Place: Tania Gooley and Pauline Manser-Australia
5th Place: Laura Bruschini and Annamaria Solazzi-Italy

FORTALEZA BRAZIL
October 31st-November 5th, 2000

Just as at the first FIVB Women's World Tour Brazilian event in Vitoria Brazil, the large crowd at the 2000 Women's FIVB $150,000.00 Brazil Open were subdued during the "Gold-Medal" match, in Fortaleza Brazil, when the American team of Holly McPeak and Misty May controlled the match against the Brazilian team of Sandra Pires and Adriana Samuel. In the championship match, McPeak and May out-played Pires and Samuel to capture the "Gold-Medal" along with the $26,000.00 first place check. The runner-ups shared $18,000.00. In the USA vs Brazil "Bronze-Medal" match, the USA team of Nancy Mason and Leanne Schuster McSorley dealt the Brazilian team of Adriana Behar and Shelda Bede a loss, earning $14,000.00 in the process.

3rd Place: Nancy Mason and Leanne McSorley-USA
4th Place: Shelda Bede and Adriana Behar-Brazil
5th Place: Adriana Bento Buczmiejuk and Magda Lima-Brazil
5th Place: Maria Clara Salgado Rufino and Jackie Silva-Brazil

TOP PHOTOS: Left: Danalee Bragado reaches to make the shot. **Center:** Holly McPeak shows great form while setting the ball. **Right:** Barbra Fontana gets ready to make the play.

MIDDLE PHOTOS: Left: Kerri Poppinga (left) and Ali Wood (right) joust for the balL. **Center:** Lisa Arce reaches above the net for the block. **Right:** Angela Rock gets ready fo chase-down the ball.

2000 WOMEN'S BEACH VOLLEYBALL ACTION

BOTTOM PHOTOS: Left: Marla O'Hara gets "down and dirty" to make the dig. **Center:** Gabby Reece gets above the net for the attack. **Right:** Liz Masakayan is ready for action.

Top and Middle Photo's Courtesy of the AVP. Bottom Photo's Courtesy of "Couvi"

ADDITIONAL VOLLEYBALL INFORMATION 2000

FORT WAYNE INDIANA
May 6th, 2000

On the campus of Indiana Purdue Fort Wayne (IPFW), the UCLA Bruins defeated the Ohio State Buckeyes to take home their 18th NCAA Men's Volleyball Championship. In the championship match, the Bruins out-lasted the Buckeyes by scores of 15-8, 15-10 and 17-15. The NCAA Tournament All-Star Team included Ohio State players Angel Aja, Chris Fash and Chris Fash. They were joined by UCLA players Seth Burnham, Evan Thatcher and the tournament MVP, Brandon Taliaferro.

HERMOSA BEACH CALIFORNIA
June 25th, 2000

Beach volleyball player Eric Fonoimoana launched the "Dig for Kids" Foundation. Fonoimoana formed the Dig for Kids Foundation to promote excellence in youth sports and academics. John Paul Mitchell Systems was the first to pledge sponsorship for the Dig for Kids charitable organization. The initial vision for Dig for Kids is to have donations pledged for each "dig" that Fonoimoana achieves during a volleyball tournament. The donations will fund school and community youth volleyball programs. The larger vision of Dig for Kids includes additional professional beach volleyball players participating, special events such as a Celebrity Charity Golf Tournament with professional beach volleyball players, and expanded benefits including scholarships and support for other children''s charities.

ESTERO BEACH MEXICO
2000

The 2000 Estero beach volleyball tournament was won by Jason Dudley (Portland OR) and Zach Small (San Francisco, CA). In the championship match, they defeated Pepe De la Hoz (San Diego, CA) and Juan Padronieto (Puerto Vallarta, MEX). The third place tie went to the teams of Alex Torres (San Diego/Puerto Rico) and John Sandemeyer (San Diego CA) along with Randy Hughes (Carlsbad, CA) and Aaron Genereaux (Hermosa Beach, CA).

3rd Place: Randy Hughes and Aaron Genereaux
3rd Place: John Sandmeyer and Alex Torres
5th Place: John Ward and Mark Ostrom
5th Place: Justin Warren and Howie Silagi
5th Place: Matt Sheeler & David Dinwiddie
5th Place: Steve Heywood and Eric Christianson

ASPEN COLORADO
September 4th, 2000

The 2000 MotherLode tournament was staged over another Labot-Day weekend. The winner's of the Men's Open division were AVP players Dax Holdren (Hermosa Beach, CA) and Ian Clark (Boulder, CO). In the championship match, Holdren and Clark out-lasted fellow AVP players, Matt Unger (Santa Monica, CA) and Albert Hanneman (Hermosa Beach, CA) for the title. The third spot was occupied by Joe Samuelu (Salt Lake City, UT) and Jake Gibb (Salt Lake City, UT).

The winner's of the Women's Open division were AVP players Leanne Schuster McSorley (Chicago, IL) and Nancy Mason (Phoenix AZ). In the championship match, McSorley and Mason out-scored AVP peers, Kristen Schritter (Del Mar, CA) and Jennifer Meredith (Los Angeles, CA) for the title. Pat Keller-Killiany (San Diego, CA) and Allison Block (Santa Barbara, CA) finished in third place.

ERIC FONOIMOANA
In 2000, prominent AVP player, Eric Fonoimoana launced the "Dig For Kids" foundation to promote excellence in youth sports and academics. Above photo, Fonoimoana makes a dig on the court.
Photo Courtesy of "Couvi"

NANCY MASON
Avp players, Nancy Mason and Leanne Schuster McSorley, paired-up to win the 2000 MotherLode event in Aspen Colorado. Above photo, Mason gets in the sand to pass the ball.
Photo Courtesy of John Pryor-Official MotherLode photographer

MEN'S BEACH VOLLEYBALL
2001

2001 marked a turning point in the young history of beach volleyball. The sport was permanently placed in the Olympic Games.

AVP

In 2001, the AVP Pro-Beach Volleyball tournament schedule included eight AVP Tour events. Five of the AVP Tour events were for both men and women. The total prize money was at $550,000.00. In 2001 there were four California events with the four additional events staged in four different States. Virginia, Michigan, and New Jersey all staged one AVP Tour event. The fourth event was the King and Queen of the Beach event staged in Las Vegas Nevada.

There were two teams that won two events on the 2001 AVP Men's Tour. Brent Doble and Lee LeGrande won the Muskegon Michigan and Belmar Beach New Jersey events, while earning over $40,000.00 in prize money. Stein Metzger and Kevin Wong won the Santa Barbara and Manhattan Beach events, while earning over $30,000.00 in prize money. There were three additional AVP Tour tournament champions in 2001. Scott Ayakatubby and Eduardo Bacil won the Huntington Beach Men's Open. Dax Holdren and Todd Rogers won the Hermosa Beach Men's Open. Aaron Boss and Colin Smith won the Virginia Beach Men's Open. Kevin Wong was "Crowned" the 2001 King of the Beach.

The following rules were used for the 2001 AVP Pro Beach Volleyball Tour:
1. Each match will be the best of three rally-scoring sets.
2. First two sets are to 21 points.
3. Third eventual set is to 15 points. When the first team reaches 14 in the third eventual set, side out scoring will be used until one team has scored the 15th point or wins by two points.
4. Must have a two-point advantage to win any set.
5. No caps for all sets.
6. Two timeouts per set with a duration of 30 seconds each.
7. Injury timeout - only one injury timeout per match is allowed per player.
8. A side change will occur every 10 points in the first two sets and every five (5) points in the third eventual set. The side changes will be direct without delay.
9. Time between sets will be one (1) minute.
10. Court dimensions are 8-meter (26-feet, 3-inches) by 8-meter per side.
11. The AVP has approved the implementation of "Let serve in play" for all events in 2001.

BRENT DOBLE
In 2001, Brent Doble paired-up with Lee LeGrande to win two AVP Tour events and over $40,000.00 in prize money. Above photo, Doble gets above the net to reject the hit by Stein Metzger.
Photo Courtesy of "Couvi"

SCOTT AYAKATUBBY
Scott "Ack" Ayakatubby was ready to celebrate after winning the 2001 AVP Tour event in Huntington Beach CA. with Eduardo Bacil. Above photo, Ack celebrating his win in Huntington Beach.
Photo Courtesy of Frank Goroszko

2001 INDIVIDUAL AVP TOURNAMENT FINISHES

Player	1st	2nd	3rd	4th	5th
Scott Ayakatubby	1	0	0	2	0
Eduardo Bacil	1	0	0	2	1
Paul Baxter	0	0	0	0	2
Dain Blanton	1	1	1	0	0
Aaron Boss	1	0	0	0	2
Bill Boullianne	0	0	0	0	1
Daniel Cardenas	0	0	0	1	1
Canyon Ceman	0	2	3	0	0
Ian Clark	0	1	0	0	1
Scott Davenport	0	0	0	0	1
Brent Doble	2	0	1	1	1
Eric Fonoimoana	2	1	1	0	0
Matt Fuerbringer	0	0	0	0	2
Albert Hannemann	0	1	2	1	0
Nick Hannemann	0	0	1	0	2
John Hayden	0	0	0	1	0
Matt Heath	0	0	0	0	1
Rob Heidger	0	1	0	1	0
Carl Henkel	0	0	0	0	1
Dax Holdren	2	2	0	1	1
Adam Jewell	0	1	1	0	0
Mike Lambert	0	0	0	1	1
Dan Landry	0	0	0	1	0
Lee LeGrand	2	0	0	0	1
Matt Lyles	0	0	0	1	0
Gaston Macau	0	0	0	0	1
Chip McCaw	0	0	0	1	0
Stein Metzger	1	1	2	0	0
Jim Nichols	0	0	0	1	1
Jeff Nygard	0	0	0	0	1
Jason Ring	0	0	0	0	1
Adam Roberts	0	0	1	0	0
Todd Rogers	2	2	0	1	0
Sean Rosenthal	0	0	0	0	1
Brian Saldano	0	0	1	0	0
Sean Scott	0	1	2	1	1
Colin Smith	1	0	0	1	2
Sinjin Smith	0	0	0	0	1
David Swatik	0	0	0	0	2
Mark Williams	0	0	0	0	1
Chad Turner	0	0	0	0	1
Mike Whitmarsh	0	2	3	0	0
Kevin Wong	2	1	1	0	0
Eric Wurts	0	0	0	0	1

(Above list includes 2 BVA finishes)

BVA

In 2001 there were two Men's BVA Tour events staged. The 2001 Men's BVA Tour events were staged in Clearwater Beach Florida and Oceanside California. Dax Holdren and Todd Rogers won the Clearwater Beach event while Dain Blanton and Eric Fonoimoana won the Oceanside event.

FIVB

For the first time, on the Men's and Women' FIVB Tour's, the players were treated with complete equality when both tours scheduled the same number of events, as well as equal prize money from the $4,550,000.00 that was distributed. $2,275,00.00 each, for men and women). The twenty-four FIVB Tour events of the 2001were covered with a particularly large television exposure creating more and more interest for a spectacular sport, proved at the Sydney Games 2000. There were eight TV channels that broadcast in 98

LEE LeGRANDE
Lee LeGrande used every move that he had to gain a couple of championship victories on the 2001 AVP Tour. Above photo, On his way to a victory, LeGrande uses the unusual "Up-side-down" digging technique.

Photo Courtesy of "Couvi"

DAIN BLANTON & ERIC FONOIMOANA
On the 2001 AVP and BVA Tour's, Dain Blanton and Eric Fonoimoana teamed-up to advance to 2 finals, winning once. Above photo, Blanton makes the block attempt while Fonoimoana is ready on defense.

Photo Courtesy of "Couvi"

countries: "Eurosport" covered 60 countries, ESPN Star produced the TV signal for 32 countries in Asia, TV Globo for Brazil, Denmark Radio TV for Denmark, Channel 4 for Great Britain, Mainichi Gaora for Japan and two general channels, SNTV and CNN mainly for USA and the "Anglo-Saxon" world in general. After two successful years in Volleyball, the Rally Point System (RPS) was started in Beach Volleyball. The matches were/are played in two sets of 21 points and an eventual third decisive set with 15 points. In order to prolong spectacular rallies, the playing court's new dimensions of 16x8m (instead of 18x9m) reducing it to 8x8m per side, was instituted to be tested for one year, and by 2004 it was still in use. The Men's FIVB 2001 World Tour of Beach Volleyball staged twelve events, including the Goodwill Games in Brisbane Australia. There were events in eleven countries with a total purse of over one million dollars. The FIVB events were staged in Tenerife Spain, Gstaad Switzerland, Berlin Germany, Stavanger Norway, Lignano Italy, Marseille France, Espinho Portugal, Klagenfurt Austria (World Championship), Ostende Belgium, Brisbane Australia (Goodwill Games), Mallorca Spain and Vitoria Brazil.

The top team, on the 2001 FIVB Men's World Tour, was Brazil's Emanuel Rego and Tande Ramos. They advanced to six "Gold-Medal" matches, winning five times, while earning nearly one-quarter of a million dollars. Argentina's Martin Conde and Mariano Baracetti were the number two team on the 2001 FIVB Men's Tour. Conde and Baracetti advanced to five "Gold-Medal" Matches, winning three times, while earning over $200,000.00. Another Brazilian team was in the top three as Jose Loiola and Ricardo Santos advanced to six "Gold-Medal" matches, winning twice, while earning $180,000.00. There were three additional teams that each won one "Gold-Medal" on the 2001 FIVB Men's World Tour. The American team of Stein Metzgar with Kevin Wong, Australian's Julien Prosser and Lee Zahner as well as the Russian team of Vladimir Kostioukov and Dmitri Barsouk.

EMANUEL REGO SCHAEFER
Emanuel Rego Schaefer teamed-up with Alexandre Tande Ramos to advance to 6 FIVB Tour championship matches, winning 5 times. Above photo Rego attacking the block of compatriot Z-Marco de Melo.
Photo Courtesy of the FIVB

2001 INDIVIDUAL FIVB TOURNAMENT FINISHES

Player	1st	2nd	3rd	4th	5th
Dain Blanton	0	0	0	1	1
Mariano Baracetti	3	2	1	1	1
Bjorn Berg	0	0	0	0	1
John Child	0	0	0	2	2
Martin Alejo Conde	3	2	1	1	1
Simon Dahl	0	0	0	0	1
Markus Diechmann	0	0	0	0	1
Sergey Ermishin	0	0	0	1	3
Klepper Feitosa	0	0	0	1	0
Eric Fonoimoana	0	0	0	2	1
Mark Heese	0	0	0	2	2
Rob Heidger	0	0	0	2	1
Patrick Heuscher	0	0	0	1	1
Jody Holden	0	0	0	1	1
Dax Holdren	0	0	0	0	1
Jorre Kiemperud	0	0	1	0	3
Stefan Kobel	0	0	0	1	1
Mikhail Kouchnezev	0	0	0	1	2
Martin Laciga	0	5	2	0	3
Paul Laciga	0	5	2	0	3
Conrad Leinemann	0	0	0	1	1
Jose Loiola	2	4	0	1	0
Roberto Lopes	0	0	1	0	2
Chip McCaw	0	0	0	1	0
Stein Metzger	1	0	2	1	2
Jose Franco Vieira Neto	0	0	1	0	1
Jose Z-Marco Melo Ferreira Nobrega	0	0	1	1	1
Oliver Oeteke	0	0	0	0	1
Julien Prosser	1	0	0	0	2
Jonas Reckermann	0	0	0	0	1
Todd Rogers	0	0	0	0	1
Ricardo Alex Costa Santos	2	4	0	1	1
Emanuel Rego Scheffer	**5**	**1**	**4**	**0**	**1**
Andreas Scheuerpflug	0	0	0	0	1
Rogrio "Para" Ferrirs de Souza	0	0	1	0	1
Alexandre Tande Ramos	**5**	**1**	**4**	**0**	**1**
Murilo Toscano	0	0	0	1	0
Kevin Wong	1	0	2	1	2
Lee Zahner	1	0	0	0	2

(Above list includes results from 2001 Goodwill Games)

MEN'S TOURNAMENT RESULTS
2001-AVP

HERMOSA BEACH CALIFORNIA
June 8th-10th, 2001

The $75,000.00 Mervyns Beach Bash AVP Sideout Hermosa Beach Open, was staged on the north side of the Pier. The top-seeded team of Dax Holdren and Todd Rogers captured the $16,750.00 first-place prize by defeating third-seeded Dain Blanton and Eric Fonoimoana 21-18, 16-21 and 17-15 in the 62-minute men's final. After splitting the first two games in the title match, Holdren and Rogers rallied from 9-3 and 13-7 deficits to win the event. This was the eighth career win for the Holdren and Rogers partnership and their first-ever at Hermosa Beach. In the match for third place, sixth-seeded Stein Metzger and Kevin Wong scored a 22-20 and 21-17 win over eighth-seeded Brent Doble and Matt Lyles for the $8,200.00 third-place prize. Doble, who was scheduled to play this weekend with Karch Kiraly, and Lyles shared $6,200.00 for fourth-place. Kiraly, a three-time Olympic Gold Medallist in Volleyball, withdrew Thursday with a left calf injury. A record 106 men's and women's teams entered this tournament. FOX Sports Net tape delayed the action for TV.

3rd Place: Stein Metzgar and Kevin Wong
4th Place: Brent Doble and Matt Lyles
5th Place: Albert Hannemann and Sean Scott
5th Place: Aaron Boss and Ian Clark

HUNTINGTON BEACH CALIFORNIA
June 15th-17th, 2001

Sixty-two (62) teams entered the $62,500.00 Paul Mitchell AVP Huntington Beach Men's Open, presented by Michelob Light. The event was staged on the south side of the Pier. The fifth-seeded team of Scott Ayakatubby and Eduardo Bacil captured the $14,000.00 first-place prize by defeating top-seeded Canyon Ceman and Mike Whitmarsh 21-16, 21-23 and 16-14 in the 58-minute men's final. The runner-ups split $9,250.00. In the 35 minute match for third place, number two seeds, Adam Jewell and Nick Hanneman scored a 21-19 and 21-15 win over nineteenth-seeded Mike Lambert and Colin Smith, for the $6,600.00 third-place prize. FOX Sports Net tape delayed the action.

3rd Place: Nick Hannemann and Adam Jewell
4th Place: Mike Lambert and Colin Smith
5th Place: Brent Frohoff and David Swatik
5th Place: Larry Witt and Andy Witt

DAX HOLDREN
On the 2001 AVP and BVA Tour's, Dax Holdren teamed-up with Todd Rogers to advance to 4 championship, winning twice. They won in Hermosa Beach on the AVP Tour and in Clearwater on the BVA Tour. Above photo, Holdren makes a nice diving-dig.
Photo Courtesy of Frank Goroszko

SCOTT AYAKATUBBY
Scott "Ack" Ayakatubby teamed-up with Brazilian Eduardo Bacil to win the 2001 AVP Tour event in Huntington Beach CA. Ack had not won a tournament since winning twice, with Brian Lewis, in 1996. Above photo, Ack gets over the net for the block attempt.
Photo Courtesy of "Couvi"

MUSKEGON MICHIGAN
July 13th-15th, 2001

The 2001 AVP Men's Sunkist Pro Beach Volleyball event, in Pere Marquette Park, in Muskegon Michigan was won by Brent Doble and Lee LeGrande. Seeded fourth in the men's main draw, Doble and LeGrande won all six of their matches on the Pere Marquette Park courts to capture the $14,000.00 first-place prize. In the championship match, they captured their second pro beach title together with a 21-16 and 23-21 win in 49 minutes over second-seeded Canyon Ceman and Mike Whitmarsh. Ceman and Whitmarsh shared $9,250.00 for second. Albert Hannemann and Sean Scott shared $6,600.00 for winning the third-place match by defeating Daniel Cardenas and Jim Nichols 21-17 and 21-10. Brighton Entertainment of New York, N. Y., taped the action for replay on FOX Sports Net.

3rd Place: Albert Hannemann and Sean Scott
4th Place: Daniel Cardenas and Jim Nichols
5th Place: Paul Baxter and Jason Ring
5th Place: Aaron Boss and Colin Smith

BELMAR BEACH NEW JERSEY
July 20th-22nd, 2001

On a picture perfect afternoon, the 2001 AVP Men's $62,500.00 Sunkist Pro Beach Volleyball event, at Fourth Avenue on Belmar Beach New Jersey was won by Brent Doble and Lee LeGrande. This title was the second-straight for Doble and LeGrande, In the championship match, second-seeded Doble and LeGrande increased their Association of Volleyball Professionals (AVP) winning streak to 12 matches after defeating fourth-seeded Albert Hannemann and Sean Scott 21-16, 20-22 and 15-9. Doble and LeGrande won all six of their matches at this event. Doble and LeGrande shared the $14,000.00 first-place prize while Hannemann and Scott split $9,250.00 for second-place. Mike Whitmarsh, the reigning AVP "King of the Beach", and Canyon Ceman captured the 35 minute third-place match and the $6,600.00 prize with a 21-18 and 21-18 win over Scott Ayakatubby and Eduardo Bacil.

3rd Place: Canyon Ceman and Mike Whitmarsh
4th Place: Scott Ayakatubby and Eduardo Bacil
5th Place: Daniel Cardenas and Jim Nichols
5th Place: Nick Hannemann and David Swatik

MIKE WHITMARSH & CANYON CEMAN
Mike Whitmarsh and Canyon Ceman paired-up on the 2001 AVP Tour. They finished within the top three on 5 occasions, including 2 second place finishes. Above photo, Ceman hits a set from Whitmarsh, through the block of Eric Fonoimoana.
Photo Courtesy of "Couvi"

ALBERT HANNEMANN
Albert Hanneman teamed-up with Sean Scott to advance to the finals of the 2001 AVP Tour event in Belmar NJ, where they finished in second place. Above photo, Hannemann challenges the block of Dain Blanton.
Photo Courtesy of "Couvi"

VIRGINIA BEACH VIRGINIA
June 27th-29th, 2001

Aaron Boss and Colin Smith netted their first pro beach volleyball title at the $62,500.00 AVP Paul Mitchell Open, on the beach at 600 Atlantic Avenue, in Virginia Beach Virginia. In the championship match, the fifth-seeded Boss and Smith avenged an early morning loss to score a 21-19 and 21-19 win over eighth-seeded Ian Clark and Adam Jewell. The 38-minute title match was played in a driving rainstorm. Boss and Smith collected the $14,000.00 first-place prize. In the match for third place, Albert Hannemann teamed with Sean Scott for a 21-14 and 21-12 over fourth-seeded Scott Ayakatubby and Eduardo Bacil.

3rd Place: Albert Hannemann and Sean Scott
4th Place: Scott Ayakatubby and Eduardo Bacil
5th Place: Paul Baxter and Matt Fuerbringer
5th Place: Brent Doble and Lee LeGrande

SANTA BARBARA CALIFORNIA
August 17th-19th, 2001

With 108 teams forming the largest field in the history of the Association of Volleyball Professionals (AVP), The $62,500.00 Michelob Light Open, on East Beach, near the Cabrillo Bathhouse, in Santa Barbara was won by the team of Stein Metzgar and Kevin Wong. In the 41 minute championship match, they upset top-seeded and local favorites Dax Holdren and Todd Rogers 21-14 and 21-19. Before collecting their $14,500.00 first place check, Metzger and Wong posted an 8-1 match mark and had to win five-straight elimination matches to reach the final two rounds. Canyon Ceman and Mike Whitmarsh defeated Albert Hannemann and Sean Scott 21-13 and 22-20 in the 41-minute third-place match to share $9,750.00.

3rd Place: Canyon Ceman and Mike Whitmarsh
4th Place: Albert Hannemann and Sean Scott
5th Place: Scott Davenport and Jeff Nygard
5th Place: Sean Rosenthal and Mark Williams

MANHATTAN BEACH CALIFORNIA
August 24th-26th, 2001

Before an overflowing crowd of 5,000, on the south side of the Manhattan Beach Pier, in Manhattan Beach California, fifth-seeded Stein Metzger and Kevin Wong won the men's Michelob Light Open Manhattan Beach title. In the, over one-hour, championship match, Metzger and Wong defeated eighth-seeded Eric Fonoimoana and Rob Heidger 21-17, 18-21 and 15-10. For the second-straight week, Metzger and Wong advanced through the elimination bracket to reach this AVP Pro Beach Volleyball Tour finale. The winners shared the $17,400.00 first place check for their efforts. Canyon Ceman and Mike Whitmarsh captured the men's third-place match by scoring a 21-18 and 21-15 over Dax Holdren and Todd Rogers. Echo Entertainment of Studio City, California, taped the events action for tape-delay broadcast on FOX Sports Net.

3rd Place: Canyon Ceman and Mike Whitmarsh
4th Place: Dax Holdren and Todd Rogers
5th Place: Matt Fuerbringer and Davis Swatik
5th Place: Eduardo Bacil and Mike Lambert

LAS VEGAS NEVADA
September 6th-9th, 2001

Kevin Wong, playing in the Paul Mitchell King of the Beach competition at the Hard Rock Hotel and Casino, in Las Vegas Nevada, after arriving from the Goodwill Games in Australia four days earlier, didn't let lingering jet lag keep him from claiming the King of the Beach crown. Wong's final match was with his regular season partner Stein Metzger. Wong took his victory lap after the first game. All Wong needed was a win in the first game against Brent Doble and Mike Whitmarsh, the defending champion. Wong and Metzger triumphed 21-19, 21-15, but it was after the first game, which Wong ended with a sharp kill, when the 6-foot-7 Hawaiian native was able to stake claim to his first-place check of $21,000.00. In the final match, Wong played exceptional beach volleyball, accumulating match-high totals of 18 kills and five blocks. The final match was the third victory for Wong on Sunday, when only the final four qualifiers competed. In the opener, Wong and Doble defeated Metzger and Whitmarsh, 21-16, 21-18. Wong and Whitmarsh, who is also 6-foot-7, then defeated Metzger and Doble, 21-13, 22-20. Wong was followed in the prize money category by men's runner-up Whitmarsh, who claimed $12,000.00, and Metzger, who earned $11,000.00. Final standings:

1. Kevin Wong-$21,000.00
2. Mike Whitmarsh-$12,000.00
3. Stein Metzger-$11,000.00
3. Brent Doble-$7,500.00
5. Dax Holdren-$8,000.00
6. Todd Rogers-$6,000.00
7. Canyon Ceman-$2,750.00
8. Lee LeGrande-$750.00
9. Eric Fonoimoana-$1,000.00
10. Albert Hannemann-$1,000.00

AARON BOSS
Aaron Boss paired-up with Colin Smith to win their first pro-beach event on the AVP Tour. They won the 2001 Virginia Beach VA event. Above photo, Boss attempts to poke the ball over the block of David Swatik
Photo Courtesy of "Couvi"

MEN'S TOURNAMENT RESULTS
2001-BVA

CLEARWATER BEACH FLORIDA
April 20th-22nd, 2001

Dax Holdren and Todd Rogers captured their second Florida title, in the last year, at the BVA $75,000.00 Volleyhut Clearwater Beach Men's Invitational, on Clearwater Beach in Florida. In the men's "Gold-Medal" match, third-seeded Holdren and Rogers defeated fourth-seeded Stein Metzger and Kevin Wong 21-15 and 21-16 in 35 minutes to share the $15,000.00 first-place prize. In the 40 minute "Bronze-Medal" match, Dain Blanton and Eric Fonoimoana notched a 21-16 and 21-18 over Rob Heidger and Chip McCaw. This opening domestic event on the 2001 BVA Pro Beach Volleyball Tour was taped for television replay on ESPN-2.

3rd Place: Dain Blanton and Eric Fonoimoana
4th Place: Rob Heidger and Chip McCaw
5th Place: Carl Henkel and Sinjin Smith
5th Place: Bill Boullianne and Colin Smith

OCEANSIDE CALIFORNIA
May 26th-27th, 2001

The Men's BVA $50,000.00 VolleyHut.com Oceanside Invitational was won by the team of Dain Blanton and Eric "Fonoi" Fonoimoana. They collected $5,000.00 along with the win. In the championship match, against Dax Holdren and Todd Rogers, Blanton and Fonoi won the first match 21-19 and 21-15, forcing a second match in this double-elimination final. This second match was just one game to 21, instead of best of three match, Blanton and Fonoi won 21-18. In the match for third place Adam Roberts and Brian Soldano outlasted John Hyden and Dan Landry, 21-19 and 21-19.

3rd Place: Adam Roberts and Brian Soldano
4th Place: John Hyden and Dan Landry
5th Place: Gaston Macau and Chad Turner
5th Place: Matt Heath and Eric Wurts

KEVIN WONG & STEIN METZGER
Kevin Wong and Stein "Steino" Metzger paired-up on both the AVP and BVA Tours, advancing to 3 championship matches, winning twice on the AVP Tour. Above photo, Wong hits a set from "Steino" into the block of Scott Ayakatubby.
Photo Courtesy of "Couvi"

TODD ROGERS & DAX HOLDREN
On the 2001 AVP and BVA Tours, Todd Rogers and Dax Holdren advanced to 4 championship matches, winning once on each tour. Above photo, Holdren hits a set from Rogers, towards the block of Mike Whitmarsh.
Photo Courtesy of "Couvi"

MEN'S TOURNAMENT RESULTS 2001-FIVB

TENERIFE SPAIN
June 13th-17th, 2001

The Men's FIVB $180,000.00 Spain Open, on the Canary Islands, in Tenerife Spain was won by the Brazilian team of Tande Ramos and Emanuel Rego. In the "Gold-Medal" match, they outplayed the Swiss team of Martin Laciga and Paul Laciga, in only 31 minutes to win the championship 21-19 and 21-14. The winner's split $27,000.00, while the runner-ups shared $18,000.00. In the "Bronze-Medal" match, Mariano Baracetti and Martin Conde, from Argentina, earned $14,000.00, by defeating Canadians John Child and Mark Heese, by scores of 21-15 and 25-23.

3rd Place: Mariano Baracetti and Martin Conde-Argentina
4th Place: John Child and Mark Heese-Canada
5th Place: Jose Loiola and Ricardo Santos-Brazil
5th Place: Stein Metzger and Kevin Wong-USA

GSTAAD SWITZERLAND
June 20th-24th, 2001

The last day of the Men's FIVB $180,000.00 Swiss Open, in Gstaad Switzerland was as warm and sunny as all the previous days. The event was won by the American team of Stein Metzger and Kevin Wong. In the "Gold-Medal" match, Wong and Metzger were the victors of this first men's World Tour in Switzerland. The American duo beat the top Swiss duo Paul and Martin Laciga by scores of 21-17 and 22-20. During the medal ceremony, while standing on the winner's podium, the Americans won the hearts of the 4,000 spectators with storms of applause when they expressed their conviction "we love Switzerland, we love Gstaad, the cows, the beautiful setting, and we love you all." The winner's split $27,000.00, while the runner-ups shared $18,000.00. In the "Bronze-Medal" match, the two newly formed Brazilian teams of Emanuel Rego with Tande Ramos and Ricardo Santos with Jose Loiola were face to face. The winners from Teneriffe, Emanuel and Tande were the victors as they took the match in two straight sets, 22-20 and 21-17, earning $14,000.00 for their efforts.

3rd Place: Tande Ramos and Emanuel Rego-Brazil
4th Place: Jose Loiola and Ricardo Santos-Brazil
5th Place: John Child and Mark Heese-Canada
5th Place: Mariano Baracetti and Martin Conde-Argentina

PAUL & MARTIN LACIGA
Paul and Martin Laciga played some very competitive beach volleyball on the 2001 FIVB World Tour. They advanced to the finals of 5 events, finishing as the runner-ups each time. Above photo, Martin (kneeling) and Paul (standing) celebrate a win.
Photo Courtesy of the FIVB

STEIN METZGER & KEVIN WONG
Stein Metzger and Kevin Wong stepped-up to receive the "Gold-Medal" at the 2001 Men's FIVB World Tour event in Gstaad Switzerland. Above photo, Metzger hits a set from Wong, past the out-stretched arms of Dain Blanton.
Photo Courtesy of "Couvi"

BERLIN GERMANY
June 27th-July 1st, 2001

Julien Prosser and Lee Zahner gave Australia its first International Men's "Gold-Medal" at the 2001 Men's FIVB $180,000.00 German Open, in Berlin Germany. In the surprising "Gold-Medal" match, they outplayed the Swiss team of Martin Laciga and Paul Laciga, in a nerve-racking three sets final 18-21, 28-26 and 22-20. Although the Swiss team had 6 match-points in the second they lost when Martin Laciga received a "Red-Card" for pulling down the net in anger. 7000 spectators were very excited by the tremendous play in this match. The winner's split $27,000.00, while the runner-ups shared $18,000.00. Earlier in the tournament, the Australians defeated the top seeded team of Emanuel Rego and Tande Ramos, in the semi-final by 28-26,14-21 and 15-11. In the all Swiss semi-final Paul and Martin Laciga triumphed over their countryman Stefan Kobel and Patrick Heuscher by 27-25 and 26-24. In the "Bronze-Medal" match, the Swiss team of Kober and Heuscher presented themselves as fearless opponents against the favored team of Emanuel and Tande from Brazil. In the end however the Brazilian team won in two games 21-16 and 21-18. During the five day event 32.000 spectators joined exciting matches on all days of the tournament. Warm days and hardly any clouds made for perfect conditions for the German Open 2001. Once more downtown Berlin presented as much beach feeling as any coastal City.

3rd Place: Tande Ramos and Emanuel Rego-Brazil
4th Place: Patrick Heuscher and Stefan Kobel-Switzerland
5th Place: John Child and Mark Heese-Canada
5th Place: Ze Marco de Melo and Rogerio Para-Brazil

STAVANGER NORWAY
July 4th-8th, 2001

The Brazilian combination of Emanuel Rego and Tande Ramos dominated the finals of the Men's FIVB $180,000 Philips Norway Open in Stavanger Norway. In the "Gold-Medal" match, they defeated the Swiss team of Martin Laciga and Paul Laciga, 21-19 and 21-15. The winner's split $27,000.00, while the runner-ups shared $18,000.00. During the tournament, a light rain was falling, but the capacity crowd of 3500 spectators was not deterred from enjoying some great beach volleyball. The Brazilian's dominated the tournament going through undefeated. So dominate was their performance that they only lost one set in three days of competition. Early in the day they gave advanced notice of the great form that they were in, by defeating compatriots Ze Marco de Melo and Rogerio Para in the semi final to advance directly to the "Gold-Medal" game. In the "Bronze-Medal" match, Brazil's Ze-Marco de Melo and Rogerio Para, earned $14,000.00, by defeating Canadians John Child and Mark Heese, by scores of 21-17 and 21-15.

3rd Place: Ze Marco de Melo and Rogerio Para-Brazil
4th Place: John Child and Mark Heese-Canada
5th Place: Vegard Hoidalen and Jorre Kjemperud-Norway
5th Place: Oliver Oetke and Andreas Scheuerpflug-Germany

BRAZIL vs ARGENTINA
On the 2001 Men's FIVB World Tour, Brazilian teams faced-off, in "Gold-Medal" matches, against the Argentine team of Mariano Baracetti and Martin Conde at five different tournaments. The Argentine team won five of these match-ups. While the Brazilan teams of Jose Loiola with Ricardo Santos and Emanuel Rego with Tande Ramos, each winning one time. Above photo, Barcetti hits a set from Conde, over the block of Santos, towards the defense of Loiola.

Photo Courtesy of the FIVB

LIGNANO ITALY
July 11th-15th, 2001

New champions were crowned in Lignano Sabbiadoro Italy when the Argentine team of Mariano Baracetti and Martin Conde were crowned champions of the 2001 Italy Open. This was the first victory for the new team of Baracetti and Conde in 2001. In the 40 minute "Gold-Medal" match, the Argentinean pair defeated Ricardo Santos and Jose Loiola, from Brazil, 21-17 and 21-16. The crowd of over 12,000 spectators enjoyed the perfect sunny weather along with the beautiful scenery of Lignano Sabbiadoro and the spectacular play of the best beach volleyball players in the world. Mariano Baracetti was awarded the Speedo Trophy as the best player of the tournament. The winner's split $27,000.00, while the runner-ups shared $18,000.00. In the 38 minute "Bronze-Medal" match, Brazil's Emanuel Rego and Tande Ramos were victorious against the American team of Kevin Wong and Stein Metzger, by scores of 21-19 and 21-12. This bronze medal was the fifth consecutive medal for Emanuel and Tande in five FIVB World Tour events in 2001.

3rd Place: Tande Ramos and Emanuel Rego-Brazil
4th Place: Stein Metzger and Kevin Wong-USA
5th Place: Martin Laciga and Paul Laciga-Switzerland
5th Place: Jody Holden and Conrad Leinemann-Canada

JOSE LOIOLA
Brazilian Jose Loiola teamed-up with Ricardo Santos for success on the 2001 FIVB World Tour. They advanced to 6 "Gold-Medal" matches, winning twice. Above photo, Loiola attacking with a jump serve.
Photo Courtesy of the FIVB

MARSEILLE FRANCE
July 17th-22nd, 2001

The Men's FIVB $180,000.00 Grand Slam French Open, in Marseille France, was staged in front of a big and enthusiastic crowd, supporting the best beach volleyball players in the world, under a hot sun. The winner's were the team of Mariano Baracetti and Martin Conde, from Argentina. In the "Gold-Medal" match, the Argentinean pair defeated Brazil's Tande Ramos and Emanuel Rego, when they made some crucial defensive plays at the end of both games to win the match and the French Grand Slam title 21-19 and 21-19. During the "Bronze-Medal" match, the French audience had the chance to see an excellent match between two American teams for the third place. Kevin Wong and Stein Metzger outlasted their countrymen Dain Blanton and Eric Fonoimoana 33-31, 13-21 and 15-11.

3rd Place: Stein Metzger and Kevin Wong-USA
4th Place: Dain Blanton and Eric Fonoimoana-USA
5th Place: Martin Laciga and Paul Laciga-Switzerland
5th Place: Sergey Ermishin and Mikhail Kouchnerev-Russia

ESPINHO PORTUGAL
July 25th-29th, 2001

In a jam-packed stadium filled with an enthusiastic crowd under warm and sunny skies, Brazil's Ricardo Santos and Jose Loiola won the title at the 2001 FIVB World Tour Portugal Men's Open played in the beautiful Praia da Baia in Espinho Portugal. In the electrifying "Gold-Medal" match, Santos and Loiola faced the Laciga brothers, Paul and Martin, from Switzerland, who were vying to win their first World Tour Tournament. They didn't go higher than the 2nd place, losing to the Brazilians in three games 11-21, 21-17 and 19-17. This match didn't start very well for the Brazilians. In the first game, losing 11-21 in 20' minutes. The rest of the match was a totally different story. The Brazilian team won the remaining two games. The Swiss team had match-point at 14-13, but the Brazilians saved the match and had four match-points at 15-14, 17-16 and 18-17. A successful attack from Jose Loiola gave the 19th point and the victory to the Brazilians. Third place was taken by Brazil's Emanuel Rego and Tande Ramos, the number one Team in the World Ranking, when they outlasted the Canadian team of Jody Holden and Conrad Leinemann, in three games 27-25, 18-21 and 15-8. This was a very tight and exciting match as the Canadians, ranked number twenty in the World, gave a hard time to the Brazilian's. But in the end, Emanuel and Tande were more effective, winning the "Bronze-Medal." match.

3rd Place: Tande Ramos and Emanuel Rego-Brazil
4th Place: Jody Holden and Conrad Leinemann-Canada
5th Place: Vegard Hoidalen and Jorre Kjemperud-Norway
5th Place: Sergey Ermishin and Mikhail Kouchnerev-Russia

KLAGENFURT AUSTRIA
August 1st-5th, 2001

Capacity crowds inspired the players at the Men's FIVB $250,000.00 Beach Volleyball World Championships in Klagenfurt, Austria. The event was won by the Argentine team of Mariano Baracetti and Martin Conde. In the "Gold-Medal" match, they out-pointed the Brazilian team of Jose Loiola and Ricardo Santos, to pocket the

$47,000.00 purse. The runner-ups collected $35,000.00. In the "Bronze-Medal" match, the team of Vegard Hoidalen and Jorre Kjemperud, from Norway, edged the unexpected team from America, Chip McCaw and Rob Heidger, to earn the $21,000.00 third place check.

3rd Place: Vegard Hoidalen and Jorre Kjemperud-Norway
4th Place: Rob Heidger and Chip McCaw-USA
5th Place: Tande Ramos and Emanuel Rego-Brazil
5th Place: Martin Laciga and Paul LacigaS-witzerland
5th Place: Dain Blanton and Eric Fonoimoana-USA
5th Place: Dax Holdren and Todd Rogers-USA

OSTENDE BELGIUM
August 8yh-12th, 2001

In front of another large beach volleyball crowd, the Brazilian team of Emanuel Rego and Alexander Tande Ramos utilized their tournament experience in winning the 2001 FIVB World Tour Spa Beach Volley Ostend Open. In the all-Brazilian "Gold-Medal" match Rego and Tande, after losing the first game to Ricardo Santos and Jose Loiola, played some great defense along with spectacular blocking to go on to a three set victory. The scores were 19-21, 21-16 and 15-9. The winner's received $27,000.00 for their efforts and the runner-ups collected $18,000.00. In the "Bronze-Medal" match, the Swiss brothers, Paul and Martin Laciga, advanced to their sixth podium finish of the season but had not won a "Gold-Medal" after winning a 2 game "Bronze-Medal" victory over the Argentine team of Mariano Baracetti and Martin Conde, 21-18 and 21-11.

3rd Place: Martin Laciga and Paul Laciga-Switzerland
4th Place: Mariano Baracetti and Martin Conde-Argentina
5th Place: Stein Metzger and Kevin Wong-USA
5th Place: Julien Prosser and Lee Zahner-Australia

BRISBANE AUSTRALIA
August 29th-September 4th, 2001

The Men's 2001 FIVB $150,000.00 Goodwill Games were staged in Brisbane, Australia. The second-seeded team of Jose Loiola and Ricardo Santos, from Brazil won the "Gold-Medal" by defeating FIVB World Champions Mariano Baracetti and Martin Conde of Argentina in the men's title match. Loiola and Ricardo scored a 21-14 and 21-13 win in 35 minutes over the top-seeded Baracetti and Conde. The winner's split the $30,000.00 first-place prize while the Argentineans settled for $24,000.00 along with the "Silver-Medal." In the "Bronze-Medal" match, the United States captured its third straight Goodwill Games medal when fourth-seeded Stein Metzger and Kevin Wong defeated their American rivals Eric Fonoimoana and Rob Heidger 23-21 and 21-19 in 52 minutes.

3rd Place: Stein Metzger and Kevin Wong-USA
4th Place: Eric Fonoimoana and Rob Heidger-USA
5th Place: Julien Prosser and Lee Zahner-Australia

MALLORCA SPAIN
September 12th-16th, 2001

The extremely high level of the competition provided by the entrants, completely satisfied the crowd that filled up the stadium on Santa Ponca Beach. In the extremely competitive match, the top seeded Brazilian's Emanuel Rego and Tande Ramos became the first champions in Mallorca Spain, at the 2001 FIVB Men's $180,000.00 Spain Open. During the "Gold-Medal" match, in one of the best finals of this season, the top two seeded teams of Emanuel Rego and Tande Ramos, from Brazil and the 2001 World Champions, from Argentina, Mariano Baracetti and Martin Conde battled out a 78 minute epic grand final, saving a match-point in the third set being down 13-14. Rego rallied with some amazing defense and they fought back to gain match point twice on the opposition. The team from Argentina saved the match by leveling the score at 18-18. Tande made a successful spike for another match-point at 19-18. Rego, after making a nice defensive play, earned the victory, in this exciting match, with a hard-driven spike. Emanuel Rego received the Speedo "Player of the Tournament" award. In the "Bronze-Medal" match, it was another Brazilian success as veterans Roberto Lopes and Franco Neto made the best finish of the 2001 season, winning over the Russian team of Sergey Ermishin and Mikhail Kouchnerev, 21-17 and 26-24. The 4th place was also the best finish for the Russain team in this 2001 season. This event had everything to make the Mallorcan crowd come alive on the last day of competition. Even though it was played without the usual music and entertainment activities, out of respect to the victims of the "911" New York tragedy. The extremely high level of the competition offered by the players, completely satisfied the crowd inside the filled up stadium on Santa Ponca Beach and proved that Beach volleyball is enjoyed in Spain.

3rd Place: Roberto Lopes and Franco Neto-Brazil
4th Place: Sergey Ermishin and Mikhail Kouchnerev-Russia
5th Place: Patrick Heuscher and Stefan Kobel-Switzerland
5th Place: Bjorn Berg and Simon Dahl-Sweden

VITORIA BRAZIL
November 27th-December 2nd, 2001

The 2001 Men's FIVB $180,000.00 Brazil Open, staged on Camburi Beach, Vitoria, Espirito Santo, in Vitoria Brazil, was won by Tande Ramos and Emanuel Rego. In an all-Brazilian final, top-seeded Tande and Emanuel fought back from one game down to defeat second-seeded team of Jose Loiola and Ricardo Santos 18-21, 24-22 and 15-12 in 78 minutes, to win the "Gold-Medal" match. The Swiss brother-pairing of Martin and Paul Laciga, defeated Brazilians Klepper Feitosa and Murilo Toscano 21-18 and 25-23 to claim the "Bronze-Medal" match and in the process, eclipsed World Champions Mariano Baracetti and Martin Conde for the second spot of the FIVB Tour's years-end rankings.

3rd Place: Martin Laciga and Laciga-Switzerland
4th Place: Klepper Feitosa and Murilo Toscano-Brazil
5th Place: Roberto Lopes and Franco Neto-Brazil
5th Place: Markus Dieckmann and Jonas Reckermann-Germany

TOP PHOTOS: Left: Kevin Wong attacking the ball. **Center:** Brian Lewis stirs-up the sand while making a dig. **Right:** John Anselmo smashing the ball past the block of Mike Whitmarsh.

MIDDLE PHOTOS: Left: Eric Fonimoana reaching above the net for the spike. **Center:** Karch Kiraly ready to make the defensive play. **Right:** Lee LeGrande follows-through after attacking the ball.

2001 MEN'S BEACH VOLLEYBALL ACTION

BOTTOM PHOTOS: Left: Scotty Lane reaches over the net for the block attempt. **Center:** Stein Metzger gets above the net for the block attempt. **Right:** Todd Rogers gets over the net to make a block.

Photo's Courtesy of "Couvi"

WOMEN'S BEACH VOLLEYBALL
2001

AVP

The 2001 Women's AVP Tour was comprised of five events that were staged congruently with the men's AVP events. The five stops on the women's tour were in Hermosa Beach CA, Muskegon MI, Santa Barbara CA, Manhattan Beach CA and the Queen of the Beach event in Las Vegas Nevada. The women's prize money pool was over $300,000.00.

There were five different champions at the five Women's AVP Tour events in 2001. Linda Hanley and Sara Straton won the Muskegon Michigan event. Lisa Arce and Holly McPeak won the Hermosa Beach Women's Open. Diane DeNochea and Liz Masakayan won the Santa Barbara event. Elaine Youngs and Barbra Fontana won the Manhattan Beach Women's Open. Lisa Arce was "Crowned" the 2001 Queen of the Beach. Arce collected over $20,000.00 with her crown.

2001 INDIVIDUAL WOMEN'S AVP TOURNAMENT FINISHES

Player	1st	2nd	3rd	4th	5th
Lisa Arce	2	2	0	1	1
Lynda Johnson Black	0	0	0	1	0
Carrie Busch	0	0	0	1	3
Stephane Cox	0	0	0	0	2
Dianne DeNeochea	1	0	0	3	1
Katy Eldridge	0	0	0	0	2
Barbra Fontana	2	1	2	0	0
Linda Hanley	1	0	0	2	1
Karen Helyer	0	0	0	0	1
Jen Holdren	0	1	0	0	0
Denise Koelliker	0	0	1	0	0
Tammy Leibl	0	0	0	1	0
Liz Masakayan	1	1	0	2	1
Nancy Mason	0	0	2	0	1
Misty May	1	0	0	0	0
Holly McPeak	1	3	1	1	0
Leanne Schuster McSorley	0	0	2	0	1
Jen Meredith	0	1	1	0	2
Jen Pavley	0	0	0	0	2
Tammy Pelski	0	0	0	0	1
Tammy Rau	0	0	0	0	1
Wendy Stammer	0	1	1	1	1
Sara Straton	1	0	0	3	1
Karen Trussel	0	0	1	0	0
Teri VanDyke	0	0	0	0	1
Rachel Wacholder	0	1	0	1	2
Kerri Walsh	1	0	0	0	0
Elaine Youngs	2	2	2	0	0

(Above list includes 2 BVA finishes)

SARA STRATON
Australian Sara Straton paired-up with Linda Hanley to win the 2001 Women's AVP Tour event in Muskegon MI. Above photo, Straton challenges the block of Liz Masakayan, while Barbra Fontana stays alert on defense.
Photo Courtesy of "Couvi"

NANCY MASON & LEANNE McSORLEY
Nancy Mason and Leanne Schuster McSorley provided ample competition on the 2001 AVP and BVA Tours. Mason and McSorley finished in third place twice. Above photo, Holly McPeak challenges the block of Mason. McSorley is ready on defense.
Photo Courtesy of "Couvi"

BVA

In 2001 there were two Women's BVA Tour events staged. The 2001 Women's BVA Tour events were staged in Clearwater Beach Florida and Oceanside California. Elaine Youngs and Barbra Fontana won the Clearwater Beach event while Misty May and Kerri Walsh won the Oceanside event.

FIVB

The Women's FIVB 2001 World Tour of Beach Volleyball staged twelve events, including the Goodwill Games in Brisbane Australia. There were events in ten countries with a total purse of over $600,000.00. The FIVB events were staged in Macau China, Cagliari Italy, Gstaad Switzerland, Gran Canaria Spain, Marseille France, Espinho Portugal, Klagenfurt Austria (World Championship), Osaka Japan, Maoming China, Hong Kong China, Brisbane Australia (Goodwill Games) and Fortaleza Brazil.

The top team, on the 2001 FIVB Women's World Tour, was Brazil's Shelda Bede and Adriana Behar. They advanced to eleven "Gold-Medal" matches, winning seven times, while earning over $300,000.00. American's Elaine Youngs and Barbra Fontana were the number two team on the 2001 FIVB Women's Tour. Youngs and Fontana advanced to four "Gold-Medal" Matches, winning twice, while earning nearly $200,000.00. Another Brazilian team was in the top three as Sandra Pires and Tatiana Minello advanced to three "Gold-Medal" matches, winning once, while earning nearly $175,000.00. Another American team was within the top four, as Misty May and Kerri walsh advanced to three "Gold-Medal" matches, winning once. There were two additional teams that each won one "Gold-Medal" on the 2001 FIVB Women's World Tour. They were Australian's Kerri-Ann Pottharst with Natalie Cook and China's Rong Chi with Zi Xiong.

2001 INDIVIDUAL FIVB TOURNAMENT FINISHES

Player	1st	2nd	3rd	4th	5th
Lisa Arce	0	0	1	0	4
Shelda Kelly Bruno Bede	5	4	1	0	0
Adriana Brandao Behar	5	4	1	0	0
Danalee Bragado	0	0	0	0	1
Laura Bruschini	0	0	0	0	1
Bento Buczmiejuk	0	0	0	0	1
Eva Celbova	0	0	1	1	0
Rong Chi	0	0	0	1	1
Natalie Cook	1	1	1	4	0
Dianne DeNecochea	0	0	1	0	0
Sonja Dosoudilova	0	0	1	0	0
Barbra Fontana	2	2	3	2	1
Daniela Gattelli	0	0	1	0	0
Dalixia Fernandez Grasset	0	0	0	0	3
Rebbekka Kadijk	0	0	0	1	0
Vasso Karadassiou	0	0	0	0	1
Chiaki Kusuhara	0	0	0	0	1
Marrit Leenstra	0	0	0	1	0
Liz Masakayan	0	0	1	0	0
Misty May	1	2	2	0	0
Holly McPeak	0	1	2	0	4
Tatiana Minello	1	2	1	3	3
Claudia Oliveria	0	0	0	0	4
Tamara Larrea peraza	0	0	0	0	3
Lucilla Perrotta	0	0	1	0	0
Sandra Tavares Pires	1	2	1	3	3
KerriAnn Pottharst	1	1	1	4	0
Efi Sfyri	0	0	0	0	1
Jacqueline "Jackie" Cruz Silva	0	0	0	0	3
AnnaMaria Solazzi	0	0	0	0	1
Jia Tian	0	0	0	0	1
Ryo Tokuno	0	0	0	0	1
Kerri Walsh	1	3	1	0	0
Fei Wang	0	0	0	0	1
Ali Wood	0	0	0	0	1
Zi Xiong	0	0	0	1	1
Elaine Youngs	2	2	3	2	1

SHELDA BRUNO BEDE
Brazilian Shelda Bede teamed-up with compatriot Adriana Behar as the top team on the 2001 Women's FIVB World Tour. They advanced to the "Gold-Medal" match at 11 events, winning 7 times. Above photo, Bede gets in the sand to make a dig.
Photo Courtesy of the FIVB

LIZ MASAKAYAN & LINDA HANLEY
In 2001, at the AVP event in Manhattan Beach CA, Liz Masakayan and Linda Hanley announced their retirement from the Women's AVP Tour. Above photo, Masakayan hits a set from Hanley, past the block of Kerri Walsh.
Photo Courtesy of "Couvi"

WOMEN'S TOURNAMENT RESULTS
2001-AVP

HERMOSA BEACH CALIFORNIA
June 8th-10th, 2001

The 2001 AVP $75,000.00 Women's Union Bay Hermosa Beach Open, at The Pier in Hermosa Beach California was won by the team of Lisa Arce and Holly McPeak. In the 57 minute championship match, second-seeded, Arce and McPeak captured the $16,750.00 first-place prize by defeating top-seeded Barbra Fontana and Elaine Youngs 21-19, 17-21 and 17-15. The championship was the 15th for the Arce and McPeak partnership as the pair were playing in their first event together since the 1998 season. For McPeak this win was the fourth time she won a pro beach event in Hermosa as she claimed her 56th career title. Arce won for the first-time in Hermosa and for the 19th-time in her career. In the match for third place, the third-seeded team of Nancy Mason and Leanne Schuster out-lasted eighth-seeded Linda Hanley and Sarah Straton 30-28 and 21-19 in 47 minutes. Mason and Schuster split $8,500.00 while Hanley and Straton shared $6,500.00.

3rd Place: Nancy Mason and Leanne Schuster
4th Place: Linda Hanley and Sarah Straton
5th Place: Stephanie Cox and Katy Eldridge
5th Place: Dianne DeNecochea and Wendy Stammer

MUSKEGON MICHIGAN
July 13th-15th, 2001

The world's best players from the AVP Tour competed in a three-day professional 2-person beach volleyball tournament, on six sand courts at Pere Marquette Park, in Muskegon Michigan. The 2001 Sunkist Muskegon Open was won by seventh-seeded Linda Hanley and Sarah Straton. This was their first Association of Volleyball Professionals' women's title together. The 41 year-old Hanley, who is believed to be the oldest woman to ever win a pro beach title, and Straton had to win two elimination matches early Sunday to advance to the semi-finals where they scored a 12-21, 21-17 and 16-14 over second-seeded Barbra Fontana and Elaine Youngs. In the championship match, Hanley and Straton claimed the $14,000.00 first-place prize with a 23-21, 15-21 and 18-16 win in 75 minutes over top-seeded Lisa Arce and Holly McPeak, who split $9,250.00 for second. Fontana and Youngs, who had won four-straight matches this season over Hanley and Straton, shared the $6,600 third-place prize with a 21-11 and 21-12 win over ninth-seeded Dianne DeNecochea and Wendy Stammer. DeNecochea and Stammer

2001 WOMEN'S AVP ACTION - HERMOSA BEACH

The 2001 AVP Hermosa Beach Women's Open was won by the team of Holly McPeak and Lisa Arce. The exciting championship match was played in-front of a packed beach volleyball stadium. Arce and McPeak out-lasted Elaine Youngs and Barbra Fontana, by the scores of 21-19, 17-21 and 17-15. Above photo, During the 2001 Hermosa Beach event, McPeak hits a set from Arce, towards the defense of Youngs (left) and Fontana (right).

Photo Courtesy of "Couvi"

shared $4,850 for fourth-place as the pair posted their best pro beach finish. Brighton Entertainment of New York, N. Y., taped the action for replay on FOX Sports Net.

3rd Place: Barbra Fontana and Elaine Youngs
4th Place: Dianne DeNecochea and Wendy Stammer
5th Place: Jen Meredith and Jenny Pavley
5th Place: Carrie Busch and Rachel Wacholder

SANTA BARBARA CALIFORNIA
August 17th-19th, 2001

The 2001 Michelob Light $62,500.00 Women's Open, presented by Paul Mitchell on East Beach in Santa Barbara California was won by the team of Dianne DeNecochea and Liz Masakayan. DeNecochea and Masakayan split the $14,500.00 first-place prize. While DeNecochea was winning her first pro beach title, Masakayan was winning her 45th. The Santa Barbara title was Masakayan's first domestic win since 1999 as Masakayan won three times in 2000 in Brazil, Portugal and China. In the 49 minute championship match, DeNecochea and Masakayan outlasted Jen Meredith and Wendy Stammer 21-19 and 22-20. Meredith and Stammer, who were playing in their first pro beach final, split $9,750.00 for second-place. In the, over one-hour, third-place match, Barbra Fontana and Elaine Youngs defeated Lisa Arce and Holly McPeak 15-21, 21-17 and 15-13, to win the $6,800.00 prize.

3rd Place: Barbra Fontana and Elaine Youngs
4th Place: Lisa Arce and Holly McPeak
5th Place: Carrie Busch and Rachel Wacholder
5th Place: Nancy Mason and Leanne Schuster McSorley

MANHATTAN BEACH CALIFORNIA
August 24th-26th, 2001

The 2001 Michelob Light $75,000.00 Women's Manhattan Beach Open was won by the top-seeded team of Barbra Fontana and Elaine Youngs. They collected $17,400.00 along with the title. In the championship match, they defeated second-seeded Lisa Arce and Holly McPeak 21-17 and 21-19 in 49 minutes. Fontana won her 20th pro beach title and Youngs her 14th. The win also earned Fontana and Youngs another $7,500.00 for winning the "Michelob Light California Swing" title by each compiling 786 points for events in Hermosa Beach, Santa Barbara and Manhattan Beach. In a 53 minute third place match, Jen Meredith and Wendy Stammer defeated Dianne DeNecochea and Liz Masakayan 17-21, 21-14 & 15-13.

3rd Place: Jen Meredith and Wendy Stammer
4th Place: Dianne DeNecochea and Liz Masakayan
5th Place: Linda Hanley and Sarah Straton
5th Place: Stephanie Cox and Katy Eldridge

LAS VEGAS NEVADA
September 6th-9th, 2001

The 2001 "Queen of the Beach" $75,000.00 tournament was staged on the man-made beach, fabricated on the parking lot of the Hard Rock Hotel and Casino, in Las Vegas Nevada. The 2001 champion was Lisa Arce. She wore the crown as she collected over $20,000.00 for her efforts. The final 2001 "Queen of the Beach" standings and prize money were as follows:

1. Lisa Arce-$20,250.00
2. Elaine Youngs-$16,250.00
3. Holly McPeak-$10,750.00
4. Sarah Straton-$4,250.00
5. Liz Masakayan-$6,125.00
5. Barbra Fontana-$3,125.00
7. Wendy Stammer-$2,750.00
8. Leanne McSorley-$5,500.00
9. Carrie Busch-$1,000.00
10. Jennifer Meredith-$1,000.00

JEN MEREDTH & WENDY STAMMER
Jen Meredith and Wendy Stammer played well enough to advance to the championship match at the 2001 Women's AVP Santa Barbara event. Above photo, Meredith hits a set from Stammer, past the block of Sara Straton.
Photo Courtesy of "Couvi"

LISA ARCE & KEVIN WONG
Lisa Arce and Kevin Wong were crowned the AVP's 2001 King and Queen of the Beach, on the sands of the Hard Rock Hotel and Casino, in Las Vegas NV. Above photo, Arce (left) and Wong (right) in all their crowning glory.
Photo Courtesy of "Couvi"

WOMEN'S TOURNAMENT RESULTS
2001-BVA

CLEARWATER BEACH FLORIDA
April 20th-22nd, 2001

The $150,000.00 BVA Volleyhut 2001 Clearwater Beach Invitational was won by the team of Barbra Fontana and Elaine Youngs. In the championship match, the top-seeded Fontana and Youngs overcame a first game loss in the best of three match to capture the $15,000.00 first-place prize by defeating third-seeded Holly McPeak and Rachel Wacholder. After losing the first game by a score of 21-18, Fontana and Youngs rallied to win the next two games 21-10 and 15-7 to conclude the 55-minute title match against McPeak and Wacholder. Fontana and Youngs concluded the weekend with a 5-0 match mark to net their first pro beach volleyball title in only their second event together. In the match for third place, Nancy Mason and Leanne Schuster McSorley scored a 21-17 and 21-17 win in 39 minutes over Linda Hanley and Sara Straton. Mason and Schuster shared $7,500.00 for the third-place finish. This opening domestic event on the 2001 BVA Pro Beach Volleyball Tour was taped for television replay on ESPN-2.

3rd Place: Nancy Mason and Leanne Schuster McSorley
4th Place: Linda Hanley and Sara Straton
5th Place: Lisa Arce and Carrie Busch
5th Place: Jennifer Meredith and Jenny Pavley

OCEANSIDE CALIFORNIA
May 26th-27th, 2001

Just over one year ago, in the scenic City of Oceanside California, next to the Oceanside Pier is where it all started for Beach Volleyball America and at the pier is apparently where the BVA Tour ended as the $22,750.00 Women's 2001 BVA VolleyHut.com Oceanside Invitational was played-out. Misty May and Kerri Walsh won this final BVA tournament before it was absorbed by the new version of the AVP. In the championship match, May and new partner Walsh, in only their second event together, looked like the future of women's beach volleyball, when they out-pointed Liz Masakayan and Jen Holdren (the wife of Dax Holdren), 21-19 and 21-19. Masakayan and Holdren were occasionally able to exploit Walsh's lack of experience and speed, but Walsh's ability at the net and May's ability virtually everywhere else was too hard to beat. The winner's pocketed $5,000.00 while the runner-ups collected $3,500.00. In the match for third place, Denise Koelliker and Karin Trussel outscored Lynda Johnson-Black and Tammy Leibl, to earn $3,000.00.

3rd Place: Denise Koelliker and Karin Trussel
4th Place: Lynda Johnson-Black and Tammy Leibl
5th Place: Tammy Pelski and Tammy Rau
5th Place: Karen Helyer and Teri Van Dyke

RACHEL WACHOLDER
Rachel Wacholder advanced to the championship match, at the 2001 BVA Clearwater Beach FL event, with Holly McPeak. They finished in second place. Above photo, Wacholder bump-setting the ball.
Photo Courtesy of Ken Delgado

MISTY MAY & KERRI WALSH
Misty May and Kerri Walsh showed their future potential when they won the 2001 BVA event in Oceanside CA. They also won the 2001 FIVB event in Espinho Portugal. Above photo, Walsh hits a set from May, past the block of Liz Masakayan.
Photo Courtesy of "Couvi"

WOMEN'S TOURNAMENT RESULTS
2001-FIVB

MACAU CHINA
April 4th-8th, 2001

At the 2001 Women's FIVB $180,000.00 China Open, in Macau China, the Australian team of Natalie Cook and Kerri-Ann Pottharst proved that the Sydney 2000 Olympic "Gold-Medal" was no fluke when they won the "Gold-Medal" and the $27,000.00 first place check. In the championship match, they out-lasted the Brazilian team of Shelda Bede and Adriana Behar by the scores of 28-26 and 21-13. The runner-ups shared $18,000.00. In the all-American "Bronze-Medal" match, Holly McPeak and Misty May defeated compatriots Elaine Youngs and Barbra Fontana by the scores of 26-24, 20-22 and 15-10 earning $14,000.00 with the victory.

3rd Place: Misty May and Holly McPeak-USA
4th Place: Barbra Fontana and Elaine Youngs-USA
5th Place: Jia Tian and Fei Wang-China
5th Place: Tatiana Minello and Sandra Pires-Brazil

CAGLIARI ITALY
June 13th-17th, 2001

The exciting "Gold-Medal" match was the magnificent conclusion of the challenging 2001 Women's FIVB $180,000.00 Italian Open, staged on Poetto Beach in Cagliari Italy. The American team of Barbra Fontana and Elaine Youngs won the event and the $27,000.00 first place prize. In the championship match, Fontana and Youngs were able to defeat the 2000 Olympic Gold Medalists, Australians Kerri-Ann Pottharst and Natalie Cook, in three games, 10-21, 21-19 and 15-11. The exciting match kept all 3,500 spectators in the packed stadium. In the "Bronze-Medal" match, Brazilians Adriana Behar and Shelda Bede defeated their compatriots Sandra Pires and Tatiana Minello, 22-20 and 21-12, to collect the $18,000.00 third place prize. A festive award ceremony kept all spectators in place, applauding all contestants for their performances. The "Best Player" award for the event was earned by Barbara Fontana, who received the special "SPEEDO TROPHY."

3rd Place: Shelda Bede and Adriana Behar-Brazil
4th Place: Tatiana Minello and Sandra Pires-Brazil
5th Place: Lisa Arce and Holly McPeak-USA
5th Place: Claudia Oliveira and Jackie Silva-Brazil

GSTAAD SWITZERLAND
June 19th-23rd, 2001

In a fairy tale setting in the Swiss Alpine town of Gstaad Switzerland, the Finals of the 2001 Women's FIVB $180,000.00 Swiss Open took place in perfect conditions. The Brazilian team of Adriana Behar and Shelda Bruno were the "Gold-Medal" winners as well as

FEI WANG & JIA TIAN
The Chinese team of Fei Wang and Jia Tian began to show their potential on the 2001 Women's FIVB World Tour with a fifth place finish at the 2001 FIVB event in Macau China. Above photo Wang hits a set from Tian, towards the block of Elaine Youngs.
Photo Courtesy of "Couvi"

BARBRA FONTANA & ELAINE YOUNGS
Barbra Fontana and Elaine Youngs collected first place checks on on the 2001 AVP, BVA and FIVB Tour's. Above photo, Fontana (left) and Youngs (right) collect their first place check at the 2001 Manhattan Beach Open, from "Bud-Ron."
Photo Courtesy of "Couvi"

recipients of the $27,000.00 first place check. In the championship match, they were able to win the women's final, by scores of 21-15 and 22-20 against the American duo of Barbara Fontana and Eliane Youngs. In the "Bronze-Medal" match, the American duo of Kerri Walsh and Misty May won against the Brazilians Sandra Pires and Tatiana Minello, 21-15 and 21-16. As was now traditional the winning three teams received real and genuine Swiss cow bells as souvenirs.

3rd Place: Misty May and Kerri Walsh-USA
4th Place: Tatiana Minello and Sandra Pires-Brazil
5th Place: Lisa Arce and Holly McPeak-USA
5th Place: Dalixia Fernandez Grasset and Tamara Larrea Peraza-Cuba

GRAN CANARIA SPAIN
July 4th-8th, 2001

On a day that was perfect for beach volleyball and a stadium packed with enthusiastic spectators to go with beautiful sunny weather, some of the best athletes in the world participated in the 2001 Women's FIVB $180,000.00 Spanish Open, staged at Playa del Ingles in Gran Canaria Spain. Adriana Behar and Shelda Bede, from Brazil were champions for the second consecutive weekend. In the "Gold-Medal" match, Behar and Bede dominated the American team of Elaine Youngs and Barbra Fontana 21-16 and 21-16, in front of the capacity crowd of 2500. The winner's collected a check for $27,000.00. Brazilian's Sandra Pires and Tatiana Minello took the "Bronze-Medal" match 21-15 and 21-18 over Eva Celbova and Sona Dosoudilova, from the Czech Republic. The top three ranked teams on the 2001 Women's FIVB World Tour that participated in this event finished 1-2-3. Shelda Bede was named the Speedo "Player of the Tournament" in recognition of her outstanding play.

3rd Place: Tatiana Minello and Sandra Pires-Brazil
4th Place: Eva Celbova and Sona Dosoudilova-Czech Republic
5th Place: Lisa Arce and Holly McPeak-USA
5th Place: Dalixia Fernandez Grasset and Tamara Larrea Peraza-Cuba

MARSEILLE FRANCE
July 16th-22nd, 2001

On a hot day, for the woman's finals of the 2001 FIVB Beach Volleyball $225,000.00 French Grand Slam in Marseille France, the stadium was crowded with enthusiastic fans. The event was won by the American team of Barbra Fontana and Elaine Youngs. During the "Gold-Medal" match, with Youngs guarding the net, they were never in danger of defeat against the Brazilian team of Adriana Behar and Shelda Bede, who were supported by a large coalition of Brazilians who live in Marseille. The scores were 21-13 and 21-14. The winner's split the first place check of $32,000.00 while the runner-ups shared $22,000.00. The "Bronze-Medal" match was won by the American team of Holly McPeak and Lisa Arce when the Australian team of Natalie Cook and Kerri-Ann Pottharst forfeited because of an injury. McPeak and Arce collected $18,000.00 for their third place finish.

3rd Place: Lisa Arce and Holly McPeak-USA
4th Place: Natalie Cook and Kerri-Ann Pottharst-Australia
5th Place: Tatiana Minello and Sandra Pires-Brazil
5th Place: Dalixia Fernandez Grasset and Tamara Larrea Peraza-Cuba

ESPINHO PORTUGAL
July 24th-28th, 2001

The Women's 2001 FIVB $180,000.00 Portugal Open, staged on warm and pleasant day, with the Stadium filled to capacity, in Praia da Baia, Espinho Portugal, the team of Kerri Walsh and Misty May, of the United States, finished on the "top-of-the-heap." This was the first ever World Tour "Gold-Medal" for this American team. The championship match, against Brazil's Shelda Bede and Adriana Behar, was a close and exciting match that included several lead changes. The final scores of 22-20 and 24-22 illustrate the closeness of the match. The winner's shared $27,000.00 while the runner-ups split $18,000.00. In the Bronze-Medal" match, another team from the United States, Barbra Fontana and Elaine Youngs, experienced another exciting match, winning in three games against the Australian team of Natalie Cook and Kerri-Ann Pottharst 21-15, 11-21 and 15-13.

3rd Place: Barbra Fontana and Elaine Youngs-USA
4th Place: Natalie Cook and Kerri-Ann Pottharst-Australia
5th Place: Tatiana Minello and Sandra Pires-Brazil
5th Place: Lisa Arce and Holly McPeak-USA

KLAGENFURT AUSTRIA
August 1st-4th, 2001

The Women's 2001 FIVB $250,000.00 Beach Volleyball World Championships, staged in Klagenfurt, Austria, was won by the Brazilian team of Shelda Bede and Adriana Behar. They collected the "Gold-Medal" and the $47,000.00 first place check. In the all-Brazilian championship match, they out-scored compatriots Tatiana Minello and Sandra Pires, 21-16 and 21-18, in 39 minutes. The runner-ups shared $35,000.00. During the finals, the party atmosphere reached fever pitch as the fans screamed and put their special Austrian stamp on the proceedings by performing the unique "slow wave" to the tune of the Blue Danube Waltz. In the "Bronze-Medal" match, Eva Celbova and Sona Dosoudilova, from the Czech Republic defeated Americans Lisa Arce and Holly McPeak, 21-17 and 21-19, earning $21,000.00 for their third place finish. This year the World Championships attracted some 100,000 spectators

DR. RUBEN & MALU ACOSTA
FIVB President Dr. Rubin Acosta and his wife Malu were in attendance at the 2001 FIVB World Tour event in Klagenfurt Austria. Above photo, Mr. and Mrs. Acosta enjoying the atmosphere of an FIVB World Tour event.
Photo Courtesy of the FIVB

over the five days of competition, including visits by the FIVB President Dr. Ruben Acosta and his wife Malu.
3rd Place: Eva Celbova and Sona Dosoudilova-Czech Republic
4th Place: Barbra Fontana and Elaine Youngs-USA
5th Place: Claudia OliveiraJackie Silva-Brazil
5th Place: Rong Chi and Zi Xiong-China
5th Place: Laura Bruschini and Annamaria Solazzi-Italy
5th Place: Danalee Bragado and Ali Wood-USA

OSAKA JAPAN
August 8th-12th, 2001

The Women's 2001 FIVB $180,000.00 Beach Volleyball World Championships, staged in Osaka Japan, was won by the Brazilian team of Shelda Bede and Adriana Behar. They collected the "Gold-Medal" and the $27,000.00 first place check. In the over one hour championship match, Behar and Bede and the young U.S. team of Kerri Walsh and Misty May fought head-to-head in the first game with Brazilians narrowly winning 23-21. In the second game Walsh and May came out hard in the second game to even the match at one game each, but only after a 30-28 marathon win. After the Americans took an 11-6 lead, the Brazilians came-back and took the "Gold-Medal" with a 15-13 exhausting third game. The runner-ups shared $18,000.00. In the "Bronze-Medal" match, Americans Barbra Fontana and Elaine Youngs out-scored Natalie Cook and Kerri-Ann Pottharst, from Australia, 21-14 and 21-14, earning $14,000.00 for their third place finish.
3rd Place: Barbra Fontana and Elaine Youngs-USA
4th Place: Natalie Cook and Kerri-Ann Pottharst-Australia
5th Place: Lisa Arce and Holly McPeak-USA
5th Place: Claudia Oliveira and Jackie Silva-Brazil

MAOMING CHINA
July 18th-22nd, 2001

A packed stadium at the 2001 Women's FIVB $180,000.00 China Open, in Maoming China witnessed a fine "Gold-Medal" performance by the Brazilian team of Shelda Bede and Adriana Behar. In the 66 minute championship match, the crowd enjoyed a thrilling match, which turned victorious again for the 2001 World Champions Behar and Bede when they faced their compatriots Sandra Pires and Tatiana Minello, in the three game match 21-18, 18-21 and 17-15. There was also a very entertaining "Bronze-Medal" match when the Australian team of Natalie Cook and Kerri-Ann Pottharst defeated the Chinese host country favorites Rong Chi and Zi Xiong 21-19, 19-2 and 15-11.
3rd Place: Natalie Cook and Kerri-Ann Pottharst-Australia
4th Place: Rong Chi and Zi Xiong-China
5th Place: Dalixia Fernandez Grasset and Tamara Larrea Peraza-Cuba
5th Place: Vasso Karadassiou and Efi Sfyri-Greece

HONG KONG CHINA
August 22nd-26th, 2001

Brazilians Adriana Behar and Shelda Bede continued with their record-breaking streak and season, in Hong Kong China, with their fourth consecutive victory at the 2001 Women's FIVB $180,000.00 Hong Kong Open. In the semi-finals, there was a fight between two Brazilian

LISA ARCE & HOLLY McPEAK
Lisa Arce and Holly McPeak played well on the AVP, BVA and FIVB Tour's in 2001, They advanced to 3 championship matches, winning once on the AVP Tour. Above photo, Arce (left) and McPeak (right) get advice from the legendary Gene Selznick.
Photo Courtesy of "Couvi"

NATALIE COOK
Australian Natalie Cook played well on the 2001 FIVB Women's World Tour. She advanced to 2 "Gold-Medal" matches, winning the Macau China event with compatriot Kerri-Ann Pottharst. Above photo, Cook challenges the block of Fei Wang from China.
Photo Courtesy of "Couvi"

teams, Sandra Pires with Tatiana Minello and Adriana Behar with Shelda Bede, to decide which team would go into the finals. Bede and Behar moved-on to the "Gold-Medal" match. In the other semifinal, the young USA team of Kerri Walsh and Misty May, defeated the Italian team of Daniela Gattelli and Lucilla Perrottal, to earn a spot in the "Gold-Medal" match. In the 45 minute championship match, the Brazilians defeated the Americans in two straight games, earning $27,000.00 in the process. Walsh and May settled on the $18,000.00 second place check. In the "Bronze-Medal" match, the Italians defeated the Brazilians in two straight games, 21-15 and 21-16.

3rd Place: Daniela Gattelli and Lucilla Perrotta-Italy
4th Place: Tatiana Minello and Sandra Pires-Brazil
5th Place: Dalixia Fernandez Grasset and Tamara Larrea Peraza-Cuba
5th Place: Chiaki Kusuhara and Ryo Tokuno-Japan

BRISBANE AUSTRALIA
August 29th-September 4th, 2001

Before a sellout crowd at the South Bank Piazza, the 2001 Women's FIVB $150,000.00 Goodwill Games, in Brisbane, Australia saw Brazil's Tatiana Minello and Sandra Pires capture the "Goodwill-Gold-Medal" when they upset the two-time FIVB World Champions, compatriots Adriana Behar and Shelda Bede. In the championship match, they defeated their Brazilian rivals, 20-18 and 23-21 in 47 minutes. Behar and Bede were the defending Goodwill Games Gold Medallists after winning the 1998 crown in New York's Central Park by defeating Pauline Manser and Pottharst in the finals. Minello and Pires shared the $30,000.00 first-place prize while Behar and Bede split $24,000.00 for the "Silver-Medal" win. In the "Bronze-Medal" match, third-seeded Barbra Fontana and Elaine Youngs of the United States captured the $19,500.00 third-place prize by defeating top-seeded Natalie Cook and Kerri Pottharst of Australia 21-12 and 25-23 in 46 minutes. The Aussies, the Sydney 2000 Olympic Gold Medallists, split $15,500.00 for fourth.

Fifth-seeded Lisa Arce and Holly McPeak of the United States outlasted the seventh-seeded Zi Xiong and Rong Chi of China 28-26 and 23-21 in 49 minutes. With the win, Arce and McPeak placed fifth in the competition to split $12,500.00 for winning three of four Goodwill Games matches. Arce and McPeak were competing in their second Goodwill Games after securing the Bronze Medal in 1998 at New York. The Chinese team placed sixth to share $9,500.00. Eighth-seeded Daniela Gattelli and Lucilla Perrotta of Italy placed seventh to share the $8,000.00 prize. The Italians outlasted sixth-seeded Daxilia Larrea Peraza and Tamara Fernandez Grosset of Cuba 21-13, 15-21 and 15-11 in 50 minutes. The Cubans split $7,000.00 for finishing eighth. Final standings for the 2001 Goodwill Games Women's Beach Volleyball:

1st Place: Tatiana Minello and Sandra Pires-Brazil
2nd Place: Shelda Bede and Adriana Behar-Brazil
3rd Place: Barbra Fontana and Elaine Youngs-USA
4th Place: Natalie Cook and Kerri-Ann Pottharst-Australia
5th Place: Lisa Arce and Holly McPeak-USA
6th Place: Zi Xiong and Rong Chi-China
7th Place: Daniela Gattelli and Lucilla Perrotta-Italy
8th Place: Daxilia Larrea Peraza and Tamara Fernandez Grosset-Cuba

FORTALEZA BRAZIL
October 30th-November 4th, 2001

The atmosphere, created by 5000 enthusiastic fans was electrifying, at the 2001 Women's FIVB $180,000.00 Brazil Open in Fortaleza Brazil, when Adriana Behar and Shelda Bede finished a perfect season with another "Gold-Medal" in the last event of the 2001 FIVB Beach Volleyball World Tour. During the championship match, undefeated up to the final, Americans Holly McPeak and Kerri Walsh did not have enough in reserve to take on the Brazilian team. The Fortaleza winds and/or the Fortaleza fans in Shelda's hometown, were too-much for the team from the U.S.A. as they went down in two straight games, by scores of 21-19, 19-21 and 22-20, in 48 minutes. The win, for the Brazilian's was their twenty-seventh international title, gave Shelda and Adriana Behar another record, that of being the most successful team ever on the FIVB World Tour, with $1,141,600.00 in career prize money. Bede and Behar collected $27,000.00 along with the win. In the 44 minute "Bronze-Medal" match, Americans Liz Masakayan and Dianne DeNecochea outlasted Rebekka Kadijk and Marrit Leenstra, from the Netherlands, 22-20 and 21-19.

3rd Place: Dianne DeNecochea and Liz Masakayan-USA
4th Place: Rebekka Kadijk and Marrit Leenstra-Netherlands
5th Place: Barbra Fontana and Elaine Youngs-USA
5th Place: Adriana Bento Buczmiejuk and Claudia Oliveira-Brazil

TATIANA MINELLO AND SANDRA PIRES
Brazilians Tatiana Minello and Sandra Pires won the "Gold-Medal" at the 2001 Goodwill Games in Brisbane Australia. They also advanced to two additional FIVB finals in 2001. Above photo, Minello (back) and Pires (facing) celebrate a victory.
Photo Courtesy of the FIVB

TOP PHOTOS: Left: Misty May is in position to pass the ball. **Center:** Barbra Fontana gets low to make the dig. **Right:** Holly McPeak reaches high for the pokie.

MIDDLE PHOTOS: Left: Brazilian Tatiana Minello makes a diving effort for the ball. **Center:** Brazilian Sandra Pires attacking the ball. **Right:** Rebekka Kadijk, from the Netherlands, reaches above the net to hit the ball.

2001 WOMEN'S BEACH VOLLEYBALL ACTION

BOTTOM PHOTOS: Left: Marla O'Hara reacting to the hit. **Center:** Nancy Mason reaches above the net to slice the ball. **Right:** Linda Hanley is ready to make the defensive play.

Top Photos Courtesy of Frank Goroszko. Middle Photos Courtesy of the FIVB. Bottom Photos Courtesy of "Couvi".

ADDITIONAL VOLLEYBALL INFORMATION 2001

NEWPORT BEACH CALIFORNIA
October 13th-14th, 2001

AVP star Brian "Lewy" Lewis instituted a new beach volleyball event called "Da Dunes Pro-Am Tournament" which was staged on four new beach volleyball courts on the waterfront resort of Newport Dunes in the "Upper Newport Bay" area of Newport Beach California. The event was financed by various sponsors and with the help of fellow volleyball standout's Steve Timmons and Tim Hovland the inaugural Da Dunes Pro-Am Tournament included 30 four-man teams and 10 four-woman teams. Most teams were outfitted in theme apparel. The event lured some of the top names in pro beach volleyball. Legendary pro beach volleyball player Randy Stoklos, along with Hovland and Olympic gold medalists Timmons and Ricci Luyties as well as Scott Ayakatubby, Sean Rosenthal, Misty May, Kerri Walsh, Mike Dodd and others. The inaugural Da Dunes Pro-Am Beach 4-Person Volleyball Tournament saw Scott Ayakatubby direct his "Blue Water Grill" team to a victory over "Heateme" 15-7, in the men's final. Ayakatubby was the MVP in the men's competition. "Blue Water Grill" had defeated "Wrap It Up" 15-11, in a semifinal game, while "Heateme" beat "Peridian" 15-4, to advance to the final. In the women's final, the "Zebras" beat "Carnival" 16-14, 15-8, in the double elimination contest. The "Zebras" were down by four points early in the first game, but rallied for the win. The team's only loss of the tournament came in an earlier match against "Carnival" 17-15. Kerri Walsh was named the MVP in the women's competition. Approximately 2,000 people attended the tournament.

MOTHERLODE VOLLEYBALL TOURNAMENT HISTORY

Labor Day Weekends, 1973-2001 (and still going) Transplanted from Newport Beach, California, all Howard Ross and Gordon Whitmer, the co-owners of the MotherLode Restaurant, in Aspen, were trying to do was to have a little fun and provide themselves and their friends with a beach volleyball "fix" on a quiet Labor Day Weekend. They set-up courts in Wagner Park, provided food for a barbecue, brought in a keg of beer, and played volleyball. The winners of that first "informal" tourney were none other than beach legends Chester and Steve Goss, from San Diego living in Aspen. It was fun! So…they decided to do it again the next year. And, a few more teams showed-up. The next thing they knew, they had, without the benefit, or effort, of advertising and promotion, a full-blown tourney on their hands. In those early years, registrations were taken by the restaurant's bar tenders; was produced by one of their waiters (Andy Hanson, originally from San Diego); and, t-shirts were produced and sold by another waiter. The tournament had grown from 14 teams to over 160 teams and had supplanted the Colorado Open, held in Boulder, as the toughest tourney in Colorado. As well, they were starting to draw teams from outside the State, especially from the beaches of California. And…it was getting too big for the restaurant to handle. In 1981, Ross and Whitmer brought in local volleyball player, coach, and event promoter Leon Fell to produce and coordinate the schedule of events surrounding the tournament. Fell, who was, at that time, producing the series of events pertaining to the Subaru/Aspen Winternational World Cup Skiing (America's Downhill) week, in Aspen, asked them if they were interested in doing what it took to make the 'MotherLode' (as it was becoming called) into a National tourney. They laughed and said "sure" thinking that that was something that could never be. The next year, Fell hired regional tournament organizer Tim Weiand as Tournament Director and set-up a new infrastructure for marketing and promotion, MotherLode Volleyball Productions. He utilized his gregarious nature and his growing contacts within the volleyball world and proceeded with his dream to make the landlocked beach tournament one of the most renowned events in beach volleyball, all the while trying to maintain the original flavor of that first tourney. Over the years, the

SCOTT AYAKATUBBY
Scott Ayakatubby played inspirational volleyball to earn the MVP award at the inaugural Brian Lewis "Da-Dunes" Pro-Am tournament in Newport Beach CA. Above photo, Ayakatubby is in position to make the perfect pass.
Photo Courtesy of "Couvi"

Event has grown to become the most comprehensive beach doubles volleyball tournament in North America; including upwards of 700 teams coming from all over the United States to participate in, and celebrate, what Volleyball Magazine has termed "the social event of the outdoor volleyball season." It has expanded from a one-day tourney to a five-day Event. And, from one division to 17 divisions of play ranging from Men's and Women's Open to Women's B - with Men's and Women's Senior's and Master's divisions in between. It has drawn players such as the 2000 Sydney, Australia Olympic Beach Volleyball Champion Dain Blanton to the likes of other current AVP players such as Mike Whitmarsh, Canyon Ceman, Adam Jewell, Dax Holdren, Albert Hanneman, Linda Hanley, Leanne Schuster Mc Sorley, Nancy Mason, Danalee Bragado, Liz Pagano, and Rachel Wacholder. Ex-AVP and USA National team players such as Pat Powers, Jon Stanley, Byron Shewman, Danny Patterson, Shawn Fallowfield, Jon Stevenson, Steve Timmons, Roger Clark, Craig Moothart, Tom Duke, Mark Tanner, Rudy Dvorak, Leif Hansen, Rob Heidger, Curtis Griffin, Erik, Moore, Ryan Post, Andrew Cavanaugh, Larry Benecke, Larry Mear, Eric Wurts, Pono Ma'a, Janice Opalinsky, Elaine Rogue, Hillary Johnson, Kim Harsch-Bird, Christine Schaefer, Gayle Stammer, Laurel Brassey, Valinda Hilleary, Pat Keller, and Canadian star Garth Pischke have graced the "Lode's" main championship courts. As well, beach legends Jon Lee, George Zebot, Dan Salyer, Chester and Steve Goss, David King, Scott Steele, Bob Pape, and Monty McBride have continued their storied careers here. The MotherLode has been the proving ground for many rookie AVP players and the feeling of satisfaction for many other amateur players from around the Country. More than quite a few volleyball relationships have been made at "the "Lode" as well as many marriages and anniversaries. For nearly 30 years now, the MotherLode is, still, that fun little tournament held every Labor Day Weekend in the mountain hamlet of Aspen, Colorado. For additional information about this highly successful and hugely popular beach doubles volleyball event at the premier summer/winter resort, please visit the Motherlode Volleyball Classic website at: **www.motherlodevolleyball.com.**

ASPEN COLORADO
August 30th-September 3rd, 2001

Featuring both sand and grass court competition, the 29th annual Motherlode Volleyball Classic was staged over a five day period. This event is rated the top "Pro-Am tournament" in North America, the 29th MotherLode Volleyball Classic attracted over 700 teams from all over the nation competing in what has been called the "toughest amateur tournament in the United States" and "the most exciting 'non-tour' professional event going." There were 17 divisions of play in men's (8 classes), women's (5) and co-ed (4), the Motherlode Volleyball Classic is the "most comprehensive" beach volleyball tournament in North America with some of the best beach volleyball east of the Pacific Coast Highway. Produced by MotherLode Volleyball Productions of Aspen, "The 'Lode" incorporates the best of traditional beach volleyball creating the "old time" sense of joy and excitement for the sport. It is a "must attend" event for the serious volleyball aficionado - providing an exciting, competitive end-of-the-season volleyball event surrounded by the beauty and excitement of Aspen.

The 2001 Motherlode Volleyball Classic's "open" classes for both men and women featured the United States' top pro beach volleyball players competing on the main championship sand courts at Koch Lumber Park. In addition to the 1,400 participants, the Motherlode Volleyball Classic attracted thousands of spectators that flocked to the Aspen-area over Labor Day weekend for the best volleyball party in the country. The defending "open" champions were Ian Clark and Dax Holdren (men) and Nancy Mason and Leanne Schuster McSorley (women). The 2001 Motherlode "Open-Class" results:

Men's Open:
1 Canyon Ceman and Adam Jewell of Hermosa Beach, CA
2 Ryan Post of Denver CO and Dane Hansen of Lakewood CO
3 Shawn Garus of Colorado Springs and Chad Turner of Clearwater, FL

Women's Open:
1 Alicia Scott of Evergreen CO and Daven Allison of Santa Barbara, CA
2 Terri McNair of Greeley CO and Aimee Sorensen of Denver CO
3 Shannon Williams and Patti Smith of Dallas TX

ADAM JEWELL
Adam Jewell paired-up with fellow AVP player, Canyon Ceman to win the 2001 MotherLode event in Aspen CO. Above photo, Jewell gets past the block, utilizing his "left-handed-whip" to score a point.

Photo Courtesy of Tim Andexler

MEN'S BEACH VOLLEYBALL
2002

AVP

By 2002, the BVA was out of business and the AVP was the only domestic professional beach volleyball circuit in operation for the top players in the U.S.A. In 2002, the AVP Pro-Beach Volleyball tournament schedule included seven AVP Tour events. All seven of the AVP Tour events were for both men and women. The total prize money was at $1,000,000.00 . In 2002 there were four California events with the three additional events staged in three different states. The three Non-California events were staged in New Jersey, Illinois and Nevada. They all staged one AVP Tour event.

The top team on the 2002 Men's AVP Your was Dax Holdren and Eric Fonoimoana. They advanced to six championship matches, winning four of them. Their wins came in Huntington Beach, Manhattan Beach, North Beach in Chicago and the Las Vegas Nevada event. The three remaining AVP Tour events were won by three different teams. Albert Hannemann and Jeff Nygard won the Hermosa Beach Men's Open. Canyon Ceman and Mike Whitmarsh won the Belmar Beach Men's Open in New Jersey. Karch Kiraly won his 143rd career championship with Brent Doble at the 2002 Santa Barbara Men's Open.

The 2002 AVP Tour featured newly signed corporate partnership agreements with the likes of Nissan, Xbox, Aquafina, Michelob Light, Gatorade, Paul Mitchell, Wilson and Sports Illustrated, the 2002 AVP tour marked the launching of the "new" AVP. The 2002 AVP tour was be highlighted by two live broadcasts on NBC, Manhattan Beach and Chicago. Five events were broadcast on Fox Sports Net and five women''s finals broadcast on The Oxygen Network.

2002 INDIVIDUAL AVP TOURNAMENT FINISHES

Player	1st	2nd	3rd	4th	5th
Scott Ayakatubby	0	0	1	0	1
Eduardo Bacil	0	1	3	0	1
Paul Baxter	0	0	0	0	1
Canyon Ceman	1	3	0	0	1
Scott Davenport	0	0	0	0	1
Brent Doble	1	0	4	0	1
Eli Fairfield	0	0	0	0	1
Eric Fonoimoana	**4**	**2**	**0**	**0**	**1**
Albert Hannemann	1	0	0	0	1
Carl Henkel	0	0	1	0	0
Dax Holdren	**4**	**2**	**0**	**0**	**1**
Casey Jennings	0	0	1	0	0
Karch Kiraly	1	0	4	0	0
Mike Lambert	0	0	3	0	2
Lee LeGrand	0	0	3	0	1
Brian Lewis	0	0	1	0	1
Stein Metzger	0	1	2	0	1
Jeff Nygard	1	0	0	0	1
Todd Rogers	0	0	0	0	4
Sean Scott	0	0	0	0	4
Fred Souza	0	1	3	0	1
Alika Williams	0	0	0	0	1
Mike Whitmarsh	1	3	0	0	1
Kevin Wong	0	1	2	0	1

2002 AVP MEN'S ACTION-MANHATTAN BEACH CALIFORNIA

By 2002, the BVA was out of business and the AVP was the only domestic professional beach volleyball circuit in operation for the top players in the U.S.A. In 2002, the AVP Pro-Beach Volleyball tournament schedule included seven AVP Tour events. All seven of the AVP Tour events were for both men and women. The total prize money was at $1,000,000.00. Above photo, In-front of a large crowd, Mike Whitmarsh hits a set from Canyon Ceman, past the block of Dax Holdren, towards the defense of Eric Fonoimoana. Action took place during the championship match of the 2002 AVP event in Manhattan Beach California.

Photo Courtesy of Frank Goroszko

FIVB

The Men's FIVB 2002 World Tour of Beach Volleyball staged ten events. There were events in nine countries with a total purse of $3.3 million (split with the Women's 11 event FIVB World Tour). The Men's FIVB events were staged in Berlin Germany, Gstaad Switzerland, Stavanger Norway, Montreal Canada, Marseille France, Espinho Portugal, Klagenfurt Austria, Cadiz Spain, Mallorca Spain and Fortaleza Brazil. The World Tour kicked off on June 5, 2002 in Madrid, Spain and concluded on November 26 at the Brazilian resort of Vitoria, branding this new Olympic sport as a truly global affair. This was the first year that the women's tour featured more events (11 events) and more prize money, than the men's tour (10 events).

The top team, on the 2002 FIVB Men's World Tour, was Jose Loiola and Ricardo Santos. They advanced to four "Gold-Medal" matches, winning three times, while earning over $100,000.00. Argentina's Martin Conde and Mariano Baracetti were the number two team on the 2002 FIVB Men's Tour. Conde and Baracetti advanced to three "Gold-Medal" matches, winning twice, while earning nearly $100,000.00. The Swiss team of Paul Laciga and Martin Laciga were in the third spot as they advanced to two "Gold-Medal" matches, winning both times, while earning over $80,000.00. Another Brazilian team was in the top four as Marcio Araujo and Benjamin Insfran advanced to three "Gold-Medal" matches, winning twice. There were three additional teams that each won one "Gold-Medal" on the 2002 FIVB Men's World Tour. The American team of Kevin Wong and Stein Metzger advanced to two "Gold-Medal" matches, winning once. Two additional Brazilian teams also won "Gold-Medals" they were Emanuel Rego with Tande Ramos and Rogerio Para with Harley Marques.

The level of 2002 events and the number of countries was maintained at the present level, with the International Volleyball Federation (FIVB), the sport's world governing body, opting in the coming year to invest more in the promotion of this popular sport of the 21st century, such as state of the art television and new-media production. Included in the FIVB plans were the

JOSE LOIOLA & RICARDO SANTOS
The top team, on the 2002 FIVB Men's World Tour, was Jose Loiola and Ricardo Santos. They advanced to four "Gold-Medal" matches, winning three times, while earning over $100,000.00. In the above photo, Loiola hits a set from Ricardo, past the block of Argentina's Mariano Baracetti. Baracetti was teamed-up with compatriot Martin Conde to earn the second spot on the 2002 FIVB World Tour. Conde and Baracetti advanced to three "Gold-Medal" Matches, winning twice, while earning nearly $100,000.00. .
Photo Courtesy of the FIVB

launching of two annual world championship events, one for the under-21 age group and another for under-18 years. The 2002 season featured two Grand Slam World Tour Events at Marseilles, France and Klagenfurt, Austria, with $200,000.00 in prize money for both men and women. Another incentive feature of the Grand Slams was the higher-ranking points for teams.

2002 Men's World Tour Calendar:

Berlin Germany June 13th-16th
Gstaad Switzerland June 19th-23rd
Stavanger Norway July 3rd-7th
Montreal Canada July 10th-14th
Marseille France July 17th-21st
Espinho Portugal July 24th-28th
Klagenfurt Austria July 31st-August 4th
Cadice Spain August 7th-11th
Mallorca Spain September 4th-8th
Fortaleza Brazil October 29th-November 3rd

2002 INDIVIDUAL FIVB TOURNAMENT FINISHES

Player	1st	2nd	3rd	4th	5th
Jorg Ahmann	0	0	0	0	2
Franco Alvarez	0	1	0	0	2
Marcio Araujo	1	3	1	1	1
Mariano Baracetti	1	1	1	2	1
Bjorn Berg	0	0	0	0	1
Javier Bosma	0	0	0	0	1
John Child	0	0	0	2	2
Martin Alejo Conde	1	1	1	2	1
Antonio Contrino	0	0	0	0	1
Simon Dahl	0	0	0	0	1
Juca Dultra	0	0	0	1	0
Markus Diechmann	0	0	1	0	1
Markus Egger	0	1	0	0	1
Axel Hager	0	0	0	0	2
Mark Heese	0	0	0	2	2
Sascha Heyer	0	1	0	0	1
Patrick Heuscher	0	0	1	0	0
Jody Holden	0	1	0	0	2
Vegard Hoidalen	0	0	1	0	1
Iver Horrem	0	0	0	0	2
Benjamin Insfran	1	3	1	1	1
Jorre Kiemperud	0	0	1	0	1
Stefan Kobel	0	0	1	0	0
Richard de Kogel	0	0	0	0	1
Martin Laciga	**2**	**0**	**0**	**0**	**1**
Paul Laciga	**2**	**0**	**0**	**0**	**1**
Conrad Leinemann	0	1	0	0	2
Jose Loiola	**2**	**1**	**0**	**0**	**0**
Roberto Lopes	0	0	0	1	0
Bjorn Maaseide	0	0	0	0	2
Harley Marques	1	0	0	2	2
Stein Metzger	1	1	1	0	1
Paulao Moreira	0	0	0	0	1
Sander Mulder	0	0	0	0	1
Jose Franco Vieira Neto	0	0	0	1	0
Maurizio Pimponi	0	0	0	0	1
Julien Prosser	0	0	0	0	3
Alexandre Tande Ramos	1	0	2	0	1
Andrea Raffaelli	0	0	0	0	1
Jonas Reckermann	0	0	1	0	1
Todd Rogers	0	0	0	0	1
Miguel Rosell	0	1	0	0	2
Ricardo Alex Costa Santos	**2**	**1**	**2**	**0**	**0**
Andrew Schachi	0	0	0	0	2
Emanuel Rego Scheffer	1	0	4	0	1
Paulo Emilo Silva	0	0	0	0	1
Josh Slack	0	0	0	0	2
Sean Scott	0	0	0	0	1
Rogrio "Para" de Souza	1	0	0	2	2
Kevin Wong	1	1	1	0	1
Lee Zahner	0	0	0	0	3

MARKUS EGGER & SASCHER HEYER
Norwegiens, Markus Egger and Sascha Heyer provided plenty of beach volleyball competition on the 2002 FIVB World Tour. Egger and Heyer advanced to the "Gold-Medal" match of the FIVB event staged in Klagenfurt Austria, where they finished in 2nd place. Above Left Photo, Egger attacking the ball. Above Right Photo, Heyer makes an all-out effort to make the dig.
Photos Courtesy of "Couvi"

MEN'S TOURNAMENT RESULTS
2002-AVP

HUNTINGTON BEACH CALIFORNIA
May 24th-26th, 2002

The 2002 AVP $62,500.00 Michelob Light Huntington Beach Men's Open, was staged on the south side of the Pier in Huntington Beach California. The tournament format for this event as well as the remainder of events, was double elimination, rally-scoring, two-games to 21, win-by-two-points, no cap with a third game tie-breaker to 15 points, if necessary. The event was won by the third-seeded team of Dax Holdren and Eric Fonoimoana. In the 49 minute championship match they downed the fourth-seeded team of Canyon Ceman and Mike Whitmarsh by a scores of 21-18 and 21-14. The winner's earned $14,500.00 while the runner-ups collected $9,750.00.

3rd Place: Stein Metzger and Kevin Wong
3rd Place: Brent Doble and Karch Kiraly
5th Place: Todd Rogers and Sean Scott
5th Place: Scott Ayakatubby and Brian Lewis

HERMOSA BEACH CALIFORNIA
June 7th-9th, 2002

The AVP 2002 Hermosa Beach Men's Open, presented by Michelob Light as part of the fourth annual Mervyn's Beach Bash, in Hermosa Beach California, was won by the surprising team of Albert Hannemann and Jeff Nygard. In the championship match Hannemann and Nygard upset the top seeded duo of Stein Metzger and Kevin Wong in an intense 100 minute final to pick up their first AVP tour victory. In the hotly contested match, they out-lasted Metzger and Wong 18-21, 29-27 and 27-25, with 17 lead changes in the final game. After Hannemann and Nygard got their first lead at 10-9 neither team ever had more than a one-point advantage. Hannemann and Nygard had their first match point at 14-13, and then had to stave off three match points by their opponents before getting another opportunity at 18-17. Failing to convert, Metzger and Wong had six chances to win the match, but couldn't convert. Battling back,

HERMOSA BEACH CALIFORNIA
The championship match of the 2002 AVP Tour event in Hermosa Beach CA was played before a packed-house. Abovr photo, During the final, Kevin Wong is ready at the at the net as Stein Metzger serves to Jeff Nygard (left) and Albert Hannemann (right).
Photo Courtesy of Frank Goroszko

ALBERT HANNEMANN
Albert Hanneman teamed-up with Jeff Nygard as they both captured their first championship victories on the AVP Tour. Above photo, Albert Hannemann follows through after spiking the ball towards the defense of Stein Metzger.
Photo Courtesy of Frank Goroszko

2002 MEN'S AVP TOUR BEACH VOLLEYBALL ACTION

TOP PHOTO: Brent Doble hits a set from Karch Kiraly, past the block of Eric Fonoimoana, towards the defense of Dax Holdren. Action took place during the 2002 AVP Tour stop in Hermosa Beach CA. **BOTTOM PHOTO:** Brian Lewis hits a set from Scott Ayakatubby. into the block of Dax Holdren. Eric Fonoimoana is ready on defense. Action took place during the 2002 AVP Tour stop in Huntington Beach CA. Holdren and Fonoimoan were the eventual winner's of the tournament.

Photos Courtesy of "Couvi"

2002 MEN'S BEACH VOLLEYBALL ACTION-HERMOSA BEACH CALIFORNIA

TOP LEFT PHOTO: Todd Rogers spikes the ball into the block of Scott Ayakatubby, while Brian Lewis is ready on defense. **TOP RIGHT PHOTO:** Lee LeGrande makes the difficult "Chester" dig. **BOTTOM LEFT PHOTO:** Scott Ayakatubby hits a set from Brian Lewis, past the block of Jeff Nygard, towards the defense of Albert Hannemann. **BOTTOM RIGHT PHOTO:** Brent Doble hits a set from Karch Kiraly, towards the block of Eric Fonoimoana. All of the above actio took place at the 2002 AVP Tour event staged in Hermosa Beach CA.

Photos Courtesy of "Couvi"

Hannemann and Nygard finally closed out the championship point on their fourth opportunity at 26-25. The winner's split the $17,400.00 first place check and the runner-ups shared $11,700.00. Earlier in the tournament, a quad injury to Brian Lewis in game two, against Hannemann and Nygard ended Brian Lewis and Scott Ayakutubby's semi-final match. Lewis and Ayakutubby had won game one and were leading game two when the injury occurred.
3rd Place: Eduardo Bacil and Fred Souza
3rd Place: Brian Lewis and Scott Ayakutubby
5th Place: Eric Fonoimoana and Dax Holdren,
5th Place: Brent Doble and Karch Kiraly

SANTA BARBARA CALIFORNIA
June 14th-16th, 2002

The 2002 AVP $62,500.00 Michelob Light Santa Barbara Men's Open, presented by Paul Mitchell, was staged on East Beach in Santa Barbara California. The event was won by the fifth-seeded team of Brent Doble and Karch Kiraly. This win was the 143rd career leading championship victory for Karch Kiraly. In the nearly one hour championship match they downed the second-seeded team of Eric Fonoimoana and Dax Holdren, by the scores of 21-12 and 21-18. The winner's earned $14,500.00 while the runner-ups collected $9,750.00.
3rd Place: Eduardo Bacil and Fred Souza
3rd Place: Mike Lambert and Lee LeGrande
5th Place: Stein Metzger and Kevin Wong
5th Place: Adam Jewell and Collin Smith

BELMAR NEW JERSEY
June 28th-30th, 2002

The pattern remained the same at the $62,500.00 AVP 2002 Belmar Men's Open, as the fourth different AVP team was crowned. In the championship match Sixth-seeded Canyon Ceman and Mike Whitmarsh won their third AVP Belmar Open title together by upsetting top-seeded Eric Fonoimoana and Dax Holdren 21-18 and 21-16 in the 50-minute men's final. The winner's shared $14,500.00, while the runner-ups split $9,750.00. Whitmarsh, who tied Kent Steffes' record of five titles on this Jersey Beach, and Ceman had now posted a 16-5 mark for the season while Fonoimoana and Holdren were 23-5, including 20-4 on the AVP Tour. This title was the 28th of Whitmarsh's pro beach career. Ceman

KARCH KIRALY
Karch Kiraly teamed-up with Brent Doble to capture his 143rd career championship victory at the 2002 Santa Brabara AVP Tour event. Above photo, Karch utilizes his perfect passing technique while passing the ball during a 2002 AVP Tour event.
Photo Courtesy of Frank Goroszko

ERIC FONOIMOANA
Eric Fonoimoana teamed-up with Dax Holdren for the best record on the 2002 AVP Tour. They advanced to the finals of 6 events, winning 4 events. Above photo, Fonoimoana is in position to make a nice overhand dig.
Photo Courtesy of Frank Goroszko

claimed his sixth overall event title and third with Whitmarsh.
3rd Place: Stein Metzger and Kevin Wong
3rd Place: Brent Doble and Karch Kiraly
5th Place: Mike Lambert and Lee LeGrande
5th Place: Scott Davenport and Eli Fairfield

MANHATTAN BEACH CALIFORNIA
August 8th-11th, 2002

Manhattan Beach, California was the place to be for the fifth stop on the 2002 Michelob Light AVP Tour. During the championship match, an estimated 6,000 people filled the stands, lined the pier and crowded the bike path to take in Eric Fonoimoana and Dax Holdren's finals victory over Mike Whitmarsh and Canyon Ceman. This victory allowed Fonoimoana and Holdren's names to be place on the Manhattan Beach Pier's "Beach Volleyball Walk of Fame." Their names were placed in the company of beach volleyball legends such as Mike O'Hara, Ron Von Hagen, Sinjin Smith, Mike Dodd and Karch Kiraly (Just to name a few). The top-seeded Fonoimoana and Holdren became the first two-time winner on the 2002 Association of Volleyball Professionals Tour by defeating fourth-seeded Ceman and Whitmarsh 21-15 and 21-18, in 60 minutes, claiming the $20,000.00 first-place prize. The men's final was televised "live" by NBC. This title was the second for the Fonoimoana and Holdren partnership.

Ceman and Whitmarsh shared $14,000.00 for second-place finish.
3rd Place: Brent Doble and Karch Kiraly
3rd Place: Eduardo Bacil and Fred Souza
5th Place: Todd Rogers and Sean Scott
5th Place: Paul Baxter and Alika Williams

CHICAGO ILLINOIS
August 23rd-25th, 2002

The top seeded team of Eric Fonoimoana and Dax Holdren defeated Eduardo Bacil and Frederico Souza of Brazil 21-18 and 21-16 to win the Nissan U.S. Championships of Beach Volleyball presented by Xbox before a standing room only crowd on North Avenue Beach in Chicago Illinois. After a season of relative parity on the 2002 AVP Tour, Fonoimoana and Holdren, clearly become the dominate men's team on the beach, picking up their second consecutive victory and third overall on the 2002 AVP Tour. They were the only men's team this season to win more than one event. They have also been in the "Final-Four" in five of six events in 2002. Finishing tied for third was the fourth ranked team of Mike Whitmarsh and Canyon Ceman. Carl Henkel and Casey Jennings, the 16th ranked team, also picked up a third. For Jennings, it was his first appearance ever in a "Final-Four" match.
3rd Place: Mike Lambert and Lee LeGrande
3rd Place: Carl Henkel and Casey Jennings
5th Place: Canyon Ceman and Mike Whitmarsh
5th Place: Sean Scott and Todd Rogers

ERIC FONOIMOANA & DAX HOLDREN
Eric Fonoimoana and Dax Holdren claimed a "Bronze-Plaque" on the Manhattan Beach Pier, with their championship victory over Canyon Ceman and Mike Whitmarsh, at the 2002 Manhattan Beach Men's Open. Above photo, Dax Holdren hits a set from Eric Fonoimoana directly into the huge block of Mike Whitmarsh. Canyon Ceman is on defense. Action took place, on the south-side of the Manhattan Beach Pier, during the finals of the 2002 Manhattan Beach Men's Open.

Photo Courtesy of "Couvi"

2002 MEN'S BEACH VOLLEYBALL ACTION-MANHATTAN BEACH CALIFORNIA
TOP LEFT PHOTO: Eric Fonoimoana attacking the block of Mike Whitmarsh. **TOP RIGHT PHOTO:** Scott Ayakatubby slices the ball past the block of Carl Henkel. **BOTTOM PHOTO:** Canyon Ceman hits a set from Mike Whitmarsh, towards the block of Dax Holdren. Eric Fonoimoana is on defense. All of the above action took place on the south-side of the Manhattan Beach Pier, during the 2002 Manhattan Beach Men's Open..

Photos Courtesy of "Couvi"

LAS VEGAS NEVADA
September 5th-7th, 2002

The AVP Tour made its seventh and final stop, on the 2002 schedule, at the Hard Rock Hotel & Casino under the lights in a single-elimination format competition. The top eight ranked men's and women's teams competed in the Paul Mitchell AVP Shoot Out. The top-seeded team of Eric Fonoimoana and Dax Holdren proved that their top ranking was legitimate by winning the $150,000.00 (men and women) AVP Paul Mitchell Shootout. In the championship match, Fonoimoana and Holdren captured their fourth title this season by beating second-seeded Canyon Ceman and Mike Whitmarsh 26-24 and 21-18 in the 52-minute match. Fonoimoana and Holdren shared the $30,000.00 first-place prize while Ceman and Whitmarsh split $15,000.00. Fonoimoana and Holdren, who won four of five matches against Ceman and Whitmarsh this season, also became the first AVP Tour team to win four titles in a season since 1999 when Adam Johnson and Karch Kiraly captured four crowns together. Fonoimoana and Holdren also became the first team to win three-straight AVP titles since Johnson and Kiraly accomplished the feat near the end of the 1998 season. Kiraly also became the first $3-million winner during this event when he reached $3,001,258.00 with his third place finish.

This event also staged a "novelty-match" when beach volleyball legends, Matt Gage and Jim Menges won the Paul Mitchell AVP Shoot Out "Battle of the Sexes" by defeating McPeak and Youngs 17-21, 21-19 and 15-10 in the 60-minute exhibition on the Hard Rock sand. Menges, winner of 46 career tournament titles, and Gage, who captured 26 open tournament crowns, last played competitively in 1982 when they won three tournaments. Gage and Menges were both over the age of 50 during "Battle of the Sexes" match.

3rd Place: Brent Doble and Karch Kiraly
3rd Place: Mike Lambert and Lee LeGrande
5th Place: Eduardo Bacil and Fred Souza
5th Place: Stein Metzger and Kevin Wong
5th Place: Todd Rogers and Sean Scott
5th Place: Albert Hannemann and Jeff Nygard

2002 LAS VEGAS "SHOOT OUT"
At the Hard Rock Hotel & Casino, under the lights, the top eight ranked teams competed in the Paul Mitchell AVP Shoot Out. Above photo, Under the lights Kevin Wong hits a set from Stein Metzger, over the block of Brent Doble. Karch Kiraly is on defense.
Photo Courtesy of "Couvi"

KARCH KIRALY
Karch Kiraly became beach volleyball's first $3 million dollar winner when he placed third, with Brent Doble, at the 2002 Las Vegas Shoot Out. Above photo, Kiraly accepts the check from AVP CEO Leonard Armato.
Photo Courtesy of "Couvi"

2002 MEN'S BEACH VOLLEYBALL ACTION

TOP LEFT PHOTO: An unidentified AVP fan shows his approval of the action. **TOP RIGHT PHOTO:** AVP qualifier Mike "Bud" Wilkinson enjoying the action during the finals an AVP event. **MIDDLE LEFT PHOTO:** The Laker-Girls leading the AVP fans to a thunderous noise level. **MIDDLE RIGHT PHOTO:** Hecklers Mike "Barney" Ferris and Joe Rumsey doing what they do best. **BOTTOM LEFT PHOTO:** Mike Lambert singing the "AVP Song" **BOTTOM RIGHT PHOTO:** AVP fans Mike Igalo and Texas Steve Simpson enjoying the action at an AVP event.

Photo's Courtesy of "Couvi"

MEN'S TOURNAMENT RESULTS
2002-FIVB

BERLIN GERMANY
June 12th-16th, 2002

More than 1,500 tons of sand were brought to Berlin, Germany's Capitol, to set up the Center Court on Alexanderplatz, "Alex" as it is popularly known, one of the biggest squares in the city. Some 31,000 spectator supported the World's best Beach Volleyball players in the arena despite tough weather conditions during the week with rain and chilly temperatures. Downtown Berlin was treated to an all South American final at the $150,000.00 Berlin Open, the first stop of the 2002 FIVB Men's World Tour, when Brazilians Harley Marques and Rogerio Para stole the show and the "Gold-Medal" by defeating Argentinean World Champions Mariano Baracetti and Martin Conde, in an exciting final. In the championship match, Para and Harley won in three nerve-racking games 25-23, 19-21, 15-10, to collect the $22,500.00 first place prize. This was only their second international tournament together. Both teams treated the crowd with an array of hard spikes and impressive jump serves. Brazil's Harley won the "Player of the Tournament" award. In the "Bronze-Medal" match, the German team of Markus Dieckmann and Jonas Reckermann conquered the Canadian team of John Child and Mark Heese to win an exhilarating match. The German's rallied to win the three game match with hard serving and great blocking, by the scores of 21-12, 18-21 and 15-13. This Berlin Open featured 63 teams from 37 countries and also produced some surprises and jubilation for the German fans.

3rd Place: Markus Dieckmann and Jonas Reckermann-Germany
4th Place: John Child and Mark Heese-Canada
5th Place: Julien Prosser and Lee Zahner-Australia
5th Place: Francisco Alvarez and Juan Rosell-Cuba
5th Place: Maurizio Pimponi and Andrea Raffaelli-Italy
5th Place: Martin Laciga and Paul Laciga-Switzerland

GSTAAD SWITZERLAND
June 19th-23rd, 2002

Argentinean World Champions Mono Baracetti and Martin Conde swept to victory at the $150,000.00 FIVB 200 Swiss Open, staged in the Swiss alpine resort of Gstaad Switzerland. In the "Gold-Medal" match, the Argentine's defeated the Brazilian team of Marcio Araujo and Benjamin Insfran, in two straight games, by the scores of 21-14 and 21-15. The winner's collected $22,500.00 for their efforts. The American team of Kevin Wong and Stein Metzger won the "Bronze-Medal" when they beat Roberto Lopes-Franco Neto of Brazil, in two games 21-18 and 21-14.

3rd Place: Stein Metzger and Kevin Wong-USA.
4th Place: Roberto Lopes and Franco Neto-Brazil
5th Place: Tande Ramos and Emanuel Rego-Brazil
5th Place: Julien Prosser and Lee Zahner-Australia
5th Place: John Child and Mark Heese-Canada
5th Place: Markus Egger and Sascha Heyer-Switzerland

HARLEY MARQUES
Brazilian Harley Marques teamed-up with compatriot Rogerio Para de Souza to win the first stop, on the 2002 Men's FIVB World Tour, in Berlin Germany. Above photo Marques throws his body while making an all-out effort to dig the ball.
Photo Courtesy of "Couvi"

KEVIN WONG & STEIN METZGER
Kevin Wong and Stein Metzger teamed-up on the 2002 Men's FIVB World Tour. They advanced to the "Gold-Medal" match of two events, winning Espinho Portugal event. Above photo, Wong (left) and Metzger are ready for action.
Photo Courtesy of "Couvi"

STAVANGER NORWAY
July 3rd-7th, 2002

The beach volleyball fans, in the packed stadium, at the Men's 2002 FIVB $150,000.00 Norway Open, on the docks of Norway's fourth largest city, Stavanger, were treated to an all-Brazilian final when last year's top-ranked team of Emanuel Rego and Tande Ramos, stopped compatriots Ricardo Santos and Jose Loiola in the final of this FIVB World Tour event. More than 80,000 spectators came to watch over the six days of the competition. In the over one-hour "Gold-Medal" match, Emanuel and Tande, needed five match points to finish off the match. The first game was tight at 22-20, then Ricardo and Loiola tied the match a game each, taking the second game 21-18 In the final game Emanuel and Tande outlasted Ricardo and Loiola 19-17. The "Bronze-Medal match went to Swiss team Patrick Heuscher and Stefan Kobel after Brazilians Para and Harley withdrew and forfeited the match. Para suffered heart rhythm problems and indicated that he had to quit half way through the first set. He received some medical treatment and was told to relax.

3rd Place: Patrick Heuscher and Stefan Kobel-Switzerland
4th Place: Harley Marques and Rogerio Para-Brazil
5th Place: Vegard Hoidalen and Jorre Kjemperud-Norway
5th Place: Markus Dieckmann and Jonas Reckermann-Germany
5th Place: Jorg Ahmann and Axel Hager-Germany
5th Place: Andrew Schacht and Josh Slack-Australia

MARSEILLE FRANCE
July 17th-21st, 2002

The Plage du Prado in Marseille France was the site for the Men's FIVB $200,000.00 French Grand Slam. This was the first Grand Slam stop on the 2002 FIVB Beach Volleyball World Tour. During the championship match, French beach volleyball aficionados were treated to a Brazilian vs Cuban final, between Ricardo Santos with Jose Loiola and Francisco Alvarez with Miguel Rosell. The spirit of the Brazilian Salsa triumphed over the passion of the Cuban Samba in an exciting and fervent final, where Ricardo and Loiola pulled off the game victory 19-21, 21-16 and 15-9 to capture the first Grand Slam title. The victors split $30,000.00 while the runner-ups shared $20,000.00. In the "Bronze-Medal" match, Brazilian's Emanuel Rego and Tande Ramos, won in two sets over the Argentine team of Mariano Baracetti and Martin Conde, 21-15 and 26-24.

3rd Place: Tande Ramos and Emanuel Rego-Brazil
4th Place: Mariano Baracetti and Martin Conde-Argentina
5th Place: Marcio Araujo and Benjamin Insfran-Brazil
5th Place: Harley Marques and Rogerio Para-Brazil
5th Place: Julien Prosser and Lee Zahner-Australia
5th Place: Stein Metzger and Kevin Wong-USA

JORRE KJEMPERUD & VEGARD HOIDALEN
Norwegians Jorre Kjemperud and Vegard Hoidalen provided some worthy competition on the 2002 Men's FIVB World Tour. Their best finish was a third in Klagenfurt Austria. Above photo, Hoidalen hits a set from Kjemperud at France's Stephane Canet.
Photo Courtesy of "Couvi"

JOSH SLACK & ANDREW SCHACHT
Australia's Josh Slack and Andrew Schacht managed a couple of top five finishes on the 2002 Men's FIVB World Tour. Above photo, Schacht hits a set from Slack, away from the block of American Brent Doble.
Photo Courtesy of "Couvi"

ESPINHO PORTUGAL
July 24th-28th, 2002

In-front of 5,000 enthusiastic spectators, the Men's 2002 FIVB $150,000.00 Portugal Open, on the Atlantic coast of Portugal on "Praia da Baia" beach in Espinho, was won by the American team of Kevin Wong and Stein Metzger. This was their second-ever major FIVB tournament career victory. In the "Gold-Medal" match, they out-lasted the Brazilian team of Marcio Araujo and Benjamin Insfran, in a three-set thriller, 17-21, 24-22 and 15-12,. The Brazilian's utilized strong serves for a fast start, winning the first game and lasting until the end of the second game, when after three tries at match-point they lost to the Americans. This was the first tournament victory for a Non-South-American team in the last fourteen FIVB events. The winner's split $22,500.00 and the second place team collected $15,000.00. Kevin Wong was named the "Speedo Player of the Tournament." In the "Bronze-Medal" match, defending Champions Ricardo Santos and Jose Loiola of Brazil, out-pointed Mariano Baracetti and Martin Conde of Argentina, 22-20 and 21-10.

3rd Place: Jose Loiola Ricardo Santos-Brazil.
4th Place: Mariano Baracetti and Martin Conde-Argentina
5th Place: John Child and Mark Heese-Canada
5th Place: Todd Rogers and Sean Scott-USA
5th Place: Andrew Schacht and Josh Slack-Australia
5th Place: Jody Holden and Conrad Leinemann-Canada

KLAGENFURT AUSTRIA
August 1st-4th, 2002

Heavy rain showers in the morning did not thwart the spirit and enthusiasm of the thousands of beach volleyball fans that filled the stadium for the Men's 2002 FIVB $200,000.00 Austria Grand Slam, in Klagenfurt Austria. Their persistence was rewarded when skies cleared and the thermometer soared in the afternoon for the "Gold-Medal" match, won by the Brazilian team of Jose Loiola and Ricardo Santos. In the 47 minute action-packed championship match, they won in straight sets, 21-16 and 21-18 over the Swiss team of Markus Egger and Sascha Heyer. Appearing in the final was a career first for the Swiss team. The winner's of this Grand-Slam event won $30,000.00 while the runner-ups took home $20,000.00. In the "Bronze-Medal" match, the "Viking" duo of Jorre-Andre Kjemperud and Vegard Hoidalen took their second consecutive third place in Austria when they demolished Brazilians Marcio Araujo-Benjamin Insfran 21-18 and 21-14.

3rd Place: Vegard Hoidalen and Jorre Kjemperud-Norway
4th Place: Marcio Araujo and Benjamin Insfran-Brazil
5th Place: John Child and Mark Heese-Canada
5th Place: Nikolas Berger and Clemens Doppler-Austria
5th Place: Roberto Lopes and Franco Neto-Brazil
5th Place: Iver Horrem and Bjorn Maaseide-Norway

CADIZ SPAIN
August 7th-11th, 2002

In-front of more than 3,000 enthusiastic beach volleyball fans, the Swiss team Paul and Martin Laciga, seized the "Gold-Medal" at the Men's 2002 FIVB $150,000.00 Spain Open. The event was staged on "La Victoria" beach in Cadiz Spain, In the championship match, they out-played Canadian's Jody Holden and Conrad Leinemann, in an outstanding final, 21-18 and 21-17. The winner's collected $22,500.00 and the runner-ups took home $15,000.00. Paul Laciga was named Speedo player of the tournament. In the third-place match, Brazil's Emanuel Rego and Tande Ramos grabbed the "Bronze-Medal" by defeating Marciano Baracetti and Martin Conde of Argentina in two sets 21-17 and 21-18.

3rd Place: Tande Ramos and Emanuel Rego-Brazil
4th Place: Mariano Baracetti and Martin Conde-Argentina
5th Place: John Child and Mark Heese-Canada
5th Place: Francisco Alvarez and Juan Rosell-Cuba
5th Place: Iver Horrem and Bjorn Maaseide-Norway
5th Place: Richard de Kogel and Sander Mulder-Netherlands

MALLORCA SPAIN
September 4th-8th, 2002

In Palmade Mallorca Spain, on the island that has even seduced the King of Spain, the largest of the Balearic Islands was the host to the top beach volleyball players on the FIVB World Tour. The 2002 FIVB Mallorca Open was captured by the Swiss brother duo of Paul and Martin Laciga. In the "Gold-Medal" match, on "Playa de Palma" they won a tough battle, over the Brazilian team of Marcio Araujo and Benjamin Insfran, 21-17 and 27-25. The winner's pocketed $22,500.00 while the runner-ups collected $15,000.00. The "Bronze-Medal" match was won by another Brazilian pair as Emanuel Rego and Ricardo Santos defeated compatriots Harley Marques and Rogerio Para, 21-15 and 24-22.

3rd Place: Emanuel Rego and Ricardo Santos-Brazil
4th Place: Harley Marques and Rogerio Para-Brazil
5th Place: Mariano Baracetti and Martin Conde-Argentina
5th Place: Jody Holden and Conrad Leinemann-Canada
5th Place: Javier Bosma and Antonio Cotrino-Spain
5th Place: Bjorn Berg and Simon Dahl-Sweden

VITORIA BRAZIL
October 1st-6th, 2002

Fortaleza, the capital of the Brazilian state Cearáá, on the eastern Brazilian coast, was the site of the 2002 FIVB Brazilian Open. In-front of a huge crowd, in a carnival-like atmosphere, the winner's were Marcio Araujo and Benjamin Insfran, from Brazil. In the nearly one-hour "Gold-Medal" match, they defeated the American team of Kevin Wong and Stein Metzger, 22-20 and 21-17. The winner's collected $22,500.00 and the second place team took home $15,000.00. In the "Bronze-Medal" match, Brazilians Emanuel Rego and Ricardo Santos were the winners over compatriots Jefferson Bellaguarda and Juca Dultra.

3rd Place: Emanuel Rego and Ricardo Santos-Brazil
4th Place: Jefferson Bellaguarda and Juca Dultra-Brazil
5th Place: Harley Marques and Rogerio Para-Brazil
5th Place: Iver Horrem and Bjorn Maaseide-Norway
5th Place: Jorg Ahmann and Axel Hager-Germany
5th Place: Paulao Moreira and Paulo Emilio Silva-Brazil

TOP PHOTOS: Left: Lee LeGrande follows-through after hitting the ball. **Center:** Canyon Ceman with a crowd pleasing dig. **Right:** George Roumain attacking the ball.

MIDDLE PHOTOS: Left: Dax Holdren attacking the ball. **Center:** Sean Rosenthal getting above the net for the block attempt. **Right:** Todd Rogers challenges the block of Scott Ayakatubby. Brian Lewis is on defense.

2002 MEN'S BEACH VOLLEYBALL ACTION

BOTTOM PHOTOS: Left: Brian Lewis doing what he does best, digging the ball. **Center:** Scotty Lane challenging the block of Mike Whitmarsh. **Right:** Eric Fonoimoana attacking the ball.

Photo's Courtesy of "Couvi"

WOMEN'S BEACH VOLLEYBALL
2002

AVP

By 2002, the BVA was out of business and the AVP was the only domestic professional beach volleyball circuit in operation for the top players in the U.S.A. On the 2002 Women's AVP Tour, Holly McPeak and Elaine Youngs teamed-up to advance to the championship match of all seven events. They won all but two of the events, while earning nearly $120,000.00 in prize money. Their wins came at Huntington Beach, Hermosa Beach, East Beach in Santa Barbara and Belmar Beach in New Jersey. The only other team to win a tournament on the 2002 Women's AVP Tour was Jenny Johnson Jordan and Annette Davis. They advanced to four championship matches, winning two events. Jordan and Davis won at the Manhattan Beach Women's Open and the event on North Beach in Chicago Illinois. They earned over $80,000.00 in prize money. The team of Dianne DeNecochea and Barbra Fontana were able to advance to three championship matches in 2002, but were unable to win a tournament.

2002 INDIVIDUAL AVP TOURNAMENT FINISHES

Player	1st	2nd	3rd	4th	5th
Angie Akers	0	0	0	0	3
Lisa Arce	0	0	3	0	4
Carrie Busch	0	0	5	0	1
Stephane Cox	0	0	0	0	1
Annette Buckner-Davis	2	2	3	0	0
Dianne DeNeochea	0	3	1	0	2
Katy Eldridge	0	0	0	0	2
Barbra Fontana	0	3	1	0	2
Linda Hanley	0	0	3	0	4
Jen Holdren	0	0	0	0	1
Jennifer Johnson Jordan	2	2	3	0	0
Nancy Mason	0	0	2	0	3
Holly McPeak	**5**	**2**	**0**	**0**	**0**
Leanne Schuster McSorley	0	0	5	0	1
Jen Meredith	0	0	0	0	2
Jen Pavley	0	0	0	0	3
Wendy Stammer	0	0	0	0	1
Rachel Wacholder	0	0	2	0	2
Elaine Youngs	**5**	**2**	**0**	**0**	**0**

ELAINE YOUNGS & HOLLY McPEAK
Elaine "EY" Youngs and Holly McPeak were the top team on the 2002 Women's AVP Tour. They advanced to 7 finals, winning 5 times. Above photo, EY hits a set from McPeak, over the block of Jenny Jordan, towards the defense of Annette Davis.
Photo Courtesy of "Couvi"

JENNY JORDAN & ANNETTE DAVIS
Jenny Jordan and Annette Davis were the number-two team on the 2002 Women's AVP Tour. They advanced to 4 finals, winning twice. Above photo, Jordan hits a set from Davis, towards the block of Dianne DeNecochea.
Photo Courtesy of "Couvi"

FIVB

The Women's FIVB 2002 World Tour of Beach Volleyball staged eleven events. There were events in ten countries with a total purse of $3.3 million (shared with the Men's FIVB World Tour). The Women's 2002 FIVB events were staged in Madrid Spain, Gstaad Switzerland, Stavanger Norway, Montreal Canada, Marseille France, Rhodes Greece, Klagenfurt Austria, Osaka Japan, Maoming China, Mallorca Spain and Vitoria Brazil.

The top team, on the 2002 FIVB Women's World Tour, was the American team of Kerri Walsh and Misty May. They advanced to eight "Gold-Medal" matches, winning five times, while earning nearly $200,000.00. American's Elaine Youngs and Holly McPeak were the number two team on the 2002 FIVB Women's Tour. Youngs and McPeak advanced to five "Gold-Medal" Matches, winning four times, while earning nearly $150,000.00. The Brazilian team of Shelda Bede and Adriana Behar was the third best team on the 2002 Women's FIVB World Tour. Bede and Behar advanced to five "Gold-Medal" matches, winning twice, while earning nearly $150,000.00. The Australian team of Kerri-Ann Pottharst and Natalie Cook was within the top four, as they advanced to two "Gold-Medal" matches, without a championship victory. There were not any additional teams that won a Women's FIVB World Tour championship in 2002.

Women's FIVB World Tour Schedule:

Madrid Spain June 5th-9th
Gstaad Switzerland June 18th-22nd
Stavanger Norway July 2nd-6th
Montreal Canada July 9th-13th
Marseille France July 16th-20th
Rohdes Greece July 24th-28th
Klagenfurt Austria July 30th-August 3rd
Osaka Japan August 7th-11th
Maoming China August 14th-18th
Mallorca Spain September 3rd-7th
Vitoria Brazil November 26th-December 1st

KERRI WALSH & MISTY MAY

Americans Kerri Walsh and Misty May were the top team on the Women's 2002 FIVB World Tour. They advanced to 8 "Gold-Medal" matches, winning 5 times. Above photo, May hits a set from Walsh, away from the block of Carrie Busch.
Photo Courtesy of "Couvi"

2002 INDIVIDUAL FIVB TOURNAMENT FINISHES

Player	1st	2nd	3rd	4th	5th
Leila Barros	0	0	0	0	6
Shelda Kelly Bruno Bede	2	3	1	3	1
Adriana Brando Behar	2	3	1	3	1
Laura Bruschini	0	0	0	0	1
Carrie Busch	0	0	0	0	3
Eva Celbova	0	0	0	1	2
Angela Clarke	0	0	0	0	2
Ana Paula Connolly	0	2	2	0	4
Natalie Cook	0	3	4	1	1
Dianne DeNecochea	0	0	0	0	2
Sonja Dosoudilova	0	0	0	1	2
Alexandra Fonseca	0	0	0	2	3
Barbra Fontana	0	0	0	0	2
Daniela Gattelli	0	0	0	0	4
Suzanne Glesnes	0	0	0	0	2
Tania Gooley	0	0	0	0	2
Rebbeka Kadijk	0	0	0	2	2
Vasso Karadassiou	0	0	1	0	2
Chiaki Kusuhara	0	0	0	1	0
Marrit Leenstra	0	0	0	2	2
Kathleen Maaseide	0	0	0	0	2
Misty May	**5**	**3**	**1**	**1**	**0**
Holly McPeak	4	1	2	0	1
Leanne Schuster McSorley	0	0	0	0	3
Tatiana Minello	0	2	2	0	4
Lucilla Perrotta	0	0	0	0	4
Sandra Tavares Pires	0	0	0	0	6
Stephane Pohl	0	0	0	0	2
Kerri Ann Pottharst	0	2	4	1	1
Okka Rau	0	0	0	0	2
Monica Rodrigues	0	0	0	2	3
Nicole Sanderson	0	0	0	0	1
Anna Maria Solazzi	0	0	0	0	1
Anette Huygens Tholen	0	0	0	0	1
Jia Tian	0	0	0	0	3
Ryo Tokuno	0	0	0	1	0
Kerri Walsh	**5**	**3**	**1**	**1**	**0**
Fei Wang	0	0	0	0	3
Linda Yanchulova	0	0	0	0	1
Petia Yanchulova	0	0	0	0	1
Elaine Youngs	4	1	2	0	1

WOMEN'S TOURNAMENT RESULTS
2002-AVP

HUNTINGTON BEACH CALIFORNIA
May 24-26th, 2002

The "new" partnership of Elaine Youngs and Holly McPeak paid immediate returns at the Pier in Huntington Beach California, as they won the 2002 AVP $62,500.00 Huntington Beach Women's Open, presented by Michelob Light. In the over one-hour championship match, they out-lasted Dianne DeNecochea and Barbra Fontana 21-18, 20-22 and 15-9. The winner's split $14,500.00 while the runner-ups shared $9,750.00. The television carrier was FOX Sports Net.

3rd Place: Lisa Arce and Linda Hanley
3rd Place: Annette Davis and Jenny Johnson Jordan
5th Place: Nancy Mason and Wendy Stammer
5th Place: Carrie Busch and Leanne Schuster McSorley

HERMOSA BEACH CALIFORNIA
June 7th-9th, 2002

The 2002 Women's AVP $75,000.00 Hermosa Beach Open, presented by Michelob Light at the Mervyn's Beach Bash, was won by the team of Holly McPeak and Elaine Youngs. They collected $17,400.00 for their efforts. In the championship match, in-front of a packed stadium, Youngs and McPeak easily defeated Dianne DeNecochea and Barbra Fontana, 21-15 and 21-14. The runner-ups shared $11,700.00.

3rd Place: Annette Davis and Jenny Johnson Jordan
3rd Place: Carrie Busch and Leanne McSorley
5th Place: Lisa Arce and Linda Hanley
5th Place: Katy Eldridge and Jennifer Meredith

SANTA BARBARA CALIFORNIA
June 14th-16th, 2002

East Beach, in Santa Barbara California, was the site of the 2002 Women's AVP $62,500.00 Michelob Light Santa Barbara Open, presented by Paul Mitchell. The event was won by the team of Holly McPeak and Elaine Youngs. They collected $14,500.00 for their efforts. In the championship match, in-front of a loyal beach volleyball crowd, Youngs and McPeak, for the third week in a row, defeated Dianne DeNecochea and Barbra Fontana. The runner-ups shared $9,750.00.

3rd Place: Annette Davis and Jenny Johnson Jordan
3rd Place: Carrie Busch and Leanne McSorley
5th Place: Lisa Arce and Linda Hanley
5th Place: Angie Akers and Jenny Pavley

BELMAR NEW JERSEY
June 28th-30th, 2002

New Jersey's Belmar Beach was the site of the annual Belmar Beach Bash, presented by Paul Mitchell. This 2002 Women's AVP $62,500.00 Belmar Open was won by Holly McPeak and Elaine Youngs as they captured their fourth-straight women''s domestic title. In the championship match, McPeak and Youngs scored a 16-21, 21-14 and 15-12 win in 60 minutes over third-seeded Annette Davis and Jenny Johnson Jordan. The championship team shared the $14,500.00 first-place prize. McPeak and Youngs extended their Association of Volleyball Professionals (AVP) Tour winning streak to

WOMEN'S AVP TOUR ACTION - HERMOSA BEACH CALIFORNIA
The 2002 Women's AVP Tour was staged in-front of large crowds at all of the venues. The 2002 Hermosa Beach event was no exception, as witnessed by the large crowd in the above photo. The event was won by the team of Holly McPeak and Elaine Youngs, when they defeated Dianne DeNecochea and Barbra Fontana, by the scores of 21-15 and 21-14. In the above photo, in-front of the large Hermosa Beach crowd, Youngs hits a set from McPeak, over the block of DeNecochea, towards the defense of Fontana.
Photo Courtesy of "Couvi"

20-straight matches with this win.
3rd Place: Carrie Busch and Leanne McSorley
3rd Place: Nancy Mason and Rachel Wacholder
5th Place: Lisa Arce and Linda Hanley
5th Place: Angie Akers and Jenny Pavley

MANHATTAN BEACH CALIFORNIA
August 8th-10th, 2002

The 2002 Women's AVP $87,500.00 Michelob Light Manhattan Beach Open, presented by Xbox, was won by the second-seeded team of Annette Davis and Jenny Johnson Jordan. In the nearly one-hour championship match, they surprised the top-seeded team of Holly McPeak and Elaine Youngs, 13-21, 23-21 and 15-9.
3rd Place: Carrie Busch and Leanne McSorley
3rd Place: Lisa Arce and Linda Hanley
5th Place: Dianne DeNecochea and Barbra Fontana
5th Place: Nancy Mason and Rachel Wacholder

CHICAGO ILLINOIS
August 22nd-24th, 2002

On North Beach, in Chicago Illinois, the 2002 Women's AVP $75,000.00 Nissan US Championships of Beach Volleyball, presented by Xbox, was won by the second-seeded team of Annette Davis and Jenny Johnson Jordan. In the over one-hour championship match, for the second week in a row, they surprised the top-seeded team of Holly McPeak and Elaine Youngs, 19-21, 21-16 and 18-16.
3rd Place: Carrie Busch and Leanne McSorley
3rd Place: Nancy Mason and Rachel Wacholder
5th Place: Lisa Arce and Linda Hanley
5th Place: Dianne DeNecochea and Barbra Fontana

LAS VEGAS NEVADA
September 5th-7th, 2002

The 2002 Women's $75,000.00 Paul Mitchell AVP Shootout, in Las Vegas, Nevada was staged on the parking lot of the Hard Rock Hotel and Casino. Under the lights, the top-seeded team Holly McPeak and Elaine Youngs validated their top ranking by winning the title. In the championship match, McPeak and Youngs avenged defeats in the past two Association of Volleyball Professionals (AVP) Tour events in Manhattan Beach, and Chicago, by defeating second-seeded Annette Davis and Jenny Johnson Jordan 21-15 and 21-11 in 41 minutes. McPeak and Youngs split the $30,000.00 winner''s check while Davis and Johnson Jordan shared $15,000.00. This final marked the fourth-straight event that the 2002 AVP Tour's top two teams played for the title as McPeak and Youngs defeated Davis and Johnson Jordan for the Belmar crown after losing the championship matches in the nationally-televised Manhattan Beach and Chicago events to Davis and Johnson Jordan. The final standings with prize money:
1. Holly McPeak and Elaine Youngs-$30,000.00
2. Annette Davis and Jenny Johnson Jordan-$15,000.00
3. Dianne DeNecochea and Barbra Fontana-$7,500.00
3. Lisa Arce and Linda Hanley-$7,500.00
5. Nancy Mason and Rachel Wacholder-$3,750.00
5. Katy Eldridge and Jennifer Meredith-$3,750.00
5. Angie Akers and Jenny Pavley-$3,750.00
5. Stephanie Cox and Jennifer Holdren-$3,750.00

ANGIE AKERS & JEN PAVLEY
Angie Akers and Jen Pavley played well enough to finish within the top five at three 2002 Women's AVP Tour events. Above photo, Akers (left) and Pavley (right) are both ready on defense to dig the hit by Jenny Jordan.

Photo Courtesy of "Couvi"

NANCY MASON & RACHEL WACHOLDER
Nancy Mason and Rachel Wacholder finished within the top three at two 2002 Women's AVP Tour events. In the above photo, Elaine Youngs hits a set from Holly McPeak, into the block of Nancy Mason. Wacholder is on defense.

Photo Courtesy of "Couvi"

WOMEN'S TOURNAMENT RESULTS
2002-FIVB

MADRID SPAIN
June 5th-9th, 2002

The 2002 Women's FIVB $150,000.00 Spain Open, in Madrid, the Spanish capital of Spain was won by the U.S. team of Misty May and Kerri Walsh. They shared the first place prize of $22,500.00. This was, the first event on the 2002 FIVB Women´s Beach Volleyball World Tour. The crowds streamed into the Casa de campo stadium complex to watch the "Gold-Medal" match as Walsh and May swooped to victory over Ana Paula Connelly and Tatiana Minello of Brazil. May and Walsh won in straight sets 23-21 and 21-14. During the match, the rangy Walsh played awesome defense as she dug seemingly impossible balls, providing the perfect complement for partner May´s agility on the court. The first game was a hard-fought battle with each team exchanging the lead back and forth, until May and Walsh took the victory and went on to a commanding lead early in the second game and went on to wrap up the final in just 35 minutes. The winner's shared $22,500.00 while the runner-ups split $15,000.00. The "Bronze-Medal" match was decided in a hard fight between Olympic Champions Kerri Pottharst and Natalie Cook and the Brazilian qualifiers Alexandra Fonseca and Monica Rodrigues. The veteran Aussies won the match with great shots and spectacular digs resulting in a 21-10 and 21-17 victory.

3rd Place: Natalie Cook and Kerri-Ann Pottharst-Australia
4th Place: Alexandra Fonseca and Monica Rodrigues-Brazil
5th Place: Daniela Gattelli and Lucilla Perrotta-Italy
5th Place: Eva Celbova and Sona Dosoudilova-Czech Republic
5th Place: Laura Bruschini and Anna-Maria Solazzi-Italy
5th Place: Stephanie Pohl and Okka Rau-Germany

GSTAAD SWITZERLAND
June 18th-22nd, 2002

With sizzling temperatures in the mountains of the Alps, the 2002 Women's FIVB $150,000.00 Swiss Open, in Gstaad Switzerland, was won by the American team of Misty May and Kerri Walsh. The hot summer temperatures combined with exciting crowds and the picturesque scenery of the Swiss Alps made for a great day of "Alpine Beach Volleyball." In the "Gold-Medal" match, Walsh and May won in straight sets against the

ANA PAULA CONNELLY
Brazilian Ana Paula Connelly paired-up with compatriot Tatiana Minello to advance to 2 "Gold-Medal" matches, on the 2002 Women's FIVB World Tour. They were the runner-ups twice. Above photo, Connelly challenges the block of Kerri Walsh, USA.
Photo Courtesy of "Couvi"

SANDRA PIRES
Brazilian Sandra Pires was teamed-up with compatriot Leila Barros on the 2002 Women's FIVB World Tour. They compiled 6 fifth place finishes. Above photo, Pires loses the "Joust" with American Kerri Walsh.
Photo Courtesy of "Couvi"

Brazilian team of Adriana Behar and Shelda Bede 21-17 and 21-17 as they confirmed in an impressive way, as to why they are the current holders of the Speedo "Gold-Tops" (worn by the top team on the Women's FIVB Tour). With their aggressive style of beach volleyball, Walsh and May lost only one game during the this competition in Gstaad. In the "Bronze-Medal" match, between Australians Kerri Pottharst and Natalie Cook, and Alexandra Fonseca and Monica Rodrigues of Brazil, the Aussies won in a hard fought match 21-19 and 21-15.

3rd Place: Natalie Cook and Kerri-Ann Pottharst-Australia
4th Place: Alexandra Fonseca and Monica Rodrigues-Brazil
5th Place: Ana Paula Connelly and Tatiana Minello-Brazil
5th Place: Holly McPeak and Elaine Youngs-USA
5th Place: Daniela Gattelli and Lucilla Perrotta-Italy
5th Place: Leila Barros and Sandra Pires-Brazil

STAVANGER NORWAY
July 2nd-6th, 2002

Despite the cool temperatures, there was a large excited crowd for the 2002 Women's FIVB $150,000 Norway Open, in Stavanger Norway. The event was won by Americans Holly McPeak and Elaine Youngs as they won the first women's title in this historic port city of Norway. In the "Gold-Medal" match, they marched to victory over Aussies Kerri Pottharst and Natalie Cook. McPeak and Youngs had to fight for three tough sets 21-17, 16-21 and 15-11, while gaining the victory. In the "Bronze-Medal" match between Brazilians Adriana Behar and Shelda Bede vs Americans Kerri Walsh and Misty May, the Brazilian's out-lasted the American's 11-21, 21-17 and 15-13.

3rd Place: Shelda Bede and Adriana Behar-Brazil
4th Place: Misty May and Kerri Walsh-USA
5th Place: Ana Paula Connelly and Tatiana Minello-Brazil
5th Place: Dianne DeNecochea and Barbra Fontana-USA
5th Place: Leila Barros and Sandra Pires-Brazil
5th Place: Angela Clarke and Tania Gooley-Australia

JIA TIAN & FEI WANG
China's Jia Tian and Fei Wang were able to collect three top five finishes on the 2002 Women's FIVB World Tour. Above photo, Wang hits a set from Tian.
Photo Courtesy of "Couvi"

MONTREAL CANADA
July 9th-13th, 2002

Organizers said some 14,000 were in the stadium during the finals of the 2002 Women's FIVB $150,000.00 Canadian Open, in Montreal Canada. This was the first time that the FIVB Beach Volleyball World Tour made an appearance in the Stade du Maurier in Montreal. Some 2,730 tons of sand were brought in to create the Center Court and six side courts, here where some of the world's tennis stars have played. During this event, a crowd of 30,000 spectators watched some 200 matches featuring 244 athletes from 27 countries. The event was won by Americans Kerri Walsh and Misty May when they outplayed the Brazilian team of Adriana Behar and Shelda Bede. In the action-packed "Gold-Medal" match, the young duo defeated the Brazilians, 21-18 and 25-23. Kerri Walsh for the second time this year was voted Speedo player of the tournament. In a hard-fought "Bronze-Medal" match, another American two-some, Holly McPeak and Elaine Youngs made fewer mistakes as they pulled off a victory over Australians Kerri Pottharst and Natalie Cook, 21-16, 20-22 and 15-12.

3rd Place: Holly McPeak and Elaine Youngs-USA
4th Place: Natalie Cook and Kerri-Ann Pottharst-Australia
5th Place: Ana Paula Connelly and Tatiana Minello-Brazil
5th Place: Daniela Gattelli and Lucilla Perrotta-Italy
5th Place: Annette Huygens Tholen and Nicole Sanderson-Australia
5th Place: Carrie Busch and Leanne McSorley-USA

MARSEILLE FRANCE
July 16th-20th, 2002

The 2002 Women's FIVB $200,000.00 French Grand Slam event in sunny Marseille France, was won by American's Holly McPeak and Elaine Youngs. In the all-American "Gold-Medal" match, they pulled no punches in their bid for gold as the duo powered their way to a 21-19 and 21-12 victory over compatriots Kerri Walsh and Misty May. In the "Bronze-Medal" match, Australian's Natalie Cook and Kerri Pottharst dismissed Brazilians Adriana Behar and Shelda Bede in two sets 21-13, 22-20.

3rd Place: Natalie Cook and Kerri-Ann Pottharst-Australia
4th Place: Shelda Bede and Adriana Behar-Brazil
5th Place: Ana Paula Connelly and Tatiana Minello-Brazil
5th Place: Leila Barros and Sandra Pires-Brazil
5th Place: Eva Celbova and Sona Dosoudilova-Czech Republic
5th Place: Suzanne Glesnes and Kathrine Maaseide-Norway

RHODES GREECE
July 24th-28th, 2002

The 2002 Women's FIVB $150,000.00 Hellas Open, in Rhodes Greece, was won by Americans Holly McPeak and Elaine Youngs. In the Championship match, they stole the "Gold-Medal" from Australian Olympic Champions Natalie Cook and Kerri Pottharst. The "Gold-Medal" match, staged on this popular Greek island resort was an explosive confrontation that included hard hitting from the Australians and incredible blocks from the American side of the net. In the "Bronze-Medal" match, two local heroes from Greece, Vasso 'Vicky' Karadassiou and Efi Syfri, defeated the team of Rebekka Kadijk and Merrit Leenstra, from the Netherlands. The Greek supporters filled the Stadium to the last seat, with more crowds waiting outside of the arena as well as on the top of some surrounding

buildings to get a glimpse of the Greek player as they defeated the Dutch team 21-17 and 25-23.
3rd Place: Vasso Karadassiou and Efi Sfyri-Greece
4th Place: Rebekka Kadijk and Marrit Leenstra-Netherlands
5th Place: Shelda Bede and Adriana Behar-Brazil
5th Place: Leila Barros and Sandra Pires-Brazil
5th Place: Alexandra Fonseca and Monica Rodrigues-Brazil
5th Place: Dianne DeNecochea and Barbra Fontana-USA

KLAGENFURT AUSTRIA
July 31st-August 3rd, 2002

The stands at the Center Court here in southern Austria were packed with some 8,000 ecstatic fans. They cheered and danced under hot summer temperatures during the 2002 Women's FIVB $200,000.00 Austria Grand Slam, in Klagenfurt Austria The event was won by Americans Kerri Walsh and Misty May, as they won their fourth World Tour title of the season and their first Grand Slam of the 2002 FIVB Beach Volleyball World Tour. In the "Gold-Medal" match, they pulled off a two set victory over Brazilian's Adriana Behar and Shelda Bede, 21-19 and 21-18 as Shelda was visibly handicapped by an injured ankle. In the battle for third place, the "Bronze-Medal" went to another US team as Holly McPeak and Elaine Youngs defeated Japan's Chiaki Kusuhara and Ryo Tokuno Japan 21-17 and 21-15.
3rd Place: Holly McPeak and Elaine Youngs-USA
4th Place: Chiaki Kusuhara and Ryo Tokuno-Japan
5th Place: Ana Paula Connelly and Tatiana Minello-Brazil
5th Place: Jia Tian and Fei Wang-China
5th Place: Carrie Busch and Leanne McSorley-USA
5th Place: Rebekka Kadijk and Marrit Leenstra-Netherlands

OSAKA JAPAN
August 7th-11th, 2002

Beach Volleyball was in the land of the rising sun for the 2002 Women's FIVB $150,000.00 Japan Open, in Osaka Japan. The event was won by the Brazilian team of Adriana Behar and Shelda Bruno Bede. In the all-Brazilian "Gold-Medal" match, they out-lasted compatriots Ana Paula and Tatiana Minello 21-17, 14-21 and 18-16. The "Bronze-Medal" match went to American's Kerri Walsh and Misty May who beat Marrit Leenstra and Rebekka Kadijk, of the Netherlands, 18-21, 21-12 and 15-8.
3rd Place: Misty May and Kerri Walsh-USA
4th Place: Rebekka Kadijk and Marrit Leenstra-Netherlands
5th Place: Leila Barros and Sandra Pires-Brazil
5th Place: Jia Tian and Fei Wang-China
5th Place: Vasso Karadassiou and Efi Sfyri-Greece
5th Place: Stephanie Pohl and Okka Rau-Germany

MAOMING CHINA
August 14th-18th, 2002

The 2002 Women's FIVB $150,000.00 China Open, in Maoming China, was won by Americans Kerri Walsh and Misty May as they captured their fifth "Gold-Medal" this year, by defeating compatriots Holly McPeak and Elaine Youngs. In the all-American "Gold-Medal" match, May and Walsh out-lasted Youngs and McPeak 13-21, 21-15 and 19-17. This was the third time in four FIVB Beach Volleyball World Tour meetings this season, that May and Walsh proved to be the top United States team on foreign sand, The holders of the Speedo "Gold-Tops" underlined once more that they were the uncontested number one pair this year. The championship match was a real thriller with spectacular rallies on both sides. In the first game, Walsh and May went down quickly, but then fought back in the second. In the tiebreaker they were tested to the limit as they won 19-17, after five match-point tries. The "Bronze-Medal" went to Australian's Natalie Cook and Kerri Pottharst who knocked out Brazilian's Adriana Behar and Shelda Bruno Bede 21-17 and 22-20.
3rd Place: Natalie Cook and Kerri-Ann Pottharst-Australia
4th Place: Shelda Bede and Adriana Behar-Brazil
5th Place: Jia Tian and Fei Wang-China
5th Place: Daniela Gattelli and Lucilla Perrotta-Italy
5th Place: Lina Yanchulova and Petia Yanchulova-Bulgaria
5th Place: Angela Clarke and Tania Gooley-Australia

MALLORCA SPAIN
September 3rd-7th, 2002

The Last European Beach stop of the season was in Spanish Mallorca for the 2002 Women's FIVB $150,000.00 Spanish Open, in Palma de Mallorca. The event was won by Brazilians Adriana Behar and Shelda Bruno Bede. In the "Gold-Medal" match, they out-pointed Americans Kerri Walsh and Misty May in an action packed match, 21-13, 17-21 and 16-14. The "Bronze-Medal" match went to another Brazilian pair when Ana Paula and Tatiana Minello knocked out Czech duo Eva Celbova and Sonia Dosoudilova 21-10 and 21-19.
3rd Place: Ana Paula Connelly and Tatiana Minello-Brazil
4th Place: Eva Celbova and Sona Dosoudilova-Czech Republic
5th Place: Rebekka Kadijk and Marrit Leenstra-Netherlands
5th Place: Alexandra Fonseca and Monica Rodrigues-Brazil
5th Place: Vasso Karadassiou and Efi Sfyri-Greece
5th Place: Carrie Busch and Leanne McSorley-USA

VITORIA BRAZIL
September 18th-22nd, 2002

The last Women's Beach stop of the 2002 season was the Women's FIVB $150,000.00 Brazil Open, in Vitoria Brazil. The winner's were Holly McPeak and Elaine Youngs, from the United States. In the all-American "Gold-Medal" match, McPeak and Youngs defeated compatriots and World Tour title winners Kerri Walsh and Misty May 21-13, 19-21 and 15-10. Both teams started the match tentatively as they each made uncharacteristic errors, but McPeak and Youngs were able to overcame the shaky start and win the first game. Walsh and May then fought back to win the second game, but lost their momentum in the third game, settling for the "Silver-Medal" The title here in Brazil earned McPeak and Youngs a fourth place on the 2002 FIVB World Ranking. The "Bronze-Medal" match was an all-Brazilian affair that went to Ana Paula Connelly and Tatiana Minello, when they out-scored compatriots Adriana Behar and Shelda Bruno Bede 21-17 and 21-18.
3rd Place: Ana Paula Connelly and Tatiana Minello-Brazil
4th Place: Shelda Bede and Adriana Behar-Brazil
5th Place: Natalie Cook and Kerri-Ann Pottharst-Australia
5th Place: Leila Barros and Sandra Pires-Brazil
5th Place: Alexandra Fonseca and Monica Rodrigues-Brazil
5th Place: Suzanne Glesnes and Kathrine Maaseide-Norway

TOP PHOTOS: Left: Leanne Schuster McSorley is ready to make the play on defense. **Center:** Fei Wang attacking with her jump serve. **Right:** Barbra Fontana chases-down the overset.

MIDDLE PHOTOS: Left: Lisa Arce follows-through after spiking the ball. **Center:** Misty May attacking the block of Linda Hanley. **Right:** Linda Hanley attacking the block of Elaine Youngs.

2002 WOMEN'S BEACH VOLLEYBALL ACTION

BOTTOM PHOTOS: Left: Liz Masakayan gets above the net for the block attempt. **Center:** Jenny Jordan reaches above the net for the pokie. **Right:** After attacking the ball, Holly McPeak coils with the follow-through.

Photo's Courtesy of "Couvi"

ADDITIONAL VOLLEYBALL INFORMATION
2002

BEACH VOLLEYBALL "SCREEN" GAMES

"DEAD OR ALIVE XTREME BEACH VOLLEYBALL"

Dead or Alive Xtreme Beach Volleyball, also known as DOAX Beach Volleyball, throws the hot girls from the Dead or Alive fighting series into skimpy bathing suits and has them battling it out in high-powered volleyball matches. Not just your standard volleyball game, Dead or Alive Xtreme Beach Volleyball requires you to make nice with your partner. You can even make your rival's partner fond of you so she'll be less aggressive on the court. For this end, the game features an extensive lineup of items that can be bought as gifts, from new bathing suits to accessories like sunglasses or even desserts. Also includes mini-game diversions, like pool hopping and casino games. For up to two players.

"BUMP! SET! SPIKE!"

Bump! Set! Spike! SEGA's Beach Spikers delivers intense beach volleyball action for up to four players and showcases beautiful female athletes as they battle it out under the fierce summer sun. Gamers' will have to cooperate and compete as they take control of bikini-clad beauties and go two-on-two at the net.

FIVB BEACH VOLLEYBALL WORLD CHAMPIONSHIPS

Nearly one hundred players form all over the world began their quest for excellence at the 2002 FIVB Under-18 Beach Volleyball World Championships, at the northern Peloponnese resort of Xylokastron. This was the first ever edition of this event, in which the FIVB has great aspirations for the development of the sport. The Main Draws of each of the two genders featured six pools of four teams. Pool play had the top two teams in each pool, plus the four best-ranked amongst the third placed teams advancing to the 16-team single elimination bracket.

SAN DIEGO CALIFORNIA
September 14th-15th, 2002

The Cal-King Volleyball Tour 2002 event in San Diego California was a "King of the Beach" tournament. The event was won by Mike Bruning. Bruning edged-out the runner-ups, "Pepe" Delahoz and Mike Desjardens who finished with an equal point total. Jeff Smith was in fourth place. The fifth place tie went to Said Souikane and LaVelle Carter.

THE WORLD-WIDE INTERNET
June 04, 2002

A new beach volleyball web-site: "Beach Volleyball Database" provided by Dennis "Dr. Ono" Wagner at http://www.bvbinfo.com/, became the source for all things beach volleyball (men's and women's). The front page provides database statistics, "Today in Beach Volleyball History," upcoming tournament information, and the latest news. The top of the page gives you several different ways to search the database, including players, tournaments, and seasons. Search results for players include name, country, home town, date of birth, and height. (not all information is available for all players.) Click on the name of the player and get a page of information on the player, including career summary and best finish. There are also photos provided by famed beach volleyball photographer Carl Schneider's "ShotFile" collection.

Also available on this site is a time-line of beach volleyball history provided from the book "Sands Of Time" The History of Beach Volleyball" at www.volleyballbooks.net, as well as tour news (via a drop-down menu at the top of the screen), and a list of player birthdays.

ASPEN COLORADO
September, 2002

The 2002 MotherLode tournament in Aspen Colorado was another fun-filled Labor-Day weekend of volleyball. The winner's of the men's open division were Skylar Davis (Irving TX) and Brian Soldano (Irving TX). In the championship match, they out-classed Bryan Gibson (Birmingham AL) and Keith Jones (Hendersonville TX) by the score of 15-6. There were 67 teams entered in this division.

3rd Place: Rob Baily (Annandale VA) and Jason Robertson (Reston VA)
4th Place: Justin Hersey (Denver CO) and Vince Robbins (Aurora CO)
5th Place: Adam Roberts and Gaston Macau (Myrtle Beach SC)
5th Place: Joe Stollings (Carrollton TX) and Dana Camacho (Ft Lauderdale)

The winner's of the women's open division were Angela Knopf (Fort Collins CO) and Krista Schwartzendruber (Thornton CO). In the championship match, they out-lasted Natalie Sime (Denver CO) and Dawn Tischauser (Denver CO) by the score of 18-16. There were 26 teams entered in this division.

3rd Place: Samantha Meador (Houston TX) and Julie McGann (Houston TX)
4th Place: Kelly Rowe (LA CA) and Catie Fleischer (LA CA)
5th Place: Shannon Williams (Dallas TX) and Yolanda Muññoz (Dallas TX)
5th Place: Erin Galli (San Diego CA) and Pat Keller (Cardiff CA)

MEN'S BEACH VOLLEYBALL
2003

AVP

The AVP 2003 tour schedule had expanded from seven tournaments in 2002 to ten and concluded with an Olympic qualifying AVP/FIVB event in September. The AVP/FIVB event was held at the newly constructed Home Depot Center in Carson, California. All ten AVP Tour "Nissan Series" Tournament stops featured men's and women's competition and offered more than $1 million in prize money. In 2003 there were five California events with the five additional events staged in five different states. Fort Lauderdale Florida, Tempe Arizona, Belmar New Jersey, Chicago Illinois and Las Vegas Nevada all staged one AVP Tour event. See tournament and event schedule below:

The top team on the 2003 Men's AVP Your was Dain Blanton and Jeff Nygard. They advanced to four championship matches, winning three of them. Their wins came at Mariners Point in San Diego CA, North Beach in Chicago and the AVP Shootout in Las Vegas Nevada. The six remaining AVP Tour events were won by six different teams. Eric Fonoimoana and Dax Holdren won the Fort Lauderdale event. Canyon Ceman and Mike Whitmarsh won in Tempe. Scott Ayakatubby and Brian Lewis won the Hermosa Beach Men's Open. Canton Larry Witt and Sean Rosenthal won the Belmar Beach Men's Open in New Jersey. Eric Fonoimoana and Kevin Wong won the prestigious Manhattan Beach Open. Karch Kiraly won his 144th career championship with Brent Doble at the 2003 Huntington Beach Men's Open. The AVP/FIVB event in Carson CA was won by the Brazilian team of Ricardo Santos and Emanuel Rego.

2003 AVP TOURNAMENT SCHEDULE

Fort Lauderdale, Florida	April 4-6	Cable TV
Tempe, Arizona	April 25-27	Cable TV
Hermosa Beach, California	June 6-8	Cable TV
San Diego, California	June 13-15	Cable TV
Belmar Beach, New Jersey	July 25-27	Cable TV
Manhattan Beach, California	August 7-10	LIVE NBC
Huntington Beach, California	August 14-17	LIVE NBC
Chicago, Illinois	August 28-31	LIVE NBC
Las Vegas, Nevada	September 4-6	Cable TV
Carson, California	September 19-21	Cable TV

DAIN BLANTON & JEFF NYGARD
Dain Blanton and Jeff Nygard earned the most tournament championships on the 2003 AVP Tour. They advanced to the championship match 4 times, winning 3 events. Above photo, Blanton hits a set from Nygard, during the 2003 Tempe AZ event.
Photo Courtesy of "Couvi"

SCOTT AYAKATUBBY & BRIAN LEWIS
Scott Ayakatubby and Brian Lewis were the top point earners on the 2003 Nissan AVP Tour. They advanced to 2 championship matches, winning the Hermosa Beach event. Above photo, Larry Witt challenges the block of Ayakatubby. Lewis is on defense.
Photo Courtesy of "Couvi"

2003 INDIVIDUAL AVP TOURNAMENT FINISHES

Player	1st	2nd	3rd	4th	5th
Scott Ayakatubby	1	1	3	0	2
Eduardo Bacil	0	1	0	0	0
Paul Baxter	0	0	1	0	0
Dain Blanton	**3**	**1**	**0**	**0**	**0**
Canyon Ceman	1	1	0	2	3
Brent Doble	1	0	2	0	5
Eric Fonoimoana	2	0	2	0	1
Jake Gibb	0	0	1	0	1
John Hayden	0	0	0	0	1
Carl Henkel	0	0	1	0	0
Dax Holdren	1	0	2	0	0
Casey Jennings	0	4	1	0	1
Adam Jewell	0	0	1	0	1
Karch Kiraly	1	0	2	0	5
Brian Lewis	1	1	3	0	2
Jose Loiola	0	1	0	0	0
Stein Metzger	0	0	1	0	3
Jeff Nygard	**3**	**1**	**0**	**0**	**0**
Jason Ring	0	0	1	0	0
Todd Rogers	0	1	2	0	2
Sean Rosenthal	1	0	2	0	1
Sean Scott	0	1	2	0	2
Mike Whitmarsh	1	1	2	0	3
Andy Witt	0	0	0	0	1
Larry Witt	1	0	2	0	1
Kevin Wong	1	0	1	0	4
Scott Wong	0	0	1	0	0

FIVB

The Men's FIVB 2003 World Tour of Beach Volleyball staged eleven events, including the XIV Pan American Games in Santo Domingo and four "Grand Slam" events as well as the World Championships. The World Championships, played on Copa Cabana in Rio de Janeiro Brazil, offered $800,000.00 in prize money. There were events in eleven countries with a total purse of $2,500,000.00. The FIVB events were staged in Rhodes Greece, Gstaad Switzerland, Berlin Germany, Stavanger Norway, Marseille France, Espinho Portugal, Klagenfurt Austria, Santo Domingo Dominican Republic, Mallorca Spain, Los Angeles California U.S.A. and Rio de Janeiro Brazil. FIVB events from January 2003 until July 2004 are part of the Olympic qualification process. Also groundbreaking agreement with the USA's Association of Volleyball Professionals (AVP), opened the way for a Grand Slam event in Los Angeles that was a season highlight. The FIVB calendar also include Challenger and Satellite events. The demand for Challenger and Satellite events was a sign of the growing popularity of beach volleyball in many countries. Challenger and Satellite tournaments are a perfect launching pad for up-and-coming players to gain international experience.

SEAN ROSENTHAL
Sean Rosenthal teamed-up with Larry Witt, for their first career championship, at the 2003 Belmar New Jersey AVP event. They also had three third place finishes. Above photo, Rosenthal challenging the block of Scott Ayakatubby.
Photo Courtesy of "Couvi"

RICARDO SANTOS & EMANUEL REGO
Brazilians Ricardo Santos & Emanuel Rego were the top team on the 2003 FIVB World Tour. They advanced to 5 "Gold-Medal" matches, winning all five. Above photo, Rego slices a set from Santos, away from the block of Switzerland's Sascha Heyer.
Photo Courtesy of "Couvi"

The top team, on the 2003 FIVB Men's World Tour, was Brazil's Emanuel Rego and Ricardo Santos. They advanced to five "Gold-Medal" matches, winning all five times, while earning nearly one quarter of a million dollars. Brazil's Marcio Araujo and Benjamin Insfran were the number two team on the 2003 FIVB Men's Tour. Araujo and Insfran advanced to four "Gold-Medal" Matches, winning three times, while earning nearly $180,000.00. There were four additional teams that won "Gold-Medals" on the 2003 FIVB World Tour, including the Swiss team of Stefan Kobel and Patrick Heuscher, American's Dain Blanton with Eric Fonoimoana, Brazilians Franco Neto and Harley Marques along with the Cuban team of Juan Rosell and Francisco Alvarez.

The Men's 2003 FIVB World Tour will be remembered for the success of a number of new combinations. The men's World Tour ranking winner was a new team. Brazil's Ricardo Alex Costa Santos and Emanuel Rego had only played two tournaments together in 2002 (collecting bronze on each occasion) before claiming five gold, including the World Championship and a bronze in 2003. Another new men's duo was Stein Metzger and Dax Holdren, from the USA, finished second to Ricardo and Emanuel at the men's World Championship. As a shorter team, Metzger and Holdren utilize quickness and ball control in order to play competitively. Ricardo and Emanuel crowned a magnificent first full season together by beating the American's in the final on a sun-drenched Copa Cabana Beach. It was particularly fitting for the Brazilians to finish off their excellent year in front of their own fans who lined up to watch their local favorites in action.

2003 INDIVIDUAL FIVB TOURNAMENT FINISHES

Player	1st	2nd	3rd	4th	5th
Franco Alvarez	1	0	0	0	1
Marcio Araujo	3	1	1	0	2
Mariano Baracetti	1	1	1	2	1
Jefferson Bellaguarda	0	0	0	1	0
Nikolas Berger	0	0	1	2	1
Dain Blanton	1	0	1	1	1
Pedro Brazao	0	0	0	0	1
Joao Brenha	0	0	0	1	0
Stephan Canet	0	0	0	0	1
Canyon Ceman	0	0	1	0	0
John Child	0	0	0	1	0
Martin Alejo Conde	0	2	1	0	1
Luizao Correa	0	1	0	0	0
Clemens Doppler	0	0	1	2	1
Christopher Diechmann	0	0	0	1	1
Markus Diechmann	0	2	0	1	3
Juca Dultra	0	0	0	1	0
Markus Egger	0	1	0	0	4
Eric Fonoimoana	0	0	0	0	1
David Fischer	0	0	0	1	0
Christian Garcia	0	0	0	0	1
Mathieu Hamel	0	0	0	0	1
Mark Heese	0	0	0	1	0
Ramon Hernandez	0	0	1	0	0
Thomas Hernandez	0	0	0	0	1
Patrick Heuscher	0	0	2	0	3
Sascha Heyer	0	1	0	0	4
Jody Holden	0	1	0	0	3
Dax Holdren	0	1	0	0	2
Vegard Hoidalen	0	0	1	0	3
Juan Rodriguez Ibarra	0	0	0	0	1
Benjamin Insfran	3	1	1	0	2
Jorre Kjemperud	0	1	0	0	3
Stefan Kobel	0	0	2	0	3
Martin Laciga	0	1	0	0	8
Paul Laciga	0	1	0	0	8
Djordje Ljubieic	0	0	0	0	1
Luis Maia	0	0	0	1	1
Harley Marques	1	0	0	1	2
Jeovanny Medrano	0	0	0	0	1
Stein Metzger	0	2	0	0	2
Jose Franco Vieira Neto	0	0	0	1	2
Jeff Nygard	1	0	1	1	1
Raul Papaleo	0	0	1	0	0
Julien Prosser	0	0	1	0	0
Andrea Raffaelli	0	0	0	0	1
Jonas Reckermann	0	2	0	1	3
Todd Rogers	0	0	0	0	1
Miguel Rosell	0	1	0	0	2
Alejandro Salas	1	0	0	0	1
Ricardo Alex Costa Santos	5	0	1	0	2
Andrew Schacht	0	0	0	0	1
Emanuel Rego Scheffer	5	0	1	0	2
Andreas Scheuerpflug	0	0	0	1	1
Sean Scott	0	0	0	0	1
Paulo Emilo Silva	0	1	0	0	0
Josh Slack	0	0	0	0	1
Michael Slean	0	0	0	0	1
Fred Souza	0	0	0	0	1
Brad Torsone	0	0	0	1	0
Rafael Vargas	0	0	0	0	1
Jose Vieira	1	0	0	0	0
Mike Whitmarsh	0	0	1	0	0
Mark Williams	0	0	1	0	0
Kevin Wong	0	1	0	0	1

MARKUS EGGER & SASCHA HEYER
The Swiss team of Markus Egger and Sascha Heyer provided ample competition on the 2003 FIVB World Tour. They had a best finish of second place in Los Angeles CA. Above photo, Heyer hits a set from Egger, towards the block of Brazils Ricardo Santos.
Photo Courtesy of "Couvi"

MEN'S TOURNAMENT RESULTS
2003-AVP

FORT LAUDERDALE FLORIDA
April 4th-6th, 2003

The 2003 AVP "Nissan Series" $62,000.00 Men's tournament results, for the first event of the season saw Eric Fonoimoana and Dax Holdren split $14,500.00 for their first place finish at the Fort Lauderdale Men's Open. Matt Fuerbringer and Casey Jennings split $9,750.00 for their second place finish. In the championship match, Fonoimoana and partner Holdren held off Fuerbringer and Jennings 21-14, 26-28, 22-20. In this exciting AVP final, Fonoimoana captured his 12th title while Holdren secured his fifth. The men's finals lasted 84 minutes and saw 15 match points throughout the competition. Fonoimoana and Holdren notched their 21st straight match victory, with their last loss occurring June 30th, 2002.

3rd Place: Canyon Ceman and Mike Whitmarsh
3rd Place: Paul Baxter and Carl Henkel
5th Place: Brent Doble and Karch Kiraly
5th Place: Stein Metzger and Kevin Wong

TEMPE ARIZONA
April 25th-27th, 2003

The 2003 AVP "Nissan Series" $62,000.00 tournament results, for the second event of the season saw Mike Whitmarsh and Canyon Ceman split $14,500.00 for their first place finish at the Tempe Arizona Men's Open. Dain Blanton and Jeff Nygard split $9,750.00 for their second place finish. In the championship match, second seeded Canyon Ceman and Mike Whitmarsh held off thirteenth seeds Dain Blanton and Jeff Nygard by a score of 21-17, 18-21, 15-12. This was the first meeting between these two teams and the fourth AVP title for Ceman and Whitmarsh. With this victory, Mike Whitmarsh notched his 28th career title.

3rd Place: Scott Ayakatubby and Brian Lewis
3rd Place: Eric Fonoimoana and Dax Holdren
5th Place: Brent Doble and Karch Kiraly
5th Place: Stein Metzger and Kevin Wong

HERMOSA BEACH CALIFORNIA
June 6th-8th, 2003

The 2003 AVP "Nissan Series" $75,000.00 tournament in Hermosa Beach California, Presented By Bud Light at Target/Mervyn's Beach Bash, was won by the team of Scott Ayakatubby and Brian Lewis. In the championship match, they out-pointed Matt Fuerbringer and Casey Jennings. The winners shared $17,400.00, while the runner-ups split $11,700.00 for their efforts. An excited crowd witnessed a grueling men's finals. AVP vets Scott Ayakatubby and Brian Lewis won a hard-fought three game matche in front of a packed stadium near the

SCOTT AYAKATUBBY & BRIAN LEWIS

Scott "Ack" Ayakatubby and Brian "Lewey" Lewis stepped-up for a championship victory at the 2003 AVP event in Hermosa Beach CA. In the championship match, they out-lasted Casey Jennings and Matt Fuerbringer, by the scores of 21-18, 16-21 and 22-20. In the above photo, during a semi-final match, Ayakatubby slices a set from Lewis, away from the block of Brent Doble. Karch Kiraly is on the right, playing defense. Ack and Lewey won the match 21-15, 16-21 and 15-13.

Photo Courtesy of "Couvi"

Hermosa Beach Pier. In the Sideout men's final, fourth seeds Ayakatubby and Lewis, as a team, won their first AVP title since 1997 by knocking off sixth seeded Matt Fuerbringer and Casey Jennings 21-18, 16-21, 22-20. The third and decisive game featured a total of seven match points for both teams. With this victory, Ayakatubby and Lewis notched their third career title. This was the second time in three AVP tournaments this year that Fuerbringer and Jennings had reached the finals, both times finishing in second place, and losing the deciding game by a 22-20 score.

3rd Place: Brent Doble and Karch Kiraly
3rd Place: Jake Gibb and Adam Jewell
5th Place: Sean Rosenthal and Larry Witt
5th Place: Stein Metzger and Kevin Wong

SAN DIEGO CALIFORNIA
June 13th-15th, 2003

In front of a large crowd at Mariners Point, San Diego pro beach volleyball fans welcomed back the AVP Nissan Series with loud cheers as they were treated an exciting men's championship match. The San Diego Open presented by Bud Light was the fourth event of the 2003 Nissan Series. This $62,500.00 event was won by the team of Dain Blanton and Jeff Nygard. They collected the winner's check for $14,500.00. The final match showcased two hot teams, sixth seeds Matt Fuerbringer and Casey Jennings vs Blanton and Nygard. Blanton and Nygard were making their second appearance in the finals this season, while Fuerbringer and Jennings were in their third appearance. The championship match featured several awe-inspiring rallies as Blanton and Nygard out lasted Fuerbringer and Jennings 21-16, 13-21, 15-12 to capture their first title this year on the 2003 AVP Nissan Series. Blanton's last title was in May of 2001 while Nygard's last win was in June 2002. This match marked the third time this season that the duo of Fuerbringer and Jennings had lost in the finals in a tough three game matche. The runner-ups shared a check for $9,750.00.

3rd Place: Stein Metzger and Kevin Wong
3rd Place: Todd Rogers and Sean Scott
5th Place: Scott Ayakatubby and Brian Lewis
5th Place: Brent Doble and Karch Kiraly

BELMAR BEACH NEW JERSEY
July 25th-27th, 2003

The boisterous crowd at the AVP Nissan Series Belmar Open observed an exciting final as the eighth seeded team of Sean Rosenthal and Larry Witt captured their first win on the AVP Nissan Series. In the championship match they defeated the fourth seeded team of Matt Fuerbringer and Casey Jennings 21-17, 21-11, 15-12 in a exhausting three game match. This was the fourth finals appearance for Fuerbringer and Jennings this season. The winners split the first place check in the amount of $14,500.00.

3rd Place: Brent Doble and Karch Kiraly
3rd Place: Jason Ring and Scott Wong
5th Place: Canyon Ceman and Mike Whitmarsh
5th Place: Jake Gibb and Adam Jewell

SCOTT AYAKATUBBY & BRIAN LEWIS vs SEAN ROSENTHAL & LARRY WITT
During the 2003 Nissan AVP Tour, the teams of Scott "Ack" Ayakatubby with Brian "Lewy" Lewis and Larry "Dizzel" Witt with Sean "Rosie" Rosenthal went head-to-head in some of the most exciting matches of the year. At the Hermosa event, Ack & Lewy scored a 15-21, 31-29 and 17-15 comback victory over Rosie and Dizzel. **LEFT PHOTO:** Scott Ayakatubby challenging the block of Sean Rosenthal. **RIGHT PHOTO:** Larry Witt attacking the ball against the block of Brian Lewis.

Photo's Courtesy of "Couvi"

Good Luck SCOTT AYAKATUBBY
From Your Friends On 16th & 17th Street

2003 MEN'S BEACH VOLLEYBALL ACTION-HERMOSA BEACH CALIFORNIA
TOP PHOTO: Scott Ayakatubby gets a little support from his 16th & 17th street fans. **MIDDLE LEFT PHOTO:** Brian Lewis (left) and Scott Ayakatubby (right) enjoy the moment after winning the 2003 AVP Tour event in Hermosa Beach California. **MIDDLE RIGHT PHOTO:** Brian Lewis (right) shows his approval of Scott Ayakatubby's play. **BOTTOM PHOTO:** Brian Lewis (left) and Scott Ayakatubby (right) have a little fun with "Rosie's-Raiders" after winning a tough match, 15-21-31-29 and 17-15, against Sean Rosenthal and Larry Witt.

Photo's Courtesy of "Couvi"

MANHATTAN BEACH CALIFORNIA
August 7th-10th, 2003

The AVP Nissan Series completed an action-packed weekend of pro beach volleyball with a splendid championship match at the 2003 Manhattan Beach Men's Open. The stands were packed with scores of fans and the pier was topped-off with gawkers watching the seventh seeds and new teammates Eric Fonoimoana and Kevin Wong capture the championship title over the ninth seeded team of Eduardo Bacil and Jose Loiola 23-25, 21-18, 15-13. The match was highlighted by numerous rallies which incited the crowd to bestow several standing ovations, while the cameras were rolling for the NBC TV coverage. This was the first tournament together for the new team of Fonoimoana and Wong. Both had won Manhattan Beach titles in previous seasons. Fonoimoana won last year with Dax Holdren, while Wong won two years ago in 2001 with Stein Metzger. The winner's shared $17,400.00.

3rd Place: Canyon Ceman and Mike Whitmarsh
3rd Place: Matt Fuerbringer and Casey Jennings
5th Place: Brent Doble and Karch Kiraly
5th Place: Scott Ayakatubby and Brian Lewis

HUNTINGTON BEACH CALIFORNIA
August 14th-17th, 2003

The championship match of the $150,000 Huntington Beach Open, presented by Bud Light, was played in front of 6,500 fans crammed on center court to see three-time Olympic Gold Medalist Karch Kiraly and partner Brent Doble capture the AVP Nissan Series Huntington Beach Open title, with a 21-16, 21-16 win over ninth-seeded Todd Rogers and Sean Scott. With this victory, at an age of 42 years, nine months and 14 days, Kiraly broke his own record for oldest players to win an AVP tournament. Doble displayed his power around the net, finishing with 18 kills, while Kiraly's relentless defense helped catapult them to the championship. Kiraly and Doble dominated at times, fighting off every comeback attempt by Rogers and Scott. Scott's play was affected when he aggravated a back injury, which he had developed in a previous match. The Huntington Beach Open win was the first title of 2003 for Kiraly and Doble. Kiraly increased his all-time record of most tournament wins to 144. This marked the seventh different men's team to win on the 2003 AVP Tour. This was also the first men's final in 2003 that didn't go to a third and deciding game.

3rd Place: Scott Ayakatubby and Brian Lewis
3rd Place: Sean Rosenthal and Larry Witt
5th Place: Canyon Ceman and Mike Whitmarsh
5th Place: Eric Fonoimoana and Kevin Wong

BRENT DOBLE & KARCH KIRALY
On the 2003 Nissan AVP Tour, Brent Doble and Karch Kiraly struggled for consistancy. During the 2003 season, they only advanced to one championship match. They won the Huntington Beach event, earning Kiraly his 144 career leading championship. Above photo, Kiraly hits a set from Doble, over the block of Kevin Wong, towards the defense of Stein Metzger.
Photo Courtesy of "Couvi"

2003 MEN'S BEACH VOLLEYBALL ACTION-MANHATTAN BEACH CALIFORNIA

TOP PHOTO: During the 2003 MB semi-finals, Casey Jennings slices a set from Matt Fuerbringer, past the block of Jose Loiola, towards the defense of Eduardo Bacil. Loiola and Bacil prevailed by scores of 21-19, 25-27 and 15-13. **BOTTOM PHOTO:** In front of a capacity crowd, during the finals of the 2003 Manhattan Beach Open, Eduardo bacil hits a set from Jose Loiola, towards the block of Kevin Wong. Eric Fonoimoana is on defense. Wong and Fonoimoana won the exciting match and the event by the scores of 23-25, 21-18 and 15-13.

Photo's Courtesy of "Couvi"

2003 MEN'S BEACH VOLLEYBALL ACTION

TOP LEFT PHOTO: Kevin Wong challenging the block of Mike Whitmarsh. **TOP RIGHT PHOTO:** Sean Scott hits a set from Todd Rogers, past the block of Brent Doble, towards the defense of Karch Kiraly. **BOTTOM LEFT PHOTO:** Jeff Nygard challenges the block of Mike Whitmarsh. **BOTTOM RIGHT PHOTO:** Emanuel Rego braces himself for action. All of the above action took place on the 2003 Men's AVP Nissan Series Tour.

Photo's Courtesy of Frank Goroszko

CHICAGO ILLINOIS
August 28th-31st, 2003

The 2003 AVP Nissan Series $150,000 Chicago Open ($75,000.00 for Men and $75,000.00 for Women), presented by Bud Light, was won by Dain Blanton and Jeff Nygard. In the championship match, Blanton the 2000 Olympic Gold Medalist and Nygard outlasted Canyon Ceman and Mike Whitmarsh 21-18, 27-25. Blanton and Nygard were the first team to repeat as winners on the 2003 AVP Nissan Series. They won earlier in the season at the AVP San Diego Open. Both teams made it to the finals coming through the contender's bracket. This marks Blanton's ninth career victory and Nygard's fourth. Today's confrontation was a rematch of the AVP Tempe Open Finals in which Ceman and Whitmarsh were victorious. Blanton and Nygard received $17,400.00 for their efforts.

3rd Place: Brent Doble and Karch Kiraly
3rd Place: Scott Ayakatubby and Brian Lewis
5th Place: Todd Rogers and Sean Scott
5th Place: John Hyden and Andy Witt

DAIN BLANTON & JEFF NYGARD
Under the lights, in Las Vegas NV, Dain Blanton and Jeff Nygard outplayed Scott Ayakatubby and Brian Lewis, to win the 2003 AVP Shoot-Out by scores of 21-13 and 21-19. Above photo, Blanton hits a set from Nygard, towards the block of Ayakatubby.
Photo Courtesy of "Couvi"

LAS VEGAS NEVADA
September 4th-6th, 2003

Dain Blanton and Jeff Nygard were the champions at the Men's $75,000.00 Las Vegas Aquafina AVP Shootout. In the championship match, of the 2003 AVP Nissan Series, Blanton and Nygard defeated Scott Ayakatubby and Brian Lewis 21-13, 21-19 to capture the Shootout title. This win gave Blanton and Nygard their third title this season and back to back victories as the tandem captured the title last week in Chicago. Blanton and Nygard remained as the only team this season to win multiple titles. Ayakatubby and Lewis ended the season as the AVP Nissan Series overall title winners and were able to take home a Nissan automobile of their choice for the title. As is the current tradition, there were a couple of "Special" matches played durin the Las Vegas Shoot-Out. Sinjin Smith and Randy Stoklos outplayed Brent Frohoff and Ricci Luyties in one match. In the other match, Elaine Youngs and Holly McPeak devastated Steve Obradovich and Jim Menges.

3rd Place: Sean Rosenthal and Larry Witt
3rd Place: Eric Fonoimoana and Dax Holdren
5th Place: Brent Doble and Karch Kiraly
5th Place: Canyon Ceman and Mike Whitmarsh
5th Place: Todd Rogers and Sean Scott
5th Place: Matt Fuerbringer and Casey Jennings

STEVE OBRADOVICH & JIM MENGES
Steve "OB" Obradovich and Jim Menges tried to re-live their legendary moments of glory, but Ealine Youngs and Holly McPeak helped the "Sands of Time" keep though's moments locked in history. Above photo, OB hits a set from Menges, past the block of Youngs, towards the defense of McPeak.
Photo Courtesy of "Couvi"

MEN'S TOURNAMENT RESULTS 2003-FIVB

RHODES GREECE
June 3rd-8th, 2003

The FIVB World Tour was on the Island of Rhodes Greece, to launch the 2003 Tour with a flourish. This event, on this picturesque Greek island was won by the American team of Dain Blanton and Jeff Nygard. The court was set up, under the lights, in a historic square just adjacent to the beach. In the magnificent Mediterranean evening, the championship match came down to a contest between the new partnership of Blanton and Nygard against the highly-experienced Brazilian team of Benjamin Insfran and Marcio Enrique Barroso Araujo. But it was the American's who finished on top, winning the "Gold-Medal" with a 22-20 and 21-18 championship victory. Blanton's inspired defense helped him win the Speedo Most Valuable Player Award. This event launched the FIVB's new partnership with title sponsor Swatch, the world's biggest manufacturer of time keeping and timing devices and was enhanced by animated electronic score boards and a speed measuring device that revealed some players can serve at more than 50 miles per hour.

3rd Place: Nikolas Berger and Clemens Doppler-Austria
4th Place: John Child and Mark Heese-Canada
5th Place: Martin Laciga and Paul Laciga-Switzerland
5th Place: Harley Marques and Franco Neto-Brazil
5th Place: Vegard Hoidalen and Jorre Kjemperud-Norway
5th Place: Markus Egger and Sascha Heyer-Switzerland

GSTAAD SWITZERLAND
June 18th-22nd, 2003

Brazil's Benjamin Insfran and Marcio Enrique Araujo secured their first gold medal of the 2003 SWATCH-FIVB World Tour at the Men's FIVB $150,000 Gstaad Switzerland Open In the "Gold-Medal" match they overcame the brave challenge of Germany's Markus Dieckmann and Jonas Reckermann to win 23-25, 21-13 and 15-10. Germany's Dieckmann won the Speedo Most Valuable Player Award. The Swiss fans were given a boost when Stefan Kobel and Patrick Heuscher claimed the bronze medal thanks to a 21-18, 19-21 and 15-10 victory over Austrians Clemens Doppler and Niki Berger. Switzerland's Patrick Heuscher won the SWATCH Fastest Speed Award after having one of his "spikes" clocked at 97.2 mph.

3rd Place: Patrick Heuscher and Stefan Kobel-Switzerland
4th Place: Nikolas Berger Clemens and Doppler-Austria
5th Place: Martin Laciga and Paul Laciga-Switzerland
5th Place: Markus Egger and Sascha Heyer-Switzerland
5th Place: Mariano Baracetti and Martin Conde-Argentina
5th Place: Francisco Alvarez and Juan Rosell-Cuba

PATRICK HEUSCHER
Switzerland's Patrick Heuscher teamed-up with compatriot Stefan Kobel to advance to the "Bronze-Medal" match at the 2003 FIVB event in Gstaad Switzerland. Heuscher was awarded the "Swatch Fasted Speed" award with a spike clocked at 97.2 MPH.
Photo Courtesy of the FIVB

JEFF NYGARD
American Jeff Nygard was paired-up with fellow American, Dain Blanton, on the 2003 FIVB World Tour. They won a "Gold-Medal" on the island of Rhodes Greece, the site of the 2004 Olympics. Above photo, Nygard gets above the net for the spike.
Photo Courtesy of "Couvi"

BERLIN GERMANY
June 25th-29th, 2003

The winner's of the Swatch FIVB $300,000.00 Berlin Grand Slam was the Brazilian team of Harley Marques Silva and Franco Jose Vieira. In the "Gold-Medal" match, they downed Argentina's Mariano Baracetti and Martin Conde 21-18 and 21-16. It was an dramatic and fully-deserved victory for the pair and gave Franco his first World Tour title since 1996, the year he finished on top of the rankings. The "Bronze-Medal" went to another Brazilian pair, Ricardo Alex Costa Santos and Emanuel Rego, who silenced the packed Schlossplatz City Beach stadium in Berlin by defeating local favorites Markus Dieckmann and Jonas Reckermann 21-15 and 21-16. The winner's received $22,500.00 in prize money for their victory. Reckermann won the SWATCH Fastest Serve Award with a speed of over 60 mph.

3rd Place: Emanuel Rego and Ricardo Santos-Brazil
4th Place: Markus Dieckmann and Jonas Reckermann-Germany
5th Place: Marcio Araujo and Benjamin Insfran-Brazil
5th Place: Martin Laciga and Paul Laciga-Switzerland
5th Place: Vegard Hoidalen and Jorre Kjemperud-Norway
5th Place: Eric Fonoimoana and Dax Holdren-USA

STAVANGER NORWAY
July 2nd-6th, 2003

Brazil's Ricardo Alex Costa Santos and Emanuel Rego secured their first SWATCH-FIVB World Tour title together at the Norway Open. In the "Gold-Medal" match they downed Argentina's Mariano Baracetti and Martin Conde in a arousing final. The Brazilians, playing their first full season together, fought back from a set down to defeat last year's World Tour champions 16-21, 21-16 and 15-12 in front of a packed stadium. This championship gave Rego his third consecutive Norway Open title, his fourth in all. He also won in 1999, 2001 and 2002 with different partners. Rego was voted the Speedo Most Valuable Player.

3rd Place: Julien Prosser and Mark Williams-Australia
4th Place: Jefferson Bellaguarda and Juca Dultra-Brazil
5th Place: Martin Laciga and Paul Laciga-Switzerland
5th Place: Harley Marques and Franco Neto-Brazil
5th Place: Stein Metzger and Kevin Wong-USA
5th Place: Patrick Heuscher and Stefan Kobel-Switzerland

MARSEILLE FRANCE
July 16th-20th, 2003

Brazil's Ricardo Alex Costa Santos and Emanuel Rego won their second consecutive "Gold-Medal" on the 2003 SWATCH-FIVB World Tour when they won the Men's FIVB $300,000.00 France Grand Slam. In the "Gold-Medal" match, in front of a packed stadium, they scored a captivating 21-18, 20-22 and 15-13 win against Swiss brothers Martin and Paul Laciga. Third place went to American Olympic champion Dain Blanton and Jeff Nygard, who fought back from a set down to defeat Germany's Christopher Dieckmann and Andy Scheuerpflug 19-21, 21-15 and 15-8. Ricardo also won the SWATCH Fastest Service Award with a time of nearly 60 mph.

3rd Place: Dain Blanton and Jeff Nygard-USA
4th Place: Christopher Dieckmann and Andreas Scheuerpflug-Germany
5th Place: Vegard Hoidalen and Jorre Kjemperud-Norway
5th Place: Markus Dieckmann and Jonas Reckermann-Germany
5th Place: Patrick Heuscher and Stefan Kobel-Switzerland
5th Place: Joao Brenha and Luis Maia-Portugal

MARIANO BARACETTI & MARTIN CONDE
Mariano Baracetti and Martin Conde, from Argentina, played well on the 2003 FIVB Worls Tour. They advance to the "Gold-Medal" match at 2 events, finishing second twice. Above photo, Baracetti slices a set from Conde, away from the block of Todd Rogers.
Photo Courtesy of the FIVB

RAMON HERNANDEZ
Portugal's Ramon Hernandez was teamed-up with compatriot Raul Papaleo when they won the "Bronze-Medal" at the 2003 Men's FIVB XIV Pan American Games. Above photo, Hernandez challenges the block of Austria's Nikolas Berger.
Photo Courtesy of "Couvi"

ESPHINO PORTUGAL
July 23rd-27th, 2003

The Brazilian team of Ricardo Alex Costa Santos and Emanuel Rego won their third consecutive "Gold-Medal" on the 2003 Men's World Tour when they won the $150,000.00 Portugal Open in Esphino. In the "Gold-Medal" match, Ricardo and Rego fought back from a game down to defeat Norway's Jorre Andre Kjemperud and Vegard Hoidalen in a thrilling final. The dauntless Norwegian pair fought-off four match points, as well as having a match point of their own, before falling 21-23, 21-14 and 20-18 in front of full-house in this Atlantic coastal resort. Ricardo, was voted the Speedo Most Valuable Player (MVP). Norway's Jorre Hoidalen received the SWATCH Fastest Service Award after being timed at nearly 60 mph.

3rd Place: Andrew Schacht and Josh Slack-Australia
4th Place: Marcio Araujo and Benjamin Insfran-Brazil
5th Place: Martin Laciga and Paul Laciga-Switzerland
5th Place: Markus Egger and Sascha Heyer-Switzerland
5th Place: Todd Rogers and Sean Scott-USA
5th Place: Stephan Canet and Mathieu Hamel-France

KLAGENFURT AUSTRIA
July 31st-August 3rd, 2003

Brazil's Benjamin Insfran and Marcio Enrique Araujo claimed their second title of the 2003 SWATCH-FIVB World Tour by winning the "Gold-Medal" at the Men's FIVB $260,000 A-1 Austria Grand Slam in Klagenfurt Austria. In the championship match they earned a straight-sets victory over Americans Stein Metzger and Kevin Wong in, front of a capacity center-court crowd in this Austrian lakeside resort. The Brazilian's secured the gold with a 22-20 and 21-17 victory. Benjamin and Araujo managed to defuse the blocking threat of Wong with a powerful service game supported with some exceptional ball control during side-outs. The "Bronze-Medal" went to the Swiss pair of Patrick Heuscher and Stefan Kobel, who fought back from a set down to defeat Olympic champion Dain Blanton and Jeff Nygard of the U.S.A. 19-21, 21-19 and 15-8.

3rd Place: Patrick Heuscher and Stefan Kobel-Switzerland
4th Place: Dain Blanton and Jeff Nygard-USA
5th Place: Emanuel Rego and Ricardo Santos-Brazil
5th Place: Markus Dieckmann and Jonas Reckermann-Germany
5th Place: Nikolas Berger and Clemens Doppler-Austria
5th Place: Markus Egger and Sascha Heyer-Switzerland

SANTO DOMINGO DOMINICAN REPUBLIC
August 2nd-9th, 2003

The 2003 Men's FIVB XIV Pan American Games, staged in Santo Domingo, Dominican Republic was won by the Cuban team of Francisco Alvarez and Juan Rosell. In the "Gold-Medal" match, they defeated the Brazilian team of Luizao Correa and Paulo Emilio Silva 23-25, 21-11 and 15-12 for the title.

3rd Place: Ramon Hernandez and Raul Papaleo-Puerto Rico
4th Place: David Fischer and Brad Torsone-USA
5th Place: Djordje Ljubicic and Michael Slean-Canada
5th Place: Tomas Hernandez and Juan Rodriguez Ibarra-Mexico
5th Place: Jeovanny Medrano and Rafael Vargas-El Salvador
5th Place: Christian Garcia and Alejandro Salas-Dominican Republic

ANDRE KJEMPERUD & VEGARD HOIDALEN
Norway's Andre Kjemperud and Vegard Hoidalen provided some worthy competition on the 2003 Men's FIVB World Tour. They had a best finish of second place, after losing the "Gold-Medal" match to Brazil's Ricardo Santos and Emanuel Rego, at the 2003 World Tour event staged in Esphino Portugal. Above photo, Hoidalen hits a set from Kjemperud, past the block of Santos.
Photo Courtesy of the FIVB

MALLORCA SPAIN
September 3rd-7th, 2003

The Brazilian team of Benjamin Insfran and Marcio Enrique Araujo collected their third "Gold-Medal" of the 2003 FIVB season, in the World of Tui Open de Mallorca, at the Men's FIVB $150,000.00 Men's Spain Open. In the championship match, they fought back from a game down to defeat Germany's Markus Dieckmann and Jonas Reckermann in one of the longest and most electrifying finals in the history of the SWATCH-FIVB World Tour. The Brazilians deprived the Germans of what would have been their first title on the World Tour with a memorable 19-21, 21-19 and 34-32 victory that had the capacity stadium crowd on the edge of their seats for one hour and 38 minutes. The Brazilians needed 12 match points before winning their sixth title together on the World Tour, while Dieckmann and Reckermann also had eight match points to secure what would have been Germany's first men's victory on the FIVB World Beach Volleyball Tour.

3rd Place: Mariano Baracetti and Martin Conde-Argentina
4th Place: Harley Marques and Franco Neto-Brazil
5th Place: Emanuel Rego and Ricardo Santos-Brazil
5th Place: Martin Laciga and Paul Laciga-Switzerland
5th Place: Christoph Dieckmann and Andreas Scheuerpflug-Germany
5th Place: Andrew Schacht and Josh Slack-Australia

LOS ANGELES CALIFORNIA U.S.A.
September 18th-21st, 2003

The 2003 Men's FIVB World Tour event was won by the Brazilian team of Ricardo Alex Costa Santos and Emanuel Rego. The 2003 season was a "Gold Rush" for Ricardo and Rego, claiming their fourth title of on the 2003 SWATCH-FIVB World Tour. In the championship match, they outclassed Switzerland's Sascha Heyer and Markus Egger in a one-sided final at this $300,000 Nissan Grand Slam event. The dominant Brazilians extended their lead at the top of the FIVB World rankings as Ricardo produced a supreme display of blocking on the way to a 21-11 and 21-18 victory over their struggling Swiss opponents. American Beach veteran Mike Whitmarsh and Canyon Ceman captured the bronze medal with a 22-20 and 21-16 conquest over Niki Berger and Clemens Doppler of Austria.

3rd Place: Canyon Ceman and Mike Whitmarsh-USA
4th Place: Nikolas Berger and Clemens Doppler-Austria
5th Place: Marcio Araujo and Benjamin Insfran-Brazil
5th Place: Markus Dieckmann and Jonas Reckermann-Germany
5th Place: Martin Laciga and Paul Laciga-Switzerland
5th Place: Dax Holdren and Stein Metzger-USA

RIO DE JANEIRO BRAZIL
October 14th-19th, 2003

The 2003 Beach Volleyball World Championships, presented by SWATCH on a sun-drenched Copacabana Beach, in front of a huge crowd, was won by the Brazilian team of Ricardo Alex Costa Santos and Emanuel Rego. This "Gold-Medal" capped off a brilliant first full season together for Rego and Santos. In the championship match, Rego and Santos defeated American's Dax Holdren and Stein Metzger 21-18 and 21-15. It was the Brazilian teams fifth championship victory.

3rd Place: Marcio Araujo and Benjamin Insfran-Brazil
4th Place: Joao Brenha and Luis Maia-Portugal
5th Place: Martin Laciga and Paul Laciga-Switzerland
5th Place: Patrick Heuscher and Stefan Kobel-Switzerland
5th Place: Dain Blanton and Jeff Nygard-USA
5th Place: Pedro Brazao and Fred Souza-Brazil

EMANUEL REGO & RICARDO SANTOS
Brazilians Emanuel Rego and Ricardo Santos won five "Gold-Medal" matches on the 2003 FIVB World Tour. Included in their win list was a one-sided "Gold-Medal" performance against the Swiss team of Sascha Heyer and Markus Egger, during the final at the $300,000.00 World Tour event in Carson California U.S.A. They outclassed Heyer and Egger by scores of 21-11 and 21-18.
Photo Courtesy of "Couvi"

2003 MEN'S BEACH VOLLEYBALL ACTION-CARSON CALIFORNIA-U.S.A.

TOP LEFT PHOTO: Brazils Ricardo Santos hits the ball off the block of Switzerland's Sascha Heyer. Markus Egger is on defense. **TOP RIGHT PHOTO:** Brazils Ricardo Santos hits a set from Emanuel Rego, off the block of Argentina's Mariano Baracetti. **BOTTOM PHOTO:** Austria's Clemens Doppler slices a set from compatriot Nokolas Berger, past the block of Brazil's Ricardo Santos, towards the defense of Emanuel Rego. All of the above action took place during the 2003 FIVB World Tour event, in the city of Carson, near Los Angeles California U.S.A.

Photo's Courtesy of "Couvi"

2003 MEN'S BEACH VOLLEYBALL ACTION-CARSON CALIFORNIA-U.S.A.

TOP LEFT PHOTO: Germany's Charles Dieckmann hits the ball off the block of Argentina's Martin Conde, away from the defense of Mariano Baracetti. **TOP RIGHT PHOTO:** Austria's Nick Berger hits a set from compatriot Clemens Doppler, towards the block of Brazil's Emanuel Rego. **BOTTOM LEFT PHOTO:** Dain Blanton challenges the block of Dax Holdren. Both players are from the United States. **BOTTOM RIGHT PHOTO:** America's Scott Ayakatubby is ready for action. All of the above action took place during the 2003 FIVB World Tour event, in the city of Carson, near Los Angeles California U.S.A.

Photo's Courtesy of "Couvi"

2003 MEN'S BEACH VOLLEYBALL ACTION-CARSON CALIFORNIA-U.S.A.
TOP PHOTO: American Canyon Ceman gives an all-out effort to dig the ball. **MIDDLE PHOTO:** Brazil's Franco Jose Vieira lays-out in an effort to get the ball-up for partner Harley Marques. **BOTTOM PHOTO:** American Casey Jennings grouvels in the sand in an effort to get to the ball. All of the above action took place during the 2003 FIVB World Tour event, in the city of Carson, near Los Angeles California U.S.A.
Photo's Courtesy of "Couvi"

2003 MEN'S BEACH VOLLEYBALL ACTION

TOP LEFT PHOTO: During 2003 Hermosa Beach event, Matt Fuerbringer hits a set from Casey Jennings, towards the block of Scott Ayakatubby. **TOP RIGHT PHOTO:** Brian Lewis attacking the ball during the 2003 Huntington Beach event. **BOTTOM PHOTO:** Veterens Scott Ayakatubby and Brian Lewis are one of the best ball-control teams on the AVP Tour. They utilized their ball-control to earn the most points on the 2003 Nisan AVP Tour. They won a Nissan car of their choice for their efforts. Above photo, Lewis (right) passing the ball to Ayakatubby (left), during play at the 2003 AVP Tour event in Hermosa Beach California.

Photo's Courtesy of "Couvi"

2003 MEN'S BEACH VOLLEYBALL ACTION
TOP LEFT PHOTO: Kevin Wong hits a set from Eric Fonoimoana, away from the block of Jose Loiola and away from the defense of Eduardo Bacil. Action took place during the championship match of the 2003 Manhattan Beach Open. **TOP RIGHT PHOTO:** Adam Jewell challenges the block of Sean Rosenthal, during the 2003 AVP event in Huntington Beach. **BOTTOM PHOTO:** Upstarts Larry Witt and Sean Rosenthal represent the new-breed of players on the AVP Tour. In 2003 they collected their first career AVP Tour championship at the Belmar NJ event. Above photo, Rosenthal (right) passing the ball to Witt (left), during action at the 2003 AVP Tour event in Manhattan Beach California.
Photo's Courtesy of "Couvi"

 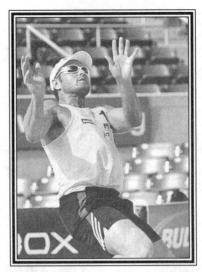 

TOP PHOTOS: Left: Canada's Ahren Cadieux slicing the ball over the net. **Center:** Australia's Andrew Schacht is ready to make the dig. **Right:** Brazil's Harley Marques is in position to dig the ball.

MIDDLE PHOTOS: Left: Niklas Rademacher, from Germany challenging the huge block of Canadian Rich Van Huizen. **Center:** Jose Pedrosa, from Portugfal challenges the big block of American Matt Fuerbringer. **Right:** Sascha Heyer, from Switzerland, attacking the ball.

2003 MEN'S BEACH VOLLEYBALL ACTION

BOTTOM PHOTOS: Left: Puerto Rican Raul Papaleo goes-up for the block attempt. **Center:** Brazil's Ricardo Santos is enormous at the net. **Right:** Brazilian Franco Neto reaches above the net to make the block.

Photo's Courtesy of "Couvi"

TOP PHOTOS: Left: While participating in his 27th Manhattan Beach Open, Kevin Cleary attacks the block of Colin Kaslow. **Center:** Brent Doble challenging the block of Scott Ayakatubby. **Right:** Brian Lewis acknowledging an intelligent play by his partner.

MIDDLE PHOTOS: Left: Casey Jennings gets-up high to spike the ball. **Center:** Karch Kiraly does his imitation of a line judge as he calls the ball out. **Right:** Chris Marlowe is still prominent on the beach volleyball scene as a TV announcer.

2003 MEN'S BEACH VOLLEYBALL ACTION

BOTTOM PHOTOS: Left: Carl Henkel reaches over the net to make the block. **Center:** Sean Rosenthal gets above the net to attack the ball. **Right:** Larry Witt attacking the ball.

Photo's Courtesy of "Couvi"

WOMEN'S BEACH VOLLEYBALL
2003

AVP

The AVP 2003 tour schedule has expanded from seven tournaments to ten and concluded with an Olympic qualifying AVP/FIVB event in September. The AVP/FIVB event was held at the newly constructed Home Depot Center in Carson, California. All ten AVP Tour "Nissan Series" Tournament stops featured men's and women's competition and offered more than $1 million in prize money. In 2003 there were four California events with the five additional events staged in five different states. Fort Lauderdale Florida, Tempe Arizona, Belmar New Jersey, Chicago Illinois and Las Vegas Nevada all staged one AVP Tour event.

The top team on the 2003 Women's AVP Tour was Kerri Walsh and Misty May. They entered eight AVP Tour Events, including the AVP/FIVB event in Carson CA. They advanced to eight AVP Tour championship matches and won all eight times, while earning nearly $150,000.00. Elaine Youngs and Holly McPeak were the only other team to win an event on the Women's AVP Tour when they won the San Diego CA event. Youngs and McPeak advanced to a total of eight championship matches on the 2003 Women's AVP Tour, while earning over $100,000.00 in prize money. There were only two additional teams that advanced to the finals of an AVP event in 2003. The two teams were Annette Davis with Jenny Jordan and Dianne DeNecochea with Nancy Mason.

2003 INDIVIDUAL AVP TOURNAMENT FINISHES

Player	1st	2nd	3rd	4th	5th
Angie Akers	0	0	0	0	3
Lisa Arce	0	0	2	0	6
Carrie Busch	0	0	3	0	3
Annette Buckner-Davis	0	1	5	0	3
Dianne DeNeochea	0	1	4	0	1
Linda Hanley	0	0	1	0	3
Jennifer Johnson Jordan	0	1	5	0	3
Liz Masakayan	0	0	1	0	3
Nancy Mason	0	1	1	0	1
Misty May	**8**	**0**	**0**	**0**	**0**
Holly McPeak	1	7	1	0	0
Leanne Schuster McSorley	0	0	3	0	3
Jen Meredith	0	0	2	0	1
Wendy Stammer	0	0	2	0	1
Sara Straton	0	0	0	0	3
Kerri Walsh	**8**	**0**	**0**	**0**	**0**
Rachel Wacholder	0	0	2	0	6
Elaine Youngs	1	7	1	0	0

KERRI WALSH & MISTY MAY
The top team on the 2003 Women's AVP Tour was Kerri Walsh (left) and Misty May (right). They entered eight AVP Tour Events as well as the AVP/FIVB event in Carson CA. They advanced to eight AVP Tour championship matches and won all eight times.

Photo Courtesy of "Couvi"

ELAINE YOUNGS
Elaine Youngs paired-up with Holly McPeak to advance to 8 championship matches on the 2003 AVP Tour. They were only able to win the event in San Diego CA. Above photo Youngs rejects the spike from Kerri Walsh.

Photo Courtesy of Frank Goroszko

FIVB

The Women's 2003 FIVB World Tour of Beach Volleyball staged thirteen events, including the XIV Pan American Games in Santo Domingo and four Grand Slam events. There were events in thirteen countries with a total purse of $2,500,000.00. The Women's FIVB events were staged in Rhodes Greece, Gstaad Switzerland, Berlin Germany, Marseille France, Klagenfurt Austria, Santo Domingo Dominican Republic, Osaka Japan, Lianyungang China, Bali Indonesia, Milan Italy, Los Angeles California U.S.A. and Rio de Janeiro Brazil.

The top team, on the 2003 FIVB Women's World Tour, was American's Kerri Walsh and Misty May. They entered eight events and advanced to six "Gold-Medal" matches, winning five times, while earning over one quarter of a million dollars. Brazilian's Sandra Pires and Ana Paula Connelly were the number two team on the 2003 FIVB Women's Tour. Pires and Connelly entered ten events and advanced to eight "Gold-Medal" Matches, winning four times, while earning nearly one quarter of a million dollars. Jia Tian and Fei Wang, from China, entered twelve events and advanced to two "Gold-Medal" matches, winning each time, while earning nearly $120,000.00. The team of Tamara Larreea Peraza and Dalixia Fernandez Grasset won the "Gold-Medal" match at the XIV Pan American Games. The team of Rebekka Kadijk and Marrit Leenstra, from the Netherlands, was the only other team on the 2003 Women's FIVB Tour to win a "Gold-Medal" when they won the event in Lianyungang China, after entering eleven events.

Above all, the 2003 Women's FIVB World Tour will be remembered for the success of a number of new combinations. The American team of May and Walsh, had an excellent year claiming the World Championship and winning three (France, Austria and USA) of the four Grand Slam legs, only missing out in Germany where they finished fourth. The Brazilian combination featuring Olympic and two-time world champion Sandra Pires Tavares and Ana Paula Connelly collected an amazing four gold and four silver medals.

2003 WOMEN'S FIVB WORLD TOUR ACTION-CARSON CALIFORNIA U.S.A.
The American team of Holly McPeak and Elaine Youngs provided plenty of competition on the 2003 Women's FIVB World Tour. The Americans advanced to the final of the Berlin Germany event, where they lost to Brazil's Ana Paula Connelly and Sandra Pires, in a thriller, 20-22, 29-27 and 15-13. The Chinese team of Jei Wang and Jia Tian advanced to 2 "Gold-Medal" matches in 2003, winning both times. Above photo, During the 2003 Carson event, Youngs hits a set from McPeak towards the defense of Wang (left) and Tian (right).
Photo Courtesy of "Couvi"

2003 INDIVIDUAL FIVB TOURNAMENT FINISHES

Player	1st	2nd	3rd	4th	5th	Player	1st	2nd	3rd	4th	5th
Andrea Ahmann	0	0	0	0	1	Simon Kuhn	0	0	0	1	3
Maria Arago	0	0	0	0	1	Suzanne Luhme	0	1	0	0	1
Lisa Arce	0	0	0	0	1	Marrit Leenstra	1	0	0	1	2
Ethel Julie Arjona	0	0	0	0	1	Summer Lochowicz	0	0	0	0	2
Vassiliki Arvaniti	0	0	0	0	2	Annie Martin	0	0	0	0	1
Leila Barros	0	0	0	0	1	Nancy Mason	0	0	1	0	1
Shaylyn Bede	0	0	0	0	1	**Misty May**	5	1	1	1	0
Shelda Kelly Bruno Bede	0	4	5	0	0	Holly McPeak	0	1	0	2	1
Adriana Brando Behar	0	4	5	0	0	Tatiana Minello	0	0	0	1	2
Nicole Benoit	0	0	0	1	3	Michelle Morse	0	0	0	0	1
Eva Celbova	0	0	1	0	3	Danja Musch	0	1	0	0	1
Angela Clarke	0	0	0	0	2	Katerina Nikolaidou	0	0	0	0	1
Ana Paula Connolly	4	4	0	0	1	Liz Pagano	0	0	0	0	1
Natalie Cook	0	0	4	1	1	Tamara Larrea Peraza	1	1	0	1	1
Annete Davis	0	0	0	2	4	Lucilla Perrotta	0	0	0	0	1
Dominque Deevlovic	0	0	0	0	1	Sandra Tavares Pires	4	4	0	0	1
Dianne DeNecochea	0	0	1	0	1	Stephane Pohl	0	0	0	0	3
Patricia Diaz	0	0	0	0	1	Kerri Ann Pottharst	0	0	0	0	2
Xinia Diaz	0	0	0	0	1	Okka Rau	0	0	0	0	3
Sonja Dosoudilova	0	0	1	0	3	Esteves Ribarta	0	0	0	0	1
Guylaine Dumont	0	0	0	0	1	Renata Ribeiro	0	0	0	0	1
Alexandra Fonseca	0	0	0	1	2	Ana Richa	0	0	1	0	0
Larissa Franca	0	0	1	0	0	Monica Rodrigues	0	0	0	0	2
Myra Garcia	0	1	0	0	1	Nicole Sanderson	0	0	4	1	1
Daniela Gattelli	0	0	0	0	1	Efi Sfyri	0	0	0	0	4
Hilda Gaxiola	0	1	0	0	1	Jia Tian	2	0	0	1	3
Kyle Gerlic	0	0	0	0	2	Ryo Tokuno	0	0	0	0	1
Sylvana Gomez	0	0	0	0	1	Maria Tsiartsian	0	0	0	0	1
Nancy Gougeon	0	0	0	1	0	Tiansol Villablanca	0	0	0	0	1
Wanda Guennette	0	0	0	1	0	Jana Vollmer	0	0	0	0	1
Daxila Grasset	1	1	0	1	1	Rachel Wacholder	0	0	0	0	1
Linjun Ji	0	0	0	0	1	**Kerri Walsh**	5	3	1	1	0
Jenny Jordan	0	0	0	2	4	Fei Wang	2	0	0	1	3
Rebbeka Kadijk	1	0	0	1	2	Jei Wang	0	0	0	0	1
Virginia Kadjo	0	0	0	0	1	Lu Wang	0	0	0	1	0
Vasso Karadassiou	0	0	0	0	4	Wenhui You	0	0	0	1	0
Efthalia Koutroumanidou	0	0	0	0	2	Elaine Youngs	0	1	0	2	1

2003 WOMEN'S FIVB WORLD TOUR ACTION-CARSON CALIFORNIA U.S.A.

The top two teams on the 2003 Women's FIVB World Tour were Misty May with Kerri Walsh, from the United States of America and Brazilians Ana Paula Connelly with Sandra Pires. The Americans advanced to 8 "Gold-Medal" matches, winning five times. The Brazilians also advanced to 8 "Gold-Medal" matches, winning 4 times. Above action, during the 2003 Carson event, Connelly hits a set from Pires, over the block of Walsh, towards the defense of May.

Photo Courtesy of "Couvi"

WOMEN'S TOURNAMENT RESULTS
2003-AVP

FORT LAUDERDALE FLORIDA
April 4th-6th, 2003

At the 2003 AVP $62,500 Paul Mitchell Fort Lauderdale Women's Open, the new AVP team of Misty May and Kerri Walsh collected $14,500.00 for winning the championship match against Holly McPeak and Elaine Youngs. McPeak and Youngs split $9,750 3.00 for their second place finish. The women's final produced a highly anticipated rivalry between the number one seeded team of McPeak and Youngs and the number two seeded team of May and Walsh. The championship match had numerous lead changes and came down to a 15-12 third game tiebreaker. In their semifinal match, May and Walsh outlasted Dianne DeNecochea and Nancy Mason 21-18 and 22-20. The other semifinal saw McPeak and Youngs beat third seeds Annette Davis and Jenny Johnson-Jordan 21-11 and 21-15, leaving Davis and Johnson-Jordan to finish in third place along with Dianne DeNecochea and Nancy Mason.

3rd Place: Annette Davis and Jenny Johnson Jordan
3rd Place: Dianne DeNecochea and Nancy Mason
5th Place: Carrie Busch and Leanne Schuster McSorley
5th Place: Lisa Arce and Rachel Wacholder

TEMPE ARIZONA
April 25th-25th, 2003

At the 2003 AVP Nissan Series $62,000.00 Tempe Women's Open, top seeded Misty May and Kerri Walsh collected $14,500.00 for winning the championship match against Annette Davis and Jenny Johnson Jordan. Davis and Jordan split $9,750 3.00 for their second place finish. The top seeded AVP newcomers, May and Walsh won a hard-fought match to capture the title in front of a packed house at Tempe Beach Park. The women's finals saw May and Walsh win their second consecutive title match by outlasting number three seeds Davis and Jordan 21-16, 18-21 and 15-13. This was only the second meeting between these two teams with May and Walsh winning the previous contest. Since making their AVP debut this season, May and Walsh now have a 10-0 match record, with only two game three tiebreakers.

3rd Place: Holly McPeak and Elaine Youngs
3rd Place: Linda Hanley and Liz Masakayan
5th Place: Lisa Arce and Rachel Wacholder
5th Place: Angie Akers and Sarah Straton

MISTY MASY & KERRI WALSH
Misty May and Kerri Walsh won all eight 2003 Women's AVP Tour events that they entered. They earned nearly $150,000.00 for their winning efforts. Above photo, May (left) and Walsh (right) show the hustle that enabled them to enjoy so much success in 2003.
Photo Courtesy of Frank Goroszko

JENNY JOHNSON JORDAN
Jenny Johnson Jordan paired-up with Annette Davis to provide some stiff competition on the 2003 Women's AVP Tour. They fininshed within the top three on 6 occasions. Above photo, Jordan challenges the block of Kerri Walsh.
Photo Courtesy of Frank Goroszko

HERMOSA BEACH CALIFORNIA
June 6th-8th, 2003

The Women's AVP $75,000 Hermosa Beach Open, presented by Bud Light at the Target/Mervyn's Beach Bash's Mossimo women's final, was captured by Misty May and Kerri Walsh. This was their third consecutive AVP title. In the championship match, they outlasted the number three seeds, Holly McPeak and Elaine Youngs, 21-15, 18-21 and 16-14, in a match that featured several breath-taking rallies. McPeak and Youngs were at match point, leading 14-12, when the aggressive tandem of May and Walsh fought back to win four points in a row to secure the victory. This was the second meeting in the finals between these two teams on the AVP Nissan Series, with May and Walsh winning both. Since making their AVP debut this season, May and Walsh now have a 15-0 match record. The winner's split $17,400.00, while the runner-ups shared $11,700.00.

3rd Place: Annette Davis and Jenny Johnson Jordan
3rd Place: Lisa Arce and Rachel Wacholder
5th Place: Dianne DeNecochea and Nancy Mason
5th Place: Linda Hanley and Liz Masakayan

DIANNE DeNECOCHEA
Dianne DeNecochea paired-up with Nancy Mason, on the 2003 Women's AVP Tour for some success. They finished within the top three on 5 occasions. Above photo, DeNecoches attacking the ball.

Photo Courtesy of Frank Goroszko

SAN DIEGO CALIFORNIA
June 13th-15th, 2003

Before a packed crowd at Mariners Point, San Diego pro beach volleyball fans welcomed back the AVP Nissan Series with roars and cheers as they were treated to an exciting women's $62,000.00 championship match. The San Diego Open presented by Bud Light was the fourth event of the 2003 Nissan Series. The women's final brought together the top seeded team of Holly McPeak and Elaine Youngs and fourth seeds Dianne DeNecochea and Nancy Mason. This was DeNecochea and Mason's first appearance in the finals this season. The top seeded tandem of McPeak and Youngs easily defeated DeNecochea and Mason 21-17 and 21-14. This was McPeak's 66th victory bringing her one closer to tying the all time record of 67 held by Karolyn Kirby. The winner's split $14,500.00 while the runner-ups split $9,750.00.

3rd Place: Annette Davis and Jenny Johnson Jordan
3rd Place: Lisa Arce and Rachel Wacholder
5th Place: Carrie Busch and Leanne McSorley
5th Place: Jennifer Meredith and Wendy Stammer

HOLLY McPEAK & ELAINE YOUNGS
Holly McPeak and Elaine "EY" Youngs grabbed a championship at the 2003 AVP Tour event in San Diego CA. Above photo, During the 2003 SD event, EY hits a set from McPeak into the block of Dianne DeNecochea.

Photo Courtesy of "Couvi"

2003 WOMEN'S BEACH VOLLEYBALL ACTION-HERMOSA BEACH CALIFORNIA
Winner's of the 2003 AVP Tour event in Hermosa Beach were Kerri Walsh and Misty May. In the thrilling championship match, they defeated Holly McPeak and Elaine Youngs by the scores of 21-15, 18-21 and 16-14. **TOP LEFT PHOTO:** Misty May challenging the block of Annette Davis. **TOP RIGHT PHOTO:** Jenny Jordan attacking the block of Misty May. Kerri Walsh is on defense. **BOTTOM PHOTO:** During the finals of the 2003 HB event, Holly McPeak hits a set from Elaine Youngs into the block of Kerri Walsh. Misty May is ready on defense.
Photo's Courtesy of "Couvi"

BELMAR NEW JERSEY
June 25th-27th, 2003

The Women's AVP $62,500.00 Belmar Open was won by Kerri Walsh and Misty May. They shared the first place prize of $14,500.00. In the championship match, the top seeds dispatched the second seeded team of Holly McPeak and Elaine Youngs in workmanlike fashion, by the scores of 21-17 and 21-11. This was the third meeting in the finals between these two teams on the AVP Nissan Series, with May and Walsh winning each contest. Since making their AVP debut this season, May and Walsh now had a 19-0 match record.

3rd Place: Dianne DeNecochea and Nancy Mason
3rd Place: Carrie Busch and Leanne McSorley
5th Place: Annette Davis and Jenny Johnson Jordan
5th Place: Lisa Arce and Rachel Wacholder

MANHATTAN BEACH CALIFORNIA
August 7th-9th, 2003

The 2003 Women's AVP $75,000 Manhattan Beach Open was won by the team of Kerri Walsh and Misty May. In the championship match, in front of a packed crowd at the Manhattan Beach Pier, the dynamic duo of May and Walsh captured their first Manhattan Beach Open title. The top-seeded May and Walsh outlasted second seeds Holly McPeak and Elaine Youngs 21-16 and 21-19 in a punishing battle that was televised "live" on NBC, the first ever for a women's final. It was the fifth straight championship title for May and Walsh in five opportunities this year on the AVP Nissan Series. With the victory, May and Walsh kept their unbeaten streak alive, running their match record to 26-0 this year on the AVP. Beach volleyball legends Liz Masakayan and Linda Hanley announced their retirements at this event.

3rd Place: Dianne DeNecochea and Nancy Mason
3rd Place: Carrie Busch and Leanne McSorley
5th Place: Annette Davis and Jenny Johnson Jordan
5th Place: Lisa Arce and Rachel Wacholder

HUNTINGTON BEACH CALIFORNIA
August 14th-16th, 2003

The AVP Nissan Series $75,000.00 Huntington Beach Open, presented by Bud Light was another victory for Kerri Walsh and Misty May. The championship match entertained thousands of cheering fans to a highly anticipated and strenuous match. The top-seeded duo of May and Walsh clinched their sixth AVP title by out-pointing their second-seeded rivals Holly McPeak and Elaine Youngs 22-24, 21-17 and 15-7. May and Walsh needed a third and deciding game to seal the win as both teams were effective as they displayed their awe-inspiring skills before a "live" NBC audience. With the

2003 MANHATTAN BEACH WOMEN'S OPEN
The 2003 Women's AVP Tour event, in Manhattan Beach CA, was won by Misty May and Kerri Walsh. Above photo, during the finals of the 2003 MB event, in front of a large crowd, May hits a set from Walsh towards the defense of Youngs (left) and McPeak (right).
Photo Courtesy of "Couvi"

JENNIFER MEREDITH
Jennifer Meredith teamed-up with Wendy Stammer to provide some stiff competition for the top teams on the 2003 Women's AVP Tour. They finished within the top three twice. Above photo, Meredith challenging the block of Kerri Walsh.
Photo Courtesy of Frank Goroszko

victory, May and Walsh had now beaten McPeak and Youngs all five times on the 2003 AVP Tour. The Huntington Beach title gave May and Walsh their sixth consecutive championship title in six opportunities on the AVP 2003 Nissan Series. They also keep their unbeaten streak alive on the AVP, running their match record to an incredible 31-0.

3rd Place: Annette Davis and Jenny Johnson Jordan
3rd Place: Jennifer Meredith and Wendy Stammer
5th Place: Carrie Busch and Leanne McSorley
5th Place: Linda Hanley and Liz Masakayan

CHICAGO ILLINOIS
August 28th-30th, 2003

The $75,000.00 Chicago Open, presented by Bud Light was another victory for Kerri Walsh and Misty May. They continued their winning streak by capturing their seventh title on the AVP Nissan Series Chicago Open. In the championship match, May and Walsh defeated the second seeded team Holly McPeak and Elaine Youngs 21-11 and 21-17. They also keep their unbeaten streak alive on the AVP, running their match record to an remarkable 36-0.

3rd Place: Dianne DeNecochea and Nancy Mason
3rd Place: Jennifer Meredith and Wendy Stammer
5th Place: Annette Davis and Jenny Johnson Jordan
5th Place: Lisa Arce and Rachel Wacholder

LAS VEGAS NEVADA
September 4th-6th, 2003

The 2003 Women's $75,000 Las Vegas Aquafina AVP Shootout, presented by Bud Light, showcased the final women's match of the 2003 AVP Nissan Series. In this final championship match of 2003, Misty May and partner Kerri Walsh captured their seventh title of the year and finished with a perfect season by defeating Holly McPeak and Elaine Youngs 21-16 and 21-13. This event was staged in the man-made sand court that was created on the parking lot of the Hard Rock Hotel and Casino in Las Vegas Nevada. May and Walsh went 39-0 during the 2003 season which is an AVP Tour record. By winning the Aquafina Shootout, not only did May and Walsh take home the first place purse of $30,000.00, but they clinched the AVP Nissan Series overall title which entitles them to choose a new Nissan automobile of their choice as their bounty.

3rd Place: Annette Davis and Jenny Johnson Jordan
3rd Place: Carrie Busch and Leanne McSorley
5th Place: Jennifer Meredith and Wendy Stammer
5th Place: Lisa Arce and Rachel Wacholder
5th Place: Linda Hanley and Liz Masakayan
5th Place: Angie Akers and Sarah Straton

LINDA HANLEY & LIZ MASAKAYAN
Linda Hanley and Liz Masakayan competed in their last AVP Tour event at the 2003 Las Vegas Shoot-Out, where they finished in fifth place. Above photo, during the 2003 LV event, Hanley hits a set from Masakayan, past the block of Elaine Youngs.
Photo Courtesy of "Couvi"

LEANNE McSORLEY & CARRIE BUSCH
Leanne Schuster McSorley and Carrie Busch paired-up for three third place finishes on the 2003 Women's AVP Tour. Above photo, during the 2003 LV event, Misty May attacks the block of McSorley. Busch is on defense.
Photo Courtesy of "Couvi"

WOMEN'S TOURNAMENT RESULTS
2003-FIVB

RHODES GREECE
June 11th-15th, 2003

The 2003 SWATCH-FIVB World Tour $150,000.00 Women's Hellas Open, in Rhodes Greece, was won by the Brazilian team of Ana Paula Connelly and Sandra Pires Tavares. In the all Brazilian "Gold-Medal" match, played in front of a large and excited crowd, they defeated compatriots Adriana Brando Behar and Shelda Kelly Bruno Bede. The new Brazilian pair of Pires and Connelly, fought from a game down to secure the $22,000.00 winner's purse with a three-game 21-23, 21-19 and 15-12 victory. Americans Misty May and Kerri Walsh, World Tour champions in 2002, took the bronze after beating the Cuban team of Larrea Peraza and Fernandez Grasset 21-15 and 25-23. As with the men's event, the quarter-finals, semifinals and final were broadcast live on local Rhodes television.

3rd Place: Misty May and Kerri Walsh-USA
4th Place: Dalixia Fernandez Grasset and Tamara Larrea Peraza-Cuba
5th Place: Leila Barros and Monica Rodrigues-Brazil
5th Place: Vasso Karadassiou and Efi Sfyri-Greece
5th Place: Linjun Ji and Jie Wang-China
5th Place: Vassiliki Arvaniti and Efthalia Koutroumanidou-Greece

VASSO KARADASSIOU
Vasso Karadassiou, from Greece, provided some competition on the 2003 Women's FIVB World Tour. She paired-up with compatriot Efi Sfyri for four fifth place finishes in 2003. Above photo, Karadassiou consentrates while passing the ball.
Photo Courtesy of the FIVB

GSTAAD SWITZERLAND
June 17th-21st, 2003

The Women's FIVB $150,000.00 Swiss Open was captured by the Defending champions, Misty May and Kerri Walsh of America. In the "Gold-Medal" match they gained a "sweet victory" over Brazilian rivals Ana Paula Connelly and Sandra Pires Tavares, by the scores of 23-21 and 21-15. After an exciting and closely fought first set, the American's dominance at the net and exceptional defense allowed them to control the Brazilians who had only been together as a team for two events. The bronze medal went to Brazil's Adriana Brando Behar and Shelda Kelly Bruno Bede after they defeated American wildcards Jennifer Jordan and Annette Davis 21-15 and 21-15. Kerri Walsh won the Speedo Most Valuable Player Award.

3rd Place: Shelda Bede and Adriana Behar-Brazil
4th Place: Annette Davis and Jenny Johnson Jordan-USA
5th Place: Alexandra Fonseca and Tatiana Minello-Brazil
5th Place: Rebekka Kadijk and Marrit Leenstra-Netherlands
5th Place: Eva Celbova and Sona Dosoudilova-Czech Republic
5th Place: Dianne DeNecochea and Nancy Mason-USA

NANCY MASON & DIANNE DeNECOCHEA
Nancy Mason and Dianne DeNeccohea played well on the 2003 Women's FIVB World Tour. Their best finish in 2003 was a third place in Milan Italy. Above photo, Mason hits a set from DeNecochea.
Photo Courtesy of "Couvi"

BERLIN GERMANY
June 24th-28th, 2003

The 2003 SWATCH-FIVB World Tour $300,000.00 Berlin Women's Grand Slam was won by the Brazilian team of Ana Paula Connelly and Sandra Pires. In the "Gold-Medal" match, they fought back from match point down with a thrilling victory over America's Holly McPeak and Elaine Youngs. The Brazilians lost a close first set 20-22, but kept their chances alive by saving match point at 21-22, in a marathon second set, which they finally won 29-27. Connelly and Pires won the third game and the gold with a 15-13 victory in the tie-break. The winner's collected the $45,000.00 winner's check. Third place went to another Brazilian team, Adriana Brando Behar and Shelda Bruno Bede. They ousted the American duo of Misty May and Kerri Walsh 21-18 and 21-19 in the bronze medal playoff.
3rd Place: Shelda Bede and Adriana Behar-Brazil
4th Place: Misty May and Kerri Walsh-USA
5th Place: Annette Davis and Jenny Johnson Jordan-USA
5th Place: Alexandra Fonseca and Tatiana Minello-Brazil
5th Place: Rebekka Kadijk and Marrit Leenstra-Netherlands
5th Place: Stephanie Pohl and Okka Rau-Germany

STAVANGER NORWAY
July 1st-5th, 2003

The stadium was filled to capacity at the 2003 SWATCH-FIVB World Tour Women's FIVB $150,000.00 Norway Open. The event was captured by Brazil's Ana Paula Connelly and Sandra Pires Tavares. In the championship match, they won their third "Gold-Medal" of the 2003 FIVB Tour by defeating America's Misty May and Kerri Walsh 21-19 and 21-15. The Brazilians had now won three of the four World Tour events this season. Third place went to Adriana Brando Behar and Shelda Kelly Behar as the Brazilian pair won their third bronze medal of the season with a 21-13 and 21-17 victory over American defending champions Holly McPeak and Elaine Young.
3rd Place: Shelda Bede and Adriana Behar-Brazil
4th Place: Holly McPeak and Elaine Youngs-USA
5th Place: Jia Tian and Fei Wang-China
5th Place: Natalie Cook and Nicole Sanderson-Australia
5th Place: Dalixia Fernandez Grasset and Tamara Larrea Peraza-Cuba
5th Place: Kylie Gerlic and Summer Lochowicz-Australia

MARSEILLE FRANCE
June 15th-20th, 2003

The Women's FIVB $300,000.00 Marseille French Grand Slam is where America's Misty May and Kerri Walsh won their second "Gold-Medal" of the 2003. In the "Gold-Medal" match they demolished Brazil's Ana Paula Connelly and Sandra Pires Tavares. In a surprisingly one-sided final, the Americans produced a near-flawless performance to secure the $40,000.00 winners' prize with a 21-10 and 21-13 victory. The bronze medal went to Brazilian duo Adrian Brando Behar and Shelda Kelly Bruno after they downed Aussie Olympic champion Natalie Cook and Nicole Sanderson 21-18 and 21-14.n.
3rd Place: Shelda Bede and Adriana Behar-Brazil
4th Place: Natalie Cook and Nicole Sanderson-Australia
5th Place: Annette Davis and Jenny Johnson Jordan-USA
5th Place: Eva Celbova and Sona Dosoudilova-Czech Republic
5th Place: Jia Tian and Fei Wang-China
5th Place: Stephanie Pohl and Okka Rau-Germany

KLAGENFURT AUSTRIA
July 30th-August 2nd, 2003

The Women's FIVB $260,000.00 Austria Grand Slam was won by the American team of Kerri Walsh and Misty May. In the "Gold-Medal" match, May and Walsh successfully defended their A1 Klagenfurt Grand Slam title by devastating arch-rivals Ana Paula Connelly and Sandra Pires Tavares of Brazil in another surprisingly one-sided final. The 2002 World Tour champions collected their third title of the season, and their second in succession, with a 21-17 and 21-12 victory over the Brazilians. May and Walsh also collected $40,000.00 for their first place effort. Third place went to Adriana Brando Behar and Shelda Kelly Bruno as the Brazilian duo acquired the bronze with a 21-17 and 21-18 victory over American's Holly McPeak and Elaine Youngs.
3rd Place: Shelda Bede and Adriana Behar-Brazil
4th Place: Holly McPeak and Elaine Youngs-USA
5th Place: Annette Davis and Jenny Johnson Jordan-USA
5th Place: Eva Celbova and Sona Dosoudilova-Czech Republic
5th Place: Andrea Ahmann and Jana Vollmer-Germany
5th Place: Vasso Karadassiou and Efi Sfyri-Greece

SANTO DOMINGO DOMINICAN REPUBLIC
August 2nd-9th, 2003

The 2003 Women's FIVB XIV Pan American Games, staged in Santo Domingo, Dominican Republic was won by the top seeded Cuban team of Dalixia Fernandez Grasset and Tamara Larrea Peraza. In the "Gold-Medal" match, they defeated the Mexican team of Mayra Garcia and Hilda Gaxiola 21-16 and 21-15 for the title. Fourth-seeded Larissa Franca and Ana Richa Medeiros of Brazil defeated Nancy Gougeon and Wanda Guenette 21-6 and 21-9 for the "Bronze-Medal."
3rd Place: Larissa Franca and Ana Richa-Brazil
4th Place: Nancy Gougeon and Wanda Guenette-Canada
5th Place: Michelle Morse and Liz Pagano-USA
5th Place: Patricia Diaz and Xinia Diaz-Costa Rica
5th Place: Dominique Deevlovic and Tiansol Villablanca-Chile
5th Place: Maria Arago and Sylvana Gomez-Guatemala

OSAKA JAPAN
August 6th-10th, 2003

In front of a sun-drenched crowd, the Women's FIVB $150,000.00 Japan Women's Open was seized by the Brazilian team of Ana Paula Connelly and Sandra Pires Tavares. In the "Gold-Medal" match, Connelly Pires won their fourth "Gold-Medal" of the 2003 SWATCH-FIVB World Tour when they defeated compatriots Adriana Brando Behar and Shelda Kelly Bruno, in the three game final. The victorious duo resisted a brave fight back from their fellow Brazilian's to secure the $22,000.00 first place check, with a 21-18, 19-21 and 15-13 victory. The "Bronze-Medal" went to the Australian team of Nicole Sanderson and Natalie Cook as the Aussie pair downed Brazilian's Alexandra Fonseca Da Silva and Tatiana Minello 21-18, 15-21 and 15-10. Sanderson posted a career-best finish on the FIVB World Tour when she stepping-up to the podium for the first time.
3rd Place: Natalie Cook and Nicole Sanderson-Australia
4th Place: Alexandra Fonseca and Tatiana Minello-Brazil
5th Place: Leila Barros and Monica Rodrigues-Brazil
5th Place: Nicole Benoit and Simone Kuhn-Switzerland
5th Place: Vasso Karadassiou and Efi Sfyri-Greece
5th Place: Katerina Nikolaidou and Maria Tsiartsiani-Greece

LIANYUNGANG CHINA
August 13th-17th, 2003

The Women's FIVB $150,000.00 China Open was captured by Rebekka Kadijk and Marrit Leenstra of the Netherlands. In the "Gold-Medal" match Kadijk and Leenstra won their first "Gold-Medal" on the SWATCH-FIVB World Tour. They defeated Germany's Suzanne Lahme and Danja Musch as it drizzled, in the exciting final The Dutch pair ignored the increasingly wet and overcast conditions to down their opponents 21-15, 17-21 and 15-13. The final match attracted a full house to the center court that was located on Lianyungang's pacific coast. This was the first "Gold-Medal" for the 24-year-old Kadijk since joining the World Tour six seasons ago, and for the 29-year-old Leenstra it was her first gold since turning professional in 2001. The Dutch pair collected $22,000.00 for the win. The "Bronze-Medal" match was won by the Australian team of Natalie Cook and Nicole Sanderson when the Aussie duo saved three match points to apprehend their second "Bronze-Medal" in as many weeks with a 17-21, 26-24 and 18-16 victory over the Swiss pair Nicole Schnyder-Benoit and Simone Kuhn. It should be noted that there were no American or Brazilian teams entered in the tournament.

3rd Place: Natalie Cook and Nicole Sanderson-Australia
4th Place: Nicole Benoit and Simone Kuhn-Switzerland
5th Place: Jia Tian and Fei Wang-China
5th Place: Angela Clarke and Kerri-Ann Pottharst-Australia
5th Place: Vasso Karadassiou and Efi Sfyri-Greece
5th Place: Guylaine Dumont and Annie Martin-Canada

BALI INDONESIA
August 22nd-24th, 2003

The Women's FIVB $150,000.00 Bali Indonesia Open was won by China's Tian Jia and Wang Fei as they wrote their names into the Beach Volleyball history books when they became the first Chinese team to win a gold medal on the SWATCH-FIVB World Tour. In the "Gold-Medal" match they defeated the Cuban team of Tamara Larrea Peraza and Dalixia Fernandez Grasset. The Chinese produced a near flawless display to down their Cuban opponents 21-17 and 21-19 Jia and Fei mixed a powerful service game with strong defense and some to secure the $22,000.00 winner's purse. Top seeds Eva Celbova and Sona Novakova of the Czech Republic finished third after defeating You Wenhui and Wang Lu of China 21-15 and 21-10 in the "Bronze-Medal" match.

3rd Place: Eva Celbova and Sona Dosoudilova-Czech Republic
4th Place: Lu Wang and Wenhui You-China
5th Place: Angela Clarke and Kerri-Ann Pottharst-Australia
5th Place: Mayra Garcia and Hilda Gaxiola-Mexico
5th Place: Milagros Crespolmara and Esteves Ribalta-Cuba
5th Place: Kylie Gerlic and Summer Lochowicz-Australia

MILAN ITALY
September 3rd-7th, 2003

The Women's FIVB $150,000.00 Italy Open, staged in Milan, was won by China's golden girls Jia Tian and Fei Wang, winning for the second week in a row. After becoming the first team from the world's most populated country to win a "Gold-Medal" on the World Tour by winning the Bali Open the previous week. The two 22-year-old's won the championship match again after fighting back from one game down to beat the Brazilian second seeds Adriana Behar and Shelda by scores of 17-21, 22-20 and 15-11. The young Asian duo performed with remarkable consistency all tournament long. Jia Tian was the tournament's Most Valuable Player. The USA team of Nancy Mason and Dianne DeNecochea completed their best finish on the 2003 SWATCH-FIVB World Tour when they beat the Netherlands duo of Rebekka Kadijk and Marrit Leenstra in two straight games 21-16 and 21-13 in the playoff for the "Bronze-Medal."

3rd Place: Dianne DeNecochea and Nancy Mason-USA
4th Place: Rebekka Kadijk and Marrit Leenstra-Netherlands
5th Place: Suzanne Lahme and Danja Musch-Germany
5th Place: Daniela Gattelli and Lucilla Perrotta-Italy
5th Place: Nicole Benoit and Simone Kuhn-Switzerland
5th Place: Ethel Julie Arjona and Virginie Kadjo-France

LOS ANGELES CALIFORNIA U.S.A
September 18th-21st, 2003

The 2003 Women's FIVB World Tour event, staged in Carson California U.S.A. was won by the American team of Kerri Walsh and Misty May. They won their third consecutive SWATCH-FIVB World Tour final against Brazil's Ana Paula Connelly and Sandra Pires Tavares, when they produced a stunning comeback to defeat their arch-rivals at this $300,000.00 Nissan Grand Slam. In the "Gold-Medal" match, staged on center court of the "Home-Depot" sports center complex, Walsh and May, the reigning World Tour champions, lost a tough first game 22-24. They went on to win the second game 22-20. In the third game they needed to rally from a deficits of 1-4 and 7-10 to close out the match 15-12. Australia's Natalie Cooke and Nicole Sanderson won the "Bronze-Medal" when they ended the medal-winning run of China's Tian Jia and Wang Fei with a 23-21 and 21-18 triumph.

3rd Place: Natalie Cook and Nicole Sanderson-Australia
4th Place: Jia Tian and Fei Wang-China
5th Place: Annette Davis and Jenny Johnson Jordan-USA
5th Place: Stephanie Pohl and Okka Rau-Germany
5th Place: Lisa Arce and Rachel Wacholder-USA
5th Place: Vassiliki Arvaniti and Efthalia Koutroumanidou-Greece

RIO DE JANEIRO BRAZIL
October 7th-12th, 2003

The Women's FIVB $400,000.00 World Championship, staged on Copacabana Beach in Rio de Janeiro, Brazil, was won by the USA's Misty May and Kerri Walsh as they left nobody in any doubt as to their standing as the premier team, in women's beach volleyball. In the "Gold-Medal" match, they defeated Brazil's Adriana Brando Behar and Shelda Kelly Bruno 21-19 and 21-19. The duo claimed their fifth title of the 2003 FIVB World Tour. It was their fourth title in succession on the World Tour and complimented their remarkable form on the American domestic circuit during which they went unbeaten on the way to winning eight events.

3rd Place: Natalie Cook and Nicole Sanderson-Australia
4th Place: Annette Davis and Jenny Johnson Jordan-USA
5th Place: Ana Paula Connelly and Sandra Pires-Brazil
5th Place: Nicole Benoit and Simone Kuhn-Switzerland
5th Place: Holly McPeak and Elaine Youngs-USA
5th Place: Shaylyn Bede and Renata Ribeiro-Brazil

2003 WOMEN'S BEACH VOLLEYBALL ACTION-CARSON CALIFORNIA-U.S.A.
TOP LEFT PHOTO: Australia's Nicole Sanderson hits a set from compatriot Natalie Cook, into the block of China's Jia Tian. **TOP RIGHT PHOTO:** Brazil's Sandra Pires hits a set from partner Ana Paula Connelly, topwards the block of American Kerri Walsh. **BOTTOM LEFT PHOTO:** China's Jai Tian challenging the block of the USA's Elaine Youngs. **BOTTOM RIGHT PHOTO:** Holly McPeak, from the United States of America, challenges the block of China's Fei Wang. All of the above action took place during the 2003 FIVB World Tour event, in the city of Carson, near Los Angeles California U.S.A.

Photo's Courtesy of "Couvi"

TOP PHOTOS: Left: Germany's Suzzane Lahme reaches for the ball. **Center:** Brazil's Ana Paula Connelly braces herself for the dig. **Right:** Brazil's Sandra Pires gets into position to make the play.

MIDDLE PHOTOS: Left: Eva Celbova, from the Czech Republic, challenges the block of Elaine Youngs, from the USA. **Center:** America's Misty May makes an all-effort while diving for the dig. **Right:** China's Jia Tian follows through after attacking the ball.

2003 WOMEN'S BEACH VOLLEYBALL ACTION

BOTTOM PHOTOS: Left: Australia's Pauline Manser challenges the block of Mist May, from the USA. **Center:** Australia's Nicole Sanderson pounds the ball through the net. **Right:** China's Fei wang follows-through with her jump serve.

Photo's Courtesy of "Couvi"

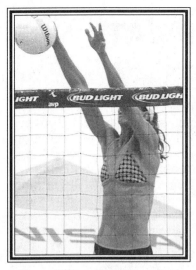

TOP PHOTOS: Left: Dianne DeNecochea gets above the net to make a successful block of the ball. **Center:** Lisa Arce hits the ball past the block of Sara Straton. **Right:** Holly McPeak is in the right spot to make another dig.

MIDDLE PHOTOS: Left: Misty May challenging the block of Carrie Busch. **Center:** Liz Masakayan (left) and Linda Hanley (right) anounced their retirement from the AVP Tour. **Right:** Misty May challenges the block of Liz Masakayan.

2003 WOMEN'S BEACH VOLLEYBALL ACTION

BOTTOM PHOTOS: Left: Elaine Youngs rejects the ball. **Center:** Nancy Mason pokes the ball over the block of Lisa Arce. **Right:** Kerri Walsh gets above the net for the spike.

Photo's Courtesy of "Couvi"

ADDITIONAL VOLLEYBALL INFORMATION 2003

HOLYOKE MASSACHUSETTS
October 25th, 2003

The Volleyball Hall of Fame in Holyoke, Massachusetts inducted four international Beach Volleyball players. They included legend Sinjin Smith, Japanese volleyball player Jungo Morita and coaches Julio Velasco of Italy and the late Givi Akhvlediani of Russia. Smith, who is currently the President of the Beach Volleyball World Council, was known as "King of the Beach" in his playing days, which spanned 23 years from 1977. He was the first professional player to reach 100 career victories and won 11 International and World Championships and placed fifth at the 1996 Olympics in Atlanta. Japanese legend Morita was a true innovator and part of the national team that won Olympic Gold in 1972 while Akhvlediani and Velasco, who both recently received "Special 20th Century Awards" by the Federation Internationale de Volleyball (FIVB) when it considered Volleyball's best coaches, had been pioneers in the sport. Akhvlediani coached the USSR men's team to World Championship glory in 1960 and 1962 before taking the women's team to gold medals at the 1968 and 1972 Olympics. Velasco, who currently coaches the Coprasystel club in Italy, fashioned the Italian men's team into one of the most dominant teams in the 1990s, winning two World Championships, five consecutive World League titles and an Olympic silver medal in 1996. Velasco coached the "Best Men's Team of the 20th Century," according to the FIVB.

LAUSANNE SWITZERLAND
January 27th, 2003

Lausanne, January 27, 2003 - A groundbreaking research project into injuries in professional Beach Volleyball indicated that professional Beach Volleyball is a safe sport and the rate of acute time-loss injuries is considerably lower than most other team sports. The researchers, Dr. Ronald Bahr and Dr. Jonathan Reeser conducted their research at the 2001 Beach Volleyball World Championship in Klagenfurt, Austria, and the incidence of injuries was measured at five other FIVB World Tour events in 2001. They are both members of the FIVB Medical Commission. The study, the first of its kind that pays special attention to professional Beach Volleyball, was published in the March 2003 issue of the American Journal of Sports Medicine. It showed that the injury pattern in the sport resembles that of indoor volleyball, but with fewer ankle injuries. Researchers found, however, that more than one in every three players reported having sought medical attention for an overuse injury during the 7.5-week study period, mainly for knee, shoulder, and low back pain. Beach Volleyball has been an Olympic discipline since the 1996 Atlanta Olympic Games. About the authors Ronald Bahr, MD PhD, Secretary of the FIVB Medical Commission is a professor of sports medicine and Chair of the Oslo Sports Trauma Research Center and the Department of Sports Medicine at the University of Sport and Physical Education. Dr. Jonathan Reeser, Member of the FIVB Medical Commission, is from the Department of Physical Medicine, Marshfield Clinic, Marshfield, Wisconsin, USA. Read the report online The Research is available online at the Oslo Sports Trauma Research Center web-site (in English and Norwegian)

ASPEN COLORADO
August 28th-September 1st, 2003

Concluding its 31st year, the MotherLode is, still, that fun little tournament held every Labor Day weekend in the mountain hamlet of Aspen, Colorado. Event Producer/Director Leon Fell provided the 31st Annual MotherLode Volleyball Classic results. In the championship match, of the Men's Open, Chris Hannemann (Seal Beach CA) and Dana Camacho (Fort Lauderdale FL) out-pointed Randy Meador (Houston TX) and Riley Salmon (Houston TX) by the score of 25-17. There were 69 teams entered in this division.

3rd Place: Colin Kaslow (Austin TX) and Tim Wooliver (Austin TX)
4th Place: Dave Smith (Culver City CA) and Skyler Davis (Dallas TX)
5th Place: Dane Hansen (Raleigh NC) and Curtis Griffin (Boulder CO)
5th Place: Ryan Post (Denver CO) and Jamey Martin (Denver CO)

In the championship match, of the Women's Open, Krista Schwartzendruber (Thornton CO) and Angela Knopf (Fort Collins CO) overwhelmed Wendy Martin (Tampa FL) and Mel Karwowski (San Antonio TX), by the scores of 21-18 and 21-16. There were 30 teams entered in this division.

3rd Place: Samantha Meador (Houston TX) and Julie McGarr (Houston TX)
4th Place: Kris Bredehoft (Englewood CO) and Tanya Bond (Aurora CO)
5th Place: Dawn Tischauser (Denver CO) and Natalie Sime (Denver CO)
5th Place: Kristie LoDolce (Redmond WA) and Brandi Travess (Redmond)

MOTHERLODE ACTION
Over the years, the annual MotherLode beach volleyball tournament has been attracting players of all abilities to play in front of large crowds in a party atmosphere. The MotherLode began in 1973 and is always played over Labor-Day weekend.
Photo Courtesy of Aspen Times

MOTHERLODE CLASSIC OPEN CHAMPIONS
MEN'S & WOMEN'S SINCE 1973

Year	Men's Champions
2003	Chris Hannemann/Dana Camacho
2002	Skyler Davis/Brian Soldano
2001	Canyon Ceman/Adam Jewell
2000	Ian Clark/Dax Holdren
1999	Dane Hansen/Ryan Post
1998	Curtis Griffin/Erik Moore
1997	Curtis Griffin/Erik Moore
1996	Curtis Griffin/Erik Moore
1995	Curtis Griffin/Erik Moore
1994	Leif Hanson/Rob Heidger
1993	Tom Duke/Jeff Williams
1992	Matt Perry/Pat Powers
1991	Larry Mear/Eric Wurts
1990	Pono Ma'a/Pat Powers
1989	Roger Clark/Shawn Fallowfield
1988	Roy Gerlits/Scott Steele
1987	Craig Moothart/Scott Steele
1986	Rudy Dvorak/Shawn Fallowfield
1985	Marty Gregory/Scott Steele
1984	John Cook/Gary Stevenson
1983	Tim Hill/Mike Wirsing
1982	Jack Hinton/Garth Pischke
1981	Larry Benecke/Garth Pischke
1980	Dale Pruce/Rob Quinlan
1979	Garth Pischke/Jon Stanley
1978	Results not available
1977	Called for darkness
1976	Rainout
1975	Rainout
1974	Bruce Downing/Bob Pape
1973	Chester Goss/Steve Goss

Year	Women's Champions
2003	Angela Knopf/Krista Swartendruber
2002	Angela Knopf/Krista Swartzendruber
2001	Daven Casad-Allison/Alicia Scott
2000	Nancy Mason/Leanne Schuster
1999	Valinda Hilleary/Pat Keller
1998	Nancy Mason/Leanne Schuster
1997	Valinda Hilleary/Pat Keller
1996	Shannon Misek/Gina Pilitere
1995	Kristine Bailey/Danalee Bragado
1994	Kristine Bailey/Christine Schaefer
1993	Valinda Hilleary/Pat Keller
1992	Shawn Hoover/Erin Deiter
1991	Kim Harsch-Bird/Chris Miller
1990	Shawn Hoover/Kim Harsch-Bird
1989	Shawn Hoover/Kim Harsch-Bird
1988	Janice Opalinski, Elaine Roque
1987	Lynn Bulig/Mary Diamond
1986	Shawn Hoover/Debbie Main
1985	Shawn Hoover/Debbie Main
1984	Shawn Hoover/Debbie Main
1983	Shawn Hoover/Debbie Main
1982	S. Hoover/Laurel Brassey-Kessel
1981	Hillary Johnson/Julie Morgan
1980	Hillary Johnson/Jerrie McGahan
1979	Suzanne Murphy/Patty O'Brien
1978	Results not available
1977	Linda Dahle/Linda Smith
1976	Susan Daily/Ann McKay
1975	Susan Daily/Ann McKay
1974	Laurie Buck/Susan Daily
1973	None

ERIK MOORE & CURTIS GRIFFIN
With 4 championships, the team of Curtis Griffin and Erik Moore are the most prolific Men's Open Division winner's in the history of the MotherLode tournament. Above photo, Moore challenges the block, during action at a 1990's MotherLode tournament.
Photo Courtesy of John Pryor, MotherLode Photographer

DANA CAMACHO & CHRIS HANNEMANN
The 2003 MotherLode Men's Open Division champions were Dana Comacho and Chris Hannemann. In the championship match they defeated Randy Meador and Riley Salmon. Above photo, Camacho hits a set from Hanneman.
Photo Courtesy of John Pryor, MotherLode Photographer

The Annual MotherLode Tournament
Men

Photos Courtesy of John Pryor, MotherLode Photographer

The Annual MotherLode Tournament Women

Photos Courtesy of John Pryor, MotherLode Photographer

MOTHERLODE BEACH VOLLEYBALL ACTION-ASPEN COLORADO
TOP LEFT PHOTO: Early 1970's MotherLode action, with Bobby Kaiser challenging the block of Marshall Savage. Tim Oliver is on defense. **TOP RIGHT PHOTO:** With eight championship victories (5 with Debbie Main), Shawn Hoover is the all-time winner of the MotherLode's Women's Open Division. Above photo, Hoover is ready to make the play. **BOTTOM LEFT PHOTO:** Matt Unger challenging the block of Neil Rooney. Kyle Schultz is on defense. **BOTTOM RIGHT PHOTO:** Valinda Hillary is just one of the many "Pro" beach players that have participated in the MotherLode tournament. Above photo, Hillary attacks a set from Pat Keller. All of the above action took place, over the years, during various MotherLode tournaments in Aspen Colorado.
Top Photos Courtesy of the Aspen Times. Bottom Photos courtesy of John Pryor, MotherLode Photographer

MEN'S BEACH VOLLEYBALL
2004

AVP

In 2004, the Men's AVP Nissan Series included twelve stops, featuring over $1 million in total prize money, for both men and women playing each event for equal purses. The 2004 Tour visited all ten of the 2003 stops, with the addition of two new sites. The new sites were in Austin, Texas and Honolulu Hawaii. The remaining ten stops included five stops in California. The California stops were in Huntington Beach, Manhattan Beach, San Diego, Hermosa Beach, and the Los Angeles Invitational in Carson. The remaining five stops were in Fort Lauderdale Florida, Tempe Arizona, Belmar New Jersey, Chicago Illinois and Las Vegas Nevada. The 2004 AVP Pro Beach Volleyball Tour, the 21st consecutive season, took a hiatus during August as two qualifying men's and women's teams competed in the 2004 Summer Olympics in Athens, Greece. In addition, NBC increased its network coverage from last season with the Belmar NJ, Hermosa Beach CA, Chicago IL, Las Vegas NV and Honolulu HI. The remainder of the season was scheduled for telecasts via Fox Sports Net.

The 2004 Men's AVP Tour began, as it left-off in 2003, showcasing "Team-Parity" with the first three events delivering a different champion. At the first event, in Fort Lauderdale Florida, Casey Jennings and Matt Fuerbringer were once again (for the fifth time) in the championship match where they lost to Sean Rosenthal and Larry Witt. The next event in Tempe Arizona, Sean Scott and Todd Rogers were the winners over Karch Kiraly and Mike Lambert. The third event, in Austin Texas, produced the third different champion when Adam Jewell and Jake Gibb won their first career championship by defeating Sean Scott and Todd Rogers in the championship match. Huntington Beach California was the site of the fourth AVP Tour event in 2004, where the winners were George Roumain and Jason Ring, keeping the trend alive by having the fourth different champion in as many events. The trend continued when Karch Kiraly and Mike Lambert won the Manhattan Beach event. Kiraly and Lambert put an end to the trend when they won again in San Diego California. The AVP "Team-Parity" trend" was on again when Casey Jennings and Matt Fuerbringer entered their sixth career championship match, on Belmar Beach NJ, where they finnaly captured their first career title by defeating Adam Jewell and Jake Gibb.

MIKE LAMBERT & KARCH KIRALY
The new team of Mike Lambert and Karch Kiraly showed some potential when they won "back-to-back" tournaments on the 2004 AVP Tour. First they won the Manhattan Beach Open then they follwed it up by winning the championsahip match on Mariners Point in San Diego California. The MB event was Kiraly's 145 career title and the 8th time Kiraly had won the MB Open. The SD event was the 146th title for Karch. Above photo, Karch hits a set from "Lambo" past the block of Matt Fuerbringer, towards the defense of Casey Jennings.
Photo Courtesy of "Couvi"

2004 INDIVIDUAL AVP TOURNAMENT FINISHES

Player	1st	2nd	3rd	4th	5th
Eduardo Bacil	0	0	0	0	1
Paul Baxter	0	0	0	0	2
Dain Blanton	0	0	3	0	1
Canyon Ceman	0	0	1	0	1
Eli Fairfield	0	0	0	0	1
Eric Fonoimoana	0	0	1	0	1
Matt Fuerbringer	1	2	0	0	1
Jake Gibb	1	1	2	0	0
John Hayden	0	0	0	0	1
Dax Holdren	0	0	1	0	2
Casey Jennings	1	2	0	0	1
Adam Jewell	1	1	2	0	0
Karch Kiraly	**2**	**1**	**2**	**0**	**0**
Mike Lambert	**2**	**1**	**2**	**0**	**0**
Stein Metzger	0	0	1	0	2
Chad Mowrey	0	0	0	0	1
Jeff Nygaard	0	0	3	0	1
Ed Ratledge	0	0	0	0	1
Jason Ring	1	0	2	0	2
Todd Rogers	1	1	1	0	0
George Roumain	1	0	2	0	2
Sean Scott	1	1	1	0	0
Mike Whitmarsh	0	0	1	0	0
Andy Witt	0	0	0	0	1
Larry Witt	1	2	1	0	1
Kevin Wong	0	0	1	0	1
Scott Wong	0	0	0	0	2

(**Note:** The above tournament finishes include 2004 results for events up to and including the July 11th final of the Belmar New Jersey tournament)

FIVB

In Lausanne, Switzerland, the International Volleyball Federation (FIVB) increased the schedule for the 2004 Swatch-FIVB World Tour, with five more events than the 2003 schedule. The 2004 season was a landmark for Beach Volleyball, with an impressive 27 tournaments (15 men and 12 women), worth $5,480,000.00 in Prize Money and Bonus Pool. FIVB President IOC member Dr. Ruben Acosta said: "It confirms the positive decisions made by the FIVB and its partners and creates a solid platform to further promote Beach Volleyball at all levels and all over the world." For the first time the Swatch-FIVB World Tour, included a three-leg Grand Slam series that began in Germany and was followed by legs in France and Austria. The 2004 season was scheduled over seven months starting in March and explored new territories over five continents. Men's and women's open events were contested on some of the world's most famous beaches in Greece, South Africa, France, Portugal, Puerto Rico and Spain and in the glamorous cities of Shanghai, Lianyungang, Osaka, Berlin, Stavanger, Montreal, Klagenfurt, Milan, and Stare Jablonki as well as the Gstaad Open in the enchanting mountains of Switzerland in Gstaad.

Early in 2004, the FIVB staged a "Country vs Country" event, in Rio de Janeiro Brazil, where the United States' Dain Blanton and Jeff Nygard scored a victory over the Brazilian world champion pair of Ricardo Santos and Emanuel Rego, as the USA walked away with the "Country vs Country" title. The 2004 FIVB Men's World Tour began in Salvador Brazil with the Brazilian team of Emanuel Rego and Ricardo Santos, beginning where they left-off at the 2003 World Championship, in Rio de

KARCH KIRALY
Karch Kiraly was "pumped-up" on the 2004 AVP Tour. Kiraly teamed-up with Mike Lambert and at the half-way-point of the season, they had advanced to 3 finals, winning 2 events. Above photo, Kiraly gets "pumped-up" at the 2004 Huntington event.
Photo Courtesy of Ken Delgado

JEFF NYGARD & DAIN BLANTON
Jeff Nygard and Dain Blanton, began the 2004 season where they left-off the 2003 season, with a win at the FIVB "Country-vs-Country" event, staged in Rio de Janeiro Brazil. Above photo, Nygard cuts a set from Blanton, at the block of George Roumain.
Photo Courtesy of "Couvi"

Janeiro Brazil, winning another "Gold-Medal" match. This time against the Swiss "brothers" team of Martin and Paul Laciga. Santos and Rego also won the events in Lianyungang China, Budva Serbia Montengro, Espinho Portugal and Stavanger Norway. The 2004 event staged in Cape Town South Africa was won by the Brazilian team of Franco Neto and Tande Ramos. Brazil's Pedro Henrique Cunha paired-up with compatriot Paráá Ferreira to win the men's "Gold-Medal" match on Carolina Beach in Puerto Rico. The Swiss team of Paul and Martin Laciga won in Santa Ponsa Mallorca, while their compatriots, Patrick Heuscher and Stefan Kobel won the event in Gstaad Switzerland. The German team of Jonas Reckermann and Markus Dieckman won in Berlin Germany.

The highlight of the 2004 FIVB Tour was to be the 24 men and 24 women's teams at the Olympic Games in Athens, Greece, August 14-25. World Tour events that were staged before July 13, 2004 were part of the Olympic qualification process, which started in June, 2003. The best eight results of each pair based on World Ranking points including the results of the recognized continental finals were used to determine the best 24 teams per gender (with a maximum of two teams per country) for the Olympic Games in Athens. A double elimination playing format was implemented for the 2004 Swatch-FIVB World Tour, as well as Challenger and Satellite events. The pool play format followed by single elimination, which had been used for the past two years, will only be used at the Olympics Games in Athens to better accommodate the needs of broadcasters and media.

2004 INDIVIDUAL FIVB TOURNAMENT FINISHES

Player	1st	2nd	3rd	4th	5th
Franco Alvarez	0	0	0	0	1
Marcio Araujo	0	0	1	1	2
Mariano Baracetti	0	1	2	1	0
Javier Bosma	1	0	0	0	1
John Child	0	0	0	0	1
Martin Alejo Conde	0	1	2	1	0
Pedro Henrique Cunha	1	0	1	0	0
Christopher Diechmann	0	0	0	1	1
Markus Diechmann	1	2	0	2	0
Markus Egger	0	1	0	0	2
Rogerio Para Ferreira	1	0	1	0	0
Eric Fonoimoana	0	0	0	0	1
Peter Gartmayer	0	0	0	1	0
Mark Heese	0	0	0	0	1
Patrick Heuscher	1	1	1	0	2
Pablo Herrea	1	0	0	0	1
Sascha Heyer	0	1	0	0	2
Dax Holdren	0	0	0	1	0
Vegard Hoidalen	0	1	0	0	0
Iver Horrem	0	0	0	0	1
Benjamin Insfran	0	0	2	1	0
Kristian Karis	0	0	0	1	0
Jorre Kjemperud	0	1	0	0	0
David Klemperer	0	1	0	0	0
Stefan Kobel	1	1	1	0	2
Martin Laciga	1	1	0	0	2
Paul Laciga	1	1	0	0	2
Bjorn Maaseide	0	0	0	0	1
Amiraldo Magalhaes	0	0	1	0	0
Harley Marques	0	0	1	1	0
Stein Metzger	0	2	0	0	2
Jose Franco Vieira Neto	1	0	2	0	1
Robert Nowotny	0	0	0	1	0
Julien Prosser	0	0	0	0	2
Niklas Rademacher	0	1	0	0	0
Tande Ramos	1	0	2	0	1
Jonas Reckermann	1	2	0	2	0
Todd Rogers	0	0	0	1	1
Miguel Rosell	0	0	0	0	1
Ricardo Alex Costa Santos	**4**	**2**	**1**	**1**	**0**
Andrew Schacht	0	0	0	0	1
Emanuel Rego Scheffer	**4**	**2**	**1**	**1**	**0**
Andreas Scheuerpflug	0	0	0	1	1
Sean Scott	0	0	0	1	1
Paulo Emilo Silva	0	0	1	0	0
Josh Slack	0	0	0	0	1
Fred Souza	0	0	0	1	0
Rivo Vesik	0	0	0	1	0
Mark Williams	0	0	0	0	2
Kevin Wong	0	0	0	0	1

Note: The above tournament finishes include 2004 results for events up to and including the July 11th final of the Santa Ponsa Mallorca event)

EMANUEL REGO
In 2004, Emanuel Rego was still teamed-up with Ricardo Santos and began where they left-off in 2003, by winning the first FIVB World Tour event in Salvador Brazil, followed by 4 additional titles. Above photo, Rego is ready to chase-down the ball on defense.
Photo Courtesy of Ken Delgado

PATRICK HEUSCHER & STEFAN KOBEL
The Swiss team of Patrick Heuscher and Stefan Kobel stepped-up to win the "Gold-Medal" at the 2004 FIVB World Tour event in Gstaad Switzerland. Above photo Heuscher hits a set from Kobel, away from the block of Mike Whitmarsh.
Photo Courtesy of "Couvi"

MEN'S TOURNAMENT RESULTS
2004-AVP

FORT LAUDERDALE FLORIDA
April 2nd-4thth, 2004

The first 2004 Men's AVP Nissan Series event was at South Beach Park, in Fort Lauderdale Florida. The winner's of the event were Sean "Rosie" Rosenthal and Larry "Dizzel" Witt. After facing each other in the semifinals earlier in the day, center court featured Rosenthal and Witt against last year's second-place finishers Matt Fuerbringer and Casey Jennings. Rosie and Dizzel out-played the runner-ups, 21-17 and 21-14. The winner's split $14,500.00 while the runner-ups shared $9,750.00. Earlier in the semifinals, Rosenthal and Witt lost to Fuerbringer and Jennings 21-15, 19-21, 15-13. Fuerbringer and Jennings qualified for the finals after coming through the contender's bracket. The pair beat the new team of George Roumain and Jason Ring 23-21, 21-19. Earlier, Roumain and Ring had two major upsets when they defeated the teams consisying of Olympic Gold Medalist Eric Fonoimoana and Olympian Kevin Wong and Olympic Gold Medalist Dain Blanton and Olympian Jeff Nygard.

3rd Place: Todd Rogers and Sean Scott
3rd Place: Jason Ring and George Roumain
5th Place: Dax Holdren and Stein Metzger
5th Place: John Hyden and Andy Witt

TEMPE ARIZONA
April 23rd-25th, 2004

A sell-out crowd of more than 6,000 watched America''s finest beach volleyball players, compete at the Men's Association of Volleyball Professionals $62,500.00 Men's Tempe Open. After three days of competition, in 95°F heat and only six percent humidity, in the "purpose-built" stadium court, the team of Todd Rogers and Sean Scott captured the championship. In the 79 minute crowd-pleasing final, Rogers and Scott denied three-time Olympic gold medalist Karch Kiraly another title in his brilliant career with a hard fought, three-set 15-21, 25-23 and 18-16, over Kiraly and his partner Mike Lambert. The win was the first of Scott's career while Rogers was winning for the ninth time.

3rd Place: Jason Ring and George Roumain
3rd Place: Jake Gibb and Adam Jewell
5th Place: Dax Holdren and Stein Metzger
5th Place: Chad Mowrey and Ed Ratledge

AUSTIN TEXAS
April 30th-May 2nd, 2004

The 2004 Men's AVP Nissan Series $62,500.00 Austin Open at Auditorium Shores Park in Austin Texas was won by the hard hitting Adam Jewell and the tough

LARRY WITT & SEAN ROSENTHAL
Larry "Dizzel" Witt and Sean "Rosie" Rosenthal stepped-up to win the first AVP Tour event in 2004, when they won the Fort Lauderdale Florida championship. Above photo, Rosie hits a set from Dizzel, towards the defense of Aaron Boss.
Photo Courtesy of Ken Delgado

TODD ROGERS & SEAN SCOTT
In 2004, Todd Rogers and Sean Scott won the second AVP Tour event of the season by winning the Tempe Arizona championship. Above photo, Scott hits a set from Rogers, away from the block of Brent Doble. Karch Kiraly is on defense.
Photo Courtesy of Ken Delgado

blocking Jake Gibb. In the championship match, Jewell and Gibb earned their first AVP Pro Beach Volleyball Tour title by defeating last weekend's Tempe Open winners Todd Rogers and Sean Scott 21-12 and 21-18. The finals were staged in front of packed stands as the fans of Austin cheered the return of the tournament after an 11-year interruption. This was the first time in Gibb's two-year career that he has made it to the finals. He and Jewell lost against Rogers and Scott earlier in the day 19-21 and 19-21 and then arrived in the finals after coming through the contender's bracket.

3rd Place: Dain Blanton and Jeff Nygard
3rd Place: Dax Holdren and Stein Metzger
5th Place: Sean Rosenthal and Larry Witt
5th Place: Matt Fuerbringer and Casey Jennings

HUNTINGTON BEACH CALIFORNIA
May 28th-30th, 2004

Rising Stars Jason Ring and George Roumain captured their first championship victory at the AVP Huntington Beach Nissan Series event. In-front of the crowded stadium, the first-time tournament title for the up-and-coming team of Ring and Roumain. As the number three seeds, out-distanced the first-seeded team of Sean Rosenthal and Larry Witt 21-12, 21-16. The winner's split $14,500.00 while the runner-ups shared $9,750.00. Ring and Roumain arrived at the finals after defeating three-time Olympian Karch Kiraly and his partner Olympian Mike Lambert 21-17, 17-21, 21-19, in the semifinals, where the losers were relegated to third place ties. In the other semifinal match, Rosenthal and Witt out-lasted Dain Blanton and Jeff Nygaard 22-20 and 21-19. This event was missing some of the top Olympic-contenders including Dax Holdren and Stein Metzger, Tempe Open winners Todd Rogers and Sean Scott and 2000 Olympians Eric Fonoimoana and Kevin Wong were all in Budva on the coast of Serbia and Montenegro, for an FIVB World Tour event. These teams were each attempting to get the edge, over each other, in gaining qualifying points for the 2004 Olympics in Athens Greece.

3rd Place: Karch Kiraly and Mike Lambert
3rd Place: Dain Blanton Jeff Nygaard
5th Place: Paul Baxter Scott Wong
5th Place: Eduardo Bacil Eli Fairfield

MANHATTAN BEACH CALIFORNIA
June 4th-6th, 2004

The stands, south of the Manhattan Beach Pier, as well as on the Pier, were filled to capacity, during a weekend of records, as three-time Olympian Karch Kiraly, the oldest player on the AVP Tour, won his 145th career tournament championship and his eighth Manhattan Beach Open, with partner Olympian Mike Lambert. In the championship match, Kiraly and Lambert outplayed Matt Fuerbringer and Casey Jennings 21-15, 21-18 to win the 2004 Manhattan Beach Men's Open. It was the first AVP title for Lambert. The winner's collected $14,500.00 for their efforts while the runner-ups shared $9,750.00. Kiraly and Lambert won their 65 minute semi-final match against Eric Fonoimoana and Kevin Wong by the scores of 22-20, 17-21 and 15-13. Fuerbringer and Jennings won their 70 minute semi-final match against Dain Blanton and Jeff Nygaard, by the scores of 21-15, 21-23 and 15-13

3rd Place: Dain Blanton and Jeff Nygaard
3rd Place: Eric Fonoimoana and Kevin Wong
5th Place: Canyon Ceman and Mike Whitmarsh
5th Place: Jason Ring and George Roumain

JAKE GIBB & ADAM JEWELL
Jake Gibb and Adam Jewell teamed-up to win the third AVP Tour event in 2004. They were the first place winners in Austin Texas. Above photo, Jewell hits a set from Gibb, towards the block of Ty Loomis.
Photo Courtesy of "Couvi"

JASON RING & GEORGE ROUMAIN
Jason Ring and George Roumain each won their first tournament championship at the 2004 AVP Tour event in Huntington Beach California. Above photo, Ring hits a set from Roumain, away from the block of Jeff Nygard.
Photo Courtesy of "Couvi"

SAN DIEGO CALIFORNIA
June 11th-13th, 2004

The 2004 AVP Nissan Series Tour event on Mariners Point in San Diego California was won by three-time Olympian Karch Kiraly and partner Olympian Mike Lambert. In the championship match, Lambert and Kiraly defeated Sean Rosenthal and Larry Witt 21-18, 14-21 and 15-8. For Kiraly this weekend in San Diego marked his record-extending 146th win and Lambert's second on the Tour. Kiraly and Lambert took 50 minutes to defeat Adam Jewell and Jake Gibb 23-21 and 21-11 in their semi-final match. In a quick 34 minute semi-final match, Rosenthal and Witt made short work of Canyon Ceman and Mike Whitmarsh, 21-19 and 21-15. The men's teams of Jeff Nygaard with Dain Blanton, Stein Metzger with Dax Holdren, and Todd Rogers with Sean Scott were not entered in this weekend's tournament. They were all playing in an FIVB Tour Olympic qualifier in Puerto Rico.

3rd Place: Adam Jewell and Jake Gibb
3rd Place: Canyon Ceman and Mike Whitmarsh
5th Place: Eric Fonoimoana and Kevin Wong
5th Place: Jason Ring and George Roumain

BELMAR NEW JERSEY

July 8th-11th, 2004 The 2004 Men's AVP Nissan Series Belmar Open, presented by Bud Light was won by Crowd-pleasers Matt Fuerbringer and Casey Jennings when they took home their first AVP title on the sands of Belmar, New Jersey. In their seventh career championship match appearance, Fuerbringer and Jennings finally seized their first title, when they out-scored Jake Gibb and Adam Jewell 21-14, 21-19. During the match, Jewell fought-off the pain of leg cramps in a valiant effort to block Fuerbringer and Jennings quest for the title. The winner's collected $20,000.00 for their efforts while the runner-ups shared $14,000.00.

3rd Place: Karch Kiraly and Mike Lambert
3rd Place: Sean Rosenthal and Larry Witt
5th Place: Paul Baxter and Scott Wong
5th Place: Dain Blanton and Jeff Nygaard

Additional events scheduled for 2004 included Hermosa Beach CA, Chicago IL, Las Vegas NV, Waikki HI and Carson CA.

MIKE LAMBERT & KARCH KIRALY
Mike Lambert and Karch Kiraly were the first two-time winner's on the 2004 AVP Tour. They won the Manhattan Beach and San Diego events. Above photo, Lambert gets above the net for the block attempt and Kiraly is "ever-ready" on defense.
Photo Courtesy of "Couvi"

CASEY JENNINGS & MATT FUERBRINGER
Casey Jennings and Matt Fuerbringer were first-time winner's when they won the 2004 Belmar NJ event. They had advanced to five previous finals prior to this victory. Above photo, Jennings hits a set from Fuerbringer, past the block of Mike Whitmarsh.
Photo Courtesy of "Couvi"

MEN'S TOURNAMENT RESULTS
2004-FIVB

SALVADOR BRAZIL
March 16th-21st, 2004

The first stop on the 2004 SWATCH $180,000.00 FIVB World Tour was in Salvador Brazil. There was a jam-packed center court crowd of more than 4,000 in front of the at the Catussaba Resort Hotel, where Emanuel Rego and Ricardo Santos captured the "Gold-Medal" match. In the championship match, Emanuel and Ricardo defeated the top-seeded team of Stefan Kobel and Patrick Heuscher of Switzerland. Emanuel and Ricardo, who captured the 2003 SWATCH-FIVB World Tour's final two events in Los Angeles and Rio de Janeiro, scored a 21-19 and 21-18 win over the sixth-seeded Kobel and Heuscher to claim the $27,000.00 first-place prize. Emanuel and Ricardo never trailed in the 22-minute first game as they had leads of 5-2, 7-3, 13-8 and 15-9 before the Swiss used a 5-1 run to make it 20-19. In the 21-minute second game, the Swiss tandem raced to a 6-1 lead by scoring four points on their serve. Emanuel and Ricardo caught Kobel and Heuscher at 10-10 as the match was tied seven more times. After being tied at 18, the Brazilians scored the final three points, including the final score on an Emanuel serve that fell in front of the diving Swiss team. For their "Silver-Medal" finish, the Swiss split $18,000.00 for their best finish-ever in a FIVB "Open" event. The re-occurrence of an abdominal strain for Germany's Markus Dieckmann led to the forfeiture the "Bronze-Medal" with partner Jonas Reckermann, against the 11th-seeded Mariano Baracetti and Martin Conde, from Argentina.

3rd Place: Mariano Baracetti and Martin Conde-Argentina
4th Place: Markus Dieckmann and Jonas Reckermann-Germany
5th Place: Franco Neto and Tande Ramos-Brazil
5th Place: Francisco Alvarez and Juan Rosell-Cuba

CAPE TOWN SOUTH AFRICA
March 23rd-28th, 2004

The second stop on the 2004 SWATCH $180,000.00 FIVB World Tour was in Cape Town South Africa. Brazil's Tande Ramos and Franco Neto "surprised" the international beach volleyball community by capturing the South African Open "Gold-Medal" match. In that championship match, they upset the top-seeded Emanuel Rego and Ricardo Santos, in an All-Brazilian finale at Camps Bay before an over-flowing crowd of more than 2,000 beach volleyball fans. Seeded 12th in the 32-team Main Draw and playing in only their second SWATCH-FIVB World Tour event together, Tande and Franco scored a 27-25, 14-21 and 15-12 win over Emanuel and Ricardo to snap the top-ranked team's 25-match winning streak. With the win, Tande and Franco shared the $27,000.00 first-place prize, while Emanuel and Ricardo split $18,000.00 for the "Silver-Medal" finish. During the final the third and deciding game was tied nine times with Tande and Franco never trailing after taking a 2-1 lead. Tied at 8, 9, 10, 11 and 12, the winners took possession on a side out and scored the final two points on a hitting error and then Franco's block of Emanuel at the net. Another Brazilian team, Benjamin Insfran and Harley Marques consummated their brief two-event partnership by capturing the "Bronze-Medal" for a Brazilian podium sweep. The third-seeded Benjamin and Harley scored a 21-11 and 21-15 win in 41 minutes over 26th-seeded Robert Nowotny and Peter Gartmayer of Austria. Benjamin and Harley shared $14,000.00 for third-place.

3rd Place: Benjamin Insfran and Harley Marques-Brazil
4th Place: Peter Gartmayer and Robert Nowotny-Austria
5th Place: Christoph Dieckmann and Andreas Scheuerpflug-Germany
5th Place: Javier Bosma and Pablo Herrera-Spain

FRANCO NETO
Brazil's Franco Neto teamed-up with compatriot Tande Ramos to win the 2004 FIVB World Tour event in Cape Town South Africa. Above photo, Neto gets above the net in the block attempt of fellow countryman Luizao Correa.
Photo Courtesy of "Couvi"

LIANYUNGANG CHINA
May 19th-23rd, 2004

Following a late change of venue for the China Women's Open from Maoming to Lianyungang in 2003, due to the SARS epidemic, Beach Volleyball in this popular coastal town was a huge success as China staged international men's Beach Volleyball for the first time when the stars of the Swatch-FIVB Men''s World Tour arrived to partake in the $180,000.00 China Open. In the "Gold-Medal" match, playing before a full capacity crowd of 3,700 at the newly built Lianyungang Stadium, two tandems split the first two sets, forcing a tiebreaker, as the twelfth seeds Javier Bosma and Pablo Herrera of Spain upset top seeds and world number-one tandem Ricardo Santos and Emanuel Rego. The winner's survived three match points to outlast Ricardo and Emanuel 15-21, 21-19 and 21-19 for their second win in two days over the 2003 FIVB world champions. In the third game, the Brazilians were ahead 14-11 when Ricardo suddenly lost his momentum, failing to side out on two consecutive opportunities, allowing the Spaniards to overtake the lead at 18-17 and clinch the match in 66 minutes. Earlier in the tournament, Bosma and Herrera upset Ricardo and Emanuel 24-22 and 21-19 in a winner's bracket match. With the win, Bosma and Herrera shared the $27,000.00 first-place prize while Ricardo and Emanuel split $18,000.00 for the "Silver-Medal" finish.

3rd Place: Pedro Cunha Rogerio Para Brazil
4th Place: Todd Rogers and Sean Scott-USA
5th Place: Eric Fonoimoana Kevin Wong-USA
5th Place: Patrick Heuscher and Stefan Kobel-Switzerland

BUDVA SERBIA and MONTENEGRO
May 28th-30th, 2004

On the stunning beaches, with warm friendly people and mythological tales, a packed stadium watched as Ricardo Santos and Emanuel Rego of Brazil took the 2004, Swatch FIVB Serbia and Montenegro Open title in Budva. In the 43 minute "Gold-Medal" match Ricardo and Emanuel took two straight from Markus Diekmann and Jonas Reckermann of Germany by scores of 21-18 and 21-19. The winner's split $27,000.00 and the runner-ups shared $18,000.00. In the "Bronze-Medal" match, Patrick Heuscher and Stefan Kobel of Switzerland, triumphed over Kristjan Kais and Rivo Vesik of Estonia. The game scores of the 41 minute match were 21-17 and 21-18.

3rd Place: Patrick Heuscher and Stefan Kobel-Switzerland
4th Place: Kristjan Kais and Rivo Vesik-Estonia
5th Place: Martin Laciga and Paul Laciga-Switzerland
5th Place: Julien Prosser and Mark Williams-Australia

ESPINHO PORTUGAL
June 2nd-6th, 2004

In perfect conditions for beach volleyball, the 2004, Swatch - FIVB World Tour Portugal Open in Espinho was won by World Champions, Brazilians Ricardo Santos and Emanuel Rego. In the "Gold-Medal" match they faced Norwegian's Vegard Hoidalen and Jorre Andre Kjemperud, winning in two games, as the Brazilians were on fire, scoring 21-12 and 22-20 wins in a 38 minute match. Rego and Santos raced into a 10-2 first game lead, as they battered their opponents with astounding blocking from Santos and exceptional digging from Rego. In the second game, Hoidalen and Kjemperud managed to stay in touch with the eventual winners, however, with the score at 16-14, a crucial moment arrived when Ricardo rose to produce a thunderous spike that appeared to crush the Norwegian's resolve and from that point the outcome seemed inevitable. In the "Bronze-Medal" match, Brazilian's Benjamin Insfran and Marcio Araujo out-played Germany's Markus Dieckmann and Jonas Reckermann by 21-16 and 21-15.

3rd Place: Benjamin Insfran and Marcio Araujo-Brazil
4th Place: Markus Dieckmann and Jonas Reckermann-Germany
5th Place: John Child and Mark Heese-Canada
5th Place: Julien Prosser and Mark Williams-Australia

CAROLINA BEACH PUERTO RICO
June 9th-13th, 2004

The Carolina Open, the sixth stop on the 2004 SWATCH-FIVB World Tour, presented by Claxo Smith Kline was won by the second youngest player ever to win an FIVB World Tour event when Brazil's Pedro Henrique Cunha paired-up with compatriot Paráá Ferreira to win the men's "Gold-Medal" match. In the "Gold-Medal" match, just three days removed from his 21st birthday, Cunha along with Paráá, out-lasted seventh-seeded Mariano Baracetti and Martin Conde of Argentina 21-17 and 35-33 in the 58-minute final of this $180,000.00 event. With the win, the 12th-seeded Brazilians shared the $27,000.00 first-place check while Baracetti and Conde left the stadium splitting $18,000.00 for second-place. Brazil's Andre Lima was the youngest player ever to win an "open" SWATCH-FIVB World Tour event by capturing a July 29, 1990 event in Sete, France with Guilherme Marquez. Lima was only five days younger than Cunha at 20 years, 11 months and 29 days. In the "Bronze-Medal" match, second-seeded Franco Neto and Tande Ramos, also from Brazil, defeated Dax Holdren and Stein Metzger of the United States 22-20 and 21-19. The Brazilians shared $14,000.00 for their third place finish while the Americans split $11,000.00 with their fourth place finish.

3rd Place: Franco Neto and Tande Ramos-Brazil
4th Place: Dax Holdren and Stein Metzger-USA
5th Place: Benjamin Insfran and Marcio Araujo-Brazil
5th Place: Andrew Schacht and Josh Slack-Australia

GSTAAD SWITZERLAND
June 16th-20th, 2004

The beach volleyball fans were out in full-force, on the summer slopes of Gstaad in the Swiss Alps, for the 2004 Swatch FIVB World Tour's $360,000.00 "One-To-One Energy" Switzerland Open. The Swiss team of Patrick Heuscher and Stefan Kobel were the "Gold-Medal" winners. In the championship match they were able to solve their German rivals, Markus Dieckmann and Jonas Reckermann, as the Swiss pair captured their first-ever Beach Volleyball "open" title. Dieckmann and Reckermann, the 2004 European champions, played tough during the 54-minute match, but Heuscher and Kobel withstood a late charge by the Germans to score a 21-18 and 27-25 win to share the $27,000.00 first-place prize. Dieckmann and Reckermann split $18,000.00 for their "Silver-Medal" performance. This "Gold-Medal" match marked only the second-time in 154 "open" Swatch-FIVB World Tour events that two teams from Europe competed for an international title. The win also gave Switzerland their first "Gold-Medal" since the Laciga brothers (Martin and Paul) accomplished the feat in Spain and Mallorca at the end of the 2002 season. The last time two teams from Europe played for a SWATCH-FIVB World Tour "Gold-Medal" match was in 1994 in Marseille France, when Norway's Jan Kvalheim and Bjorn Maaseide defeated J. P. Jodard and Christian

Penigaud of France in the finals. In the all-Brazil "Bronze-Medal" match, the top seeds, Emanuel Rego and Ricardo Santos defeated fourth-seeded Benjamin Insfran and Marcio Araujo 21-18 and 21-16 in 41 minutes. Emanuel and Ricardo, shared $14,000.00 for third.

3rd Place: Emanuel Rego and Ricardo Santos-Brazil
4th Place: Benjamin Insfran and Marcio Araujo-Brazil
5th Place: Paul Laciga and Martin Laciga-Switzerland
5th Place: Sascha Heyer and Markus Egger-Switzerland

BERLIN GERMANY
June 23rd-27th, 2004

The city of Berlin Germany is now considered a firm promoter of Beach Volleyball. Berlin has now hosted highly-successful men's World Tour events for the past ten years. This year the Swatch FIVB World Tour returned with a total prize money of $600,000.00, for both men and women, in the first "Grand-Slam" event of 2004. To the enjoyment of the German fans, the German team of Markus Dieckmann and Jonas Reckermann claimed the top spot on the podium, capturing the "Gold-Medal" and sharing the $43,000.00 first-place prize. In the championship match, the third seeded team of Dieckmann and Reckermann rallied from a first game defeat to score a 20-22, 21-19 and 16-14 win in 66 minutes over the fifth-seeded team of Paul and Martin Laciga, from Switzerland. The Lacigas overcame a 12-11 deficit in the first game to lead 14-12. The Germans tied it at 20-20 and then the Swiss team scored the last two points. Dieckmann and Reckermann led 10-5 in the second game before the Swiss tied the game at 12, 13 and 14 points each. Three-straight German points led to a 17-14 lead and control of the second game. The Germans led 3-0, 6-2 and 9-4 in the third-and-deciding game before the Swiss tied it at 12 and 14 points each. The Swiss brothers split $29,500.00 for their second-place finish. In the "Bonze-Medal" match, Mariano Baracetti and Martin Conde, from Argentina, defeated top-ranked Emanuel Rego and Ricardo Santos of Brazil 21-12, 16-21 and 15-12 in 52 minutes.

3rd Place: Mariano Baracetti and Martin Conde-Argentina
4th Place: Emanuel Rego and Ricardo Santos-Brazil
5th Place: Benjamin Insfran and Marcio Araujo-Brazil
5th Place: Patrick Heuscher and Stefan Kobel-Switzerland

STAVANGER NORWAY

July 1st-4th, 2004 The Brazilian team of Ricardo Santos and Emanuel Rego were the "Gold-Medal" winners at the 2004 FIVB World Tour Conoco Phillips Open, staged in Stavanger Norway. This was the sixth consecutive year that a beach volleyball team from Brazil captured this event. In the championship match, the top seeded Ricardo and Rego won the 37-minute title match 21-15 and 21-17, over the German team of Niklas Rademacher and David Klemperer as the 26th-seeded Germans could not overcome the experience of top-seeded team. Emanuel and Ricardo split the $27,000.00 first-place prize. For the young Germans, who were playing in their first-ever "final four" on the SWATCH-FIVB World Tour, the "Silver-Medal" netted them $18,000.00. In the "Bronze-Medal" match, Brazil's Franco Neto and Tande Ramos defeated Germany's Christoph Dieckmann and Andreas Scheuerpflug by scores of 18-21, 21-18 and 15-10. The Brazilians shared $14,000.00 for third-place while the Germans split $11,000.00.

3rd Place: Franco Neto and Tande Ramos-Brazil
4th Place: Christoph Dieckmann and Andreas Scheuerpflug-Germany
5th Place: Sascha Heyer and Markus Egger-Switzerland
5th Place: Sean Scott and Todd Rogers-USA

SANTA PONSA MALLORCA
July 7th-11th, 2004

It was an all-Swiss final at the 2004 FIVB $360,000.00 Mallorca Open, staged in on the largest of the Balearic isle of Mallorca, in Santa Ponsa. Switzerland snared the top two podium spots for the first-time ever at an international Beach Volleyball event when the Laciga brothers, Paul and Martin, won for the third-time on this Mediterranean island by defeating compatriots Sascha Heyer and Markus Egger. In the 33 minute "Gold-Medal" match, Laciga and Laciga out-pointed Heyer and Egger, 21-14 and 21-13. The winner's split $27,000.00 and the runner-ups shared $18,000.00 for their efforts. Mariano Baracetti and Martin Conde, from Argentina, were scheduled to battle the Brazilian team of Amiraldo Magalhaes and Paulo Emilio Silva, in the "Bronze-Medal" match, but the match was canceled when Baracetti had to retire due to a sore right shoulder. Magalhaes and Paulo Emilio earned their first-ever podium placement together and shared $14,000.00 for third-place while the Argentineans split $11,000.00.

3rd Place: Amiraldo Magalhaes and Paulo Emilio Silva-Brazil
4th Place: Mariano Baracetti and Martin Conde-Argentina
5th Place: Fred Souza and Harley Marques-Brazil
5th Place: Iver Horrem and Bjorn Maaseide-Norway

ADDITIONAL 2004 FIVB EVENTS SCHEDULED

MARSEILLE FRANCE
July 14th-18th, 2004

STARE JABLONKI POLAND
July 21st-25th, 2004

KLAGENFURT AUSTRIA
July 28th-31st, 2004

ATHENS GREECE-XVIII OLYMPIC GAMES
August 14th-24th, 2004

MALLORCA SPAIN
September 1st-5th, 2004

RIO DE JANEIRO BRAZIL
September 21st-26th, 2004

TOP PHOTOS: Left: John Anselmo passing the ball. **Center:** Brian Lewis scrambles to make the play. **Right:** Trevor and Nick teamed-up, to shag some volleyballs (with a little help from Shane). The boys and girls that shag for the AVP help to keep the action going.

MIDDLE PHOTOS: Left: Joel Jones shows that he's "still got game." **Center:** Eric Fonoimoana avoids the block of Aaron Boss. **Right:** Jason Ring attacking the ball.

2004 MEN'S BEACH VOLLEYBALL ACTION

BOTTOM PHOTOS: Left: Casey Jennings deals with the block of Mike Lambert. **Center:** Eli Fairfield reaches above the net for the shot. **Right:** Jeff Nygard opposing the block of George Roumain.

Photo's Courtesy of "Couvi"

TOP PHOTOS: Left: Andy Witt faces the block of his brother, Larry Witt. **Center:** Karch Kiraly confronts the block of Eric Fonoimoana. **Right:** George Roumain getting "pumped-up" during a match.

MIDDLE PHOTOS: Left: Scott Wong challenging the block of Mike Lambert. **Center:** Kevin Wong attacking the block of Mike Whitmarsh. **Right:** Jason Ring attacks a set from George Roumain.

2004 MEN'S BEACH VOLLEYBALL ACTION

BOTTOM PHOTOS: Left: Aaron Boss attacking the block of Matt Olson and the defense of Jimmy Nichols. **Center:** Canyon Ceman avoids the block of Kevin Wong. **Right:** Dain Blanton testing the block of Scott Wong.

Photo's Courtesy of Ken Delgado

WOMEN'S BEACH VOLLEYBALL 2004

AVP

In 2004, the Women's AVP Nissan Series included twelve stops, featuring over $1 million in total prize money, for both men and women playing each event for equal purses. The 2004 Tour visited all ten of the 2003 stops, with the addition of two new sites. The new sites were in Austin, Texas and Honolulu Hawaii. The remaining ten stops included five stops in California. The California stops were in Huntington Beach, Manhattan Beach, San Diego, Hermosa Beach, and the Los Angeles Invitational in Carson. The remaining five stops were in Fort Lauderdale Florida, Tempe Arizona, Belmar New Jersey, Chicago Illinois and Las Vegas Nevada. The 2004 AVP Pro Beach Volleyball Tour, the 21st consecutive season, took a hiatus during August as two qualifying men's and women's teams competed in the 2004 Summer Olympics in Athens, Greece. In addition, NBC increased its network coverage from last season with the Belmar NJ, Hermosa Beach CA, Chicago IL, Las Vegas NV and Honolulu HI. The remainder of the season was scheduled for telecasts via Fox Sports Net.

The 2004 Women's AVP Tour began, as it left-off in 2003, showcasing the superiority of one team. The team of Kerri Walsh and Misty May, who won all nine 2003 AVP events that they entered (including a 39-0 match record), began the 2004 season by winning the first three events. At the first event, in Fort Lauderdale Florida, as was the case in most 2003 events, they were in the championship match against Holly McPeak and Elaine Youngs and as was the case in 2003 they defeated McPeak and Youngs. The next event in Tempe Arizona, May and Walsh were again winner's over McPeak and Youngs. The third event, in Austin Texas, produced another championship for May and Walsh. This time it was against Jenny Jordan and Annette Davis. Walsh and May's championship victory in Austin was also a landmark in beach volleyball. They tied the teams of Jim Menges with Greg Lee and Karch Kiraly with Kent Steffes, for the record of 13 tournament championships in a row. They also set the record for most consecutive match victories ever, at 74 (which they raised to 80 on the FIVB World Tour). In Huntington Beach Walsh and May continued their dominance by extending their record to 86 straight matches and 15 consecutive tournament titles when they out-pointed Barbara Fontana and Jennifer Kessy in the finals of the AVP Huntington Beach Nissan Series 21-16, 21-15. Earlier in the day, May and Walsh beat the newly-formed team of Angie Akers and Rachel Wacholder 21-15, 21-16. During a semifinal match, at the 2004 Manhattan Beach Open, May and Walsh were finally defeated by the team of Jenny Jordan and Annette Davis 21-19 and 21-19. Davis and Jordan then lost in the finals to Holly McPeak and Elaine Youngs 21-19, 16-21 and 15-12.

ELAINE YOUNGS & HOLLY McPEAK

Elaine Youngs and Holly McPeak became the first team, other than Misty May and Kerri Walsh, to win an AVP Women's Tour event, since Youngs and McPeak won the San Diego event on June 7th, 2003. In the championship match, Mc Peak and Youngs defeated Jenny Jordan and Anette Davis 21-19, 16-21 and 15-12. Earlier, in the semifinals, Jordan and Davis had ended Misty May and Kerri Walsh's nine tournament AVP win streak, by the scores of 21-19 and 21-19. Above photo, Youngs hits a set from McPeak, over the block of Davis, towards the defense of Jordan. Above action took place during the championship match of the 2004 AVP event in Manhattan Beach CA.

Photo Courtesy of "Couvi"

This was McPeak's 68th career championship, moving her ahead of Karolyn Kirby's 67 and to the top of the all-time career win list. McPeak and Youngs won again the following week in San Diego California, increasing McPeak's total to 69. McPeak and Youngs also won an FIVB event in Stavanger Norway which was followed by another AVP title in Belmar NJ, bringing her career championship total to 71.

2004 INDIVIDUAL AVP TOURNAMENT FINISHES

Player	1st	2nd	3rd	4th	5th
Angie Akers	0	0	1	0	1
Lisa Arce	0	0	2	0	4
Gracie Santana Baeni	0	0	0	0	1
Carrie Busch	0	0	4	0	1
Annette Buckner-Davis	0	3	3	0	0
Diane DeNeochea	0	0	0	0	1
Barbra Fontana	0	1	2	0	3
Tyra Harper	0	0	0	0	1
Jennifer Johnson Jordan	0	3	3	0	0
Jennifer Kessy	0	1	2	0	3
Tammy Leibl	0	0	0	0	2
Heather Lowe	0	0	0	0	1
Nancy Mason	0	0	4	0	1
Misty May	4	0	1	0	0
Holly McPeak	3	2	1	0	0
Leanne Schuster McSorley	0	0	2	0	4
Jen Meredith	0	1	0	0	0
Jenny Pavley	0	0	0	0	1
Paula Roca	0	0	0	0	1
Sara Straton	0	0	0	0	1
Rachel Wacholder	0	0	1	0	1
Kerri Walsh	4	1	1	0	0
Makare Wilson	0	0	0	0	1
Elaine Youngs	3	2	1	0	0

(**Note:** The above tournament finishes include 2004 results for events up to and including the July 11th final of the Belmar New Jersey tournament)

FIVB

In Lausanne, Switzerland, the International Volleyball Federation (FIVB) increased the schedule for the 2004 Swatch-FIVB World Tour, with five more events than the 2003 schedule. The 2004 season was a landmark for Beach Volleyball, with an impressive 27 tournaments (15 men and 12 women), worth $5,480,000.00 in Prize Money and Bonus Pool. FIVB President IOC member Dr. Ruben Acosta said: "It confirms the positive decisions made by the FIVB and its partners and creates a solid platform to further promote Beach Volleyball at all levels and all over the world." For the first time the Swatch-FIVB World Tour, included a three-leg Grand Slam series that began in Germany and was followed by legs in France and Austria. The 2004 season was scheduled over seven months starting in March and explored new territories over five continents. Men's and women's Open Events were contested on some of the world's most famous beaches in Greece, South Africa, France, Portugal, Puerto Rico and Spain and in the glamorous cities of Shanghai, Lianyungang, Osaka, Berlin, Stavanger, Montreal, Klagenfurt, Milan, and Stare Jablonki as well as the Gstaad Open in the enchanting mountains of Gstaad Switzerland.

Early in 2004, the FIVB staged a "Country vs Country" event in Rio de Janeiro Brazil, where the United States' Kerri Walsh and Misty May, favorites for the 2004 Athens

KERRI WALSH & MISTY MAY
In 2004, Kerri Walsh and Misty May continued their winning ways on the AVP Women's Tour. They won four out of the first five AVP events that they participated in as well as the three FIVB events that they participated in. Above photo, Walsh hits a set from May, over the block of Davis, towards the defense of Jordan.
Photo Courtesy of Ken Delgado

ANGIE AKERS & RACHEL WACHOLDER
Angie Akers and Rachel Wacholder teamed-up for some success on the 2004 Women's AVP Tour. At the half-way mark of the 2004 tour, their best finish was a third in Huntington Beach. Above photo, Wacholder hits a set from Akers, towards the block of Makare Wilson.
Photo Courtesy of Ken Delgado

Olympic "Gold-Medal," beat Brazil's Queen of the Beach Vanilda dos Santos Leãão and her partner Gerusa da Costa Ferreira, as the USA walked away with the "Country vs Country" title.

The winner's of the first seven 2004 Women's FIVB World Tour events were as follows:
Fortaleza Brazil-Misty May and Kerri Walsh-USA
Rhodes Greece-Misty May and Kerri Walsh-USA
Shanghai China-Holly McPeak and Elaine Youngs-USA
Osaka Japan-Shelda Bede and Adriana Behar-Brazil
Gstaad Switzerland-Misty May and Kerri Walsh-USA
Berlin Germany-Shelda Bede and Adriana Behar-Brazil
Stavenger Norway-Holly McPeak and Elaine Youngs-USA

The highlight of the 2004 FIVB Tour was to be the 24 men and 24 women's teams at the Olympic Games in Athens, Greece, August 14-25. World Tour events that were staged before July 13, 2004 were part of the Olympic qualification process, which started in June, 2003. The best eight results of each pair based on World Ranking points including the results of the recognized continental finals were used to determine the best 24 teams per gender (with a maximum of two teams per country) for the Olympic Games in Athens. A double elimination playing format was implemented for the 2004 Swatch-FIVB World Tour, as well as Challenger and Satellite events. The pool play format followed by single elimination, which had been used for the past two years, was only be used at the Olympics Games in Athens to better accommodate the needs of broadcasters and media.

2004 INDIVIDUAL FIVB TOURNAMENT FINISHES

Player	1st	2nd	3rd	4th	5th
Andrea Ahmann	0	0	0	0	1
Shaylyn Bede	0	0	0	0	1
Shelda Kelly Bruno Bede	2	2	2	0	0
Adriana Brando Behar	2	2	2	0	0
Nicole Benoit	0	0	1	0	1
Eva Celbova	0	0	1	0	0
Angela Clarke	0	0	0	0	1
Ana Paula Connolly	0	0	0	1	1
Natalie Cook	0	1	0	0	0
Annete Davis	0	2	0	1	0
Sonja Dosoudilova	0	0	1	0	0
Guylaine Dumont	0	0	0	1	0
Larissa Franca	1	0	1	0	2
Daniela Gattelli	0	0	0	0	2
Kyle Gerlic	0	0	0	0	1
Daxila Grasset	0	1	0	0	1
Nila Ann Hakedal	0	0	0	0	1
Jenny Jordan	0	2	0	1	0
Vasso Karadassiou	0	0	0	1	0
Simon Kuhn	0	0	1	0	1
Chiaki Kusuhara	0	0	0	0	1
Suzanne Lahme	0	1	0	1	2
Summer Lochowicz	0	0	0	1	2
Annie Martin	0	0	0	1	0
Misty May	3	0	0	0	0
Holly McPeak	2	1	2	0	0
Danja Musch	0	1	0	1	2
Tamara Larrea Peraza	0	1	0	0	1
Lucilla Perrotta	0	0	0	0	2
Sandra Tavares Pires	0	0	0	1	1
Kerri Ann Pottharst	0	0	0	1	2
Renata Ribeiro	0	0	0	0	1
Nicole Sanderson	0	1	0	0	0
Efi Sfyri	0	0	0	1	0
Juliana Felisberta Silva	1	0	1	0	2
Jia Tian	0	0	0	1	0
Ryo Tokuno	0	0	0	0	1
Ingrid Torlen	0	0	0	0	1
Jana Vollmer	0	0	0	0	1
Rachel Wacholder	0	0	1	0	0
Kerri Walsh	3	0	1	0	0
Fei Wang	0	0	0	1	0
Lu Wang	0	0	0	1	0
Wenhui You	0	0	0	1	0
Elaine Youngs	2	1	2	0	0

(**Note:** The above tournament finishes include 2004 results for events up to and including the July 11th final of the Santa Ponsa Mallorca event)

KERRI WALSH & MISTY MAY
Kerri Walsh and Misty May won three of the four 2004 FIVB World Tour events that they entered. The event that they did not win, they had to retire from competition, due to an abdominal muscle injury to May. Above photo, May hits a set from Walsh over the block of Brazil's Ana Paula Connelly.
Photo Courtesy of "Couvi"

ELAINE YOUNGS & HOLLY McPEAK
Elaine Youngs and Holly McPeak stepped-up to win a "Gold-Medal" at the 2004 FIVB World Tour event in Shanghai China. They also advanced to the "Gold-Medal" match in Rhodes Greece, where the finished in second place. Above photo, McPeak attacking a set from Youngs.
Photo Courtesy of "Couvi"

WOMEN'S TOURNAMENT RESULTS
2004-AVP

FORT LAUDERDALE FLORIDA
April 2nd-4thth, 2004

The first 2004 Women's AVP Nissan Series event was at South Beach Park, in Fort Lauderdale Florida. The winner's of the event were Misty May and Kerri Walsh. In the championship match, the stands were filled to capacity as they witnessed another victory by the dynamic duo of May and Walsh in the 2004 AVP Nissan Series season opener. In a what is becoming an almost automatic championship match-up, May and Walsh met Holly McPeak and Elaine Youngs on center court. May and Walsh demolished McPeak and Youngs, in two straight games, 21-11 and 21-11. The winner's collected $14,500.00 and the runner-up's shared $9,750.00. This victory extended Walsh and May's winning streak to 63 straight matches on both the domestic AVP Nissan Series and the international FIVB Tour. The 13th seeded team of local favorites, Paula Roca and Gracie Santana-Baeni used the home-court advantage to upset Davis and Johnson Jordan in the second round and was one win away from the final four. Their fifth-place finish marked a career best for both players. Tanya Fuamatu and Heide Ilustre survived a long weekend of play, winning three matches on Friday in the qualifier, then three more in the main draw as they tied their career bests by finishing ninth.

3rd Place: Carrie Busch and Nancy Mason
3rd Place: Annette Davis and Jenny Johnson Jordan
5th Place: Lisa Arce and Leanne McSorley
5th Place: Paula Roca and Gracie Santana-Baeni

TEMPE ARIZONA
April 23rd-25th, 2004

A sell-out crowd of more than 6,000 watched America's finest beach volleyball players, compete at the Women's Association of Volleyball Professionals $62,500.00 Women's Tempe Open. After three days of competition, in 95°F heat and only six percent humidity, in the "purpose-built" stadium court, the team of Misty May and Kerri Walsh captured the women's championship. Competing in the second domestic event of the season, the top-seeded May and Walsh, were again in total control of the final match, when they out-scored Holly McPeak and Elaine Youngs 21-12 and 21-19 for the women's title, earning the $14,500.00 first-place prize. May had now won 28 pro beach events, including 23 with Walsh. May and Walsh extended their incredible victory string to 69 matches, including 49-straight on the domestic tour. They were now winners of 12-straight event titles since losing in a SWATCH-FIVB World Tour event in Norway last July. Also, May and Walsh had now defeated McPeak and Youngs 10-straight times, including nine times in domestic finals. May and Walsh lead the series 13-2 with McPeak and Youngs while being 6-0 against Davis and Johnson Jordan. May and Walsh, who also won their second-straight Tempe Open title after defeating Davis and Johnson Jordan in last year''s finals.

3rd Place: Annette Davis and Jenny Johnson Jordan
3rd Place: Lisa Arce and Leanne McSorley
5th Place: Carrie Busch and Nancy Mason
5th Place: Barbra Fontana and Jennifer Kessy

JENNIFER KESSY & BARBRA FONTANA
Jennifer Kessy and Barbra Fontana progressively improved during the first half of the 2004 Women's AVP Tour. Their best finish was a 3rd in San Diego at the 6th event of the year. Above photo, Fontana hits a set from Kessy into the block of Kerri Walsh.
Photo Courtesy of Ken Delgado

CARRIE BUSCH & NANCY MASON
Carrie Busch and Nancy Mason were competitive during the first half of the 2004 AVP Tour. They placed within the top five at five out of six events, including 4 third place finishes. Above photo, Busch slices a set from Mason past the block of Elaine Youngs.
Photo Courtesy of "Couvi"

AUSTIN TEXAS
April 30th-May 2nd, 2004

The 2004 Women's AVP Nissan Series $62,500.00 Austin Open at Auditorium Shores Park in Austin Texas was won by the top women's team in the world, Kerri Walsh and Misty May. In the championship match, May and Walsh were able to capture their record-tying 13th-straight tournament title when they out-played the third-ranked team of Olympians Annette Davis and Jenny Johnson Jordan 21-17 and 21-12. May and Walsh now had 74 consecutive victories on the AVP and FIVB Pro Beach Volleyball Tour's. Although, not in the championship match, May and Walsh did face Holly McPeak and Elaine Youngs in the semifinals when they out-scored them 21-12 and 21-16. Davis and Jordan's win over Lisa Arce and Leanne McSorley in the semifinals secured their spot in the women's finals for the first time of the 2004 season.

3rd Place: Holly McPeak and Elaine Youngs
3rd Place: Lisa Arce and Leanne McSorley
5th Place: Dianne DeNecochea and Tammy Leibl
5th Place: Barbra Fontana and Jennifer Kessy

HUNTINGTON BEACH CALIFORNIA
May 28th-30th, 2004

In Huntington Beach, Kerri Walsh and Misty May continued their dominance by extending their record to 86 straight matches and 15 consecutive tournament titles when they out-pointed Barbara Fontana and Jennifer Kessy in the finals of the AVP Huntington Beach Nissan Series 21-16, 21-15. The winner's shared the first place prize of $14,500.00 and the runner-ups split $9,750.00. Earlier in the semifinals, May and Walsh beat the newly-formed team of Angie Akers and Rachel Wacholder 21-15 and 21-16. In the other semifinals match, where the losers were also relegated to a third place tie, Fontana and Kessy out-lasted Carrie Busch and Nancy Mason 19-21, 21-16 and 18-16. This event was missing some of the top Olympic-contenders including two of the three top teams on the women's side of the 2004 AVP Tour. Four-time MVP Holly McPeak and Olympian Elaine Youngs, as well as Olympians Annett Davis and Jenny Jordan Johnson, were in Shanghai China. Both teams were currently competing internationally to qualify for the second spot at the 2004 Olympics in Athens Greece.

3rd Place: Carrie Busch and Nancy Mason
3rd Place: Angie Akers and Rachel Wacholder
5th Place: Lisa Arce Leanne McSorley
5th Place: Tyra Harper Makare Wilson

LEANNE McSORLEY
On the 2004 AVP Tour, Leanne McSorley was paired-up with Lisa Arce. During the first half of the season, they had finished within the top five at all six events. Above photo, McSorley challenges the block of Angie Akers and the defense of Rachel Wacholder.
Photo Courtesy of "Couvi"

ANGIE AKERS & RACHEL WACHOLDER
Angie Akers and Rachel Wacholder provided a great deal of competition, to the top teams, on the 2004 Women's AVP Tour. Above photo, during the 2004 Huntington Beach event, Akers hits a set from Wacholder, towards the block of Misty May.
Photo Courtesy of Ken Delgado

MANHATTAN BEACH CALIFORNIA
June 4th-6th, 2004

There was a "packed-house" at the 2004 Women's AVP Nissan Series Manhattan Beach Open. It was a day for record watchers as Holly McPeak captured her 68th pro beach volleyball title to set the women''s career record for tournament wins as she teamed with Elaine Youngs to win their second-straight event together in as many weeks. In breaking the career win's tie with Karolyn Kirby, McPeak now owned all three of the women''s major career marks for event titles with 229 tournaments played and earnings as she increased her all-time winnings to $1,213,451.00, including $607,729.00 domestically and $605,722.00 internationally. In 38 pro beach events together, McPeak and Youngs had now captured 12 titles. In the record-breaking championship match, McPeak and Youngs out-lasted the team of Annette Davis and Jenny Johnson Jordan by scores of 21-19, 16-21 and 15-12 in the 76 minute match. The second-seeded team this week, McPeak and Youngs scored a 21-14 and 21-19 win over Carrie Busch and Nancy Mason to advance to their third-straight event final. In their semifinal match Davis and Jordan ended the record 15-event and 90-match winning streaks for Misty May and Kerri Walsh, with a 21-19 and 21-19 victory over Walsh and her injured partner May. (May was suffering from an abdominal muscle injury). McPeak and Youngs, shared $14,500.00 for this week''s title.

3rd Place: Carrie Busch and Nancy Mason
3rd Place: Misty May and Kerri Walsh
5th Place: Lisa Arce and Leanne McSorley
5th Place: Barbra Fontana and Jennifer Kessy

LISA ARCE & LEANNE McSORLEY
Lisa Arce and Leanne Schuster McSorley, played well enough to finish within the top three, two times during the first half of the 2004 Women's AVP Tour. Above photo, Arce hits a set from McSorley, past the block of Mary Bailey.
Photo Courtesy of "Couvi"

SAN DIEGO CALIFORNIA
June 11th-13th, 2004

Presented by Bud-Light, in front of a jammed-packed stadium, the 2004 Women's AVP Nissan Series Tour staged a "Beach-Party" on Mariner's Point in San Diego California. Two-time Olympian Holly McPeak and partner Olympian Elaine Youngs took home their second consecutive tournament title this weekend as McPeak increased her career win record to 69 tournament championships. In the championship match, McPeak and Youngs defeated Davis and Jordan 22-20 and 21-18. Misty May and Kerri Walsh, currently the number-one ranked women's professional beach volleyball team, did not compete this weekend as May was currently recovering from a strained abdominal muscle. McPeak and Youngs earned their way into the finals with a 21-11 and 21-18 win over Carrie Busch and Nancy Mason in their semi-final match. Jordan and Davis won their semi-final match over Barbra Fontana and Jennifer Kessy, 28-26 and 21-14.

3rd Place: Barbra Fontana and Jennifer Kessy
3rd Place: Carrie Busch and Nancy Mason
5th Place: Lisa Arce and Leanne McSorley
5th Place: Jenny Pavley and Heather Lowe

MISTY MAY
Misty May, paired-up with Kerri Walsh, seemed invincible on the 2004 AVP Tour. They won every event they entered, until the MB, event when an abdominal muscle strain to May contributed to defeat. Above photo, May test the block of Rachel Wacholder.
Photo Courtesy of Ken Delgado

BELMAR NEW JERSEY
July 8th-11th, 2004

The 2004 Women's AVP Nissan Series Belmar Open, presented by Bud Light was won by three-time Olympian Holly McPeak and two-time Olympian Elaine Youngs, as they captured their third consecutive title of the AVP Nissan Series. In the championship match, McPeak and Youngs defeated Jennifer Meredith and Kerri Walsh 21-15, 21-17. Walsh's normal partner Misty May was recovering from a strained abdominal muscle. The winner's split $20,000.00 and the runner-ups shared $14,000.00.

3rd Place: Annett Davis and Jenny Johnson Jordan
3rd Place: Barbra Fontana and Jennifer Kessy
5th Place: Angie Akers and Rachel Wacholder
5th Place: Tammy Leibl and Sarah Straton

ADDITIONAL AVP EVENTS SCHEDULED FOR 2004

HERMOSA BEACH CALIFORNIA
July 22nd-25th, 2004

CHICAGO ILLINOIS
September 2nd-5th, 2004

LAS VEGAS NEVADA
September 9th-11th, 2004

WAIKIKI HAWAII
September 22nd-25th, 2004

CARSON CALIFORNIA
October 15th-17th, 2004

DIANNE DeNECOCHEA
At the start of the 2004 Women's AVP Tour, Dianne DeNecochea was still around to cause some trouble for the top teams on the tour. Above photo, DeNecochea closes the door on Misty May's hit. Kerri Walsh is ready to cover the block.
Photo Courtesy of Ken Delgado

ANNETTE DAVIS & JENNY JORDAN
By the middle of the 2004 AVP Tour's season, Annette Davis and Jenny Jordan were the number three team on the tour. They reached three finals, finishing second each time. Above photo, Jordan hits a set from Davis, towards the block of Elaine Youngs.
Photo Courtesy of Ken Delgado

WOMEN'S TOURNAMENT RESULTS
2004-FIVB

FORTALEZA BRAZIL
March 9th-14th, 2004

There was an overflowing crowd of more than 4,000 beach volleyball aficionados, on the Praia de Iracema center court, where lines for stadium entrance were formed at 5 a.m. to watch the action in the first Women's Beach stop of the 2004 season, the Women's FIVB $180,000.00 Brazil Open, in Fortaleza Brazil. The winner's were the top-seeded team of Misty May and Kerri Walsh, from the United States. In the "Gold-Medal" match, May and Walsh used a "strong" service game to defeated Shelda Bede and Adriana Behar of Brazil 21-10 and 21-18 to win the 2004 SWATCH-FIVB World Tour season opener. In the 37-minute match, May and Walsh scored 26 points on their serves as compared to 12 by the Brazilians. In the first game, May and Walsh scored the first four points and used a seven-point run to take an 11-3 lead on their way to victory. In the second game, there were five ties and two lead changes with the Americans using a 6-0 run to take a 13-8 lead. Trailing 17-11, Shelda and Adriana used a 7-2 run to get back into the match. With the Brazilian trailing by one after scoring two points on their serve, May then ended the action with two kills. The American's shared the $27,000.00 first-place prize while Bede and Behar split $18,000.00 for the "Silver-Medal" finish. The winner's had now won 34-straight matches on the FIVB World Tour. In the "Bronze-Medal" match, Larissa Franca and Juliana Felisberta Silva of Brazil completed their "remarkable" week on the Praia de Iracema by defeating fourth-seeded Jia Tian and Fei Wang of China 24-22 and 21-9 to capture third place.

3rd Place: Juliana Felisberta Silva and Larissa Franca-Brazil
4th Place: Jia Tian and Fei Wang-China
5th Place: Ana Paula Connelly and Sandra Pires-Brazil
5th Place: Nicole Benoit and Simone Kuhn-Switzerland

RHODES GREECE
May 19th-23rd, 2004

The 2004 Women's FIVB $180,000.00 Hellas Open, in Rhodes Greece, was won by Americans, Kerri Walsh and Misty May. In the all-American "Gold-Medal" match, they out-classed Holly McPeak and Elaine Youngs 21-17 and 21-13. During the first set of this final an upset looked possible as Walsh and May made several errors while McPeak and Youngs appeared strong and determined, but May and Walsh slowly began pulling

TOP AMERICAN TEAMS ON THE FIVB
After six FIVB Women's World Tour events, the two American teams to qualify for the 2004 Olympiad in Athens Greece had been determined. After winning the "Gold-Medal" at three of the first six events in 2004, Kerri Walsh and Mist May were on top, ahead of all teams, from all countries. With one "Gold-Medal" a second and two thirds, the second American team to qualify was Elaine Youngs and Holly McPeak. Above photo, May makes a dig for Walsh, while Youngs (left) and McPeak (right) are ready for the play.
Photo Courtesy of "Couvi"

their game together and eventually forged ahead to win the first game as well as the second. The winner's split $27,000.00 while the runner-ups shared $18,000.00. In the "Bronze-Medal" match, Adriana Behar and Shelda Bede of Brazil captured third place by the scores of 23-25, 21-16 and 15-11, over another team from the USA, Annette Davis and Jennifer Jordan.

3rd Place: Shelda Bede and Adriana Behar-Brazil
4th Place: Annett Davis and Jenny Johnson Jordan-USA
5th Place: Juliana Felisberta Silva and Larissa Franca-Brazil
5th Place: Chiaki Kusuhara and Ryo Tokuno-Japan

SHANGHAI CHINA
May 26th-30th, 2004

The 2004 Women's FIVB World Tour's Chinese Open was staged in Shanghai, also called in short in Chinese "Hu" or "Shen" Situated in the middle of China's east coastline, the delightful climate of Shanghai with its four distinct seasons and population over 13 million served Beach Volleyball and the athletes well. The winner's were Holly McPeak and Elaine Youngs, from the United States of America. The "Gold-Medal" match was played in light rain at the Jinshan Beach Volleyball Complex before an over-flowing crowd of 4,000. McPeak and Youngs sailed past compatriots Jenny Johnson Jordan and Annette "Nette" Davis 21-17 and 21-13. This was McPeak's 67th career title, tying her with countrywoman Karolyn Kirby for most career wins, the longest-standing record in Beach Volleyball. McPeak and Youngs shared the $27,000.00 first-place prize while Jordan and Davis split $18,000.00 for the "Silver-Medal" finish. In the "Bronze-Medal" match, Brazil's Adriana Behar and Shelda Bede outlasted China's Lu Wang and Whenhui You 24-22 and 21-17 to place in the third spot.

3rd Place: Adriana Behar and Shelda Bede-Brazil
4th Place: Lu Wang and Whenhui.You-China
5th Place: Larrea Peraza and Fernandez Grasset-Cuba
5th Place: Suzanne Lahme and Danja Müüsch-Germany

OSAKA JAPAN
June 2nd-6th, 2004

Tannowa Beach, in Osaka Japan staged the 2004 Women's FIVB World Tour's Japan Open. Brazil's Shelda Bede and Adriana Behar were the winner's. In the "Gold-Medal" match, the top seeded Bede and Behar captured their sixth Japan Open title when Australian's Natalie Cook and Nicole Sanderson were forced to retire, after losing the first game 21-12, when Cook was unable to continue because of a shoulder injury. The winner split $27,000.00 while the runner-ups shared $18,000.00. In the "Bronze-Medal" match, third-seeded Nicole Schnyder-Benoit and Simone Kuhn of Switzerland earned their first podium finish together on the SWATCH-FIVB World Tour by defeating 21st-seeded Vasso Karadassiou and Efi Sfyri of Greece 21-13 and 21-14.

3rd Place: Nicole Schnyder-Benoit and Simone Kuhn-Switzerland
4th Place: Vasso Karadassiou and Efi Sfyri-Greece
5th Place: Suzanne Lahme and Danja Musch-Germany
5th Place: Summer Lochowicz and Kerri-Ann Pottharst-Australia

KERRI WALSH & MISTY MAY vs HOLLY McPEAK & ELAINE YOUNGS

Kerri Walsh and Misty May vs Holly McPeak and Elaine Youngs, made for an interesting "All-American" final at the FIVB Women's World Tour event, staged in Rhodes Greece. The "Gold-Medal" was taken by Walsh and May. Above photo, May hits a set from Walsh, past the block of Youngs, towards the defense of McPeak.

Photo Courtesy of "Couvi"

GSTAAD SWITZERLAND
June 15th-19th, 2004

The beach volleyball fans were out in full-force, on the summer slopes of Gstaad in the Swiss Alps, for the 2004 Swatch FIVB World Tour's $360,000.00 "One-To-One Energy" Switzerland Open. The USA's Misty May and Kerri Walsh won the "Gold-Medal" match. There were cool and damp conditions for the championship match that saw the top-seeded May and Walsh score a 26-28, 21-17 and 15-10 win in 61 minutes over second-seeded Adriana Behar and Shelda Bede of Brazil. The 61-minute title match saw Adriana and Shelda score a 28-26 first-game win in 26 minutes. The opening game had five lead changes, 19 ties with the Brazilian's winning on their eighth-set point as May hit a cut shot into the net. The American's never trailed in the second game and scored six of the last nine points. In the third and deciding game, May and Walsh led 4-2, 6-3 and 10-6 before the Brazilian's closed the deficit to 10-9 by scoring three-straight points. Then, May and Walsh closed the match by scoring five of the last six points. Along with the "Gold-Medal" the American's shared the $27,000.00 first-place prize and won the 1to1 Energy Open "cow bell" for the third-straight year. The Brazilians split $18,000.00 for placing second. Holly McPeak and Elaine Youngs of the United States shared $14,000.00 for earning the "Bronze-Medal" when Ana Paula Connelly and Sandra Pires forfeited the third-place match due to injuries.

3rd Place: Holly McPeak and Elaine Youngs-USA
4th Place: Ana Paula Connelly and Sandra Pires-Brazil
5th Place: Felisberta Silva and Larissa França-Brazil
5th Place: Summer Lochowicz and Kerri Ann Pottharst-Australia

BERLIN GERMANY
June 22nd-26th, 2004

Adriana Behar and Shelda Bede won the $600,000.00 FIVB Smart Grand Slam "Gold-Medal" at the 2004 FIVB World Tour event in Berlin Germany. In the 45 minute championship match, they out-scored the Cuban team of Dalixia Fernandez Grasset and Tamara Larrea Peraza, 21-16 and 21-17.

The Brazilian's posted a 6-0 match record for this event. In addition to sharing the $43,000.00 first-place prize, Adriana and Shelda used the 600 team points to become the second-ranked team on the FIVB Olympic qualifying list behind Misty May and Kerri Walsh of the United States. The Cubans split $29,500.00 for second-place.

After trailing 1-0 in the first game, the Brazilians took command with leads of 9-6, 11-7 and 12-9. Then the Cubans came out of a "technical time-out" to pull within one point at 12-11. After ten straight sideouts, Adriana and Shelda closed out the scoring with four-straight points to win the 23-minute game. Grasset and Peraza jumped to a 6-2 lead in the 22-minute second game. The Brazilians got back into the game with three-straight points to make it 6-5. Adriana and Shelda gained the lead for good at 13-12 and continued to pressure the Cubans by taking 15-13, 17-14 leads before closing out the match with two-straight points. In the "Bronze-Medal" match, third-seeded Holly McPeak and Elaine Youngs of the United States scored a 21-13 and 21-16 win in 38 minutes over ninth-seeded Suzanne Lahme and Danja Müüsch of Germany. McPeak and Youngs split the $23,000.00 third-place prize.

3rd Place: Holly McPeak and Elaine Youngs-USA
4th Place: Suzanne Lahme and Danja Müüsch-Germany
5th Place: Lucilla Perrotta and Daniela Gattelli-Italy
5th Place: Andrea Ahmann and Jana Vollmer-Germany

STAVANGER NORWAY
June 30th-July 3rd, 2004

The 2004 FIVB World Tour Conoco Phillips Open, staged in Stavanger Norway, was won by the American team of Holly McPeak and Elaine Youngs. They were joined by two additional American teams on the "Medal-Podium" as this was the first time in 112 SWATCH-FIVB World Tour events, that the women from the United States captured all three podium spots. Jenny Johnson with Annette Davis were the "Silver-Medal" and Kerri Walsh with Rachel Wacholder were the "Bronze-Medal" winners. In the championship match, McPeak and Youngs scored a 21-17, 16-21 and 15-10 win in 49 minutes over third-seeded Davis and Jordan in the All-American final on the Vaagen Harbour centre court. This was McPeak's 70th career tournament championship, ranking her in the number-one spot, ahead of Karolyn Kirby's mark of 67. In the match for third place, playing in their first-ever beach volleyball event together, the second-seeded Walsh and Wacholder rallied to defeated 12th-seeded Guylaine Dumont and Annie Martin of Canada 18-21, 21-18 and 15-11. Wacholder was filling in for Walsh's regular partner Misty May, who is sidelined with an abdominal strain. McPeak and Youngs shared the $27,000.00 first-place prize while Davis and Johnson Jordan split $18,000.00 for second-place. Davis also captured the SWATCH "fastest" serve award. The "Bronze-Medal" winners shared $14,000.00 while Dumont and Martin, who are the first Canadian women's team to appear in a FIVB "final four," split $11,000.00.

3rd Place: Kerri Walsh with Rachel Wacholder-USA
4th Place: Guylaine Dumont and Annie Martin-Canada
5th Place: Nila Ann Hakedal and Ingrid Torlen Norway
5th Place: Renata Ribeiro and Shaylyn Bede-Brazil

SANTA PONSA MALLORCA
July 6th-10th, 2004

There was another Brazilian women's team atop the podium at the 2004 FIVB $360,000.00 Mallorca Women's Open, staged in on the largest of the Balearic isle of Mallorca, in Santa Ponsa, but it was not the familiar Beach Volleyball names of Bede with Behar, Pires with Silva or Rodrigues with Samuel. In the 39 minute "Gold Medal match, Brazil's Juliana Felisberta Silva and Larissa Franca scored a 21-17 and 21-12 over second-seeded Suzanne Lahme and Danja Musch of Germany. The winner's split $27,000.00 and the runner-ups shared $18,000.00 for their efforts. In the 56 minute "Bronze-Medal" match, the Czech team of Eva Celbova and Sonja Novakova Dosoudilvoa scored a 21-14, 19-21 and 18-16 win over Australian's Summer Lochowicz and Kerri Ann Pottharst. The Czech team shared the $14,000.00 third-place prize while the Aussies split $11,000.00 for fourth-place.

3rd Place: Eva Celbova and Sonja Dosoudilvoa-Czech Republic
4th Place: Summer Lochowicz and Kerri Ann Pottharst-Australia
5th Place: Lucilla Perrotta and Daniela Gattelli-Italy
5th Place: Angela Clarke and Kylie Gerlic-Australia

TOP PHOTOS: Left: Rachel Wacholder confronts the block of Annette Davis. **Center:** Elaine Youngs (left) "Joust" with Nancy Mason. **Right:** Annette Davis attacking the ball.

MIDDLE PHOTOS: Left: Tiffany Rodriguez reaches above the net to make a cut shot. **Center:** Nancy Mason attacking the ball. **Right:** Jenny Johnson Jordan confronts the block of Elaine Youngs.

2004 WOMEN'S BEACH VOLLEYBALL ACTION

BOTTOM PHOTOS: Left: Lisa Arce demonstrates her version of the "Kong" block. **Center:** Holly McPeak follows through after spiking the ball. **Right:** Carrie Busch reaches for the shot.

Photo's Courtesy of "Couvi"

TOP PHOTOS: Left: Hawaiian Tanya Fuamatu hits a set from Heidi Ilustre into the block of Misty May. **Center:** Kerri Walsh test the block of Leanne McSorley. **Right:** Leanne McSorley evades the block of Kerri Walsh.

MIDDLE PHOTOS: Left: Leanne McSorley test the block of Kerri Walsh. **Center:** Jennifer Kessy encounters the block of Kerri Walsh. **Right:** Barbra Fontana confronts the block of Kerri Walsh.

2004 WOMEN'S BEACH VOLLEYBALL ACTION

BOTTOM PHOTOS: Left: Dianne DeNecochea gets-up high to attack the ball. **Center:** Suzanne Stonebarger hustles for the ball. **Right:** Jennifer "JJJ" Johnson Jordan " (left) Joust" with Holly McPeak.

Top Photo's Courtesy of "Couvi" Middle and Bottom Photo's Courtesy of Ken Delgado

ADDITIONAL VOLLEYBALL INFORMATION
2004

Additional Women's 2004 FIVB events scheduled were in Marseille France, Klagenfurt Austria, Milan Italy, Rio de Janeiro Brazil and the Olympics in Athens Greece.

AROUND THE WORLD
2004

Not just in Southern California or Brazil! When the subject of beach volleyball comes-up, it usually starts with discussions about "hot beds" of competition at the beaches in Southern California or on Copacabana in Rio de Janeiro. To the causal observer, the top players must come from the United States or Brazil. The USA has a long history of legendary beach volleyball players such as Sinjin Smith and Randy Stoklos as well as 1996 Olympic "Gold-Medalist" Karch Kiraly and Kent Steffes. But all of these players, with the exception of Kiraly, are retired from the game. Also, it is true that Brazil had three of the top-ranked teams on the SWATCH-FIVB World Tour in 2003, but the Swiss matched the South American country with three pairs listed among the top 10 tandems on the international beach volleyball tour. The first Swiss team to break through on the beach, was Paul Laciga and Martin Laciga. At the end of the 2003 SWATCH-FIVB World Tour, the Laciga brothers were ranked third internationally behind two teams from Brazil and ahead of Swiss rivals Stefan Kobel and Patrick Heuscher. Sascha Heyer and Markus Egger is the third team from Switzerland ranked in the top ten.

RIO DE JANEIRO BRAZIL
February 16th, 2004

The USA won the men's round of the "Country vs Country" playoff, on the captivating sands of Ipanema Beach, in Rio de Janeiro, Brazil, In the men's match of the "Country vs Country Challenge" Dain Blanton and Jeff Nygard broke a two-year American drought to beat the world champion pair of Ricardo Santos and Emanuel Rego from Brazil, in a three set match, by scores of 22-20, 20-22 and 15-13 on Sunday. Previously in 2002 Brazil's Ricardo Santos and Jose Loiola beat the USA's Kevin Wong and Stein Metzger and in 2003 Brazil won again when Brazil's Guto and Jorge beat Americans Dax Holdren and Eric Fonoimoana. During the championship match, playing in front of a packed passionate and noisy local crowd, the Americans showed right from the opening whistle that they were not going to aid the Brazilian party and proceeded to claim the honors in this annual event.

RIO DE JANEIRO BRAZIL
February 23rd, 2004

The USA also won the women's round of the "Country vs Country" playoff when the USA's Kerri Walsh and Misty May sealed the series for USA in Rio de Janeiro. In the championship match, the American women's pair, favorites for the 2004 Athens Olympic "Gold-Medal" took only 41 minutes, in two straight games, to beat Brazil's Queen of the Beach Vanilda dos Santos Leãão and her partner Gerusa da Costa Ferreira by scores of 21-7 and 21-16, allowing the USA to walk away with the "Country vs Country" title. The Brazilian team tried to put pressure on Walsh but she was up to the task. Several times her outstanding attack "nailed" the Brazilian block, which even caused the local 1,500 strong crowd to cheer and applaud the talent of Walsh and May. This series was contested between two of the best Beach Volleyball nations. And in the end the height advantage and overall skill of the world champions was too much for the Brazilians who were playing for the first time together.

ASPEN COLORADO
2004

Early in 2004, Leon Fell, the producer of the annual MotherLode beach volleyball tournament, began arrangements for the 32nd year of this fun little tournament held every Labor Day Weekend in the mountain hamlet of Aspen, Colorado. There were not any results available at the time that this book was published, but it is a sure thing that the it was competitive and that players at all levels enjoyed the MotherLode experience.

LEON FELL
The producer of the annual MotherLode "Pro-Am" tournament, Leon Fell has also competed in the event as a player. Above photo, Leon Fell reaches above the net to spike the ball.
Photo Courtesy of the Aspen Times

MEN'S BEACH VOLLEYBALL RECORDS
1944-2004

The following document list the available beach volleyball tournament records, from 1944 up to July of 2004, of all the male players, that competed in this era and placed fifth or higher, in events that were of the uppermost classification of their era, ie: AVP, BVA, FIVB, Parks and Recreation "A" - "AAA" etc.

(Note: "Oral-History" accounts were utilized for some of the early players, when actual written records were not available)

Player	1st	2nd	3rd	4th	5th	Player	1st	2nd	3rd	4th	5th
Jose Luis Salema Abrantes	0	0	1	0	2	Bob Ballard	0	0	0	0	1
Eduardo "Duda" Pintode Abreau	0	0	1	0	3	Mariano Baracetti	7	5	4	7	5
Osvaldo Agustine Archer Abreu	0	0	0	0	1	Bobby Barber	0	0	0	1	0
Jim Adams	0	1	0	0	4	Mark Barber	0	1	4	2	8
Jorge Ahmann	0	2	2	0	8	Jim Barclay	0	0	0	1	0
Vince Ahmann	0	0	1	1	4	Greg Barnett	0	0	1	0	0
Andy Aitken	0	0	0	0	1	Mike Barton	0	0	0	1	0
Skip Allen	0	2	3	0	1	Fabrizio Bastianelli	0	0	0	0	1
Mike Allio	0	0	0	1	0	Paul Baxter	0	0	1	0	5
Marlosde Almeida	0	0	0	0	1	Dan Bearer	0	2	2	0	3
Claudino Aloizio	0	0	0	2	3	Bruce Bearer	0	1	0	0	0
Francisco Alvarez	3	2	1	2	8	Ed Becker	0	0	1	1	0
Mike Anapol	0	2	3	1	3	Jefferson Bellaguarda	0	0	1	2	1
John Anderson	0	1	1	0	0	Joe Bena	4	1	0	1	0
Phil Anderson	0	1	1	0	0	Dan Bennett	0	0	0	1	0
Marcio Araujo	7	7	3	3	7	Bjorn Berg	0	1	0	0	2
John Archer	0	0	0	0	1	Nikolas Berger	0	0	1	2	2
Bob Arges	0	1	0	0	0	Sam Berger	0	0	0	0	1
Leonard Armato	0	0	0	2	2	Henry Bergman	15	9	3	2	3
Pete Aroncheck	1	0	2	0	2	Dan Berry	0	0	0	0	1
Brazil's Atila	0	0	0	0	1	Philippe Blain	0	0	0	1	0
Dave Avazon	0	0	1	0	0	Dain Blanton	10	11	21	10	22
Scott Ayakatubby	19	30	35	28	49	Dave Boardwell	2	0	0	1	0
Bob Ayelsworth	1	0	0	0	0	Spike Boarts	0	2	3	1	2
Paulo Emilo Silva Azevedo	5	3	4	8	9	Javier Bosma	1	3	3	2	11
Eduardo "Anjinho" Bacil	2	13	16	17	32	Aaron Boss	1	0	0	1	7
Scott Bailey	0	0	0	0	1	Bill Boullianne	2	5	16	12	36
Larry Baldwin	0	0	1	0	0	Paul Boyd	0	0	0	0	1

KARCH KIRALY & SINJIN SMITH

Karch Kiraly and Sinjin Smith were the two most prolific winner's in the history of beach volleyball. The all-time leader is, Kiraly at 146 career championships. In 2004, Kiraly was still competing on the AVP Tour and may very well add to his total. Sinjin Smith is in the second spot with 139 career championships. At an early age, Kiraly and Smith began to amass their victories together as a team. Above photo, Karch hits a set from Sinjin, towards the defense of Gary Hooper (left) and Steve Obradovich (right). Action took place at the 1980 Santa Barbara Men's Open. Kiraly and Smith were the champions. It was Kiraly's eighth title and the tenth for Smith.

Photo Courtesy of Bob Van Wagner

Player	1st	2nd	3rd	4th	5th
Eric Boyles	0	0	1	1	1
Ernie Brach	0	0	0	0	1
George Brackel	0	1	0	0	0
John Brajevic	0	0	0	0	2
John Brame	1	1	0	0	0
Pedro Brazao	0	0	0	0	1
Joao Brenha	2	0	0	6	7
Carlos Briceno	0	3	2	2	1
Mike Bright	16	18	6	1	2
Woody Brooks	0	0	0	5	0
Barry Brown	2	3	1	0	0
Steno Brunicardi	0	1	0	0	0
Pete Bryan	0	0	0	1	0
Tom Bryan	0	0	0	1	0
Andrew Burdin	0	0	1	3	3
Jack Cameron	1	1	0	0	0
Stephan Canet	0	0	0	0	1
Larry Cantor	0	0	0	0	1
Daniel Cardenas	0	0	0	1	2
Mike Carey	1	12	7	4	9
George Carey	0	0	0	0	1
Rand Carter	2	4	3	1	2
Scott Carter	1	0	0	0	0
Chris Casebeer	0	0	0	0	1
Dan Castillo	0	0	0	1	5
Canyon Ceman	7	13	18	14	20
Tom Chamales	12	13	8	4	5
Robert Chavez	0	1	1	4	10
John Child	1	5	10	9	19
Rocky Ciarelli	0	0	0	0	1
Ian Clark	1	2	4	4	25
Roger Clark	0	0	1	5	13
Kevin Cleary	1	2	2	7	21
Bob Clem	9	11	3	3	4
Bill Clemo	0	0	0	1	0
Denny Cline	0	0	0	0	2
Altie Cohen	1	2	0	1	1
Pete Colbert	2	6	0	1	0
Bud Colette	1	3	0	0	0
Martin Alejo Conde	9	12	10	14	15
Ray Cone	2	0	0	0	0
Bob Conrad	1	0	0	0	3
Antonio Contrino	0	0	0	0	1
Dave Cook	0	0	0	1	0
Jeff Cook	0	0	0	0	1
John Cook	0	0	0	1	0
Dick Cooper	1	0	0	0	0
Luizao Correa	0	1	0	0	0
Roberto Lopesda Costa	15	11	16	8	12
Mike Cram	0	0	0	1	1
Bob Ctvrtik	0	0	0	2	2
Robert Anthony Curci	0	0	0	0	1
Simon Dahl	0	0	0	0	5
Scott Davenport	0	0	0	0	2
Bob Davis	0	2	0	0	0
Dick Davis	1	3	1	1	0
George Davis	1	0	0	0	0
Shawn Davis	0	0	1	0	1
Pepe DeLaholz	0	0	0	0	1
David Denitz	0	1	1	0	5
Mark Denitz	0	1	1	0	4
Mike Desrochers	0	0	0	0	2
Carlos Eduardo Garrido Dias	0	4	4	4	13
Roberto Moreira Durate Dias	0	3	2	3	4
Christoph Dieckmann	0	0	0	1	3
Markus Dieckmann	0	3	1	3	7
Mike Diehl	0	0	0	0	1
Fabio Diez	0	1	2	1	4
Brazil's Dionisio	0	0	0	0	1
Brent Doble	5	0	13	2	17
Mike Dodd	75	83	73	36	47
Bill Dolby	0	0	1	0	0
Kurt Donaldson	0	1	0	1	2
Clemens Doppler	0	0	1	2	1
Kent Dorwin	1	1	0	0	1
Edward "Eddie" Drakich	0	0	0	1	1
Denniees Duggan	0	2	1	0	0
Rich Duke	0	0	1	0	0

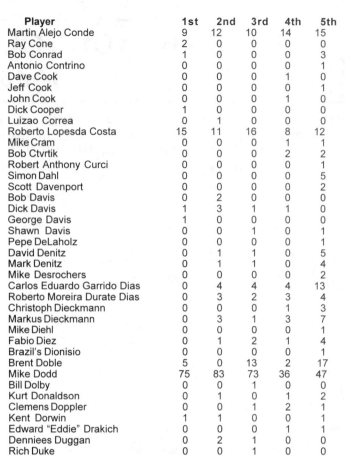

RANDY STOKLOS
With 122 career championships, Randy Stoklos is number three on the all-time career wins list. Above photo, Stoklos slices the ball away from the defense of Gary Hooper. Action took place at the 1979 Santa Barbara Men's Open.
Photo Courtesy of Bob Van Wagner

KENT STEFFES
During his beach volleyball career, Kent Steffes won 110 tournament championships to put him in the fourth spot on the all-time career wins list. Above photo, Steffes follows through after attacking the ball during a 1990's AVP Tour event.
Photo Courtesy of the AVP

Player	1st	2nd	3rd	4th	5th
Juca Dultra	0	0	0	2	0
Don Duncan	0	0	0	0	2
Doug Dunlap	0	1	2	1	6
Bob Duran	1	0	0	0	0
Dusty Dvorak	0	0	1	1	3
Rudy Dvroak	0	1	0	1	14
John Eddo	1	3	1	4	6
Peter Eden	0	0	0	1	0
Markus Egger	0	4	3	0	6
Peter Ehrman	1	0	1	0	0
Carl Eissmann	0	0	0	0	1
Doug Eisemann	0	0	0	0	1
Mark Eller	4	5	4	4	21
Ed Ellison	1	0	0	0	0
Tom Englen	0	0	0	0	1
Keith Erickson	3	3	2	2	2
Sergey Ermishin	0	0	1	1	4
Jerry Escallier	0	2	0	0	0
Gordon Evans	3	0	2	0	1
Alain Fabian	0	0	0	1	0
Fred Fachus	0	0	1	0	1
Eli Fairfield	0	0	0	0	3
Sean Fallowfield	0	5	1	2	8
Klepper Feitosa	0	0	0	1	0
James Fellows	0	1	0	0	0
Pete Fields	0	0	0	0	1
David Fischer	0	0	0	1	0
Andy Fishburn	20	33	24	13	14
Dana Fitzgerald	0	0	1	0	0
John Fitzgerald	0	0	0	0	1
Mike Fitzgerald	0	1	1	1	0
Chris Fletcher	0	0	0	0	1
Mike Floyd	0	0	0	0	1
Eric Fonoimoana	13	12	22	18	45
Doug Foust	0	0	0	0	5
Emanuele Fracascia	0	0	0	0	1
Craig Freeburg	1	1	2	2	9
Scott Friederichsen	0	1	6	8	37
Butch Friedman	0	0	2	1	1

Player	1st	2nd	3rd	4th	5th
Brent Frohoff	19	34	49	32	72
Matt Fuerbringer	1	6	1	0	4
Matt Gage	26	25	21	13	13
Karlis Galens	0	0	0	0	1
Bob Garcia	0	1	1	1	2
Christian Garcia	0	0	0	0	1
Mike Garcia	0	0	0	0	1
Adriano Dias Garrido	1	1	0	0	1
Carlos Eduardo Garrido	0	4	4	4	13
Brian Gatzke	0	0	1	0	10
Giovane Gavio	0	0	1	0	3
Dick Geary	0	1	0	0	0
Andrea Ghiurghi	0	2	1	0	6
Jake Gibb	1	1	3	0	1
Bob Gill	0	1	0	0	0
Jim Glaesier	0	0	0	0	1
Andre Faria Gomes	2	1	5	2	5
John Gonzales	0	1	3	2	2
Wally Goodrick	0	0	2	6	3
Chester Goss	0	0	0	1	1
Steve Goss	0	0	2	1	0
Digger Graybill	0	1	0	0	0
Marty Gregory	0	0	0	0	1
Nicola Grigolo	0	0	0	0	2
Lee Grosscup	0	2	2	1	0
Art Grossman	0	0	2	0	1
Glenn Gundert	0	0	0	0	2
Gary Gysin	0	0	1	0	1
Axel Hager	0	2	2	1	8
Tom Haine	0	0	0	1	0
Mathieu Hamel	0	0	0	2	2
Glen Hamilton	0	0	0	0	1
Reid Hamilton	0	0	0	0	1
John Hanley	16	29	38	36	36
Albert Hannemann	1	2	3	2	6
Nick Hannemann	0	1	3	0	6
Eric Hansen	0	0	0	0	1
Jay Hanseth	5	13	14	13	18
Gene Hanson	1	0	0	0	0

GENE SELZNICK
Gene Selznick played during an era when there were not a lot of organized tournaments, but he was without a doubt one of the all-time most prolific winner's on the beach. Above photo, During the 1959 State Beach Open, Selznick hits a set from Bob Vogelsang.
Photo Courtesy of Kevin Goff

RON LANG
Ron Lang also played during an era when there were not a lot of organized tournaments, but he is also one of the all-time most prolific winner's on the beach. Above photo, During the 1954 State Beach Open, Lang hits a set from Dick Davis.
Photo Courtesy of Dave Heiser

Player	1st	2nd	3rd	4th	5th
Leif Hanson	3	6	9	7	25
Bill Hansyrd	0	0	0	0	1
Dennis Hare	5	10	8	0	12
Al Harris	1	2	0	0	0
John Hayden	0	0	0	1	1
Matt Heath	0	0	0	0	1
Mark Heese	1	5	10	8	19
Rob Heidger	1	5	13	7	22
Carl Henkel	0	6	3	4	12
Jack Henn	0	0	0	1	0
Ramon Hernandez	0	0	1	0	0
Thomas Hernandez	0	0	0	0	1
Patrick Heuscher	0	0	3	1	4
Sascha Heyer	0	2	0	0	5
Mike Higer	2	3	2	1	2
Jack Hilton	0	0	0	0	1
Henry Hitchcock	1	0	1	0	1
Bob Hogan	2	6	4	2	2
Pete Hogan	3	7	4	2	2
Vegard Hoidalen	1	5	2	4	8
Jody Holden	1	2	1	1	8
Dax Holdren	13	11	6	8	26
Bob Holland	0	0	1	1	0
Dane Holtzman	1	5	1	2	1
Bernie Holtzman	29	5	4	1	0
Gary Hooper	11	6	10	15	23
Iver Horrem	0	0	0	0	3
Tim Hovland	60	62	55	23	36
Tom Howlett	3	0	1	0	0
Clyde Hyatt	0	1	0	0	0
Jim Iams	0	1	0	0	0
Juan Rodriguez Ibarra	0	0	0	0	2
Bill Imwalle	4	6	10	6	4
Benjamin Insfran	7	7	4	3	7
Chris Irvin	0	0	1	0	0
Keith Iverson	0	0	0	0	1
Bryan Ivie	0	0	1	1	4
Bob Jackson	4	9	5	2	8
Dick Jackson	1	0	1	0	0

Player	1st	2nd	3rd	4th	5th
Jeff Jacobs	0	0	0	0	2
Al Janc	1	2	5	7	22
Al Jansci	0	0	0	0	1
Rick Jeffs	0	0	0	0	1
Charlie Jenkins	0	1	0	0	0
Rick Jennings	0	0	0	0	1
Casey Jennings	1	6	2	0	2
Adam Jewell	1	3	4	0	5
Sixto Jiminez	0	1	1	0	4
Jean Philippe Jodard	1	1	2	6	8
Pete Johnson	0	0	0	0	1
Adam Johnson	44	37	34	30	41
Bob Jones	1	3	1	3	3
Charlie Jones	0	0	0	0	1
Ike Jones	0	1	0	0	0
Joel Jones	0	0	2	2	3
Jeff Jordan	0	0	0	4	5
John Kalin	1	0	1	2	0
Lee Kammerdiner	0	0	1	0	0
Dave Kaplan	1	5	5	0	1
Dmitri Karasev	0	0	0	0	2
Bill Kasmerek	0	0	0	0	1
Jim Kaufman	0	2	1	1	1
Chuck Keller	0	2	0	0	0
Ev Keller	4	2	0	0	0
Glen Keller	0	2	0	0	0
Bill Kelter	1	0	0	0	0
Mark Kerins	2	1	3	5	8
Jorre Kiemperud	1	5	2	4	8
Christian Kiernan	0	0	0	0	1
Greg Kiernan	0	0	0	0	2
Kirk Kilgore	0	2	2	1	3
Karch Kiraly	**146**	**54**	**45**	**13**	**38**
Jorre Andre' Kjemperud	1	2	0	3	4
Kerry Kleppinger	0	0	0	0	1
Phil Klorer	1	0	0	0	0
Tom Klorer	0	1	0	0	1
Stefan Kobel	0	0	3	1	4
Richardde Kogel	0	0	0	0	1

RON VON HAGEN
Even though he won 62 Open tournaments, Ron Von Hagen was another player that played during an era when there were not very many events scheduled. He is number six on the all time career win list. Above photo, Von Hagen poised/posed to serve the ball.
Photo Courtesy of Brian Lewis Sr.

JIM MENGES
Jim Menges, like the previous players mentioned, played during an era when there were only a few tournaments scheduled each year. Menges had 48 career wins to his credit. Above photo, Menges in his classic overhand defensive stance.
Photo Courtesy of Bruce Hazelton

Player	1st	2nd	3rd	4th	5th
Mikhail Kouchnezev	0	0	1	1	4
Hannes Kronthaler	0	0	0	0	1
Premysl Kubala	0	0	0	1	0
Yasunori "Kuma" Kumada	0	0	0	0	1
Jan Kvalheim	7	2	10	9	10
Jim Kwinac	1	0	0	0	0
Micha l "Palda" Palinek	0	0	0	2	3
Martin Laciga	5	12	5	9	30
Paul Laciga	5	12	5	9	30
Ken LaDuke	2	4	2	2	0
Horace Lambden	1	0	0	0	0
Mike Lambert	2	1	5	1	2
Dan Landry	0	0	0	1	0
Ron Lang	53	19	9	2	3
Martin Lebl	0	0	0	1	0
Eugene LeDuff	0	0	1	0	1
Brent Lee	0	0	0	0	1
Greg Lee	28	9	7	4	10
Jon Lee	0	3	4	6	7
Bob Leebody	1	0	0	0	0
Bill Leeka	0	1	0	1	0
Lee LeGrande	4	1	6	2	12
Conrad Leinemann	1	1	1	1	6
DionisioDio Lequaglie	0	1	1	1	3
Jeff Leroy	1	0	0	0	0
Brian Lewis, Sr.	1	0	0	0	0
Brian Lewis	8	28	36	19	48
Brazil's Lezaburo	0	0	0	0	1
Andre Perlingeiro Lima	1	4	5	1	1
Ricardo "Riccardino" Lione	0	0	1	0	2
Dick Livingston	1	5	0	0	0
Djordje Ljubieic	0	0	0	0	1
Jose Loiola	55	44	26	17	25
Roberto Costa Lopes	15	11	16	8	12
Carlos "Alemao" Galletti Loss	1	2	2	1	9
Tom Lubisich	1	0	0	0	0
Ricci Luyties	8	17	20	39	60
Matt Lyles	0	0	1	1	2
Bjorn Maaseide	7	2	10	9	14

Player	1st	2nd	3rd	4th	5th
Gaston Macau	0	0	0	0	1
Eric Macias	0	0	0	1	3
Ted Mahan	0	0	1	1	0
Gordie Mahon	0	1	2	0	1
Luis Miguel Barbosa Maia	2	0	0	6	7
Jud Mallard	1	0	0	0	0
Mitch Malpee	0	3	2	1	1
Chris Marlowe	8	4	3	6	9
Steven Marlowe	0	0	0	0	1
Harley Marques	2	0	1	3	5
Luiz Guilherme Marques	8	19	12	6	11
Butch Martin	0	0	0	1	0
Kevin Martin	0	0	2	2	12
Eduardo Esteban Martinez	3	7	7	8	12
Guliberto Chavarry Martins	0	0	1	0	0
Gianni Mascagna	0	0	0	2	0
Butch May	3	3	2	0	4
John May	0	0	0	0	1
Benjamin Vicedo Mayor	0	0	0	0	1
Chip McCaw	0	0	0	2	0
Doug McClure	0	1	0	0	0
Russ McCollum	0	1	0	0	0
Bill McElroy	1	0	0	0	0
Bruce McFarland	0	0	1	0	3
Dana McFarland	0	1	3	3	6
Dan McFarland	0	0	1	0	1
Duncan McFarland	0	1	0	0	2
Ron McHenry	0	0	0	0	1
Dave McKay	2	0	0	0	0
Owen McKibbin	0	0	1	1	2
Paul McLaughlin	0	1	0	0	0
Don McMahon	8	9	3	1	1
Warren McMillin	1	0	0	0	0
Jack McShane	1	0	0	0	0
Larry Mear	0	3	3	4	35
Jeovanny Medrano	0	0	0	0	1
John Meehan	0	0	0	1	1
John Meek	0	2	1	0	0
Phil Melese	0	0	1	0	0

MIKE DODD
During his beach volleyball career, Mike Dodd won 75 tournament championships, ranking him at number five on the all-time career win list. Above photo, Dodd is in position to pass the ball.
Photo Courtesy of Frank Goroszko

TIM HOVLAND
Tim Hovland had a successful career on the beach. Hovland won 60 tournament championships, which ranks him at number seven on the all time career win list. Above photo, Hovland slips the ball through the block of Randy Stoklos.
Photo Courtesy of Dennis G. Steers

Player	1st	2nd	3rd	4th	5th
Jim Menges	48	21	14	7	10
George Mesic	0	1	0	0	0
Stein Metzger	4	7	13	2	21
Rich Mielkey	0	1	0	0	1
Juan Miguel Rosell Milanes	2	2	1	2	8
Delmer Miller	1	0	0	0	0
George Miller	0	1	0	0	0
Greg Miller	0	0	0	1	0
John Miller	1	0	0	0	0
Larry Milliken	0	0	0	2	3
Ralph Mine	0	0	0	0	1
Javier Bosma Minguez	1	3	3	2	11
Al Mirabito	0	1	0	0	0
Craig Moothart	0	0	3	6	22
Curt Moothart	0	0	0	0	1
Keith Morehart	1	0	0	0	0
Craig Morehouse	0	0	0	0	1
Dave Morehouse	0	0	0	0	1
Paulo Robert Dacosta Moreira	7	3	4	9	8
Roberto Duarte Dias Moreira	0	3	2	3	4
Deforest Most	2	0	0	0	0
Sander Mulder	0	0	0	0	1
JavierYuste Muniz	0	0	0	0	2
Steve Neptune	0	0	0	0	1
John Nesbitt	0	0	0	0	1
Jose Franco Vieira Neto	17	13	18	10	19
Fred Newcomb	1	1	0	0	0
Bob Newkirk	0	0	0	1	0
Jim Nichols	0	0	0	3	1
Randy Niles	0	0	0	2	1
Jose Z-Marco Melo Nobrega	26	16	14	6	12
Mike Normand	1	2	3	2	4
Jeff Nygard	5	1	4	1	4
Dick O'Brien	0	1	0	0	0
Mike O'Hara	21	22	9	4	1
Steve Obradovich	9	9	21	27	43
Oliver Oetke	0	0	0	2	2
Rick Olmstead	0	1	0	0	0
Marco Ortega	0	1	1	3	2
Peter Ott	0	1	1	0	0
Frank Page	0	0	0	0	1
Marco "Pako" Pakosta	0	0	0	0	1
Marek Pakosta	0	0	0	0	1
Michal Palinek	0	0	0	2	1
Raul Papaleo	0	0	1	0	4
Bob Pape	0	0	1	2	3
Joe Pappas	1	0	0	0	0
Denny Gomes Paredes	0	0	0	0	2
Dodge Parker	1	0	1	0	0
Nate Parrish	0	0	1	0	1
Dan Patterson	0	0	1	0	1
Christian Penigaud	1	1	2	6	8
Joao Brenha Alves Pereira	2	0	0	6	7
Justin Perlstrom	0	0	0	0	1
Fredrik "Figge" Peterson	0	0	0	0	1
Gene Pflueger	1	9	6	3	4
Maurizio Pimponi	0	0	0	0	3
Stan Pinky	0	0	1	0	0
Mike Pomeroy	0	0	0	0	1
Maxim Popelov	0	0	0	0	1
Greg Porter	0	0	0	2	3
Stefan Potyka	0	0	0	0	1
Jack Power	1	1	0	0	0
Pat Powers	13	12	14	19	38
Dan Prall	1	0	0	0	0
Jim Prather	1	0	0	0	0
Miguel Angel Martin Prieto	0	0	0	2	2
Julien Prosser	1	0	8	6	18
Larry Prowd	1	0	2	2	0
Jason Pursley	0	0	0	1	1
Leland Quinn	0	0	0	0	1
Andrea Raffaelli	0	0	0	1	3
Alexandre Tande Ramos	7	2	8	0	7
Niel Rasmussen	0	1	1	0	0
Jonas Reckermann	0	3	1	3	5
Don Reynolds	0	0	0	0	1
Nolan Riddle	0	0	0	1	0
Rich Riffero	0	1	2	1	3

JOSE LOIOLA

With 55 career tournament championships, Brazilian Jose Loiola is the most proflic non-American to compete on the beach volleyball circuit. He ranks number eight on the all time win list. Above photo, Loiola is ready for action.

Photo Courtesy of Eric Barnes

EMANUEL REGO

With 51 career tournament championships, Brazilian Emanuel Rego Schaefer is the second most proflic non-American to compete on the beach volleyball circuit. He ranks number ten on the all time win list. Above photo, Rego diving for the ball.

Photo Courtesy of "Couvi"

Player	1st	2nd	3rd	4th	5th
Matt Rigg	0	0	0	1	0
Jason Ring	0	0	1	0	1
Wilfredo Sombra Garcia Rizo	0	0	0	0	1
Adam Roberts	0	0	1	0	0
Johnny Robinson	1	0	0	0	0
Jeff Rogers	0	1	1	0	8
Todd Rogers	8	9	6	8	29
Miguel Rosell	0	2	0	0	4
Sean Rosenthal	2	2	3	0	3
Chester Ross	0	0	1	0	0
Brazil's Rossard	0	0	0	0	1
Steve Rottman	0	0	0	1	5
Daryl Rucco	0	0	0	0	1
Larry Rundle	13	8	2	1	1
Henry Russell	1	1	3	1	4
Bill Ryan	0	0	0	1	0
Mike Ryan	0	0	0	0	1
Manny Saenz	13	2	1	0	0
Alejandro Salas	1	0	0	0	1
Brian Saldano	0	0	1	0	0
Jose Salema	1	0	1	1	2
Clarence Sandstrum	0	1	0	0	0
Ricardo Alex Costa Santos	24	15	8	5	9
Mark Savage	0	0	0	0	1
Marshall Savage	1	2	4	4	5
Tony Sayler	0	0	0	0	1
Andrew Schacht	0	0	0	0	3
Todd Schaffer	0	1	1	0	1
Emanuel Rego Schaeffer	51	25	29	3	13
Andreas Scheuerpflug	0	0	0	2	4
Walt Schiller	1	0	4	1	0
Mike Schlegel	0	0	0	0	1
Carl Schllig	0	0	1	0	0
Bill Schmittey	0	1	0	0	0
Bob Schumacker	0	0	0	1	0
Todd Schumons	0	0	0	0	1
Beryl Schwartz	0	0	1	1	1
Larry Scott	3	0	0	2	0
Sean Scott	0	2	4	1	9
Pete Sebastian	1	0	0	0	0
Kenny Seese	0	1	0	0	0
Fred Seger	2	1	0	0	0
Wayne Seliqson	0	0	1	0	2
Dane Selznick	13	26	18	21	24
Gene Selznick	50	28	4	3	1
Don Shaw	1	1	5	2	9
Randy Shaw	0	1	0	0	0
Rick Shaw	1	4	6	7	14
Paul Siano	1	0	0	0	0
Paulo Emilo Azevedo Silva	5	3	5	8	9
Luiz "Lula" Barbosada Silva	0	1	0	0	0
Carl Silvkoff	0	0	0	1	1
Steve Sims	2	5	7	5	10
Josh Slack	0	0	1	0	4
Michael Slean	0	0	0	0	1
Jim Slivkoff	0	0	0	1	0
Alika Smith	0	1	0	0	0
Andrew Smith	3	13	13	32	71
Bob Smith	0	0	1	0	0
Colin Smith	1	0	0	1	3
Noble Smith	0	0	1	0	2
Sinjin Smith	139	73	40	18	38
Jerry Smolinsky	0	0	0	0	1
Tom Smuz	0	0	1	0	0
Bill Smythe	0	0	0	1	0
Marco "Sollu" Solustri	0	0	1	4	1
Matt Sonnichsen	0	0	0	1	1
Jeff Southcott	1	2	2	4	12
Federico "Fred" Doriade Souza	0	1	5	2	8
Rogrio "Para" Ferrirsde Souza	7	14	6	7	12
Tim Spees	0	0	2	3	5
Oliver Stamm	0	0	0	0	1
Jon Stanley	0	1	0	0	0
Scott Steele	0	0	1	1	4
Don Steere	1	0	0	0	0
Kent Steffes	110	34	22	12	22
Bill Stetson	0	1	0	0	0
Bob Stevenson	1	0	0	0	0
Clint Stevenson	1	0	0	0	0
Jon Stevenson	19	31	29	33	34
John Stimpfig	0	0	1	1	0
Charlie Stinnett	0	0	1	0	2
Raqndy Stoklos	122	86	53	28	37
Carl Stuart	1	0	0	0	0
Fred Sturm	6	4	4	7	7
Bill Suwara	0	0	0	0	1
Ernie Suwara	2	5	3	0	0
Rudy Suwara	1	1	2	1	2
Buzz Swartz	10	6	6	8	10
David Swatik	4	3	5	5	21
Troy Tanner	0	10	13	5	25
John Taylor	0	2	1	0	0
Ed Teagle	1	0	0	0	0
Tulio Teixeira,	0	1	0	0	1
Eugenio Telles	0	0	0	0	1
Craig Thompson	0	0	0	2	1
Bill Thompson	0	0	1	0	0
Steve Timmons	1	1	3	3	8
Lloyd Tolman	1	0	0	0	0
Gonzalo Manuel Torres	0	0	0	0	1
Brad Torsone	0	0	0	1	0
Murilo Toscano	0	0	0	1	0
Toshi Toyoda	0	1	3	1	0
John Treman	0	1	0	1	0
Chad Turner	0	0	0	0	1
Matt Unger	0	0	0	1	6
John Vallely	8	2	1	2	1
Ron Van Horsen	0	0	0	1	1
Bruk Vandeweghe	1	4	9	12	13
Kiki Vandeweghe	0	0	0	0	1
Rafael Vargas	0	0	0	0	1
Bernhard Vesti	0	0	0	0	1
Jose Vieira	1	0	0	0	0
Bob Vogelsang	1	9	4	7	5
Ron Von Hagen	62	31	12	5	12
Dan Vrebalovich	6	7	20	19	54
George Wagner	2	1	0	0	1
Dick Wainright	2	0	0	0	0
Stu Waite	0	0	0	0	1
Tim Walmer	8	6	10	20	50
Bill Wardrop	0	0	1	1	1
Fred Warren	0	0	1	0	0
Darrow Weeks	0	0	0	1	0
Wes Welch	0	0	5	3	11
Ray Weldie	1	1	0	0	0
Jay Whalen	0	0	1	0	3
Sel White	0	1	0	0	0
Mike Whitmarsh	28	49	39	26	53
Bill Wieand	2	0	0	0	0
Mark Williams	0	0	0	0	1
Jeff Williams	0	3	3	2	1
Alika Williams	0	0	0	0	1
Mark Williams	0	0	2	2	2
Mike Wilton	0	1	0	0	0
Larry Witt	2	2	4	0	6
Andy Witt	0	0	0	0	3
Kevin Wong	7	7	10	3	23
Scott Wong	0	0	1	0	2
Karvel Wortham	0	0	0	1	0
Eric Wurts	1	6	4	4	28
Mike Yniguez	0	0	1	1	0
Chris Young	0	1	0	0	5
Lee Zahner	1	0	6	3	16
George Zebot	0	0	0	0	1
Fred Zuelich	8	8	15	5	10

KARCH KIRALY
Karch Kiraly is the all time career leader for tournament championships. Kiraly has 146 career wins to his credit. Above photo, Kiraly passing the ball.

Photo Courtesy of Tim Andexler

WOMEN'S BEACH VOLLEYBALL RECORDS 1970-2004

The following document list the available beach volleyball tournament records, from 1970 up to July of 2004, of all the female players, that competed in this era and placed fifth or higher, in events that were of the uppermost classification of their era, ie: AVP, BVA, FIVB, Parks and Recreation "A" - "AAA" etc.

(Note: "Oral-History" accounts were utilized for some of the early players, when actual written records were not available)

Player	1st	2nd	3rd	4th	5th	Player	1st	2nd	3rd	4th	5th
Jen Adams	0	0	1	0	0	Judy Bellomo	0	2	4	4	10
Andrea Adamson	0	1	0	0	0	Nicole Benoit	0	0	0	1	3
Andrea Ahmann	0	0	0	0	1	Janet Benton	0	0	0	0	3
Angie Akers	0	0	0	0	7	Rosie Bergin	0	1	0	1	1
Karen Ambler	0	0	0	1	0	Anna Biller	0	0	1	1	2
Chris Anderson	0	0	0	2	0	Lori Biller	0	0	0	1	4
Marie Anderson	1	0	0	2	2	Brooke Binley	0	0	0	1	0
Tiffany Anderson	0	0	0	0	2	Mary Binley	0	2	3	0	4
Maria Arago	0	0	0	0	1	Paula Birney	0	0	0	1	0
Lisa Arce	21	17	22	12	40	Allison Bisantz	0	1	0	0	0
EthelJulie Arjona	0	0	0	0	1	Mona Bishop	0	0	0	0	2
Vassiliki Arvaniti	0	0	0	0	2	Chris Black	0	0	0	0	1
Krista Atkinson	0	0	0	0	2	Debbie Black	0	0	1	0	2
Pam Ayakatubby	0	0	0	0	2	Donna Black	0	0	0	0	1
Colleen Bailey	0	0	0	0	1	Lynda Johnson Black	0	0	0	1	0
Darlene Bailey	2	2	5	6	3	Krista Blomquist	0	0	3	3	10
Ollette Bailey	0	0	1	0	0	Julie Bowser	0	0	0	1	0
Amy Baltus	0	1	1	0	1	Danalee Bragado	0	3	1	3	9
Laura Bandel	0	0	0	0	1	Andrea Brat	0	0	0	1	0
Teresa Bandel	0	0	0	0	1	Leslie Brewer	0	0	0	1	0
Patty Barrett	8	2	2	1	2	Bonnie Bright	0	0	0	0	1
Leila Barros	0	0	0	0	8	Patti Bright	0	1	2	3	7
Maria Isabel Salgado Barroso	1	3	2	2	2	Debbie Brockman	0	0	0	0	1
Kay Bay	0	0	1	0	1	Jaynette Brown	0	0	0	1	0
Pat Bearer	0	2	1	1	0	Jean Brunicardi	32	0	1	0	1
Shelda Kelly Bruno Bede	31	21	18	7	4	Laura Bruschini	0	0	0	2	7
Paula Bee	0	0	0	1	8	Stacy Buck	0	0	0	1	0
Adriana Brando Behar	31	21	19	9	7	Adriana Benito Buczmiejuk	0	0	0	0	2

HOLLY McPEAK
With 71 career titles to her credit, Holly McPeak is the most prolific winner in the history of women's beach volleyball. In 2004, McPeak was still competing on the AVP Tour and may very well add to her total. Above photo, McPeak passing the ball.
Photo Courtesy of Frank Goroszko

KAROLYN KIRBY
With 67 career tournament championships to her credit, Karolyn Kirby is number two on the all-time career wins list. She was surpassed by Holly McPeak during the 2004 season. Above photo, Kirby gets sandy in order to make the dig.
Photo Courtesy of Frank Goroszko

Player	1st	2nd	3rd	4th	5th
Beate Buhler	1	1	1	2	2
Lynn Buhlig	0	1	0	2	7
Marsha Burns	0	0	0	0	1
Carrie Busch	1	0	9	2	12
Margie Bushey	0	0	0	0	1
Donna Bydonsky	0	0	0	0	2
Sheri Caldwell	0	0	1	0	0
Jackie Campbell	0	0	0	0	5
Chris Cantu	0	1	0	0	1
Elaine Cantu	0	0	0	0	1
Kathy Cantu	0	0	1	1	0
Becky Carey	0	1	0	1	0
Debbie Carey	0	0	1	0	1
Linda Carrillo Chisholm	39	30	19	27	21
Gail Castro	6	22	23	27	56
Mary Caudino	0	0	0	2	0
Eva Celbova	0	0	3	2	7
Cammy Chamlers	0	0	0	0	1
Betsey Chavez	0	0	0	1	2
Rong Chi	0	0	2	1	1
Cammy Ciarelli	14	8	15	11	6
Eileen Clancy	3	6	6	3	3
Rosey Clark	0	0	1	0	0
Angela Clarke	0	0	1	0	7
Claire Clem	0	0	1	0	0
Ilga Clemens	0	1	0	0	0
Cindy Cochrane	1	3	2	5	4
Nancy Cohen	17	2	5	1	3
Susie Condon	0	0	1	0	0
Evlyn Conley	0	1	1	0	1
Ana Paula Connolly	5	6	5	0	10
Edie Conrad	0	3	1	1	2
Natalie Cook	3	7	15	14	23
Stephanie Cook	0	0	1	0	0
Wendy Cook	0	1	1	0	0
Tania Cooley	0	0	0	0	2
Denise Corlette	0	1	0	1	10
Jan Corley	0	0	1	0	0
Mary Corraugh	0	0	1	1	2
Laurie Costello	0	0	0	0	1
Stephane Cox	0	0	1	0	7
LuAnn Crawford	0	0	0	0	1
AnnCroaker	0	1	0	0	0
Jan Crow	0	0	1	0	0
Ann Cunningham	4	4	5	8	5
Annete Buckner Davis	8	17	17	6	11
Raffa Davita	0	0	0	0	1
Dominque Deevlovic	0	0	0	0	1
Angie DeGroot	1	0	0	0	0
Dianne DeNeochea	1	4	7	3	8
Mary Ann Deutschman	0	0	0	0	1
Mary Diamond	0	3	0	1	0
Patricia Diaz	0	0	0	0	1
Xinia Diaz	0	0	0	0	1
Debbie Dick	0	1	0	0	1
Patty Orozco Dodd	14	13	20	22	26
Kathy Dombroski	1	0	0	0	0
Torrie Dorrell	0	4	2	4	1
Sonja Novakova Dosoudilvoa	0	0	4	2	8
Kathy Drumboski	0	0	0	1	0
Peggy Dulay	0	1	0	0	0
Guylaine Dumont	0	0	0	0	1
Rose Duncan	5	2	1	1	3
Jan Dunn	0	0	0	0	2
Jill Durkee	4	11	5	11	13
Diedre Dvorak	0	0	0	0	1
Wendy Dvorak	0	0	1	0	0
Mary Dwight	0	0	0	0	1
Gail Edison	1	0	0	0	1
Katy Eldridge	0	0	1	0	8
Jackie Elmer	0	0	0	0	1
Berta Kaize Engel	0	0	0	0	1
Beth Engman	0	0	0	0	1
Liane Fenwick	0	1	2	0	4
Mona Fether	0	0	0	2	1
Rose Finnager	0	0	1	0	0
Mary Fischer	0	0	0	0	1
Bonnie Fisk	0	0	0	0	2
Ginny Fitzgerald	0	2	0	2	1
Wendy Fletcher	0	0	2	2	11
Jan Flora	0	1	0	0	1
Junice Flora	0	0	0	0	1
Bev Floyd	0	0	0	0	2
Valerie Foley	0	0	1	0	0
Debbie Fonoimoana	0	1	1	2	1
Alexandra Fonseca	0	0	0	3	5
Barbara Fontana.	20	36	33	21	43
LoriKotas Forsythe	9	22	28	27	42
Betty Alysworth Fraker	0	2	1	1	3
Larissa Franca	1	0	1	0	0
Maike Friedrichsen	0	3	0	2	8
Debbie Fromme	0	0	0	0	1
Jo Fry	0	0	0	0	1
Sachika Fujita	0	0	0	1	2
Camilla Funck	0	0	0	0	1
Jean Gaertner	2	2	2	1	2
Karta Gainer	0	1	0	0	0
Amy Galbraith	0	0	0	0	1
Myra Garcia	0	1	0	0	1
Kengelin Gardiner	0	0	0	0	2
Karla Garner	0	0	1	0	0
Lisa Garritty	0	0	0	0	1
Georjean Garvey	2	2	6	1	2
Daniela Gattelli	0	0	1	0	6
Hilda Gaxiola	0	1	0	0	1
Paula Gehley	0	0	0	0	1
Karen Geraldson	0	0	1	0	0
Kyle Gerlic	0	0	0	0	3
Betty Ann Ghormley	0	1	0	0	2
Connie Gibbon	0	0	0	0	1
Sandy Gillespie	0	1	0	0	0
Marie Gingras	0	0	1	1	0
Sue Glamboski	0	1	0	0	1
Sheryl Glenwinkle	0	0	0	1	2
Suzanne Glesnes	0	0	0	0	2
Jill Goldberg	0	0	1	0	0
Sandy Goldberg	0	0	0	0	1
Nancy Goldpaper	0	1	0	0	0
Jeanne Goldsmith	0	0	0	0	1
Laura Golub	0	0	0	1	3
Sylvana Gomez	0	0	0	0	1
Pam Gomillion	0	0	0	1	1
D'Ney Goodfellow	0	1	1	2	3
Tania Gooley	0	1	0	0	7
Nancy Gougeon	0	0	0	1	0
Sue Gozarsky	0	0	0	0	1
Dalixia Fernandez Grasset	1	1	0	1	8
Kathy Gregory	58	38	9	4	6
Mariao Grisanti	1	0	0	0	0
Wanda Guennette	0	0	0	1	0
Mabelle Guitierez	0	1	0	0	0
Karen Gysin	0	1	1	1	0
Robin Gysin	0	0	1	0	0
Heather Medina Hafner	2	3	6	7	14
Cathy Hahn	0	1	0	0	0
Christi Hahn	2	0	2	2	3
Lindsey Hahn	2	0	0	0	0
Lucy Hahn	0	1	0	0	2
Dale Hall	1	3	5	6	4
Sacha Hall	0	0	0	0	1
Kathy Hanley	21	17	12	16	16
Linda Robertson Hanley	46	41	33	25	35
Ann Hanson	1	0	0	1	3
Lois Haraughty	0	1	2	1	3
Janice Opalinski Harrer	25	39	22	15	26
Maya Hashimoto	0	0	0	0	1
Missy Hauter	0	0	0	0	1
Sally Heiser	0	0	0	1	3
Karen Helyer	0	0	0	0	1
Vickie Hill	0	0	0	1	0
Valinda Hilleary	0	0	1	2	10
Hillary Hinwood	0	0	0	0	1
Lima Hirahara	0	0	0	0	1
Mary Hiuvn	0	0	0	0	1
Jen Holdren	0	1	0	0	0
Sue Holmes	0	1	0	1	1
Norma Weier Holtzman	3	2	0	0	1
Muriel Horak	0	1	1	2	3
Jill Horning	1	0	0	0	0
Marsha Hunt	0	0	0	0	2
Robin Irvin	1	1	0	1	3
Lynn Irwin	0	0	1	1	2
Yukikio Ishizaka	0	1	0	0	1
Mary Isley	0	0	1	1	0
Donna Janulitis	0	0	1	1	1
Gerusa Ferreirde Jesus	0	0	0	0	1
Linjun Ji	0	0	0	0	1
Mary Jo Peppler	1	2	3	4	7
Alison Johnson	0	1	0	6	7
Hilary Johnson	1	2	3	2	4
Fran Jones	0	0	0	1	2
Susie Jones	4	11	8	7	8

Player	1st	2nd	3rd	4th	5th
JennyJohnson Jordan	8	17	17	6	11
Ninja Jorgensen	0	0	1	2	3
Pernille Jorgensen	0	0	0	0	1
Debora Schoon Kadijk	0	0	0	0	3
Rebbekka Kadijk	1	0	0	4	7
Virginia Kadjo	0	0	0	0	1
Vasso Karadassiou	0	0	1	0	8
Kathy Kehoe	0	0	0	1	0
Connie Keller	3	0	1	1	2
Pat Keller	0	1	1	3	10
Dale Keough	1	6	6	5	6
Mary Kerwin	0	0	0	0	1
Jennifer Kessy	0	1	2	0	3
Bev King	0	0	0	0	1
Margie Kingras	0	0	0	0	1
Eri Kinugasa	0	0	0	0	1
Karolyn Kirby	67	22	26	9	18
Mary Lou Kirby	1	0	0	0	1
Roberta Kisselburgh	0	0	0	2	0
Sue Klein	0	1	0	2	3
Fran Knapkiewicz	0	0	1	0	1
Dennie Schupyt Knoop	0	3	11	21	24
Denise Koelliker	0	0	1	0	0
Shaunna Koening	1	0	0	0	0
Debbie Koppel	0	1	0	0	0
LoriForsythe Kotas	9	22	28	27	42
Efthalia Koutroumanidou	0	0	0	0	2
Simon Kuhn	0	0	0	1	3
Chikako Kumamae	0	0	0	0	1
Darleen Kurby	0	0	0	0	1
Chiaki Kusuhara	0	0	0	1	1
Jan Kyle	0	0	0	1	0
Grace LaDuke	0	3	2	1	2
Suzanne Lahme	0	2	0	1	3
Karen Lane	0	0	0	1	0
Johnette Latreille	21	4	2	1	1
Marrit Leenstra	1	0	0	4	4
Linda Lehde	0	0	0	0	0
Tammy Leibl	0	0	0	1	1
Bev Lidyoff	1	0	2	2	2
Magda Rejane FalcoDe Lima	0	0	1	2	6
Sue Lipps	0	0	0	0	1
Summer Lochowicz	0	0	0	1	2
Joann Loos	0	2	3	1	2
Suzanne Luhme	0	1	0	0	1
Kathy Lynch	0	0	0	1	1
Lisa Strand Ma'a	0	8	7	5	20
Kathleen Maaseide	0	0	0	0	2
Mary Machado	0	1	2	2	1
Beane MacLaurie	0	0	0	0	1
Cynthia Mahar	0	1	0	0	0
Sandy Malpee	5	2	5	5	8
Janet Mammon	0	0	0	0	1
Pauline Manser	0	3	1	1	4
Annie Martin	0	0	0	1	1
Donna Martin	0	0	1	1	0
Kim Martin	0	0	1	0	0
Liz Masakayan	47	16	23	21	36
Nancy Mason	0	2	14	2	8
Nina Grouwinkel Matthies	50	26	24	9	16
Barbara Grubb May	2	6	3	1	1
Misty May	31	13	6	3	3
Kathy Mayer	0	0	0	0	1
Jackie McCabe	0	0	0	0	1
Susan McCall	0	0	0	0	1
Ann McCampbell	2	2	6	4	1
Claire McCarty	1	2	3	6	3
CarolPier McCaslin	2	2	7	1	2
Carolyn McDonald	0	0	0	0	1
Miki McFadden	16	5	2	2	3
Jessie McGahan	0	0	1	0	0
Roberta McGann	0	1	1	0	0
Aggie McHugh	0	0	0	1	0
Marion McMahon	1	3	1	1	3
Roxanne McMillen	0	0	0	1	0
Lisa McNally	1	0	0	0	0
Holly McPeak	**71**	**43**	**31**	**19**	**29**
Martha McPhaooca	0	1	0	0	0
Marilyn McReavy	0	0	1	1	2

JEAN BRUNICARDI
Jean Brunicardi played during an era when there were not a lot of organized Women's tournaments, but she was without a doubt one of the all-time most prolific winner's on the beach. Above photo, during a 1961 Sorrento event Brunicardi gets into position.
Photo Courtesy of Kevin Goff

KATHY GREGORY
Kathy Gregory also played during an era when there were not a lot of organized Women's tournaments, but she is also one of the all-time most prolific winner's on the beach. Above photo, during a 1977 Marine Street event, Gregory is all smiles after a victory.
Photo Courtesy of Bruce Hazelton

Player	1st	2nd	3rd	4th	5th
Leanne Schuster McSorley	1	1	13	3	16
MariaRicha Medeiros	0	0	0	1	1
JeannieGoldsmith Meltzer	0	1	7	7	11
Donna Menty	0	0	0	0	1
Jennifer Meredith	0	3	6	0	9
Silke Meyer	0	1	0	0	1
Marsha Miller	0	0	0	0	1
Shannon Miller	0	0	0	0	5
Marie Millsom	0	0	0	0	1
Tatiana Minello	1	4	3	4	9
Charlotte Mitchell	0	0	0	2	6
Linda Mohr	0	0	1	1	1
Janis Morgan	0	0	0	1	0
Junko Moriyama	0	0	0	0	1
Michelle Morse	0	0	0	0	1
Lisa Murphy	0	0	0	0	1
Danja Musch	1	5	1	4	12
Teruko "Peko" Nakano	0	0	0	0	1
Jan Nathan	0	0	0	0	1
Ricky Neal	0	0	0	0	1
Zoanne Neff	1	1	1	1	3
Linda Nelson	1	0	0	0	0
Katerina Nikolaidou	0	0	0	0	1
Sherry Norman	0	0	1	0	1
Marla O'Connell	0	1	2	1	5
Marla O'Hara	1	0	5	3	27
Kathy O'Keefe	0	1	0	0	0
Fran Oliver	0	0	1	2	4
Monique Oliver	1	0	1	4	6
Claudia Oliveria	0	0	0	0	4
Jane Orgar	1	0	0	0	1
Gail O'Rourke	0	0	0	3	5
Liz Pagano	0	0	0	0	1
Andrea Paiducci	0	0	0	0	1
Laurie Pairmont	0	0	0	0	2
Anita Palm	0	0	0	0	9
Allison Palmer	0	0	0	0	1
RenataCosta Palmier	0	0	0	0	1
Monica Park	0	0	0	1	0
Kathy Parker	0	1	0	1	2
Lisa Pate	0	0	1	0	0
Fran Paulson	0	0	0	0	1
Helena Pavels	0	0	0	0	1
Jenny Pavley	0	1	1	0	6
Katie Peden	0	0	0	0	2
Tammy Pelski	0	0	0	0	1
Pauline Penline	0	0	0	0	1
Mary Jo Peppler	1	2	3	5	7
Tamara Larrea Perazza	1	1	0	1	5
Christina Pereria	0	0	0	2	0
Lucilla Perrotta	0	0	1	0	6
Mary Perry	1	0	1	1	2
Diane Pestolesi	0	0	0	2	4
Sharon Peterson	0	0	0	1	1
Linda Pettit	1	0	0	0	0
Diane Phair	0	1	0	0	0
Keri Pier	0	0	2	0	1
Sandra Tavares Pires	22	17	20	13	17
Stephane Pohl	0	0	0	0	5
Karrie Trieschmann Poppinga	0	1	5	8	27
Wendy Porter	0	0	0	1	0
Lisa Pote	0	0	0	0	1
Kerri Ann Pottharst	3	9	11	16	20
Anna Proussalis	3	7	7	13	8
Erin Prouty	0	0	0	1	1
Adriana Samuel Ramos	7	14	8	10	11
Sue Rampe	0	0	0	1	1
Marie Rasmussen	0	1	0	0	0
Okka Rau	0	0	0	0	5
Tammy Rau	0	0	0	0	1
Gabrielle Reece	0	0	2	0	2
Jeanne Reeves	0	0	0	1	1
Lima Falcãão De Magda Rejane	0	0	1	2	6
Nancy Reno	38	28	25	13	18
Donna Reynolds	0	0	1	0	0
Esteves Ribarta	0	0	0	0	1
Renata Ribeiro	0	0	0	0	2
Ana Richa	0	0	1	0	0

NINA GROUWINKEL MATTHIES
Nina Grouwinkel Matthies was another player from an era that did not provide very many women's tournaments, and she is also one of the all-time most prolific winner's on the beach. Above photo, During a 1979 event, Nina passing the ball.
Photo Courtesy of Bruce Hazelton

LIZ MASAKAYAN
During her beach volleyball career, Liz Masakayan won 47 tournament championships, ranking her at number six on the all-time career win list. Above photo, Masakayan spikes the ball over the net.
Photo Courtesy of Frank Goroszko

Player	1st	2nd	3rd	4th	5th
Lisa Richards	0	1	0	0	0
Rhondell Richards	0	0	0	0	1
Deb Richardson	0	7	16	14	24
Joan Rickward	0	0	0	0	1
Charlotte Roach	0	0	0	0	3
Kenui Rochlen	1	0	1	1	0
Angela Rock	27	35	19	26	23
Monica Rodriguez	6	11	6	7	18
Adriana Bento Rodrigues	0	0	0	0	5
Beth Rogers	0	1	1	2	3
Elaine Roque	6	36	27	32	37
Rita Crockett Royster	1	6	12	11	18
Melanie Russell	0	1	1	0	3
Regan Ruth	0	0	1	0	0
Mika Teru Saiki	0	1	2	1	4
Maria Isabel Barroso Salgado	0	0	0	0	1
Nicole Sanderson	0	1	4	1	4
Roseliane Dos Santos	0	0	1	0	0
Jan Saunders	0	0	0	0	1
Tracy Saying	0	1	3	1	1
Julie Thornton Schaar	2	12	7	5	16
Christine Schaefer	1	0	8	5	9
Ulrike Schmidt	0	0	0	0	2
Kristen Schritter	0	0	0	0	1
Liz Schwarz	0	0	0	0	1
Margie Schwarz	0	0	0	1	1
Susan Schwartz	0	0	0	1	1
Diane Sebastian	2	2	0	1	1
Efi Sfyri	0	1	2	1	8
Vickie Shea	0	5	0	0	2
Steph Sieg	0	0	0	0	1
Juliana Felisberta Silva	1	0	1	0	2
JacquelineLouiseCruz Silva	60	23	33	12	19
Patty Smith	0	2	0	0	1
Lane Smith	0	0	1	0	0
Mary Jane Smith	0	1	0	0	1
Anna Maria Solazzi	1	0	0	4	8
Siomara Marciade Souza	0	0	0	0	2
Dawn Spurlock	0	0	1	0	0
Gayle Stammer	1	2	2	7	25
Wendy Stammer	0	1	3	1	4
Gudula Staub	0	0	0	0	2
Patty Steer	0	1	2	3	4
Mary Stephenson	0	0	0	1	2
Cookie Stevens	0	0	0	1	0
Wendy Stevenson	0	0	0	1	1
Rhonda Stoklos	0	0	1	0	1
Georgia Storm	0	0	0	1	1
Evie Stoten	0	1	1	2	2
Lisa Strand	0	0	0	2	0
Kathy Strand	0	0	0	1	0
Barbie Stranksy	0	0	0	0	1
Sara Straton	1	0	2	3	6
Karen Swabeck	1	0	0	0	0
Laura Sweeney	0	0	1	0	0
Michelle Sweet	0	0	1	0	0
Wendy Swenson	0	0	0	0	1
Dagmara Szyszczak	0	0	1	2	0
Kim Tackas	0	0	0	0	1
Yukiko Takashi	0	1	0	2	6
Chris Talunas	0	1	3	0	0
Ann Taylor	0	0	0	0	1
Lou Ann Terheggen	0	0	1	0	1
Maya Thiene	1	1	0	4	1
Anette Huygens Tholen	0	0	0	0	3
Jia Tian	2	0	0	2	7
AnaRoseli Timm	1	3	3	2	1
Ryo Tokuno	0	0	0	1	2
Cathy Tonne	0	0	0	0	2
Elaine Torvinen	1	0	0	0	0
Bonnie Toth	2	0	4	3	3
Donna Townsend	1	1	1	1	0
Nancy Townsend	1	1	1	1	2
Jenelle Trant	0	0	0	0	1
Beth Trekman	0	1	0	0	0
Nancy Tresselt	0	2	1	1	2
Karen Trussel	0	0	1	0	0
Maria Tsiartsian	0	0	0	0	1
Kaori Tsuchiya	0	0	0	1	0
Consuelo Tureita	0	0	0	1	0
Jackie Twisdale	0	0	0	0	1
Carol Ushijama	0	0	1	1	2
Kelly Van Winden	0	0	1	1	1
Lisette VanDeVen	0	0	0	0	1
Tanya Vandeweghe	1	0	1	0	3
Teri VanDyke	0	0	0	0	1
Roxanne Vargas	0	5	4	6	7
Kathy Vaughn	0	0	0	1	0
Veronica Velez	0	1	0	1	3
Tiansol Villablanca	0	0	0	0	1
Julie Vocke	0	0	0	0	1
Dana Volmer	1	0	0	0	0
Jana Vollmer	0	0	0	0	1
Jacqui Vukosa	0	0	0	0	2
Rachel Wacholder	0	2	6	2	12
Kerri Walsh	20	10	4	3	0
Fei Wang	2	0	0	2	7
Jei Wang	0	0	0	0	1
Lu Wang	0	0	0	2	0
Jane Ward	0	3	1	1	3
Beverly Watson	0	0	0	0	1
Wendy Weat	0	0	0	0	1
Rose Wegrich	0	2	4	1	3
Paula Weisoff	0	1	2	1	5
Wendy Whitting	0	0	1	0	0
Christine Wilson	0	0	0	0	1
Pat Wilson	0	0	0	0	1
Peely Wilson	3	0	1	1	1
Pattie Woiemberg	0	0	0	1	1
Gayle Wolze	0	1	0	0	5
Ali Wood	0	1	1	3	7
Torrie Woods	0	1	0	0	1
Monica Worthy	0	0	0	0	1
Johanna Wright	0	0	0	1	2
Marci Wurts	0	0	0	1	1
Zi Xiong	0	0	0	1	1
Barb Yakely	0	0	0	0	1
Pam Yakely	0	0	0	0	1
Linda Yanchulova	0	0	0	0	1
Petia Yanchulova	0	0	0	0	1
Wenhui You	0	0	0	1	0
Lia Young	0	0	0	0	2
Elaine Youngs	29	21	14	10	11
Ni Putu Tim Rahayu Yudhani	0	0	0	0	1
Sharky Zartman	2	1	4	7	19
Lori Zeno	0	0	0	0	1
Laurie Zenow	0	0	0	0	1

JACKIE SILVA
With 60 career tournament championships, Brazilian Jackie Silva is the most proflic non-American to compete on the women's beach volleyball circuit. She ranks number three on the all time win list. Above photo, Silva makes a spectacular dig.
Photo Courtesy of Frank Goroszko

USA Volleyball 75th Anniversary Beach All-Era Players
Courtesy of Paul Soriano

Men's Beach All-Era Players
1928-1987

Manny Saenz – Saenz won his first major tournament at the 1948 "Pacific Coast Outdoor Volleyball Championships" with Al Harris. Later, Saenz teamed-up with Bernie Holtzman to win just about every match that they played in together, including both pick-up games and tournaments. Saenz went on to win 12 beach tournaments during a period when there were only one or two tournaments a year. He was also credited for creating a method of determining when teams changed sides, during games, so as to even out the effects of wind and sun conditions. In the early days teams would switch sides one time: when the first team reached a score of eight. Saenz used his influence on the beach to persuade the other players that teams should change sides when the total of each teams scores were divisible by five, i.e., 5-5, 13-7, etc. He was also a very successful indoor player and coach, as evidenced by his selection to two different USA Volleyball 75th Anniversary All-Era teams as a player (Men's 1928-52) and coach (Women's 1949-77).

Bernie Holtzman – Holtzman, who once said that "Volleyball is God's gift to the beach bum," first started to play volleyball on the beach in 1935—when he was just 13-years-old. His first tournament championship came when he paired-up with Manny Saenz at the 1948 State Beach Men's Open. They formed a nearly unbeatable combination. Together, they won virtually every event that they entered, during a period when there were only two or three "Open" tournaments a year. Holtzman and Saenz ended-up with 10 "Open" titles together. Holtzman later teamed with Gene Selznick, forming another "almost" unbeatable combination. Together, Selznick and Holtzman won 18 championship matches together. Holtzman also excelled in the indoor game and was honored as a member of the USA Volleyball 75th Anniversary Men's 1928-52 All-Era team earlier this year.

Gene Selznick – Selznick was one of the best to ever play beach volleyball in the "early years." A true innovator, he is credited with bringing the "spike" to the beach game. Although other players used to spike the ball occasionally on the beach, Selznick was the first to use it as his main weapon. His first "Open" tournament win came with Everette "Ev" Keller at the 1950 State Beach Men's Open. Selznick later enjoyed a great deal of sand success with Don McMahon, Bernie Holtzman, and Ron Lang. With Holtzman and Lang combined, he won

MANNY SAENZ
"All-Era" player Manny Saenz won his first major beach tournament in 1948 with Al Harris. Later, Saenz teamed-up with Bernie Holtzman to win just about every beach match that they played in together (pick-up games and tournaments). Above photo Saenz collects a trophy with Al Harris.
Photo Courtesy of Bernie Holtzman

BERNIE HOLTZMAN & GENE SELZNICK
"All-Era" player Bernie Holtzman won his first beach championship with Manny Saenz. They won virtually every beach event that they entered. "All-Era" player Gene Selznick won his first "Open" beach event with "Ev" Keller. Selznick later enjoyed a great deal of sand success with Bernie Holtzman. Above photo Holtzman (left) and Selznick (right) collect trophies
Photo Courtesy of Kevin Goff

more than 40 events. Selznick also passed on his knowledge as a highly successful coach. At the 1996 Atlanta Olympic Games, he coached Sinjin Smith and Carl Henkel to a near upset of eventual gold-medal winners Karch Kiraly and Kent Steffes. In 2000, he helped Misty May and Holly McPeak qualify for the Olympic Games in Sydney, Australia. Selznick, who was inducted into the Volleyball Hall of Fame in 1988, was also one of the best indoor volleyball players. He was named the Most Valuable Player of USA Volleyball's 75th Anniversary Men's 1953-77 All-Era Team.

Ron Lang – Lang started his beach volleyball career on Hermosa Beach—in the early 1950s—when he noticed a group playing volleyball and decided to give it a try. He liked the game immediately and the rest is beach volleyball history. Eventually he paired-up with Gene Selznick and later Ron Von Hagen to form two of the most successful partnerships of all time. Lang won more than 50 "Open" tournaments during his career, most of them with Selznick and Von Hagen. With Selznick, he earned over 20 tournament championships. With Von Hagen, he won 28 events. Lang was also an indoor volleyball All-American from 1957-1968 and a member of the 1964 Olympic Team. A member of three National Championship teams in (1960, 1966 and 1968), Lang was also honored as a member of the USA Volleyball 75th Anniversary Men's 1953-77 All-Era team.

Greg Lee – Lee was primarily known for his basketball abilities at UCLA, where he played with the great Bill Walton. He never played volleyball while at UCLA but was lured to the sand by older brother, Jon, who had a "AAA" rating on the beach. In 1972, Greg Lee played in his first "Open" at the Laguna Beach Open and finished second with Ron Von Hagen. His first "Open" victory came with Tom Chamales at the 1972 Santa Barbara Open. Lee's enjoyed the most success when he teamed-up with Jim Menges. From 1973-1982, Lee and Menges played in 28 tournaments together, winning 25 of them and finishing second in the other three. They were in the finals of every tournament that they entered together. Lee had additional victories with Von Hagen and Jay Hanseth. In all Lee entered a total of 37 "Open" tournaments and reached the finals all 37 times while collecting 29 tournament titles.

Jim Menges – Menges, tied for ninth on the all-time wins list with 48, started playing beach volleyball in 1968 at Santa Monica's Sorrento Beach. He went to the beach with a group of friends and they all learned by watching the greats, such as Ron Von Hagen and Ron Lang. He started playing on the "outside courts" and eventually graduated to the "first court," playing with Tom Chamales, Greg Lee and Randy Niles. His first "Open" win came at the 1973 Marine Open, with Greg Lee. From 1973-1982, Menges and Lee played in 28 tournaments together, winning 25 of them and finishing second in the other three. They were in the finals of every tournament that they entered together. Menges teamed-up with Matt Gage for 17 events, winning eight of them. This team was also in the finals of every tournament that they entered together. Menges enjoyed success with all of his partners through 1982, winning with Chris Marlowe five times and once each with Von Hagen, Chamales, Gary Hooper, Sinjin Smith, Randy Stoklos and Jon Stevenson.

Mike O'Hara – O'Hara was a prominent beach volleyball player who started to play the game in the early 1950s. His first "Open" victory came with Don McMahon at the 1954 State Beach Men's Open. After a fairly successful partnership with McMahon (and others) he eventually teamed-up with Mike Bright in 1960 for a win at the Laguna Beach Men's Open. O'Hara and Bright went on to win 13 tournaments together, including the first five Manhattan Beach Opens. O'Hara's career included a total of 20 championship victories. O'Hara was also an indoor volleyball star as evidenced by seven first-team All-America and two Player of the Year honors. He was a member of the 1964 Olympic Team and was recognized as a member of the USA Volleyball 75th Anniversary Men's 1953-77 All-Era team earlier this year. In 1989, O'Hara was inducted into the Volleyball Hall of Fame.

Ron Von Hagen – At 6-feet-1 and 190 pounds, Von Hagen was one of the first players to include weight training in his workout program. He was also one of the first players to train for beach volleyball year around. Most volleyball enthusiasts agree that Von Hagen had more desire—and was in better shape physically—than any of the other players. Von Hagen won his won his first tournament with Clyde Grosscup and his first Open tournament with Rand Carter. The "Open" win was the 1964 Laguna Men's Open. Later in his career, Von Hagen teamed-up with Ron Lang to form one of the most successful partnerships in the history of beach volleyball. Nearly half of his victories (28) would come with Lang. Von Hagen was able to adapt to the styles of different partners as he went on to win 62 open tournaments from 1964 through 1977. During an incredible, 100 Open tournament stretch, Von Hagen won 60 times, was second 23 times and took the third spot seven times. He won his final tournament at the age of 38 years and nine months.

MIKE O"HARA, RON VON HAGEN & RON LANG
"All-Era players Mike O'Hara, Ron Von Hagen and Ron Lang were all top players during their era's on the beach volleyball circuit. O'Hara teamed-up with Mike Bright for great success. As a team, Von Hagen and Lang were synonymous with winning. Above photo, O'Hara hits the ball towards the defense of Von Hagen (left) and Lang (right).
Photo Courtesy of Bob Van Wagner

Women's Beach All-Era Players
1928-1987

Johnette Latreille – In 1955 Latreille showed up at Sorrento Beach and noticed a group of people playing "doubles beach volleyball." She decided to see if she could play. Eventually, Latreille met her future husband, Dave Heiser, who was instrumental in her increased involvement with the beach game. While she was still learning the game, Heiser taught her many good basics of the game and helped her move from the Sorrento Beach "D" court to "C" and eventually up to the "B" court. Later on in her career, Latreille was coached by Bernie Holtzman and then Gene Selznick. She went on to become one of the best women's beach players of her era. Teamed with Jean Brunicardi, Latreille was one-half of the top women's team of the late 1950's and early 1960's. Latreille was also a top mixed-double's player on the beach and an accomplished indoor player. She played on four-straight national championship teams (1963-66) and earned honorable mention All-America honors twice.

Jean Brunicardi – In 1956 Brunicardi started playing beach volleyball in Santa Monica, Calif., where she was tutored by Manny Saenz to become the first "beach queen" of beach volleyball. Brunicardi played outstanding defense, had the ability to read her opponent's shots like no other player and she moved through the sand with unmatched effectiveness. Her stamina was also unmatched by any of her opponents. Brunicardi was successful with nearly all of her partners. When Brunicardi paired-up with Johnette Latreille, they formed one of the most successful female duos ever. They won virtually every pick-up game and tournament that they were involved in together. In 1974, prior to the State Beach Women's Open, the 42-year-old Brunicardi was approached by 14-year-old Nancy Cohen to play with her. This was to be Cohen's first-ever open tournament. In the championship match, Brunicardi and Cohen defeated Barbara (Grubb) May and Eileen Clancy to become both the oldest and the youngest players to ever win an open women's doubles tournament.

Kathy Gregory – The number speaks for itself. With 49 career victories in the sand, Gregory ranks fourth in overall wins and is tied for second in domestic wins. She enjoyed most of her success with a trio of partners. Gregory, who embarked on a beach career in the 1960s, earned 14 tournament wins with Miki McFadden, 13 victories with Nancy Cohen and 12 "W's" with Kathy

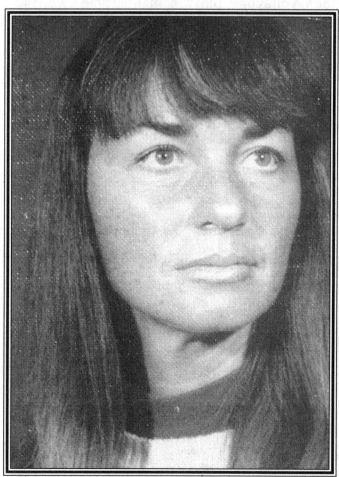

JOHNETTE LATREILLE
"All-Era" player Johnette Latreille was one of the best women's beach players of her era. Teamed with Jean Brunicardi, Latreille was one-half of the top women's team of the late 1950's and early 1960's. Latreille was also a top mixed-double's player on the beach and an accomplished indoor player. Above photo, Latreille poses for the camera.
Photo Courtesy of Kevin Goff

JEAN BRUNICARDI
"All-Era" player Jean Brunicardi's stamina was unmatched by any of her opponents. Brunicardi was successful with nearly all of her partners. When Brunicardi paired-up with Johnette Latreille, they formed one of the most successful female beach duos ever. They won virtually every beach pick-up game and tournament that they were involved in together.
Photo Courtesy of Jean Brunicardi

Hanley. She also captured half-a-dozen titles with Janice Harrer. On the court Gregory was a talkative dynamo who would interact with the beach crowd as well as her opponents. After being awarded Women's Beach Tournament Player of the Year honors in 1976, 1977, 1978, 1981 and 1983, Gregory was crowned "Queen of the Beach." Gregory excelled at the indoor game as well. A former member of the USA national team and the recipient of numerous All-America honors, she became only the third woman to be inducted into the Volleyball Hall of Fame in 1989. Earlier this year, she was selected to the USA Volleyball 75th Anniversary Women's (1949-77) All-Era Team. Since 1975 Gregory has been the highly successful head coach of the UC Santa Barbara women's volleyball program. She was named National Coach of the Year in 1993 and began the 2003 season ranked sixth all-time in NCAA Division I victories.

Eileen Clancy – Clancy starred in the sand at an early age, teaming up with Butch May to dominate the mixed-doubles scene when she was only 12-years-old. The tandem played—and won—together for 10 years. In 1995, Clancy was inducted into the California Beach Volleyball Hall of Fame.

Nina Grouwinkel Matthies – Matthies, one of the best beach volleyball players of her time, won 43 tournaments during her legendary career with a variety of partners but enjoyed a majority of her success with Linda Hanley. Together, Matthies and Hanley earned 30 tournament titles to rank No. 1 on the all-time team victory list along with Brazil's Adriana Behar and Shelda Bede. For her career, Matthies played in 139 events with 43 championships, 26 runner-up finishes and 24 third-place results. The 43 titles place Matthies seventh on the all-time individual wins list. She was a force off the sand as well. Matthies spearheaded a successful effort in the mid-1980's to create the Women's Professional Volleyball Association (WPVA)—an organization which laid the foundation for the dramatically enhanced national visibility of the women's beach tour. Matthies was inducted into the WPVA's "Hall of Fame" in 1995 and was honored as one of the "20 Legends of Beach Volleyball" in a ceremony at UCLA in 1997. Matthies, a former member of the USA women's national team, is currently in her 21st year as the head coach of the Pepperdine women's volleyball program.

Mary Jo Peppler – Peppler is acclaimed for helping to establish women's volleyball in the United States. At 6-foot-1 and 125 pounds, the southpaw also probably had the greatest physical talent of any women's player (beach or indoor) during her time. Her success at the indoor game has been well documented. Peppler, a 1964 Olympian, earned numerous All-America honors and played on numerous national championship teams. She was inducted into the Volleyball Hall of Fame in 1990 and honored as a member of the USA Volleyball 75th Anniversary Women's (1949-77) All-Era Team earlier this year. But Peppler had a successful career on the beach playing with various partners. She was also an outstanding coach who was known as an innovator, visionary and crusader. Peppler later coached one of the top women's beach volleyball teams of all time when she coached Karolyn Kirby and Liz Masakayan.

Jane Ward – Ward did not discriminate; she excelled at both beach and indoor volleyball. Ward was a force to be reckoned with outdoors in the late 1950s and early 1960s. In recognition of her talents with the indoor game, Ward was inducted into the Volleyball Hall of Fame in 1988 and honored as the Most Valuable Player and one of three coaches of USA Volleyball's 75th Anniversary Women's (1949-77) All-Era Team earlier this year.

Norma Weir – Weir was one of the top players of her generation during the 1950s. She partnered with Lois Haraughty and later Jean Gaertner to win a number of early tournaments, including the Women's "AAA" Tournament in Santa Monica in 1950, the Pacific Coast Championship in Santa Barbara in 1957 and the Sorrento Women's Open in Santa Monica in 1958.

KATHY GREGORY & NINA GROUWINKEL MATTHIES
"All-Era" players Kathy Gregory and Nina Grouwinkel Matthies were the top two beach players of their era. Gregory and Grouwinkel teamed-up together, but mostly they battled it out against each other, taking turns winning tournaments. Above photo, Grouwinkel spikes the ball towards the defense of Gregory.
Photo Courtesy of Suzie Jones

JANE WARD
"All-Era" player Jane Ward was a top indoor player, as well as a top player on the beach. She was also successful on the mixed-doubles beach circuit. Above photo, Ward delivers a nice set to Spike Boarts, hitting the ball towards the defense of Steno Brunicardi (left) and Jean Brunicardi (right), during a 1960's event on Sorrento Beach in Santa Monioca CA.
Photo Courtesy of Kevin Goff

FUTURE BEACH VOLLEYBALL BOOKS:

"THE PERSONALITY OF BEACH VOLLEYBALL"
The 1915 through Present Day

This book dwells into the personality and personalities of beach volleyball. The atmosphere of the game is analized from its inception to present day. The book includes stories and anecdotes concerning humorous incidents, the characters and fans of the game. There is also a section regarding the "Specialty Tournaments" that have taken place over the years. Included are nearly 200 photographs of the various events described in the book.

"THE GREAT PERFORMANCES OF BEACH VOLLEYBALL"
The 1915 Through Present Day

This book highlights the best of beach volleyball includig the great performances and perforrmers of the game. The book focuses in on the best: hitters, blockers, diggers, setters, and servers that have played beach volleyball from its inception to present day. The book also covers the best rallies, saves, comebacks, tournaments as well as additional subjects. Included are nearly 200 photographs of the various events described in the book.

"THE MANHATTAN BEACH OPEN"
1960 Through Present Day

The book discusses the history and events that concern the "Wimbeldon" of all the beach volleyball tournaments, the Manhattan Beach Open. This book covers the players, winners, fans, characters, changes, high-lights and low-lights of this prestigious beach volleyball event. Included are nearly 200 photographs of the various events described in the book.

Future books will be available along with previously published books, from:

INFORMATION GUIDES
HERMOSA BEACH, CA 90254

PHONE: 1-800-347-3257

E-MAIL: firebks@gte.net

WEB SITE: www.volleyballbooks.net

THREE VOLUMES OF :
"SANDS OF TIME"
THE HISTORY OF BEACH VOLLEYBALL

VOLUME #1
"SANDS OF TIME"
THE HISTORY OF BEACH VOLLEYBALL
1895-1969

This volume consist of four Chapters that fill nearly **300** pages with Beach Volleyball stories and anecdotes, of some of the most unbelievable events in the history of the game, along with tournament results and **500**, classic and rare, some never before seen, photographs of the events, venues, characters, players and legends of Beach Volleyball.

In Chapter #1, the first 50 years of volleyball's growth is discussed. The remaining **244** pages, beginning with Chapter #2, cover Beach Volleyball, revealing the games "Birth" and illustrating how the indoor game contributed to the "conception" of the beach game.

In the third Chapter, you are guided up to and through beach volleyball's "Golden" years of the 1950's.

Chapter #4 covers the 1960's, referred to as the "Adolescent" years of Beach Volleyball.

Each of the preceding Chapters include a summary of Men's, Women's and Mixed-Doubles beach volleyball, with recorded events, information, anecdotes and tournament results, along with photos that integrate with the events.

AVAILABLE NOW

VOLUME #2
"SANDS OF TIME"
THE HISTORY OF BEACH VOLLEYBALL
1970-1989

This volume of the book: "Sands of Time" consist of two large Chapters that fill nearly **600** pages, with over **1,200** beach volleyball photographs.

Chapter #1 covers The "Spirited" years of beach volleyball, 1970-1979. This Chapter includes a summary of Men's, Women's and Mixed-Doubles beach volleyball. Each year's beach volleyball events (1970-1979), information, anecdotes and tournament results are recorded along with over **600** photographs that intregate with the events.

Chapter #2 covers The "Transitional" years of beach volleyball, 1980-1989. This Chapter includes a summary of Men's, Women's and Mixed-Doubles beach volleyball. Each year's beach volleyball events (1980-1989), information, anecdotes and tournament results are recorded along with another **600+** photographs that integrate with the events.

This book includes Department of Recreation, CBVA, AVP, WPVA, and FIVB beach volleyball information and results.

AVAILABLE NOW

VOLUME #3
"SANDS OF TIME"
THE HISTORY OF BEACH VOLLEYBALL
1990-2004

This volume of the Sands of Time will consist of two large Chapters that fill nearly **500** pages and over **1000** photos. Chapter #1 covers The "Prosperous" years of beach volleyball, 1990-1999. This chapter includes a summary of Men's and Women's beach volleyball. Each year's beach volleyball events, information, anecdotes and tournament results are recorded along with over **600** photographs that intregate with the happenings.

Chapter #2 covers "Beach Volleyball: 2000 and Beyond." This chapter includes a summary of Men's and Women's beach volleyball for the 200-2004 seasons. Each year's beach volleyball events, information, anecdotes and tournament results are recorded along with over **400** photographs that intregate with the events.

This book includes information regarding the AVP, WPVA, CBVA, BVA, U.S.A., FIVB, International tournaments, four-person beach volleyball, the Olympics, as well as additional information that relates to the history of beach volleyball.

AVAILABLE NOW